D1174268

Yale Historical Publications

Fallen Women, Problem Girls

Unmarried Mothers
and the
Professionalization
of Social Work
1890–1945

Regina G. Kunzel

Yale University Press
New Haven & London

Published under the direction of the Department of History of Yale
University with assistance from the income of the Frederick John
Kingsbury Memorial Fund.

Copyright © 1993 by Yale University. All rights reserved. This
book may not be reproduced, in whole or in part, including
illustrations, in any form (beyond that copying permitted by
Sections 107 and 108 of the U.S. Copyright Law and except by
reviewers for the public press), without written permission from
the publishers.

Set by Keystone Typesetting, Inc. Printed in the United States of
America by Edwards Brothers, Ann Arbor, Michigan.

Library of Congress Cataloging-in-Publication Data
Kunzel, Regina G., 1959–
Fallen women, problem girls : unmarried mothers and the
professionalization of social work, 1890–1945 / Regina G. Kunzel.
    p.   cm. — (Yale historical publications)
  Includes bibliographical references and index.
  ISBN 0-300-05090-9 (alk. paper)
  1. Unmarried mothers—United States—History. 2. Maternity
homes—United States—History. 3. Unmarried mothers—
Services for—United States—History. I. Title. II. Series: Yale
historical publications (Unnumbered)
HV700.5.K86 1993
362.83'92'0973—dc20   93-10013

A catalogue record for this book is available from the British
Library.

The paper in this book meets the guidelines for permanence and
durability of the Committee on Production Guidelines for Book
Longevity of the Council on Library Resources.

10   9   8   7   6   5   4   3   2   1

362.8392
K96

94-1131
27768414

Contents

Illustrations

Acknowledgments

Throughout the course of writing this book, I have received encouragement and assistance from a great number of friends, teachers, and colleagues, and I take great pleasure in acknowledging them here. My first thanks go to Nancy Cott. The ideas from which this book grew were sparked in her graduate seminar, and she has encouraged the twists and turns they have taken in years since. I feel fortunate to have had the benefit of her searching criticism and thank her for her generous and strong support. I am grateful as well to the other members of my dissertation committee, David Montgomery and Jean-Christophe Agnew, for their enthusiasm and guidance. I would also like to acknowledge teachers I encountered early on, especially Estelle Freedman, who taught me to begin to think critically about gender and history.

A number of friends and colleagues read this manuscript at various stages. Jacqueline Dirks, Kathryn Oberdeck, and Catherine Stock nurtured these ideas from the beginning, read several versions of each chapter, and inspired, challenged, and supported me in countless and important ways. Susan Johnson's careful and astute reading of an early draft of the manuscript encouraged me to rethink some of its assumptions; I am grateful for her friendship and support. I owe a special debt to Joanne Meyerowitz for her insightful and generous suggestions concerning chapter 6. For their helpful reading of specific chapters, I am very grateful to Steve Lassonde, Jane Levey, Laurie Maffly-Kipp, Mark Naison, Kathleen Nilen, Peggy Pascoe, Patricia Tracy, and Susan Yohn. I am indebted to Mary Renda and Stuart Clarke for their thoughtful comments and sustaining friendship. For much-appreciated help at different points along the way, I would like to thank Sherri Broder, George Chauncey, Allison Coleman,

Dana Frank, Lori Ginzberg, Yukiko Hanawa, Gail Hershatter, Daniel Letwin, Katherine Morrissey, Karin Shapiro, and Sarah Wilson. I would also like to thank my colleagues in the History Department and Women's Studies Program at Williams College; among them, Paige Baty, Jeanne Bergman, Carol Ockman, Jana Sawicki, Karen Swann, Chris Waters, Joel Wolfe, and Scott Wong have kept my spirits up and sharpened my thinking.

Librarians and archivists have provided crucial aid in my research. In particular, I would like to thank Judith Johnson, formerly at the Salvation Army Archives and Research Center, for granting me permission to use the case records in the collection. Susan Mitchem's knowledge of Salvation Army history and her enthusiasm for my project were an enormous help in the final stretch. David Klaassen at the University of Minnesota's Social Welfare History Archives offered guidance in the National Florence Crittenton Mission papers and shared his considerable knowledge of early-twentieth-century social welfare. Many thanks also to the staff of the Library of Congress, the National Archives, the Sophia Smith Collection, the New York Academy of Medicine, the Old Dominion University Library, the Chicago Historical Society, the Columbia University Archives, the Rutgers University Library, and Yale University's Sterling Memorial Library.

Generous funding from several sources made researching and writing this book possible. I would like to express my appreciation to the Mrs. Giles Whiting Foundation, the Woodrow Wilson Foundation, the John D. Rockefeller Foundation, the American Historical Association, and Yale University. A summer research stipend and a year-long fellowship from the National Endowment for the Humanities funded additional research and provided me with valuable time to think and write. I finished this book on a leave graciously granted and funded in part by Williams College.

Chuck Grench, my editor at Yale University Press, has been helpful and encouraging at every step. Eliza Childs and Otto Bohlmann helped me navigate the passage from manuscript to book, and Cecile Rhinehart Watters's careful editing greatly improved the finished product. I also want to thank the *Journal of Social History* for permission to use material from my article, "The Professionalization of Benevolence: Evangelicals and Social Workers in the Florence Crittenton Homes, 1915 to 1945," *Journal of Social History* 22 (Fall 1988): 21–43.

My parents, Klonie and Fritz Kunzel, made history an integral part of my growing up. I thank them here for encouraging me all along the way. My sister, Karen, read the entire manuscript and offered her keen thoughts as well as her support; my brothers, Paul and Fritz, reminded me of life beyond the book.

My deepest thanks go to Siobhan Somerville. Every chapter has benefited in immeasurable ways from her insightful reading and comments. She has been exceedingly generous with her time, her ideas, and her good humor. Her own work has enriched my writing and thinking, and she has sustained me throughout.

To write this book, I relied on sources that revealed the secrets of women and girls who might have been uneasy at the prospect of becoming historical subjects. I analyze stories that they told in confidence and sometimes under coercion. As interested as I am in the ways in which single pregnancy has been socially constructed, these sources constantly reminded me that real lives and painful struggles lay behind them. I hope that my profound respect for these women is reflected in the pages that follow.

Introduction

> Against the background of history, too prominent to escape the observation from which it shrinks, stands a figure, mute, mournful, and indescribably sad. It is a girl holding in her arms the blessing and burden of motherhood, but in whose face one finds no trace of maternal joy or pride. . . . Who is this woman, so pitiable, yet so scorned? It is the mother of the illegitimate child. By forbidden paths she has obtained the grace of maternity, but its glory is for her transfigured into a badge of unutterable shame.
> —Albert Leffingwell, *Illegitimacy: A Study in Morals*

In 1919, social worker J. Prentice Murphy called on these melodramatic words by British reformer Albert Leffingwell to represent the unmarried mother. Shrinking against the "background of history," she was a timeless figure who resisted description and eluded understanding. But even as Murphy wrote, he and his colleagues were refiguring unmarried motherhood from a transhistorical inevitability to one of the most compelling and urgent "problems" of the day. Struggling to discover its "causes," reformers and social workers rushed to fill in the explanatory gaps suggested by the unmarried mother's alleged "muteness," the "indescribability" of her sadness, and the "unutterability" of her shame.

Among the first to draw attention to out-of-wedlock pregnancy were evangelical reform women who founded maternity homes to "redeem" and "reclaim" unmarried mothers in the late nineteenth and early twentieth centuries. Heirs to a long tradition of female benevolence, evangelical women brought to the homes the skills of sisterhood, sympathy, and piety, well honed in nineteenth-century female reform efforts. Styling the homes as places of rehabilitation and, they hoped, of conversion, evangelical women treated women they considered their "fallen sisters" with the maternal, religious, and domestic influence that made up the redemptive tonic of womanly benevolence.[1]

Although by the 1920s evangelical women could boast a national network of more than two hundred maternity homes, they increasingly had to compete for the authority to define unmarried motherhood and eventually, and most painfully, to control the homes they had founded. As social workers sought to establish themselves as professionals, they claimed "illegitimacy" to be within their realm of expertise and eventually demanded places of central importance in homes for unmarried mothers. In order to distance themselves from evangelical reform and to dissociate their own work from the earlier style of benevolence so heavily informed by "feminine" values, they described work with unmarried mothers in a very different light. "Success," one caseworker wrote in 1921, "is achieved in inverse ratio to the degree of emotion involved."[2] Trading the explicitly gendered language of evangelical reform for the ostensibly gender-neutral, objective, rational, and scientific language of professionalism, social workers articulated the reform outlook of a new generation of women. Maternity homes—which were once shelters dedicated to the redemption and reclamation of "fallen women"—were now redefined by social workers as places of scientific treatment. Rather than unfortunate "sisters" to be "saved," unmarried mothers became "problem girls" to be "treated."

The transition from benevolent reform to professional casework with unmarried mothers, from 1890 to 1945, provides the frame for this book. For historians, this transition moves from a familiar and well-traveled terrain to one that is considerably less well mapped. Although nineteenth-century women's reform work and ideology have been richly documented and thoughtfully analyzed, much less is understood about this impulse in its twentieth-century incarnation, when faith in Christian motherhood and redemptive "feminine" virtue was giving way to a new faith in science and secular reform. Historians have analyzed in sophisticated and illuminating detail how women reformers used the rhetoric of maternity and domesticity to define and justify their place in reform, to explain their unique and necessary role in benevolent work, and eventually to carve out careers for themselves in social welfare.[3] After 1920, however, this familiar female reform tradition was on the wane, and the women who moved into social welfare and casework agencies are largely unknown to us. Barely resembling their predecessors, this new generation of women complicates the framework within which we understand women's reform efforts.

I take these complications as points of departure. Given our conceptualization of the history of women's reform efforts, how do we understand women who viewed unmarried mothers not as "erring daughters" in need of salvation but as "social units" in need of "adjustment"?[4] How are we to approach women who spoke as fluently and with as much conviction as their male colleagues in the language of professionalism? If our understanding of female reformers is framed in terms of "social housekeeping," what are we to make of women who accepted the imperatives of a professional ideology that devalued the work of their predecessors as too "female" to be reliable and effective?

Although historians of social welfare have more fully explored the professionalization of benevolence and the rise of the "expert," they offer few answers to questions concerning the meaning of gender to that transition. A number have chronicled the inevitable and, to some, laudable march of professionalization, resulting in the victory of "objective" and "scientific" experts over the moralistic "ladies bountiful" and the eclipse of the ideology of womanly benevolence by the new, more secular ideology of professional social work.[5] Others less inclined to celebrate this transition tell a story in which the new professionals wrested control of benevolent work from proto-feminist female reformers. Both approaches characterize the professionalization of social welfare as a smooth transition, marked by the easy substitution of one set of values with another—the victory of omnipotent professionals who quickly and readily dispensed with the long-standing tradition of nineteenth-century benevolence and replaced it with their own. Tending to underplay the roughness of this transition, these studies obscure the resistance and resilience of the older tradition and exaggerate the power and hegemony of the new.

This book argues that professionalization was not a simple linear progression but an embattled and protracted transfer of power from evangelical women to social workers. More important, I propose that these moments of contest—specifically, the terms of debate between evangelical women and social workers over unmarried motherhood and the purposes of maternity homes—reveal the ways in which gender figured powerfully in the process by which a coalition of male and female reformers claimed to free themselves from gendered meanings.[6]

Taking gender into account in the study of professionalization adds a new dimension to the historical understanding of the devaluation of the amateur and the rise of the expert and substantially shifts the terms of larger historical debates on the meaning and purpose of professionalization. Whereas sociologists have concerned themselves primarily with identifying structural characteristics shared by professionals (high ethical standards, educational credentials, specialized skills, and so on), some historians have suggested that professionalization could be better understood as an occupational strategy that legitimated an elite class's claims to power.[7] Historians addressing women's experience in the professions have made an important contribution to our understanding of professionalization by revealing that process to be fundamentally and pervasively gendered. Those who have focused on male-dominated professions trace the grim story of sex discrimination and conclude that professionalism was structurally biased against female achievement.[8] In her study of women in science, for example, Margaret Rossiter posits the ideological congruence of professionalism and "masculinity." Rossiter argues convincingly that the professionalization of science constituted a backlash against the perceived threat of "feminization" that male leaders believed would compromise professional excellence and prestige. Increasingly allied with values coded as "masculine," professionalism served to oust women from the most prestigious and visible positions in science, restricting them to a narrow band of stereotypically "feminine" jobs.[9] Other historians who document the strategies undertaken by women in the "female professions" of teaching, nursing, and librarianship similarly argue that full professional privilege was denied women in the low-paying, low-prestige occupations in which they were concentrated.[10]

Most histories of women and the professions, then, portray women as excluded from or at the margins of the professions. Some women, however, took an active part in professionalization, shaping its precepts and reaping its rewards. Because the transfer of power from evangelical workers to professional social workers in maternity homes took place between two groups of women, it adds a new and complicated dimension to the history of professionalization. The experience of the two generations of women in maternity homes between 1890 and 1945 illuminates the gender tensions and conflicts accompanying the professionalization of benevolence and adds as well to our understanding of the importance of gender in larger shifts accompanying the transition to "modern" twentieth-century culture.[11] Historians have identified the rise of expertise and the growth of secularization and rationalization as defining characteristics of modern America. I argue not only that women participated in the process but that the transition itself was shaped and structured by gender.[12]

The professionalization of the field of illegitimacy entailed more than a transformation of the ideology of reform and a change in the personnel of maternity homes. One of the central projects of this book is to trace the shifting constructions of out-of-wedlock pregnancy that accompanied this transition. The multiple and changing understandings of the unmarried mother—as innocent victim, sex delinquent, unadjusted neurotic—suggest that evangelical women and social workers inscribed their own anxieties and those of their time and place in the narratives of out-of-wedlock pregnancy they popularized and promoted. This book explores the ways in which those narratives became legitimizing vehicles, first for evangelical women and later for social workers and policymakers, in their larger struggles for cultural authority from 1890 to 1945.

Although struggles to define, represent, and control female sexuality have often been waged by and between men, illegitimacy became a site for women's contests for power and authority.[13] The competition between evangelical women and social workers for authorship of popular understandings of out-of-wedlock pregnancy, for recognition as legitimate authorities, and for control of maternity homes raised larger questions of how female sexuality would and could be represented and understood. This book explores the ways in which the "problem" of the unmarried mother drew different generations and classes of women into a public discussion of sexuality, and the possibilities and constraints imposed on that discussion by their shifting and relative positions of power.

Competing discourses of illegitimacy also illuminate a struggle for authority over issues of sexuality and the family that transcended the contest for professional status. Touching different nerves in different periods and cultural contexts, unmarried motherhood has long engaged fears about class, race, ethnicity, sexuality, and the family. Throughout the period from 1890 to 1945, out-of-wedlock pregnancy functioned as a language through which people might seek to contain, contest, and resolve issues of social change and sexual, racial, and class conflict far more sweeping than the issue of illegitimacy. Those who struggled to discover the "cause" of out-of-wedlock pregnancy were engaged in an effort to understand weightier, more disconcerting, and less comprehensible issues. This book, then, considers the development of work with unmarried mothers in the context of a broad social and cultural history of sexuality, gender, class, and race.[14]

At times, unmarried mothers seemed strangely peripheral to the cacophony of voices raised to represent, "redeem," and "treat" them. One of my primary intentions is to bring unmarried mothers from the periphery to the center, not simply out of a desire to draw a fuller picture of the history of single pregnancy, but with the conviction that neither the struggle between evangelical women and social workers nor the shifting construction of unmarried motherhood can be understood otherwise. Unmarried mothers were not simply objects of Christian benevolence or of professional social service; rather, as historical agents in their own right, they were active participants in the relationships of reform. As evangelical women and social workers sought to realize their different visions of the homes, unmarried mothers came to them with self-conscious strategies of their own and, in turn, shaped the attitudes, expectations, and boundaries of possibility for those in charge.[15]

To address the professionalization of maternity homes from the perspectives of evangelical women, social workers, and unmarried mothers, I have examined a wide range of sources. Evangelical women and social workers wrote extensively about what they did, what they thought, and why. To understand the world created by evangelical reformers in maternity homes, I have drawn principally on the records of the two largest chains of homes—those founded by the Salvation Army and the National Florence Crittenton Mission. Evangelical ideas are well documented in annual reports, promotional pamphlets, and personal accounts. Social workers were at least as prolific as evangelical women. Answering the call of their profession to measure, diagnose, quantify, and analyze, they conducted scores of investigations of out-of-wedlock pregnancy in cities and towns across the country. Their views also appear in their many professional journals, the records of the large centralized bureaus they established, and other writing, published and unpublished.

Considering out-of-wedlock pregnancy from the perspective of the third group of women in this triangle—the unmarried mothers—was a more complicated task. Attempting to write about unmarried mothers in 1910, Evangeline Booth of the Salvation Army voiced her frustration: "Figures you can have and bare statements, but anything further you must wrestle for!"[16] For the historian, foregrounding the perspective of unmarried mothers in the first half of the twentieth century involves its own process of "wrestling" and raises a number of methodological challenges.

The most obvious and immediate challenges are material. Few single mothers in this period wrote willingly of their experience of out-of-wedlock pregnancy, and most tried to cover their tracks. But those who went to social agencies or maternity homes were interviewed, and the notes on their "cases" were recorded in maternity home logbooks and social case files. Casework followed a step-by-step procedure of collecting information about a client's experiences and background, or "investigation," followed by "diagnosis" and "treatment" of the client's problem. The keeping of case records in maternity homes, which accompanied the professionalization of social work, began in the early twentieth century and became more thorough as social workers' scrutiny of those homes intensified. By the 1920s, most homes had moved from a logbook system to a standard form in which they kept records of each resident.[17]

Although many case records are detailed, others often are abbreviated or fragmented. It is frustrating to realize that, as one Salvation Army matron admitted, "the best and most telling incidents never got into print; nay, some of them never got any farther than the Matron-mother's sitting room."[18] Yet, even if all such stories had been recorded in their entirety, it would not change the fact that case records were written by maternity home matrons and social workers and created for their own use. As one astute sociologist wrote in 1928, "the characters in case records do not speak for themselves. They obtain a hearing only in the translation provided by the language of the social worker."[19] The experience of unmarried mothers as presented in case records, then, was mediated several times over—shaped by the kinds of questions asked, by who was asking, by the unmarried mother's relationship with the social worker, and by what that worker considered important enough to record. Consequently, case records often reveal as much, if not more, about those conducting the interviews as they do about the unmarried mothers themselves.

Occasionally, however, case records provide glimpses into maternity home life from their residents' perspective, sometimes revealing more than their authors intended about the relationship between worker and client, the attitudes of single mothers toward their "keepers," and the strategies they employed to pursue their own needs and agendas. Using case records from several sources, this book explores how women negotiated the crisis posed by out-of-wedlock pregnancy, why they turned to maternity homes, how they experienced life in them, and how they used them to their own ends. A rich and largely unexamined set of documents, case records reveal unmarried mothers as active and resourceful agents rather than as docile recipients of the reforming intentions of evangelical women and social workers.[20]

Unmarried mothers were asked the question, "How did you become pregnant?" often repeatedly, by women who sought to learn the "true story" behind their pregnancy. At the same time that case records shed light on the experience of single pregnancy and the social relations of maternity home life, they draw attention to the inextricability of that experience from the linguistic and narrative means by which unmarried mothers represented it. Unmarried mothers' stories were shaped by the complex interaction of power between women in the casework process; as historian Mary Poovey has written in another context, case records stand "as texts that mark the passage of women from objects of another's discourse to women as subjects of their own."[21] They illuminate as well the broader systems of power within which those exchanges between women took place. The process of casework both enabled and set limits to ways in which women might counter dominant and often pathologizing constructions of out-of-wedlock pregnancy. This book explores the relationship between unmarried mothers as historical agents and as discursive figures, between unmarried motherhood as lived experience and as a constructed social problem.[22]

Case records not only pose methodological challenges but also select and determine the group of unmarried mothers who become visible to the historian. Those single pregnant women who were able to evade the view of social agencies and maternity homes escape the historian's view, as well. As Clara Laughlin noted in 1915, "girls whose families are able and willing to protect and shield them never become known as mothers of unlegalized children."[23] The unmarried mothers who appear in the case records of maternity homes and social agencies were typically those whose financial and familial circumstances made it impossible to remain anonymous and who, voluntarily or not, came under the purview of evangelical matrons and social workers.

Maternity homes, then, were charged sites, bringing together evangelical women, professional social workers, and working-class "problem girls." In its broadest sense, this book argues that their negotiations and struggles distilled larger generational and cross-class conflicts among women in the first half of the twentieth century. It explores unmarried motherhood, not against history's background, but as a historically changing construction fraught with multiple contests for authority over the meaning of gender, sexuality, motherhood, and the family between 1890 and 1945.

1

The

Maternity Home

Movement

Kate Waller Barrett often told the story of how she was first called to rescue work with unmarried mothers. Late one night, a young woman came to see Barrett's husband, a minister. The woman had been out all night and arrived at the Barretts' doorstep cold and wet, "clasping in her arms a fatherless child." After inviting her in and talking with her, Barrett was moved by the deep bond she felt with the woman and struck by their essential similarity. "She, too, was a country girl. She, too, had loved, but alas! for her, she had loved unwisely while I had loved wisely; she had loved a bad man and I a good one. That seemed to me about the only difference in our stories in the beginning, but how different the end." From that moment, Barrett recalled, "there entered a God-given purpose in my heart, which has never left me from that day to this, that she should have a chance." Compelled by an empathetic bond of sisterhood and angered at the injustice of a sexual double standard that labeled such women "fallen," Barrett vowed to spend her life "trying to wipe out some of the inequities that were meted out to my sisters who were so helpless to help themselves."[1]

The story of Kate Barrett's calling contains the most compelling features of evangelical work with unmarried mothers in the late nineteenth and early twentieth centuries. Religious purpose and sisterly sympathy combined to shape the way evangelical women viewed unmarried mothers and to inform the institutional responses to out-of-wedlock pregnancy that they sought to create in maternity homes. Under the auspices of the National Florence Crittenton Mission, the Salvation Army, the Door of Hope, and various religious denominations, women constructed a national network of "protection and rescue shelters" to reclaim and redeem their "less fortunate sisters." A maternity home movement of considerable proportion took shape in the rich ideological and organizational context of womanly benevolence. Their vision would not long remain uncontested, but at the time of their founding of the movement and for several decades thereafter, evangelical women held sway in homes that were their exclusive province.

ORGANIZED WOMANHOOD AND THE MATERNITY HOME MOVEMENT

The women who founded and staffed maternity homes were generally not the elite reformers of the Gilded Age (although the philanthropic elite would eventually be well represented on the rosters of the Florence Crittenton Circles and boards), but rather were part of a larger "organized womanhood" drawn from the ranks of predominantly white middle-class evangelically oriented Protestant women.[2] Women came to maternity homes with experience as missionaries, teachers, or benevolent volunteers and many boasted overlapping membership in the Women's Christian Temperance Union (WCTU) or the YWCA. Nettie Stray Bliss's career offers a good example of the paths of many women who traveled in and out of reform activism before going to work in a maternity home. Noting that she had always had "a sort of missionary instinct," Bliss described first working at age eighteen among the Iroquois on a reservation in western New York and then joining the WCTU before she came to work with unmarried mothers at the Chicago Florence Crittenton Anchorage in 1892.[3] Women came and left maternity homes from foreign missionary work as well. The "Personals" section of the *Florence Crittenton Magazine* that charted the comings and goings of Crittenton workers listed several in 1901 "who leave us to go to the foreign field" and others who returned, including a Miss O'Neill, who left a missionary post in Africa to minister to the "wayward" residents of the Los Angeles Crittenton home.[4]

Identifying themselves as evangelicals, women came to maternity homes after "hearing the call" and described their commitment to rescue work as religiously inspired and motivated. Emma Whittemore, founder of the Door of Hope maternity homes, described deliberating with God over the best work for her: "Most earnestly did I desire to know what would be most to His glory. Suddenly the girls on the street came to my mind so forcibly that it was not difficult to almost imagine I could hear the tramp of number-less feet going straight to perdition."[5] The call of the Salvation Army won out over the disapproval of Agnes Wright Dickinson's relatives; from the time she was fifteen, Dickinson felt "that God was calling," and that "there was no other way I could go."[6]

Unmarried mothers were only one among many groups of women deemed by nineteenth-century women reformers to be in need of protection. Whether ministering to prostitutes, widows, homeless women, or single mothers, evangelical women understood their work to be a collective and emphatically missionary effort and one that they were uniquely suited to as women. Over the course of the late eighteenth and nineteenth centuries, piety, virtue, and morality had come to be identified as female qualities, and ones that especially equipped women for benevolent work. Distinguishing this tradition was a belief in the redemptive potential of white middle-class models of domesticity and a desire to translate "feminine" virtues into social policy. Many historians have noted how nineteenth-century female reformers in temperance activism, moral reform societies, and the suffrage movement turned the dominant ideology of gender difference to their advantage, using the rhetoric of domesticity to explain women's unique contribution to social change and, paradoxically, to justify extrafamilial activities and to stake claims to "public" work and space. Seeking to expand their moral guardianship from the home to society, female reformers used the nineteenth-century conflation of "femininity" and "morality" to create a place for themselves in the work of benevolence.[7]

Evangelical women drew on this nineteenth-century tradition to define their own identities and to design maternity homes. When a Crittenton worker in New Haven stated in a promotional pamphlet of 1913 that "the matron carried a mother's heart into her work," or when the Boston Salvation Army home matron celebrated "the value of pure and noble womanhood" as "inestimable to any community," they invoked a gendered language of benevolence and a belief in a uniquely feminine means of reform that was, by then, decades old.[8] More specifically, Kate Barrett argued that training in domestic skills equipped women to run rescue homes when she suggested that "the internal affairs of an institution are largely of a character with which women are more familiar than men," and proclaimed women "superior to men" in "making home-like and proper surroundings in the proper attention and care of children and in the many small details which go to make up the perfection of the whole."[9] The matron of the Philadelphia Crittenton home cited female piety itself as the essential qualification for benevolent work. "It is rather difficult to tell people how to do this work," she wrote. "My only plan is to remember Jesus and His love, and then to act naturally."[10]

For women interested in reform, then, it was enough to "act naturally" and to pursue their instinctive affinity for benevolence. Evangelical women granted men their place as trustees of the homes and in the upper echelons of both the Salvation Army and the National Florence Crittenton Mission, but when one man wrote to Kate Barrett to inquire as to the place of men in rescue work, she responded that although the work attracted the interest of "the best men in the world," even these "best men" should "thoroughly understand the limitations" imposed by their sex and leave the work to women.[11] At times, evangelical women in maternity homes could test the boundaries of domestic ideology, and their rhetoric sometimes resonated with a more self-consciously feminist notion of reform. Writing in 1913, Edith Livingston Smith related her work with unmarried mothers to "the so-called 'Feminist Movement,'" defining that movement as motivated by the belief "that a better world can be made if women generally cooperate in our moral and social problems."[12]

Like other nineteenth-century female reformers, maternity home workers proclaimed their sisterhood with the women under their care. Women active in the social purity and antiprostitution movements had long declared themselves protectors and defenders of the "unfortunate" of their own sex. Self-consciously defining their endeavor as "women's work for women" and articulating an ideology of kinship with all women, evangelical women referred to unmarried mothers as "sisters" and proposed to forge bonds across lines of class and reputation, stressing in their writing their equality with the women under their care.[13] As rescue worker Mary Tinney wrote in 1920, "we are not so far removed morally from these sisters of ours, and who knows how red our sins may be?" Tinney asked evangelical women to "appreciate the fact that under the same given circumstances, we might be as weak as they."[14]

Evangelical women's rhetoric of sisterhood, of course, obscured the hierarchical nature of their relationship with the women under their care. Indeed, although sisterhood suggested an equal relationship across a horizontal divide, Kate Barrett's appeal to "reach down and clasp the hand of some sister and help her to struggle up" revealed the chasm of difference that evangelical women believed separated them from their charges and that would come to complicate their relationship with them.[15] At the same time, their proposal to cross the boundary that separated the "fallen" from the "pure" marked a bold transgression of the Victorian equation of a sexual "fall" with moral and often physical "ruin."

Although evangelical women went to explicit and sometimes exhaustive lengths to underline the gendered nature of reform, they were noticeably mute on the ways in which race, as well as gender, inflected the theory and practice of womanly benevolence and shaped their understanding of themselves and their charges. Hazel Carby has argued perceptively and persuasively that the nineteenth-century "cult of true womanhood" was as much a racial as a gender ideology, operating to define "the parameters within which women were measured and declared to be, or not to be, women," and to mystify the way in which those parameters were set by race.[16] White evangelical reformers invoked racial representations of themselves as sexually pure and refined and their predominantly white charges as redeemable, even as their declarations of a cross-class sisterhood obscured the racial homogeneity of that proposed sorority.

At the same time, however, African-American women founded benevolent institutions for "unprotected women" in their own communities. In her study of black and white visions of social welfare, historian Linda Gordon documents some areas of shared emphasis amid the considerable differences in orientation between black and white women activists, writing that "neither group questioned 'sexual purity' as an appropriate goal for unmarried women."[17] In 1909, W. E. B. Du Bois listed eight homes dedicated "to rescue girls who are already fallen into vice, or liable to."[18] Most notable and enduring among refuges for black single mothers was the Katy Ferguson Home, a New York City shelter founded in 1920. Some African-American women worked within the National Florence Crittenton Mission (NFCM) as well; in 1901, the NFCM president noted that the Alexandria, Virginia, Crittenton home was "the only organized work we have among colored people," but added that "one of the most hopeful features of this work" was that it was "carried on entirely by colored people."[19]

Rescue and maternity homes took their place in a long history of organizing in African-American communities, much of which was initiated and sustained by black women. As Gordon points out, black women reformers' attention to the purity of young women "had profoundly different meanings" than that of white women, and their attempt to aid and protect black single mothers was inseparable from their efforts to "uplift the race."[20] Efforts to provide services to African-American communities—including settlement houses, schools, homes for the elderly, and community centers—intensified in the late nineteenth and early twentieth centuries to fill in the gaps in such services that widened with the expansion of Jim Crow segregation in the South and racism in the North.[21]

Although evangelical women claimed maternity homes as part of the ever-expanding "women's sphere," the largest organization of homes was initiated in 1882 by a man. Known as the "millionaire evangelist," Charles Nelson Crittenton had earned his fortune in the pharmaceutical business but received a divine call to devote himself to rescue work following the death of his young daughter, Florence. Establishing the first home, the Florence Night Mission, in New York City's red-light district, Crittenton held nightly religious services for "outcast girls" to give "spiritual redemption to the most despised of all throughout the centuries—the girl of the street."[22]

Crittenton built his chain of homes through extensive revival tours. Crisscrossing the nation in his personal railroad car, the "Good News," Crittenton proselytized for rescue work with "fallen women" along with more general evangelical fare, and women in several cities were inspired to establish homes in their communities. His close connection with the Women's Christian Temperance Union also generated interest in the Crittenton maternity home movement. An energetic supporter of the temperance movement, Crittenton ran for mayor of New York City in 1883 on the Temperance party ticket. In gratitude for his contributions to the cause, Frances Willard, president of the WCTU, granted him an office in the organization—the first offered to a man—and graciously bestowed upon him the title "Brother of Girls." In 1892, at the WCTU national convention, Crittenton offered to donate five thousand dollars to open five new WCTU rescue homes if they would adopt the Florence Crittenton name.[23] Through this arrangement, Crittenton added homes in Chicago, Denver, Fargo, Norfolk, and Portland to the fourteen homes then in existence; by 1909, the chain had grown to seventy-eight. In 1918, these homes were incorporated into the National Florence Crittenton Mission, and a special act of Congress provided them with a national charter—the first granted to a charitable organization.[24]

As the Crittenton chain was expanding, the Salvation Army, which would build the second largest network of homes for unmarried mothers, was embarking on its own evangelical crusade. William Booth, an itinerant Wesleyan preacher, broke from the Methodist church in 1865 and founded the Salvation Army in England, with the commitment to bring the church to the people through street-corner evangelism. In February 1880, George Railton and "seven Army lassies" formed the first contingent of missionary bands to lead the "United States invasion."[25] By 1890, the Army had spread across the country, with 410 corps in thirty-five states.[26]

Combining religious and social services, the Salvation Army styled itself as both a religious society, with a formal body of doctrines and form of worship, and a community welfare organization. As Commander Eva Booth wrote, "the Salvation Army early in its career realized that an empty stomach and a shivering form were not the citadel for thoughts of Christianity and salvation. It has followed the plan of first putting the body in a condition in which such divine conceptions would be accepted."[27] This dual sense of purpose, and the belief that care of the body necessarily precedes salvation of the soul, shaped the ideology of the Salvation Army's rescue homes, the first of which were founded in England for prostitutes. In 1887, Mrs. Bramwell Booth, daughter-in-law of the Army's founder and wife of the chief of staff, sent one of her officers to the United States to assist in the opening of the first American rescue home in Brooklyn, New York. Within seven years, the Salvation Army had opened fifteen homes in the United States.[28]

Both the Crittenton and the Salvation Army homes were initially loosely defined as rescue homes, sheltering women who were deemed to have been victimized by a range of circumstances. Open to any woman "wishing to leave a Crooked Life," the Florence Night Mission welcomed prostitutes, "wayward girls," and women suspected of "sexual misconduct," as well as unmarried mothers. The Salvation Army homes cast a similarly wide net, catering to "the drunkard, the drug addict, the homeless, the prostitute," and offered shelter "to any girl who needs its protection and who otherwise would be forced along the paths to which only heartbreak, despair, and disgrace can point."[29]

Since evangelicals could not always count on women knocking on rescue home doors, many of the early homes accepted women and girls sent by the courts. Functioning either as temporary houses of detention for women awaiting trial or as places of referral for courts to send delinquent and "predelinquent" girls, some Crittenton and Salvation Army homes formed a quasi-official partnership with the court system by providing an alternative to jail or reform school. The Florence Crittenton Mission of New York City, for example, employed an all-night missionary, who sat in on the night court sessions regularly to "see what service she can render to any of the cases." "Frequently," the mission reported, "she is called upon by the Judge to advise as to the proper disposition to make of the case."[30] This practice became more common as judges accrued discretionary power during the Progressive Era; in some cases, judges were permitted to sentence women to Florence Crittenton and Salvation Army homes.[31]

Maternity home workers valued an alliance with the court for several reasons, not least of which was the legitimacy that such an alliance conferred upon their homes. Evangelical women had reason to hope that a relationship with the court would give their work good publicity. Noting in 1914 that one quarter of all the women received in the Crittenton homes had been referred by the courts, the NFCM president remarked that "this fact should be far reaching in influencing people to assist us in carrying on the work"; it would demonstrate that "the judges and officers of the courts, which always represent the highest degree of intelligence in a community," valued the services of Crittenton homes.[32] Because it ensured a steady flow of clients, an arrangement with the court made financial sense as well, allowing many homes to supplement their income. The New Haven Florence Crittenton home, for example, collected $3.50 a week from the court as board for each woman sent there.[33] Most rescue homes in the early twentieth century relied on private fund-raising and contributions; the weekly stipends provided by the courts could make their financial standing less precarious.

With the exception of women delivered to the homes by the courts, rescue home clientele had to be actively recruited. Workers often left the homes in the early evening and toured the city until two or three o'clock in the morning, appealing to prostitutes and women on the streets to return with them. Emma Whittemore, founder of the Door of Hope homes, adopted a kind of cross-class disguise in her nightly forays onto city streets, explaining that "it was desirable to dress as near like these depraved people themselves as possible; otherwise their inbred suspicion would have resented our appearance and approach."[34] Salvation Army and Crittenton workers stationed themselves at places where women traditionally "went wrong," and in 1913, the Florence Crittenton League of Boston employed a street matron "to look after the girls on the streets, Commons, and other public places."[35] Rescue work offered middle-class women access to city streets otherwise unsanctioned by turn-of-the-century gender and class codes of behavior, and their descriptions of these nightly tours of the urban underworld ring with the excitement of exploring dangerous and foreign terrain.[36]

Both the Crittenton and Salvation Army homes turned from rescue work primarily with prostitutes to cater almost exclusively to unmarried mothers in the early decades of the twentieth century. Kate Waller Barrett played a leading role in hastening this change in the NFCM. Trained as a physician at the Women's Medical College of Georgia, Barrett had done pastoral work with local prostitutes in her husband's Episcopal parish in Kentucky. Describing her first meeting with an unmarried mother as a sort of conversion experience, she opened a maternity home in Atlanta in 1893. Barrett had met Charles Crittenton that year at a Christian workers convention in Atlantic City, New Jersey, and appealed to him for building funds. Crittenton contributed five thousand dollars to Barrett's home, which became the fifth in the growing Florence Crittenton chain.

With this deal, Crittenton and Barrett forged a partnership. Crittenton asked Barrett to help him organize his homes into a national organization, and in 1896, Barrett became the superintendent of the newly formed National Florence Crittenton Mission, of which Crittenton was president. Busy with his national revival tour, Crittenton left Barrett to supervise and guide the homes, and when he died in 1909, she took charge. As president of the NFCM from then until her death in 1925, Barrett shifted the emphasis of the homes from the rescue and redemption of prostitutes to residential and maternity care for single mothers.[37] Since their founding, Crittenton homes had admitted unmarried mothers; under Barrett's direction, maternity care became the organization's primary function. The Crittenton homes did not make this transition alone. Most rescue homes that began as shelters for prostitutes shifted to maternity care for unmarried mothers in the years between 1910 and 1920.[38]

The practical, bottom-line fact of empty beds explains in part the shift from serving prostitutes to helping unmarried mothers. Rescue workers had to rely either on prostitutes committing themselves voluntarily to the homes, which apparently did not occur often enough to ensure a steady supply of clients, or on the power of evangelical persuasion during nightly walking tours of brothel districts. Even if they were successful in appealing to prostitutes to return to the homes with them, rescue workers had a difficult time persuading them to stay for the length of time deemed necessary for redemptive efforts to take hold. One Crittenton worker recalled that "the money and effort involved were found to be all out of relation to the tangible results achieved," and for this reason, "the workers turned more and more toward the erring girl rather than to the confirmed professional."[39] Rather than soliciting prostitutes on the streets, evangelical women had reason to hope that unmarried mothers would solicit them. The superintendent of the Norfolk Crittenton home who wrote in 1926 that "women do not voluntarily restrict their own liberty unless forced to do so by illegitimate pregnancy" revealed the pragmatic thinking behind the transition from rescue to maternity work.[40] Unlike prostitutes, unmarried mothers offered, in the minds of rescue workers at least, a compliant population more amenable to a longer stay in the homes and, once there, more receptive to the evangelical message.

The shift from rescue work with prostitutes to maternity care for unmarried mothers is more fully understood in the broader ideological context of

the antiprostitution crusade and the changes in that movement that occurred around the First World War. As anxiety about sexual morality
accelerated to a fever pitch in the 1910s, public concern turned toward the
problem of illegitimacy, in part out of fear of rising illegitimacy rates
overseas and the potential threat of an increase in the number of illegitimate children at home. Fearing that the patriotic appeal of men in uniform
would swell the ranks of unmarried mothers, Salvation Army and Crittenton workers shifted into high gear during the war.[41] At such an unsettled,
emotional time, one Crittenton worker warned, "any agency whose work is
primarily to deal with those who are drifting from their moorings is sure to
find its work doubled."[42]

The wartime specter of the syphilitic prostitute also encouraged rescue
workers to turn their attention to unmarried mothers. Historian Ruth
Rosen has described the ways in which prostitution stood at the center of a
matrix of Progressive Era anxieties, including disease, urban crime, and
commercialization. As the image of the prostitute shifted from tragic victim
of a bad environment and lustful men to predatory disease-carrier, hardened harlot, and domestic enemy, the state moved in to deal with prostitutes not in the evangelical style of rescue workers but in the coercive
style of the police. With the criminalization of prostitution and the closing of
red-light districts, rescue workers joined in the general rejection of the
prostitute and turned to another fallen woman—the unmarried mother—
who better conformed to their notions of the role.[43]

The wartime campaign that targeted prostitutes as threats to the fitness
of America's fighting men also spurred "protective" work aimed at the "girl
problem" that reflected widespread anxiety about the danger posed by
female sexuality unleashed. Maternity home evangelicals invoked the com-
plementary watchwords of the war era—prevention and protection—to
redefine their mission, and they raised the twin specters of prostitution and
venereal disease to emphasize the importance of their preventive work. As
a Boston Crittenton worker wrote, maternity homes existed to protect
society "from moral and physical contagion. We do not wish immorality to
spread, nor do we wish venereal disease to become more prevalent."[44] The
Chicago Florence Crittenton Anchorage's slogan, "Every girl saved is a
public asset. Every girl lost is a public menace," resonated with the fears of
the day and testified to the fundamental shift in the aim of rescue homes
from saving the girl to saving society.[45]

But even as reformers turned their attention to unmarried mothers,
prostitution remained their central point of reference. In describing their
work as preventive, evangelicals posited a slippery slope theory that linked

their new attention to unmarried mothers to their rescue work with prostitutes. According to the most popular scenario, unmarried mothers were the victims of failed love affairs, who, condemned by society and family, with no resources and no place to turn for help, would inevitably descend by degrees into prostitution. One woman articulated this new theory of causation in 1915, claiming that "they do not become mothers because they have become depraved, but they frequently become depraved because they have become mothers. The 'underworld' is full of women whom society cast out because they bore children without society's license to do so."[46] Kate Barrett agreed, writing that "the vast majority of street girls began their downward course by being deceived, and no door being opened to them. . . . they fell deeper and deeper."[47]

Evangelical workers in rescue homes now aimed to open that door or, as one put it, "a sort of side *trap* . . . to catch the girls that are going so surely down to perdition."[48] Salvation Army officer Mrs. Bramwell Booth stated in 1921, "It is far better . . . to prevent people from falling into the abyss than to rescue them when they have fallen." Work with prostitutes served as "the ambulance at the foot of the precipice"; attention to unmarried mothers could provide "the fence at the top to keep them from falling down."[49] Robert South Barrett, son of Kate Barrett and president of the NFCM after his mother's death in 1925, cast preventive work with unmarried mothers in similar terms: "No longer must we be content to simply mop up the floor but must turn off the spigots. No longer must we be the ambulance and relief corps that care for the victims that fall off the cliff but must put guards at the top of the cliff to warn the passersby of the dangers that confront them."[50]

The metaphors that abounded in evangelical descriptions of the plight of unmarried mothers—cliff edges, floods, slippery slopes—underlined the precariousness of female respectability and the stakes involved in its maintenance. By these descriptions, evangelical workers contributed to the construction of a new boundary that divided good women from bad. Not yet fallen, but standing dangerously close to the edge, unmarried mothers supplanted prostitutes as the object of evangelical ministrations.

"THE OLD, OLD STORY": THE EVANGELICAL SCRIPT OF SEDUCTION
AND ABANDONMENT

Evangelical women might have reasonably hoped that unmarried mothers would compose a more compliant clientele than prostitutes. Nevertheless, like prostitutes, unmarried mothers were living embodiments of illicit sex;

indeed, pregnancy rendered their transgression disturbingly visible and inarguable. Perhaps before evangelical women could contemplate the task of building institutions to rescue unmarried mothers, they faced the problem of understanding their new charges and representing them to the public. Evangelical women struggled mightily to incorporate the illicit sexuality of single mothers into an ideology of female benevolence that emphasized sisterly sympathy and solidarity.

They did so, in part, by returning to a familiar reference point and reading from an old script. The melodramatic tale of seduction and abandonment that charted the trials of virtuous women at the hands of villainous men—one of the most popular themes of street literature, the penny press, and scandal journalism—had been a narrative strategy used by female reformers earlier in the nineteenth century in their efforts to reclaim and redeem prostitutes. In an effort to garner sympathy for "fallen women," reformers popularized an image of the prostitute as the victim of male lust forced to live a life of shame.[51] Stressing the sexual victimization of women by men and criticizing the double standard that forced women to pay the moral price for a fall surely initiated by a man, women reformers turned the literary convention of seduction and abandonment to reform purposes.

Having worked in homes that had served prostitutes, Crittenton and Salvation Army reformers were fluent in the narrative convention of seduction and abandonment. The change in their clientele, then, required no substantial discursive leap. In fact, the story of seduction and abandonment might more easily have accommodated the unmarried mother than the prostitute, since her sexual transgression could be (and, in its literary representation, usually was) limited to a single episode. Appearing mainly in publicity brochures but also in the unpublished records of maternity homes, these stories, emphasizing female sexual vulnerability and passivity in the face of male sexual aggressiveness and will, were virtually interchangeable. All drew heavily on melodramatic conventions of plot, style, and characterization, with good and evil sharply drawn.[52] The unmarried mother who had been "lured into sin, robbed of her virtue, and left by the man who pretended he loved her, either to live or die whatever her lot chanced to be," formed the model for countless stories in this hyperbolic genre of male sexual irresponsibility and aggressiveness and female vulnerability and victimization.[53] When a Salvation Army matron wrote in 1912 that "one night, the old, old story of a strong man and a weak girl was repeated," she began a tale told and retold by maternity home workers, and assumed that her evangelical sisters would be able to fill in the gaps.[54] Less abbreviated renditions of the "old, old story" repeated catch-phrases—unmarried mothers were "more sinned against than sinning," they "loved not wisely but too well"—that suggested that when confronted by out-of-wedlock pregnancy, evangelical women might comfort themselves with familiar lines. As a worker in the Los Angeles Florence Crittenton home confidently wrote of one woman's story, "it differed not a whit from hundreds of stories. She had loved too well and trusted overmuch."[55]

Unqualified passivity on the part of the woman marked all these stories. Although they occasionally were descriptions of rape, these tales more often blurred the line between coercion and consent. Significantly, however, the woman in the story of betrayal who was "lured into sin by a pretense of love and the promise of a happy home" was as fully absolved from responsibility and devoid of sexual agency as in a case of rape.[56] Writing in 1910, reformer Annie Allen compared the degree of responsibility of the unmarried mother to that of "a baby" who "may wreck a railroad train and not even be naughty." She explained that "choice—volition—must enter into a wrong deed before the doer can be called wicked."[57] And in these stories, female volition rarely made an appearance. As Salvation Army Major Julia Thomas asserted, "Natural womanhood is modest and virtuous, but there are circumstances, conditions, and temptations that entrap and drag downward."[58] Women who found their way into maternity homes and into the stories of their evangelical keepers had been lured, ensnared, and deceived into out-of-wedlock pregnancy.

Underscoring this female passivity, evangelical women told many tales in which drugs, potions, alcohol, and knock-out drops compromised the resolve and often the consciousness of their heroines. "Girls are often given drugged drinks," the NFCM reported in 1927, and "chlorodyne is said to be widely used and is very accessible."[59] Portentously resonant in this period, the specters of drugs and drink recalled the genre of white slave narratives and exaggerated the images of innocent womanhood and male villainy.[60]

Inseparable from the heroine's passivity was her respectability. The women depicted by evangelicals were, at heart, good girls. The Salvation Army in 1903 thus characterized the residents of their homes as "carefully reared, most of them innocent of all pre-conceived evil," and made it clear that the ranks of "womanhood's army of the fallen" might include "somebody's sisters, somebody's daughters, once pure as the driven snow."[61] The matron of the San Francisco Crittenton home took care to point out in 1918 that "our girls come from the well-ordered home" and share "good principles, right intentions."[62]

But how did good girls become single mothers? Betrayal was the explanatory and unifying theme in these stories. Crucial to every melodrama, and present in nearly every story of seduction and abandonment told by evangelical women, was the villain. These tales were filled with rogues, scoundrels, and unscrupulous cads who typically promised to marry the woman, lured her into sex "by the most infamous treachery," and then callously abandoned her.[63] Counterposed against the dormant sexuality of women, male sexuality was animalistic, brutalizing, and predatory. By the logic of the evangelical equation, "man is nearly always, in the first instance, the tempter, woman the tempted. The motive that impels him is the lowest kind of animal indulgence, while the motives that impel her seldom descend to the low level of his."[64]

Although evangelical women's depiction of seduction and abandonment as an "old, old story" characterized male sexual aggression and female sexual passivity as transhistorical, historically specific circumstances led them to represent out-of-wedlock pregnancy in these terms. The story of seduction and abandonment offers clues as to how they understood their work in maternity homes and the women under their care. Some historians have focused on the depiction in melodrama of class difference and the tension between the country and the city.[65] Rooted as they were in the tradition of nineteenth-century popular melodrama, many of these narratives staged dramas of class exploitation, pairing the respectable working-class girl with the irresponsible and evil aristocrat. They were often populated by wealthy libertines, as rich in worldly knowledge as they were in the resources to lure young women of few worldly goods. In one story told in a Crittenton journal, class inequity occupied center stage. When "Lettie," a farm girl pregnant by her beau "Lemont Ferrier," a "stylish, well-dress gentleman," asks him whether he will marry her, Ferrier responds, "'My dear girl! What nonsense you are talking! Of course I won't. How could I? You must remember, Lettie, I have a position to maintain. My parents would not consent to it even if society would.'" And in case the reader failed to discern the class message of this tale, Ferrier explained further: "'You see, my girl, I belong to what they call an *aristocratic clique*—a certain class of well-to-do people who entertain the most ideal ambitions for their kind, especially in matrimony.'"[66]

As in the story of Lettie and Lemont, the battle between rural innocence and urban corruption, so popular in nineteenth-century fiction, persisted in many of these tales. In some, the city was as severely indicted as the villain, sometimes replacing his role as the dark seductive force that dragged the girl downward. The heroines of these stories were often from the farm: "The prospects and allurements of the city here in many cases brought them away from associations and restraining influences whose value they discover only after bad company has led them astray," one Salvation Army worker noted.[67] Another Salvation Army matron told a similar story in 1914: "Henrietta grew up from childhood as almost any young woman might. Nothing transpired to change her simple, country-bred existence until suddenly, like thousands of others, she decided to live in a distant city . . . and soon she found herself, suddenly and without warning, swept into a life of sin and shame."[68]

Although maternity home evangelicals generally stayed within the lines of conventional melodrama, they imbued those narratives with meanings of their own, and their "old, old story" was as marked by gender as by class. Transforming melodrama from a language of class protest into a politicized discourse to express anger at male sexual license and to denounce the injustices of the sexual double standard, evangelical women railed against the convention that labeled women "fallen" while absolving men of all guilt.[69] The NFCM in 1899 called for "a change in public sentiment," from one in which "society closes its doors in her face and points the finger of scorn as she passes by" while receiving the man in good society.[70] Evangelical women named seduction and abandonment "not a crime against the woman, but a crime against the sex," and proclaimed their sisterhood with "fallen women."[71] Turner spared no sympathy for men responsible for out-of-wedlock pregnancy when she declared, "Let them suffer. If there are to be trials, what sacred exemption has man over woman, that he alone should escape them? What right has he to secure his bodily comfort at such a cost to her in body and soul?" Turner decried the injustice of a society in which "he whose conduct is the baser by all this difference at risk, is allowed to keep his place in society only mildly blamed, while she is . . . crushed by a punishment so cruel, so pursuing, so inexorable, that a return to virtue is almost impossible."[72]

The script of seduction and abandonment also allowed evangelical women to dramatize their solidarity with their working-class "sisters" under their care. Whereas men appeared in conventional melodramatic tales as fathers, protectors, and rescuers, evangelical women appropriated those brave and benevolent roles for themselves, transforming the narratives from stories in which "the seduced maiden became only a cipher in conflicts between men" into tales in which they cast themselves as the saviors of their betrayed sisters.[73] Melodramatic tales emphasized the bond between fallen women and their rescuers and at the same time situated evangelical women in a hierarchy that would inform and pervade their relationship with unmarried mothers.

Since many of these stories appeared in publications intended to solicit donations for maternity homes, evangelical women undoubtedly exploited them for their promotional appeal. Raising funds for the controversial work of caring for unmarried mothers was a difficult undertaking at the turn of the century, and evangelical women hoped that the stories would inspire sympathy on the part of potential donors. But melodrama was the private as well as the public language used by evangelical women, and the fact that they invoked the same literary conventions in their private writing suggests that the meaning of the "old, old story" went beyond public relations.

Historian Judith Walkowitz offers a way to understand the profound appeal of the story of seduction and abandonment to evangelical women. In her study of the Men and Women's Club in late-nineteenth-century England—a group of "middle-class radical-liberals, socialists, and feminists" who came together to "talk about sex"—Walkowitz argues that the club's female members called on a melodramatic script of sexual danger to aid in the difficult project of constructing a public female language of sexuality.[74] There is some evidence that the "old, old story" offered evangelical women a way to talk about what, to their generation and class, was literally "unspeakable." At their annual conference of 1928, for example, NFCM workers looked back to the time of their founding some three decades earlier, when "it was well nigh impossible to discuss sex problems in public or before mixed audiences. The topic of illegitimacy was tabooed and people dared to talk only in whispers about evidences of immorality and vice. The words 'prostitute,' 'illegitimate,' 'bastard,' and similar expressions found no place in the vocabulary of people of breeding."[75] Women who had trouble speaking about the women under their care found the words in the language of melodrama. In his introduction to Lillian Yeo's memoirs of her work at the House of Mercy, a book filled with seduced maidens, Bishop Alfred Harding explained that "it is because she has adopted this way of telling about her work that she has been able to handle as she has a subject in itself so delicate, with entire faithfulness to the facts, but at the same time with such womanly reserve and tenderness and sympathy as her little book reveals."[76] Melodrama authorized Yeo and other women like her, quite literally, to speak about illicit sex and, at least as important, to create and control a public discourse of sexuality.

Of course, some aspects of maternity home life fit awkwardly and sometimes not at all within the boundaries of the "old, old story." In composing the selection criteria for maternity homes, evangelical women implicitly acknowledged that not all unmarried mothers had been seduced. Rules against accepting "second offenders" and references to women whose "highly sexed" nature unsuited them for maternity home life make clear their recognition that some women did not fit the melodramatic convention of female passivity and innocence. Although the story also depended on sisterly ties between evangelicals and unmarried mothers, relations with maternity home residents often stretched sisterhood to its limits and beyond. One worker at the Jersey City Door of Hope admitted reluctantly, "It is easy to love the babies, but it is not always so easy . . . to love some of the unloveable mothers."[77] Indeed, the story of seduction and abandonment itself was riddled with contradictions, the most glaring of which threatened to call the maternity home enterprise itself into question: if unmarried mothers were as blameless and sexually passive as the tales made them out to be, why were they in such dire need of the kind of redemption offered by evangelical women? These contradictions pointed to a troubling ambivalence on the part of evangelical women about those under their care: were unmarried mothers good girls or bad? Not least among its uses, the melodramatic narrative offered to smooth over and contain these contradictions or at least to hold them in check.

In addition to the discursive and ideological functions melodrama served, it is important to remember that there was a literalness to the script of seduction and abandonment. However stylized, these stories resonated as deeply as they did, in part, because of the very real sexual vulnerability of women, a vulnerability that probably increased with the combination of geographical mobility, urban anonymity, and the new styles of courtship being forged by urban working-class men and women at the turn of the century.[78] The matron of the Des Moines Salvation Army home testified to this vulnerability in 1901 when she admitted a new resident into the home, pregnant by "a young man who makes it his business to ruin every girl he can." She went on, "This is the third girl we have had that he is the father of the child. I don't think Edna has been a bad girl. What shall be done with such men!"[79] Confronted by the victims of this vulnerability, and, more disturbingly, by the changing sexual mores of working-class women under their care, evangelical women used the script of seduction and abandonment to fix single women's sexuality firmly within the comprehensible lineaments of the "old, old story" that might explain women who had ruptured the conventional narrative of nineteenth-century femininity. In the language of melodrama, evangelicals found a way to transform a changing and unsettling world into comprehensible patterns.

"HOMES IN THE TRUEST SENSE": MATERNITY HOMES AND THE
ARCHITECTURE OF REDEMPTION

Evangelical women drew on the nineteenth-century tradition of womanly benevolence in constructing their own identity as reformers and that of their charges as seduced and abandoned. That tradition also provided them with a blueprint for creating a redemptive environment in the homes they founded and staffed. Emotion, intuition, empathy, and piety had come to be considered particularly feminine qualities, and these were the tools of the trade that evangelical women brought to maternity homes. They were confident that, given a steady diet of religious and domestic training, sisterly sympathy, motherly care, and middle-class guidance, their charges could be saved and returned to "the glory of their womanhood."[80]

Evangelical women conceived of maternity homes as primarily redemptive. "Little or no gain is effected in the removal of a woman from the outward conditions of a vicious life, if her heart remains unchanged," explained Evangeline Booth, who judged rescue work a failure "unless it creates in them a burning desire for a new and altogether different life."[81] Evangelical women set out not only to shelter but to reclaim and redeem their "less fortunate sisters."

"If in the set-up of your work you have not given God first place in rebuilding the character of these girls," Mrs. W. E. F. Taylor wrote in 1933, "you are simply helping them build their house upon the sand, and when the winds of criticism and adversity blow, and the storms of temptation and trial beat upon their house, it will fall."[82] Religion was the foundation on which evangelical women built their redemptive program, and maternity home workers measured their own success by the rate of religious conversion confessed by the unmarried mothers under their care. Crittenton workers matched Salvationists in evangelical fervor, declaring that "our Florence Crittenton homes will never reach their highest ideals unless they are *Christian* homes. . . . They are failures unless they send out from their doors girls and young women who have Christ in their hearts and who will be sustained in their battle with the world by His power."[83]

Religion informed every aspect of maternity homes, from their overarching purpose to the details of everyday life within their walls. As the superintendent of the Boston Crittenton home explained in 1915, "the goal of our effort is a life rounded out into Christian womanhood, and all our equipment, our daily regime in its minutest detail, are but the means to that supreme end."[84] Days spent by unmarried mothers in early-twentieth-century maternity homes were punctuated by religious services. In Salvation Army homes in 1912, "short prayer-meetings are held night and morning, and on Sunday afternoon a special meeting is convened, when the girls are particularly pleaded with to confess and forsake their sins."[85] Although NFCM president Robert Barrett believed that "mechanical or rote memorizing of songs, psalms, or chapters, without understanding, had better be avoided," he advised that religious services in Crittenton homes "should consist of morning and evening prayers, grace or recitation of Scripture verses at the meals, and a Sunday afternoon service."[86]

Maternity home schedules suggest that when unmarried mothers were not praying they were working. Kate Barrett testified to the close connection between work and religion in the redemptive scheme of maternity homes when she declared laundry "a means of grace."[87] Boasting that "there are no drones in our Home," and that "every girl is expected to do her share in each department of the work unless she is physically disabled from doing so," Barrett advised Crittenton workers to fill the days of the women under their care with constant activity.[88] Expected to do the basic work of the homes, including cooking, cleaning, and laundering, maternity home residents were subjected to a fairly heavy regime, usually spending seven to ten hours a day in domestic chores.

Evangelical women found that the redemptive and the remunerative functions of work often conveniently coincided, and some used profits from the work of the mothers to support the running of their homes. Many maternity homes took in sewing from the outside, and Boston Crittenton workers took great pride in generating enough money through the laundry work of their residents to pay all the running expenses of the home except rent. Work in maternity homes varied by region. Homes in northeastern cities took in sewing and laundry, and the Salvation Army home in Birmingham, Alabama, located on the outskirts of the city, kept a cow, chickens, and a large garden, all of which were worked for profit.[89]

Work in maternity homes was also useful in simply keeping the residents busy and out of trouble. "There is nothing that settles a restless, high-strung spirit like weariness of the flesh," Kate Barrett wrote, adding that "much of the restlessness and many of the mischievous pranks which bring our homes into ill repute would be prevented if we were wiser in utilizing the animal spirits of our charges in some useful and profitable manner."[90] The Chicago Florence Crittenton Anchorage took Barrett's advice; the board noted in 1913 that "all felt if the girls could be employed at something there would be less trouble and less mischief among them" and decided to employ a woman to teach the girls sewing and "fancy work."[91]

Evangelical women were quick to point out that life in maternity homes included more than work and prayer, and most of the homes boasted carefully planned recreation programs. Few workers in early-twentieth-century homes elaborated on the details of these programs—some mentioned libraries full of edifying books, music hours, and exercise yards—but all invested play with redemptive and reformative purpose. Recreation

was intended to reorient unmarried mothers from heterosocial to homosocial activities and to introduce them to quieter, more decorous forms of
leisure than those they were presumably familiar with. Kate Barrett encouraged Crittenton workers to interest unmarried mothers in "the simple
Home pleasures that we give them," with the goal that they would eventually be "entirely weaned from the reckless life of excitement in which
they have lived in the past."[92]

Domesticity also occupied a central place in the redemption of unmarried
mothers. Believing family and home to be especially curative for women
who "have never known what it was to have a home in the truest sense"
and who had so radically flouted domestic conventions, evangelical women
sought to construct physical facilities that would contribute to their redemption and refinement.[93] Like other reformers of their day, evangelical women were anxious to avoid an association with the cold and incarcerational "institution." Seeking instead to make each home "a home in
the truest sense," evangelical women envisioned and designed maternity
homes in ways that reflected their faith in the redemptive power of domesticity.[94] Kate Barrett thus instructed those who wished to establish a
Crittenton home to select a structure "which breathes 'Home' from every
angle," advising Crittenton workers to "remember with what fastidious
care we try to keep our own daughter's room the most attractive in the
house." Reminding them that "the purity of the furnishings" was "emblem-
atic of the purity of her who accepts it," Barrett urged workers to use "the
same watchful care" when planning and decorating the bedrooms of unmarried mothers.[95]

Descriptions of the homes testify to close attention to domestic detail.
Leading an imaginary visitor through a Salvation Army home, an evangelical tour guide lovingly described the "polished floors and snowy beds and
stiff pillow shams, gipsy tables bearing pot plants, and white curtained windows."[96] Indeed, the homes appealed so strongly to the tastes of middle-
class women that "a leading woman of the Professional Women's League"
was so enthusiastic after her four-day tour of a Salvation Army maternity
home that she declared, "I'm almost tempted to do something to be sent
here!"[97]

For those women who had done something to be sent to maternity
homes, domesticity demanded their energetic participation. Training in the
womanly arts supplemented training in religion and industrial habits to
complete the evangelical strategy of redemption, and lessons in cooking,
sewing, laundering, ironing, and child care were offered in every home.
Evangelical women measured single mothers' progress toward true wom-

anhood according to their acquisition of these domestic skills. "We believe that every lady should know how to cook, wash, and iron," Kate Barrett explained, "and since we expect our girls to be ladies in the highest and truest sense, they must learn to do these things and do them well."[98]

If maternity homes were to be "homes in the truest sense," evangelical women believed that their residents must become "in a true sense family."[99] Stretching the domestic metaphor still further, the workers sought to create surrogate families in the homes, envisioning themselves as "mothers" to their "children," the inmates. Evangelical women often described unmarried mothers as "motherless," metaphorically, if not literally. A New Haven Crittenton worker claimed that "surely the primary reason for illegitimacy is lack of true motherhood, most of our girls being motherless or worse than motherless since babyhood."[100] The matron of the Baltimore Crittenton home thus recommended that a matron be "a mother to these lost girls. In all her dealings with them she should make this question the test of her actions: What would I do were it my own daughter?"[101] The language of maternity at once naturalized and disguised relations of power. In prescribing these familial roles, evangelical women sanctioned a hierarchical relationship of authority and discipline as well as love and nurture; as one Crittenton matron noted, the evangelical "mother" must "love well enough to chide sometimes for the good of the children."[102]

Of course, it was much easier to take good, essentially respectable girls into the family that evangelical women imagined they were creating. And the selection criteria in most maternity homes, giving preference to those women who could most easily pass as the real daughters of evangelicals, were designed to separate the "good" from the "bad." Attempting to limit their clientele to young, usually white women who were, in the terms of the matrons, "first offenders," evangelical women tried to weed out those who might have tested the limits of their sisterly generosity.

Evangelicals endeavored to keep their clientele as homogeneous as possible. Robert Barrett stressed the difficulty of doing "good permanent work" with women of widely differing ages. Arguing that those over twenty-five years "have problems that are entirely different from girls of sixteen or eighteen," and were "more difficult to control, are unwilling to stay the prescribed period, and cannot be trained as effectively as the younger girl," Barrett advised restricting Crittenton homes to unmarried mothers under twenty-five years of age.[103]

The early homes also strived to be racially homogeneous. The NFCM noted that "the handling of girls of mixed races in the same institution is difficult" and declared it "wise to restrict admission to girls of one color."[104]

This one color, with very few exceptions, was white. Some homes admitted black women on a quota basis, such as the Chicago Salvation Army home, which noted that although "colored cases are accepted," an attempt was made to "keep the number comparatively low," usually four or five.[105]

Selection was perhaps most carefully dictated by sexual experience and morality. Because most evangelical women agreed with the Crittenton worker in Little Rock, Arkansas, who asserted that "certain types of girls should not be brought into contact with deserving girls who have unfortunately erred," most maternity homes made it their policy to accept only "first offenders."[106] Kate Barrett explained that it was Crittenton policy not to receive a woman with a second illegitimate child, "mainly because of the bad influence which this might have upon girls who are in the institution for the first time, also because it is questioned whether a worker can handle a girl satisfactorily a second time if she fails the first time to leave an impress which would prevent a second lapse."[107] Bramwell Booth got at the heart of the rationale behind the Salvation Army selection policy when he wrote that "the greatest care must be taken to prevent the use of the Army's institutions by unprincipled women who may wish to use them when in distress or difficulty, but who have no intention to reform their lives."[108]

These criteria of selection recalled older distinctions made by private and public charitable organizations between the "worthy" and the "unworthy," the "deserving" and the "undeserving" poor. Embedded in the selection policies of maternity homes, as with these earlier distinctions, were pragmatic considerations of success rates. Emma Booth Tucker of the Salvation Army proposed that preference be given to those "most likely to respond to the loving call of our blessed Lord and Master."[109] Despite Booth's insistence that "this does not imply that those cases which appear easy to help are to be preferred," the admission policies functioned to limit the clientele to a group of women who seemed most promising, most easily reconcilable with evangelical notions of fallen women, and most receptive to the redemptive message of the homes. Preferring to admit women "who can best profit by the help rendered" and who expressed "a genuine desire to do right," workers tried to select women who were predisposed to success, as measured by the evangelical standard of religious conversion.[110]

Maternity home rules followed from this broad-reaching redemptive program. Although Evangeline Booth insisted that "we have no cast-iron rules," and that "our Home in no sense partakes of the nature of a reformatory, house of correction, or prison," the lives of the residents were governed by a welter of regulations, the most basic, universal, and ultimately contentious of which concerned length of stay.[111] Believing "the upbuilding of character" to be "slow work," most maternity homes required the women to stay as long as necessary for redemption to take hold and stick.[112] In the early years, the length of time was typically indeterminate but long. The Florence Crittenton Anchorage of Chicago noted in 1928 that "if a girl remains six months, or a year if it is necessary, the work will be more permanent."[113] Many homes required unmarried mothers to sign an agreement to remain in the institution for a given period as a condition of admission.[114]

A maternity home resident could expect most aspects of her life—the way she wore her hair, the visitors she received, her mail—to come under the close scrutiny of her matron. Some homes permitted no visitors, others only female relatives; residents ordinarily could not leave the grounds unchaperoned. In the Wauwatosa, Wisconsin, Salvation Army home, unmarried mothers had to sign a form stating, "For the better protection of myself and others, while I am an inmate of the Salvation Army Women's Home and Hospital, I agree that my letters and all other mail matter directed to me, shall be opened and read by the superintendent in charge and all improper letters shall be withheld. I also agree that all letters written by me, shall be subject to like inspection."[115] The regulation and censorship of letters was a common practice; evangelical women in most homes read and often withheld incoming and outgoing mail.

Even the habits, style, and dress of residents came under evangelical jurisdiction. "Profane language, slang phrases, and all coarse jesting are strictly prohibited," the NFCM dictated, suggesting that the purpose behind some rules was to strip women of a working-class style that middle-class matrons associated with moral and sexual laxity.[116] Although they viewed dress through judgmental middle-class lenses, their attention to its significance was not completely off the mark, for as historian Christine Stansell has argued, "fancy dress signified a rejection of proper feminine behavior and duties. For the girl who donned fine clothes, dress was an emblem of an estimable erotic maturity."[117] Regulations regarding dress were accordingly strict. Kate Barrett, reminding Crittenton workers that "a fondness for dress has often been the cause of a woman's downfall, and in no way is her looseness of morals shown in a more pronounced manner than in her style of dress after her downfall," called for "simplicity of dress, with extreme neatness."[118] Lillian Yeo of the House of Mercy agreed, writing that "of course we put our foot down good and hard on anything that smacks of studied conspicuousness: silk stockings, extreme arrangement of the hair, paint, powder, jewelry, and the like."[119] Convinced that a working-class "excess" in dress and style was causally related to the circumstances that brought women to maternity homes, evangelical women envisioned uniforms as middle-class correctives. The blue dress, white apron, and cap worn by Inwood House residents, and that of Crittenton residents, tailored of "a seven-cent gingham, neatly made, rustling in its spic and spanness," reflected the hope that a change of clothes might help change the woman.[120]

Despite their faith in their elaborate redemptive program, evangelical women looked with some foreboding to the time when the unmarried mother would leave the home. Even if, through a regime of religion, work, and domesticity, workers succeeded in "changing the heart" of a resident, there was no guarantee that she would be able to resist temptation after she left. Thus, evangelical women worked to extend their influence beyond the walls of the maternity home and to fortify the unmarried mother for life after her departure.

"To bring about marriage with the men who were the occasions of their downfall . . . has always been one of the methods of securing the future of our girls," the Florence Crittenton Mission of New Haven recorded in 1913, and "in almost every case it has proved to be the wise and happy solution of all difficulties."[121] Until the mid-1910s, many maternity homes viewed marriage as the ultimate guarantor of redemption. It was, of course, ideal if the father of the child "stepped forward to do the right thing," but marriage to almost any man, it seems, was preferable to no marriage at all. In 1904, the New Haven Florence Crittenton home celebrated the marriage of one of their inmates "brought about in a most unlooked for manner." A man answering an advertisement placed by the home seeking jobs as domestic servants for its residents told the matron that he was not in the market for a maid, "'but it is a wife I want.'" The matron arranged for him to meet the residents of the home, he made his choice, and "the marriage was brought about within a very short time."[122] Most homes, however, in the early twentieth century abandoned the practice of encouraging women to marry the fathers of their children. As one Salvation Army matron wrote in 1915, "I seldom advise the marriage of the girl to her betrayer, for . . . a life of misery is sure to follow," as "deceit is a poor foundation for good marriage."[123] Although most women left maternity homes single, some matrons dispensed wedding rings and advised the mother to assume a married name.[124]

If maternity home residents could not be redeemed through marriage, they might still benefit from the purifying influence of motherhood, seen by evangelical women as a powerful rehabilitative tool. Convinced that nurturing the maternal bond was one of the most effective methods of guaranteeing that unmarried mothers would conduct themselves responsibly and avoid moral relapse once released from the home, evangelicals insisted that every effort be made to keep mother and child together. "It is a dangerous thing to take an infant away from a mother of this type," asserted Lilian Clarke in 1913. "It is saving her *reputation* at the expense of her *character*. If deprived of this powerful motive and influence toward an upright life, a daily safeguard from temptation, the empty, craving heart is like the house swept and garnished, ready for the evil spirits to come in and take possession."[125] Even though conceived out of wedlock, then, a baby—"nature's rescue- and miracle-worker"—might facilitate the ultimate redemption of the unmarried mother and deter another fall.[126] "There is a God-implanted instinct of motherhood in every woman's heart that needs only to be aroused to be one of the strongest incentives to right living," Barrett maintained.[127] Similarly, the Salvation Army found that "responsibility for her baby is one of the best steadying and uplifting influences that can be brought to bear on the mother."[128]

Some evangelicals believed that encouraging unmarried mothers to keep their babies might do more than arouse redeeming maternal instincts. When sterilization gained popularity in the 1920s and 1930s in the eugenic campaign to control the spread of "feeblemindedness," NFCM General Superintendent Reba Smith opposed sterilizing "normal" girls not because doing so would deprive them of their right to have children but because "the demands and pleasures of family life drive out such things as the sex urge more than anything else."[129] Both Crittenton and Salvation Army homes required the prospective resident to sign a contract promising to keep her child before being admitted.[130] This commitment to keep mother and child together—one of the most sacred of maternity home policies—could and presumably often did take coercive forms, but it also gave evangelical sanction to a potentially radical alternative to the patriarchal family. Although Kate Barrett held foremost "that Trinity which God intended, father, mother, and child," she advanced a second option—"that beautiful Trinity which is so potent—Mother, Child, and Home."[131]

Endorsing fatherless families was a bold gesture on the part of evangelical women in the early twentieth century, but the economic vulnerability of a woman who had to support herself and a baby presented no small practical problem. Maternity home workers made an effort to secure paid employment for unmarried mothers when they left the homes, though, of course, not just any occupation would do. The Door of Hope matron who, in 1921, pronounced the employment prospects of a resident "poor, except in her own line of vaudeville actress," suggested that evangelical women had specific occupations in mind for unmarried mothers after they left the home.[132] Many evangelicals believed that the domestic training given in maternity homes could serve the vocational as well as redemptive needs of former residents, offering perhaps the only employment that would allow a woman to keep a small child with her. Thus, the occupation had both ideological and practical appeal. Female reformers had long expounded the virtues of domestic service as rehabilitative work for prostitutes and orphan girls.[133] But in the context of the late-nineteenth-to-early-twentieth-century job market, with expanding opportunities for women in factories, department stores, and offices, evangelical women's insistence on placing unmarried mothers in domestic service took on a different cast. Evangelicals valued domestic work for precisely the reasons that working women disliked it; it effectively removed women from the temptations of city life and limited their independence in ways that young women found constraining and reformers found reassuring. Providing a healthy example of middle-class home life, the household in which the woman worked could extend the protection of the maternity home; the watchful eye of an employer would replace that of the home's matron. The ideological appeal of domestic service to evangelical women and the close connections in their minds among domesticity, safety, and respectability allowed them to overlook the irony of this strategy: many studies indicated that domestic servants were disproportionately represented among populations of unmarried mothers, prostitutes, and delinquent girls.[134]

The practice of placing unmarried mothers as domestic servants gained further support from market demand. At a time when middle- and upper-class women complained of a "servant problem," maternity homes could supply an increasingly rare commodity—white, English-speaking women, trained in domestic skills and willing to live in.[135] One woman who made a practice of employing unmarried mothers as servants, going through three in five years, found in these women "the solution of the problem I have had of late," and recommended unmarried mothers to "couples requiring only one servant. A woman of this class," she explained, "is generally so glad to get a good home where she can keep her child with her that gratitude makes her an ideal servant."[136] Other women also found single mothers an answer to their servant problem; many homes reported receiving more requests for domestics than they could fill.[137]

Evangelical women celebrated the great success of their redemptive strategy. Although some measured that success in terms of conversion rates, most defined success more broadly; a Boston Crittenton worker noted with pride that "less than fifteen percent of the girls who come to the

Home become second offenders."[138] Although this meant that 15 percent of the women "sink back into the byways of the underworld and are never heard from again," 85 percent reportedly left the home as "fine, law-abiding young women." However they calculated their rate of success, most evangelical women in maternity homes shared the opinion of the Salvation Army matron who reported a percentage "so overwhelming that it leaves not the slightest doubt of the worth of the enterprise."[139]

Nineteenth-century female reformers had fashioned an ideology of benevolence that celebrated the unique contribution of women to benevolence, promoted sisterly bonds across the lines of class and reputation, and promised to redeem "fallen women" through domesticity, religion, and womanly sympathy. The women who founded homes for unmarried mothers in the late nineteenth and early twentieth centuries—in their sense of themselves as natural reformers, their understanding of unmarried mothers as seduced and abandoned, and their strategy of redemption and reclamation in the homes—described their work in the gendered and religious language of their predecessors. Forces were at work, however, that would challenge evangelical women on all fronts. Their sense of themselves as pioneers in the field of illegitimacy, their vision of the homes as places of redemption, their view of unmarried mothers as passive victims of evil men—all were to come under attack in the years to come. Once the exclusive province of evangelical women, maternity homes would become contested terrain in the battle between two generations of women over control of the discourse of illegitimacy and, more broadly, over the proper relationship of gender and reform.

2

The New Experts

and the

"Girl Problem"

A few years after her first encounter with an unmarried mother, Kate Waller Barrett became president of the National Florence Crittenton Mission and the many homes under its auspices. In 1908, Barrett boasted that "if any organization today wants to know anything about the condition of unfortunate girls . . . they send to the headquarters of the NFCM."[1] The early-twentieth-century antiprostitution crusade and the First World War focused national attention on illegitimacy, boosting the confidence of evangelicals and galvanizing public support for maternity homes. In the 1910s and 1920s, when "everywhere throughout the country the great problem of illegitimacy is confronting those who interest themselves in welfare work," the women who had founded large national chains of maternity homes "before it became a fad" wore their decades of experience like badges that proudly proclaimed their place at the forefront of the field.[2]

Yet while evangelical women claimed authority over the care of unmarried mothers, expertise was being defined quite differently in other circles. Beginning in the late 1910s, unmarried mothers attracted the attention of social workers, who, with the emergence and growth of their profession in the early twentieth century, claimed illegitimacy to be within their ever-expanding domain.

The agenda that women in social work brought to illegitimacy sharply distinguished them from evangelical women. Few social workers considered unmarried mothers their "unfortunate sisters" and fewer still harbored any missionary impulse to "save" them. Turning from the nineteenth-century tradition of female reform to the legitimizing rhetoric of science, they cast themselves not as social housekeepers, moral guardians, or home missionaries but as experts. Their attempt to professionalize social welfare would significantly reshape ideas about illegitimacy and attitudes toward single mothers. At the same time, their efforts to redefine expertise illuminate the dilemma this new generation of women faced in attempting to negotiate the contradictory and vexed identity of "woman professional."

"THE EXPERTS IN SCIENTIFIC SOCIAL PROGRESS"

"You no longer refer to your calling as one of philanthropy, nor of charity nor of altruism nor of mutual aid. You speak of a type of *work*, as though you were engaged in a sort of engineering," William Ernest Hocking congratulated social workers in 1925.[3] The early twentieth century witnessed tremendous growth and transition in social work, and social work practitioners energetically took to the task of transforming benevolence into a profession.

This task began before social welfare's heyday of professionalization in the 1920s. Professional social work claimed nineteenth-century roots in the charity organization society (COS) movement, which began in the 1870s. Drawing on ideas about scientific philanthropy and efficient reform promoted by the Civil War Sanitary Commission, and daunted by demands placed upon a disorganized, decentralized charity apparatus by the depression of 1873–78, philanthropic workers initiated the movement to rationalize and systematize benevolence. Charity organizers opposed what they saw as the sentimental, morality-laden, and indiscriminate relief offered by their predecessors and sought to bring order to "the anarchy of charity."[4] The COS was intended not to distribute relief but to coordinate the philanthropic resources of its community and to refer "deserving" applicants to the appropriate agency. In this way, the COS sought to prevent duplication of services, to protect philanthropic coffers from people who applied to more than one agency, and to rein in the material aid that COS workers deemed excessive and believed encouraged dependency. The COS movement advocated secular, rational, and scientific charity and repudiated sentimental benevolence in favor of a more efficient, systematic philanthropy ruled by the head rather than by the heart.[5]

Twentieth-century social workers inherited charity organizers' aspirations and extended their commitment to scientific benevolence. The COS had introduced the idea that philanthropy was most efficiently administered by skilled, trained, and paid agents assisted by a corps of volunteer "friendly visitors." Continuing the effort of the COS movement to create a profession out of "doing good," social workers established professional associations to affirm and codify their new conceptions of expertise. The largest and most inclusive of the professional associations, the American Association of Social Workers (AASW), established in 1921, took as its most important task "the study of professional problems which must underlie all successful work to raise professional standards."[6] Aspiring to the status of doctors, lawyers, and engineers, whose associations enforced standards of competence and monitored membership requirements, social work leaders envisioned the AASW as their new profession's gatekeeper. Aiming to differentiate the skilled worker from those "poorly trained workers who considered themselves full fledged members of the profession," the AASW continually redefined its own membership requirements along ever more stringent lines.[7]

Schools of social work joined professional associations in the creation of a professional subculture.[8] Nineteenth-century charity workers had learned their trade as apprentices, but by the early twentieth century the apprenticeship system seemed to social work leaders an anachronistic throwback to an earlier time, lacking scientific substance and consistency. The school of social work, on the other hand, promised to "give its graduates a professional attitude of mind," teaching the student "to apply knowledge and experience to the ancient impulse of neighborliness."[9] Social work education had its beginnings in a six-week summer training course for charity workers sponsored by the New York COS in 1898; within the next two decades, seventeen schools of social work had been founded.

At first glance, social workers would appear to have achieved many of the prerequisites for professional status. They had followed what historian Jean-Christophe Agnew describes as the formulaic story of professionalization—"a narrative of academic entrepreneurship and institution building; a story of journals, associations, and foundations, of examinations and degrees; in short, a story of technical and cultural gatekeeping and awarding credentials."[10] If one takes their impressive number of associations and schools as a barometer of professionalization, as many historians of social welfare have done, social work appeared to be fast on its way to the status it coveted. In 1929, the federal census recognized social workers' achievements by removing them from the category of "religious and charity workers"—a "semi-professional pursuit" that included fortune tellers, hypnotists, healers, officials of lodges, and theater owners—and classifying them as "professional."[11]

Many social workers, however, were far from secure in this status. For every proud proclamation of having joined the professional club, there was a frustrated admission that they were not yet recognized as full members. Social workers' anxiety deepened with a landmark session on professional standards at the National Conference on Charities and Corrections (NCCC) in 1915. In his address at that conference, Abraham Flexner provoked social workers' worst fears when he informed them that they lacked the basic criteria of a profession. Having surveyed the field of medicine several years before, Flexner had established himself as an expert not on any particular profession but on the process of professionalization itself.[12] Holding social work to his own test, Flexner found it lacking on a number of counts. The social worker was not an autonomous professional but "mediated" among other professions. Since social work utilized and complemented the other professions—medicine, law, education, ministry—in the performance of its duties, Flexner judged it "not so much a definite field than an aspect of work in many fields."[13] His declaration dealt a devastating blow to social workers. "His assessment of social workers as mediators among *real* professionals made them out to be little more than errand boys and girls in the world of social altruism," historian Don Kirschner writes. "As a result, he not only denied that they were professionals, but he implied strongly that they would never be professionals, because social work was inherently nonprofessional."[14]

Flexner's comments elicited a flood of responses from social workers, including some angry rebuttals. Mary Richmond recalled that "as we listened to Mr. Flexner we were more or less aware that quietly and behind his back . . . there was developing a skill quite different in method and in aim from the work that he described. We were not all behaving like the telephone girl at the switchboard who pulls out one plug and pushes in another."[15] But Flexner's denouncement haunted social workers for decades and set the stage for long-lasting professional self-consciousness and self-doubt. Social workers would spend the next twenty years responding to Flexner, directly and indirectly. Having proclaimed themselves professionals, they nervously measured themselves against the yardstick established by medicine and law.

As damaging as social workers felt outside opinion to be—and some believed themselves targets of "a sort of guerilla warfare of criticism"— at least as much criticism came from within their own ranks.[16] Anxiety over their professional status led social workers to take frequent self-inventories, but the statistics they gathered on their practitioners offered them little solace. In a canvass of 1,258 social workers in 1921–22, the AASW found that 60 percent of the men and 40 percent of the women were college graduates and that only 7 percent could claim at least a full year in a school of social work.[17] Frank Bruno noted in 1929 that although the thirty to forty training centers for social work turned out four hundred graduates a year, the twenty thousand practicing social workers in the country suggested that "the day-by-day tasks of social work are done by amateurs or apprentices, or by untrained people."[18] By many accounts, it seemed that the gap between the ambitions of social work leaders and the realities of social work practitioners was wide indeed.

Social workers betrayed their anxiety about their professional status in a number of ways, perhaps most obviously by endlessly comparing themselves to established, high-status professionals. The medical analogy, which held the social worker to be a sort of doctor to society, was probably the most frequently drawn. The position of the social worker, Homer Folks stated in his presidential address to the National Conference of Social Work (NCSW) in 1923, "is precisely that of the true practitioner of scientific medicine."[19] Engineering analogies ran a close second, supplying social workers with a powerful metaphoric title—"social engineers"—with which they strove to prove that "the principles of social organization and social procedure can be learned with some precision just as truly as mechanical principles can be learned."[20]

Like doctors and engineers, social workers struggled to prove themselves rigorously and unassailably scientific. The key to cultural authority in the early twentieth century, scientific knowledge carried promises of objectivity, expertise, empiricism, reliability, and neutrality—values intimately associated with the authority of professional expertise.[21] Social work theorists like Virginia Robinson knew that "to differentiate social case treatment in the technical sense from the more-or-less haphazard, unscientific 'influencing'" was a task in which social workers must make some headway if they were to rank with those professions "firmly founded in scientific method."[22] Beginning in the late nineteenth century and accelerating in the early twentieth, social work leaders struggled to align their work with that of the scientist. "What are the chances of ever making social work more exact and reliable, and what is the likelihood for social work ever becoming a real profession?" Karpf asked in 1931, directly linking professional success with scientific expertise.[23] Karpf went on to make this connection clearer. Since faith in science "characterizes the professionally trained practitioner in other professions," he asserted, "faith in the possibilities of science and a belief in its applicability to social problems should be essential for the professionally trained social worker."[24] Social workers placed extravagant faith in scientific expertise and took every opportunity to attach its precepts to their purposes.

Scientific metaphors and analogies abounded in social workers' writing, but occasionally, one would make clear the instrumentality behind their devotion. Halbert explained that he included "scientific standards" in his definition of social work "in order to exclude things which are meant well but do not really do any good and may even do harm. Its effect," he noted candidly, "is to exclude quacks."[25] Science, then, not only offered to confer legitimacy on social work but might also draw tighter boundaries around the occupation, insulating the true professional from the unscientific pretender and excluding those who might damage the professional image social workers sought to project.

Social workers claimed to be specialists in the science of social problems. But what exactly did they do? How did their insistence on the scientific foundation of their work translate into their day-to-day activities? Flexner's address prompted a self-conscious preoccupation with social work method and initiated a broad effort to define the skill shared by all trained social workers. Growing out of earlier efforts to make record keeping and friendly visiting more scientific, casework emerged as a specialized skill shared by all social workers and analogous to services offered by doctors and lawyers. As Kate Claghorn wrote, "good 'case work' is just as much better than the uninstructed, impulsive, old-fashioned 'charity' as the care given the sick person by the doctor and the trained nurse is better and more effective than the ministrations of the loving but uninstructed friend."[26] Social workers were still engaged in what Karl DeSchweinitz called "the art of helping people out of trouble"; through casework, they aimed to raise that art to a science.

Defined as "a developing science of the socialized personality," casework was a broad and generic term, usually referring to a process that included detailed interviewing of the client and often the client's family, "diagnosis" of the problem, and "treatment."[27] Its procedure, as outlined in 1917 in Mary Richmond's classic exposition of casework *Social Diagnosis* and elaborated and embellished for decades afterward, was to follow that of scientific method. Virginia Robinson explained that casework moved through three stages: "observation and assembling of facts; hypothetical investigation of these facts; and control of the facts for new ends."[28] Robinson's repeated and defensive insistence on the centrality of "facts" to the business of casework revealed her attempt to somehow make objective the inevitably subjective process of assessing an individual's problems. Believing scientific method to be as applicable to the solution of human problems as to physics and chemistry, social workers claimed that social and individual life could be subjected to controlled experimentation. "Scientific work," of course, "must base itself upon facts," and the facts to be considered and analyzed by the social worker were those collected in the process of casework—"all the facts and conditions of social life."[29]

Casework was as much a code word of professionalism as a social work methodology. Not least among its virtues, *casework* provided aspiring social work professionals with an esoteric language—a professional jargon comprehensible only to those trained to understand it. Indeed, the lengths social workers went to detail its intricacies suggested that the exact meaning of *casework* occasionally confounded its own practitioners. Some historians and sociologists have underlined the importance of language in the project of professionalization. "The jurisdictional claim of [professional] authority derived from . . . a command over the profundities of a discipline," Burton Bledstein has argued. "The professional person possessed esoteric knowledge about the universe which if withheld from society could cause public harm."[30] Social workers labored to persuade the public that casework was such a skill; at the same time, they used casework as a kind of litmus test to separate professionals from amateurs and to advertise their professional status to a skeptical public.

Many took great heart in these developments. To the optimistic, social work seemed by the 1920s to be "sloughing off its non-professional attributes and finding its permanent professional justification."[31] The voices of the frustrated, however, continued to sound. To some, it seemed that no number of comparisons to prestigious professions, no amount of reciting the incantation of casework, would turn them into real professionals. However confidently social workers announced themselves experts in the science of social problems, the public seemed unwilling to make the leap with them—unable to understand social welfare not as old-fashioned charity but as a profession on a par with medicine and law.

In 1921, Edwin Smith wrote cryptically that "'social work' connotes things which social workers do not like to have connoted."[32] In the context of the virulent red-baiting of the postwar years, Smith could have been referring to the taint of radicalism that clung to social workers. Although even the most moderate reform affiliations appeared "pink" when viewed through the anticommunist lenses of the day, in some cases, the term *radical* was well earned. In 1917, just a few years before Smith wrote, social workers gathered at a conference in Pittsburgh to discuss socialism, the single tax, anarchism, syndicalism, and the IWW. "The attendance at these meetings," wrote one who was there, "demonstrated a deep interest by social workers in radical movements," and, the writer speculated, "in all likelihood more of them will be held in the future."[33] By 1921, however, such interests would have quickly pushed adherents to the margins of the profession or out entirely. In 1927, social worker Beulah Weldon reported with some relief that the contemporary student of social work "is analytical and diagnostic rather than revolutionary or reformatory."[34]

Social workers' discomfort with the proclivities of their past, however, seemed to involve more than their association with radical causes, and many delved more deeply into social work's roots to find the source of the damning connotations. Many social work leaders located that source in their regrettable ancestor, nineteenth-century benevolence and its unfortunate affiliation with social reform that suggested a partisanship that true professionals were expected to shun in favor of neutrality and objectivity. Historian Don Kirschner views the new generation of social workers as "embarrassed by the moral heat generated by their predecessors. It was unscientific; it was unprofessional; it was almost indecent."[35] Throughout the early twentieth century, social workers battled the public's association of social work with nineteenth-century benevolence and voiced frustration over the disparity between the public image of social work as sentimental charity and their self-image of a profession offering skilled service. As a group, one of them despaired, social workers were viewed as "now sentimentalists, now reformers, now philanthropists . . . never the experts in scientific social progress."[36] Haunted by their history as do-gooders, social workers endeavored to convince the public (and probably themselves) that their work was something different from the friendly visiting of the past.

The effort to distinguish social work from its philanthropic predecessors was most fully and famously expressed by Porter R. Lee in his presidential address to the National Conference of Social Work in 1929. Although Lee paid tribute to social welfare pioneers, he announced that social workers had entered a new era. Once a "cause," social work was now more appropriately understood as a "function"—a formula Lee used to counsel social workers to channel their energies from activism to administration and to turn their attention from social evils to more internal professional dictates. Whereas the "cause" had called for "zeal," "the emblazoned banner," and "the flaming spirit," the "function" demanded "intelligence," "standards and methods," and "an efficient personnel."[37] Promoting an image of the social worker as trained technician rather than crusader, Lee urged social workers to turn away from their preoccupation with social reform to give more careful consideration to technique and method.[38]

Lee's remarks were descriptive as well as prescriptive, for by the late 1920s, the social work establishment had already begun charting a new course. Rather than looking to environmental causes to explain a person's problem, social workers were increasingly inclined to look to "maladjustment" on the part of the individual. In the 1920s, in a fury of concern over professional progress that was part of a new interest in psychiatric methods and an increasingly conservative political climate, social work leaders urged practitioners to focus less on promoting social justice and more on adjusting the individual to the environment. Although social workers were a heterogeneous lot, some still holding to reform goals after the First World War, by the mid-1920s, those who emphasized social over individual change found themselves outside the mainstream of the profession.

If a perceived excessive involvement in reform held social workers back in their quest for professional status, their vigorous efforts in the 1920s to distance themselves from that legacy should have been enough to quell the skeptics. It seemed, though, that social work was hampered by more than its inauspicious association with doing good. The ghost of "Lady Benevolence" that haunted social workers was not only "old-fashioned"; she was female. In their defensive polemics, social workers revealed their fear that what compromised their professional status was not simply their reform past but their reputation as a female profession. As James H. Tufts bluntly decreed in 1923, "from the point of view of improvement of professional standards . . . it is highly desirable that the profession should not be regarded as exclusively a woman's profession."[39] Of course, social workers' fight against a feminized reputation was closely linked to their retreat from reform, for purging themselves of their association with nineteenth-century charity involved purging the female tradition of reform upon which that charity was based. By invoking the talismans of professionalization—objectivity, efficiency, rationality—social workers may have sought to cool the fires of reform in the 1920s, but they hoped as well to place professionalism at a safe remove from the sentiment and sympathy of female benevolence.

Extolling the virtues of efficiency, objectivity, and expertise, social work leaders disparaged the values aligned with nineteenth-century benevolence as overly sentimental, embarrassingly anachronistic, and suggestive of professional immaturity. In condemning the qualities of emotion, sentiment, and intuition, social workers occasionally gave way to a more explicit rejection of earlier benevolence as excessively feminine. The true nature of social problems, Arthur Todd wrote in 1919, "cannot be seen clearly by eyes dimmed with easy tears; nor can the calls to constructive social work be heard above the thumping of a fluttery heart." Todd demanded that social work not capitulate to "the apostles of softness."[40] Another social worker blamed "misplaced and misguided charity" for holding back the profession and regretted that "the woman who thinks her duty to her less fortunate sisters done if she drives . . . once a month to her pet settlement 'in the slums' has not yet disappeared from our thoroughfares."[41] Stuart Alfred Queen encouraged social workers to eliminate "the 'sob sisters,' the Ladies Bountiful, the *poseurs*," and turn the work over to true professionals, for whom "social work was not . . . an interesting diversion for spare time, but a profession, a 'man's job.'"[42] And Elizabeth Kemper Adams, who instructed young women considering social work to "train for it!" wrote that "'a sweet Christian character and a mother herself' are inadequate qualifications." Adams spoke for many who sought to end the day when "true womanhood" was the primary qualification for benevolent work.[43]

The attempt to defeminize social work went beyond rhetorical appeals. Some social work leaders believed that recognition as real professionals would require more than a masculinizing linguistic turn. Perhaps the lesson of medicine, law, and engineering—the professions that social workers so envied—was that the majority of the practitioners of a profession should be men. The goal of raising standards in social work often seemed to translate into a search for men to join the profession. Writing on social work education, Tufts asked anxiously, "is our present system of education and training for social work doing all that the field requires in the way of attracting men to the profession?"[44] Buell complained in 1920 that "social work is not making an adequate appeal to the new groups of men in particular, who are leaving our colleges each year," and suggested luring those men to social work with salaries two or three times those offered women.[45] In 1925, a Committee on the Recruiting and Training of Men was created under the auspices of the American Association for Organizing Family Social Work.[46] Recruiting men in the name of "higher standards" linked the concepts of prestige, status, and professionalism ever more closely to masculinity and male participation.

Since social work continued to be numerically dominated by women despite the many appeals to men, the notion that it was compromised by femininity was a troubling conclusion to reach. As reported in the federal census of 1930, over 70 percent of the twenty thousand social workers were women. Contemporary observers were often less conservative in their estimates; some claimed that women composed up to 90 percent of all paid caseworkers. Whatever the exact proportion, most acknowledged that "so far as their numbers go, social work is largely in the hands of women."[47] Some sought to solve social work's "female problem" by demarcating separate areas in the profession for men and women. Women, Tufts contended, "are undoubtedly better fitted to visit homes, to unravel tangled domestic situations, care for little children, counsel the growing girl, minister to many special types of need"; men more appropriately worked within the larger public arenas of government and industry, an arrangement that effectively relegated women to the positions in social work lowest in prestige and salary.[48] To some extent, occupational segregation by sex along these lines prevailed. Although some claimed that the fact that the names of Jane Addams, Mary Richmond, Florence Kelley, and Julia Lathrop "come at once to mind as representative leaders" in social work indicated that "the higher reaches are not altogether barred to women," others observed that positions filled by women remained low in autonomy, prestige, and pay and that the highest positions of power were usually occupied by men.[49]

Women in social work did not accept these conditions without complaint. Some protested being treated as second-class citizens in a profession in which they predominated numerically and over which they allegedly wielded such control. Esther L. Brown noted in 1935 that inferior male candidates were given preference over superior women, "a situation that has aroused much bitterness among the latter."[50] Confessing to "considerable boredom with the discussions of whether social work is a woman's or a man's profession," Neva Deardorff was unusually candid in her protest. Citing the profession's formidable female pantheon—"Jane Addams, Mary Richmond, Mary Follett, Miss Breckenridge and the Abbotts"—Deardorff declared that she was "not ashamed of its record so far . . . even though some young college boys do not see a future in it." Deardorff condemned the practice of offering men a short cut to executive jobs and salaries as "a rank injustice" and called for "the modification of that attitude of mind which assumes, when a job paying more than three thousand dollars is to be filled, that an ordinary man will be worth that much, but it will take a whale of a woman to earn it."[51]

Although these protests may have allowed some women in social work to express discontent with what Deardorff termed "the suspicious interior circumstances" of their profession, they did not offer a solution to a thornier problem.[52] What was the place for women in a professional culture that prized values and characteristics associated with masculinity and privileged male participation? Low salaries and occupational segregation were only symptoms of a more fundamental paradox: how were women to negotiate the contradiction apparently inherent in the identity "woman professional"?[53]

Women in social work tried to define professionalism in a way that would allow them to join that exclusive club. They were not, of course, alone in this effort; women had struggled to construct professional identities in other fields as well. Regina Morantz-Sanchez has described the way in which women doctors combined traditionally feminine and professional values—sympathy and science—to make a place for themselves in the heavily male-dominated profession of medicine, a strategy that allowed them "to participate fully in an important segment of professional activity while maintaining their identity as women."[54] Women in nineteenth-century benevolent work had pursued a similar strategy. In 1891, Virginia Smith could claim before the NCCC that "we mothers know how to do some things more naturally than men."[55] Smith declared women's inherent fitness for benevolent work and portrayed it as a logical extension of women's roles as mother and keeper of morals—merely homemaking on a larger scale.

Although women had once traded on the alleged fit between feminine values and benevolence to create careers for themselves, this strategy would only exacerbate the near-epidemic anxiety over professional status that raged in the social work establishment by the 1920s. Indeed, as early as the time of her address, Smith's suggestion that feminine instinct alone qualified one for social work touched sensitive nerves among some social workers. Mary Richmond's response—that "men can do personal work as well as women, sometimes better," and that "it is only fair that we should insist that in all parts of the work it is not a question of sex, but of capacity"—presaged a time when appeals on the basis of sex equality would drown out those based on sex difference.[56]

Women seeking professional status as social workers, then, faced a different set of problems than women in medicine, science, and law. Those in male-dominated professions so strongly violated nineteenth-century norms for female behavior that they had to turn their femininity into a defense, to prove themselves womanly.[57] Women in social work, on the other hand, strongly *met* those norms, but emphasizing femininity in an already feminized profession would only reinforce social work's subordination in the professional hierarchy. Many social workers believed that being taken seriously as professionals required dissociating themselves entirely from a tradition of womanly benevolence, understanding, correctly, that their professional aspirations were incompatible with its ethos. They sought to define their work in terms more consonant with professional imperatives. A telling description of the role of the caseworker held that "the skilled listener submerges all consciousness of individuality or sex. She becomes little more than a piece of furniture, an 'itself' rather than a 'herself.' "[58]

In undertaking the difficult task of transforming a "woman's occupation" into a "true profession," then, women in social work would not exploit the nineteenth-century conflation of femininity and reform, as had their predecessors, but rather would attempt to unglue the connection between gender and benevolence. By so doing, they hoped to de-gender the act of helping, to transform it from a religious, feminine calling into a profession worthy of broad respect, legitimacy, and remuneration. In her study of women and benevolent work in the nineteenth century, historian Lori Ginzberg has argued that ideologies of gender sameness, marshaled against those of gender difference, "could support either a radical call for women's equal rights or a conservative alliance with the men in the emerging professional elite."[59] In the first decades of the twentieth century, when the belief in biologically based sexual difference was coming under intellectual assault and when both working-class and middle-class women were moving into new sectors of the economy, some women in social work seemed acutely aware of the conservativism inherent in the strategy of naturalizing sexual differences.[60] And the appeal of an ostensibly gender-neutral discourse that would grant them authority equal to men is easy to understand.[61] Women social workers sought to trade the moral authority of a gender-based benevolence for the secular authority of a scientifically based professionalism. By joining their male colleagues in posing professionalism and femininity as mutually exclusive, however, they participated in the process of gendering professionalism in a way that equated professionalism with masculinity.

THE NEW EXPERTS AND THE "GIRL PROBLEM"

In 1937, one social worker complained that though "Lady Bountiful has been pretty well replaced in other fields of social work, she still holds a powerful grip in this field."[62] The field she referred to was work with unmarried mothers. In the eyes of the new professionals, no work appeared more steeped in sentimentality than that practiced in maternity homes. To social workers, the field of illegitimacy seemed an "eddy" in the larger "stream" of professional progress, and the maternity home the last holdout of the old-fashioned benevolence they were trying so hard to abolish.[63]

Illegitimacy captured the attention of some of the most notable social workers of the day, including the "mother of casework" Mary Richmond, casework theorist Ada Sheffield, and U.S. Children's Bureau officers Emma O. Lundberg, Katherine Lenroot, and Maud Morlock. To them and their colleagues, professionalizing the field of illegitimacy posed no small challenge. Mapped out and claimed by evangelical women as distinctly female territory and celebrated as monuments to "women's work for women," maternity homes presented social workers with the problem of professionalization writ large. Because illegitimacy was particularly fraught with the associations of female benevolence that social workers believed compromised their status as professionals, it threw the dilemma of the woman professional into sharp relief. If social work was perceived to be too feminine to take its place among the serious professions of medicine, science, and law, how were women to claim status as dispassionate and objective professionals in the field of illegitimacy, bounded as it was by the gendered watchwords of sympathy, sisterhood, and sentiment?

Beginning in the 1910s, and increasing in the 1920s and 1930s, social work leaders formed a united front against maternity homes such as those associated with the Florence Crittenton Mission and the Salvation Army and were harshly critical of the evangelical women who ran them. Social worker Alice Bailey, for example, proclaimed the work performed in some Crittenton homes "the most unimaginative and unprogressive of any social work done."[64] Some characterized work in maternity homes as generally "crude" or "shoddy," and denounced it as "backward."[65] One social worker chastised evangelical women in Crittenton homes: "You have stood still while the whole profession of social workers have been marching onward. A new science has grown up and you have not opened a book."[66]

Although "backwardness" was a serious charge in the context of heightened self-consciousness over the precarious status of the profession, it does not sufficiently account for the intensity of the assault that the social work establishment unleashed on evangelical women in maternity homes. Calling for a "thorough-going scientific effort without preconceived bias," Maxfield denounced work in maternity homes as "philanthropic hysteria."[67] Murphy described work with unmarried mothers as "steeped and saturated in a superheated emotional atmosphere of psuedo-moral indignation" and urged that the work be removed "from the field of emotional action in which it so largely rests at the present time."[68] Hewins charged evangelical workers with "maudlin sentimentality," and Sheffield criticized their response to unmarried mothers as "emotional rather than analytic."[69]

Evangelical women, by social workers' account, seemed to be guilty of something more serious than professional immaturity. The terms and temper of this critical onslaught suggest that the social work establishment viewed maternity homes and the evangelical work done within them as worse than unprofessional. At its heart was a devaluation of maternity homes as too closely allied to an earlier style of benevolence understood as feminine. Laying bare the gender-specificity of the professional project, the social workers' critique suggested that the purpose of professionalization was to masculinize social work by stigmatizing the "feminine" values of the older model of benevolence.

As in the field of social work more generally, social workers sought to do more than masculinize the rhetoric of benevolence; they worked as well to encourage a literal and visible male presence in positions of authority in work with unmarried mothers. Community Chests pushed maternity homes to place more men on their boards; the Chest in Little Rock, Arkansas, required the local Crittenton home to elect a "men's advisory board."[70] In planning the meeting of the Committee on Illegitimacy at the 1919 NCSW, social worker Ada Sheffield wrote to Children's Bureau officer Emma Lundberg to ask for suggestions for a male speaker for the panel. "The second speaker would have to be a man," Sheffield wrote, because "we do not want too much femininity in the program."[71] Although Lundberg agreed that the idea of having a man on the program was "excellent," she could not think of one to recommend—a telling indication of the predominance of women in the field.

If evangelical women did not meet professional standards in their treatment of the unmarried mother, social workers stood ready to step in and fill the void. Marking illegitimacy as a field in which "the difficulties encountered are so great that it is hazardous for any but the most skilled and experienced case workers to perform the services required," social workers labored to define it as a national problem requiring a professional curative.[72] Appointing themselves the new experts, social workers sought to claim the field of illegitimacy as their proper domain.

Not surprisingly, out-of-wedlock pregnancy looked different when refracted through the lens of professional social work than through that of evangelical benevolence. Whereas evangelical women located the problem of illegitimacy in a society that endangered young women and a sexual double standard that condemned them, social workers placed unmarried mothers at the vortex of a constellation of larger social problems that revolved around the state of morality and family life. By various interpretations, the unmarried mother functioned as cause or effect of those problems; that she was embroiled in this maelstrom, however, was uncontested.

To Judge Benjamin Lindsey, for instance, unmarried mothers "are in society a part of its problem and its filth. They are responsible for many of the divorce cases, for its broken homes, desertions, sorrow, misery, blighted faith, despair, and the great mass of social ills which infect society."[73] In Lindsey's view, shared by many of his contemporaries, unmarried mothers were not victims but rather *agents* of larger social problems. Taking up the issue of out-of-wedlock pregnancy, social workers began to see unmarried mothers not as endangered but as dangerous.

In part, social workers' urgency was fueled by what they saw as a dramatic rise in illegitimacy rates. Since many states did not register births in the early twentieth century and others did so only sporadically, we have no way of accurately gauging this rise. Some historians, however, suggest that in fact, illegitimacy did begin to increase in the late nineteenth century, albeit modestly, after a century-long slump. From an eighteenth-century high, illegitimacy fell in the nineteenth century and probably increased slightly between 1870 and 1920.[74] If the apparent rise in the rate of illegitimacy goes some distance in explaining the new concern for the unmarried mother, however, it is not sufficient to explain the near-apocalyptic language used to express that concern. Social workers may have been responding to a real rise in illegitimate births, but their construction of its meaning granted out-of-wedlock pregnancy a symbolic significance that far outran its numbers.

Viewing illegitimacy as a problem of frightening dimensions, social workers sounded a note of urgency. The new importance they attached to the problem makes sense only when viewed against a background of widespread concern over the state of moral life in an urban industrial society, a concern that coalesced around the future of the family. Few issues were as charged for Progressive reformers and social critics in the 1910s and 1920s.[75] "Family breakdown" seemed to be heralded in rising divorce rates and falling birthrates among "the better sort," and many also saw its imminence in rising illegitimacy rates and counted unmarried mothers among the casualties of the family's demise. Indeed, "poor homes" appeared at the top of the lists of causes of illegitimacy compiled by surveyors. Mary Brisley noted that "given an unmarried mother . . . one may fairly safely predict a home broken in fact or in spirit, usually the former."[76]

To some, unmarried mothers were among the many victims of the demise of the family, but to others, they appeared more blameworthy than blameless. Many believed that unmarried mothers were dangerous to the extent that they threatened the maintenance of conventional family life and charged them with leveling a direct hit at an already beleaguered institution. Sociologist Dr. James Q. Dealey, for example, contended that "everything that makes for the gratification of the sex instinct apart from family responsibility strikes at the very root of the family itself."[77]

A major reconceptualization of illegitimacy and redefinition of the problem of the unmarried mother accompanied social workers' efforts to claim the field as their own. Writing unmarried mothers out of the evangelical script of seduction and abandonment, social workers created new scripts within which to comprehend out-of-wedlock pregnancy. Once "seduced and abandoned," unmarried mothers were characterized first as "feebleminded" and later as "sex delinquents." Together, the related discourses of feeblemindedness and sex delinquency marked the boundaries of the social work establishment's understanding of illegitimacy from 1910 through the 1930s.

"Feeblemindedness," a diagnostic category that enjoyed enormous popularity beginning in the 1910s, seemed to social workers to provide a useful explanation for out-of-wedlock pregnancy. Social workers debated the exact meaning of feeblemindedness, which, in its ambiguity, served as a catchall term for those whose intelligence, as measured by newly designed tests, was "subnormal." As historian Barbara Meil Hobson has pointed out, other even more subjective standards were employed in the diagnosis, including "untruthfulness."[78] But confusion over the definition of feeblemindedness did nothing to deter social investigators from embracing it as a diagnosis, and beginning in the 1910s and continuing into the 1920s, social workers agreed on the strong link between illegitimacy and feeblemindedness.[79] Although Winifred Richmond believed the problem of illegitimacy to be "by no means identical" with that of feeblemindedness, she found them to "overlap largely" and claimed that "there is no doubt that the former would be materially lessened if mental defect could be eradicated."[80] Emma Lundberg insisted that "it is not difficult to demonstrate the importance of inferior mentality and psychopathic traits as predisposing factors" of out-of-wedlock pregnancy, and many agreed with the 1911 Senate Report that concluded that feebleminded women, "if left unrestricted, will inevitably become mothers of illegitimate children."[81] To social workers, the connection was clear: feebleminded women stood "in constant danger of becoming pregnant," and most unmarried mothers were feebleminded.[82] According to this circular logic, feeblemindedness both caused illegitimacy and could be deduced from the fact of out-of-wedlock pregnancy.

In bearing the title of "feebleminded," unmarried mothers were in considerable if not necessarily good company. Social workers' use of this category to describe the unmarried mother was part of a much larger concern with the problem of "feeblemindedness" in this period, and unmarried mothers were one group among many who were found to be disproportionately feebleminded. Armed with the Simon and Binet test, developed in 1908, by which mental capacity could presumably be accurately and objectively measured, criminologists, social workers, and psychiatrists journeyed to prisons and reformatories to test their theories. Expecting to find feeblemindedness among these populations, they found it with a vengeance, linking almost every variety of antisocial behavior to inherited mental defect and reporting alarming rates of feeblemindedness among prostitutes, tramps, criminals, and paupers.[83]

Both men and women could be "feebleminded," but the symptoms were markedly gendered. While feeblemindedness in men seemed to correlate with criminal activity and inability to succeed economically, feeblemindedness in women was defined almost exclusively in sexual terms.[84] According to the coalition of the new experts, the feebleminded woman was highly likely to engage in "promiscuous" behavior. Most attributed this tendency to the abnormally passive and yielding nature of the feebleminded woman. Social workers who linked illegitimacy with feeblemindedness explained the close connection in this way: "Feeblemindedness and mental imbalance doubtless greatly increase the probability of an irregular sex life, involving as they do, lack of foresight, weakened powers of inhibition, and tendency to yield to the impulse of the moment."[85]

In some ways, the conceptualization of unmarried mothers as feebleminded overlapped with the evangelical understanding of them as victims of seduction. The unmarried mother of the evangelicals' narrative yielded out of her natural feminine nature to love and to trust, and the feebleminded woman, out of "her suggestibility, defective judgment, and poor powers of inhibition." Both were victims—"easy prey of designing or unscrupulous men."[86] Yet their likeness ended there. Although feebleminded women were understood to be victims of a sort, these new victims were no longer blameless; the victims of defective genetics rather than the guiles of a villain were met not with sympathy but with fear and punishment. Social workers generally concurred that no solution short of close supervision, permanent institutionalization, and in some cases sterilization would suffice, for "unless placed in a carefully chosen environment, [feebleminded women] are almost sure to come to grief again and again."[87] In 1930, the social worker at the Norfolk, Virginia, Crittenton home claimed that "sterilization is a wonderful blessing to the feeble-minded girl who is bound to become a repeater" and remarked that "just this week we are sending one of these unfortunates to the hospital for the operation."[88]

Unlike the discourse on seduction and abandonment, which usually ended with the rescue and redemption of the victim, social workers' narratives of the feebleminded were darkly pessimistic. Eugenics added this pessimistic edge to the fear of the feebleminded, raising disquieting questions about the difficulty of control and provoking horrifying prophecies of the rapid proliferation of feeblemindedness and contamination of the national gene pool. The belief that feeblemindedness was hereditary led to what historian Mark Haller has termed "the myth of the menace of the feebleminded."[89] Given these fears, it is not difficult to understand why many perceived unmarried mothers to be particularly menacing members of the larger feebleminded population: in giving birth to illegitimate children, they had presumably added to that population by transmitting their defective traits. Social worker Mildred Mudgett thus grimly concluded that "a mental examination of any girl after she reaches a maternity hospital is like trying to repair the dam after the flood has occurred."[90]

To social workers who saw a causal link between feeblemindedness and illegitimacy, early detection, institutionalization, and sterilization promised to stem the tide of out-of-wedlock pregnancy. But what of those unmarried mothers who could not be labeled feebleminded? Even those social workers who identified feeblemindedness as the primary cause of out-of-wedlock pregnancy acknowledged that "many unmarried mothers are normally intelligent and relatively well-balanced young women."[91] How were social workers to account for women whose scores on intelligence tests presumably exempted them from relegation to the feebleminded—a category of women whose sexual behavior could be understood as "a stupid drifting in the direction of least resistance"—and who therefore presumably engaged in illicit behavior voluntarily? As historian Elizabeth Lunbeck writes, "if immoral women were too intelligent to be feebleminded, they were still too defective to be normal."[92] In these cases, social workers arrived at a new understanding of the unmarried mother as "sex delinquent."

This reconceptualization took place within the larger context of heightened public interest in delinquency. Delinquency had long been identified as a problem associated with boys; indeed, boys had been a "problem" for decades, and organizations like the YMCA and the Salvation Army committed many of their resources to keep boys and young men on the "right track."[93] Fueled by new theories of adolescence promoted by G. Stanley Hall and others, which posited adolescence as a vitally important and turbulent stage of life, and alarmed by what they saw as a significant deterioration of morality, Progressive reformers turned their attention to female delinquency.[94]

Like the diagnosis of feeblemindedness, the definition of delinquency was deeply gendered. Unlike the delinquency of boys, which most often referred to theft and criminality, female delinquency was virtually synonymous with sexual impropriety. As one social worker put it, "immorality comes near taking among these girls the place larceny holds among boys."[95] Even if a young woman's delinquency manifested itself in ways not overtly sexual, social workers believed that "they are nearly always found associated with the instinctive urge."[96] Female delinquents were, almost by definition, "immoral," and sex delinquency was perceived to be, also by definition, female. "Who has ever heard of a 'fallen boy'?" one social worker asked.[97] Indeed, the logic of the period rendered a male sex delinquent a contradiction in terms. Social workers were candid in acknowledging that "when we speak of a delinquent girl we mean one thing, and when we speak of a delinquent boy we mean another," and that "when we speak of the delinquent girl we usually have in mind the sex offender."[98]

Unlike social workers, evangelical reformers had always been careful to distinguish unmarried mothers from delinquents. Privately characterizing delinquent girls as "riffraff," they feared that they might exert a bad influence on unmarried mothers and made great efforts to segregate the two groups.[99] "The hardened delinquent girl, especially one who has been an inmate of a state reformatory, has no permanent place in a maternity home," the NFCM stated in 1929.[100] By setting aside Ivakota Farms, their estate in rural Virginia, for delinquent girls, the NFCM sought to reserve maternity homes for presumably nondelinquent unmarried mothers.[101]

To social workers, however, the line between unmarried mothers and sex delinquents progressively blurred. *Sex delinquency* was a general term, defined broadly enough to include girls and women who participated in "illicit sexual behavior" as well as those who looked as if they might be considering it—a definition that left little doubt that unmarried mothers would be included.[102] The beginning of the inclusion of unmarried mothers in the category of sex delinquency appeared in Emma Lundberg's schema of 1920, in which she divided unmarried mothers into the following types: "a) The mentally subnormal girl who lacks controlling inhibitory instincts and is an easy victim because of helplessness; b) the young, susceptible girl, unprotected from dangers . . .; c) the more mature young woman of good character who is led by false promises . . .; d) the really delinquent girl or woman, who knowingly chooses antisocial conduct, her illegitimate maternity being only an incidental evidence of repeated immorality." Lundberg warned that "the last type is undoubtedly recruited to a considerable extent from the preceding ones."[103] Social workers eroded and eventually collapsed this boundary between unmarried mothers and delinquents until, by many accounts, they were synonymous. Five years later, a social worker included in the category of sex delinquent: "a) Those who have had but one sexual experience (i.e., in rape cases or when seduction was accomplished under promise of marriage); b) those who had been repeatedly immoral with the same person . . .; c) those who had been promiscuous . . .; d) prostitutes; and e) homosexual perverts."[104] In its hierarchy of sex delinquency, this new typology included those previously absolved of all sexual agency by virtue of seduction and abandonment.

Social workers, then, came to posit a continuum of sex delinquency in which, as one wrote, "illegitimate maternity is part of a career of immorality and other delinquencies."[105] In 1911, the Senate Report on the Relation between Occupation and Criminality of Women concluded that "no hard and fast line can be drawn between the unmarried mother who [has] not made a trade of vice," "the girl who leaves and regains the accepted path without any general knowledge of her deviations," "the occasional prostitute," and "the professional immoral woman."[106] By the 1930s, some social workers were using the terms *illegitimacy* and *delinquency* interchangeably.[107] No longer imbued with melodramatic images of seduction and abandonment, single pregnancy marked just one more variety of female sexual activity that could be subsumed under the inclusive rubric of "sex delinquency." The massive literature on female delinquency in this period suggests that women's delinquency was sexualized. The social work discourse on illegitimacy indicates, in turn, that unmarried female sexuality was increasingly labeled delinquent.

The social workers' sex delinquent differed in most respects from the seduced victim of the evangelicals' imagination. Whereas unmarried mothers were marked in evangelical narratives by their vulnerability and victimization, and feebleminded women by "their incapacity for self-direction," female sex delinquents were distinguished by their *aggressive* self-direction.[108] Although social workers did not depart from the conviction that normal women were sexually passive, unmarried mothers could no longer claim membership in those ranks. Indeed, in replacing the notion of female passivity with female sexual aggressiveness, social workers essentially reversed the earlier construction of unmarried mothers. From helpless victims, they became women who willfully violated moral sanctions; once essentially passive, they were now dangerously sexual.[109]

Male villains went the way of female victims in the new script of out-of-wedlock pregnancy. "We have to a certain extent outgrown the easy assumption . . . that all unmarried fathers are conscienceless rakes," Mary Brisley wrote in 1939.[110] Many social workers criticized evangelicals for creating villains out of unmarried fathers, arguing that viewing men in this way was stereotyped and rigid, and Brisley went so far as to admit a "sneaking admiration for and sympathy with" the man accused. Since, as she explained, "there is no way that a man can be sure he is the father of a child, other than his belief in its mother," she was reluctant to "'saddle' a young man with the support of a child which may prevent his marriage to someone for whom he cares."[111] With this assessment, social workers had completed the reversal of the evangelical script. Out-of-wedlock pregnancy no longer ruined women's chances for marriage, but those of men. Social workers had shifted the burden of guilt for illegitimacy from men to women.

It is clear that in the social work literature of the 1910s to 1930s, illegitimacy had acquired a meaning dramatically different from that ascribed to it by evangelical women. The unmarried mother who had once embodied the traits of the "good girl" had decidedly entered the ranks of the bad. What had happened with the shift in power and authority from evangelicals to social workers to alter so profoundly the vision of the unmarried mother? What function did this new explanation of out-of-wedlock pregnancy serve?

At least in part, the propensity of social workers to label the behavior of single mothers as sexually delinquent can be understood as their response to the revolution in sexual mores taking place among working-class youth in early-twentieth-century cities.[112] As we know, the "girl problem" did not reside entirely in the imaginations of social workers. Historians Kathy Peiss, Joanne Meyerowitz, and others have suggested that during this period some working-class women were forging new standards of sexual behavior. Although middle-class sexual mores set chastity against promiscuity, some working-class women held to a more fluid definition of respectability that could include varying degrees of sexual experience. Concerned observers noted the new appearance of the young woman who "tends to live without a sense of ethic, and what is worse, without a desire for one," and labeled it "the girl problem."[113] Social workers understood unmarried mothers to be a particularly vexing and serious aspect of the girl problem and placed illegitimacy within "the very much larger problem of sex experimentation and freedom, which characterizes our present era."[114] In a way, the social workers' endless effort to explain the unmarried mother seems to have served a function similar to evangelical women's tireless retelling of the story of seduction and abandonment: each was an attempt to comprehend a working-class female sexuality increasingly incomprehensible to middle-class observers.

Working-class women pioneered this new sexuality in the dance halls, movie theaters, and amusement parks springing up in the early twentieth century. They flocked to places where "the dancing floor is good, there are always plenty of men, and there are laughter and liberty galore."[115] These commercial amusements—landscapes of gregarious heterosociality and heterosexual desire—provided the young urban wage-earning woman with public arenas for independence and sexual expressiveness. But this combination was predictably the stuff of nightmares for reformers. Where working-class women saw vistas of autonomy, romance, and pleasure, social workers saw promiscuous sexuality and inappropriate *delinquent* behavior.[116] The eroticism of movies "lurid with temptation," the darkness of theaters, the stimulation of amusement parks, and "the aphrodisiac effects of the immoderate consumption of alcohol—all of these factors tend to place undue emphasis upon the whole question of sex."[117] Armed with "a good deal of evidence that for many people sex irregularities may be traced pretty directly to unsupervised dance halls, amusement parks, low-grade theaters, and excursion steamers," social reformers made recreation a high priority, infiltrating and investigating places of amusement and writing books with such titles as *The Lure of the Dance* and *From the Ball Room to Hell*.

Given the association of working-class recreation with sexual impropriety, it is not surprising that commercial amusements loomed large in the social workers' lists of causes leading to out-of-wedlock pregnancy. Some unmarried mothers seemed drawn to the evils of several forms of debauching recreation. One resident of the Jersey City Door of Hope in 1930, for example, was "very much of a movie fan and she likes to dance and has visited parks a great deal."[118] This list became a kind of shorthand for sexual impropriety, and social workers called on "sex delinquency" to explain a female sexual agency that was visible, even flaunted in these new venues. Shocked to find so many unmarried mothers pregnant by "chance acquaintances," social workers were appalled at how many met their partners at dance halls and movie theaters. Mabel Mattingly noted that almost one-third of the unmarried mothers in her study mentioned that "illicit intercourse first occurred after the couple had attended a dance."[119] Another study of unmarried mothers in Connecticut found that a scant 20 percent had "met in ways that could be considered fairly normal" and that most of the rest had met on the street, in parks, in theaters, and at dances.[120] In social workers' eyes, women who traded sexual favors, ranging from flirtation to intercourse, for men's "treats" to a night out could hardly lay claim to the status of seduced victims. The behavior of women who told stories not of seduction and abandonment but of meeting men in movie theaters, parks, or on the street, who often did not know the man's last name, who were listed in the case records of maternity homes as "dance case," suggested not female sexual passivity and innocence but a sophistication and sexual assertiveness that social workers found profoundly troubling.[121]

Evangelical women had not shut their eyes to the new commercial amusements. Indeed, their concern for the threat posed by these places at least matched that of social workers. Their particular apprehension, however, derived from their construction of female sexual passivity and still followed the lines of the script of seduction and abandonment. To evangelical women, dance halls were dangerous gathering places for unscrupulous men who patronized them "for the sole purpose of meeting attractive girls and persuading them to surrender their virtue"; in the dance halls, there was "always a chance for exploiting the young, inexperienced girl." Similarly, movie theaters were places "haunted by the male sex who seem to care not how they tread, and they always stand ready to wield their powers over their weaker companions, caring not for the result."[122] To social workers, on the other hand, the woman who frequented urban commercial amusements seemed at least "equal in delinquent experience to the man," and in some accounts, women appeared as the aggressors.[123] One social worker documented women's active participation in movie theater courtship: "Girls go into these places, take seats in the darkest corners, preferably against the wall and in front of the men whom they wish to attract."[124]

What unmarried mothers did at work seemed to social workers to be as fraught with problems as how they spent their time afterward. Social workers' concern about working-class women's sexual independence was linked to their larger concern about the meaning of their new opportunities for paid employment. Anxiety over women working for pay outside the home was certainly not new in the early twentieth century. What *was* new was what was seen as the increased opportunity for moral harm accompanying employment in the manufacturing and service sectors. Social workers cataloged and analyzed the occupations of unmarried mothers in their search for clues to the causes of illegitimacy. Individually, they singled out specific occupations that were especially worrisome; together, they managed to condemn as unsafe every occupation open to women. Kammerer alone detailed the moral dangers of factory work; department stores, where "we find the girl whose days are spent . . . confronted with very distinct temptations"; office work, where "they are thrown into direct relation with a very few people with whom they quickly get on terms of

intimacy"; and hotels and restaurants, where "the physical hardships endured . . . are infinitely lighter than the moral dangers to which they are
exposed."[125] Danger inhered not just in these occupations, according to
Kammerer, but in a woman's entrance into the industrial city. At this point,
he wrote, "her personality expands with almost startling rapidity. She
assumes a 'grown-up' attitude, and affects a spirit of bravado. At this time
also, she . . . enters into such free associations with men that the delicacy
of her moral reserve is often in danger."[126] The unmarried mother symbolized the worst-case scenario—the horrifying though logical outcome of
the larger changes that propelled young working women into the urban
world. Social workers' understanding of unmarried mothers as sex delinquents was marked by their overriding preoccupation with urban threats to
female morality and with the alleged breakdown in female moral standards
in the "revolution in manners and mores" that seemed to accompany the
movement of women onto city streets and into urban employment.

Anxiety regarding working-class women's work and recreation was part
of the still more portentous problem of female independence. Many social
workers were convinced that out-of-wedlock pregnancy was the result of
women living apart from their families. Concern about "women adrift" ran
through studies of illegitimacy, and social workers drew close connections
between "unconventional" living arrangements and single pregnancy. The
social worker of the Detroit Crittenton home explained the connection by
charting a typical course: "Girls leave home to secure work to care for
themselves and perhaps other members of their family. Because of their
inability to provide themselves with a better mode of living, they crowd
together in cheap rooming houses, or rent single rooms, where a high
standard of living is not maintained, and no moral suasion is apparent, and
finally the girl becomes a sex delinquent."[127]

The class and ethnic background of women frequenting commercial
amusements and earning wages in the city, as well as the activities they
engaged in there, also made it easier for social workers to brand their
behavior "delinquent." Their impression was that unmarried mothers were
disproportionately foreign-born and poor. Social workers alerted the country to high illegitimacy rates among working-class and immigrant populations, enlisting the new category of "sex delinquency" to describe unmarried mothers.

Sex delinquency most clearly followed a geography of class. Some social
workers were moved to render this coincidence graphically; Mabel Wiley,
for example, actually mapped out the correspondence of New Haven's
"delinquency districts" and working-class neighborhoods.[128] Most social

workers would have agreed with Anne Bingham, who wrote that "low standards of personal morality are general in many neighborhoods and it may be perfectly true as the girl will say when asked that all the girls whom she knows will 'go with fellows.'"[129] Writing of an unmarried mother in an Illinois study, Beatrice Mann noted that "she comes from an environment of low social status, where it is likely that illicit sex relations are not considered to be seriously delinquent, or may even be accepted as normal."[130] Evangelical women might explain away the sexual agency of native-born white women, but social workers felt no such compunction when faced with the task of explaining the sexuality of working-class women.

Social workers were also struck by the predominance of foreign-born women or the daughters of the foreign-born among unmarried mothers. Kammerer noted that "so large a part does the girl who has recently immigrated play in a study of the unmarried mother that considerable space must be given to causes illustrating her special condition."[131] Although convinced of the connection between foreignness and illegitimacy, social workers disagreed about the direction of causation. Some stressed "natural licentiousness," thinly disguised in the terms of cultural relativism. "Among certain classes abroad," investigators in 1911 discovered, "premarital relations seem to be common, and not to be looked upon as objectionable." They concluded that among people of these unspecified nationalities, "it is too much to expect them to make over their whole code of morality in a single generation."[132] Anne Bingham remarked that "the idea commonly accepted in Germany and Austria of regarding a betrothal as sufficient ground for men and women to live together . . . is undoubtedly reflected in the opinions commonly heard from our girls that there is no impropriety in sexual intercourse if a promise of marriage has been made or may be reasonably expected."[133] Others attributed the alleged connection to too-rapid Americanization, or the foreign-born girl "coming into contact with the freedom of life and ideals of America."[134] Noting a high percentage of foreign-born and second-generation women in her study of delinquent girls, Bingham found that "the desire to become Americanized as quickly as possible is felt by practically all the girls" and "in a desire to appear sophisticated a girl may indulge in impulsive acts of recklessness which involve a total change in her habits of life."[135] Whether these habits were brought to the United States from a more licentious homeland or were nurtured in the process of adapting to new surroundings, foreignness and illegitimacy neatly intersected in the minds of many social workers. Feeble-mindedness, too, seemed to social workers to follow lines of class, race, and ethnicity. Harold Phelps, for example, pointed to the high incidence of feeblemindedness among blacks in his study and to "the greater concentration of the lower mental types in the casual and unskilled occupations."[136]

At the same time that social workers called on feeblemindedness and sex delinquency to both describe and condemn working-class women's premarital sexual activity, they used these constructions in other ways that were at least as important. To understand their dramatic reconceptualization of the unmarried mother, one must remember that social workers were fighting internal as well as external battles. Professional status hinged on their success in dissociating their work from old-fashioned female benevolence. In this context, it is not surprising that the evangelical script of seduction and abandonment, filled as it was with hyperbolic emotionalism and stylized sentimentality, held little appeal for social workers. To the new professionals, evangelical women understood the unmarried mother according to "no scientific habit of thought or observation," but rather to "their own impressions and conclusions as to the causes of her errancy."[137] Rheta Childe Dorr wrote plainly that "no scientific study of delinquent girls ever came out of a philanthropic or religious institution."[138] It was clear to social workers that melodrama—a narrative strategy that not only filled evangelical publications but also sold theater tickets and dime novels— lacked the scientific substance to serve as a professional explanation for illegitimacy. Resonating with scientific reliability and certainty, diagnoses of "feeblemindedness" and "sex delinquency" carried assurances of objectivity and neutrality essential to professional identity. With the development of intelligence tests, "feeblemindedness" could ostensibly be scientifically and objectively measured. Eager to prove the connection between feeblemindedness and illegitimacy, social workers subjected unmarried mothers to batteries of tests and then published papers packed with statistical "proof."[139] Similarly, sex delinquency's appeal to social workers lay in its alleged basis in science, objectivity, and rationality; it too invited testing, typological ordering, and elaborate diagnostic schemes. Both feeblemindedness and sex delinquency afforded great opportunities to impose order on the disorderliness of "bad girls"; assigning unmarried mothers to "types," the resulting classification schemes signaled the culmination of rigorous research and testing.[140] To social workers, replacing the melodramatic story of seduction and abandonment with feeblemindedness and sex delinquency took illegitimacy out of the emotional, moralistic world of old-fashioned benevolence and into the objective, empirical realm of science.[141]

Professional status was boosted through these associations with science, but professional authority was ultimately expressed in the practitioner-client relationship. Professionalization demanded that this relationship be impersonal, objective, impartial. The melodramatic script had linked unmarried mothers and evangelical women in a bond of sisterhood. A professional relationship, however, was marked by distance, not identification. By discarding the story of seduction and abandonment, social workers made certain that no one could accuse them of maintaining a sisterly relationship with unmarried mothers. Diagnoses of feeblemindedness and sex delinquency widened the distance between the two groups and demonstrated that social workers could cultivate the proper objectivity required of professionals, recasting as clients those who were once sisters.[142]

In removing unmarried mothers from the evangelical narrative and placing them within the scientific scripts of feeblemindedness and sex delinquency, social workers had gone a considerable distance toward achieving recognition as experts in the field of illegitimacy. They had garnered a sort of representational authority—the right to define unmarried mothers and to explain out-of-wedlock pregnancy—and this was no small victory. As sociologist Magali Larson explains, experts obtain power when they appropriate a field and establish it as their own domain. She emphasizes the discursive nature of that appropriation when she writes that "monopolized discourse exerts effective influence silently and invisibly. Its effects are measured in the non-physical constraint of accepted definitions, of internalized moral and epistomological norms."[143] The discourses of feeblemindedness and sex delinquency served social workers in precisely this way. Whereas evangelical women had struggled to exercise what historian Peggy Pascoe has termed "female moral authority," women in social work aspired to the broader cultural authority of professional legitimacy.[144] Donning the mantle of science helped legitimize social workers' expertise.

In addition to boosting social workers' professional stature, discourses of feeblemindedness and sex delinquency provided them with material to construct a "modern" identity. Social workers called on that powerful combination—sex and science—to measure the distance they had traveled from nineteenth- to twentieth-century womanhood and to revel in their difference from their mothers and grandmothers. By becoming experts in the treatment of sex delinquents, social workers declared themselves New Women—quintessentially modern, secular, scientific, objective, willing to confront sexuality head-on, and unburdened with sentimental notions of sisterhood.

Women social workers' appropriation of scientific discourses was at once boldly transgressive and deeply conservative. In authoring scientific scripts to explain out-of-wedlock pregnancy, they subverted what feminist theorists have described as "the historic conjunction of science and masculinity" and "the equally historic disjunction between science and femininity."[145] Mary Jacobus, Evelyn Fox Keller, and Sally Shuttleworth have argued that "for women, scientific discourse has been especially crucial in constructing reality as something they can embody but not know. . . . In this scheme, women can never be meaning makers in their own right."[146] The story of the professionalization of social work, however, suggests a more complicated relationship between scientific language and gender. By becoming the authors of meaning about illegitimacy, the new generation of women in social work assumed the right to scientific authority.

Social workers established that authority at the expense of the objects of those scientific meanings through the act of claiming the right to diagnose other women. As bold as social workers were in joining their male colleagues in transforming benevolence into science, they were blind to the ways in which doing so contributed to the process—one that accelerated in the early twentieth century—by which "scientific discourses [had] come to articulate the authoritative social theories of the feminine body."[147] The task of inventing their own modern, professional identities led social workers to contribute to new sexual discourses that stigmatized working-class women's sexuality as pathological and criminal. Social workers who purported to bring objectivity to the study of unmarried mothers and the problem of illegitimacy ultimately crystallized public sexual discourse around normality and deviance and widened the disciplinary regime under which unmarried mothers were more aggressively and intrusively scrutinized.

In one sense, social workers created themselves as professionals and as New Women by constructing unmarried mothers. But unmarried mothers were not merely the inventions of social workers or of evangelical women; rather, they participated actively in constructing their own identities. The next two chapters turn from the construction of the "girl problem" to the "problem girls"—to consider the ways women negotiated single pregnancy in the first half of the twentieth century.

3

The "Secret Sisterhood": Unmarried Mothers in Maternity Homes

In 1900, Kate Barrett narrated the story of the admission of a new "inmate" into a maternity home. A resident of the home first showed her into the drawing room, where she found "every evidence of the fact that this is a true home—God's home," in which "the very atmosphere of love seems to breathe forth." She was then greeted by the matron, who began not by asking "a long string of questions" but by simply inquiring "'can I be of any help to you?'" In a few moments, Barrett wrote, "touched by the tenderness of her tone, the girl has sobbed out her sin."[1] As soon as possible, the new resident would be immersed in the religious and domestic regimen of the home, structured around the assumption that the birth of her child would awaken maternal instincts that would hasten her redemption.

A woman arriving at a maternity home thirty years later would undoubt-edly have been similarly greeted by an evangelical matron, but within a week or so, the home would have arranged for her to meet a caseworker. In her first interview, she would be asked detailed questions about the circum-stances that led to her pregnancy, the identity of the "putative father," how long she had known him, and how many times they had had sex. To properly diagnose the etiology of her delinquency, the social worker would inquire about the nature of her living situation, her occupation, the character of her companions, what she did for recreation, whether or not she smoked or drank, and the names and addresses of parents, relatives, and friends who could verify the truthfulness of her answers. The social worker would probably administer an intelligence test to determine whether she was "feebleminded." Regardless of the results, the fact that she was unmarried would be evidence enough that she was unfit to be a good mother to her child, and the social worker would begin to encourage her to place it for adoption.

The responses of evangelical women and social workers to unmarried mothers were informed by the narratives each constructed to render single motherhood comprehensible—discourses of out-of-wedlock pregnancy that encoded their fears and anxieties and at the same time underwrote their authority over unmarried mothers. Chances were good, however, that an unmarried mother would recognize herself in neither the evangelical nor the professional script of out-of-wedlock pregnancy. The next two chapters turn from the authors to the subjects of those narratives, focusing on unmarried mothers in maternity homes. This chapter considers the crisis that single pregnancy posed to women in the first half of the twentieth century and examines the range of alternatives available to single pregnant women. It explores the reasons that some turned to maternity homes, traces the routes they traveled there, and attempts, as fully as possible, to illuminate the social relations among the residents in the homes. Finally, it considers the strategies unmarried mothers employed to pursue their own ends.

THE CRISIS OF OUT-OF-WEDLOCK PREGNANCY

Had the young woman Barrett described in 1900 found herself in similar circumstances two centuries earlier, her experience of single pregnancy and motherhood would have been quite different. Never an easy status to bear, unmarried motherhood conferred different social meanings over time that determined changing responses. Although out-of-wedlock pregnancy was "a particularly trying experience for the young woman who was unfortunate enough to face it in colonial New England," for example, historian Ellen Fitzpatrick argues that "she could count on the community to support her and her offspring in at least some rudimentary way."[2]

Some historians suggest that illegitimacy became a crisis of new proportions—familial and personal—in the course of the nineteenth century.[3] Maternity home case records were written hurriedly and often in sentence fragments; yet even in their abbreviation, they testify to the trauma that out-of-wedlock pregnancy continued to pose to many women and their families in the first decades of the twentieth century. When Marya Lenol's parents discovered in 1920 that their daughter was pregnant, they told a social worker that they "feel the disgrace so that they plan to move into another neighborhood."[4] "I am nearly frantic with grief and shame," wrote one woman in 1926 to the Des Moines Salvation Army home, requesting that the home accept her daughter.[5] To explain her absence from home, one resident of the Jersey City Door of Hope in 1945 told her brother that she was in jail, preferring that her family think she had been arrested than to know that she was pregnant.[6]

Illegitimacy tested and stretched family ties, sometimes to the breaking point. When Elizabeth, a nineteen-year-old factory worker, became pregnant in 1929, her older sister told her to "go and not come back." The Salvation Army matron reported that Elizabeth "had then wanted to do away with herself. Threw herself in front of car, and taken to Salvation Army."[7] Many records suggest that Elizabeth was not alone, and that the families of young women living at home often rejected their pregnant daughters. Women who were thrown out of their homes were also thrown out of the family economy and onto their own often limited resources, making single pregnancy an economic as well as an emotional crisis. Wage-earning women living apart from their families either left their jobs or could expect to be dismissed when their employer discovered that they were pregnant. Dorothy told the New York Family Welfare Office in 1942 about being fired from her clerical job: "She explained that the manager of the company had questioned her as to whether she was able to work and when she replied in the affirmative, he asked if she were married and upon receiving a negative answer, asked whether she should be. She had said 'yes' to this question and had been discharged."[8]

Out-of-wedlock pregnancy prompted some young women to move away not only from their families but out of their communities. Maternity home workers were aware that a large proportion of unmarried mothers traveled long distances to the homes. "The preponderance of traffic is cityward," George Mangold wrote of unmarried mothers, many of whom migrated from rural to urban areas in search of a solution to their problem.[9] Cities had long offered a refuge to those seeking anonymity, and certainly many unmarried mothers left rural villages and small towns to escape the condemnation of family and community. For the unmarried pregnant woman, larger towns and cities also offered a greater range of choices. Maternity homes were one option, but only a small proportion of single pregnant women elected to go to one.

Ironically, the women who left the fewest historical traces were not working-class women but middle- and upper-class women who had the resources—financial and familial—with which to keep their pregnancies private. Although few sources exist, stories of the middle-class girl who left school to spend time with her aunt and uncle on the farm or of the upper-class girl sent on a European tour retained enough popular currency to suggest their importance as class-specific strategies of handling single pregnancy. Of course, these options were accessible to few women. Depending on their financial resources and familial circumstances, women whose families would not or could not care for them responded to out-of-wedlock pregnancy in one of a variety of ways: they sought abortions, delivery in a hospital, or care in a commercial institution or maternity home.

Both evangelical matrons and social workers were aware that the migration of unmarried mothers to larger cities could signal their search for an illegal abortion rather than for a maternity home. Whereas abortion in the nineteenth century was probably most widely used by white, married, Protestant, native-born women of the middle and upper classes who wished to delay or control their childbearing, by the early twentieth century, unmarried mothers were seeking abortions in greater numbers.[10] One observer in 1923 attested to the number of unmarried mothers who succeeded in procuring abortions when he estimated that "if every physician who even once in his career—under the stress of tragic circumstances, in order to save the life and reputation of a young girl and the happiness of her parents—performed an abortion is a murderer; then 75 percent, nay, probably 90 percent of the medical profession are murderers."[11] Another investigator speculated that "a great number of potential cases of illegitimacy are avoided each year in this country through the efforts of abortionists."[12]

Evangelicals and social workers alike envisioned the maternity home as an alternative to abortion. One woman warned in 1944 that if unmarried mothers "are not assured an opportunity to bear their babies away from prying inquisitiveness, in the decent, wholesome surroundings that befit an enlightened twentieth century, then they would swell the abortion racket far beyond its already alarming heights of 1943."[13] Some women who applied for residence in maternity homes reported having had abortions for previous pregnancies, and clues in case records suggest that many women who turned to the homes did so after attempting to get abortions.[14] Social worker Mary Tinney noted that "practically every other girl who has come into the office has told of some attempt to prevent the birth of her child" and speculated that "if we do not attempt to solve the problem of our unmarried mother quickly and with some degree of success, . . . our girls are going to be educated along lines which we would shudder to contemplate."[15]

It was probably not lack of education but lack of money or nerve that deterred more pregnant single women from procuring abortions. Social workers recognized that fees for this service were prohibitive, making abortions most readily available to women who had both the financial resources to afford them and relationships with doctors who would perform them.[16] Women who sought illegal abortions also risked legal persecution, medical complications, and even death. In her study of state investigations of illegal abortions in Chicago, historian Leslie Reagan finds that though women were not arrested for having abortions, they were punished through intrusive investigations and public exposure.[17] Although most women survived their abortions, Reagan also found the number of deaths following illegal abortions to be "significant."[18]

If a woman either could not afford an abortion or did not want to face the risks of an illegal and often dangerous procedure, she might still choose from several alternatives to the charitable maternity home. Some whose families were willing and able to care for them through their pregnancies joined the increasing number of married women who went to hospitals to have their babies.[19] But even into the twentieth century, many hospitals refused to admit unmarried mothers for maternity care, and a single woman who wanted a hospital delivery often had to lie about her marital status.[20] Still, one observer in 1939 noted that unmarried mothers in Philadelphia turned to hospitals at a rate higher than married women to give birth.[21] For a fee, the unmarried mother who had her child in a hospital was able to receive medical care, at least at the time of delivery, while avoiding the investigation, supervision, and lengthy stay required by most maternity homes. Some hospitals assisted in placing the baby for adoption.

In addition to procuring an abortion or giving birth in a hospital, an unmarried mother with some money at her disposal could choose from a variety of privately run lying-in homes. Florence Crittenton and Salvation Army homes competed with retreats that ran advertisements such as the one placed in the *Denver Post* in 1942 that read "Fairmount Maternity— SECLUSION sanitarium for unmarried girls. Low rates. Confidential."[22] Typically quite expensive, commercial homes covered the hospital and medical care for mother and child and sheltered the mother before and after her delivery. Since many of these homes existed to supply infants to a black market in adoption, the homes made arrangements to place the baby as well.[23]

Associated with "baby farming" and high infant mortality rates, commercial homes came under widespread attack in the early twentieth century. Evangelical women and social workers who led the charges against them deplored lying-in homes for precisely the reasons many unmarried mothers were attracted to them: they placed a premium on secrecy, paid little attention to "character-building," and arranged quiet and quick adoptions. Kate Waller Barrett worried that unmarried mothers who went to commercially run homes "would not likely meet a Christian man or a Christian woman." Should her own daughter get pregnant, Barrett declared, "I would rather she would not have a cent in her pocket than to have her come to this city with a thousand dollars," explaining that "if she was a poor girl she would have to go to Christians to help her. . . . She could go to a dozen institutions" where "everything would be done to upbuild her moral character."[24] The costliness of abortions, hospital care, and lying-in homes meant that only unmarried mothers with money could afford the privilege of giving birth to a child out of wedlock while avoiding close scrutiny of their characters and souls.

The woman who "had only two dollars in the world" or the one who traveled from her small town to New York City with "about eight dollars in my pocketbook" could scarcely afford any of these options.[25] For them, there were few choices other than a charitable maternity home such as those run by the Salvation Army and the NFCM. For several decades after their founding, Florence Crittenton homes maintained a policy of refusing to take money from residents regardless of their financial circumstances. Evangelical women characteristically represented this policy as a humanitarian gesture to the girl in trouble, but a roundtable discussion at the 1903 national conference of the NFCM revealed that control as well as altruism underlay the practice. "I thought it was dreadful to think of taking girls in for pay and allowing them to go right out afterwards," Mrs. Robertson of the Washington, D.C., Crittenton home commented. "I feared the influence in the Home might be bad and that we would not be able to exact obedience to the rules from girls who were independent of us."[26]

As distasteful or disruptive as some evangelical matrons thought the practice would be, they apparently grew accustomed to the idea of charging residents, and by the 1920s, most maternity homes had set standard fees. The average cost of residence in a Crittenton home in 1929 was fifty dollars.[27] Still, most homes were willing to negotiate a flexible payment plan, and it remained the policy, if not always the practice, of both Crittenton and Salvation Army homes to accept women who were unable to pay. "We make no difference between the girl who pays us nothing and the girl who pays us twenty-five dollars a month," Kate Barrett claimed.[28] In 1925, the Boston Florence Crittenton League of Compassion charged residents five dollars per week for room and board and thirty dollars as a hospital fee, but insisted that "the girl who can pay nothing . . . is just as welcome and received precisely the same care and accommodations as those who are able and do pay something."[29] Some homes allowed local women to reside in maternity homes at no charge, but required out-of-town residents to pay the full fee.[30]

Race, even more than class, determined the alternatives available to unmarried mothers. Although case records offer little evidence of how out-of-wedlock pregnancy was handled in Asian-American, Latino, and Native American communities, Annie Lee Davis reported in 1948 that some maternity homes in western states accepted "some Mexican, Chinese and Indian girls," suggesting both that they were reluctant to do so and that most nonwhite single and pregnant women would have to fend for themselves.[31] These same homes refused to admit African-American women, and there is abundant evidence that black unmarried mothers faced sharply circumscribed options. Financial constraints weighed heavily on many, and they also had to contend with the discriminatory policies of maternity homes, most of which were restricted to white women.[32] The Salvation Army women's social secretary wrote in 1919 that Army homes accepted unmarried mothers "independent of creed or color, except where the national prejudice prevents. In the South," she explained, "we have had to confine our work entirely to the white girls," rationalizing the discriminatory policies of most Salvation Army homes.[33]

Evangelical women and social workers argued that the supposed lack of stigma surrounding illegitimacy in black communities justified the segregation of their homes. "The unmarried Negro mother is not looked upon as an outcast, and does not particularly stand in need of the same sort of help as the unfortunate white girl who has violated the conventions of her race," claimed NFCM president Robert Barrett, who concluded that "for the present the real field of work of protecting and reclaiming unfortunate women and girls lies with the white race."[34] Some black unmarried mothers seemed to confirm the view of maternity home workers and contemporary sociologists who held that black families were less likely than their white counterparts to stigmatize out-of-wedlock pregnancy. As Ruby, a nineteen-year-old resident of the New York City Salvation Army home put it, "'Among my people it is not such a disgrace to have a child when one is not married.'"[35] Lizzie, another single mother in the same home, wrote, "'I guess we are different from white people maybe, because we don't think about having babies as much account. We all have plenty of babies, all our friends. Some of them get married and some don't."[36] And Etta explained, "'We are used to doing differently than you do. We live more in common with each other, and mix it up more. . . . If some of the girls have babies, not much is thought about it."[37] Because these words of black unmarried mothers come to us through the report of a white social worker, it is difficult to discern to what extent these women were telling her what they thought she wanted to hear or mocking her assumptions, and to what extent they were reporting candidly on how illegitimacy was handled in black communities. In any event, social investigators seized upon comments like these as representative of what they termed a "colored attitude" toward illegitimacy.[38]

In spite of the insistence of many social workers and investigators that African-Americans were less critical of out-of-wedlock pregnancy, enough black women sought the services of charitably run maternity homes to fill the spaces allotted for them by the few integrated homes and to sustain several homes that were devoted to serving black unmarried mothers. The Jersey City Door of Hope was the only institution in New Jersey to accept African-American women until 1946 and always had a waiting list for the five spaces reserved for them. When the waiting list grew too long, Door of Hope workers compromised their six-month-stay policy and shortened the period of time black women were committed to stay in order to allow more to come. The admissions policy of 1922 stated that "because of the great need for work with the colored girl, we try to keep them on the move." Rather than requiring them to come in three months before delivery, they were not allowed to enter the home until one month before they were due, "and then we work with the social worker to try and have plans completed for her discharge at the end of her six-weeks post-partum examination."[39] The Katy Ferguson Home, a maternity home for black unmarried mothers in New York City, received so many applications that by the 1930s, it was unable to accept referrals from outside the greater New York area.

Many black unmarried mothers went to charitable maternity homes for reasons similar to those of white women: because they had nowhere else to go. Katy Ferguson Home reports were filled with applicants whose families were either unable to support them or unwilling to do so when they discovered their daughter's pregnancy. Eloise, an applicant to the Katy Ferguson Home in 1948, had been living with a sister who was "extremely religious and refused to understand Eloise's condition, so she was asked to leave the house immediately." She came to the home with "no funds, family, or friends who were willing to help her during the pregnancy."[40] Others reported similar stories of desertion or came from families too poor to help them.[41]

Some evidence suggests that maternity homes also served those black women for whom illegitimacy was particularly stigmatizing. Alongside applications to the Katy Ferguson Home from women with "no money or family" were some from either middle-class or aspiring working-class homes, for whom out-of-wedlock pregnancy threatened to undermine hard-won class status that depended on the appearance of respectability. The parents of a high school student who hoped that their daughter would train to be a nurse appealed to the Katy Ferguson Home in 1947 to help their daughter through her pregnancy "in as quiet a manner as possible so that she may resume her life along constructive lines."[42] Sally, a twelve-year-old resident of the New York Salvation Army home, wrote that her friends "'did not feel it made such a difference if a girl had a baby—lots of them that went to school had babies, and it was common.'" But, she noted, "'of course, my people felt different from the rest of the colored people,'" and added, "'my father could never get over it.'"[43]

Unmarried mothers whose meager financial and familial resources left them with few alternatives to charitable maternity homes learned of those homes through different and changing channels and traveled to them along different routes. Many heard of the existence of a home through word of mouth, and either applied themselves or were escorted by a parent or other relative. Others came to maternity homes accompanied by a friend, and occasionally a friend who had herself been a resident in the home in the past.[44] Women and girls were also referred to maternity homes by priests and ministers. One minister appealed to the Jersey City Door of Hope to accept the daughter of a family in his congregation in 1935. She had previously been a resident of the local Florence Crittenton Home, he explained, "due to the fact that someone had taken advantage of her" and "it seems she has again become pregnant."[45]

Unmarried mothers continued to turn to relatives, friends, doctors, or ministers after 1925, indicating the ongoing importance of familial, kinship, and friendship networks in dealing with unmarried pregnancy. Changes in routes taken to maternity homes, however, suggest the expansion of these networks by the 1920s, when many unmarried mothers began to be referred to homes by another social agency to which they had gone first. The authors of an investigation of unmarried mothers in Connecticut in 1927, for example, found that two-thirds of the women who went to maternity homes were referred by another agency.[46]

Another important shift occurred in the late 1930s and 1940s, when many women learned of maternity homes not from their mothers or from doctors, priests, or social workers but from popular magazines. When the new confessional magazines such as *Romantic Story* and *True Love* featured stories of unmarried mothers, popular culture began to compete with families, traditional community leaders, and social service professionals to shape the broader cultural meanings of out-of-wedlock pregnancy. Evangelical women and social workers viewed this development with some discomfort—they disdained what they considered trashy and debauching reading and probably also realized their disadvantage in the battle for the attentions of young working-class women. Perhaps a realistic assessment of the forces against them led to their decision to use confessional magazines rather than to fight them. In 1936, NFCM officers, fearing that their traditionally conservative and discreet strategies for publicizing the homes were failing to reach their audience, decided to capitalize on the large readership of these magazines by running an article in *True Story*. Prepared and probably written by Robert South Barrett, "I Was an Unmarried Mother" opened with a description of the NFCM as "the greatest philanthropic institution in the world for the care of unmarried mothers," and followed with a tale of a young woman, Virginia Day, who found herself pregnant by a married man. Considering suicide, Virginia read of the NFCM, entered the Washington, D.C., Crittenton home and, "after many thrilling experiences" appropriate to the genre of confessional fiction, led "a happy and successful life."[47] The response to the story was immediate and overwhelming. The story was published in September; by October, it had elicited thousands of applications.[48] "No publicity that the Florence Crittenton work has received in many years has brought greater results than the story," one Crittenton worker wrote.[49]

Articles in more mainstream publications followed. In 1944, unmarried mothers from all over the country flooded the Children's Bureau with letters requesting assistance when Virginia Reid's "Black Market Babies" in *Woman's Home Companion* listed the bureau's address.[50] One woman wrote to Children's Bureau worker Maud Morlock for information about maternity homes after reading the article, adding, "You see I am one of the many unmarried, soon to be mothers."[51] Another woman wrote to Morlock, "I am sick with despair, have tried to figure a way that I can have my baby without disgrace, could turn to no one, and pray that you will be able to help me."[52] For women like these, the publication of articles on maternity homes in popular magazines offered a private channel to maternity homes that relieved young women of having to confide in parents or doctors; at the same time, these articles made information about the homes public and widely accessible for the first time.

SOCIAL RELATIONS AMONG UNMARRIED MOTHERS IN MATERNITY HOMES

Women who entered philanthropic maternity homes were most likely those with little money and without family or kin that would or could support them. Yet within that broad shared profile lay a diverse group of women from a surprisingly wide range of ages, classes, occupational and educational backgrounds, and ethnic and racial identities. Although maternity home workers envisioned the residents of their homes as uniformly young, white, Protestant women of the respectable working class, the actual composition of their clientele belied that imaginary community in a number of ways. Despite the highly selective admission policies that both Salvation Army and Crittenton homes devised to elicit homogeneous groups, the communities in many of their homes were striking in their diversity. One woman commented on the women she encountered during her stay in a maternity home in 1946: "There were about twenty-five girls there when I first went there; all of us sleeping in one big room. About ten of the girls were Negroes. Some of the girls were nice, some were tramps, some were sick, some were very young, and there were four or five over forty."[53] Although maternity home workers sought to prevent the coresidence of girls and women of varying ages, the assortment of women in this home was not unusual. Maternity homes often served mothers of widely divergent ages, from twelve- and thirteen-year-old girls to forty-five-year-old women.[54]

The homes attracted an occasional nurse or schoolteacher, but until the 1940s, the vast majority of their clientele came from broadly working-class families.[55] The class background of girls and women in charitable maternity homes, at least before the 1940s, gave maternity home communities the appearance of homogeneity, but within a working-class clientele lay room for marked differences. Although the majority of Jersey City Door of Hope residents, for example, had had less than a ninth-grade education, many left high school to come to the home, and a few came with some college education.[56] Women also came to maternity homes from a variety of living situations. More than two-thirds of the Door of Hope residents claimed to live at home with parents or relatives, and a sizable number lived apart from their families, either lodging in boardinghouses or renting rooms, sometimes alone but more often sharing them with friends.[57] Religious differences as well were pronounced in some homes. Since both Salvation Army and Florence Crittenton homes were run by Protestants with decidedly evangelical goals, one might expect the communities in these homes to be characterized by religious homogeneity. Yet, although Protestants predominated in the Door of Hope—composing roughly 60 percent of the unmarried mothers from 1922 to 1945—over one-third of the residents were Catholic.[58] Racial and ethnic diversity, of course, depended greatly on the admission policy of the home and on its geographical location. Unmarried mothers in the Door of Hope were predominantly American-born of Italian parents, reflecting the ethnic character of the surrounding area.[59] But the home housed women of various ethnic backgrounds, mixing first-generation immigrants with second-generation daughters. And, as mentioned above, although the Salvation Army and the NFCM typically restricted their homes to white women, some, including the Door of Hope, were to some extent racially integrated as well.

Evangelical women, intending to accept only "good girls" of the respectable working class, nevertheless sometimes admitted women who had been in reformatories of various sorts including prison. Even after the Door of Hope made the transition from a rescue home for "wayward" women to a maternity home, the institution still occasionally accepted juvenile delinquents sent by the courts. In 1924, a juvenile court judge sent a young woman to the Door of Hope whom he described as "a fit subject for the care, discipline, and instruction of the Salvation Army Rescue Home . . . in that she is habitually incorrigible."[60] Another woman arrived at the Jersey City home after a veritable tour of New York's and New Jersey's corrective and reform agencies.[61] The most flagrant digression from selective admission policies was the apparently near-routine acceptance of women who had more than one illegitimate child. Although the majority of the Jersey City Door of Hope's resident unmarried mothers were "first offenders," the home accepted some women with two and even three illegitimate children.[62]

Homes that brought together reform school veterans and college graduates, thirteen-year-old school girls and women accustomed to living independently, were bound to engender at least occasional tension. Division and conflict among the unmarried mothers documented in case records seems often to have been precipitated by the confrontation of differences in the homes and by ethnic, racial, and class hierarchies that structured life inside as well as outside their walls.[63] In integrated homes, clashes often took place along lines of race and ethnicity. The matron of the Door of Hope anticipated racial conflict among her charges. To her list of information about the home for new residents in 1945—including rules regarding visiting hours, restrictions on phone calls, and censorship of mail—she added that they had "colored girls."[64] But she failed to forestall discord and sometimes open conflict. A Door of Hope caseworker noted in 1943 that one white woman in the home "got into many arguments with the girls in the Home" and "seemed to take a very special dislike for the colored girls."[65] One woman explained that she wanted to leave the Door of Hope "primarily because she did not have any privacy and felt that living in a dormitory with so many girls of different types, that she would be unhappy if she had to stay for a two-month period"; she told her social worker that, in particular, "she was not prepared to adjust to 'so many foreign girls.'"[66]

In homes in which the majority of unmarried mothers worked in factories, department stores, and other people's homes, the most surprising divisions may have been the ones provoked by class differences. For example, one unmarried mother explained "somewhat self-consciously, that she did not join in the social activities of the other girls, as she felt above them."[67] Another twenty-seven-year-old college graduate told her social worker that she "finds it very difficult . . . to mingle with all types of girls" in the Door of Hope where she was a resident in 1939.[68] Lila, a twenty-year-old black woman whose pregnancy interrupted her sophomore year in college, "had been accustomed to associating with persons in this college category and found much difficulty in adjusting to the environment and girls" in the Katy Ferguson Home where she was a resident in 1945.[69] Another applicant to the Katy Ferguson home wrote, "I am not a loose woman. I am the holder of an MA degree from Teacher's College Columbia University."[70] One woman, who identified herself as a "respectable, twenty-one-year-old schoolteacher," wrote that "I still couldn't believe it had happened to me. I had heard whispered stories about girls 'getting into trouble.' But it was something that just didn't happen among the nice people I knew."[71]

Most of the strained relations probably arose between working-class women and the few middle-class residents of maternity homes. Some tension between unmarried mothers, however, may have been fueled by divisions based on competing standards of respectability within the working class. Out-of-wedlock pregnancy and residency in a maternity home inevitably brought the issues of respectability and reputation to the fore, and some "respectable" unmarried mothers struggled to distinguish themselves from those they considered "rough."[72] "I'm not really a rough and tough of the street," wrote one woman in her application to the NFCM in 1939, adding, "I've not had the life that you no doubt will judge due to my condition, and I don't blame you. . . . I never have smoked or drank as a large number of my age seem to be doing to-day."[73] Families, as well, tried to distinguish their daughters from the supposed rough ranks of unmarried mothers. "I hope you don't get this wrong," one mother wrote to a social worker on her daughter's behalf. "Irene is a very fine girl. She does not indulge in liquor or smoke."[74]

Although the differences that separated unmarried mothers sometimes engendered conflict among them, the circumstances they shared could also work to forge bonds between them. Maternity homes may have housed mixed groups of women, but their residents shared the conditions of out-of-wedlock pregnancy in a society that stigmatized them and the inability to afford alternatives to maternity home care. One unmarried mother felt that she belonged to "a kind of secret sisterhood" and recounted how she had maintained friendships with women she met in a maternity home over time and great geographic distances: "From near the Canadian border, one of the girls I knew at the shelter writes me confidences she wouldn't dare breathe in her little town. Another friend, now happily married, sometimes sends dolls to Ann from her home in Texas. I exchange holiday cards with a third, who has returned to the Midwest."[75] Another woman in 1930 wrote to the Terre Haute Crittenton home where she had been a resident: "There is a comradeship between the girls which links them closely together, there is a common bond of understanding."[76]

This discourse of sisterhood among unmarried mothers perhaps in part reflected the influence of their evangelical matrons. Conceiving of themselves as belonging to a sisterhood of women reformers, maternity home workers tried to foster similar relationships among the unmarried mothers under their care. In addition to introducing them to the refining virtues of piety and domesticity, evangelical women touted the elevating influence of sisterhood, and female cooperation became a central ideal of maternity home life.[77] Kate Barrett encouraged unmarried mothers to band together: "When a new girl comes into the home it is the attitude of the girls in the home that will decide her future in the home more than anything that the superintendent or the Board are able to do," Barrett admonished Crittenton residents in 1919. "If you meet a new girl in a friendly way and remember how homesick you felt when you first came and tell her that she will find friends there, and that everything will come out right, she will start with that thought in her heart."[78] Viewing unmarried mothers as casualties of excessively heterosocial working-class amusements, evangelical matrons envisioned maternity homes as a homosocial antidote—a spatial and psychological separation from men that would free residents from their supposed preoccupation with the opposite sex. In addition to the domestic and religious regimen they imposed, evangelical women hoped that simply removing unmarried mothers from mixed-sex company and providing them with an all-female retreat might be purifying in and of itself.

Salvation Army matrons tried to institutionalize sisterly bonds among unmarried mothers that would endure after they left the homes. Former residents were invited to join "Out-of-Love Clubs," so named "as an indication of the fact that what they do now for the Home is out of love for it."[79] Some clubs provided volunteer service to the home: "loyal to the institution" and "grateful for the wonderful service rendered to them," club members "always grasp the opportunity of giving a helping hand to some other girl who has met with the same misfortune."[80] The members held weekly meetings at the home and helped to secure positions for those about to leave. Other clubs operated as social groups. In one, former residents returned to the home once a month for a dinner party.[81] Membership in some Out-of-Love Clubs allowed women to return to the home in times of need. The Chicago home, for example, set aside "a room handsomely furnished" for the use of former residents who were temporarily out of work.[82]

Undoubtedly some former maternity home residents benefited from the Out-of-Love Clubs and willingly participated in their activities. The clubs, however, were structured by evangelical matrons, and the sisterhood nurtured by them could be coercive. One Salvation Army worker explained that "when a girl loses interest in the club, which seldom occurs, Major Cowden immediately seeks her out, and after a little talk or a heart-to-heart letter, the tardy one becomes as active as ever."[83] The Salvation Army worker who characterized the Out-of-Love Club as "the Home's follow-up system" suggested that the clubs could also serve a policing function, allowing the Salvation Army to keep tabs on former residents.[84] Membership in the Out-of-Love Club "presupposes that the life she is living is all that it should be," and a lapse in membership alerted maternity home workers to a more dangerous lapse in morals.[85]

Although evangelical women cast unmarried mothers as sisters in the surrogate families they attempted to create in maternity homes, the residents could form strong and lasting bonds with each other on their own initiative and on their own terms. The most basic and potentially subversive expression of sisterhood in maternity homes revolved around unmarried mothers' shared condition. For many women, a stay in a maternity home allowed the possibility of experiencing out-of-wedlock pregnancy as a collective undertaking rather than a private crisis. One woman wrote of her stay at the Lakeview home: "One cannot overestimate the truth in the words 'misery loves company.' I imagined myself alone in a predicament of this sort and I was in desperate need of understanding and help. At Lakeview, many girls share the same problem. Although I consider my situation serious, my moods are no longer depressive or morbid, I have the opportunity of analyzing my situation thoroughly, and I hope to benefit from my own and some of the other girls' experiences."[86]

Presumably, evangelical women would have endorsed this woman's attitude as healthy and positive. Many, however, believed that the kind of sisterly bonds described by the Lakeview resident could easily shift into relationships of a less edifying nature. Social worker Helen Welsh noticed that the women at the Minneapolis maternity home she supervised "were under the impression that it was but very seldom indeed that an unmarried girl became a mother" before they came to the institution. When they came to the home, however, "they suddenly realize that there are many girls who have done what they should not, conventionally at least. They begin to think that after all their deed was not so wrong." In the process, Welsh noted with some dismay that unmarried mothers "were losing their regret and conscience-stricken feeling."[87]

As Welsh suggested, if sisterhood rooted in the common bond of out-of-wedlock pregnancy worked to rid unmarried mothers of shame, it could disrupt maternity home goals. Accordingly, most homes designed rules to prevent unmarried mothers from talking about their experiences. Kate Barrett explained that upon entering a Florence Crittenton home, the unmarried mother "is told that she must not discuss the sorrows and sins of her past, but that if any time she needs advice or comfort, she is free to come to the matron to receive it."[88] "If any questions are asked you can let the girls know kindly that you do not want to talk about yourself," a dramatic skit advised Crittenton residents in 1935.[89] And in a prize-winning essay submitted to a Florence Crittenton contest, a maternity home resident explained that "a rule of the home is that we do not tell our history to one another."[90] Sisterhood was to be encouraged among unmarried mothers, but only on the terms approved by evangelical women.

Matrons' injunctions against discussing past experiences seemed to go largely unheeded, however, and ironically, homes designed to inhibit unmarried mothers' sexuality became virtual clearinghouses of sexual information. "Boy, what an education I got there," wrote Rusty Brown of the Florence Crittenton home to which she was sent by the juvenile court in the late 1930s. She found herself in a home with "women who had been picked up for everything from pickpocketing to prostitution" and recalled that her fellow residents "were going to teach me the ropes."[91] The homes could also serve as places to exchange information regarding contraception and abortion. The Door of Hope matron sent one woman home in 1923 because "she has been telling the girls how she did away with the baby using a crochet hook. She has been explaining to them how to do it."[92] Maternity home workers were aware of the exchange of sexual information that took place in maternity homes, but there seemed to be little they could do to prevent it. Edith Livingston Smith observed that in maternity homes, "as in reformatories and prisons, the water of evil passions finds its lowest level, so where many girls are gathered together there is danger that innocent minds will acquire knowledge that coarser natures have possessed to their destruction."[93]

The bonds that unmarried mothers created out of shared experiences not only worried evangelical women; they seemed dangerous enough to some social workers to justify opposing maternity homes altogether. Struck more by the subversive than by the curative potential of sisterhood among unmarried mothers, some warned of the emotional ties nurtured in the collective experience of maternity home living. As early as 1890, a Boston Children's Aid Society worker proposed that unmarried mothers be kept from associating with one another, explaining that there was "nothing worse for people who have been guilty of misconduct than to find that plenty of other people have done the same thing."[94] Thirty-two years later, social worker Edith Baylor agreed, writing that "to my mind, the only drawback in Maternity Home Care is the grouping together of girls who have been through a common experience, and through other revolting experiences, about which they are only too ready to compare notes." She argued that maternity home friendships should be terminated at the end of the woman's stay, "as they too often result in a drifting back into the old life. I have known instances when an acquaintance acquired at the Maternity Home succeeded in undermining entirely the work of an agency."[95] Another social worker added that "in so many instances maternity homes mean the pooling of experiences with over-emphasis on the particular experience through which the mothers are passing."[96] Social workers worried that the maternity home would "permit the exchange of confidences and the forming of new and dubious friendships comparable to that in institutions of correction with effects for the individual equally harmful."[97]

Forged from shared experience, sisterhood among maternity home residents could take on more instrumental and pragmatic purposes. As such,

their relations resembled less the genteel middle-class sisterhood celebrated by evangelical matrons and more the relations based on reciprocity
and mutuality described by historians of working-class women.[98] Case
records hint at ties of interdependence between unmarried mothers that
could directly subvert authority in the homes. Residents commonly assisted each other in running away from homes, for example. When one
woman escaped from the Door of Hope in 1937, another unmarried mother
"helped her to get away by giving her a sweater."[99] Residents also routinely smuggled out mail for one another and helped arrange clandestine
meetings with boyfriends.[100] One woman who checked into the Salvation
Army home in Des Moines one morning in 1925 had made arrangements by
that evening to smuggle out a letter to her boyfriend. "Someone is slipping
this out for me," she wrote. "The woman that is going to mail this is waiting
for this so will have to close."[101] Ties between unmarried mothers in the
Crittenton home in Norfolk, Virginia, ensured that resistance to a new rule
in that home in 1898 would be collective. When the superintendent declared
a change in policy—"that no girl should leave the house without me"—she
"anticipated trouble and dissatisfaction, . . . but nothing like what did
occur." Her description of the incident left much to the imagination, but she
underlined both the collective and premeditated nature of a rebellion that
"culminated in a dreadful scene on Tuesday morning. It commenced at the
breakfast-table and must have been planned beforehand. . . . I never experienced anything like it," she wrote, "and hope never to do again. I could
not have believed it possible that women in their sober senses could act
thus. I have never seen even drunken people as bad, and when I tried to
make things calm was met with jeers and wild laughter."[102]

The possibility of sisterly ties developing into what were beginning to be
termed, in the parlance of the period, "unhealthy attachments" also concerned maternity home workers. When lesbianism became the focus of
considerable medical and sexological attention and inquiry in the 1920s and
1930s, this concern no doubt intensified. Sisterhood among "fallen women"
might have been unambivalently endorsed in the nineteenth century, but
by the early twentieth century, the new medical discourse on "inversion"
rendered homosociality, especially that nurtured in single-sex institutions,
suspect.[103] This suspicion seemed to inform Kate Barrett's recommendation in 1903 that maternity homes be designed with three-person bedrooms
rather than doubles: "If two girls are put together in a room, often unwise
friendships are formed," she stated. "The old adage 'two is company, but
three is a crowd' proves true in this case; the third one in the room forming
a kind of balance wheel for the other two."[104] In these instructions for

organizing the spatial interior of a home, Barrett raised the possibility of "unhealthy" relationships developing in the single-sex environment.

Case records are generally mute on this topic, and romantic and sexual relationships between unmarried mothers remain an especially opaque aspect of life in maternity homes. But a decision made by the board of the Chicago Florence Crittenton Anchorage in 1912 suggests that these relationships may have been of concern to Anchorage workers. At a meeting of the board, "it was moved and carried that dancing shall not be permitted in the Home." Explanation for this decision was brief; the minutes report that "Miss McNeal thinks it is a connecting link with the underworld" and added cryptically that "the subject came up because of the conduct of two girls at the reception."[105] Whether the women offended Crittenton workers simply by dancing or by dancing together, these ambiguous comments suggest that relationships between unmarried mothers often took forms that were objectionable to evangelical women.

PUTTING MATERNITY HOMES TO USE

Rather than the elevating love of middle-class evangelical sisterhood, the sisterhood shared by unmarried mothers revolved around the exchange of favors, the common experience of out-of-wedlock pregnancy, and shared information about sex. The mothers' ability to form sisterly bonds different from those envisioned for them by evangelical women was only one expression of their larger struggle to use maternity homes for their own purposes. Preceding chapters have explored the competing notions held by evangelical women and social workers regarding the appropriate function of the maternity home. In its constitution of 1934, the NFCM stated that Crittenton homes aimed "to provide for women and young girls who have led profligate lives, or having been betrayed from the path of virtue are sincerely willing to reform, temporary homes and employment until they can be returned to friends, or established in honest industry."[106] Most social workers would doubtless have preferred Maud Morlock's description of the maternity home as "a place of treatment."[107] Unmarried mothers, on the other hand, seemed to have little use for either notion of the maternity home as a place of redemption or treatment. Indeed, rehabilitation of any sort rarely entered into the residents' ideas about the homes.

Although their goals often had little to do with those of evangelicals or social workers, they were by no means identical for all women. One woman, for example, in her first interview at the Door of Hope in Jersey City in 1942, told her social worker that she was looking forward to her stay in the maternity home as a time to "relax." Not a little taken aback, the social worker registered her concern that "all Anna wanted was a place to stay until after the baby was delivered." She wondered if Anna had been apprised of "the real purpose of the home" and concluded, "This will have to be explained further."[108] Anna was not alone in imagining the home as a restful retreat. One resident stated that she "did not have to worry about a thing while in the maternity home."[109] Another agreed, adding that she especially appreciated her private room, "'where you can get away by yourself.'"[110]

Not all unmarried mothers looked to maternity homes as places to relax, but the exchange between Anna and her social worker suggests a starting point from which to explore the disjunction between the homes as their keepers wished them to be used and the actual uses to which they were put by their residents. Although evangelical women and social workers entertained fundamentally different visions of the purpose of maternity homes, neither imagined them as providing places for residents to relax. Anna's remark makes clear that unmarried mothers came to maternity homes with agendas of their own.

The main appeal of the homes to many seemed to lie in the shelter and privacy they offered. Many took refuge in them to escape the wrath—actual or feared—of their families. One woman who applied for admission to the Door of Hope in 1939 told the matron that "she was anxious to get away from home because her mother and father did not know she was pregnant and she was afraid her father would find out and he was a very high-strung hot-blooded man and he would be very angry."[111] Another woman requesting admission to the Door of Hope told the officers there that she "does not want 'her people' to know."[112]

Evangelical women, while allowing unmarried mothers to take refuge in maternity homes, insisted that this function was secondary to that of rehabilitation and redemption. Most would have agreed with Sheltering Arms worker Marie Winokur who confessed to "a horror for maternity homes that serve as a refuge only," adding that "I firmly believe that the Mother should look upon the Home as a training school and not as a refuge—only then can we reach the girl and bring the best out of her."[113] In support of a longer required period of commitment for Crittenton residents, NFCM president Robert Barrett wrote that "we must never lose sight of the fact that we are not operating lying-in hospitals, concerned largely with the physical needs of young women, who find themselves in difficulties because of their own indiscretions."[114]

Yet many unmarried mothers saw the homes in precisely those terms.

And the comments of maternity home workers make clear that some succeeded in using the homes for their own purposes rather than as their keepers wished them to be used. "I do not feel that we have accomplished very much with this girl outside of giving her shelter and protection," wrote a Door of Hope matron of one resident in 1944.[115] Invested by their evangelical founders with the best rehabilitative and redemptive intentions, maternity homes often became simply shelters in practice.

Although maternity home workers did not approve of the desire on the part of many of their residents to use the homes as retreats to wait out their pregnancies, they at least understood the motives of those who sought secrecy. And by placing a premium on privacy, they perhaps inadvertently lent the homes to those purposes. But not all unmarried mothers sought privacy, and evangelical women were baffled by those who seemed not to care about the secrecy provided by the homes. The superintendent of the Norfolk Crittenton home in 1898, for example, fought an uphill battle with two residents, Lucy and Bertha, who, by insisting on "flirting through the windows," both displayed a lack of appropriate shame regarding their condition and exhibited a troubling public sexuality.[116] The same superintendent was forced to escort two other residents on a walk outside the gates of the home. "It is one of the oddest things how some of them love to be on the street," she wrote.[117]

In addition to their important function as refuge, maternity homes also offered inexpensive or free obstetrical care. Dr. Thomas Goethals, chief of the medical staff of the Boston Crittenton home, boasted that "the girls who are admitted to the Florence Crittenton Home receive a standard of medical service which is in every respect equal to that available to the most wealthy patient."[118] Pre- and postnatal care was out of reach of most working-class women in this period, and residents of many of the homes were provided with weekly medical checkups and a hospital delivery. By the 1920s, most maternity homes had hired medical staff, and many had constructed their own maternity wards so that residents could receive medical care without leaving the premises.[119]

Although evangelical women prided themselves on the medical care provided in their homes, they were anxious to differentiate their function from that of hospitals and lying-in homes. When a social worker appealed to the Door of Hope to readmit a client into the home—a resident who had left before her child was born—the superintendent refused, explaining that "our function was not a maternity hospital. We only took girls whom we felt we could help."[120] When one unmarried mother applied for admission to the Door of Hope but objected to the rule requiring her to stay for three months after her delivery, the matron of the home told her that "she could go to any Hospital and pay the bill and come home at the end of ten days"; she explained that "that was not our work, that in order to help a girl we needed to keep her for a longer period."[121]

Again, as some unmarried mothers used the homes as refuges and places of relaxation over the objections of maternity home workers, so too did they succeed in using the homes for maternity care and little else. "We are sorry to have to report in closing this case that we feel very little was done except the physical care and treatment given to Lillian, to help her during her stay with us," the Door of Hope matron wrote in 1937; "she did not respond to any kind of help that we tried to give her."[122] The matron noted that one resident was "most cooperative, and showed a real interest in everything she did" before her child was born. But "after her hospital period, she seemed to be an entirely different person, she did not want to work, was anxious to get away from here." The matron attributed this woman's behavior to "a dual personality."[123] More probably, the woman had used the home as she needed and was ready to leave. It is difficult to conclude that the stenographer who arrived at the Door of Hope in labor and left two weeks later or the many women who stayed less than three weeks were using the home for anything other than maternity care.[124]

In contrast to the unmarried mothers who stayed for short periods of time were others who used maternity homes as long-term shelters. The Door of Hope case records show that ten women stayed longer than nine months after their babies were born, and three longer than one year. Some homes offered to board babies of the mothers after they left, again reflecting the efforts—often successful—of unmarried mothers to use the homes as they needed them. Many homes provided day care for children, and some offered long-term boarding for former residents who had gone back to work. In 1941, a Door of Hope worker explained that "in order to meet a great need in the community, we increased our services to include a boarding children's nursery."[125]

The families of unmarried mothers also used maternity homes for reasons of their own. Many sent their daughters to avoid their own embarrassment and shame. A Door of Hope worker noted that "even though the girl herself appears ungrateful, her parents, relatives, or friends have expressed their gratitude and appreciation at finding a place such as this for their girls at the time of misfortune and oftentimes real sorrow and heartache."[126] One woman appealed to New York's Jewish Board of Guardians in 1937 to help her place her daughter in a maternity home: " 'We have always been regarded as respectable and honest,'" she wrote. "'We could never live here again if people knew.'"[127]

In addition to this purpose, which often overlapped with the daughter's desire to keep her pregnancy under wraps, parents used maternity homes as places of last resort to help them control ungovernable daughters. Historians have shown how working-class families availed themselves of the juvenile court to discipline their children and shore up their waning parental authority, and some records suggest that parents and relatives of unmarried mothers used maternity homes in this way as well.[128] One woman who escorted her niece to the Door of Hope in 1942 asked the superintendent not to allow the girl out by herself and to "make her do as she was told as she needed some stern discipline in order to keep her in control."[129] A father asked the Door of Hope to admit his teenage daughter, claiming that she was "unmanageable in the home, that her mother had no control over her, and that he . . . was away from home most of the time, and was not able to control her as he desired to." He explained to the superintendent that his daughter "delights in running around with boys and staying out at nights" and that he feared that "if something isn't done she'll go from bad to worst."[130]

Not only were unmarried mothers and their families able to turn maternity homes to their own purposes (although those purposes were often at odds), but within limits, they were able to shape the policies of those homes. Maternity homes had probably long responded to the needs of unmarried mothers, but in the 1940s, the mothers seem to have gained new leverage. This shift in power was probably due in large part to a booming wartime economy, which meant that women who only a few years before might have had to go to maternity homes could now afford other alternatives. Robert Barrett consoled a Crittenton worker in Seattle in 1943 about her difficulties in attracting unmarried mothers to her home: "This is one of the conditions brought about by war and it is only a temporary one I am sure. Young women are receiving such large payments for their service in factories and offices . . . that when they get in trouble through sexual irregularities, they can afford to pay for abortions or their way in private hospitals or commercial maternity homes rather than go to charitable institutions where they are under certain restraints."[131] In 1944, the Boston Illegitimacy Committee found that an increasing number of unmarried mothers were going to private hospitals "since they had money for confinement care."[132] The homes that rescinded some of their more burdensome rules still received more applications than they could accept, but those unwilling to do so faced sharp reductions in the number of those requesting admission. Salvation Army and Crittenton workers in many homes had geared up to accommodate the domestic casualties of the dislocations of wartime, only to find themselves in many instances with empty beds.[133]

Declining admissions encouraged maternity home workers to consider changing their policies. "The girl of today cannot be helped as the girl of yesterday," one Crittenton worker noted. "Many of our methods of a generation ago cannot be used in the programs for the modern girl any more than the square peg can be fitted into the proverbial round hole. We must be able to speak her language, to interpret her reactions and view-point."[134] And it seemed that "the girl of today" was especially averse to the many rules and restrictions governing her behavior and movement while in a maternity home. Hester Brown, an officer of the NFCM, observed that "the inhibiting enforcements that are most objectionable to the mod-ern girls are censoring the mail, refusing to let girls go out unchaperoned to Church, picture shows, and shopping and with little or no freedom in receiving or returning visits from their family and friends. In other words," she noted, unmarried mothers complain of "being too long out of circulation and leading a life that is not considered normal."[135] Many homes in this period began to bend the rules. When Sara Edlin found that unmar-ried mothers in the Lakeview home "were not merely irritated but strongly resented this invasion of their privacy"—the matron's reading incoming and outgoing mail—she discontinued the practice.[136] Although social work-ers had long advocated more flexible rules in maternity homes, social worker Agnes Hanna attributed changes in maternity home policy not to their efforts but "largely to the apparent unwillingness of unmarried moth-ers to accept the restrictions imposed by many of these homes in the past, which was reflected in the decreasing requests for care."[137]

Perhaps the biggest concession to changing times was the move on the part of many maternity homes to shorten the length of stay required of unmarried mothers. One Crittenton worker knew as early as 1937 that "the modern girl is not going to sit contentedly marking time for six months, with nothing to interest her except house work and caring for babies."[138] By the 1940s, many maternity homes had responded by shortening the required length of residence. Workers directly linked this decision to the refusal of women to stay for long periods. Robert Barrett registered his disapproval of shortening residence requirements as well as his resignation to the change when he wrote in 1942 that "all homes find an unwillingness on the part of the girls to stay the period of time necessary for their physical and moral upbuilding. Consequently, some Homes have been compelled to drop the minimum stay in the Home to ninety days, or less."[139] And the director of the Crittenton home in Detroit stated in 1942 that "we felt there was a definite need for a change in our policy in order to meet the present day problems of our applicants;" she shortened the stay required in her home from three months to two. "We have now changed our policy to meet the girls' needs," she wrote.[140]

The decision of many homes to shorten the required length of stay was no small concession, for it also shortened the period of time devoted to character building and threatened to compromise the commitment of both Crittenton and Salvation Army homes to keep mother and child together. Salvation Army Brigadier Ruth Pagen informed Maud Morlock in 1944 that "we are attempting to be much more flexible concerning their requests for care for their babies. If the girl is placing her baby in adoption and does not wish to care for it during her stay with us, in most instances, it is not necessary for her to do so." Pagen added that "this is a fairly new trend in Maternity Home care."[141] And although the NFCM managed to maintain its policy of keeping mother and child together in the face of enormous pressure from social workers, many individual Crittenton homes, finding that they could not uphold this policy and survive, bowed to the demands of unmarried mothers to help them place their children for adoption.[142] As early as 1926, a Boston Crittenton officer informed the NFCM president that "you stated that whenever you heard of a Florence Crittenton Home having babies adopted, it was, in your judgment, no longer doing Florence Crittenton work. So far as I could find out practically all of the Homes consent to the adoption of babies from time to time."[143] By the 1940s, supported by the commitment of social workers to adoption, most homes were routinely arranging for the adoption of babies.

The willingness of many maternity homes to defy their national organization and arrange adoptions testifies to the power of unmarried mothers to change the policy of those homes. The persistence of these rules on the national level might demonstrate the tenacity of evangelical women in the face of challenges by social workers; nevertheless, the bending of rules in local homes illustrates the insistence of unmarried mothers that the homes suit their needs. Rather than passively submitting to the policies of maternity homes, unmarried mothers struggled to shape those policies.

Residents of charitable maternity homes were, for the most part, women for whom out-of-wedlock pregnancy was emotionally traumatic and economically devastating. Yet, despite their desperate straits, they pursued agendas in the homes that were often at odds with those of their keepers. Active participants in the homes, they formed relationships with one another different from and occasionally subversive to those envisioned for them by workers and put the homes to purposes for which they were never intended.

Unmarried mothers pushed their resourcefulness to the limits imposed by the unequal balance of power built into the homes. The next chapter explores those limits more closely, considering the ways unmarried mothers negotiated relationships with maternity home workers and responded to maternity home regimes. Finally, it considers the ways they constructed the meaning of their pregnancies for themselves.

4

"Problem Girls": Docility and Dissidence in Maternity Homes

Of her stay at the Lakeview maternity home on Staten Island, one young woman wrote, "'though to all this is a home, to some it is a prison as well, because we are not here of our own choice.'"[1] In a sentence, she captured the ambiguity inherent in the quasi-voluntary, quasi-coercive nature of charitable maternity homes, as well as in the hierarchical arrangement of power in those homes. She was probably no less resourceful than many women who struggled to put maternity homes to their own purposes. Yet those efforts were bounded by the place unmarried mothers occupied in homes that were explicitly disciplinary and implicitly incarcerational.

This chapter explores the parameters of power in the homes by considering the ways in which unmarried mothers both accommodated to and resisted the regimes of maternity homes and the visions of those who ran them. In documenting the everyday choices and practices of unmarried mothers, case records and maternity home logbooks illuminate the contours of relationships between maternity home residents and staff and deepen our understanding of the lived experience of out-of-wedlock pregnancy in the first half of the twentieth century.

The nature of that lived experience, however, was inseparable from the

ways in which it was represented in "expert" discourse and from the responses of unmarried mothers to those representations. This chapter explores the efforts of unmarried mothers to create their own meanings of out-
of-wedlock pregnancy. Drawn from a range of disparate discourses and
cultural narratives of single pregnancy, the identities they constructed for
themselves always referred to and sometimes opposed those constructed
for them.

"COMING TO AN AWFUL PLACE": BENEVOLENT INCARCERATION IN
MATERNITY HOMES

To some women, the forces arrayed against them in maternity homes were
vivid and potent indeed. Upon her arrival at the Crittenton home in Scranton, Pennsylvania, one woman believed that she was "coming to an awful
place" and recalled that she was "nearly frightened to death from things
people had said of Homes."[2] Another, whose first impression of the Crittenton home she entered in 1915 "was that of a jail," invoked a metaphor of
imprisonment that many unmarried mothers called on to describe maternity homes.[3] Some imagined the homes as prisonlike before they arrived,
perhaps influenced by popular fictional depictions of forbidding gothic institutions for girls.[4] One woman, for example, "pictured Lakeview as a
terrible institution where everyone looked upon you as if you had committed a crime."[5] Another wrote that "visions of the reform school, of the
House of the Good Shepherd—places that I had heard the girls at the
factory refer to as punitive refuges for wicked young girls—swam before
my tortured imagination."[6] Like many unmarried mothers, she expected
the maternity home to differ little from a reformatory or prison.

Although residence in maternity homes for some women contradicted
their expectations, many experienced their confinement as incarceration
for an offense. Jennie, a resident of the Lakeview home, wrote: "'Your first
impression as you walk in is of a rather large private home, but small details
bring out the fact that this is, in reality, an institution.'"[7] Of her stay in a
maternity home, another woman wrote, "it made me feel like a criminal.
And a prisoner."[8] Women commonly referred to the end of their stay in
maternity homes as "when my time is up," as if they were serving a
sentence.[9] No matter how sincerely evangelical matrons struggled to make
maternity homes "homelike," it was difficult for unmarried mothers to
comprehend institutions in which matrons required their commitment to
stay for a certain amount of time as a condition for admittance, monitored

their visitors, read their mail, and dictated what they could wear as anything other than punitive and prisonlike.

Some women described the sense of imprisonment in terms that were more literal. One Jersey City Door of Hope resident was "under the impression that this was a Home of detention" where she was being held for the crime of out-of-wedlock pregnancy.[10] Another former resident appealed to Grace Abbott of the Children's Bureau on behalf of her friend, who was in the House of Good Shepherd in St. Louis. Beginning "Dear Sister," she took the language of imprisonment several steps further, begging Abbott to intervene "to open the Doors of these Slave pens of House's of Good Shepherds where girls are put and made Slaves for their Benefit and never allowed to come out any more or allowed to see any one who goes there to see them." She explained that the matron of the home would not deliver her letters or allow her to visit her friend, and concluded, "please see if you can do something for this awful thing that is going on in these close up places where poor girls are made [to] work for the Benefit of others. . . . This is nothing but slavery. We did have Black slavery but this is white slavery."[11] For this woman, the metaphor of incarceration was not strong enough to evoke the sense of powerlessness felt by many maternity home residents. Although her invocation of slavery is startling, her characterization of the maternity home as a sort of jail was not uncommon. As one woman explained, "I know now that anyone of us could have gotten out of that place any time we wanted to. But I didn't know it then. We were all beaten."[12]

SOCIAL RELATIONS IN MATERNITY HOMES: ACCOMMODATION AND RESISTANCE

Though depictions of the homes as prisons undoubtedly disturbed maternity home workers, some acknowledged the limits of their ability to control the way unmarried mothers experienced maternity home life. Superintendent of the Lakeview home Sara Edlin, for example, knew that "no matter what our own thinking on the subject may be, . . . to them an institution is synonymous with a place of punishment, an exile to which they are banished. They look upon their coming as a jail sentence."[13] Few maternity home workers were as astute or as honest as Edlin, however, and most were inclined to emphasize what they saw as the underlying equality of their relations with women they sometimes paradoxically referred to as "inmates." As Evangeline Booth asserted in 1910, Salvation Army matrons displayed "no touch of patronage or condescension."[14] An ethic of harmony resonates through the writing of maternity home workers, whose proclamations of mutual respect denied the existence of conflict and smoothed over the rougher edges of their relationships with unmarried mothers.

Of course, harmony between maternity home staff and unmarried mothers did not exist entirely in the imaginations of evangelical matrons. Some unmarried mothers were surprised when matrons treated them with respect, dignity, and equality. A Lakeview resident initially feared that "somehow the staff would feel or show some condemnation for the girls," but she found their attitude to be "quite the reverse. It would seem to the staff that there are no bad girls, but there are girls with problems, who are not to be looked down upon because they have made a serious mistake."[15] Another resident of the home agreed: "'I feel like an equal here. Nobody says you are good, you are bad, or anything.'"[16] An unmarried mother in a Minneapolis home in 1940 found the staff there "sympathetic and helpful," and mentioned in particular that "not once had any of the workers made a comment which showed they thought themselves superior to the girls."[17]

Letters from unmarried mothers suggest that they were often intensely devoted to maternity home matrons, and many expressed sincere appreciation for care provided them in the homes. "I will never forget your goodness to me," one woman wrote to the matron of the Des Moines Salvation Army home in 1925, "and I'm hoping that sometime I'll be able to do something for you in return."[18] Some referred to evangelical women as "mothers," accepting their role as "daughters" in the homes and suggesting that the ideology of family promoted by evangelical women held some meaning for them as well. One woman wrote to the Crittenton League of New York City, where she had been a resident: "Good motherly women like you are hard to find, and as God made you He matched the position you now hold. If there were more women with human hearts like yours there would be less bad girls in this world."[19] Another former maternity home resident wrote in 1933, "The Florence Crittenton Home gave me a chance. They took me in and I stayed six months. . . . The Superintendent of that Home was an Angel. We called her 'mother,' and she was just that."[20]

Others went further still, thanking evangelical matrons for their good influence and guidance. "'I do want you to know that I appreciate and always will appreciate everything you did for me,'" one woman wrote in 1942. "'I don't think that I would have recovered as well and as far as I have if you had not been so kind and understanding.'"[21] Another went to the superintendent's office upon her departure from the Door of Hope in 1939 to thank the officers "for what had been done for her and in expressing her gratitude said the three months' stay had been of real benefit and she felt she was a much better girl for having spent this time at the Door of Hope Home."[22] In a letter to the superintendent of the home where she had been a resident, another woman recalled that, "I was a very miserable girl when I came to the Florence Crittenton Home. I have always felt that I should like to do something for the Home for it surely did everything for me. Perhaps you think I was grateful for shelter, food, and nursing care. Yes, but this was the smallest part of it. It was really the ethics of the place that got me. I absorbed your philosophy of life, your way of looking at things."[23] For Justina, a resident of the Norfolk Crittenton home in 1904, the teachings of her matron "became indelible."[24]

Evangelical women were most honored by those unmarried mothers who were moved by the religious training they received in the homes to proclaim conversion. One Door of Hope resident told the matron that after Bible class, "she had gone up to go to bed but felt she could not without telling me what the Class had meant to her, that she had been all tied up inside but something had broken down, she felt the presence of the Lord, knew He had spoken to her, and all the burden and tension seemed to be gone. . . . She was so grateful she felt she could not let me go away without knowing."[25] Another unmarried mother, though described by the matron as "rough and ill-mannered" and "probably promiscuous," attended all the religious meetings held at the home and often cried through them. Taking her tears to be an auspicious sign, the matron talked with her "about her soul," and the woman left the home professing salvation and promising to go to church.[26] Yet another told the Door of Hope matron that she "felt very keenly about leaving our Home," the matron adding that "she has learned to love the Lord since she has been here."[27]

Of course, case records reflect the experience of unmarried mothers as recorded by the staffs of maternity homes, who no doubt listened, heard, and recorded selectively. We might expect, for example, that positive expressions more readily found their way into maternity home logbooks than less-than-glowing reports. Interpreting expressions of gratitude is also complicated by the context in which they typically appeared. Many seem to have been solicited in exit interviews, which were routine in many homes and apparently invited scripted appreciation on the part of the woman leaving. And it is possible that some were wholly fabricated, so closely did they accord with evangelicals' own understanding of the homes and so well did they suit their purposes. Maternity home workers quickly turned positive letters to their own advantage, excerpting them in pamphlets advertising the homes and using the particularly glowing examples to adorn the covers of brochures year after year.

Yet, for all the repetition of appreciative phrases from letters that appeared in maternity home publicity, many were unsolicited. Some former residents continued to write friendly and thankful letters years after they had left the home. The quieter, less obviously scripted expressions of gratitude demand that we take seriously the sincerity of many of the women. In a letter informing the Door of Hope of the death of her child shortly after her departure, a former resident thanked the matrons and asked, "Was James ever Christian please tell me."[28]

One need not minimize the affection and respect that some unmarried mothers felt for maternity home workers to suggest that these relationships had other dimensions as well. To focus only on mutual respect is to flatten a much richer, more complex range of relations. Despite maternity home workers' assertions of equality, the undeniably unequal balance of power between unmarried mothers and the staff of the homes could not help but shape the relations between them. Although they could be harmonious and respectful, their relations were also often marked by tension and conflict. For all the unmarried mothers who "absorbed the ethics of the place," there were others who resisted them as strongly.

Because maternity home workers were reluctant to acknowledge dissension in their ranks, most evidence of resistance on the part of unmarried mothers surfaces in the case records in brief, telegraphic comments that allude to acts of resistance without specifying their motivation, substance, or form. "Does not cooperate to help herself get better," the matron wrote of a Door of Hope resident in 1934.[29] "Considerable trouble with Ruth," a superintendent reported in 1937, adding only that she was "impudent and ungrateful and a continual disturber of the peace."[30] Another unmarried mother at the Door of Hope "has been the source of much disturbance and unrest," and a resident of the Pittsburgh Salvation Army home in 1910 was "so unmanageable we had to ask Juvenile Court to take her away."[31]

Although maternity home workers were typically unforthcoming when it came to acknowledging dissatisfaction in the homes, those dissatisfactions were evidently compelling enough for the matron of the Detroit Florence Crittenton home in 1925 to initiate weekly meetings for unmarried mothers to air their complaints. Referred to as a "friendly family conference" by the staff and dubbed " 'Bawling Out Night' " by the residents, the meeting was intended to offer a forum for staff and residents to "talk over the regulations of the Home and the reasons therefor." The matron boasted that "we have yet to meet an incipient rebel who has not been won over to admit the fairness of our rules."[32]

Yet, just as maternity home workers were unable to dictate the terms on which the residents formed sisterly bonds, they were similarly unsuccessful in diffusing their resentments. Apparently "Bawling Out Night" and its equivalent at other homes failed to quell all incipient rebellions, for moments of conflict and acts of resistance run through the records of many homes. Occasionally, clashes erupted violently. One day in 1940, for example, a resident of the Door of Hope ran to the superintendent's office, "frantic, out of breath," to call her to the laundry room because one of the mothers "was fighting and beating" another officer. When she reached the laundry room, she found the officer fending off blows. "The girls were all crowded around but no one offered to help or separate them." The matron managed to break up the fight momentarily, but seconds later, "Mary started to argue and was ready to again strike the Lieut."[33] When Salvation Army officer Agnes Dickinson arranged for a baby's adoption without the mother's permission, she was rammed in the back by a cart of dirty dishes in the kitchen that night.[34] Others took out their hostility on maternity home property: "frequently," social worker Louise Trout wrote, "it takes the form of breaking dishes, damaging appliances, or 'messing things up.'"[35]

Conflict typically took less dramatic and overt forms, however, with the residents rarely resorting to physical violence. The most common mode of resistance to rules of the home was probably complaining. Workers often became aware of the mothers' complaints, and invited more, by reading residents' outgoing mail. From the intercepted letter of one resident, for instance, the Door of Hope matron discovered that "she strenuously objects to her mail being read, to have to attend classes, etc. . . . She was very critical about the running of the home." The matron judged her to have "a wrong attitude."[36] Another woman complained to her social worker of the food served at the Door of Hope. Unconvinced that the food was "as bad as she stated," however, the social worker informed her that "if she does not want to eat the rice and oatmeal, it is her privilege doubtless to leave them alone."[37] Complaining inside the home could make life less pleasant for workers, but it was a relatively benign form of resistance. Residents who aired their grievances outside the home, on the other hand, could embarrass the staff and damage the reputation of the home. The Door of Hope matron in 1945 worried that one unmarried mother was "telling many untrue stories about the Home and staff to whomever will listen to her."[38]

Probably the most common complaint in maternity homes was that the work required of residents was too arduous. One woman in the Door of Hope "stated that she felt she was very much put upon because she has been asked to do all the officers' uniforms and no other girl had been asked to do any and in addition she often had to iron the underwear."[39] Another woman told the superintendent of the home that "she hated housework, the scrubbing 'almost killed' her, she has to work too hard."[40] A Lakeview resident explained that it was not the difficulty of the work but the context in which it was performed that made it so burdensome: " 'The duties must be done, but because they are done in a temporary home and not your own, they are onerous. A house must be kept clean, and the modicum of work expected of the girls would tire no one, even the weakest, but here it grips and bruises you as harder work and more monotonous work in your own home would not. It all depends on the fact that you do not do things out of choice, and therefore the entire situation becomes slowly intolerable.' " For this woman, the arduousness of the work was rooted in the broader condition of lack of control occasioned by out-of-wedlock pregnancy and exacerbated in the home. She added that " 'I wish to leave, as I have never wished anything in my life.' "[41]

Chores composed one axis of conflict between workers and mothers; the recreational activities of residents, another. The unmarried mothers' attachment to popular confessional magazines like *Real Love*, *Thrilling Love*, and *Sweetheart Stories* drove maternity home workers to distraction. Offended by the reading habits of one Door of Hope resident, the matron told her "about better reading being available" and advised her of "the damage such trashy reading could do her." She warned her that reading pulp magazines would "keep her emotions stirred up, that she would meet a problem in having had aroused in her all the feelings, emotions, and passions of an adult woman before she is mature enough to know how to handle them." Giving her a copy of a respectable novel, she arranged to meet with the woman later to find out "if she liked it better than the cheap magazines." When they met to discuss it, however, the unmarried mother reported that she preferred her magazines to the book and continued to read them over the matron's protests.[42]

Some maternity home residents found evading the rules a more effective form of resistance than complaining. Although the matron of the Detroit Crittenton home reported that "the great majority" of unmarried mothers "fall into line . . . and cheerfully conform to the customs of the Home," others did not: "To some our few but necessary rules appear to be burdensome restrictions to be evaded if possible, to others, they are mere airy nothings to be lightly disregarded."[43] Some ducked compulsory attendance in classes and religious services, "offering ingenious excuses for remaining in their wards or merely absenting themselves and betraying mild surprise when taken to task. 'Oh, I did not know we *had* to go,' is the usual rejoinder in these cases."[44] Maternity home residents found the rules restricting the letters they wrote and received particularly objectionable, and many enlisted the aid of fellow residents and visitors in smuggling uncensored mail into and out of the homes. Dorothy told her social worker that "most of the girls managed to break this rule and that they had their visitors mail letters for them."[45] When the Door of Hope matron objected to "a very lover-like letter" a resident had written to her boyfriend and forbade her to mail it or to correspond any further with him, the mother returned to the office with a letter she had written to a girlfriend, in which she included messages to her boyfriend.[46]

Other residents expressed their objections to the restrictions by simply leaving before their term was completed, offering no explanation for their departure. Door of Hope case records are filled with comments such as "couldn't settle," "left before confinement," and "did not care to stay."[47] Although these abbreviated comments illuminate little about what prompted the women to leave, it is difficult not to interpret early departures as expressions of dissatisfaction and acts of resistance. Rather than complaining or evading rules, many unmarried mothers simply voted with their feet.

The few cases that elaborated on these brief notations suggest that the women left because of the restrictions imposed upon them. In 1897, two women forced open the locked gate of the Norfolk Crittenton home and escaped "because they were not allowed to use snuff in the Home."[48] More typical were those who objected to the seclusion and isolation of maternity home life. One woman departed after only one night in the Norfolk home, explaining that she "thought she would be allowed to see company."[49] Another "would have preferred to have more freedom," stating that "they all would have liked to go for walks and get away from the place more."[50] Explaining her decision to leave, another unmarried mother said that "she did not realize it would mean such a long time and seeing that she was only four or five months pregnant, the time away from her friends and everybody seemed almost more than she could bear."[51] One Door of Hope resident, brought back to the home after running away in 1934, was interviewed by the superintendent, who wrote: "She had no particular reason, except that she was tired of being confined so long to an institution and wanted to get out for a change."[52] For many, this was reason enough. It is understandable that the women, many of whom had lived alone or with friends to avoid the supervision of family, would chafe under the restrictions on their freedoms and hardly surprising that some would choose to leave homes that so strictly monitored their conduct and movement.

Although some unmarried mothers simply announced to maternity home workers that they were leaving, others felt as though they had to escape.[53] That women "escaped" from homes in which they were not legally bound to stay and usually not locked in illuminates the way some experienced their stay in them. Even as late as 1944, by which time more liberal policies required Door of Hope workers to inform each new resident that she was "under no pressure to remain but could accept our services if she felt we could offer what she needed," women continued to run away from the home rather than announce their departures.[54] Evangelical women might have been able to rationalize, accommodate, or simply ignore some forms of resistance, but it was difficult to interpret the flight of an unmarried mother as anything but a direct assault on their understanding of the homes. Some not only ran away but, in flagrant resistance to the most basic of evangelical tenets, left their babies behind.

Escapes put a damper on maternity home morale and bruised evangelical egos; they could also result in embarrassment and bad publicity. Crittenton workers in Little Rock, Arkansas, were appalled when the local newspaper published a photograph of four women after their attempted escape from the Crittenton home in New York City in 1941. Under the headline, "Their Freedom was Brief," the photograph pictured the four after they had been caught by the police, one described as "still openly defiant," and included a short caption describing their escape: "They shinnied up a fire escape and raced across rooftops before the cops caught them and returned them to the institution."[55] The matron of the Little Rock home was "very much upset over it," writing that since "we do maintain that we are Homes for the protection of our girls and are places of refuge for the unwed mother, . . . to have a piece like this to come before the public will certainly give the wrong impression of the type of work we are trying to do." She especially resented the implication that Crittenton homes "were places where Girls were locked in and allowed no privileges whatsoever," and insisted that "our Girls come to us for protection and of their own free will and accord and we are just one big family and I dislike to have any one think we are not."[56] In 1942, NFCM officer Hester Brown expressed her concern about several publicized escapes from the Crittenton home in Charleston, writing that "the Public and Health Department have heard stories of too many half-starved girls who have run away from here."[57]

Still, evangelical women themselves sometimes stumbled over the contradictions inherent in the nature of maternity homes that combined a voluntary ethos with often coercive practices. Talking to a returned "escapee" from the Door of Hope, the superintendent suggested how blurred the line between the two could be when she explained that "we were not going to lock her up or have anybody stand over her like a policeman, that the doors were still open and it would be easy for her to run away if she wanted to." But apparently in the next breath she warned her that "if she did run away a charge would be made against her for deserting her baby and that this was a criminal offense and most likely would mean that she would be put away in an institution where she would not be able to run away and be kept there for a long period."[58] Some homes were more blatantly punitive and more literally incarcerational. The Phoenix Critten-ton home's acceptance of juvenile delinquents along with unmarried moth-ers turned the home into "a virtual jail" by the director's own admission: "A seven foot woven wire fence, mounted with three strands of barbed wire sloping inward, surrounds the institution, with a padlocked iron gate, kept locked day and night."[59] Although few homes took so extreme a course, the frequency with which residents fled from the homes forced the workers to realize that coercion was inherent in incarceration of any kind, however benevolently intended, and that they were unable to keep homes in which they obliged unmarried mothers to stay from becoming jails.

Not surprisingly, patterns of gratitude, accommodation, and resistance did not end with the termination of the residents' stay. Often placed as domestic servants after their confinement, former maternity home resi-dents took responses forged in the homes to their jobs. Just as some unmarried mothers "absorbed the ethics" of homes while they were resi-dents, some were testaments to the good influence of the home after they left, and their employers sent glowing reports of their performance back to the homes that sent them. "I do not see how we could have any better help," one woman wrote to the home that had supplied her with a domestic servant; "she is exquisitely neat, a most dainty cook, and always sweet-tempered."[60] Many unmarried mothers genuinely appreciated the arrange-ments made for them. One woman saw domestic service as "the only thing I could do to keep Johnny with me, and keep my health, and make ends meet." Of her job, she wrote that "it seemed like heaven when I first moved in with them" and described her employer as "so kind, so generous, so helpful."[61]

Others, however, found the supervision and restrictions in their jobs as onerous as those in maternity homes. The Door of Hope found it necessary to take one former resident back three times, as "she did not seem to be able to adjust anywhere and we had continual complaints about her."[62] Although generally pleased with the unmarried mother she employed as a domestic servant in 1920, Ida Garrett Murphy wrote that "any direct control of her social life was out of the question."[63] Other employers had more serious trouble in that regard. One reported to the Door of Hope that "for the past two or three weeks, Dorothy has been very independent and hasn't wanted to do the things she was told and neglected even her regular work." When her employer reprimanded her, "she has either pretended she did not hear or has done things her own way." Worse still, she "has been landing home at five and six o'clock in the morning following her afternoon off and in addition she has brought men into the house and has at different times had them sitting around and staying rather late."[64] Yet another woman told the Door of Hope superintendent that the unmarried mother who had been working for her was "Boy Crazy," that she had "stayed out all the previous night," and that she "always had a lot of men callers at the place, as well as many phone calls." When her employer objected to this behavior, the woman simply left.[65] Another single mother was dismissed from her position as domestic servant when she became pregnant for the second time after coming to be "on intimate terms with the ice man." "Hester declared that she did not wish another situation," the investigator wrote: "She said that she did not mean to 'waste' her young life but that she meant to have a good time while she was still young."[66]

The range of social relations in maternity homes and the continuum of appreciation on the one hand and resistance on the other documented in logbooks and case records complicate the tendency of historians to view social welfare institutions either as humanitarian refuges or as instruments of social control. Unmarried mothers were neither universally appreciative nor universally resentful. Homes were not the harmonious retreats portrayed by evangelicals or hotbeds of protracted and explicit resistance. Gratitude and resistance existed simultaneously in the homes. Although unmarried mothers were capable of reactions at both poles, most social relations were probably negotiated in the wide and complicated territory that lay in-between.

TELLING THE STORY OF OUT-OF-WEDLOCK PREGNANCY

In complaining about work, evading rules, and leaving maternity homes before they had completed their term of stay, unmarried mothers struggled to turn the homes into places that served their purposes rather than those of evangelical matrons and social workers. Although their resistance could occasionally take dramatic forms—a daring dash across city rooftops or a fistfight in a laundry room—it was perhaps most compellingly expressed in quieter but courageous daily acts of self-presentation.

From the moment they stepped into a maternity home or social agency, unmarried mothers were asked the question, "how did you become pregnant?" Chances were good that they would be asked to tell the "story" of their pregnancy more than once, questioned again and again by maternity home matrons and social workers eager to discern the "truth" amid omissions and outright lies. Judging from the frustrated remarks of those who worked with unmarried mothers—many of whom believed that they lied with uncommon "ease and fluency"—discovering the "true story" of out-of-wedlock pregnancy was a difficult task indeed.[67] Social worker Anne Cohn worried that "there has seldom been any attempt at verification of the stories of impregnation as related by the girls to the case workers" and noted, "it has not always been possible to determine whether these stories were real or fabricated."[68]

The voracious desire of evangelicals and social workers to know how the unmarried mothers had become pregnant suggests that they were after something more than the biological facts they presumably knew. Since out-of-wedlock pregnancy ruptured the conventional narrative of married heterosexuality, they insisted that unmarried mothers supply an alternative. In so doing, they pointed to the inextricability of the material experience of out-of-wedlock pregnancy and its discursive rendering. By requiring each unmarried mother to tell her "story," evangelical women and social workers acknowledged that the "truth" of the woman's experience would always be mediated by narrative.[69]

Rather than joining social workers in the attempt to discern the truth from unmarried mothers' narratives of out-of-wedlock pregnancy—rather than peeling back the layers of fabrication and mediation in the hope of reaching an authentic core of experience—I propose to examine the narratives that appear in logbooks and case records as the linguistic means by which the women made sense of their experience. Rather than looking to unmarried mothers as the source of "real experience," upon which experts heaped alternately condescending, distorting, and pathologizing constructions, I argue that unmarried mothers were in the business of constructing out-of-wedlock pregnancy themselves. Out-of-wedlock pregnancy did not automatically confer a particular meaning or identity upon them but rather demanded explanation and interpretation.

Certainly, unmarried mothers told these stories in coercive contexts, and it is easy to understand why many experienced the constant questioning as irritating, intrusive, and occasionally punitive. Yet, at the same time, the question, "how did you become pregnant?" invited unmarried mothers to contribute their own interpretation of out-of-wedlock pregnancy, and therein lay the possibility for appropriation, subversion, and sometimes outright resistance. The stories they told were forged from this important dialectic: the demand for an explanation forced them to speak, but at the same time, allowed them to speak for themselves. Injunctions to self-disclosure were, at the same time, opportunities for self-invention.[70] Calling on a variety of competing and often contradictory discourses, women struggled to make their own sense of out-of-wedlock pregnancy.

Many of these stories suggest that evangelical reformers and unmarried mothers understood out-of-wedlock pregnancy in strikingly similar ways. When the mothers told their stories, they often used melodramatic images that echoed those used by evangelical women, emphasizing their own passivity and condemning men as rogues, cads, and villains. One unmarried mother drew on this shared language in her letter to the Children's Bureau in 1944, writing that "a scoundrel can with his smooth, deceitful lies of love and marriage, gain a girl's confidence, then ruin her life and happiness forever."[71]

As in evangelical women's stories of seduction and abandonment, knock-out drops and drugged drinks figured prominently in the mothers' narratives of their pregnancies. By their own accounts, they were drugged with considerable frequency. One former domestic servant asserted that her employer offered her some wine while his wife was away on a trip, "and she does not remember what happened to her after that."[72] Another woman accepted a ride home from a party from a man who "forced her to drink a small glass of liquid which looked like water. Afterward, felt sleepy."[73] A Door of Hope resident who rode home from a party with a man she had met there remembered that "after going out . . . to quite a lonely place she became very sleepy. Thinks she must have slept."[74] Yet another woman explained that a friend gave her a "headache powder" at a dance hall, and "from that time she knew nothing until she found herself on the steps of a rooming house."[75] Four months later she discovered that she was pregnant. Some women denied any knowledge whatsoever about the circumstances of their pregnancy. "The whole experience has her rather mystified," the Door of Hope matron wrote of one woman in 1942. "She claims she does not know how she ever became pregnant."[76]

We have some idea how seduction and betrayal and the use of knock-out drops figured in middle-class reform ideology, but how do we interpret their meaning in stories told by predominantly working-class unmarried mothers? First, the similarity of these stories suggests that evangelical women and unmarried mothers did not trade in entirely different sexual discourses. Aspirations to respectability may have shaped the stories of unmarried mothers who knew that seduction and abandonment was the way that "good" girls fell and that to acknowledge any responsibility threatened to demote them from the ranks of the respectable.[77] Those for whom respectability exerted a powerful force may have found, like evangelical women, that melodrama provided them with the only acceptable language available to talk about sex.[78] At the same time, stories of knock-out drops made it possible to keep sex unspeakable. Many women were no doubt actually plied with alcohol, but their loss of consciousness created literal black-outs in their stories that made their experience inaccessible to evangelical women and social workers.

It is also possible that the "old, old story" of seduction and abandonment enjoyed class-specific usages and was told in what historian Michael Denning calls "class accents." At the very least, it seems that evangelical reformers and unmarried mothers learned the narrative of seduction and abandonment from different sources, and these sources may have given the story dramatically different meanings. Whereas evangelical women in maternity homes turned literary narratives of seduction and betrayal to reform purposes, working-class women were probably more familiar with the convention as it appeared in the popular magazines of the period.[79] The frustrated remarks of social workers attest to the strong appeal these magazines held for them. According to one social worker, unmarried mothers "almost universally came to the maternity home armed with *True Story Magazine.*" When another, "worn out with her fight against this type of literature," asked a group why they were so attached to them, they "rallied as one girl to its defense and explained, 'Why the stories are just like us.'"[80] Sociologist William I. Thomas explained that "betrayal is the romantic way of falling, the one used in the story books and movies. Many girls have finished stories of this kind which they relate when asked to tell about their lives."[81] When the NFCM ran its serialized article, "I Was an Unmarried Mother," it drew over two thousand letters from unmarried mothers all over the country, "each telling a story similar to that of Virginia Day," the woman portrayed in the article.[82] And E. Franklin Frazier observed that the African-American unmarried mothers he interviewed "are often influenced in their attitudes toward sex by the printed page. As a rule the literature with which they are acquainted is restricted to such magazines as *True Stories* and *True Confessions.*" One woman, according to Frazier, "recounted in her life-history a story from one of those magazines that centered about the romantic career of an unmarried mother."[83]

If, as so many reported, unmarried mothers fashioned their own stories from those they read in confessional magazines, what shape did those stories take? Many of the tales of out-of-wedlock pregnancy that filled confessional magazines drew on the conventions of melodrama. In one, the woman fell "desperately in love" with a man who "pretended to return my affection, and in a few months the old, old story had been repeated again."[84] Although many of these stories were replete with familiar features— villainous men and victimized women, virtue tested and virtue redeemed— they differed from evangelical narratives at a number of important junctures. Whereas the evangelical women's "old, old story" turned on female innocence and passivity, its pulp version was more likely to counter the Victorian association of sexual desire with maleness and to accommodate some degree of female desire. Although, for example, the heroine of one story who fell in love with the handsome boarder taken into her family's home "meant to keep our wonderful love untainted, the force of human nature," rather than the man's seductive powers, changed her mind.[85] The unmarried mother of another story explained that "something in me responded to what I knew to be his terrible need," adding that "it seemed impossible to deny ourselves the satisfaction that was to be had from kisses and caresses."[86] Yet another described lying in the arms of her lover, "with his strong arms around me and our souls joined together in long, agonizing kisses," and depicted their love as "an animal thing—terrible, sweet, agonizing, irresistible."[87] If the text of the story did not contain ambiguous messages about female desire, confession magazines often juxtaposed articles in ways that did. An issue of *True Romances*, for example, featured one article, "The Way of the Transgressor" alongside another entitled "Romance in the Subway: You Never Can Tell Where Love May Be Lurking."[88] Pulp versions of the "old, old story" might have combined with new possibilities in young women's own lives to produce new narratives in which sexual desire could be expressed.

Social workers' explanation for unmarried mothers' use of melodramatic language or for their stories in which they figured as victims was that unmarried mothers lied. When Maria told the "old, old story" at her first interview at Inwood House in New York City in 1942, her social worker commented: "She briefly sketched a picture of a very young innocent girl who had fallen desperately in love with an older and quite experienced man, and was now paying for the mistake of having loved not wisely but too well. . . . But she certainly does not give the impression of being the kind of person who is so innocent and trusting that she would be easily swerved off her feet."[89] Another wrote simply that "girls do make these representations, and very often, but they are always to be discounted."[90] Noting the frequency of assault stories told by unmarried mothers, Kammerer explained that "there is a natural desire on the part of a girl when first interviewed, to throw the blame for her behavior on the man," but added that "almost inevitably these assault stories break down upon cross-examination."[91]

It is important to call to mind here the conditions and circumstances under which unmarried mothers told these stories. Most often, they were forced to explain themselves to those to whom they were appealing for shelter and help. One social worker wrote that Louise, a thirteen-year-old girl described as promiscuous, "seems to be aware that it is not in her interest to admit sexual non-conformity."[92] This kind of manipulation does not necessarily point to either cynicism or savvy on the part of unmarried mothers. They probably told their stories in the way they thought most acceptable out of fear, and a fear that was not misplaced or irrational. The record of one woman who was dismissed from a Crittenton home in 1929 because "she showed certain psychopathic tendencies, viz. undue curiosity in sex" suggested the possible consequences of telling one's story in the "wrong" way.[93] One social worker noted that unmarried mothers believed that social workers' opinions "would largely accord with the opinion of the social class to which the social workers themselves belong," and were therefore likely to "veer the explanation of their attitudes in the direction of what appears to be the prevailing mode in thought and opinion among social workers. They do this in order to gain for themselves the maximum amount to help which the agency can afford them."[94] Thus, a social worker at the Door of Hope wrote that "Mary does not seem to be entirely truthful in all the details of her statement but this may be due to fear. She gives the impression of having been advised as to what she should say."[95] An unmarried mother who initially described being drugged at a dance hall later told her social worker that the father of her baby was "an Italian boy with whom she had been going," and that "she had been afraid to tell the truth earlier."[96] The Salvation Army included in its entrance form the question, "Did the man promise marriage?" through the early 1940s and dictated that "preference in maternity homes be given to those who have been deceived and led astray under false pretenses."[97] Unmarried mothers may have known that admitting to consensual sex without promise of marriage might have compromised their chances of acceptance.

The language of melodrama may also have appealed to working-class women and girls as a way to convey their genuine economic and sexual vulnerability. Given the frequency with which formulaic tales of seduction and abandonment appear in case records, the story apparently resonated in the experience of working-class women long after social workers had abandoned it. Many unmarried mothers told reformers and social workers that they had consented to sex only after their lovers had promised to marry them.[98] One twenty-seven-year-old black unmarried mother, for example, "said that she had been intimate with only one man. . . . They had been engaged to be married for several years, but when the man learned that she was pregnant, he refused to marry her, saying that marriage would be a handicap to him in his profession."[99] Another woman wrote to NFCM general superintendent Reba Barrett Smith in 1939: "I was fooled by the man I loved he promised to get his divorce he has been separated for five years. . . . Now he thinks I can go on like this, and I am not a bad girl. I was only fooled by love as so many are."[100]

Stories such as these suggest that many unmarried mothers may simply have been following older courtship traditions that sanctioned premarital sex after engagement. In times of economic stability, a less geographically mobile population, and family and community supervision, premarital sex held fewer risks for women.[101] Where there were new opportunities for sexual expressiveness and a freer heterosociality in early-twentieth-century cities, there were possibilities as well of danger and exploitation. When courtship took place not with boys from the neighborhood or with friends of the family, upon whom pressure could presumably be brought to bear, but with strangers met in dance halls, theaters, and skating rinks, the potential for seduction and betrayal widened.[102]

The "old, old story," with its emphasis on male responsibility and female victimization, could also be modified to tell stories of sexual violence and rape. One woman who had accepted a ride from a man she had met at a dance told the Door of Hope matron that "he was supposed to take her home but instead took her to a park where he tried to choke her and sinned against her."[103] Another woman was invited by a man to a party in his apartment, and "it was not until after she got in the apartment that [she] realized that she and he were alone and she was unable to defend herself when he made advances to her."[104] Yet another woman accepted a ride from a man in a passing car on a rainy evening; he took her to a secluded spot, "beat her into a state of insensibility," and raped her.[105]

Unmarried mothers appropriated and modified the language of seduction and abandonment to express their own sexual vulnerability, to articulate experiences of sexual violence, and probably also to speak across the gulf of class that often separated them from evangelical matrons. Some stories, however, could not be accommodated within the formula of the "old, old story," and the ruptures and silences in the stories could be at least as revealing as the words themselves. Stories of women pregnant by fathers, brothers, or uncles eluded conventional narratives and were told, and heard, only with great difficulty. Although cases of family sexual abuse appear in every maternity home logbook, they are usually unadorned with the stylistic flourishes and narrative predictability of seduction and abandonment. Of one unmarried mother, for example, a Door of Hope matron wrote simply, "Susan was ruined by her father when twelve years of age. Her brother-in-law is the father of her child."[106]

Some unmarried mothers simply refused to read from the script of seduction and abandonment, stepping outside of it in ways that shocked evangelical women and baffled social workers. Those who described bargaining with their sexuality to gain entrance to the exciting world of commercial amusements through the practice of "treating," as historian Judith Walkowitz observes, "spoke the unsensational language of sexual bartering, not the melodramatic language of seduction."[107] William I. Thomas observed that "sex in these cases was used, as a coin would be used, to secure adventure and pleasure."[108] One woman told her social worker, "'I did not have much fun unless somebody took me out to parties and dances, and when you go out with a 'boy friend,' he expects you to be nice to him, and sort of pay for the treat. . . . He was kind in taking me to places and it cost him money, and I did not see any great harm in being nice to him and in doing as he asked.'"[109] A mother of two illegitimate children told her social worker that "she cannot stay at home evenings; she gets bored and likes to go out," and explained that "she likes to have dates, and if allowing sexual intercourse was the price demanded for this, she was willing." The social worker added that "the alleged father of the second child was a boy she met at a dance hall. . . . She knows nothing about him except his name."[110]

Some women described relations with men that more explicitly mixed sex with economic concerns. Historian Joanne Meyerowitz points to the "economic roots of modern sexual expression" and argues that sexual expressiveness among working-class women in the early twentieth century was motivated not simply by a search for pleasure and romance "but also out of economic need and the customary dependence of women on higher-paid men." Meyerowitz suggests that single women living apart from families formed social and economic relationships in the city to substitute for the support of family. For these women, "a sexual relationship also represented an economic strategy for alleviating poverty."[111] This seems to have been true for Fanny, a nineteen-year-old unmarried mother at the Salvation Army home in New York City, who said that "'my girl friends had visitors that helped them out with their living expenses. They told me that I could also help out with living expenses and that they would arrange for me to meet some of their nice visitors evenings and weekends when I had time.'" The father of Fanny's baby was a "chance acquaintance of a week-end," and she was "disappointed when he did not return to her friend's house the following week."[112]

Often combining romantic and economic discourses, many unmarried mothers described having sex with "pick-ups"—men they met in dance halls, movie theaters, amusement parks, or on the street. Twenty-one percent of the Door of Hope residents described meeting the fathers of their children in areas that social workers considered unequivocally un-wholesome; only 4 percent said that they had known the man "for a long time."[113] One unmarried mother "became acquainted with the father of her baby . . . on the street late one night."[114] Another who met the father of her child on the street noted that " 'all the girls do that.' "[115] In her study of black illegitimacy, Ruth Reed noted that in eighty-eight of five hundred cases "there had been promise of marriage on the part of the man which had led the girl into extra-marital sex relations," but that "by far the larger number of cases were classed as the result of chance acquaintance in which there had been no promise of marriage on the part of the man."[116] And investigators of illegitimacy in Connecticut found that "in 27 percent of the cases . . . the acquaintance began casually, a chance 'pick-up' on the street."[117]

Although the women who had been engaged to the fathers of their children might have been operating within an older tradition of courtship that deemed intercourse acceptable if it took place after engagement, many others—particularly the ones who described the fathers of their children as pick-ups—were forging new sexual standards. Some women described the behavior that led to their pregnancies as "modern," defined it against the "Victorianism" of their parents, and declared their rebellion against the conventions of an earlier generation. Lena, a fifteen-year-old resident of the Salvation Army home in New York City, explained that she "wanted to go to parties and dances," but her parents objected: " 'The hardest thing for me to do is to obey my parents. They love me but they don't understand what girls ought to be doing these days. . . . Besides things are different now.' "[118] Another unmarried mother, Marjorie, told her social worker that "her father must never know because he is a 'victorian.' She expressed some scorn at this point."[119] Like many young urban wage-earning women in this period, Marjorie differentiated her code of moral standards and behavior from that of her parents. Orchestrated in the new arenas of movie theaters, dance halls, excursion steamers, and amusement parks, new patterns of courtship sanctioned sexual experimentation with relative strangers.[120]

In trying to elicit unmarried mothers' explanations of their pregnancies, Clara Laughlin asked, "Was it because they themselves felt desire? Have you ever tried to get a girl or woman to admit that?"[121] Robert Barrett agreed that few unmarried mothers "will admit that they have been brought there by a raging sex appetite which they could not control."[122] Although most women expressed understandable ambivalence about sex when talking to their social workers, a few more explicitly rejected the dichotomy of "seduced victim" and "sex delinquent" and claimed the right to act on sexual desire. Especially in the 1930s and 1940s, more and more women identified their mistake not as "giving in" to men but as getting pregnant. A social worker wrote of one of her cases: "Although she was very much ashamed of her second pregnancy her conversation about preventing a third was always in terms of getting knowledge of contraceptives, rather than in changing her pattern of behavior."[123] Mary's social worker wrote that "she doesn't know why she let herself get pregnant. She should have done something for that but she was too dumb."[124] The superintendent of the Lakeview home observed that "many women felt that they should be as free as men in their sex lives. A few of our girls therefore had less sense of wrong-doing than the others; they felt that if a girl loved a man, she had the right to have relations with him, and to bear a child if she so desired."[125] Robert Barrett also found as early as 1929 that "within the past eight or ten years an increasing number of girls have given as a reason for their pregnancy a desire to experience sex relations."[126] One unmarried mother thus described her courtship with the father of her child: "It never occurred to me that we ought to get married before we made love."[127] Another explained in matter-of-fact language entirely lacking in melodramatic flourish: "Because of our mutual interest in each other, I have become pregnant."[128]

As unmarried mothers rejected the evangelical imperative of sexual passivity by acknowledging their own responsibility, agency, and even desire, so too did they challenge the right of social workers to label their behavior delinquent. One young woman, described as "associating with factory girls," told her social worker that "'I didn't feel particularly bad about it, because I knew many other girls were doing the same.'"[129] Another social worker, in her confusion, revealed the difference between her own standards and those of her client when she wrote that "Mary claims she has always conducted herself properly in respect to her relations with men. However, she admits she has had sexual relations with two other men besides the father of her unborn child."[130] One unmarried mother wrote poignantly, "Sometimes I lie awake at night and start wondering how this thing happened to me. I remember something bad that I did when I was a little girl and think to myself, 'That's where it began; I must have been just naturally a rebel and therefore it's only natural I'm a "bad girl" now.' Then I rebel against that and think, 'I'm not really bad.'"[131] In her self-doubt, she underlined the inextricability of her experience of out-of-wedlock pregnancy from the experts' discursive constructions of it. But by finally refusing to understand herself as a "bad girl," she suggested that unmarried mothers might draw on and help construct alternative discourses of single pregnancy.

While some women questioned and subtly subverted dominant discourses of out-of-wedlock pregnancy, others more openly upset narrative expectations of unmarried motherhood. When one social worker took the novel approach in 1928 of asking unmarried mothers not only to tell the story of their pregnancy but to identify its "cause," she was surprised by their responses. In contrast to the familiar list of causes assigned by social workers—broken homes, bad companions, hypersexuality, low mentality—over half of the women analyzed the cause of their pregnancy as "I liked the man," some qualifying, "at least at the time."[132]

CONCLUSION

"Such are the deserted, despairing, cowering victims with whom we deal," the superintendent wrote of the "unhappy girl-mothers" in the Boston Crittenton home in 1915.[133] From the records of maternity homes and published observations of social workers that portray unmarried mothers as victimized and pathetic, one might easily conclude that evangelical matrons and social workers presided over institutions of social control, where they successfully imposed middle-class standards of morality, religion, and sexuality to remold unmarried mothers in their own image. And indeed, this interpretation would not be entirely wrong. Run under the slogan "every girl saved a public asset, every girl lost a public menace" by women who believed doing laundry to be a "means of grace," maternity homes were replete with controlling impulses.[134] But despite the workers' easily documented efforts to control the clientele of maternity homes, those clients continued to pursue their own agendas and to put the homes to their own uses. Although constrained by unequal power relations in those homes, the mothers were not the docile subjects either of maternity home regimes or of "expert" constructions of unmarried motherhood. Keenly aware of the difference between moralism and service, many unmarried mothers managed, within limits, to get the care they needed and to avoid or escape from the rest. To greater or lesser degrees, many maternity home residents probably shared Marjory's willingness, noted by her social worker, to "respond to an appeal to her common sense and discretion, whereas she shows an instant rebellion against anything that suggests an authoritarian tone or manner."[135]

Case records offer abundant material for the growing body of historical work critical of arguments based on social control.[136] Yet as sources that recorded unmarried mothers' stories of out-of-wedlock pregnancy, the records raise other questions beyond the scope of that debate that are at least as important. While shedding light on the material experience of out-of-wedlock pregnancy, they also alert us to the ways in which that experience itself was shaped by its discursive rendering, illuminating the complexity of unmarried mothers' responses to dominant meanings of illegitimacy and their interpretation of their own experiences through language and narrative.

Unmarried mothers did not speak in one voice, and the stories they told served a range of purposes. Some shaped their stories to support claims to respectability and to improve their chances of getting the help they needed, appropriating and revising the traditional language of melodrama to bridge the differences between themselves and evangelical matrons and to express their own sexual vulnerability. Others searched for words to voice experiences of sexual coercion or struggled with the inadequacies of available vocabularies to speak of rape and incest. As stories of illicit sexuality, narratives of out-of-wedlock pregnancy offered ways of repressing, containing, or expressing sexual desire. Whereas some women told stories in which they denied sexual agency, others laid bold claim to it, some calling on narratives that allowed them to move beyond the boundaries of middle-class notions of femininity and to articulate a new, modern sexual subjectivity.

To be sure, unmarried mothers' self-representations made little impact on the dominant narratives of out-of-wedlock pregnancy of the time. Considered unreliable narrators, they were not acknowledged as legitimate authorities of their own experience. Still, however they answered the question, "how did you become pregnant?" they were actively involved in making meaning of their own out-of-wedlock pregnancies. Case records provide glimpses of young mothers struggling to construct their own narratives to make sense of their experiences. In their refusal to understand out-of-wedlock pregnancy in the terms dictated by evangelical women or social workers, they resisted the efforts of reformers to instill in them their code of respectability and morality. More broadly, they proclaimed a right to construct their own identities rather than assume those constructed for them.

"Rescue Officers Seeking Fallen" (Salvation Army
Archives and Research Center).

The Florence Night Mission,
opened in 1883 in New York City
(from Charles N. Crittenton, *The
Brother of Girls* [Chicago: World's
Events Co., 1910]).

Kate Waller Barrett, cofounder of
the National Florence Crittenton
Mission, with Charles N. Crittenton, in 1895 (from Charles N. Crittenton, *The Brother of Girls*
[Chicago: World's Events Co.,
1910]).

Evangeline Booth (center), commander of the American
Division of the Salvation Army, with Salvation Army of-
ficers, dedicating a new maternity home in Chicago,
April, 1924 (Salvation Army Archives and Research
Center).

Emma Whittemore, founder of the Door of Hope rescue and maternity homes, in her Door of Hope uniform. Her anchor pin bore on its cross-bar the initials P.B.F., which stood for "Past, Buried, Forgotten," the motto of the Door of Hope (from Emma M. Whittemore, *Mother Whittemore's Records of Modern Miracles* [Toronto: Missions of Biblical Education, 1931]).

Emma Whittemore dressed for rescue work in "slum dwellings" (from Emma M. Whittemore, *Mother Whittemore's Records of Modern Miracles* [Toronto: Missions of Biblical Education, 1931]).

Rules and Regulations

FOR

RESCUE OFFICERS.

BY CONSUL MRS. BOOTH-TUCKER.

Sin-stained and weary, hopeless and
  friendless,
Outcast and scorned by the whole
  world around;
Soon to pass on to that life which is
  endless,
Misery here by a fearful death
  crowned,
Fetters of darkness these lost ones
  have bound.

But there is hope for them,
  Calvary's story
Makes no exceptions, for Jesus
  has died!
Light out of dark-
ness comes, and
the full glory
Shines on Sal-
vation's sea,
boundless and
wide,
Still in God's
mercy a limit-
less tide.

    S. M. C.

"Rules and Regulations for Rescue Officers," 1897 (Salvation Army Archives and Research Center).

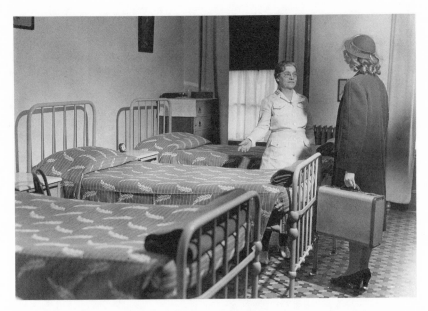

Salvation Army matron showing new resident to her
room (Salvation Army Archives and Research Center).

Salvation Army officers in nursery (Salvation Army Archives and Research Center).

Salvation Army officer consoling unmarried mother (Salvation Army Archives and Research Center).

Maternity home workers at the Evangeline Booth
Home, Cincinnati, Ohio, founded in 1917, one of the few
Salvation Army homes for African-American unmarried
mothers. In 1940, its residents and staff were integrated
into the previously all-white Catherine Booth Home and
Hospital in Cincinnati (Salvation Army Archives and
Research Center).

Prayer session, Salvation Army Booth Memorial Home and Hospital, Chicago, Illinois (Salvation Army Archives and Research Center).

Residents exercising on balcony at rear of Inwood House, on West Fifteenth Street, New York City (Courtesy Inwood House).

Recreation in the Salvation Army maternity home, Grand Rapids, Michigan (Salvation Army Archives and Research Center).

Residents sewing in early rescue home (Salvation Army
Archives and Research Center).

Residents doing dishes at the Salvation Army maternity
home, St. Louis, Missouri (Salvation Army Archives and
Research Center).

Door of Hope, Jersey City, New Jersey, founded in 1885
by Emma Whittemore and ceded to the Salvation Army
in 1905 as a gift from Whittemore (Salvation Army Archives and Research Center).

5

"Case Workers
Have Become
Necessities"

Previous chapters have introduced different sets of social actors—evangelical women, social workers, and unmarried mothers—each eager to articulate competing "truths" of out-of-wedlock pregnancy and each resting those truths on different sources of authority. Evangelical women cited religious calling and female mission, and unmarried mothers claimed the authority of experience. By the early twentieth century, however, social workers invoked the legitimizing rhetoric of science to brand evangelical women's tradition of womanly benevolence sentimental and sloppy, to pronounce unmarried mothers untrustworthy interpreters of their own experience, and to name themselves the rightful authorities over the "social problem" of unmarried motherhood. With unmistakable defensiveness, Crittenton worker Clara Marshall wrote in 1937 that "fifty-five years' work with unmarried mothers resulting in thousands of girls reconditioned to society" surely gave evangelical women "a right to speak authoritatively concerning the unwed mother and her child."[1] But after the First World War and increasingly in the 1920s and 1930s, evangelical women spoke with less authority on the topic of illegitimacy, and social workers spoke with more.

To what extent did the ability of social workers to speak with authority—to control the discourse of illegitimacy—reflect a real transfer of power in maternity homes during this period? Social workers were keenly aware that their expert status meant little as long as evangelical women continued to do the day-to-day work of caring for unmarried mothers. Meaningful authority would require social workers to move beyond criticizing evangelical women and gain control of the homes themselves. As one ambitious social worker wrote in 1921, "We can strive for such a standard that generally over the country no one will be placed in a position of power or responsibility in a society or institution doing work for unmarried mothers, who is not a trained social worker."[2]

When social workers left their professional enclaves and entered maternity homes, they met evangelical women who were as strongly dedicated to the values of sisterhood, religion, and domesticity as social workers were to those of rationality, objectivity, and science. They also encountered diverse groups of resident unmarried mothers whose agendas had little to do with either. This chapter considers the efforts of social workers to gain control over maternity homes and the persistent challenges to that control by both evangelical women and unmarried mothers. Evangelicals' and social workers' differences over maternity home policy distilled more significant struggles between two generations of women: for authority to define women's place in reform and to determine the proper relationship between gender identity and social welfare. More broadly, the struggle concerned whether what Peggy Pascoe has called "female moral authority" or professional expertise would define and preside over "social problems" concerning sexuality and the family.

At the same time, the entrance of social workers into maternity homes had dramatic consequences for unmarried mothers, transforming and widening the disciplinary regime under which they lived from one that emphasized redemption to one that stressed treatment. This chapter continues the project of the last by exploring another dimension of the relations between unmarried mothers and those who proposed to care for them.

MATERNITY HOMES COME UNDER SCRUTINY

Although maternity home matrons and social workers ordinarily traveled in different circles, evangelicals were well aware of the new understanding of expertise promoted by social workers. Maternity home workers often invited social workers to speak at their conferences, and they occasionally attended local and national professional social work meetings. Kate Barrett participated as a discussant at meetings of the National Conference of Social Work (NCSW) almost annually from 1910 until her death in 1925. Although social workers may have interpreted evangelical women's attendance at these gatherings as signaling their acquiescence to professional standards, evangelical women made clear that they went to conferences as much to teach as to learn. Anita Robb of the Salvation Army recalled that her annual trips to social work conferences "helped me to keep abreast of what was going on and to put my two cents in."[3] By meeting with the National Conference on Charities and Corrections in 1911, NFCM officers hoped to "bring our delegates in touch with a number of prominent men and women," many of whom they believed to "have a very wrong impression of Florence Crittenton work."[4] Both the NFCM and the Salvation Army maintained exhibits at the NCSW, designed to advertise their work and to convince social workers of the value of evangelically run maternity homes.

From the late nineteenth century through the 1910s, evangelical women had been able to meet social workers at occasions of their own choosing and often on their own turf. Beginning around 1920, however, the ability of evangelical women to set the terms on which they would meet social workers began to diminish. As social workers consolidated their forces and gained legitimacy, they were increasingly willing and able to scrutinize maternity homes and their evangelical matrons.

Among the first social workers to develop an interest in illegitimacy were those associated with the U.S. Children's Bureau. The founding of the bureau in 1912 to coordinate national child welfare policy marked the success of years of intensive lobbying by women active in various fields of child welfare—including settlement houses, child labor reform, and the juvenile court movement—and became, in historian Robyn Muncy's words, "the first female stronghold in the federal government."[5] The Children's Bureau's interest in out-of-wedlock pregnancy was sparked by its first investigation, which established illegitimacy as a major contributor to infant mortality, among other causes including low wages, poor housing, the employment of mothers outside the home, and large families.[6]

In an effort to learn more about the problems that unmarried mothers faced, the Children's Bureau implicitly acknowledged the authority of evangelical women by sending questionnaires to Crittenton and Salvation Army homes—the first of what would become a barrage of surveys sent to maternity homes in the 1910s and 1920s. Sponsored by social workers in various organizations interested in illegitimacy, these questionnaires quizzed evangelical women about everything from specific rules and regulations in the homes to general philosophy regarding the care of unmarried mothers. From written surveys, social workers moved to conduct in-house investigations. Beginning in the 1920s, evangelical women were visited by social workers eager to study unmarried mothers and to evaluate the standards of care provided in maternity homes. As early as 1923, one social worker conducting a study for the Children's Bureau remarked on the number and intensity of these surveys when she wrote back to headquarters, "I have the feeling that the institutions are visited to death."[7]

At the same time that investigations allowed social workers to collect information, they also promoted professionalism and showcased social work methods. Social workers acknowledged this double function, some privileging standard setting over fact finding. One Children's Bureau investigator explained that while she sought "to secure information as a basis for analysis of methods of caring for unmarried mothers and their children," she also aimed to educate agencies in the science of record keeping.[8] In their private writing, social workers admitted to using surveys and investigations as opportunities to observe maternity homes firsthand, to confirm their suspicions about the kind of work performed in them, and to sharpen their criticism of the homes. Investigations of maternity homes typically bore out social workers' expectations. In a progress report to Children's Bureau officer Ethel Waters, A. Madorah Donahue wrote of her visit to a Crittenton home: "My impression of people with narrow experience and little vision was emphasized. One [board] member told me three times that they felt they had arrived at the very best system of caring for unmarried mothers and their babies that could be devised."[9] June Hull, another researcher on this project, joked that the Children's Bureau should make a film about the Crittenton home "to illustrate to people what *not* to do."[10]

While evangelical women received questionnaires and surveys from social agencies, they were subjected to closer and often less amiable scrutiny through changes in funding that occurred around the same time. Beginning in 1913 and accelerating in the 1920s, maternity homes in many cities began to rely on Community Chests for support. Chests were established to coordinate and organize local welfare machinery by centralizing charitable donating and financing. Responsible for all fund-raising in the community, the Chest distributed collected funds to member agencies. By 1929, most cities had adopted the Community Chest system.[11]

Previously, maternity homes had raised their own funds, drawing support from a variety of sources. Emma Whittemore pronounced the Door of Hope "strictly a Faith work," and professed complete reliance on God. She listed a steady flow of prayed-for but otherwise unsolicited contributions including money, use of a rent-free building, furniture, and a piano—gifts that filled minor and major needs and always arrived the moment they were needed.[12] Most homes, however, including those in the Door of Hope chain, relied on more worldly sources of funding. Although Crittenton and Salvation Army homes received some support from their respective national organizations, it was never enough to cover their operating expenses. Maternity home workers patched together budgets through a combination of investments of endowments, voluntary and church contributions, and public and private appropriations that varied from city to city. Whereas Spokane Crittenton workers reported in 1909 that the state appropriated two thousand dollars for their home, for example, the Crittenton home in New Haven, Connecticut, supported itself entirely by setting up collections in local churches.[13] Some homes thanked local merchants for donating food and clothing.[14] Others took fees from unmarried mothers who were able to pay, and many collected the earnings of residents while in the home, using the profits from laundry work, ironing, or sewing to defray some of the home's expenses.

Although this decentralized financing of charitable organizations burdened evangelical women with the responsibility for fund-raising, it also freed them to establish their own priorities and policies. General Superintendent Reba Barrett Smith of the NFCM wistfully recalled an earlier independence when she wrote in 1941 that "in former days, we raised our own funds, set our own standards, and our Boards operated these Homes very much like privately owned institutions." The membership of maternity homes in Community Chests, however, "changed the picture altogether."[15] Although some maternity home workers interpreted the admission of their home to membership in the Community Chest as an auspicious sign heralding "the change in public sentiment" from "unfriendly aloofness" to a more positive assessment of maternity homes on the part of the social work establishment, most regretted the loss of independence and found more to condemn than to commend in the Chest system.[16]

Maternity home workers' most immediate complaints about the Chests concerned the control of money. Chests required each member agency to turn over its entire program and budget for approval and funding, and the Chest closely regulated all expenses. Although evangelical women probably welcomed the relief from constant concern with fund-raising, they often felt short-changed. The matron of the Jersey City Door of Hope, for instance, complained that "due to the failure of the Community Chest to raise its quota each year, we have along with other Agencies, never received our full budget and therefore, in spite of drastic economy have been in the 'red' at the end of each year."[17] Cincinnati Salvation Army officer Mrs. Kimble commiserated with NFCM officer Hester Brown, noting that the Chests did not pay more than half of the running expenses of their homes.[18]

Many evangelical women found more to complain about than the stinginess of the Chests. They understood that the Chests represented the interests of social workers, that they gave social workers extraordinary power, and that social workers did not hesitate to pursue a professionalizing agenda through budgetary decisions.[19] Some recognized that the generosity of the Chest was tied to social workers' evaluations of the homes. Salvation Army officer Evelyn Skinner recalled that "if you could convince the Community Chest that you were doing a quality program . . . you could gradually get them to part with funds."[20] Exerting strong pressure for "efficiency" and "rationality" in social welfare institutions, Chests used a variety of measures to induce their member agencies to professionalize.[21] Holding budgets as bargaining chips, Chests urged and eventually required allied organizations either to cooperate with local casework agencies or to hire their own caseworkers. Community Chests thus endorsed the contention of the social work establishment that the work of benevolence was the prerogative of the trained social worker and backed up that endorsement by controlling maternity home budgets.

Most maternity home workers came to resent the Chests' incursions on their authority and questioned the right of an outside body to determine policy in a field of work they had pioneered. Mrs. Ward Williams of the Little Rock, Arkansas, Crittenton home, for example, wrote to the NFCM president concerning "the very unpleasant situation brought about as a result of the action of the Community Chest in accepting the unjust and untrue report on our Home" made by "a staff of specialists" sent by the Little Rock Chest: "Although our work has been kept on the high plane established by the founder of our Mission," Mrs. Williams wrote, "it does not meet with the approval of our local social workers, who seem to have lost sight of the great need of character building among these unfortunate girls."[22]

Only when the depression cut private funding to the homes, taxing their resources and threatening many with financial collapse, were maternity home workers forced to acquiesce to the demands of Community Chests.[23] When workers in some homes were reduced to begging for food, the benefits of Chest participation seemed to outweigh the drawbacks. By 1935, Mrs. Robertson, president of the Washington, D.C., Crittenton home, reassured her colleagues that the Chests "deserve to be trusted" and instructed Crittenton workers that "in speaking of the Community Chest, of which we are a part, we should always say 'we,' not 'they.'"[24] In 1937, reflecting the pressures imposed by hard times, Reba Barrett Smith wrote that "the boogey man . . . from the Community Chests has been transformed into a friend and we realize we are not hampered but helped."[25]

By the 1930s, social workers in many cities had developed a tight network of interprofessional cooperation that allowed them unprecedented access to social welfare institutions, including maternity homes. The emergence of the Children's Bureau and the establishment of the Community Chest system had subordinated maternity homes to the decisions of an alliance of secular social agencies. Once independent, maternity homes were now closely scrutinized and evaluated according to the standards of the social work establishment. Social workers had been critical of maternity homes for years, and the Chest system had supplied them with the leverage to force the homes to respond to those criticisms. Pushing maternity homes to professionalize, Chests were able and willing to close down homes that did not comply with their directives.

The case of the Chicago Florence Crittenton Anchorage illustrates the extent to which outside social agencies could intervene in the operations of maternity homes and the power they had acquired to enforce their own standards.[26] The Anchorage was among a group of Chicago maternity homes surveyed and evaluated by the Council of Social Agencies in the late 1930s. Established by the Women's Christian Temperance Union (WCTU) in 1886, the Anchorage had been one of the first maternity homes to join the Crittenton chain in 1893. The home was an evangelical stronghold that had changed little since its founding—WCTU members continued to dominate the Anchorage board into the 1930s—and, predictably, it drew sharp censure from the council.[27] After a comprehensive evaluation of residential institutions in Chicago in the late 1930s, the council concluded that the Anchorage's program and facility were seriously deficient and insisted that the home hire a caseworker.

The Anchorage was one among many homes in Chicago to receive suggestions from the council, and most homes deferred to the council's authority. A Chicago Salvation Army matron, for example, dutifully reported in 1937 that Salvation Army supervisors had been replaced with trained social workers.[28] The Florence Crittenton Anchorage, however, was not as obliging. Perhaps Anchorage workers had taken NFCM general superintendent Reba Barrett Smith at her word in her 1938 address, when she instructed Crittenton workers to "at least take under advisement recommendations which they make for the care of the unmarried mother and her child," but at the same time urged them "not to be too hasty in putting into effect all the recommendations which come to you from no matter how authoritative a source."[29]

When the Chicago Anchorage refused to hire a social worker, the ensuing conflict with Chicago agencies grew so severe that it drew attention, mediation, and eventually reproach from the usually supportive NFCM. Although an NFCM officer, Mrs. J. Earle Collier, assured Welfare Council representative Edwina Lewis that "the National was very much discouraged about the Chicago program," privately NFCM officers wondered whether "the easiest way . . . would be to give the Board rope enough to end all and then build a new work in Chicago."[30] The censure of the professional community of Chicago was predictably more severe and carried considerably more clout. The refusal of the Anchorage to comply with the suggestion of the Council of Social Agencies to employ a trained social worker incurred the wrath of an influential network of agencies and carried devastating consequences for the Anchorage. The council advised all Chicago social work agencies to refuse to refer women to the Anchorage until they had "remedied their problems."[31] The Welfare Council determined that "the Florence Crittenton Anchorage cannot meet the membership qualifications for registering with the Social Service Exchange because it has no case work program" and threatened to drop it from membership in the council.[32] And the Referral Center, established in 1938 by the United Charities of Chicago to direct the city's unmarried mothers to homes they felt best suited their needs, refused to recommend the Anchorage for maternity care.[33] Anchorage workers had come to depend on this professional network to refer unmarried mothers to their home; by their own admission, "most of our girls come to us through these agencies."[34] When Chicago agencies boycotted the home, Anchorage beds emptied. The threat of closing provided incentive enough to persuade Anchorage workers to abide by the injunctions of the social agencies. Pushed to the limit, Anchorage workers finally agreed to hire a social worker.

The conflict in Chicago made it clear to many maternity home workers that "no matter how we may want to cling to the old ways, we do have to face the fact that Social Services have at last come under standards set by trained social workers."[35] Homes in which evangelical women had once determined their own agendas, planned their own programs, and set their own priorities now were held accountable to the social work establishment. The story of the Chicago Anchorage suggested that those who ignored the demands of an increasingly powerful and united professional community, those who were slow to cooperate with social workers and bow to their dictates, would find themselves without support. Before 1920, social workers had confined their criticisms of maternity homes to their own conferences and professional journals. By the 1930s, the professional community had acquired the power literally to put those homes out of business.

"CASE WORKERS HAVE BECOME NECESSITIES"

Crittenton officer Gladys Revelle spoke for many when she observed that "if we don't do our building from within, we are sure to be forced to from without, and that is always a bitter procedure."[36] Many evangelical women in maternity homes concluded that acquiescence to social workers was the only course that could ward off increasingly vehement criticism. Pushed from without, both the NFCM and the Salvation Army tried to professionalize from within. In 1935, the Salvation Army offered a course on social welfare to familiarize maternity home workers "with the methods, aims, and terminology employed by the professional social worker," and to help them "apply the findings of social science" to their work.[37] Similarly, the Florence Crittenton Training School, which had long emphasized religious and domestic training, began to teach its students the rudiments of social work. Reba Barrett Smith encouraged Crittenton workers to acquire some professional training and provided an example by enrolling in a university extension course in social work.[38]

Evangelical women's efforts to train themselves, however, would not satisfy the demand of the social work establishment that homes offer the services of a caseworker. Social workers were not convinced that evangelicals who had become sufficiently versed in professional jargon to pronounce themselves "Efficiency Engineers" were worthy of the name, nor were they satisfied by maternity home matrons who had taken a course in social work.[39] An incident in the Chicago Anchorage conflict revealed the gap between evangelicals' and social workers' definition of a trained social worker. When Mrs. Eaton, a young woman prominent in Chicago society, displaced a WCTU member to head the board of the Anchorage, NFCM officers hoped that, though "her progressive ways are salt in the wounds of that old WCTU Board," she would be able, "if anybody can, to build up a work that will be acceptable to Chicago Social Workers."[40] But though Mrs. Eaton may have appeared "progressive" by NFCM standards, she did not pass muster with Chicago social workers, who pronounced her understanding of casework "hazy and undeveloped."[41]

To gain the approval of the social work establishment, maternity homes would either have to ally with a local casework agency or hire their own social workers. By 1934, Reba Barrett Smith had concluded that "case workers have become necessities" in work with unmarried mothers.[42] Some homes responded to this call in a timely fashion, contacting the nearest social work school or Children's Bureau to recommend appropriate candidates. Some of the larger and better-financed homes assembled a corps of caseworkers, employing as many as three or four.[43] Most homes, however, waited until pushed, postponing the hiring of a social worker until the late 1930s or early 1940s.

The trend toward hiring professional social workers in maternity homes was vividly reflected in the employment applications received by the NFCM in the 1930s and 1940s and in the NFCM's response. Throughout this period, the NFCM received applications from women who listed qualifications that once would have stood them in good stead. Employment application files included many handwritten letters such as one that Ione Ross sent in 1934. "I am very much interested in christian work and especially with girls," Ross wrote, "having raised two of my very own that I think any mother would be very proud of, As they are both christians." She went on to apologize for an education that "is not what I would like it to be," but claimed to possess "a store of practical knowledge" and promised to "make good in this work for there can be no failure when you take Jesus as a guide."[44] Another applicant, Estelle Jewett, cited "childhood and girlhood in middle-class American home where self-discipline was taught" as her primary qualification for maternity home work, adding that "both Grandfathers were Methodist ministers." She, too, assumed that her success as a mother would help her application for work in a maternity home: "Sons are married and proudly I say 'They are good citizens' but humbly I add 'Providence walked beside me all the way.'"[45]

Maternity homes had once rewarded precisely these qualifications, but the responses to applications like Ross's and Jewett's make it clear that maternal, religious, and domestic skills no longer guaranteed a woman a place in maternity home work. When Margaret Hinchliff, a rescue work verteran with experience in both Salvation Army and Crittenton homes in the early 1900s, applied to return to maternity home work in 1942, Reba Smith replied that although "some of our Homes hold out still for those who have been trained in the work and are motivated by the love of girls," the "demand everywhere for professionally trained social workers" prevented Smith from hiring her. "I am afraid you would not find a single old friend in the work," Smith added sadly.[46] Another woman who applied in 1937 to work in the Philadelphia Crittenton home received a similar response. Smith told her that she seemed "just the type of person I love to have in Florence Crittenton work," but the social agencies of Philadelphia had insisted that the home employ a trained social worker.[47] Smith also turned down Eva Gore in 1936, explaining that "the Community Chests are demanding that we get trained social workers and have discounted such experience as you and I have had."[48]

Most homes were so financially strapped during the depression that few could hire staff members of any sort. Those women who did receive encouraging responses, however, submitted not handwritten letters listing the number of Christian children raised but long résumés detailing college education, experience as social workers, and membership in professional associations. The application form itself went through changes that encouraged a new breed of candidate. Appended to the list of inquiries as to how regularly the applicant attended church and whether she smoked or drank were new questions concerning educational background, degrees held, social work experience, and membership in the American Association of Social Workers.[49]

Although the general trend toward hiring caseworkers in maternity homes was unmistakable in the late 1920s and 1930s, the exchange of evangelical women for social workers was not as complete as the social work establishment would have liked. In fact, it was rare for social workers to assume total control of a home. More often, a maternity home reluctantly hired a social worker, and evangelical women and social workers worked alongside each other in an uneasy, competitive, and occasionally volatile partnership. Crittenton worker Irene Hunter barely tolerated her social worker superintendent, complaining that she had assumed the important responsibilities of the home, leaving Hunter with the domestic drudgery: "Since Miss Mauk has requested that I work with the girls in cleaning up the home, I feel it is most unfair, particularly since I did nothing but scrub and clean the whole month of October."[50]

Disagreements between evangelicals and social workers ranged from skirmishes over power in the homes to fundamental differences over policy rooted in conflicting visions of the purpose of the homes. Those different visions sparked perhaps the most predictable conflict between evangelical women and social workers—that over religion. Whereas evangelical women viewed Protestant Christianity as "the foundation stone . . . upon which our work was based from the very beginning," social workers criticized the "confess-and-get-saved" approach of the evangelicals, which they believe created an oppressive and coercive atmosphere in the homes.[51] Dorothy Puttee and Mary Ruth Colby, for example, in their survey of homes in Illinois, assessed each home according to "religious atmosphere," condemning the "definite and powerful religious atmospheres" in several.[52] Some social workers granted the importance of religion in rehabilitative work, but all insisted that participation in the religious program of a home be voluntary.[53] Others took their criticism of religion in the homes further; J. Prentice Murphy, for instance, saw no reason to "single out the unmarried mother for greater religious consideration than that which is given to every other patient" and declared that "a spiritual, religious approach to one's work should be a general thing, rather than a tool sharply pointed and used only against a certain group of patients."[54]

Critical of the evangelical tool of religion, social workers fashioned a more secular alternative. Although they were convinced that compelling maternity home residents "to listen to sermons and exhortations as to right conduct" did little to rebuild their characters, social workers were no less enthusiastic than evangelical women about rehabilitating unmarried mothers.[55] Rather than redeem unmarried mothers, social workers set out to treat them. At the center of their notion of treatment was the theory and practice of casework. Social workers often set casework in explicit opposition to religion and, in some instances, construed the clearheaded objectivity of casework almost as an antidote to what they saw as the excessive religious influence in maternity homes.

Although social workers would have been loath to admit it, the parallels between their use of casework and evangelicals' use of religion were often striking. The change social workers hoped to effect through casework was every bit as redemptive in tone and as conversionary in purpose as the religious transformation envisioned by evangelicals. Evangelical women hoped that religious training might create in unmarried mothers "a burning desire for a new and altogether different life"; social workers endeavored to achieve "permanent rehabilitation of the girl" through "a change in personality."[56]

The route to that rehabilitation, social workers believed, was different for each client. Central to casework was the idea of "differential diagnosis," by which social workers sought to devise a unique program of rehabilitation for each unmarried mother. Through individualized casework, they countered what they saw as a dangerous reliance on the part of evangelical women on standardized, uniform diagnosis and treatment. "Since the basic principle of case work is respect for individual differences," social workers held, "any tool used in that service must be individualized and flexible."[57]

The logical extension of social workers' insistence on individualization was what one social worker called "a determination to let rules and regulations go smash, to abolish our dependence on policies."[58] But the common-sense appeal of differential diagnosis failed to win over evangelical women, for whom an insistence on flexibility threatened to undermine two venerated policies crucial to their style of reform: the length of stay required of unmarried mothers in maternity homes and the commitment to keep mother and child together. Social workers invoked the theory of differential diagnosis to criticize the uniform policies of maternity homes generally and the length-of-stay requirement in particular. Whereas evangelical women believed "the upbuilding of character" to be "slow work" and required unmarried mothers to stay in the homes for a period generally ranging from three to six months, social workers argued that admission and dismissal regulations should be adjusted to suit individual circumstances and needs.[59]

This debate over how long unmarried mothers should stay in maternity homes posed an intrinsic threat to the other policy central to the philosophy of the Salvation Army and Crittenton homes—the commitment to keep mother and child together. Evangelically run maternity homes had been founded with the promise to encourage unmarried mothers to keep their babies, and as years went by and alternatives were raised, that commitment became a veritable litmus test of loyalty to the maternity home ethos. When a social worker applied to the NFCM for maternity home employment in 1930, Reba Barrett Smith's response testified to the strength of that commitment at the same time that it betrayed an anxious defensiveness. "I would like to know," she wrote, "whether or not you believe that a mother and child should be kept together whenever possible—that it is God's divine plan that they should not be separated, and the training and encouragement will often make it possible for a girl to keep her baby when she has previously determined to give it up and that in the long run it is better for both mother and child if an attempt is made for them to spend their lives together." She closed the letter promising to recommend the candidate to the San Francisco board only "if you feel that you could help to carry out the Florence Crittenton policy of keeping mother and child together."[60]

Evangelical women held fast to the length-of-stay requirement not only because it kept unmarried mothers in the homes for an extended period of time but because they believed that it encouraged mothers to keep their babies. A Salvation Army worker in New York City wrote that though it was the policy of the home to urge residents to keep their babies, "in most cases inducement is not necessary after she has cared for it for a few months."[61] "Experience has shown," another Salvation Army matron wrote, "that in nearly every case the chubby arms of the babe will wind themselves so tightly around the mother's heart in the three months after the baby has arrived that the mother-love will prove stronger than anything else."[62]

Early findings that breast-feeding dramatically reduced the incidence of infant mortality among illegitimate children led social workers initially to applaud the efforts of the NFCM and Salvation Army to keep mother and child together. At the urging of the Children's Bureau and other child welfare advocates, several states passed laws in the 1910s prohibiting the separation of a child younger than six months from its mother.[63] Evangelical women believed that these laws affirmed a style of reform they had pioneered. Social workers' endorsement of maternity home policy, however, stemmed not from a belief that it facilitated the unmarried mother's spiritual reclamation but from their conviction that it served the best interests of the child. As Amey Watson stated plainly, "After all, it is the child that is our real interest and it is his or her welfare that we are most vitally interested in serving."[64]

This tendency of social workers to privilege the interests of the child over those of the mother further distinguished them from evangelical women. Whereas evangelical women conceived of the baby virtually as a tool in the redemption of the mother—"one of the strongest incentives to right living"—an increasing number of social workers held that "the child is the client" and believed it necessary to subordinate the mother's interests to those of the baby.[65] When social workers' assessment of the child's best interests shifted, so did their position on the disposition of illegitimate children. Increasingly critical of the policy of keeping mother and child together, social workers declared that professional objectivity demanded a case-by-case evaluation rather than a standard policy applied uniformly. Whether to keep mother and child together or to put the child up for adoption, social workers asserted, was a decision "which only can be solved upon an individual consideration of each and every case."[66]

Ironically, however, under the guise of individualization, the social work establishment replaced the evangelicals' uniform policy with one of their own. While still insisting on differential diagnosis, social workers began to sing the praises of adoption.[67] They explained their shift by arguing that adoption served the best interests of the child. "For many years there was a rigid attitude among social workers that the baby should remain with its mother at all costs," Florence Clothier wrote in 1941. This conviction was buttressed by the belief that "the baby should serve as an anchor for the giddy girl and evoke in her some sense of responsibility." But, she continued, "I doubt if long-term statistical studies would indicate that the amount of responsibility aroused in the mother in any way justifies the emotional scars left on the personalities of the children."[68]

Although social workers professed a belief in the fundamental right of unmarried mothers to make their own decision, in practice, they often pressured them to place their babies for adoption. When a Door of Hope resident expressed her desire to keep her baby, her social worker "worked with her, trying to show her how important it would be that the child be given every possible consideration. We tried to point out to her that possibly if the child was placed for adoption, it would get things that she could not possibly give to him."[69] Another unmarried mother recognized the influence social workers could exert, even when trying to remain neutral: "'It's not what Mrs. K. says exactly, it's just that her face lights up when I talk about adoption the way it doesn't when I talk about keeping Beth.'"[70]

Social workers' new interest in adoption reflected, in part, the accelerated interest in and concern for dependent and neglected children in the Progressive era.[71] George Mangold recalled a time "when the mother received the most consideration," but noted that "recently, much sentiment has been developing in favor of removing all handicaps and granting to such children total immunity from the sins of their parents."[72] Social workers expressed their new investment in children born to single mothers by endorsing a range of provisions for their protection, including increased state supervision over adoption, uniform birth registration laws, reform and enforcement of paternity support legislation, public assistance, and changes in the wording used in birth certificates to remove the stigma of illegitimacy.[73] If, in their new construction of out-of-wedlock pregnancy, social workers had lost a victim in the unmarried mother, they seem to have gained a new one in her baby.

At least as important as social workers' shifting assessment of the best interests of the child in explaining their turn to adoption was their appraisal of unmarried mothers. The question of what to do with the baby, Children's Bureau officers Maud Morlock and Hilary Campbell declared, depended on "the kind of person" the unmarried mother was—"her relationships, what her life has been so far, and what she is likely to make of her future—particularly what kind of mother she would be under the most difficult circumstances for motherhood."[74] Committed in theory to the idea that the answer to this question was "different for each mother," many social workers nevertheless believed that out-of-wedlock pregnancy disqualified women from proper motherhood. Social workers were more likely to favor adoption because they were less inclined than evangelical women to see those who bore children out of wedlock as fit mothers. As one social worker wrote, "the majority of unmarried mothers are not strong, mature, well-adjusted people" and advised her colleagues to counsel unmarried mothers to give up their babies.[75] Another agreed, arguing that "unmarried mothers, with rare exceptions, are incapable of providing sustained care and security for their illegitimate babies."[76] "Should not social agencies look facts in the face?" Helen S. Trounstine asked, declaring the majority of unmarried mothers to be "young, ignorant, with varied grades of mental caliber and no skilled trade."[77]

The topic of illegitimacy brought attitudes toward proper family life to the fore, and the debate over the status of illegitimate children inevitably raised questions concerning the boundaries of the legitimate family. Whereas evangelical women's belief in the redemptive power of motherhood led them to endorse the potentially radical notion of a fatherless family, social workers informed more by an ideology of family and motivated by a concern about "family breakdown" tended to see unmarried mothers as "mothers in name only," unfit to raise their own children.[78] Many historians have noted social workers' dedication to preserving the normative family, and social workers themselves acknowledged the central importance of the family in their understanding of their work.[79] "Social case work with a deepening conviction bases its services on the family as essential to society," Mary Wilcox Glenn wrote in 1928. "Family relationships are studied because they are fundamental."[80] In her work on sex delinquency, Elsa Castendyck defined the task of social workers as safeguarding "the security and stability of the family."[81] Miriam Van Waters agreed, writing in 1929 that "to social workers, the family is sacred." Van Waters pointed to the incongruity between many social workers' private lives and public pronouncements when she added ironically that the family "is all the more sacred to [social workers] because they seldom have any."[82] Not only did an unmarried mother and child fail to constitute a family worthy of the name; their very existence, in the minds of some social workers, leveled "a blow at the solidarity of the family" itself.[83]

The few social workers who ventured to use the term *illegitimate family* felt compelled to justify what they feared would seem to their colleagues oxymoronic. Stuart Queen and Delbert Mann thus nervously explained their use of the term: "We are not sure that it is wholly justified, but its use is suggested by the fact that every instance of illegitimacy involves a man, a woman, and a child. In the biological sense, at least, there is a family."[84] Social workers more concerned with the ideological meanings of the family than its biological basis, however, typically banished unmarried mothers from its circle.

EVANGELICALS' RESPONSE

Evangelical women and social workers working together in maternity homes found themselves locked in acrimonious struggle on almost every maternity home policy. Still, some evangelicals transformed their homes into models of professionalism and showcases of the ideas and methods of professional social work. Professionalization of a home marked the accommodation of evangelicals to social workers' demands, often begrudgingly, but occasionally enthusiastically. Bertha Howell of the Council of Social Agencies in Oakland, California, for example, wrote to Children's Bureau officer Maud Morlock to commend Brigadier Pagen for "heading a revolution in the Salvation Army" and "making her program flexible and casework centered."[85] Pagen was joined in the Army by Josephine Deyo, praised by Morlock for her vision and eagerness "to move ahead."[86] Anita Robb, trained social worker and third-generation Salvationist, was responsible for developing a professional social service program in the Salvation Army in the late 1930s.[87] And Jane Wrieden, superintendent of the Jersey City Door of Hope through the 1940s, believed that "if Salvationists would combine an expert skill with their Christian spirit, they would be a much greater force for good.'" Wrieden ranked her decision to enroll in a school of social work in 1933 as "'the second most important turning point in my life,'" subordinated in importance only to her conversion.[88] Professionalism's allies in the NFCM included Gladys Revelle, president of the Denver Crittenton home in the 1930s who became chair of the Central Extension Committee of the NFCM in 1940, and NFCM officer Genrose Gehri, who "gave signal leadership" in the Inter-City Conference on Illegitimacy, an organization of social workers dedicated to "the advancement of standards of case work with unmarried mothers."[89] In the homes these women presided over, professionalization proceeded apace. Josephine Deyo, for example, reported to Maud Morlock "a beginning of relaxation of rules and traditional practices in our Booth Memorial Hospital" in Chicago and asked Morlock to "bear with us, I think we will be able to work this out before too long."[90]

Even those evangelical women not directly allied with social workers appreciated the seeming magic that professional language could work, and in the 1930s and 1940s, the watchwords of social work began to appear in maternity home publications. As early as 1929, the NFCM announced that "this work demands the best type of experienced social worker, just as a physician of recognized standing should be called upon for a diagnosis of the girl's physical condition."[91] And in 1933, the general secretary of the Boston Crittenton League charted the history of the home in terms designed to please social workers: "In the past century the work has shifted from the feverishly emotional type of the earlier years to a more careful and thoughtful study of every phase of the problem of helping girls. The work has become more scientific and practical in its nature."[92]

The attempt by evangelicals to graft the language of professionalism onto that of womanly benevolence, however, sometimes resulted in a confusing blend of contradictory images. The president of the Boston Florence Crittenton League embraced these contradictions, claiming that "patience and love have brought the work to a high level of efficiency."[93] Reba Barrett Smith similarly struggled to salvage the virtues of womanly benevolence while accepting the imperatives of the new professionalism, resolving to make all Crittenton homes "models of efficiency," while adding that "in so doing we will sacrifice none of that sentimentality which it is charged some of us bring into the work."[94]

These awkward efforts of evangelical women to justify their work in the eyes of professionals while retaining something of their own benevolent style inadvertently revealed the tension between the two styles of reform. Social workers were more often met by evangelical women's resistance than by their cooperation. Although a few maternity home workers allied with social workers and others bent under the pressure of Community Chests and Councils of Social Agencies, many understood the criticism of social workers to be, at base, a devaluation of their work and a challenge to their authority. In response, they steadfastly and staunchly defended their style of benevolence. "It is *work*," one Crittenton worker claimed of her duties in the Boston home; "it is not *judging* nor trading in sentimentality."[95] Defiant though she was, by invoking a discourse of work, as opposed to benevolence, female mission, or Christian calling, she framed her defense in the terms set by social workers.

Other evangelical women expressed their resistance by refusing to take up the scientific and secular language of professionalism, grounding their defense in the tradition of redemptive femininity and the belief that women were naturally suited to benevolent work. Social workers might flaunt graduate degrees and a mastery of the complexities of casework, Reba Barrett Smith stated in 1937 in language that could not have been better calculated to irritate social workers, but "I have felt that my only qualification for the position I hold is that I have an almost psychic sense of what Florence Crittenton girls feel within their hearts."[96] Smith noted in 1940 that "we have met changing conditions and made our concessions to them. But the motif of our work has never changed. It was fueled and always will be in love."[97]

Evangelical women were perfectly capable of standing up and talking back to social workers, and they sometimes explicitly rejected the very foundations of professional authority. "I do not think that all, or even the great majority of social workers are competent to handle the problem of the unmarried mother and her child," Reba Smith wrote to Mrs. Grace Knox, the director of the Houston Florence Crittenton home and social worker trained at the University of Chicago. "A Master's degree in social work does not always qualify a young woman to deal with the intricate problems of social behavior."[98] Mrs. A. J. Wilson of the Little Rock, Arkansas, Crittenton home turned the logic of professionalism on its head in a letter to the local Community Chest in 1939. "We are unwilling to lower our ideals to meet the present social trend," she wrote, as "we feel that we must uphold the standards set before us by the founder of our Mission."[99]

Some evangelical women were especially outspoken in their resistance to casework, arguing that it countenanced a level of intrusion and intervention into the lives of unmarried mothers that was unnecessary at best and dehumanizing and prurient at worst. Boston Crittenton worker Marjorie Sanderson demanded that social workers bear in mind that "the girl is a human being and not a laboratory experiment and that due consideration should be given at all times to her personal feelings and to her right to as much privacy as the situation will permit."[100] In part, evangelical women's resistance to casework derived from what Emma Whittemore termed "a reluctance to dissect sin or too closely investigate the career of the sinner," as well as a disinclination to ask questions that would force them to confront unmarried mothers' sexuality.[101] But something more than prudishness fueled their fight against casework. The Crittenton worker who wrote that "Jesus had no 'survey committee,' no place for records for the past of the individual," hinted at a more subversive form of resistance, refusing to recognize casework as a professional skill worthy of respect or to place scientific expertise above religion.[102] By rejecting the premise as well as the practice of casework—the belief that human beings could be investigated, diagnosed, and treated with scientific and objective precision—evangelical women denied that social workers possessed a skill that equipped them with greater expertise in caring for unmarried mothers. Even more heretically, some evangelical women defended their own methods as superior to those of the caseworker. "Broken lives cannot be made whole by modern case work methods alone," Hazel Tuck declared in 1929, writing that "we try to employ only that type of woman in the Social Service Department whose knowledge of the Divine friendship is such that she feels the lessons taught by Christ are the foundations on which to build character."[103]

Evangelicals also struggled to maintain organizational autonomy. Many were willing to attend social work conferences, for example, but they resisted social workers' attempts to subsume them into national professional conferences. Crittenton officers declined to hold their national conference in conjunction with the National Conference of Social Work despite repeated requests by social workers to do so, refusing to compromise their separate identity or to admit their subordinate status to the social work profession. For their part, social workers were convinced that they were being kept from participating fully in the NFCM's conferences. When Crittenton social worker Genrose Gehri was prevented from delivering her paper at that conference in 1940 because her train was late, Children's Bureau officer Maud Morlock suspected that "much more is involved than this," adding that "there was no discussion of my paper in Boston" a year earlier.[104]

Although evangelicals were capable of digging in their heels, the forms of their resistance testify to the imbalance of power between themselves and social workers. Evangelicals might edge social workers off their conference programs, but social workers, with the aid of Community Chests, could close a maternity home down if they chose. Still, by resisting social work standards and by offering their own as an alternative, and by refusing to see their own style of reform as inferior to that of professionals (and not infrequently defining it as superior), evangelical women denied the power of social workers' main legitimizing tool.

UNMARRIED MOTHERS AND CASEWORK

Professionalism not only threatened the authority of evangelicals in maternity homes; it also held complicated meanings for residents. Challenges to evangelical matrons' authority could often translate into material benefits for unmarried mothers, many of whom cheered on the changes hastened by social workers. The reforms in maternity home rules supported by Crittenton social worker Genrose Gehri, for example—"recognition of the individual differences in liking and disliking certain kinds of recreation, the right to mail and receive letters unread by others, the right to privacy in interviews or family conversations, . . . and freedom from official escorting on every outside errand"—were heartily endorsed by unmarried mothers in the Norfolk Crittenton home where Gehri was hired as superintendent.[105] Norfolk residents dedicated the first issue of their home newsletter, *Crittenton Capers*, to Gehri, noting that since her arrival, "the girls are allowed to go to the drugstore anytime and we can go to town and have company if our work is completed."[106]

The changes that social workers brought to maternity homes, however, typically went beyond the right of unmarried mothers to go for an unescorted walk or to wear their own clothes. And when unmarried mothers felt those changes to be contrary to their interests, they resisted them as strongly as they did the constraints imposed by evangelical regimes. Unmarried mothers and evangelicals clashed over the conflicts engendered by everyday life in the homes—the quality of food, the work schedule, the fairness of rules determining appropriate reading material, hair styles, and clothing. Battles between unmarried mothers and social workers, on the other hand, were fought on different fronts and over different issues. The mothers' relationships with social workers were negotiated not in the laundry room or over the dining room table but in the process of interviewing and investigation at the heart of casework.

As envisioned by social workers, casework was the process by which the worker, "by an understanding, uncensorious, and objective attitude," encouraged the unmarried mother "to discuss her difficulties and the solutions that seem possible to her." After exploring her "problem," the unmarried mother "loses much of her hostility and is freed to go ahead with constructive plans for the present and future."[107] Casework, however, often appeared markedly different to clients. Unmarried mothers experienced the interview less as an "exploration of her problem" than as an invasive interrogation that made one woman who had navigated her way through a maze of social agencies on her way to a maternity home feel that "'I've had to tell and retell my story so often, that I feel as if I'm on trial for murder.'"[108] Unmarried mothers rarely found social workers "understanding, uncensorious, and objective," but often condescending, judgmental, and eager to pursue their own agendas under the guise of objectivity.

Regardless of the nature of the client's problem, the caseworker typically asked questions regarding home conditions and her occupational, educational, and medical history. Questions on these topics alone could invade a client's privacy, but when the client was an unmarried mother, social workers added to that list a battery of questions concerning sexual experience. In a questionnaire designed in 1917 as a model for casework with unmarried mothers, Ada Sheffield instructed social workers to ask: "Has she had men callers, one or many? Have they been accustomed to go at a proper hour? Has she been given to staying out very late? Does she dress conspicuously? When did girl's or woman's sexual experiences begin? Has she had a succession of 'friends,' or has she been intimate with but one man?"[109] The language of the questions took on a more modern tone in later decades, but their content remained virtually unchanged. Given the nature and number of questions that social workers deemed necessary to ask, it is easy to see how their clients experienced casework as intrusive grilling and an invasion of their privacy, or as one put it, "a feminized third degree."[110]

Conflict between unmarried mothers and social workers was often sparked not only by the tendency of the workers to ask what the mothers considered unnecessarily personal questions, but by social workers' use of the information gleaned in the casework interview. Children's Bureau investigators Maud Morlock and Helen Campbell insisted that the relationship between caseworker and client was confidential, "guarded as carefully as that between priest and parishioner or doctor and patient."[111] Yet, many social workers believed, as one wrote, that "the girl's story alone is not enough."[112] Committed in theory to confidentiality, many social workers believed it necessary in practice to verify statements made by unmarried mothers.[113]

To an unmarried mother, a social worker's concern with "tapping every resource" to ensure a "thorough investigation" meant that her friends, her parents, and even her employer might be informed of her pregnancy.[114] Many unmarried mothers did not trust social workers to respect their privacy, and conflicts between them frequently erupted over the issue of confidentiality. Furious with her social worker for informing her brother and sister-in-law of her pregnancy, one woman spoke to the Door of Hope superintendent of "her intense irritation about the way Miss Lovett respected her as an individual," claiming simply that "she wanted to be treated like any normal human being with feelings."[115] Many unmarried mothers probably shared Pauline Leader's indignation when her social worker broke her promise of confidentiality: "I succumbed more to her smiles, her pretense of equality, of comradeship, her protestation of 'I won't tell' (which confidence she betrayed as soon as my back was turned), in short all the paraphernalia of the social service worker. She promised 'not to tell.' I told her and rested easy on her smiles and on her promises."[116] Leader's criticism of her social worker's methods was deeply ironic, of course, echoing as it did the conventional plot of seduction and betrayal.

Refusing to believe that social workers could be trusted with confidential information and fearing that they would use that information to inform relatives or employers, unmarried mothers often resorted to lying. Marjorie's social worker knew that "in spite of the free and confidential manner that Marjorie has developed . . . there is information which Marjorie does not give . . . and some of what she gives is false." She noted, for example, that her client "gave completely erroneous information" about the father of her child. Marjorie admitted later "that she had purposely given wrong information to 'throw them off the scent.'"[117] Unmarried mothers' reputation for duplicity was well established among social workers and of no small frustration to them: "Girls in serious trouble often begin the conversation by saying defiantly, 'Both my parents and *all* my relatives died when I was a baby,'" Hildegarde Dolson noted, "This invariably means that at least one parent and plenty of relatives are robustly alive, and the girl is terrified for fear they'll be told."[118] A study conducted by the United Charities of Chicago in 1936 found that unmarried mothers' case files were "filled with misrepresentations of a conscious, self-defensive nature, apparently assumed in fear of what the agency might do if it knew the facts about her age, or place of residence, or the existence of interested relatives, etc."[119]

Social workers promised not only that the casework exchange would be confidential but that their role in the interview would be impartial and objective. Considered key to casework theory, objectivity was essential to the professional status of the social worker, and theorists called on analogies to other professions to underline their commitment to its tenets. Moral judgments had "no place in case work philosophy," declared Ruth Brenner. "No obstetrician does a less competent delivery because his patient is unmarried; neither does a skin specialist adopt a moral attitude in treating his venerally infected patients. In the same way it is untenable for us to make moral judgments of our clients."[120] Before meeting a client, the social worker was to clear her mind "completely of every thought pertaining to one's own life and interests, then of all preconceived ideas or judgments about the person to be interviewed. . . . Then, with a cleared, impartial mind, one meets the client."[121] Because out-of-wedlock pregnancy raised questions of morality and propriety, social workers stressed the special importance of objectivity in working with unmarried mothers. Since social workers were themselves members and products of the culture in which "rejecting and punishing attitudes prevail against unmarried mothers and their babies," social workers asserted, "they need to be especially alert to maintain the objectivity essential to all areas of social work and to guard against subtle, disguised intrusions of their own needs and attitudes into their professional practices."[122] Thus, J. Prentice Murphy claimed that "the good social worker will refuse to consider the unmarried mother as purely a moral problem and will differ from most people in refusing to consider the unmarried mother as representing the great moral sin."[123]

Yet even some social workers themselves questioned just how different from most people they were in their attitudes toward unmarried mothers. Although casework theorists stressed the importance of objectivity, their colleagues in the field knew that maintaining objectivity in practice was difficult if not impossible. In the same way that out-of-wedlock pregnancy posed problems for social workers' commitment to confidentiality, it pushed them to consider the sincerity and practicality of their commitment to objectivity. Mary Brisley ranked illegitimacy with homosexuality as issues "in which 'inherited' and frequently unconscious social attitudes are most apt to influence even skilled workers either positively or negatively," and in 1934, she cautioned, "The one fact of the break with the accepted moral code tends . . . to obscure all other considerations except in the minds of the most experienced case workers. Emotional rather than rational attitudes; subjective identification rather than the elimination of the personal factor; . . . all spring up not only in the community but also in case workers and supervisors themselves to baffle and to perplex."[124] One social worker who acknowledged the relationship between social worker and unmarried mother as inevitably "emotionally charged" asserted that "the nature of the material itself is fraught with disturbing elements which may affect the worker personally. . . . In spite of training and experience it is difficult to throw off completely the reaction to illegitimacy which is so sharply ingrained in our cultural patterns."[125] Elizabeth Dexter prodded social workers to consider their own responses to illegitimacy and questioned their ability to be objective: "Most of us pride ourselves on being free of prejudice, but how free are we? Doesn't each of us consider some one thing as beyond the pale?"[126]

The realization of her own subjectivity led at least one social worker to question her efficacy altogether: "I wonder sometimes whether social workers have helped unmarried mothers through the years as much as they have hurt them," Marjory Embry wrote. "We are such human people, after all. We have so many emotional reactions of our own, and the best of social work training does not always prevent them from coming to the front at odd and inconvenient times. The whole question of unconventional love is so fraught with drama, with emotion and conflict and all that is the warp and woof of everyone's emotional life. Is any of us enough adjusted to meet the needs of these youngsters without defensiveness for or against them, and with that clear-eyed perspective that comes from rising above one's own immediate concerns?"[127] Unusually candid, Embry's painful self-analysis seemed to betray an anxiety about her own tenuous claim to professional legitimacy.

Most social workers, however, resisted Embry's suggestion that their subjectivity unfitted them for work with unmarried mothers, and many endeavored to turn subjectivity into a virtue. Social work theorist and educator Virginia Robinson, for example, offered caseworkers some theoretical refuge by pronouncing objectivity a "false and impossible goal of achievement" and by encouraging them to examine their own inevitable and legitimate role in the casework process.[128] Other social work theorists took up the analysis of objectivity and subjectivity in casework. Frances Potter, for example, speculated that further progress in "the art of case work" demanded "self-analysis" so that "we may determine by study and selection the mental attitudes in ourselves that evoke the desired reactions in clients."[129] Acknowledging their own subjectivity, many maintained, helped them to be more rather than less objective. Social workers aware of their biases might prevent the intrusion of those biases into casework. To Elizabeth Dexter, the social worker's first responsibility was "to study her own reactions and maintain a detachment that will keep her emotionally free."[130] By understanding their own feelings, social workers claimed, they could be all the more certain not to express them in their work. "Not one of us enjoys facing the full implications of such primitive, unconscious, and unprofessional reactions to unmarried parenthood," Ruth Brenner consoled her colleagues, but "only by recognizing the full implications of these attitudes shall we be able to modify and change them in order to function with the fine control that we need in the practice of our profession."[131] Erma Blethan wrote simply that a social worker's skills—her "ability to understand people"—depended on "an understanding of herself."[132]

The amount of ink spilled and the number of conference hours spent by social workers discovering casework to be a process in which their own ideas, desires, and preconceptions figured as strongly as those of their clients would have been ironic, even laughable, to most unmarried mothers. Social workers' revelation of their own subjectivity would hardly have been news to their clients, for whom the subjectivity of the casework relationship was usually abundantly obvious. The best indication that unmarried mothers understood casework as a forum for social workers' agendas rather than a vehicle for them to make their own decisions was the frequency with which they tried to manipulate their social workers. The social worker who "had the feeling" that her client "was trying to say all of the right things but they weren't genuine" suggested that the mothers knew that there were "right things" to say to social workers.[133] By social workers' admission, clients were adept at discerning and maneuvering around the ideas and agendas of caseworkers. Ruth Brenner, for example, noticed that one unmarried mother explained her wish for secrecy in terms she figured to be "most acceptable to the case worker," stressing "her parents' foreign birth, their lack of sympathy with American customs and with their American-born children, their expectations that she would give up her education to establish her own and their support."[134] Knowing that a social agency would withhold assistance to her if they knew that she was living with the father of her child, another woman told her social worker that "she had been deserted and was in need of care." That social worker estimated that "many who know the whereabouts of their lovers denied all such knowledge."[135]

Unmarried mothers found social workers to be most transparent in their attitudes toward children, and they seem to have been especially aware that there were "right things" to say about plans for their disposition. They knew as well that the "right things" were race-specific. Social workers' increasing insistence that white women place their babies for adoption made it difficult for white unmarried mothers to express contrary desires. In a 1926 study, on the other hand, Ruth Reed suggested that African-American unmarried mothers exploited social workers' expectations of the "mother-love" allegedly universal among black women.[136] One black unmarried mother, for example, convinced her social worker that she intended to keep her child and left the maternity home with her family, apparently persuaded to keep the baby. But "a visit some three years later disclosed the fact that the child had been placed for adoption within a few days of its return." Believing, probably correctly, that her social workers' assistance was predicated on her commitment to keep her child, the woman "pretended to acquiesce in a plan which would insure a termination of supervision."[137] If this woman's knowledge of what to say to escape the surveillance of her social worker suggested a certain canniness, it illuminated as well the pernicious way in which racism structured what could and could not be said, and the difficulty of speaking outside of the boundaries of the "right" things that social workers wanted and expected to hear.

Although many unmarried mothers' relationships with social workers were marked by conflict, others formed strong bonds, some expressing their gratitude in familial language similar to that used with evangelical matrons. "I shall never forget all you did for the baby and me," wrote Dorothy. "I can just say that it was what a *real mother* would do for a *daughter of her own* whom she loved very dearly."[138] Others thought of social workers as friends. Marjorie, for example, understood her relationship with her social worker "as that of one with a friend her own age and level," and spoke with her in a "slangy, free, off hand way."[139] When another unmarried mother heard that her social worker was to be transferred to another city, she wrote, "'I felt I again was to lose a friend someone whom I could and did turn to in all my troubles.'"[140]

Grateful and cooperative clients undoubtedly made daily life easier for their social workers. Their desire to transform social workers into friends and mothers, however, inadvertently posed a more vexing challenge than the prevarications and manipulations of their more suspicious counterparts. Clients who referred to social workers as "mothers" failed to distinguish scientific expertise from evangelical benevolence. Those who treated them as friends similarly called social workers' professionalism into question by bridging or even denying the distance between themselves and alleged experts. While social work theorists proclaimed the importance of professional detachment, practicing caseworkers struggled to negotiate the contradictory imperatives demanded of women and of professionals: maternal sympathy and nurturance on the one hand, and objectivity and dispassion on the other. Social worker Gordon Hamilton probably spoke for many when she asked in 1937, "What, in fact, is a professional friend?"[141] Social workers who anticipated battles with tenacious evangelicals and uncooperative clients seem to have been caught unaware by unmarried mothers whose kindness and responsiveness paradoxically laid bare the internal contradictions of their own strategy of professionalization.

CONCLUSION

Professionalization, in social work as in other occupations, was a process of restriction and exclusion. As Magali Larson observes, "where everyone can claim to be an expert, there is no expertise."[142] Efforts to marginalize or exclude the less acceptable members of their new profession led social workers to single out evangelical women in maternity homes for special criticism. Beginning in the 1920s, maternity homes that had once operated independently were subject to social workers' intrusions and accountable to their demands. By the 1930s, many of those homes had employed a social worker and displayed the outward signs of professionalism. By the 1940s, social workers had acquired considerable status as experts in the field of illegitimacy, publishing numerous studies and sponsoring conferences on the subject of out-of-wedlock pregnancy.

Yet, in more candid moments, social workers were less than certain of their victory. They knew what historians have been slow to appreciate: that practice did not march in lockstep with theory and that the professionalization of social welfare was at best uneven. Social workers lamented the distance between theory and practice in the field of social welfare generally. As Fern Lowry wrote in 1936, "I think this consciousness of technics may not figure as largely in our practice as it does in our vocabulary."[143] In work with unmarried mothers, the gap between theory and practice appeared wide indeed. Catherine Mathews likened the work of social workers in the field of illegitimacy to that of a fisherman "who, having lost his anchor, thinks he has arrived somewhere" only to find "that we are miles off."[144]

Even with the power of Councils of Social Agencies, Community Chests, and Welfare Councils on their side, social workers found it difficult to anchor themselves or their ideas securely in maternity homes. Despite the vigorous professionalizing efforts of the 1920s to the 1940s, some homes changed little and others not at all. Social workers were unable to transform the behavior of evangelical women in maternity homes, and evangelical work persisted in some areas long after professional social work had taken hold in others. In 1936, a social worker of the United Charities of Chicago noted that maternity homes "have such a moralistic and evangelistic atmosphere that our treatment is balked by counter-influences."[145] Social investigators Dorothy Puttee and Mary Ruth Colby declared maternity home care in Illinois in 1937 to be "a later nineteenth-century development which retains today much of the spirit of the age it represents."[146]

The records of some maternity homes testify to the incompleteness of professionalization and to the persistence and tenacity of evangelical women within them. The Salvation Army Booth Memorial Hospital in Boston asked unmarried mothers for their occupation and address "at time of Fall" into the 1940s. The matron of the Jersey City Door of Hope continued to record evidence of conversion in each case file until 1942. The NFCM's policy of keeping mother and child together survived the repeated assaults of social workers into the 1940s. And while social workers demanded that evangelicals temper the religious atmosphere of their homes, the superintendent of the Crittenton home in Trenton, New Jersey, celebrated "a real spiritual revival among our girls" in 1944.[147] She explained that "the Devil had been very active, sowing the seeds of unrest, discontent, and rebellion," but that "the spirit of God worked mightily." When one of the girls came to her room in tears to tell her that "she wanted salvation to be real in her life," others followed, and the superintendent led them in a religious revival that lasted for days. The Trenton Crittenton revival was but one example of the enduring discrepancies between what evangelical women did and what social workers wanted them to do, between the homes as social workers envisioned them and the homes as they were.

Unmarried mothers were interested in the terms of the debate between evangelical women and social workers only insofar as they were affected directly. But rather than being peripheral to the story of the changing shape and meaning of benevolence in the first half of the twentieth century, unmarried mothers participated actively in defining the terms on which that transformation would be negotiated. While evangelical women and social workers struggled between themselves over control in the homes, unmarried mothers determined for them the boundaries of possibility.

Social workers ultimately found the discourse of illegitimacy easier to control than their relationship either with evangelical women or with unmarried mothers. Although social workers had accrued considerable power, professional status ultimately hinged upon how well the would-be professionals convinced others of their expertise. Maternity home matrons who claimed a higher source of authority and unmarried mothers who found ways to maneuver around the subjective process of casework thwarted social workers in this basic task. Secularizing and professionalizing the rhetoric of benevolence had gone smoothly by comparison; professionalizing the work of benevolence proved another thing entirely.

6

White Neurosis, Black Pathology, and the Ironies of Professionalization: The 1940s

In September of 1941, Robert South Barrett sent out a warning to Crittenton workers: "I think it necessary that I should raise the storm signal to our Homes in the same way the Weather Bureau raises one at the approach of a hurricane," he wrote. "We are facing a very serious time, and I beg you to make plans now to meet a situation that is fraught with many dangers."[1] These dangers—"the lure of uniforms, the emotional disturbances produced by men being taken away from their usual habitats, the assembling of large numbers of men in military camps"—were those of the home front during wartime. Maternity home workers expected World War II to swell the illegitimacy rate and deluge the homes with applications.

Although the warnings were ominous, excitement resonates through maternity home workers' anticipation of World War II. Many harked back to World War I, which, in focusing national attention on the efforts and accomplishments of evangelical women and on the new expertise of social workers, had contained opportunity as well as challenge. The Second World War was to play as crucial a role as the first in transforming the understanding of illegitimacy and the treatment of unmarried mothers. In the course of the 1940s and 1950s, the "problem" of the unmarried mother—once cast in the singular—fractured into several "problems" along the fault lines of race and class. While class had explicitly informed early-twentieth-century discourses of illegitimacy, race had remained largely uninterrogated. Beginning in the 1940s, however, race combined with class to assume an increasingly visible, central, and defining place in constructions of out-of-wedlock pregnancy. During and after the war, black and white unmarried mothers were cast as very different figures, pregnant for different reasons and in need of the service of two different sets of experts.

Historian Rickie Solinger has documented the central importance of race in constructing the cultural meanings of out-of-wedlock pregnancy after World War II, in shaping public policies toward unmarried mothers, and in determining the ways in which women experienced single motherhood.[2] This chapter locates some beginning points for the emergence of two very different stories about black and white unmarried mothers and considers the forces behind those changes—some of which had prewar roots—to argue that these ostensibly discrete discourses were deeply interconnected and interdependent.

In addition to catalyzing new constructions of out-of-wedlock pregnancy, World War II also witnessed a more decisive shift in the balance of power between evangelical women and social workers. Professionalization continued to advance unevenly, but social workers were clearly in ascendancy, and in many ways, the 1940s witnessed the culmination of the professionalization of the field of illegitimacy. But instead of resolving the tension between female benevolence and professionalism, events of the 1940s brought that tension to the surface. Rather than constituting the clear-cut victory social workers had hoped for, the professionalization of the field magnified the ironies inherent in that strategy.

WHITE ILLEGITIMACY AND INDIVIDUAL PATHOLOGY

Those concerned with unmarried mothers had reason to sound the alarm at the onset of the war. Although in the early 1940s the illegitimacy rate rose in proportion to the general birthrate, rather than soaring dramatically as many had predicted, the relative increase in numbers of unmarried mothers still created a heavy burden for maternity homes and social agencies.[3] As early as October 1940, the NFCM reported that "there is already an increase in the number of applications for admission, and many of our Homes are filled to capacity."[4] The year 1944 witnessed the first large wartime increase in the number of illegitimate births, and many maternity homes were so overcrowded that they had to turn applicants away.[5] But to those working with unmarried mothers in the 1940s, the changing demographic profile of unmarried mothers seeking aid was as striking as their numerical increase. In contrast to the predominantly working-class clientele that had filled maternity homes in the first half of the twentieth century, maternity home staffs and social workers all over the country reported a rise in the number of white middle-class women seeking the services of homes and social agencies. Social worker Helen Perlman attributed this demographic change to marriage postponements during wartime, the rising incidence of "illicit coition," and the more frequent use of social agencies by unmarried mothers.[6] Solinger has speculated that middle-class girls and women might have turned to maternity homes in greater numbers during and after the war because out-of-wedlock pregnancy threatened the aspirations of middle-class families in a new way. Whereas the illegitimate pregnancy of a middle-class daughter was once a "private sorrow," to be attended with an appropriately private solution, the wartime and postwar family ideology rendered her a "public humiliation" that required a professional curative.[7]

Whatever the cause, the upsurge in the number of white middle-class women seeking aid drew considerable comment, and observations on the class status of unmarried mothers marked every description of the clientele of homes and agencies in the 1940s. Cases cited by social workers in the professional literature, previously populated by the paradigmatic working-class sex delinquent characterized by a fondness for the dance hall, an excessive use of makeup, and an inclination toward using slang, now pondered an altogether different unmarried mother. Social work theorist Leontine Young's description of a woman "in her mid twenties, quietly attractive, and well-dressed," who "spoke in a soft voice and with an educated accent," was filled with the signifiers of middle-class status.[8] Psychiatrist J. Kasanin and social worker Sieglinde Handschin also drew attention to the "new" unmarried mother—"a girl of good family, a good student in high school or perhaps university . . . properly brought up."[9]

Social workers were initially baffled by what to make of unmarried mothers who were "poised, calm and assured, quiet, unruffled, friendly and smiling," and to whom the conventional causes of illegitimacy did not seem to apply.[10] "They are no longer limited to the tenement dwellers," Sara Edlin noted of the wartime and postwar residents of Staten Island's Lakeview home, whose history of "overcrowding, large families, and the deprivations and struggles of poverty" had explained their condition in the past.[11] Crittenton social worker Rose Bernstein was candid in her confusion when she noted that "the extension of unmarried motherhood into our upper and educated classes in sizeable numbers further confounds us by rendering our former stereotypes less tenable. Immigration, low mentality, and hypersexuality," she wrote, "can no longer be comfortably applied when the phenomenon has invaded our own social class—when the unwed mother must be classified to include the nice girl next door, the physician's or pastor's daughter."[12]

In their departures from the stereotypical unmarried mother, those women seeking the aid of social agencies and maternity homes in the 1940s seemed to defy conventional explanations of out-of-wedlock pregnancy. The increasing presence of middle-class girls and women in maternity homes and social agencies led social workers to reevaluate the causes behind out-of-wedlock pregnancy in an attempt to remove them from the larger category of "sex delinquency." In an effort to comprehend this new group of unmarried mothers, social workers turned from explanations of illegitimacy grounded in sociology, criminology, and sexology and called instead on psychiatry. Beginning in the 1940s, social workers viewed illegitimacy among white middle-class girls and women as a symptom of unconscious needs and desires. Rather than regarding them as "delinquents, moral defectives, or prostitutes," social workers diagnosed them as neurotic.[13]

Social workers in this decade were not the first of their profession to turn to psychoanalytic explanations of behavior. The first wave of interest in psychiatry and psychoanalysis rose in the years immediately following World War I and crested in the 1920s, amounting to what historians of social work have since termed the "psychiatric deluge."[14] Especially influential in the mental hygiene movement, the child guidance movement, and the development of veterans' services, psychiatric social workers proposed an interior approach to the client's problems to replace the more sociological focus on external circumstances. As social work theory substituted personal maladjustment for environmental causes as the root of social problems, social workers proposed adjusting the individual to the environment rather than reforming that environment.[15]

Many social workers had touted the importance, even the superiority of a psychiatric approach throughout the 1920s. Mary Jarrett, one of the founders of the Smith College School for Social Work and known as the "mother of psychiatric social work," presented a paper at the National Conference of Social Work (NCSW) in 1919 entitled "The Psychiatric Thread Running through All Social Case Work," in which she proclaimed that "this *thread* constitutes the entire warp of the *fabric* of case work."[16] Jarrett and her colleagues in psychiatric social work believed themselves to be in the vanguard of social work theory. Smith alumna Rose Hahn Dawson recalled that psychiatric social work was held to be "the gospel."[17] For Jessie Taft, the NCSW held in Atlantic City in 1919 was "radiant in my memory." The psychiatric social worker made her debut at that conference—"in every section psychiatrists appeared on the program"—and Taft described a meeting devoted to discussing psychiatric social work that "burst its bounds and had to be transferred to a church a block away. Dignified psychiatrists and social workers climbed out of windows in order to make sure of a good seat."[18] Exhilarated with the new approach, Bertha Reynolds remarked that psychiatric social workers "believed themselves to have come in at the top of a new profession based upon understanding of personality, and that all other social workers would have to look up to them for the light."[19]

Psychiatric social work dominated the theoretical landscape of the profession after World War I. Yet psychoanalytic concepts seem rarely to have found their way from conference programs to casework practice. From a review of social work theoretical literature and case records from the 1920s, historian Leslie Alexander argues that "psychoanalytic theory influenced an elite minority fringe rather than the main body of theory and practice during the 1920s," and concludes that psychiatry was much less influential for both theory and practice than historians have contended.[20] Some social workers admitted as much. Helen Perlman characterized the "psychiatric deluge" of social work in the 1920s as "a myth" and recalled that when she first taught at the New York School of Social Work in 1933, "psychoanalytic theory was practically unknown in social casework *except* in the New York–Philadelphia-Boston circuit." As for social workers elsewhere, Perlman stated, "their psychodynamic knowledge . . . was minimal."[21]

Work with unmarried mothers, apparently like much social work, was largely unaffected by psychiatric ideas through the 1920s and 1930s. Yet, if the word *deluge* overstated the impact of psychiatry on social work in the early twentieth century, it can be used with little exaggeration to describe the field of illegitimacy in the 1940s. Aided by the popularization of psychiatry during World War II, psychoanalytic ideas held undisputed sway over social work theory on illegitimacy, and social workers began calling on those ideas to comprehend out-of-wedlock pregnancy among their new clientele.[22] "We have learned from psychiatry and psychoanalysis that folks have inner selves that are inextricably bound up with the outer person whom we have thought we knew," wrote Doris Brooks in 1938 in an article predicting future trends in work with unmarried mothers. Brooks and her colleagues believed that psychiatric techniques offered a way "to understand what these inner selves are saying to us, what needs are being expressed, and how to help."[23]

Some social workers, reluctant to dismiss so cavalierly the previous three decades of work on illegitimacy, proposed a bridge between psychiatric and sociological explanations. In 1938, Mandel Sherman argued that "a clear-cut differentiation cannot be made between the psychiatric and the social factors" and posited an "interrelationship" between the two.[24] But the psychological soon overwhelmed the sociological in psychiatrists' and social workers' assessments of unmarried mothers. Beginning in the 1940s, social workers joined psychiatrists and psychologists in viewing out-of-wedlock pregnancy as the unmarried mother's attempt to ease a larger unresolved psychic conflict.

The psychiatric ideas that so saturated social workers' theoretical writing on illegitimacy in the 1940s also found their way into casework practice with unmarried mothers in those years. Before 1940, psychiatry was, for the most part, irrelevant to the daily routine of maternity homes and social agencies. Historian Martha Field finds the case records of the Illinois Children's Home and Aid Society, a Chicago agency that served unmarried mothers, to have been "entirely unaffected" by psychodynamic conceptualizations of out-of-wedlock pregnancy before 1938. Between then and 1949, however, the agency's staff had grown familiar with psychoanalytic terminology and had begun using words like *neurotic* and *repressed* in their practice, "albeit imprecisely."[25] Other social workers incorporated the jargon and techniques of psychiatry into their treatment of unmarried mothers in this period as well. Dorothy Hutchinson, professor of casework at the New York School of Social Work, often used psychiatric concepts in her work with unmarried mothers in the 1940s. Judging one unmarried mother "a very neurotic girl," Hutchinson wrote that "unconsciously I feel that Marjorie was working out a love relationship with a man her father's age who represented her father to her but of all this she was totally unaware."[26] Of another client, Hutchinson proposed that "in the pregnancy situation, Jennie seems to be somehow acting out oedipus difficulties and oedipal attachment to father."[27]

Perhaps it is not surprising that a social work educator, abreast of the latest trends in her profession, would employ psychiatric terminology in her work with unmarried mothers. But even the Salvation Army's Door of Hope in Jersey City embraced the new understanding of unmarried motherhood. Jane Wrieden, Salvation Army officer and trained social worker, was principally responsible for bringing psychiatric social work to the Door of Hope, where she served as superintendent in the 1940s. Asked to assess the cause of out-of-wedlock pregnancy, Wrieden stated that "I have come to think of these pregnancies as only symptoms of more deep-seated problems," adding that "here we try to treat the person, not the symptom." To illustrate, Wrieden told the story of a Door of Hope resident, "Mary Roe," who had had an affair with a man she expected to marry. "But when she found she was pregnant, the man told her that he was not free to marry, and that he did not intend to divorce the wife of whom Mary never before had heard." Although Mary's case contained the essential ingredients of the many tales of seduction and abandonment spun by Door of Hope workers in the past, Wrieden offered a different interpretation of the meaning of Mary's pregnancy. After receiving a psychological examination at the Door of Hope, "Mary finally gained real insight into her experience, and saw her love affair and her pregnancy as related to her conflict with her own mother."[28]

Although psychiatrists and social workers agreed that illegitimacy was a neurotic symptom, they varied in their specific analyses of the deeper pathology that produced it. Explanations of out-of-wedlock pregnancy ran the gamut of psychoanalytic diagnoses, covering a range of deep-seated problems including self-punishment for forbidden sex fantasies, unresolved oedipal relationships with either or both parents, and fantasies of rape, prostitution, or immaculate conception. Many social workers believed that either a dependency upon or rejection by the mother or a seductive attachment to the father could precipitate illegitimacy.[29] Others described out-of-wedlock pregnancy as a masochistic act. "This passive-masochistic tendency probably characterizes a large proportion of unmarried mothers," psychiatrist Helene Deutsch wrote; "it is a feminine tendency, intensified by guilt feelings, that, once cruelly gratified through illegitimate motherhood, seeks repetition of the same situation." Deutsch transformed the traditional story of seduction and abandonment—"being left 'on the street' with the illegitimate child of a seducer"—into the "masochistic fantasy" of an unmarried mother.[30]

However they diagnosed its underlying cause, psychiatrists and social workers believed out-of-wedlock pregnancy to be a purposeful, albeit unconscious act on the part of a neurotic woman; although she sought pregnancy, she did so for reasons lodged deep in her unconscious. Leontine Young likened the unmarried mother to a "sleepwalker," who "acts out what she must do without awareness or understanding of what it means or of the fact that she plans and initiates the action," and claimed that "there is nothing haphazard or accidental in the causation that brought along this specific situation with these specific girls."[31]

The psychiatric reconceptualization of out-of-wedlock pregnancy was accomplished in less than a decade, so that by the mid-1940s, neurotic unmarried mothers were entirely predictable. Helene Deutsch described Ida, whose pregnancy she diagnosed as the result of "the rebellious struggle against her mother," as "a fundamentally banal story of illegitimacy."[32] In 1944, Viola Bernard remarked on the redundancy of the case of the neurotic unmarried mother: "With repetitious regularity the background histories of all the cases . . . show conspicuous maternal and paternal failure to meet the essential lifelong emotional needs of these girls."[33] By the 1940s, social workers were as little surprised to find an unmarried mother with seductive designs on her father as they had been just ten years earlier to find her the promiscuous patron of dance halls or as evangelical women before them had been to find her the victim of an unscrupulous man.

Like these earlier narratives of out-of-wedlock pregnancy, the new psychiatric understanding of the unmarried mother was heavily weighted with meaning for its authors. Despite their many gains, social workers continued to fret over the insecurity of their professional status into the 1940s. To anxious professionals, psychiatry's appeal was inescapable. Because psychiatry was invested with such cultural authority in the postwar period, it boosted social workers' claims to expertise. Even more than the earlier conceptualization of sex delinquency, the new psychiatric explanation promised to place the study of illegitimacy on the lofty level of science. Robert Fleiss, in his foreword to *Out of Wedlock*, congratulated Leontine Young for transporting out-of-wedlock pregnancy "from the nineteenth century where it had to be judged, into the twentieth century where it has to be understood."[34] Young agreed that psychiatry grounded the study of illegitimacy in science: "Not until the discoveries of Freud," she boasted, were social workers able to consider the unmarried mother "from a scientific rather than a moral point of view."[35]

The psychiatric understanding of unmarried motherhood offered social workers a discourse of illegitimacy cast in an esoteric language appropriate to the professional, filled with medical terms and cloaked in the legitimizing mantle of science. Social workers were afforded unprecedented opportunities to label and categorize and to assign unmarried mothers to "types." The new typologies, based on psychiatric categories, recalled earlier attempts to delineate various levels of sex delinquency and rivaled those classifications in their scientific pretensions. In 1938, Mandel Sherman arranged unmarried mothers into three categories: "the emotionally inadequate, the emotionally disorganized, and the neurotic."[36] By 1949, social workers had ventured more sophisticated diagnoses. In that year,

Miriam Powell classified thirty unmarried mothers according to the following categories: "Primary behavior disorder, 17; psychoneurosis, 3; schizophrenia, with excessive sexuality, 2; schizoid personality, with homosexual tendencies, 1; psychopathic personality, 3; neurotic character of the hysterical type, 1; adult maladjustment, 1; childish personality with a nonexistent ego, 1."[37] In an act of surprising humility, Powell listed one unmarried mother as "undiagnosed."

More broadly, the recasting of illegitimacy as a psychological rather than a sociological problem—the causes of which were to be sought not in environmental conditions but in individual psyches—must be understood in the context of the World War II and postwar period, when a family-centered culture and rigidly differentiated and prescriptive gender roles took shape and a therapeutic approach to social problems gained immense popularity.[38] At a time when "health" was measured in terms of how well an individual adjusted to his or her appropriate place in the nuclear family, it should come as no surprise that out-of-wedlock pregnancy was stigmatized as an "abnormal" departure from "normal" gender roles. Out-of-wedlock pregnancy thus became an index of abnormality that was defined in opposition to normal femininity. According to Marynia Farnham and Ferdinand Lundberg in their 1947 antifeminist classic *Modern Woman: The Lost Sex*, not only was the unmarried mother "a psychological mess"; she was also "a complete failure as a woman."[39] In large part, the core of the unmarried mother's failure lay in her refusal of married heterosexuality—newly sexualized, privileged, and compulsory in wartime and postwar America. "Certainly, the girl's wish to have a baby without a husband is neither an adult nor a normal desire," Young wrote, invoking two damning postwar epithets—immaturity and abnormality—in a single sentence. She continued: "The urge for a child is a fundamental biological force without which the race would not long survive, but normally that urge is an inextricable part of the love of a man and a woman for each other. . . . The serious problem of the unmarried mother is that her urge for a baby has been separated from its normal matrix, love for a mate."[40]

Social workers who believed that out-of-wedlock pregnancy placed the unmarried mother outside the bounds of mental health grew increasingly enthusiastic about "foster homes" for unmarried mothers. These homes with private families would provide more normal settings than maternity homes and would offer healthy examples of married domesticity. Maud Morlock found the main benefit of foster homes to be "the experience of normal home life." She explained that "the patterns of home life that she observes and the standards and skills that she acquires are those of normal family living and adaptable to the situations in which she is likely later to find herself."[41] Erma Blethan agreed, stating that "the placement of the unmarried mother and her child is, in effect, the placement of an atypical family group with another family group more normal in its social structure." Praising the socializing function of foster homes, she added that "each of the three foster homes now in use comprises a normal family group, with both father and mother and their own children. We are inclined to believe that such homes are most useful for our purpose."[42]

Professional aspirations of social workers and their participation in a culture that stigmatized all departures from conventional gender roles as neurotic go some distance toward explaining the rise of the neurotic unmarried mother. But the fact that not all unmarried mothers were so diagnosed suggests that class and race informed this new conceptualization in powerful ways. In large part, social workers' reframing of illegitimacy as neurotic seems to have been linked to their attempt to explain the changing demographic profile of unmarried mothers seeking aid during the war. Helen Perlman was careful to specify race when she wrote that "prevailing social work theory about the illegitimately pregnant white girl or woman is heavily dependent on psychoanalytic theory." Exploring the reasons behind the new concern for "the psychological well-being of the unmarried mothers" in the 1940s, Perlman argued that "there arose some wish to protect the 'good girl' of 'good family' who was considered to have 'made a mistake.'"[43] Diagnosing the unmarried mother as neurotic rather than as a sex delinquent offered that protection. Psychiatric explanations gave social workers a way to comprehend the illicit sexual behavior of young white women of the middle class as something other than willful promiscuity.

Accordingly, psychiatric explanations desexualized out-of-wedlock pregnancy. Branding unmarried mothers as sexual delinquents had defined them as hypersexual; diagnosing white middle-class unmarried mothers as neurotic recast them as sexually passive, even asexual. In fact, "contrary to the layman's notion," Viola Bernard reported, not one of the ten unmarried mothers in her study experienced "full sexual enjoyment," and for most of them "intercourse proved chiefly unpleasant."[44] Young also found that unmarried mothers "show much less concern and initiative in attracting men than the average girl."[45] Helene Deutsch asserted that "conception takes place under specific conditions that have nothing to do with love or sexual excitement." Of seventeen-year-old Louise, Deutsch wrote that when a man propositioned her, "she became a passive object and could not say 'No.'"[46] "The idea that all the girls are boy-crazy, oversexed, or downright bad is idiotic," Hildegarde Dolson argued in 1942. To support this claim,

Dolson noted that the unmarried mothers she observed at the Youth Consultation Service included "a nurse, a debutante, a waitress, a highschool junior, two college graduates, a young schoolteacher, and the nineteen-year-old daughter of a well-to-do businessman."[47] Dolson's assumption, shared by many of her colleagues, was that class exempted these women from the label of sex delinquency.

It is interesting to note that despite this desexualization of out-of-wedlock pregnancy, the behavior of these unmarried mothers as described by social workers and psychologists was objectively no less sexual than that of earlier women. For example, nineteen-year-old Virginia, a client of Helene Deutsch's whose "love life had its locale in restaurants and dance halls," reported having sex with a man she met at a restaurant.[48] Just a decade earlier, Virginia's manner of meeting men would have easily earned her the title of sex delinquent. Her occupation of domestic servant, which had long connoted both sexual impropriety and sexual vulnerability, would only have confirmed the label.[49] Deutsch was more interested in what she understood to be the underlying psychic causes of out-of-wedlock pregnancy than its superficial symptoms, however, and diagnosed the causes of Virginia's pregnancy as psychological, rooted in her loss of her mother at an early age.

One social worker surely spoke for many of her colleagues when she identified the sexual behavior of the unmarried mother as "one of the most difficult problems for the worker."[50] And indeed, it must have been difficult for social workers to transform behavior that had been understood as unambiguously promiscuous into behavior consistent with the sexual passivity that social workers and psychiatrists insisted was characteristic of the white middle-class unmarried mother of the 1940s. They accomplished this feat, in large part, by focusing attention on the pregnancy rather than the precipitating sexual act; the new psychiatric understanding of illegitimacy deemphasized sex and foregrounded maternity. Whereas sex with a casual acquaintance would have once marked a woman as sexually aggressive, it was now understood as a deliberate and neurotic attempt to become pregnant outside of marriage, the man in question being simply a "tool" by which to achieve the pregnancy and the steps a woman took to accomplish that end only incidentally sexual. "All the evidence points to the fact that most of the girls in this group are truly disinterested in the actual fathers of the babies," Young wrote: "For such a girl, the man is apparently a necessary biological accessory which serves only one purpose—to make her pregnant—and then is of no further interest or concern."[51] By transforming illegitimacy from a discourse of illicit sexuality into a discourse of motherhood, psychoanalytic diagnoses deemphasized the sexuality of overtly sexual women, maternalized women who flouted so many postwar family imperatives, and repositioned unmarried mothers within a structure of family relations rather than opposed to it. If their sexuality could not be contained within a nuclear family of their own formation, the understanding of illegitimacy as springing from obsession with one's mother or a desire for one's father contained unmarried mothers' sexuality within their family of origin.[52]

Interestingly, this new focus on unmarried mothers as mothers rather than as sex delinquents did not garner any more respect for their right to make their own decisions regarding the disposition of their children. Social workers had argued that sex delinquents were unfit to be mothers, and neurotic unmarried mothers were considered no more competent to care for their children. "In my experience," Young asserted, "the majority of unmarried mothers are not strong, mature, well adjusted people, and the reality is that only such a person can assume and carry out responsibility for an out-of-wedlock child without serious damage to both herself and the child."[53] In the 1940s, then, social workers took a more active role in encouraging unmarried mothers to put their children up for adoption.[54]

Finally, by subjecting unmarried mothers to individual treatment, the psychiatric approach worked to shrink the problem of the unmarried mother down to manageable proportions. In her new incarnation as neurotic, the unmarried mother appeared considerably tamer than in her older role of sex delinquent. Once an issue of national concern, illegitimacy might now be understood as the psychological problem of the individual. Leontine Young was particularly insistent that unmarried motherhood carried no grave moral consequences, criticizing the earlier tendency to view illegitimacy as posing substantial danger to the security of the family and society as "fallacious." Once devoted to assessing the damage wrought by the unmarried mother to the moral fiber of the nation and the sanctity of the family, social workers, Young wrote, now endeavored "to define the special problems which trouble them as individuals."[55]

BLACK ILLEGITIMACY AND "CULTURAL PATHOLOGY"

While illegitimacy among white middle-class women appeared less menacing when cast as a problem of individual pathology, illegitimacy among other groups began to take on a more threatening hue. "Bad girls" had not disappeared in the 1940s; on the contrary, they loomed large on the national public landscape. The psychiatric narrative of out-of-wedlock pregnancy that essentially desexualized white middle-class unmarried mothers is all the more striking when viewed in the larger context of the national preoccupation with female promiscuity that accompanied World War II. Observers in the 1940s noted with alarm "the increase in the number of footloose, unprotected girls roaming Main Street, loitering in parks, hanging around juke joints, and often getting themselves into serious trouble."[56] Much of this fear focused on the threat of venereal disease to men in the armed services and precipitated a massive drive against prostitution.[57] Many came to believe, however, that prostitution, traditionally defined as sex for money, was less a problem than "promiscuity," although contemporaries were disconcerted to find the line dividing the two "difficult, if not impossible to draw."[58] Of the girls and women who came to Hartford, Connecticut, to be near soldiers and defense workers, Helen Pigeon wrote, "They do not belong to the rank of professional prostitutes but it is evident from case histories that many are promiscuous."[59] "Sex delinquency" had been a working-class diagnosis since the 1910s, and class assumptions continued to inflect understandings of wartime promiscuity.[60] Mrs. Laura Waggoner of the Community Welfare Council of San Antonio, Texas, identified these girls and women as "almost entirely from farming and working-class homes of low economic level" and characterized them as "casual fun-seeking girls wanting male companionship, immature in judgment, sometimes lonely, unstable, and easily influenced."[61] These women who drew so much attention, condemnation, and fear from public officials and wartime media—those dubbed "Victory Girls," "khaki-wackies," and "patriotic prostitutes" who socialized with soldiers on the streets, in restaurants, and in dance halls—were not given psychiatric examinations; rather, they were rounded up by local law enforcement officials and described in the older terms of sex delinquency.[62] Race, then, did not completely eclipse class in the postwar understanding of out-of-wedlock pregnancy. The discourse of sex delinquency retained its explanatory appeal to social workers who attempted to understand the behavior of girls and women whose out-of-wedlock pregnancy still seemed to spring from familiar causes long assumed to have a working-class etiology: broken homes, bad companions, a disdain for authority, and an addiction to urban pleasures. The psychiatric understanding of out-of-wedlock pregnancy simply ensured that white middle-class unmarried mothers would no longer be cast among their ranks.

Even more than working-class white women, black unmarried mothers attracted increasingly intense concern beginning in the late 1930s and accelerating during and after the war. Social workers who went to great lengths to defuse the "problem" of the white unmarried mother drew attention to that posed by her black counterpart. While the psychiatric discourse of illegitimacy attempted to remove white middle-class unmarried mothers from the roster of problems facing postwar America, a reconceptualization of black illegitimacy catapulted African-American women to the top of that list.

Observers had commented on a disproportionately high black illegitimacy rate since the early twentieth century, but black unmarried mothers had not attracted a great deal of attention or interest before the late 1930s.[63] Indeed, in the early twentieth century, when illegitimacy among working-class white women came under such intense scrutiny, their African-American counterparts seemed hardly worthy of notice. Most of those who did investigate black illegitimacy wrote in the racist tradition that viewed out-of-wedlock pregnancy as the natural and unsurprising result of the constitutional hypersexuality and immorality believed to be characteristic of the race. Beginning in the 1920s and 1930s, however, historians, sociologists, anthropologists, and social workers moved from arguments based on racial degeneracy to new arguments that highlighted the "cultural acceptance" of illegitimacy in some black communities. Rather than providing an index of immorality, illegitimacy, these investigators argued, was better understood as an adaptation to environmental and social conditions. Some, most notably anthropologist Melville Herskovits, argued that African-American attitudes toward illegitimacy were rooted in preslavery African traditions.[64] In contrast, E. Franklin Frazier, in his pathbreaking 1939 study *The Negro Family in the United States*, argued that black family patterns were born of the conditions of enslavement in the United States.

Social workers were quick to incorporate sociological and anthropological arguments into their own investigations of black illegitimacy. Frazier, in particular, exerted enormous influence among social workers, perhaps because of his background in the profession.[65] Patricia Knapp, in a 1945 study of black unmarried mothers, assumed that "for culturally determined reasons, the morality codes of many Negroes do not include a prohibition against illegitimacy."[66] Leontine Young echoed Frazier when she wrote that "the matriarchal system and the difficulty of maintaining a strong, enduring family structure, both conditions bred and fostered in slavery, in general promoted an attitude of acceptance of the unmarried mother and her child."[67]

Before the 1940s, the argument that illegitimacy was culturally accepted in black communities led most social workers to dismiss it as a problem deserving serious concern and offered some a convenient rationalization for devoting so few resources to black unmarried mothers. Although hundreds of maternity homes across the country offered their services to unmarried mothers, the vast majority of those homes either restricted applications to white women or accepted only a very few black residents. In explanation, Ruth Reed wrote in 1926, "there is a belief held by many social workers that illegitimacy among Negroes creates few social problems which are comparable in importance with those produced among white people by unconventional birth."[68] Social workers drew support for this rationale from social scientists, some of whom concluded that the supposed acceptance of illegitimacy among blacks rendered it virtually meaningless as a concept. In his 1934 study of blacks in Macon County, Georgia, Charles Johnson suggested that because out-of-wedlock pregnancy was so much a matter of course, "there is, in a sense, no such thing as illegitimacy in this community."[69]

Beginning in the late 1930s, however, black illegitimacy came under closer scrutiny and began to appear less benign. Frazier was perhaps the first to question the casual acceptance of black out-of-wedlock pregnancy and to complicate its causes. By Frazier's own account, the necessary survival strategies adopted by black families during slavery—including a "matriarchal" family structure, "disorganized" kinship ties, and illegitimacy—took on new meaning in twentieth-century urban life. Before that time, Frazier argued, illegitimacy in rural black communities reflected "the simple and naive behavior of peasant folks"—behavior that was "not licentious and could scarcely be called immoral."[70] The new subjects that captured Frazier's attention, however, were no longer rural blacks, but those who had migrated from the rural South to southern, northern, and western cities. The migration of illegitimacy from rural areas into newly visible urban venues accompanied the geographical migration of blacks that began in the 1910s and accelerated during World War II. Historian Hazel Carby argues that African-American migration "generated a series of moral panics" about urban immorality, in which black women were targeted as "sexually dangerous and therefore socially dangerous."[71] Frazier was among the first to assert that the migration of blacks to cities rendered illegitimacy, once harmless, newly problematic: "during the course of their migration to the city, family ties are broken, and the restraints which once held in check immoral sex conduct lose their force."[72] Declaring black illegitimacy in Chicago to be "the result of family and community disorganization," Frazier argued that out-of-wedlock pregnancy was "the result of casual and impersonal contacts through which random and undisciplined impulses found expression." In its new urban incarnation, illegitimacy no longer ensued from an adaptive black family structure but rather from "an awakened imagination fed by the cheap romance of the movies and the popular magazines" that Frazier argued "led some to licentiousness and debauchery in the sex relation."[73]

The wartime migration of African-Americans to cities seemed to Frazier to reconfigure rural folkways into urban problems, and disproportionate black illegitimacy rates that had once seemed expressive of naive peasant customs now signaled a dangerously dysfunctional black family. To Frazier, illegitimacy was not only a product of unstable family relations but, more dangerously, the catalyst for "matriarchal" families, which, he claimed, "originate through illegitimacy." Illegitimacy, then, was simultaneously cause and effect of the disorganized black family. In a passage that illuminates the anxiety about black women's autonomy that underlay this characterization of the black family, Frazier wrote that "the man's or father's function generally ceases with impregnation. . . . He has no authority in the household or over his children."[74]

The manifestation of this new matriarchal autonomy most disturbing to Frazier was his belief that black women were more inclined to give up their illegitimate children, to him an important indicator of the new and dangerous character of black illegitimacy. This charge was altogether new and reflected a complete reversal in representations. For decades, social commentators had invested black unmarried mothers with instinctive maternal warmth and praised their tendency to keep their children. But by the 1940s, many observers were noting with great anxiety the desire on the part of some black unmarried mothers in urban areas to give up their children. Frazier found that, "on the whole, the unmarried mothers in the city exhibit less of the elemental maternal sympathy toward their children which one finds in rural communities in the South."[75] Frazier went so far as to accuse black single mothers of infanticide: "In the alleys of southern cities as well as in the tenements in northern cities, the unmarried mother sometimes kills her unwanted child by throwing it in the garbage can."[76]

In attempting to understand the forces generating this reconceptualization of black illegitimacy, one should note that many scholars and social workers, Frazier foremost among them, initially invoked the argument of cultural acceptance to repudiate the racist assumptions of biological theories of black family life and morality that underlay earlier prevailing explanations of black illegitimacy.[77] Frazier's analysis, for example, gave Leontine Young the ammunition to criticize those who looked for racial explanations for illegitimacy as "stupid and clearly fallacious."[78] Replacing

the natural immorality argument with one that stressed cultural acceptance allowed investigators to posit black family patterns as social rather
than biological products. As Maurine LaBarre wrote in 1940, "many social
workers attribute the problems of Negro clients to racial characteristics, as
if they were physically inherited, rather than to social and cultural factors.
We shall not find the solution to the Negro problem in physical differences
but in a study of his cultural history and situation."[79]

As eager as many sociologists and social workers were to present black
illegitimacy as culturally constructed rather than biologically ordained,
they were also concerned that distinctive African-American family patterns presented obstacles to racial integration. Thus, they found some
relief in their "discovery" that not all black Americans regarded illegitimacy with the same apparent nonchalance. Studies of urban black communities that proliferated in the 1930s and 1940s sought to show how the
family patterns of the most "advanced" black families resembled those of
the white middle class, a resemblance that was most often measured according to morality and sexuality. In her 1944 study of illegitimacy in
Durham, North Carolina, Hilda Hertz noted that middle- and upper-class
blacks "accept the same values in regard to sex behavior and family life
accepted in white society."[80] Investigators of black urban communities
turned to moral and sexual measures as often as economic indicators to map
the geography of class. Believing out-of-wedlock pregnancy to be the most
accessible index of moral values and sexual behavior, those investigators
used illegitimacy to chart the emergence of a class-stratified black urban
community. Hertz, for example, distinguished the "Negro upper and middle class" from the "lower class" by their respective "sex codes," and
psychologist Margaret Brenman cited the difference in sexual standards
and behavior between middle- and "lower-class" black teenage girls as
"probably the most reliable single criterion in establishing class membership."[81] Some residents of black communities joined investigators in describing illegitimacy in class and spatial terms. Many of the black college
students that Hertz interviewed marked illegitimacy geographically: "The
girls who are most likely to become unmarried mothers are those who stay
in the bad sections of town," one told her. Another reported that "in some
parts of the city it is the usual thing to be pregnant and not be married."[82]

This sexual cartography of class had two purposes. First, it enabled both
investigators of black communities and middle-class residents of those
communities to combat the popular notion of a homogeneous and pathological black family and to distinguish a new black bourgeoisie from its "lower-
class" neighbors. Representing this new middle class required contrasting

its assimilated manners with those of a new black proletariat.[83] Second, and at least as important, this formulation allowed sociologists to posit a hopeful trajectory: if black illegitimacy was most prevalent among recent migrants who had brought their rural ways to the city—if, as St. Clair Drake and Horace Cayton argued, illegitimacy among blacks was a reflection not of immorality but "of the incomplete urbanization of the rural southern migrants"—then perhaps the black family was moving on an evolutionary path toward the standard set by the middle-class white family.[84] The argument that illegitimacy was "culturally accepted" among blacks served the intellectual and political interests of sociologists and social workers of the 1930s and 1940s—some of whom were themselves African-American—and the class interests of a new black bourgeoisie, each of whom used this conceptualization of out-of-wedlock pregnancy to plot a liberal path toward racial integration and assimilation.

Frazier's work had a tremendous impact on social workers; it also captured the interest of a new group of "experts" in social policy. In 1935, the Carnegie Corporation commissioned a massive study of American race relations and invited Swedish economist Gunnar Myrdal to synthesize and popularize scholarly work and statistical data on African-American life. Published in 1944, *An American Dilemma* was a monument to 1940s racial liberalism. As historian David Southern explains, Myrdal understood the "American Dilemma" as "the conflict between verbally honored American ideals" of freedom and equality and "the pervasive practice of white racism."[85] Myrdal devoted an important section of his 1,400-page volume to the black family. Strongly influenced by Frazier, Myrdal credited him with offering "such an excellent description and analysis of the American Negro family that it is practically necessary only to relate its conclusions to our context and to refer the reader to it for details." In arguing that "the uniqueness of the Negro family is a product of slavery," Myrdal joined Frazier in characterizing the black family as pathological and in placing ultimate blame for "deviant" black family patterns on white racism.[86]

Postwar social policymakers and politicians were as impressed as Myrdal with Frazier's research on the African-American family and as inclined to appropriate his arguments. They were less inclined, however, to focus on the aspects of his analysis that indicted racism and more likely to name the black family itself as the dilemma that demanded national attention. As the specter of black illegitimacy that would dominate public policy debates about the black family in the 1950s and 1960s began to take shape under the weight of wartime and postwar pressures, what was once seen as "cultural acceptance" became "cultural pathology."

The principal architect of this new construction, Daniel Patrick Moynihan, positioned illegitimacy at the heart of the "tangle of pathology" of the black family.[87] Whereas Frazier had blamed white racial oppression for "pathology" and "disorganization," Moynihan suggested that the causes were intrinsic to African-American culture. Moynihan's strategy of locating the causes of problems faced by black Americans in the structure of their families served to deflect blame from broader structural problems and institutionalized racism at a time when a militant civil rights movement was directing attention to them. Invoking both Frazier and Myrdal, sometimes virtually verbatim, Moynihan's *The Negro Family: The Case for National Action*, published in 1965, articulated a view of the black family that has proved to have remarkable staying power.[88] Investigations of the "culture of poverty" nurtured by a pathological "underclass" in the 1960s and 1970s further collapsed cultural difference and cultural pathology and moved closer to attributing illegitimacy to innate immorality. In the 1980s and 1990s, the discourse of "family values" even more aggressively racialized the "decent" American family and pathologized black single mothers.

It was in a way ironic that policymakers and politicians would use an argument that sociologists and social workers posed to integrate blacks into the urban social order to further marginalize and pathologize them. As grimly as Frazier depicted black illegitimacy, he went to great lengths to locate its roots in a history of enslavement and oppression. But in many ways, Frazier lent himself to appropriations of his work that would indict the black family and black women in particular. In 1939, Frazier predicted that illegitimacy would result in "disease and in children who are unwanted and uncared for"—a double-edged warning that resonated portentously in wartime and postwar America.[89] The first reference invoked long-held racist associations between African-Americans and venereal disease and was particularly threatening in the 1940s, when fears about the health of men in the armed services ran high.[90] The second half of this warning—the specter of unwanted black children—reinforced a growing fear that black illegitimacy would drain welfare coffers. This fear was fueled in the 1940s, when, for the first time, unmarried mothers and their children became eligible for public assistance under the Aid to Dependent Children (ADC) program. Although many more white single mothers than black obtained public assistance, black women bore the brunt of white anger at increasing public welfare costs and became the targets of efforts to deny public assistance to illegitimate children.[91]

As with the psychiatric discourse of white illegitimacy, new fears surrounding black illegitimacy took shape in the larger context of the powerful familial ideology that crystallized during and after the war. It was no accident that the black family should alarm policymakers at a time when family values were being so rigidly prescribed and the normal family was portrayed as white, middle-class, male-headed, and suburban-dwelling. This hegemonic postwar family both implicitly and explicitly excluded black Americans. Mass-mediated celebrations of the American family rendered blacks all but invisible, and suburban developments restricted housing to whites. A crucial site for fighting cold war battles, the family was charged with nothing less than providing refuge from nuclear weapons, halting communist subversion, ensuring economic progress by operating as a consuming unit, and reviving conventional gender roles from the beating they had taken during the Great Depression and World War II. The stakes invested in the postwar family rendered any deviation from its norms tantamount to treason.

In the first decades of the twentieth century, class had resided at the heart of discourses about illegitimacy. By the 1940s, race had taken center stage. In 1927, social worker Henry Schumacher declared illegitimacy a "socio-psychiatric" problem.[92] During and after the war, the hyphen in that label came to separate rigidly dichotomized constructions of black and white illegitimacy. The wartime and postwar years witnessed the construction of white out-of-wedlock pregnancy as a symptom of individual pathology and the simultaneous reconceptualization of black illegitimacy as a symptom of cultural pathology. While psychiatric explanations for out-of-wedlock pregnancy were almost exclusively applied to white women, black unmarried mothers were burdened with the heavy weight of explanations that were sociological in nature.

Both constructions enlisted new groups of experts in the study of illegitimacy, and the ways in which illegitimacy was cast and recast reveal the extent to which those discourses were shaped by concern for professional legitimacy. But the fracturing of discourses on illegitimacy in the 1940s illuminates a contest over more portentous concerns about sexuality and the family. Illegitimacy had long been a lightning rod that attracted anxieties about gender, race, class, and sexuality. In the wartime and postwar years, out-of-wedlock pregnancy distilled far broader issues of social change and sexual and racial conflict. The psychiatric explanation for white middle-class out-of-wedlock pregnancy promised to forestall the "woman question," which resurfaced in the 1940s when women's sexual and economic autonomy collided with efforts to reinvigorate traditional gender roles. Mounting fears over black illegitimacy expressed larger anxieties about race relations that crystallized and intensified during and after the war. The new militancy and assertiveness on the part of blacks, expressed both in an incipient civil rights movement and in the wartime race riots of the summer of 1943, brought new urgency to the politics of race and posed the "Negro question" in new and unsettling terms that raised doubts as to its resolution. The wartime and postwar discourse on illegitimacy illuminates the way in which anxieties about gender and race were mapped onto sexuality and maternity in the larger culture.

The new constructions of illegitimacy were fraught with meaning for their authors. More difficult to gauge is the meaning of these new discourses to their subjects. On the rare occasions that the voices of unmarried mothers came through in the literature that defined them as "problems," they made clear that they were not passive recipients of others' constructions. One white woman suggested that the "experts'" understanding of illegitimacy as purposeful and neurotic bore little resemblance to her understanding of her own pregnancy: "I've been reading a book on the psychology of the unwed mother," Jean Thompson wrote in 1967. "The book says such a pregnancy is rarely accidental. It says the girl nearly always wants it—as a crutch, an excuse to fail, a way to rebel or demonstrate against her parents. . . . Phew, that sounds like a mouthful, as if the author is really looking for symptoms where there aren't any."[93] One black single mother of five told Chicago investigators that her boyfriend "wants to marry, but I don't want to be bothered. I've been my boss too long now. I go and come and do what I want to do. I can't see where I can have anyone bossing me around now."[94] Although her forthright defense might have reinforced assumptions of black matriarchal power, she made it clear that she understood out-of-wedlock pregnancy as something other than cultural pathology. Perhaps more significantly, she transformed pathology into autonomy, insisting on her own independence in the face of a construction that denied individuality to African-American women.

Yet women struggling to construct their own identities as single mothers had to contend with the terms of the dominant postwar discourses that defined them as either mentally ill or culturally deviant. Although out-of-wedlock pregnancy relegated postwar women and girls to outcast status regardless of race, "neurosis" was, in a relative sense, a privileged category. As Solinger argues, since psychiatric diagnoses made illegitimacy "contingent upon the mutable mind, rather than upon fixed, physical entities," they offered the hope of rehabilitation.[95] In short, the (white) girl could change. At the same time, however, the diagnosis subjected white middle-class girls and women to ever more intrusive scrutiny and aggressive intervention. Although the mostly white, predominantly working-class unmarried mothers who had sought the services of social workers and maternity homes before World War II had been subjected to the intrusions of casework for decades—interrogated by social workers about how many times they had had sex, with whom, and under what circumstances—the new psychiatric diagnoses, which located the cause of out-of-wedlock pregnancy not in the environment but in the mind, legitimized a widening of the scope of intrusion from women's behavior to their psyches. On the other hand, the argument that the pathological black family produced illegitimate children was used to justify public policies directed against African-American single mothers and their children, to subject them to harassment by welfare officials, to deny them public funds and services, and in some cases, to license their sterilization.[96]

Racialized discourses of out-of-wedlock pregnancy had material consequences for single mothers. For historians, they underline a phenomenon we have only begun to explore in any detail: the mutual constitution of ideologies of gender and race. Each a reference point for the other, race-specific etiologies of illegitimacy illuminate the ways in which gender and sexuality were enlisted in constructing racial hierarchies in the wartime and postwar period. Recent studies have revealed the ways in which postwar politics were profoundly gendered, but these representations of unmarried mothers suggest that race, as powerfully and pervasively as gender, determined the form and shape of the ideology of the family that stood at the heart of the postwar political agenda.

THE IRONIES OF PROFESSIONALIZATION

The wartime and postwar constructions of illegitimacy—as evidence of individual pathology on the part of white women and cultural pathology on the part of black—were developed and articulated by a new cast of experts interested in out-of-wedlock pregnancy. By the 1940s, social workers shared a field that had once been virtually their own with anthropologists, sociologists, public officials, policymakers, psychologists, and psychiatrists.

No doubt, social workers took some pride in having developed a field that attracted so much professional interest in the 1940s and in joining a team of helping professionals, scholars, and policymakers in a collective effort to study the problem of illegitimacy. At the same time, however, the composition of this team posed an obvious problem: how would social workers distinguish themselves and their work from other professionals interested in illegitimacy? Although social worker Marion Kenworthy recommended that a "careful investigation and study" of the unmarried mother's personality be undertaken by a "well-organized team of workers, including a psychiatrist, a psychologist, and a psychiatric social worker," the rules of professional hierarchy that explicitly rewarded licensing, training, and scientific knowledge and implicitly privileged male participation meant that social workers would always occupy the subordinate place on that team.[97]

This was not the first time that social workers had faced this dilemma. Psychiatric social workers anticipated a problematic relationship with psychiatrists when they pioneered their specialization in the 1910s and 1920s. One professor at the Smith College School for Social Work remarked that "it was clearly understood from the beginning that we were not to make psychiatrists and that we were not making half-doctors. These women were to be aides to experts. The first lesson that was taught all the members of the school was professional modesty."[98] Esther Cook, a former Smith social work student, recalled that "we were hung up on this idea of whether we were just handmaidens, and we didn't like to be called handmaidens."[99] Bertha Reynolds addressed the complexities of the relationship between psychiatric social worker and psychiatrist in a humorous vignette that highlighted the gendered terms of that relationship. Characterizing psychiatry as "a middle-aged man with a professional beard" and social work as "a young woman whose relationship to him is uncertain," Reynolds pondered: "I am much intrigued to know why they ever took up with each other, whether they are married or intend to be, or whether they are contemplating divorce. I do not think the young woman can support herself, but I have doubts whether Dr. Psychiatry is supporting her now. . . . She waits on him with what looks like devotion, and then when he is not around sometimes airs a poor opinion of him. Are they heading for a closer union or a break? I do not know."[100]

Reynolds recalled that although Smith graduates had had "more hours of lecture in psychiatry than were given in most medical schools," they were instructed to "*never* speak of Freud or air our psychiatric knowledge in front of doctors. . . . In spite of this warning, some of us occasionally fell into this barbed-wire fence—to our sorrow." Social workers confronted this barbed-wire fence again in the 1940s. The psychiatric understanding of illegitimacy led psychiatrists and social workers to form the closer union that Reynolds predicted, yet it was a union as fraught as ever with the gendered hierarchy of professionalism. Reynolds wrote that Mary Jarrett had told Smith social work students that "the future of our new discipline held two possibilities: we could think of ourselves as assistants in psychotherapy . . . or we could develop a profession in our own right, bringing into psychotherapy the *social* outlook and skills which would require our thinking for ourselves (not mainly following orders) and would place us alongside the psychiatrist as another different but allied professional."[101]

But the gendered assumptions of professionalism denied social workers such a choice. However they conceived their relationship with psychiatrists, the social workers' sex denied them equal stature and respect as professionals. Those who embraced a psychiatric approach to the unmarried mother situated themselves in a professional hierarchy in which they would always remain subordinate to psychiatrists. Although social workers had championed a professional ethos that celebrated the impartial authority of science and the expert, psychiatrists levied an unquestioned hold on those qualities, having firmly grounded their profession in scientific knowledge during the Progressive Era.[102]

The new understanding of the unmarried mother as neurotic granted psychiatrists the privileged position of expert. In contributing to that construction and in joining the team of professionals studying the unmarried mother, social workers yielded their position as experts in the field of illegitimacy to psychologists and psychiatrists. Ruth F. Brenner addressed social workers' subordinate status in the field when she wrote defensively in 1942, "We are not psychiatrists, but within the scope of our competence, we are concerned with our client's adaptation to the world as it exists. We cannot treat her deep-seated conflicts, but we must gain as much understanding and insight into them, with the help of psychiatric interpretation, as will enable us to deal more effectively with her conscious strivings and concerns."[103] The psychiatric reconstruction of illegitimacy that cast out-of-wedlock pregnancy as a symptom of a more serious and complex neurosis moved the social worker from the position of expert in work with unmarried mothers to that of technician. From the center of expertise in the field of illegitimacy, social workers moved further to the margins. They might help the unmarried mother reach a decision regarding the disposition of her child, but real treatment of her deeper problems demanded the attention of a trained psychiatrist. Psychiatrists, not social workers, came to occupy the highest rung of expertise and authority in the field of illegitimacy.

In 1951, Melitta Schmideberg claimed that "social work is something in its own right, and not just a poor substitute for, or an adjunct to, psychiatry. . . . Common sense, readiness to help, warmth, and efficiency are qualities not to be ashamed of. Social workers should not aim at becoming third-rate therapists."[104] But social workers had devoted their entire professional life to dissociating themselves from the "warmth" of Lady Bountifuls and had long struggled to prove that the practice of casework required training rather than "common sense." They knew that warmth, nurturance, and helping, although not qualities to be ashamed of, did not win them professional respect. Because social workers had so thoroughly distanced themselves from the rhetoric of womanly benevolence, they had no language with which to protest their loss of authority in the field of illegitimacy. It is difficult not to read their return to these virtues—the virtues of womanly benevolence that they had derided for so long—as deeply ironic.

This irony found its strongest expression in psychiatrists' and social workers' efforts to define the relationship of social worker to unmarried mother. For decades, social workers had struggled to remove their relationship with clients from the realm of the familial to the professional. The new psychiatric understanding of illegitimacy, however, dictated the proper role of social worker to be that of good mother. "Literally all the caseworker has to do is to be a good mother to the girl," wrote Young.[105] And Frances Scherz stated that "since we believe that such pregnancies are a response to an emotionally starved or distorted parental relationship, then the caseworker can become, in many situations, a parent substitute. In particular, she can become a substitute mother, an 'amended' loving mother."[106] After decades of criticizing evangelical women for their sentimental and inappropriately close relationship to unmarried mothers, social workers' assumption of the role of the "good mother" to unmarried mothers was particularly ironic. Social workers had tried to degender their profession, only to return full circle to a profoundly gendered understanding of their role in the 1940s.

Similarly, social workers yielded to academicians and policymakers in their expertise on black illegitimacy. Scholars like E. Franklin Frazier had first drawn attention to out-of-wedlock pregnancy among blacks as a social problem deserving national attention. The new association of black illegitimacy with welfare dependency, the development of a "black underclass," and the "collapse" of the black family transformed out-of-wedlock pregnancy from a casework problem to a broader concern of social policy. The Moynihan report on the black family in 1965 suggested in its subtitle— *The Case for National Action*—that the problems of the black family transcended the individual problems treated by social workers. Rather, they were matters of social policy to be attended to by policymakers.

From the 1910s to the 1940s, social workers had endeavored to remove illegitimacy from the purview of religious authority, transforming out-of-wedlock pregnancy from a moral problem to a casework problem. Understanding the unmarried mother as a subject of casework confirmed social workers' expertise. The new constructions of white and black illegitimacy—making the white unmarried mother a subject of psychiatric analysis and the black unmarried mother a subject of national social policy—ultimately worked to undermine social workers' claim to expertise. By the 1950s, social workers found themselves on the lowest rung of a professional ladder that they had helped construct, jockeying for position with professionals whose status was much more secure than their own. Authority in the field of illegitimacy passed from social workers, most of whom were women, to psychiatrists and policymakers, most of whom were men.

The advance of the professionalization of the field of illegitimacy in the 1940s should have heralded victory for social workers, and in many ways it did. In 1947, the NFCM finally surrendered its policy of keeping mother and child together, signaling the end of an era and the victory of the professional ethos of social workers over the founding ideals of evangelical women reformers. Social workers used the ideology of professionalism to carve out creative careers for themselves. More broadly, professionalism offered social workers a way to free themselves from the constraints of an ultimately conservative ideology of female benevolence that pronounced women "natural reformers."

As much as the professionalization of benevolence chronicles the story of social workers' accomplishment in claiming dominion over the field of illegitimacy, however, it also reveals the ways in which that ambition was thwarted. Despite social workers' professionalizing efforts, evangelical women protected and maintained strongholds of female benevolence in some maternity homes well into the twentieth century. Rather than bowing to the dictates of professionalism, evangelical women struggled against professional imperatives that labeled their work "old-fashioned" and, in many cases, refused to recognize the expertise of social workers. While historians have argued that the twentieth century witnessed the victory of secular, objective, and rational values over emotional, subjective, and religious ones, the tenacity of evangelical women reveals the unevenness and contentiousness of that social and cultural transition.

In one sense, the residents of maternity homes seemed to stand at a distant remove from the battles between evangelical women and social workers. Certainly unmarried mothers gave little thought to the gendered hierarchy inherent in professionalism and the dilemma it posed to women reformers. The circumstances of their lives dictated different concerns. Most immediately, they struggled to pursue their own ends in maternity homes and tried not to allow the purposes of those in charge to overwhelm or interfere too strongly with their own. Although to endow unmarried mothers with shared perceptions, identical experiences, or a uniformity of purpose would do a disservice to their diversity, case records suggest that they shared a determination to use maternity homes for purposes of their own and to make their own sense of out-of-wedlock pregnancy that was often at odds with and occasionally directly opposed to expert constructions. That determination brought them to the center of the process of professionalization. Rather than being peripheral to the story of the changing shape and meaning of benevolence in the first half of the twentieth century, unmarried mothers participated actively in defining the terms on which that transition would be negotiated.

Social workers might have anticipated the resistance of evangelical women and unmarried mothers to their professional goals, but the tendency of professionalism itself to undermine their status ultimately posed a more confounding dilemma. Eager to use professional rhetoric to distance themselves from womanly benevolence, women in social work could not escape its ambivalent meaning for themselves. Although women were attracted to professionalism's promise of neutrality and objectivity, events in the larger profession of social work suggest that professionalism promised a gender-neutrality it did not deliver. By the 1950s, the rules of professional hierarchy, which social workers had used to gain status over evangelical women, now dictated social workers' subordination to the new experts.

We must not conclude, however, that professional women were victims of "false consciousness," unknowing supporters of an ideology that would ultimately serve them poorly. Social workers did not passively imbibe the culture of professionalism; rather, they used it, as did their male colleagues, to legitimate their own authority in one of the few professions hospitable to women. As embarrassed as their male colleagues by the association of social work with sentimental womanly benevolence, women in social work strived to distance themselves from that rhetoric. Embracing the language of professionalism, they used it to criticize and transcend the language of female essentialism and female difference that seemed to them old-fashioned and self-defeating. But in the process of rejecting what seemed to them a conservative strategy—the linking of reform with womanly character—women in social work accepted definitions of professionalism that were, insidiously, as gendered as the terms they rejected.

Abbreviations

The Jersey City Door of Hope case files are referred to by code number. To preserve confidentiality, this number does not correspond to the number assigned to it in the Door of Hope case files. The key to this code is held by the Salvation Army Archives and Research Center in Alexandria, Virginia.

The following abbreviations are used to refer to other archival sources:

ASHA   American Social Health Association Collection, held at the Social Welfare History Archives, University of Minnesota, Minneapolis, Minnesota

CB   U.S. Children's Bureau Collection, Record Group 102, National Archives, Washington, D.C.

CWLA   Child Welfare League of America Collection, held at the Social Welfare History Archives, University of Minnesota, Minneapolis, Minnesota

DH   Dorothy Hutchinson papers, held in the Manuscript Division, Columbia University Library, New York, New York

FCA   Florence Crittenton Anchorage papers, held at the University of Illinois, Chicago Circle Library, Chicago, Illinois

FCL   Florence Crittenton League of Compassion papers, in-house collection located at Crittenton-Hastings Home, Boston, Massachusetts

FCS   Florence Crittenton Services, Norfolk, Virginia, papers, held at the Old Dominion University Library, Norfolk, Virginia

KF   Katy Ferguson home papers, held at the Rutgers University Library, New Brunswick, New Jersey

KWB   Kate Waller Barrett papers, held at the Library of Congress, Manuscript Division, Washington, D.C.

NFCM   National Florence Crittenton Mission Collection, held at the Social Welfare History Archives, University of Minnesota, Minneapolis, Minnesota

SAARC   Salvation Army Archives and Research Center, Alexandria, Virginia

UCC   United Charities of Chicago Collection, held at the Chicago Historical Society, Chicago, Illinois

WC   Welfare Council Collection, held at the Chicago Historical Society, Chicago, Illinois

Notes

INTRODUCTION

Epigraph: Albert Leffingwell, *Illegitimacy: A Study in Morals* (London: Swan
   Sonnenschein, 1892), pp. 1–2, quoted by J. Prentice Murphy, "Mothers, and—
   Mothers," *Survey* 42 (May 3, 1919): 171. In his preface, Leffingwell identifies
   this book as "the first treatise in the English language, upon the subject of
   Illegitimacy" (p. v).

1. I use the term *evangelical* to describe the group of women who founded maternity homes in the late nineteenth century and continued to staff them into the
   1940s. These women shared a common belief in conversion, followed by a
   changed life, and felt their commitment to work with unmarried mothers to be
   religiously inspired and motivated. They expressed a kinship with the larger
   community of predominantly white Protestant middle-class women engaged in
   temperance and social purity reform and missionary activity, with whom they
   shared a common sensibility. I will discuss this in detail in chapter 1.

2. Kenworthy, "Mental Hygiene Aspects of Illegitimacy," p. 501.

3. In her study of the ideology and work of nineteenth-century benevolence,
   historian Lori Ginzberg has located the beginning of this transformation in the
   post–Civil War period (Ginzberg, *Women and the Work of Benevolence*). The
   literature on nineteenth-century and early-twentieth-century women's reform
   efforts is too lengthy to cite in full here. Those works that have most enriched
   my understanding of female reform ideology and organization include Epstein,
   Politics of Domesticity; Ruth Bordin, *Women and Temperance: The Quest for
   Power and Liberty, 1873–1900* (Philadelphia: Temple University Press, 1981);
   Mary P. Ryan, *Cradle of the Middle Class: The Family in Oneida County, New
   York, 1790–1865* (New York: Cambridge University Press, 1981); Hewitt, *Wom-
   en's Activism and Social Change;* Freedman, *Their Sisters' Keepers;* Rosen,
   Lost Sisterhood; and Pascoe, *Relations of Rescue.*

4. Wilson, *Fifty Years Work With Girls*, p. 71.
5. See, e.g., Leiby, *History of Social Welfare*.
6. The story of the professionalization of benevolence and the rise of social work has been told in a way that curiously ignores gender. Although Roy Lubove chronicles the move toward professional identity among social workers, he fails to address the meaning of gender to the professionalization of social work (Lubove, *Professional Altruist*). Some historians have identified the need to bring professionalization and gender together in looking at social welfare after 1920. Achenbaum has called for scholars to "begin to explore systematically the issue of gender in the 'culture of professionalism,'" and to "take up the question of how the entry of predominantly middle-class women has affected the professionalization process itself," in "Agenda for Future Research in American Social Welfare History," p. 288. Cott explores these questions in her examination of the relationship between professional identity and feminism in the 1920s, in *Grounding of Modern Feminism*. Daniel J. Walkowitz has taken important steps toward bringing a gender analysis to social work in "Making of a Feminine Professional Identity." See also Glazer and Slater, *Unequal Colleagues*, chap. 5.
7. For sociological interpretations of the professions, see William J. Goode, "Community Within a Community: The Professions," *American Sociological Review* 22 (Feb. 1957): 195–200; Ernest Greenwood, "Attributes of a Profession," *Social Work* 2 (July 1957): 45–55; Howard M. Vollmer and Donald L. Mills, eds., *Professionalization* (Englewood Cliffs, N.J.: Prentice Hall, 1966); Wilbert E. Moore, *The Professions: Roles and Rules* (New York: Russell Sage, 1970); Phillip Elliott, *The Sociology of the Professions* (New York: Macmillan, 1972). For critiques of those interpretations, see Klegon, "Sociology of Professions"; Larson, *Rise of Professionalism;* and Julius A. Roth, "Professionalism." Historians of professionalization include Burton J. Bledstein, *Culture of Professionalism;* and Jerold Auerbach, *Unequal Justice: Lawyers and Social Change in Modern America* (New York: Oxford University Press, 1976).
8. See Morantz-Sanchez, *Sympathy and Science;* Mary Roth Walsh, *"Doctors Wanted: No Women Need Apply": Sexual Barriers in the Medical Profession* (New Haven: Yale University Press, 1971); Rossiter, *Women Scientists in America;* Epstein, *Women in Law;* and Moldow, *Women Doctors in Gilded-Age Washington.* Other studies of women in the professions include Rosalind Rosenberg, *Beyond Separate Spheres: Intellectual Roots of Modern Feminism* (New Haven: Yale University Press, 1982); Brumberg and Tomes, "Women in the Professions"; Hummer, *Decade of Elusive Promise;* Harris, *Beyond Her Sphere;* Barbara Solomon, *In the Company of Educated Women* (New Haven: Yale University Press, 1985); and Glazer and Slater, *Unequal Colleagues.*
9. Rossiter, *Women Scientists in America.*
10. Both Dee Garrison, in her study of librarians, and Barbara Melosh, in her study of nurses, conclude that women and professionalization were at odds. Garrison claims that "a women-dominated profession was obviously a contradiction in

terms" (Garrison, *Apostles of Culture*, p. 185). Melosh concludes similarly that "because women are the 'second sex' . . . there can be no women's profession." Nursing, then, "by definition cannot be a profession because most nurses are women" (Melosh, *"The Physician's Hand,"* p. 20). See also Reverby, *Ordered to Care;* Glazer and Slater, *Unequal Colleagues.*

11. Implicit here is my argument that tension surrounding questions of gender does not occur only in contexts in which there is a struggle between men and women.

12. My thinking here builds on the arguments of Lori Ginzberg, *Women and the Work of Benevolence*, and Peggy Pascoe, *Relations of Rescue.* Historian Joan W. Scott has encouraged historians to think about gender as a category of analysis to explore areas and realms of history that have been understood to lie outside of gender's reach. In imagining uses of this concept of gender, Scott asks, "has gender legitimized the emergence of professional careers?"—a question I engage in this book (Scott, *Gender and the Politics of History*, p. 50).

13. Mary Poovey observes that female sexuality has historically "occupied a critical place in men's contests for power and therefore in women's social oppression" (Poovey, "Speaking of the Body: Mid-Victorian Constructions of Female Desire," in *Body/Politics: Women and the Discourses of Science*, ed. Mary Jacobus, Evelyn Fox Keller, and Sally Shuttleworth [New York: Routledge, 1990], p. 30.)

14. In her thoughtful and thorough study of illegitimacy after 1945, Rickie Solinger has documented the central importance of race in constructing the cultural meanings of out-of-wedlock pregnancy after World War II, in shaping public policies toward unmarried mothers, and in determining the ways women experienced single motherhood (Solinger, *Wake Up Little Susie*). Other historians who have considered out-of-wedlock pregnancy and efforts to deal with unmarried mothers include Pascoe, *Relations of Rescue;* Joan Brumberg, "'Ruined Girls'"; Morton, "Seduced and Abandoned in an American City"; Sedlak, "Young Women and the City."

15. I am indebted to Linda Gordon's examination of the ways in which clients became active historical agents in their dealings with social welfare agents, in *Heroes of Their Own Lives.*

16. Evangeline Booth, "Rescue Work: Our Part in the Struggle for Purity," *War Cry* (June 11, 1910): 9.

17. Record keeping in maternity homes was highly uneven, however; some homes began keeping detailed records as early as the 1890s, but others recorded little more than names and dates of admission in a logbook into the 1920s. Both the Salvation Army and Crittenton homes eventually used a standard case file form, consisting of four pages to be filled out by the matron or social worker. The records noted basic biographical information, including the woman's age, residence, educational background, occupation, and religion. The form also included spaces for the social worker to record notes on the unmarried mother's sexual experience, how she met the father of the child, and information on that man.

Case forms typically left room at the end for the worker's comments. They also occasionally included correspondence, interagency memoranda, and medical records on the mother and child.

18. "The Girl Nobody Loved," *Social News* 2 (Nov. 1911): 3.

19. Ernest W. Burgess, "What Social Case Records Should Contain to be Useful for Sociological Interpretation," *Social Forces* 6 (June 1928): 527. As Linda Gordon observes, "the case records represent the caseworkers' opinions, even when they were trying to represent the clients' point of view" (Gordon, *Heroes of Their Own Lives*, p. 13). Other historians who have considered case records as historical sources include Pascoe, *Relations of Rescue;* Clarke A. Chambers, "Toward a Redefinition of Welfare History," p. 423; Brenzel, *Daughters of the State*. See also Klaassen, "Provenance of Social Work Case Records"; Parr, "Case Records as Sources for Social History."

20. Calling on case records from several sources, I drew most systematically and intensively on those from the Door of Hope in Jersey City, New Jersey, founded by Emma Whittemore in 1885 as one home in her Door of Hope chain and ceded to the Salvation Army in 1905. In addition to the 1,600 case records of the Jersey City Door of Hope from the years between 1915 and 1945, I consulted case records from several other Salvation Army and Florence Crittenton homes and social agencies. In agreement with the Salvation Army Archives and Research Center, I have changed the names of unmarried mothers that appear in the text to protect their confidentiality and have assigned code numbers to case files from the Door of Hope. The key to this code is held by the Salvation Army Archives and Research Center, Alexandria, Virginia.

21. Poovey, "Speaking of the Body," p. 29.

22. The relationship between lived experience and the discursive construction of that experience has emerged as a vexed question in recent historical scholarship (Linda Gordon, review of Scott, *Gender and the Politics of History*, and Scott's response; Scott, review of Gordon, *Heroes of Their Own Lives*, and Gordon's response, in *Signs* 15 (Summer 1990): 848–60; Scott, "Evidence of Experience"; Bryan Palmer, *Descent into Discourse: The Reification of Language and the Writing of Social History* [Philadelphia: Temple University Press 1990]). I propose here that it is possible—even necessary—to examine the unmarried mother as a figure in discourse, as well as a contributor to the discourses of unmarried motherhood, without disregarding her material presence and the material practices in maternity homes.

23. Laughlin, "Condemned Mothers and Babies," p. 230.

CHAPTER 1 THE MATERNITY HOME MOVEMENT

1. Kate Waller Barrett, *Maternity Work: Motherhood a Means of Regeneration* (Washington, D.C.: NFCM, c. 1897), p. 59.

2. Peggy Pascoe describes a wave of women's benevolent efforts that "seemed to

spring up everywhere" in the 1870s in *Relations of Rescue*, p. 5. The women who founded maternity homes are part of the tradition that Estelle B. Freedman terms "female institution building" (Freedman, "Separatism as Strategy"). See also Ryan, *Cradle of the Middle Class;* Ginzberg, *Women and the Work of Benevolence;* Hewitt, *Women's Activism and Social Change;* Carroll Smith-Rosenberg, "Beauty, the Beast, and the Militant Woman." On women's foreign missionary work, see Hill, *The World Their Household.*

3. Bliss, *A Glimpse of Shadowed Lives*, pp. 17–22.

4. "Personals," *Florence Crittenton Magazine* 2 (Feb. 1901): 280.

5. Whittemore, *Mother Whittemore's Records* p. 41. See also Dora Harris to Reba Barrett Smith, May 19, 1926, Box 7, Folder 66, NFCM; Bliss, *Shadowed Lives*, p. 17; Hazel A. Earle, "My Job: What it Demands of Me," *War Cry* (Dec. 31, 1938): 4.

6. Agnes Wright Dickinson, oral history conducted by Christina Simmons, July 28, 1982, pp. 8–9.

7. My understanding of the ideology of womanly benevolence is indebted to the recent works by Lori Ginzberg and Peggy Pascoe, who each explore the relationship of female benevolent activity, gender ideology, and class formation (Ginzberg, *Women and the Work of Benevolence;* Pascoe, *Relations of Rescue*).

8. New Haven Florence Crittenton Home, pamphlet, 1913, n.p., Sterling Memorial Library, Yale University; Evangeline Booth Maternity Home and Hospital, Boston, Massachusetts, pamphlet, 1928, n.p., pamphlet collection, SAARC.

9. K. Barrett, "The Need of Supervision for Both Public and Private Charities," National Conference for Charities and Corrections, *Proceedings* (1908): 5.

10. Sister Charlotte, "Work on the Streets and in the Halls of Ill Fame," in K. Barrett, *Fourteen Years' Work*, p. 32.

11. K. Barrett, *Some Practical Suggestions*, p. 75.

12. Smith, "Unmarried Mothers," p. 22.

13. Florence Crittenton Anchorage Board Minutes, December 5, 1912, Box 2, Folder 1, FCA. The phrase "women's work for women" was coined by women in the home and foreign mission movements. See Pascoe, *Relations of Rescue;* Hill, *The World Their Household.*

14. Mary C. Tinney, "Illegitimacy," National Conference of Catholic Charities, *Proceedings* (1920): 99–100.

15. Kate Waller Barrett to Nettie Stray Bliss, in *Our Girls*, n.d., Box 3, Folder 3, FCA.

16. Hazel V. Carby, *Reconstructing Womanhood: The Emergence of the Afro-American Woman Novelist* (New York: Oxford University Press, 1987), chap. 2.

17. Gordon, "Black and White Visions of Welfare," p. 587.

18. Du Bois, ed., *Efforts for Social Betterment*, pp. 102–03.

19. *Florence Crittenton Magazine* 3 (March 1901): 17.

20. Gordon, "Black and White Visions of Welfare," p. 587.

21. See Neverdon-Morton, *Afro-American Women of the South*, chaps. 5–9; Du Bois, ed., *Efforts for Social Betterment;* Dorothy C. Salem, *To Better Our World: Black Women in Organized Reform, 1890–1920* (Brooklyn: Carlson Pub., 1990); Ann Firor Scott, "Most Invisible of All: Black Women's Voluntary Associations," *Journal of Southern History* 56 (Feb. 1990): 3–22; Ralph E. Luker, "Missions, Institutional Churches, and Settlement Houses: The Black Experience, 1885–1910," *Journal of Negro History* 69 (Summer-Fall 1984): 101–13.

22. Florence Crittenton League of Compassion, brochure, 1948, FCL. See also Charles Crittenton, *Brother of Girls.*

23. Crittenton, *Brother of Girls*, p. 201. On ties between the NFCM and WCTU, see Martha M. Dore, "Organizational Response to Environmental Change: A Case History Study of the National Florence Crittenton Mission" (Ph.D. diss., University of Chicago, 1986), pp. 39–41; Katherine G. Aiken, "The National Florence Crittenton Mission, 1883–1925: A Case Study in Progressive Reform" (Ph.D. diss., Washington State University, 1980), p. 19.

24. For discussion of the early history of the Crittenton homes, see Crittenton, *Brother of Girls;* Nancy McConnell and Dore, *1883–1983: Crittenton Services;* Aiken, "National Florence Crittenton Mission"; Dore, "Organizational Response to Environmental Change."

25. The exact date of the Salvation Army's arrival in the United States is unclear. See Norman H. Murdoch, "The Salvation Army's U.S. Arrival," *Organization of American History Newsletter* 15 (May 1987): 12–13. Salvation Army historian Norris Magnusson notes that Railton's group was "unofficially preceded" by other Salvationists (Magnusson, *Salvation in the Slums*, p. 4).

26. Edward H. McKinley, *Somebody's Brother*, p. 2.

27. Eva Booth, "Why a Social News," *Social News* 2 (Feb. 1911): 3.

28. U.S. Department of Labor, Children's Bureau, *Maternity Homes for Unmarried Mothers: A Community Service*, Pub. No. 309, by Maud Morlock and Hilary Campbell (Washington, D.C.: Government Printing Office, 1946), p. 10. On Salvation Army rescue homes in England, see Robert Sandall, *The History of the Salvation Army*, 3:201–08.

29. "Salvation Army Services to Unmarried Parents and Their Children: Maternity Homes and Hospitals," in *Handbook of Information* (New York: Salvation Army, n.d.), p. 17. On the history of early rescue homes, see Ruggles, "Fallen Women"; Teeters, "Early Days of the Magdalen Society"; Hobson, *Uneasy Virtue*, pp. 118–21.

30. "The New York City Night Court," *Girls* 15 (Jan. 1912): 7.

31. On judicial reform in the Progressive Era, see Rothman, *Conscience and Convenience;* Schlossman, *Love and the American Delinquent.*

32. NFCM, *Annual Report* (1914): 136.

33. Ibid., p. 50. See also Robert S. Barrett to John A. Brown, Jan. 6, 1949, Box 31, Folder 3, NFCM; Florence Crittenton League of New York, *Annual Report*

(1915): 3; Worthington and Topping, *Specialized Courts*, p. 371; Magnusson, *Salvation in the Slums*, p. 83; Aiken, "National Florence Crittenton Mission," p. 104.

34. Whittemore, *Mother Whittemore's Records*, p. 155.

35. Boston Florence Crittenton League of Compassion, *Annual Report* (1916).

36. Judith Walkowitz discusses female charity workers who ventured into London's East End in the late nineteenth century, challenging what Walkowitz terms "the tradition of urban male spectatorship" and searching for "adventure, self-discovery, and meaningful work" (Walkowitz, *City of Dreadful Delight*, pp. 10, 53).

37. On Kate Waller Barrett, see Carol L. Urness, "Kate Waller Barrett," in *Notable American Women*, ed. Edward T. James (Cambridge, Mass.: Belknap Press, 1971), 1:97–99; Lundberg, *Unto the Least of These*, pp. 212–15.

38. Both Salvation Army and Crittenton homes functioned primarily as maternity homes for unmarried mothers by 1920. In that year, the Salvation Army replaced the title "Rescue Homes" with "Homes and Hospitals," reflecting this shift in emphasis and clientele.

39. "Fifty Years Work with Girls," *Florence Crittenton Bulletin* 9 (Jan. 1934): 10.

40. Superintendent's Report, 1926, Florence Crittenton Home, Norfolk, Virginia, Box 18, Fol. 6, FCS.

41. Evangelical women in many cities attested to the "many cases of soldiers and sailors" responsible for the condition of their clients. See "Report from the Los Angeles Florence Crittenton Home," NFCM, *Annual Report* (1918): 28. On concern about illegitimacy during World War I, see William Healy's introduction to Kammerer, *The Unmarried Mother*, p. ix; Tiffin, *In Whose Best Interest?* p. 172; Lundberg, "The Illegitimate Child and War Conditions."

42. "War Work in Florence Crittenton Homes," *Girls* 20 (July 1917): 1.

43. On the crusade against prostitution during World War I, see Connelly, *The Response to Prostitution in the Progressive Era*, chap. 7; Ruth Rosen, *The Lost Sisterhood: Prostitution in America, 1900–1918* (Baltimore: Johns Hopkins University Press, 1982), pp. 33–36; Hobson, *Uneasy Virtue*, chap. 7; David Pivar, "Cleansing the Nation: The War on Prostitution, 1917 to 1921," *Prologue* 12 (Spring 1980): 29–40. For an extended account of the government program against prostitution and venereal disease during World War I, see Brandt, *No Magic Bullet*, chaps. 2, 3.

44. Clarence R. Preston, "Good Care of Unmarried Mothers as an Important Phase of Preventative and Protective Work," *Journal of Social Hygiene* 17 (Feb. 1931): 96.

45. Chicago Florence Crittenton Anchorage, *Annual Report* (1920): 3.

46. Laughlin, "Condemned Mothers and Babies," p. 237. See also Dietrick, "Rescuing Fallen Women," p. 162. Historian Judith Walkowitz, in her study of prostitution in Victorian England, finds that "the stereotyped sequence of girls seduced, pregnant, and abandoned to the streets fitted only a small minority of women

who ultimately moved into prostitution" (Walkowitz, *Prostitution and Victorian Society*, p. 18).

47. K. Barrett, *Maternity Work*, p. 53.

48. "Report of Seattle Florence Crittenton Home," *Florence Crittenton Magazine* 1 (May 1899): 76.

49. Quoted in Sandall, *History of the Salvation Army*, 3:201. W. Bramwell Booth believed that white slaves were recruited from the ranks of unmarried mothers (Booth, *Orders and Regulations for Officers*, p. 285).

50. R. Barrett, "President's Address," NFCM, *Annual Report* (1928): 44.

51. See Judith Walkowitz, "Male Vice and Female Virtue"; Hobson, *Uneasy Virtue*, pp. 55–61, 70–72; Rosen, *The Lost Sisterhood*, esp. chap. 4.

52. On melodramatic structure, see Earl Bargainnier, "Melodrama as Formula," *Journal of Popular Culture* 9 (Winter 1975): 726–33; Grimsted, *Melodrama Unveiled*, chap. 8.

53. "Brief Sketches Taken from the Record of Thirty-One Years in Redemption Home," *There Is Hope* 21 (1934), p. 1, Box 8, Folder 94, NFCM. Peggy Pascoe discusses the images that rescue workers held of unmarried mothers in the Denver, Colorado, Cottage Home in *Relations of Rescue*, pp. 59–61.

54. "Help in Extremity," *Social News* 2 (Dec. 1912): 14.

55. Clara V. Eastman, "Crittenton Home Ministers to Life's Unfortunates When Other Doors Close," *Los Angeles Examiner*, March 15, 1916. These phrases originated in Shakespearean drama. The line "One that loved not wisely, but too well," comes from *Othello* V, ii, line 344, and refers to Othello himself. "I am a man/more sinned against than sinning" is from *King Lear*, III, ii, line 59, and is spoken by Lear. These lines might have wended their way from tragic male Elizabethan heroes to American unmarried mothers via Shakespeare's popularity in the United States and the fluidity between "high" and "low" culture in the nineteenth century that Lawrence Levine describes in *Highbrow/Lowbrow: The Emergence of Cultural Hierarchy in America* (Cambridge, Mass.: Harvard University Press, 1988). I am grateful to Paula Smith for drawing my attention to these citations.

56. Florence Crittenton Anchorage, pamphlet, n.d., n.p., UCC, CHS.

57. Annie W. Allen, "How to Save Girls Who Have Fallen," *Survey* 24 (Aug. 6, 1910): 692.

58. Major Julia Thomas, "What the Salvation Army IS Doing for the Unmarried Mother and Her Child," paper presented at the National Conference of Florence Crittenton Missions, July 25, 1933, p. 3, Box 11, Folder 112, NFCM.

59. "Report of the General Superintendent," NFCM, *Annual Report* (1927): 33–34. See also Charles Crittenton's address to the First Conference of the NFCM, in K. Barrett, *Fourteen Years' Work*, p. 174.

60. On white slave narratives, see Connelly, *Response to Prostitution in the Progressive Era*, chap. 6; Frederick Karl Grittner, "White Slavery: Myth, Ideology, and American Law" (Ph.D. diss., University of Minnesota, 1986).

61. *Mended Links* (1903), pp. 8, 3.

62. Report from the San Francisco Florence Crittenton Home, NFCM, *Annual Report* (1918–19): 23.

63. *Mended Links* (1903), p. 14. In the case records of the Wauwatosa, Wisconsin, Salvation Army maternity home, the putative father is referred to as "her betrayer" in the case record form until 1915. (Case Files, Booth Memorial Hospital, Wauwatosa, Wisconsin, RG 14.6, SAARC).

64. Rev. J. T. Sunderland, "Keep Yourself Pure," *Florence Crittenton Magazine* 2 (Dec. 1900): 227.

65. See, e.g., Martha Vicinus, "'Helpless and Unbefriended'," p. 128; Anna Clark, "The Politics of Seduction in English Popular Culture," p. 48; Denning, *Mechanic Accents*, pp. 94, 190.

66. T. Shelly Sutton, "A Girl Who Fell," *Florence Crittenton Magazine* 2 (April 1900): 35.

67. "A Typical Home for the Rescue of the Fallen," *Social News* 5 (Aug. 1915): 9.

68. Major M. Louise Coggeshall, "Truelove Home and Maternity Hospital," *Social News* 4 (Sept. 1914): 9.

69. See Walkowitz, *City of Dreadful Delight*, chap. 5. This had not always been the case. Anna Clark argues that nineteenth-century melodrama served as a politicized language, but one that "displaced potential anger of sexual exploitation to the level of class conflict, preventing women from publicly articulating antagonism towards men of their own class" (Clark, "Politics of Seduction," p. 49). Evangelicals drew on an older critique of the sexual double standard, articulated by female reformers working in the social purity and antiprostitution movements. See Pivar, *Purity Crusade;* Rosen, *Lost Sisterhood;* Hobson, *Uneasy Virtue;* Smith-Rosenberg, "Beauty, the Beast, and the Militant Woman."

70. "Our Appeal," *Florence Crittenton Magazine* 1 (Nov. 1899): 198.

71. Alice Lee Moque, "On the Other Side," *Florence Crittenton Magazine* 1 (April 1899): 33. See also K. Barrett, "History of the Florence Crittenton Movement," *Florence Crittenton Magazine* 2 (May 1900).

72. E. S. Turner, "An Equal Standard of Morals—Some Plain Words on a Forbidden Subject," *Philanthropist* (May 1894): 3.

73. Clark, "Politics of Seduction," p. 49. Judith Walkowitz, in her discussion of the English rescue worker Josephine Butler, makes a similar argument: "By asserting herself as a figure in the story, Butler accomplishes a series of substitutions. She replaces the wronged father of popular melodrama with an avenging mother who presents the magdalen's case to the dastardly seducer." Walkowitz goes on to argue that Butler gave "radical meaning to the melodramatic narrative of sexual danger by vindicating female activism, by dignifying the figure of the suffering fallen woman, and by inserting herself as a heroine/victim" (Walkowitz, *City of Dreadful Delight*, pp. 90, 92). Melodramas in which women appear as heroines depart from earlier seduction narratives. In his examination of George Lippard's seduction tales, Michael Denning finds that the focus of the

plot "is less on the story of the 'fallen woman' than on the struggle between good and evil men over that woman" (Denning, *Mechanic Accents*, p. 98). Susan Staves argues that the main figure in the treatment of seduction in law and literature in eighteenth-century Britain was the girl's father (Staves, "British Seduced Maidens," esp. pp. 110, 120).

74. Walkowitz, *City of Dreadful Delight*, p. 135. See esp. chap. 5.
75. NFCM, *Annual Report* (1928): 43.
76. Bishop Alfred Harding, introduction to Lillian M. Yeo, *Inasmuch*, pp. v–vi.
77. Helen Rogers, "My Job: What it Demands," *War Cry* (Nov. 5, 1938): 3.
78. See Peiss, *Cheap Amusements;* Lunbeck, "'A New Generation of Women'"; Joanne Meyerowitz, *Women Adrift*. To be discussed more fully in chapter 4.
79. Case file, 1901, Booth Memorial Hospital, Des Moines, Iowa, RG 14.2, SAARC.
80. Whittemore, *Mother Whittemore's Records*, p. 48. Peggy Pascoe discusses the structure of daily life in the nineteenth- and early-twentieth-century rescue homes in *Relations of Rescue*, pp. 76–85.
81. Evangeline Booth, "True Rescue Work," *War Cry*, no. 1736 (Jan. 9, 1915): 10; Yeo, *Inasmuch*, pp. 9–10.
82. Mrs. W. E. F. Taylor, "Putting First Things First," paper delivered at the National Conference of Florence Crittenton Missions, July 24, 1933, Box 11, Folder 112, NFCM.
83. *Florence Crittenton Bulletin* 5 (April 1930): 3–4.
84. Florence Crittenton League of Compassion, *Annual Report* (1915): 11.
85. "Help in Extremity," *Social News* 2 (Dec. 1912): 14.
86. Robert South Barrett, *Care of the Unmarried Mother*, p. 159.
87. K. Barrett, *Some Practical Suggestions*, p. 28.
88. Ibid., p. 36.
89. Evangeline Booth, "Rescue Work: Our Part in the Struggle for Purity, II" *War Cry*, no. 1498 (June 18, 1910): 9. The remunerative and redemptive aspects of work could occasionally clash. When workers at the Philadelphia Hebrew Sheltering Arms experimented with compensating unmarried mothers for their services, paying them six dollars a month for their work in the homes, they found that they compromised their own authority. As Superintendent Marie Winokur observed, "very little could be accomplished with the mothers along the lines of character building, as they considered themselves as paid workers and felt independent of our guidance. This defeated the very purpose . . . for which the girls were placed here" (Winokur to Katherine Lenroot, October 24, 1927, Box 295, Fol. 7-4-4-1, CB).
90. K. Barrett, *Some Practical Suggestions*, pp. 28–29.
91. Florence Crittenton Anchorage, board minutes, Dec. 4, 1913, FCA.
92. K. Barrett, *Some Practical Suggestions*, p. 35. Evangelicals' close attention to recreation was part of a larger concern among middle-class reformers regarding working-class leisure. See Roy Rosenzweig, *Eight Hours for What We Will: Workers and Leisure in an Industrial City, 1870–1920* (New York: Cambridge University Press, 1983); Peiss, *Cheap Amusements*, esp. chap. 7.

93. "Homes vs. Missions," *Florence Crittenton Magazine* 1 (March 1899): 24.

94. Florence Crittenton Mission of New Haven, pamphlet, 1913, n.p., Sterling Memorial Library, Yale University. See also *Mended Links* (1903), p. 17. These ideas about maternity homes took place in the context of a broad and sustained critique of most forms of long-term institutional care in the Progressive Era. See Rothman, *Conscience and Convenience;* Schlossman, *Love and the American Delinquent*, chap. 3; Freedman, *Their Sisters' Keepers;* Brenzel, *Daughters of the State.*

95. K. Barrett, *Some Practical Suggestions*, pp. 7–8.

96. "An Army Maternity Hospital," *Social News* 4 (June 1914): 11.

97. "A Refuge for the Erring," *Social News* 4 (Feb. 1914): 14.

98. K. Barrett, "How We Conduct Our Rescue Homes," *Florence Crittenton Magazine* 2 (Sept. 1900): 2.

99. K. Barrett, *Some Practical Suggestions*, p. 21.

100. New Haven Florence Crittenton Home, *Annual Report* (1901): 9–10. Peggy Pascoe discusses "maternalism" in the Denver, Colorado, Cottage Home in *Relations of Rescue*, pp. 102–03.

101. Mrs. A. D. Perry, "A Matron and Her Duties," in K. Barrett, *Fourteen Years' Work*, p. 30.

102. "Reports from Homes," *Florence Crittenton Magazine* 7 (Feb. 1906): 440.

103. *Florence Crittenton Bulletin* 4 (Jan. 1929): 5.

104. Ibid.

105. "The Salvation Army's Woman's Home and Maternity Hospital," July 1, 1930, Box 397, Folder 6, WC. Inwood House first considered admitting black unmarried mothers in 1934 and decided in 1940 to accept a few "as an experiment" (Baxter and Welter, *Inwood House*, p. 41). See also "Admissions Policy," 1923, Door of Hope, Jersey City, New Jersey, RG 14.5, SAARC. Many studies found that virtually all black unmarried mothers remained in the care of their family or friends in the late nineteenth and early twentieth centuries. See Sedlak, "Young Women and the City," p. 21.

106. Mrs. A. J. Wilson to Mr. Sam Grunfest, October 20, 1939, Box 5, Folder 35, NFCM.

107. "Committee on Illegitimacy," National Conference of Social Work, *Proceedings* (1919): 86.

108. Booth, *Orders and Regulations*, pp. 160, 162.

109. Emma Booth Tucker, "Rules and Regulations for Rescue Officers," n.d. (1897?), p. 9, pamphlet collection, SAARC.

110. Booth, *Orders and Regulations*, pp. 160–61.

111. Evangeline Booth, "Rescue Work: Our Part in the Struggle for Purity, I," *War Cry*, no. 1497 (June 11, 1910): 9.

112. "What Has the National Association Done for the Homes?" *Florence Crittenton Magazine* 1 (March 1899): 6.

113. Chicago Florence Crittenton Anchorage, *Annual Report* (1928), p. 17.

114. See NFCM Application for Admission, c. 1937, Box 10, Folder 108, NFCM. In

signing this application, the unmarried mother committed herself to remaining in the home for six months after the birth of her baby. In a survey of disposition records of one Crittenton home, Michael Sedlak finds that four- or five-year terms of stay were not uncommon (Sedlak, "Young Women and the City," p. 7). In requiring unmarried mothers to stay for six months to a year, Crittenton and Salvation Army homes distinguished themselves from "disreputable" maternity homes and lying-in hospitals that were becoming more popular in this period, where unmarried mothers could enter before giving birth and leave soon after. To be discussed more fully in chapter 3.

115. Case Files, Booth Memorial Hospital, Wauwatosa, Wisconsin, RG 14.6, SAARC. At the First General Convention of the NFCM, the Boston Crittenton home acknowledged that matrons read letters to and from the residents of the home. At this conference, the question was raised as to whether a matron had a right to open letters, and the proceedings noted that "this difficulty was obviated in one Home by having the girl herself break the seal and the matron first reading the letter" ("Report of the First General Convention of the NFCM and School of Methods," in K. Barrett, *Fourteen Years' Work*, pp. 135–36). See also Edlin, *Unmarried Mother in Our Society*, p. 50; U.S. Census Bureau, "Study of Maternity Homes in Minnesota and Pennsylvania," Pub. No. 167, by Ethel Waters (Washington, D.C.: Government Printing Office, 1926), p. 26; "Censoring Mail," Roundtable Discussion, NFCM, *Annual Report* (1925): 40–41.

116. "Rules and Regulations Suitable for Adoption in Any Florence Crittenton Home," *Florence Crittenton Magazine* 1 (June 1899): 109. Historians Kathy Peiss and Christine Stansell both discuss the significance of working-class women's dress and style (Peiss, *Cheap Amusements*, chap. 7; Stansell, *City of Women*, pp. 93–98). See also Mariana Valverde, "The Love of Finery: Fashion and the Fallen Woman in Nineteenth-Century Social Discourse," *Victorian Studies* 32 (Winter 1989): 168–88.

117. Stansell, *City of Women*, p. 187.

118. Quoted in R. Barrett, *Care of the Unmarried Mother*, p. 173.

119. Yeo, *Inasmuch*, p. 49.

120. K. Barrett, "How We Conduct Our Rescue Homes," p. 3.

121. Florence Crittenton Mission of New Haven, pamphlet, 1913, Sterling Memorial Library, Yale University, New Haven, Conn.

122. "Matron's Report," New Haven Florence Crittenton Home, *Annual Report* (1904): 10–11.

123. Annie Cowden, "Finds Hope for the Unfortunate Girl," *Social News* 5 (Jan. 1915): 10. See also *Service; An Exposition of the Salvation Army in America* (Clinton, Mass.: Colonial Press, 1937), p. 47.

124. See, e.g., *Girls* 17 (1914): 119; "Message from the General Superintendent," *Florence Crittenton Bulletin* 14 (April 1939): 2.

125. Lilian Freeman Clarke, *Story of an Invisible Institution*, p. 12.

126. Barnes, "Unmarried Mother and Her Child," p. 557.

127. K. Barrett, *Some Practical Suggestions*, p. 47.

128. *Service; An Exposition of the Salvation Army in America*, p. 50.

129. Reba Barrett Smith to Norma Beck, April 26, 1932, Box 6, Folder 50, NFCM.

130. See "The Maternity Home: How It Is Operated," *Social News* 12 (Sept. 1922): 15.

131. K. Barrett, "The Unmarried Mother and Her Child," p. 7, unpub. ms., Box 3, Folder 9, KWB.

132. Case file #121001, Door of Hope, Jersey City, N.J., RG 14.5, SAARC.

133. Brenzel, *Daughters of the State;* Pascoe, *Relations of Rescue*, pp. 166–71; Dudden, *Serving Women*, pp. 168–69.

134. See, e.g., U.S. Senate, "Relation between Occupation and Criminality of Women," vol. 15 of U.S. Senate Report on Condition of Women and Child Wage Earners, Doc. no. 645 (Washington, D.C.: Government Printing Office, 1911), esp. pp. 86–87.

135. See Brenzel, *Daughters of the State*, esp. pp. 139–41; Katzman, *Seven Days a Week*.

136. "One Solution to the Servant Problem," *Florence Crittenton Magazine* 11 (March 1908): 24. Ida Garrett Murphy also touted the virtues of employing an unmarried mother as domestic servant in "The Unmarried Mother at Work," *Survey* 43 (Feb. 28, 1920): 641–42.

137. See Cowden, "Finds Hope for the Unfortunate Girl," p. 8.

138. Florence Crittenton League of Compassion, pamphlet, 1925, p. 10, FCL. See also "Superintendent's Report," Florence Crittenton League of Compassion, *Annual Report* (1915): 12.

139. "Romance in the Out-of-Love Club," *Social News* 9 (Oct. 1919): 6.

CHAPTER 2 THE NEW EXPERTS AND THE "GIRL PROBLEM"

1. "Mrs. Barrett's Response," *Florence Crittenton Magazine* 11 (Sept. 1908): 195.

2. "Raising the Bottom!" 1917, Salvation Army pamphlet, SAARC; "Kate Waller Barrett: Nurse, Doctor, and Sociologist," *Trained Nurse and Hospital Review* 24 (April 1925): 387. NFCM President Kate Waller Barrett perhaps traded most successfully on her status as expert. An active participant in state and national conferences of Charities and Correction, Barrett was a delegate to the White House Conference for Dependent Children in 1909 that planned for the creation of the Children's Bureau. In 1914, Barrett traveled abroad as a special representative of the Bureau of Immigration of the U.S. Department of Labor to investigate the treatment of women deported on morals charges. See Urness, "Kate Waller Barrett"; "Kate Barrett's Report," NFCM, *Annual Report* (1914): 27; Lundberg, *Unto the Least of These*, p. 216.

3. William Ernest Hocking, "Osmosis: The Object of Social Work," *Survey* 55 (Dec. 15, 1925): 361.

4. D. O. Kellogg, "The Principle and Advantage of Association in Charities,"

Journal of Social Science 12 (1880): 88. Lori Ginzberg discusses the role played by the Civil War Sanitary Commission in "toughening" a generation of activists and in redefining the terms of benevolence in *Women and the Work of Benevolence*, chap. 5.

5. The charity organization movement spread rapidly. Robert H. Bremner notes that at least twenty-five cities had established COSs by 1883, and about one hundred by 1895 (Bremner, "'Scientific Philanthropy,'" p. 169). On the COS movement, see Frank Dekker Watson, *The Charity Organization Movement in the United States: A Study of American Philanthropy* (New York: Macmillan, 1922); Lubove, *Professional Altruist*, pp. 1–21; Gettleman, "Charity and Social Classes"; Kusmer, "Functions of Organized Charity"; Julia B. Rauch, "The Charity Organization Movement in Philadelphia," *Social Work* 21 (Jan. 1976): 55–62; Raymond Mohl, "The Abolition of Public Outdoor Relief, 1870–1900," in *Social Welfare or Social Control?* ed. Walter Trattner (Knoxville: University of Tennessee Press, 1983): 35–50; Michael B. Katz, *In the Shadow of the Poorhouse: A Social History of Welfare in America* (New York: Basic, 1986), chap. 3.

Closely related to the COS movement were the state charity boards. Emerging about the same time, they also promoted the goals of efficiency and rationality and pursued the ideals of scientific charity in public social service. Mohl points out that the charity boards shared analyses of the problems of dependency and public assistance as well as personnel with the COS in "Abolition of Public Relief," p. 44.

6. Porter R. Lee, "The Future of Professional Social Work," in Lee, *Social Work as Cause and Function* (New York: Columbia University Press, 1937), p. 137. Medical social workers, visiting teachers, and psychiatric social workers all formed their own professional associations between 1918 and 1921. On the growth of professional associations in social work, see Lubove, *Professional Altruist*, pp. 124–36.

7. Paul L. Benjamin, "Social Workers," *Survey* 46 (1921): 181. From the beginning, the AASW restricted membership to paid workers and stipulated four years of experience as a requirement for membership. See Lubove, *Professional Altruist*, p. 136. Leslie Leighninger examines the movement to raise membership standards within the AASW in the late 1920s in *Social Work*, chap. 3.

8. Lubove argues that the establishment of "a subculture or community whose members shared a group identity and values" was of vital importance to the professionalization of social work and was maintained and perpetuated by professional associations and schools (Lubove, *Professional Altruist*, p. 118). William Goode discusses the importance of a sense of community to the professions in "Community within a Community: The Professions," *American Sociological Review* 22 (Feb. 1957): 195–200.

9. Margaret E. Rich, "Professional Training from the Point of View of the Family Field," NCSW, *Proceedings* (1929).

10. Agnew, "A Touch of Class," p. 70. See also Veysey, "Who's a Professional?" pp. 419–20.

11. See Mary Van Kleek, "The Social Workers," *Survey* 35 (Jan. 1, 1916): 386–89.

12. Don S. Kirschner notes that as "the first specialist in specialization," Flexner was "a difficult man to ignore on the subject of professionalism" (Kirschner, *Paradox of Professionalism*, p. 54). Not all social workers jumped on the bandwagon of professionalization in the 1920s. A vocal minority greeted the trend toward professionalism with ambivalence, some lamenting the emotional distance that seemed to accompany it. See, e.g., Jane Addams, "The Spirit of Social Service," NCSW, *Proceedings* (1920): 41–43; Eduard C. Lindeman, "The Social Worker and His Community," *Survey* 52 (1924): 83–85; Abraham Epstein, "The Soulessness of Presentday Social Work," *Current History* 28 (1928): 391–92; Rev. James I. Vance, "The Message of Religion to Social Workers," NCSW, *Proceedings* (1914): 19.

13. Abraham Flexner, "Is Social Work a Profession?" NCCC, *Proceedings* (1915): 589.

14. Kirschner, *Paradox of Professionalism*, p. 55.

15. Mary Richmond, "The Social Case Worker's Task," NCSW, *Proceedings* (1917): 114. See also William Hodson, "Is Social Work Professional? A Re-Examination of the Question," NCSW, *Proceedings* (1925): 629–36. On social workers' response to Flexner, see John H. Ehrenreich, *The Altruistic Imagination: A History of Social Work and Social Policy in the United States* (Ithaca: Cornell University Press, 1985), p. 58; Glazer and Slater, *Unequal Colleagues*, pp. 173–76.

16. Alice S. Cheyney, "A Definition of Social Work" (Ph.D. diss., University of Pennsylvania, 1923), pp. 55–56. Daniel Walkowitz notes that "negative depictions of social workers in the emerging mass media of the 1920s further exacerbated the social worker's struggle to develop a positive professional identity" (Walkowitz, "Making of a Feminine Professional Identity," p. 1065).

17. Neva R. Deardorff, "The Objectives of Professional Organization," NCSW, *Proceedings* (1925): 637–38. See also Veronica O. Wilder, "Our Salaries," *Family* 3 (1922): 6–9; Walker, *Social Work and the Training of Social Workers*, p. 117.

18. Frank J. Bruno, "Training for Social Work from the Point of View of the School," NCSW, *Proceedings* (1929): 300. In fact, the majority of social work practitioners lacked the qualifications required for membership in the AASW in the 1920s. In 1930, less than one-third of the employed social workers were members of the professional associations (*Encyclopedia of Social Work*, 15th issue, p. 14).

19. Homer Folks, "Prevention Succeeds," NCSW, *Proceedings* (1923): 8. JoAnne Brown argues that professions use metaphors as their primary strategy of legitimation, borrowing authority and image from other precedent professions: "the use of metaphor to found a new enterprise upon the cultural authority of an old one" (Brown, "Professional Language," p. 39).

20. "Where Are the Social Engineers?" *Survey* 54 (Aug. 15, 1924): 524–43; Halbert, *What Is Professional Social Work?* p. 20. See also Chambers, "Creative Effort in an Age of Normalcy," p. 266.

21. On the importance of science in the professionalization of social work, see Glazer and Slater, *Unequal Colleagues*, pp. 235–37; Ehrenreich, *Altruistic Imagination*, p. 40; Carol Germain, "Casework and Science: A Historical Encounter," in *Theories of Casework*, ed. Robert W. Roberts and Robert H. Nee (Chicago: University of Chicago Press, 1970): 3–32. On the place of science in professionalization more generally, see Alfred D. Chandler, Jr., *The Visible Hand: The Managerial Revolution in American Business* (Cambridge: Harvard University Press, 1977); Louis Galambos, *The Public Image of Big Business and America, 1880–1940: A Quantitative Study in Social Change* (Baltimore: Johns Hopkins University Press, 1975), pp. 47–114; Jerold S. Auerbach, *Unequal Justice: Lawyers and Social Change in Modern America* (New York: Oxford University Press, 1976), chap. 3.

22. Virginia Robinson, "Analysis of Processes in the Records of Family Case Working Agencies," NCSW, *Proceedings* (1921): 253.

23. Maurice J. Karpf, *The Scientific Basis of Social Work: A Study in Family Case Work* (New York: Columbia University Press, 1931), p. 358.

24. Ibid., p. 368.

25. Halbert, *What Is Professional Social Work?* p. 25, p. 28. Bledstein argues that "the methods of science separated the amateur from the professional, the dilettante from the dedicated specialist" in *Culture of Professionalism*, p. 285. In medicine, the evocation of science had worked in precisely this way, raising the new trained doctors as the true practitioners of medicine and condemning those who had not been scientifically trained as "irregulars."

26. Kate Holladay Claghorn, *Social Work as a Profession for College Men and Women*, New York School of Philanthropy (1915), p. 2. See also DeSchweinitz, *Art of Helping People Out of Trouble*, p. 41; Pearl Salsberry, "Techniques in Case Work," *Family* 8 (July 1927): 153.

27. Ada E. Sheffield, "Case Records in Family Agencies," NCSW, *Proceedings* (1920): 242.

28. Robinson, "Analysis of Processes in the Records of Family Case Working Agencies," p. 253.

29. Charles A. Ellwood, "Social Facts and Scientific Social Work," NCSW, *Proceedings* (1918): 687.

30. Bledstein, *Culture of Professionalism*, p. 91. Magali Larson asserts that "the main instrument of professional advancement . . . is the capacity to claim esoteric and identifiable skills—that is, to create and control a cognition and technical base" in *Rise of Professionalism*, p. 180. See also Brown, "Professional Language," in *Professions and Professional Ideologies in America*, ed. Gerald L. Geison (Chapel Hill, N.C.: University of North Carolina Press, 1983);

Kenneth Hudson, *Jargon of the Professions;* Edelman, "Political Language of the Helping Professions."

31. Adams, *Women Professional Workers,* p. 157.

32. Edwin S. Smith, letter to editor, *Survey* 46 (Sept. 1, 1921): 654.

33. *Survey* 38 (June 16, 1917): 265.

34. Beulah Weldon, "Training for Social Work," *Survey* 58 (Sept. 1, 1927), p. 510.

35. Kirschner, *Paradox of Professionalism,* p. 55.

36. J. B. Buell, "The Challenge to Social Workers," *Survey* 45 (Oct. 30, 1920): 164. See also LeRoy E. Bowman, "What the Press Thinks of Social Work," NCSW, *Proceedings* (1923): 477–83; Dorothy E. Wysor, "How Can We Interpret Social Work to the Public?" *Family* 7 (Dec. 1926): 248; R. Clyde White, "A Strategy for Social Workers," *Compass* 25 (Nov. 1943): 21. Not all social workers applauded this change in course. Alice S. Cheyney likened the repudiation of nineteenth-century philanthropic values to "the act of a thankless child denying an unfashionable parent" (Cheyney, *Nature and Scope of Social Work,* p. 10).

37. Porter R. Lee, "Social Work: Cause and Function," NCSW, *Proceedings* (1929): 5. This dialogue in social work has shaped social work historiography. Many historians writing on social work have been primarily concerned with the relative balance, at particular historical moments, of social reform and concern for environmental causes of poverty, and emphasis on the individual and attention to method and technique. See, e.g., Lubove, *Professional Altruist;* Ehrenreich, *Altruistic Imagination;* Leighninger, *Social Work.* Robyn Muncy, on the other hand, posits an "interrelationship between the professional interests of white, middle-class women and their participation in progressive reform" (Muncy, *Creating a Female Dominion in American Reform,* p. 38).

38. Not all social workers agreed with Lee. New York social worker Daisy Lee Worthington Worcester reported that a group of social workers gathered in an "indignation meeting" following the presidential address of 1929. Worthington "resented its major assumptions" and urged social workers "to turn away from this preoccupation with techniques and functions and consider the then ominous realities of our industrial life" (Worcester, *Grim the Battles,* p. 164).

39. Tufts, *Education and Training for Social Work,* p. 70. Joan Brumberg and Nancy Tomes assert that "prestige within the professions has increasingly come to depend upon precisely those qualities least associated with the ideal 'feminine'" (Brumberg and Tomes, "Women in the Professions," p. 288).

40. Todd, *Scientific Spirit and Social Work,* pp. 105, 86.

41. "Report from the Summer School in Philanthropic Work," *Charities* 9 (July 19, 1902): 71–72.

42. Queen, *Social Work in the Light of History,* p. 88.

43. Adams, *Women Professional Workers,* p. 184. Some historical writing about social work reproduces the equation of amateur benevolence with women and professional social work with men. For example, W. Richard Scott writes that

social workers "range from the proverbial little old lady in tennis shoes, armed with good intentions and a highschool diploma . . . to the young man with a Ph.D. degree from a graduate school of social welfare engaged in a program of evaluative research on the merits of a new casework technique" (Scott, "Professional Employees in a Bureaucratic Structure: Social Work," in *The Semi-Professions and Their Organization,* ed. Amitai Etzioni [New York: Free Press, 1969], p. 83).

44. Tufts, *Education and Training for Social Work,* p. 70.

45. Buell, "The Challenge to Social Workers," p. 164. The most complete study of salaries in social work was published in 1926 by the Russell Sage Foundation. Surveying 1,258 social workers, this study revealed the national median salary for women in social work to be $1,680; for men, $3,600 (Ralph G. Hurlin, *Social Work Salaries* [New York: Russell Sage Foundation, 1926]). Louise C. Odencrantz cited an agency with 3 male caseworkers out of a staff of 27, who commented that "'we are always glad to get men, and give them preferential treatment as to salary'" in *Social Worker,* p. 57. On the discrepancy between salaries earned by men and women in social work, see also Deardorff, "The Objectives of the Professional Organization," p. 642; Van Kleeck, "The Social Workers," pp. 387–88; Mary Clarke Burnett, "Salaries for New Recruits," *Survey* 57 (Dec. 15, 1926): 395–96; Hurlin, "Measuring the Demand for Social Workers," NCSW, *Proceedings* (1926): 587–95; Fred R. Johnson, "Salary Standards in Social Work," NCSW, *Proceedings* (1920): 424–27.

46. See Odencrantz, *Social Worker,* pp. 58, 124.

47. Hatcher, ed., *Occupations for Women,* p. 465. See also Van Kleeck, "The Social Workers," pp. 386–89.

48. Tufts, *Education and Training for Social Work,* p. 73.

49. Claghorn, "Social Work as a Profession," pp. 6–7. Elizabeth Kemper Adams reported that in Minneapolis, 31.2% of the men studied were general executives of agencies and only 7.2% of the women occupied such positions (Adams, *Women Professional Workers,* p. 174). Subsequent studies of social work found that men were disproportionately represented among officers of the professional associations, deans and directors of social work schools, contributors of journal articles, and agency administrators. See Giovannoni and Purvine, "Myth of the Social Work Matriarchy"; Diane Kravetz, "Sexism in a Women's Profession," *Social Work* 21 (Nov. 1976): 421–27; George Brazer and John A. Michael, "The Sex Distribution in Social Work," *Social Casework* 50 (Dec. 1969): 545–601; Aaron Rosenblatt et al., "Predominance of Male Authors in Social Work Publications," *Social Casework* 51 (July 1970): 421–30; C. Barnard Scotch, "Sex Status in Social Work: Grist for Women's Liberation," *Social Work* 16 (July 1971): 5–11; James W. Grimm, "Women in Female Dominated Professions," in *Women Working: Theories and Facts in Perspective,* ed. Ann H. Stromberg and Shirley Harkness (Palo Alto: Mayfield, 1978), p. 303.

50. Brown, *Social Work as a Profession,* p. 110.

51. Deardorff, "Objectives of the Professional Organization," pp. 642–43. Historian Nancy Cott notes the tension between feminism and professional identity and finds that women professionals were reluctant to acknowledge discrimination. Cott argues that women had to reject the sex loyalty that was a prerequisite for feminism in order to become professionals. To charge discrimination constituted a tacit acknowledgment that professionalism's meritocracy, which stated that the professions accepted individuals on the basis of talent alone, was a sham. In this light, these public protests of women social workers are all the more remarkable. See Cott, *Grounding of Modern Feminism*, pp. 226–29.

52. Deardorff, "Objectives of the Professional Organization," p. 642.

53. Although I argue that professionalism was (and is) powerfully and pervasively laden with assumptions about gender, as well as race and class, I do not intend to pose professionalism and femininity as essentially and inevitably mutually exclusive or antagonistic. Rather, I argue that both are socially and historically constructed categories, and as such, constructed as antagonistic. Daniel J. Walkowitz discusses the difficulties social workers faced in constructing what he terms a "useable feminine professional identity," in "The Making of a Feminine Professional Identity."

54. Morantz-Sanchez, *Sympathy and Science*, p. 308.

55. Virginia Smith, "The Cooperation of Women in Philanthropic and Reformatory Work," NCCC, *Proceedings* (1891): 240.

56. Discussion following Smith, "The Cooperation of Women in Philanthropic and Reformatory Work," p. 338.

57. See Morantz-Sanchez, *Sympathy and Science*; Epstein, *Women in Law*; Walsh, *"Doctors Wanted, No Women Need Apply."*

58. Nannie E. Deihl and Robert S. Wilson, "Can Listening Become a Case Work Art?" in *Readings in Social Case Work*, ed. Lowry, p. 236. There are interesting parallels here with studies of women in other occupations dominated by women. For example, Virginia Drachman distinguishes the first generation of women doctors, who built their careers on separatism, from the second generation, who came to see female solidarity as an obstacle to their professional progress and who "minimized their womanhood in favor of their identification as doctors" in *Hospital with a Heart*, p. 152. See also Melosh, *The Physician's Hand*; Reverby, *Ordered to Care*, chaps. 7, 8.

59. Ginzberg, *Women and the Work of Benevolence*, p. 10.

60. See Rosalind Rosenberg, *Beyond Separate Spheres: Intellectual Roots of Modern Feminism* (New Haven: Yale University Press, 1982).

61. Nancy Cott describes the appeal of the professions to women: "In theory, of course, the setting of empirical, rational, and objective standards for access to and advancement within the professions . . . was of great benefit to women, whose exclusion from lucrative and influential positions resulted from customary, nonrational, and subjective limitations. If there were ascertainable standards rather than subjective criteria for training, achievement, and so on, then

women could strive to meet those standards and proceed as if they were to be judged as individuals, rather than being judged a priori on account of sex" (Cott, *Grounding of Modern Feminism*, p. 232).

62. Genrose Gehri, "The Illegitimate Family," p. 12, pamphlet, Church Mission of Help, 1937, Box 49, Folder 1, CWLA.

63. C. C. Carstens to Martha Falconer, 30 October 1922, Box 212, Fol. 7-4-0-5, CB.

64. *Florence Crittenton Bulleton* 11 (Oct. 1936): 29. See also Edith M. Baylor, "Necessary Changes"; Mary S. Brisley, "The Illegitimate Family and Specialized Treatment," *Family* 19 (May 1938): 67–76; Joanna C. Colcord, "The Need of Adequate Case Work with the Unmarried Mother," *Family* 4 (Nov. 1923): 167–72; Lawrence Cole, "The Need of the Case Work Method"; Francis V. Emerson, "The Place of the Maternity Home," *Survey* 42 (August 30, 1919): 772–74; Howland, "Illegitimate Mothers"; Lenroot, "Case Work with Unmarried Parents"; Murphy, "What Can Be Accomplished?"; Murphy, "Mothers and—Mothers"; Paul Popenoe, "Some Eugenic Aspects of Illegitimacy," *Journal of Social Hygiene* 9 (Dec. 1923): 513–27; Mary Frances Smith, "Changing Emphases in Case Work with Unmarried Mothers, *Family* 14 (Jan. 1934): 310–17.

65. George B. Mangold, *Children Born out of Wedlock*, p. 103; George L. Jones, "How Does Our Treatment of the Unmarried Mother with the Second or Third Child Differ from Our Treatment of the Unmarried Mother with Her First Child?" NCSW, *Proceedings* (1919): 82.

66. NFCM, *Annual Report* (1931): 36.

67. Maxfield, "Social Treatment of Unmarried Mothers," p. 217.

68. Murphy, "Mothers and—Mothers," p. 171; Murphy, "What Can Be Accomplished?" p. 130.

69. Katherine P. Hewins, "A Study of Illegitimacy," *Survey* 46 (April 23, 1921), p. 115; Sheffield, "What Is the Case Worker Really Doing?" p. 365.

70. E. G. Bylander to Mrs. J. Earle Collier, March 8, 1940, Box 5, Folder 35, NFCM.

71. Ada Sheffield to Emma Lundberg, March 27, 1919, Box 68, Fol. 7-4-4-0, CB; Lundberg to Sheffield, April 3, 1919, Box 68, Fol. 7-4-4-0, CB.

72. Queen and Mann, *Social Pathology*, p. 171.

73. Ben Lindsey, "When Girls Go Wrong," *Florence Crittenton Magazine* 7 (Feb. 1906): 426. See also Preston, "Good Care of Unmarried Mothers."

74. See Smith and Hindus, "Premarital Pregnancy in America"; Smith, "Dating of the American Sexual Revolution," p. 435; Vinovskis, *An 'Epidemic' of Adolescent Pregnancy?* p. 10; Smith, "The Long Cycle in American Illegitimacy," pp. 362–78. The Federal Bureau of Census began to publish statistics on illegitimacy in 1917. However, the Bureau accepted the figures reported from the various states, figures known to be inaccurate. See George B. Mangold, "The Census Statistics on Illegitimacy," CWLA, *Bulletin* 7 (Dec. 1928): 8. Therefore, although social workers reported a dramatic upswing in the rate of illegitimacy

in the 1920s, it remains unclear whether this represents an actual rise or a rise in the rate of reporting.

75. The demise of the family was a staple of sociological and social work literature beginning in the 1900s and accelerating into the 1920s. See Howard, "Sociology and the Family in the Progressive Era," pp. 39–62.

76. Brisley, "'Humble and Distracted,'" p. 231. See also Guibord and Parker, *What Becomes of the Unmarried Mother?* p. 20.

77. Inter-City Conference on Illegitimacy, *Bulletin*, in CWLA, *Bulletin* 5 (June 15, 1926): 8. See also Kammerer, *Unmarried Mother*, p. 2; William I. Thomas, *Unadjusted Girl*, p. xii; Gillin, *Social Pathology*, p. 213. Not all social workers viewed unmarried mothers as hastening the breakdown of the family. See, e.g., Brisley, "The Illegitimate Family and Specialized Treatment."

78. Hobson, *Uneasy Virtue*, p. 192.

79. See Richard W. Fox, *So Far Disordered in Mind: Insanity in California, 1870–1930* (Berkeley: University of California Press, 1978).

80. Richmond, *Adolescent Girl*, p. 73.

81. Lundberg, "The Child Mother as a Delinquency Problem," NCSW, *Proceedings* (1920): 162; U.S. Senate, "Relation between Occupation and Criminality of Women," p. 67.

82. Kammerer, *Unmarried Mother*, p. 263.

83. See Haller, *Eugenics*, pp. 100–101. On feeblemindedness and intelligence testing in the Progressive Era, see Michael M. Sokol, ed., *Psychological Testing and American Society, 1890–1930* (New Brunswick, N.J.: Rutgers University Press, 1987).

84. At the height of the term's popularity, the feebleminded woman was virtually synonymous with the prostitute. See Hobson, *Uneasy Virtue*, pp. 190–91; Rosen, *Lost Sisterhood*, pp. 21–23; Connelly, *Response to Prostitution*, pp. 41–44, 171.

85. Queen and Mann, *Social Pathology*, pp. 163–64. See also Taylor, "'Denied the Power to Choose the Good.'" Contradictions in explications of the sexual nature of the feebleminded woman suggested a deep ambivalence about the nature of female sexuality. Some social workers attributed the feebleminded woman at once with passivity and hypersexuality. To Anne T. Bingham, for example, the feebleminded woman's alleged inclination to promiscuous sexual behavior was at once "a stupid drifting in the direction of least resistance" and "the primitive gratification of an appetite" (Bingham, "Determinants of Sex Delinquency," p. 57).

86. Richmond, *Adolescent Girl*, p. 73.

87. U.S. Senate, "Relation between Occupation and Criminality," p. 89. See also Vida Francis, "The Delinquent Girl," NCCC, *Proceedings* (1906): 144; Lowe, "Intelligence and Social Background of the Unmarried Mother," p. 793; Louise Waterman Wise, "Mothers in Name," *Survey* 43 (March 20, 1920): 780; Cole, "Need of the Case Work Method in Dealing with Illegitimacy," p. 432; Jean

Weidensall, "The Mentality of the Unmarried Mother," NCSW, *Proceedings* (1917): 294.

88. Superintendent's Report, Florence Crittenton Home, Norfolk, Virginia, 1930, Box 18, Folder 7, FCS.

89. Haller, *Eugenics*, chap. 7.

90. Mildred O. Mudgett, "Results of Minnesota's Law for Protection of Children Born out of Wedlock," in U.S. Children's Bureau, "Illegitimacy as a Child-Welfare Problem," part 3, Pub. no. 128 (Washington: Government Printing Office, 1924), p. 232. Many warned of the disgenic effects of illegitimacy. See Major Leonard Darwin, "Divorce and Illegitimacy," *Eugenics Review* 9 (Jan. 1918): 286–306; Popenoe, "Some Eugenic Aspects of Illegitimacy." One of the most extreme eugenicists to write on illegitimacy, Popenoe criticized efforts to protect the welfare of illegitimate children as "eugenically a step backward," and advised that they "be accompanied by some definite eugenic measures to counterbalance it; otherwise, this humanitarian reform, like many others, will leave the race really worse off than before, in regard to the perpetration of defective strains of germ plasm" (Popenoe, "Some Eugenic Aspects," p. 518). Certainly not all social workers agreed with him. Emma Lundberg found Popenoe's suggestion that infant mortality served eugenic purposes and that support from the father was dysgenic "astounding, to say the least" (Lundberg to Katherine Hewins, 19 March 1924, Box 212, Folder 7-4-0-3, CB, NA).

91. Queen and Mann, *Social Pathology*, pp. 163–64.

92. Lunbeck argues that the diagnosis of psychopathic personality followed that of feeblemindedness to describe women who willingly engaged in sex in "'A New Generation of Women,'" esp. pp. 523–24.

93. See Joseph F. Kett, *Rites of Passage*, esp. chaps. 4–7.

94. The scientific and popular literature on female delinquency in this period is voluminous. Schlossman and Wallach include a good bibliography in "Crime of Precocious Sexuality." On theories of adolescence and the relationship to the new concern with delinquency, see Schlossman and Wallach, "Crime of Precocious Sexuality," p. 82; Demos and Demos, "Adolescence in Historical Perspective"; Lunbeck, "'A New Generation of Women,'" pp. 515–17; Kett, *Rites of Passage*, chap. 8.

95. U.S. Senate, "Juvenile Delinquency and Its Relation to Employment," p. 75. Schlossman and Wallach argue that female delinquency was defined as sexual delinquency in the Progressive Era and that girls bore a disproportionate share of the burden of juvenile justice in this period, receiving more severe punishments than boys, in "Crime of Precocious Sexuality."

96. Richmond, *Adolescent Girl*, p. 113.

97. Francis, "Delinquent Girl," p. 142.

98. Kate Burr Johnson, "Problems of Delinquency among Girls," *Journal of Social Hygiene* 12 (Oct. 1926): 385. Some social workers protested the attribution of "sex delinquency" solely to girls and women. Richmond claimed that "if boys

were brought to book for sex delinquencies as girls are, their preponderant offenses would be found to lie in the same sphere also" (Richmond, *Adolescent Girl*, p. 113).

99. Russell Cooper to NFCM, March 19, 1937, Box 4, Folder 31, NFCM.

100. *Florence Crittenton Bulletin* 4 (Jan. 1929): 7. See also Alice Albee to Mrs. Slocum, August 26, 1942, Box 2, Folder 15, NFCM; Corine A. Dieterly to Robert S. Barrett, January 21, 1943, Box 4, Folder 33, NFCM.

101. Ivakota Farms was a 400-acre farm donated to the NFCM in 1915. Located in Clifton, Virginia, it was initially used as a summer retreat for Crittenton inmates, especially from the Washington, D.C., home thirty miles away. It soon became a facility to care for female delinquents. On Ivakota Farms, see Aiken, "The National Florence Crittenton Mission," pp. 202–09; Reba B. Smith, "Description of Work at Ivakota," unidentified newspaper clipping, Box 4, scrapbook, KWB.

102. Schlossman and Wallach, "Crime of Precocious Sexuality," p. 68. "Sex delinquency" became a sort of umbrella term, encompassing prostitution, promiscuity, and homosexuality. Linda Gordon finds that, in the decades 1910–1930, victims of incest and sexual abuse were also labeled sex delinquents (Gordon, *Heroes of Their Own Lives*, p. 22).

103. Lundberg, "Children of Illegitimate Birth and Measures for Protection," p. 12.

104. Bingham, "Determinants of Sex Delinquency," p. 35. See also Lundberg, "Illegitimate Mother as a Delinquency Problem."

105. Lundberg, "Children of Illegitimate Birth and Measures for Protection," p. 14. See also Reed, *Social and Health Care of the Illegitimate Family*, pp. 76–77.

106. U.S. Senate, "Relation between Occupation and Criminality of Women," p. 82.

107. See Roror, "A Survey of Illegitimacy of Unmarried Negresses." In conducting studies of female delinquency, many social workers sampled from populations in maternity homes as often as reformatories. See, e.g., Wiley, *A Study of the Problem of Girl Delinquency.*

108. Bingham, "Determinants of Sex Delinquency," p. 60.

109. See, e.g., Kammerer, *Unmarried Mother*, p. 222. Psychiatrists in this period were formulating the category "hypersexual psychopath" to describe women whose sexuality they deemed abnormally aggressive. See Lunbeck, "A New Generation of Women."

110. Brisley, "The Unmarried Parent-Child Relationship," a paper and two discussions given at the NCSW, 1939, p. 5, pamphlet collection, CWLA. See also Hewins, "A Study of Illegitimacy," p. 115.

111. Brisley, "The Unmarried Parent-Child Relationship," p. 15. Lunbeck notes that, in the discourse on women diagnosed as psychopathic hypersexuals, "men were at best the passive recipients, or, at worst, the unwitting victims of their unwanted attentions" in "'A New Generation of Women,'" pp. 513–14.

112. See Peiss, *Cheap Amusements;* Lundberg, "'A New Generation of Women,'" Meyerowitz, *Women Adrift.*

113. Blanchard and Manasses, *New Girls for Old*, p. x. See also Martha P. Falconer, "The Girl of To-Day," *Journal of Social Hygiene* 8 (Oct. 1922): 369–74.

114. Dr. E. T. Kreuger, "Problems of Adolescence," *Florence Crittenton Bulletin* 13 (Aug. 1938): 49.

115. Belle Lindner Israels, "The Way of the Girl," *Survey* 22 (July 3, 1909): 488.

116. On Progressive reformers' concern with working-class recreation and leisure, see Peiss, *Cheap Amusements*, chap. 7; Rosenzweig, *Eight Hours for What We Will*.

117. "What Is Modesty?" *Willows Magazine* 19 (March–April, 1930): 19; Gillin, *Social Pathology*, p. 302.

118. Case file #1300027, Door of Hope, Jersey City, New Jersey, RG 14.5, SAARC.

119. Mabel Higgins Mattingly, "The Unmarried Mother and Her Child" (M.A. thesis, Western Reserve University, 1928), p. 25. Many observers drew causal links between commercial amusements and out-of-wedlock pregnancy. See, e.g., Wiley, *Girl Delinquency*, pp. 16–17; Elliott and Merrill, *Social Disorganization*, p. 637; *Study of Children Born out of Wedlock in Connecticut* (New Haven: Connecticut Child Welfare Association, 1927), p. 9; Queen and Mann, *Social Pathology*, p. 165; Bingham, "Determinants of Sex Delinquency," pp. 24–25; Kammerer, *Unmarried Mother*, chap. 5; U.S. Senate, "Relation between Occupation and Criminality," p. 91; Reeves, *Training Schools for Delinquent Girls*, p. 313; U.S. Children's Bureau, *Maternity Homes*, pp. 46–47; Lowe, "The Intelligence and Social Background of the Unmarried Mother," p. 788; Reed, *Negro Illegitimacy*, pp. 88–92.

120. *Study of Children Born out of Wedlock in Connecticut*, pp. 5–6. See also Reed, *Negro Illegitimacy*, pp. 88–92; Amey Eaton Watson, "Philadelphia's Problem and the Development of Standards of Care," in U.S. Children's Bureau, *Illegitimacy as a Child Welfare Problem*, Part 3, Pub. no. 128 (Washington, D.C.: Government Printing Office, 1924), p. 50.

121. Casebook #069, December 8, 1919, Booth Memorial Hospital, Wauwatosa, Wisconsin, RG 14.6, SAARC.

122. Barrett, *Care of the Unmarried Mother*, p. 34; NFCM, *Annual Report* (1914): 14; "Moving Pictures Downfall of Girl," *Girls* 14 (June 1911): 47.

123. Elliott and Merrill, *Social Disorganization*, p. 637.

124. Wiley, *Girl Delinquency*, p. 16.

125. Kammerer, *Unmarried Mother*, pp. 48, 49, 50, 52. By the 1920s, social workers were beginning to disabuse themselves of the illusion of safety and protection offered by domestic service.

126. Ibid., p. 103. See also Edith Livingston Smith and Hugh Cabot, "A Study in Sexual Morality," *Journal of Social Hygiene* 2 (Oct. 1916): 544; Grace Abbott, *The Immigrant and the Community*, p. 72; Enid Severy Smith, "A Study of Twenty-Five Adolescent Unmarried Mothers in New York City" (Ph.D. diss., Columbia University, 1935); Breckenridge and Abbott, *Delinquent Child and the Home*, pp. 77–79. Social workers' anxiety about women's paid employment

persisted, despite the report of a Senate committee in 1911 that found, contrary to popular opinion, that "the widening of the industrial sphere of women has not been accompanied by any proportionate increase in criminality" (U.S. Senate, "Relation between Occupation and Criminality of Women," p. 76).

127. "Report of the Detroit Florence Crittenton Home," NFCM, *Annual Report* (1925): 99. On the connection between living conditions and out-of-wedlock pregnancy, see U.S. Children's Bureau, "Illegitimacy as a Child Welfare Problem," Part 3, p. 109; *Study of Children Born out of Wedlock in Connecticut*, p. 19; Helen S. Trounstine, "Illegitimacy in Cincinnati," *Studies from the Helen S. Trounstine Foundation* 1 (Sept. 1919): 196; Lundberg, *Unmarried Mothers in the Municipal Court of Philadelphia*, p. 201. For an excellent analysis of the experience of women living apart from families and the "problem" of the "woman adrift" as constructed by reformers, see Meyerowitz, *Women Adrift*.

128. Wiley, *Girl Delinquency*. See also Fletcher, "The Problem of Illegitimacy in Pittsburgh," p. 245.

129. Bingham, "Determinants of Sex Delinquency," p. 23.

130. Beatrice Mann, "Our Philosophy in Handling Illegitimacy," paper delivered at the NFCM Conference, July 15, 1933, p. 11, Box 11, Folder 112, NFCM.

131. Kammerer, *Unmarried Mother*, p. 36.

132. U.S. Senate, "Relation between Occupation and Criminality of Women," p. 92.

133. Bingham, "Determinants of Sex Delinquency," p. 13.

134. Wiley, *Girl Delinquency*, p. 13.

135. Bingham, "Determinants of Sex Delinquency," p. 26. See also Abbott, *The Immigrant and the Community*, p. 70.

136. Phelps, *Contemporary Social Problems*, pp. 341–42. Marian Morton notes that the changed racial and ethnic background of unmarried mothers was reflected in social workers' attachment to feeblemindedness as an explanation for unmarried mothers (Morton, "Seduced and Abandoned in an American City," p. 459). On black feeblemindedness, see Mary O'Malley, "Psychoses in the Colored Race: A Study in Comparative Psychiatry," *American Journal of Insanity* 71 (1914–15): 309–37; W. M. Bevis, "Psychological Traits of the Southern Negro with Observations as to Some of His Psychoses," *American Journal of Psychiatry* 1 (1921–22): 69–78.

Although heavily implicated in the discourse of feeblemindedness, African-American unmarried mothers seemed to be largely exempted from the category of sex delinquent. For example, when Enid S. Smith cataloged the usual list of causes leading to out-of-wedlock pregnancy, she found "'colored' attitude toward pregnancy" sufficient to explain the causes of black out-of-wedlock pregnancy (Smith, "A Study of Twenty-Five Adolescent Unmarried Mothers"). Elizabeth Lunbeck suggests that while white immorality demanded an explanation, black immorality "was entirely normal. . . . The fooling with boys that was a definite symptom of psychopathy in white girls was in blacks only the expression of the natural immorality of the race" (Lunbeck, "Psychiatry in the Age of Reform," p. 154). Concern regarding black illegitimacy accelerated in the 1940s and will be discussed more fully in chapter 6.

137. Allen, "How to Save Girls Who Have Fallen," p. 685.

138. Dorr, "Reclaiming the Wayward Girl," p. 73.

139. The unmarried mothers in one study, e.g., were given the Stanford Revision of the Simon-Binet Scale, the Morgan test, the Seguin Form-board, the Healy Pictorial Completion II, the Metropolitan Achievement Series, the Pressey Interest-Attitude Test, the Kent Rosanoff Association Test, the Bernreuter Personality Inventory, and the Brown Personality Inventory for Children (Nottingham, "Psychological Study of Forty Unmarried Mothers").

140. Murray Edelman argues that "categorization is necessary to science" and is also a political tool, "establishing status and power hierarchies" (Edelman, "The Political Language of the Helping Professions," p. 300).

141. There are interesting parallels between women social workers' use of the "male" language of science and that of the early-twentieth-century New Woman, as described by Smith-Rosenberg in "The New Woman as Androgyne." Smith-Rosenberg sees subversive potential in the efforts of women modernist writers of the 1920s and 1930s to appropriate the language of male sexologists, but argues that they ultimately relinquished a critical source of identity and political strength—"the power to create language"—in that appropriation.

142. In order to cultivate the proper professional distance from clients, most social workers working with unmarried mothers, unlike evangelical women, did not live in maternity homes. One Crittenton caseworker in Baltimore who recommended that "the case worker should not live in the home" explained that "if she lives in the Home she is presumably a member of the 'family,' and therefore cannot maintain the completely objective relationships which are necessary for her success as a caseworker" (Baltimore Council of Social Agencies, "Florence Crittenton Mission of Baltimore," July 1941, p. 31, Box 6, Folder 58, NFCM). Judith Trolander notes that settlement house workers similarly began to view the practice of living in settlement houses as at odds with professionalism, in *Professionalism and Social Change*, pp. 35–38.

143. Magali Sarfatti Larson, "The Production of Expertise and the Constitution of Expert Power," in *The Authority of Experts: Studies in History and Theory*, ed. Thomas Haskell (Bloomington: Indiana University Press, 1984), pp. 35–36.

144. Pascoe, *Relations of Rescue*.

145. Keller, *Reflections on Gender and Science*, p. 4. See also Irigary, "Is the Subject of Science Sexed?"; Keller, "Women Scientists and Feminist Critics of Science"; Joan Rothschild, ed., *Machina ex Dea: Feminist Perspectives on Technology* (New York: Pergamon Press, 1983); Ruth Bleier, ed., *Feminist Approaches to Science* (New York: Pergamon Press, 1986).

146. Mary Jacobus, Evelyn Fox Keller, and Sally Shuttleworth, "Introduction," in

Body/Politics: Women and the Discourses of Science, ed. Mary Jacobus et al. (New York: Routledge, 1990), p. 7.

147. Ibid., p. 1.

CHAPTER 3 THE "SECRET SISTERHOOD": UNMARRIED MOTHERS IN MATERNITY HOMES

1. K. Barrett, "How We Conduct Our Rescue Home," *Florence Crittenton Magazine* 2 (Sept. 1900): 2.
2. Fitzpatrick, "Childbirth and an Unwed Mother in Seventeenth-Century New England," p. 747. See also Ulrich, *A Midwife's Tale*, pp. 147–60.
3. See Brumberg, "'Ruined' Girls," p. 249; Hobson, *Uneasy Virtue*, p. 59.
4. Breckenridge, *Family Welfare Work*, p. 673.
5. Letter to Brigadier Caldwell, August 14, 1926, case files, Booth Memorial Home and Hospital, Des Moines, Iowa, RG 14.2, SAARC.
6. Case file #1450075, Door of Hope, Jersey City, New Jersey, RG 14.5, SAARC.
7. Case file #1290087, Door of Hope, Jersey City, New Jersey, RG 14.5, SAARC.
8. Case of Dorothy, February 1, 1942, p. 2, Box 1, Folder 3, Dorothy Hutchinson papers, Columbia University Archives, New York, New York.
9. George B. Mangold, "Unlawful Motherhood," p. 338. Joanne Meyerowitz cites out-of-wedlock pregnancy as one cause of female migration to cities around the turn of the century, along with need for work and the changing geography of the female labor market, disruption of the family economy, and search for upward mobility (Meyerowitz, *Women Adrift*, p. 16). A Children's Bureau study found that only 53% of the unmarried mothers in eighty-five maternity homes in thirty-nine urban areas in 1937 resided in the areas in which the agency was located ("Maternity Home Care during 1937," *Child* 2 [June 1938, supplement]: 3).
10. James Mohr documents a "dramatic surge of abortion in the United States after 1840" and reveals abortion to have been a "widespread social phenomenon" into the 1870s. He detects a shift in the "social character of abortion" in the late nineteenth and early twentieth century, from middle-class married women who wished to control their fertility to "the poor, the socially desperate, and the unwed" (Mohr, *Abortion in America*, pp. 46, 240). See also D'Emilio and Freedman, *Intimate Matters*, pp. 253–54.
11. Robinson, *Sexual Problems of To-Day*, p. 157.
12. Gillin, *Social Pathology*, p. 300.
13. O'Conner, "Baby or Abortion—Which?" pp. 99–100. See also Lesik, "Bachelor Mothers," p. 35.
14. Case file #1210002, Door of Hope, Jersey City, New Jersey, RG 14.5, SAARC.
15. Mary C. Tinney, "Illegitimacy," National Conference of Catholic Charities, *Proceedings* (1920): 104.

16. See Gillin, *Social Pathology*, p. 300; Kammerer, *Unmarried Mother*, p. 2; Groves, *Social Problems and Education*, p. 182.

17. Reagan, "'About to Meet Her Maker,'" pp. 1243–44. Interestingly, Reagan finds that when an unmarried woman died as the result of an abortion, her lover was often arrested and sometimes prosecuted as an accessory to the crime (Reagan, "'About to Meet Her Maker,'" pp. 1244–45, 1261).

18. Ibid., p. 1245.

19. Richard W. Wertz and Dorothy C. Wertz find that by 1939, half of all women and 75 percent of all urban women went to hospitals to have their babies (Wertz and Wertz, *Lying-In*, p. 133). See also Leavitt, *Brought to Bed*, chap. 7.

20. Dorothy Frances Puttee and Mary Ruth Colby found that 103 of 127 hospitals in Chicago in 1937 "report that they knowingly admit unmarried women," but noted that "of the 103, there are ten hospitals that, while stating a willingness to admit unmarried mothers, have likewise stated a preference to refuse them." Puttee and Colby also noted that "a few hospitals carried the bulk of the illegitimacy work in the city of Chicago" (Puttee and Colby, *Illegitimate Child in Illinois*, pp. 125, 127). Susan Ware finds that it cost sixty-five dollars to have a baby in a New York City hospital in 1935 (Ware, *Holding Their Own: American Women in the 1930s* [Boston: Twayne, 1982], p. 7).

21. See Fletcher, "The Problem of Illegitimacy in Pittsburgh," p. 244.

22. "Personals," *Denver Post*, October 18, 1942.

23. Linda Gordon writes that "the baby farming service resembled that offered by abortionists, and the fees were similar" (Gordon, *Heroes of Their Own Lives*, p. 45). Kate Waller Barrett wrote in 1903 that private lying-in homes charged about ten to twenty dollars per week (K. Barrett, "Shall Girls Who Are Able to Pay Be Received into Florence Crittenton Homes?" *Florence Crittenton Magazine* 5 [June 1903]: 143).

24. "Shall Girls Who Are Able to Pay Be Received into Florence Crittenton Homes?" p. 143.

25. Leader, *And No Birds Sing*, p. 244; "I Kept My Baby," *American Magazine* 130 (Aug. 1940): 27.

26. "Shall Girls Who Are Able to Pay Be Received into Florence Crittenton Homes?" pp. 141–42.

27. R. Barrett, *Care of the Unmarried Mother*, p. 51.

28. Kate Waller Barrett, quoted in R. Barrett, *Care of the Unmarried Mother*, p. 148. Undoubtedly, this flexibility varied from home to home. One young woman wrote to a social worker, "To be taken into the maternity home I must pay a dollar a day and $75 at the end of my confinement. My parents are barely making ends meet. . . . Yet I am repeatedly asked how much my family can contribute for my stay in the home" (Ruth F. Brenner, "What Facilities Are Essential to the Adequate Care of the Unmarried Mother?" NCSW, *Proceedings* [1942]: 433).

29. Florence Crittenton League of Compassion, Boston, Massachusetts, pamphlet, 1925, p. 4, FCL.

30. The Chicago Crittenton home, for example, publicized a fee of fifty dollars to cover the entire cost of care regardless of how long the woman remained in the home, but did not take fees from unmarried mothers from Chicago. (See Lillian Ripple, "Facilities for the Care of the Unmarried Mother and Her Child in Chicago," Department of Statistics and Research, Council of Social Agencies of Chicago, 1942, p. 42, Box 53, Folder 42, UCC.) A 1927 study of illegitimacy in Connecticut found that in 33% of the cases, the expenses of confinement in a maternity home were assumed by the unmarried mother herself, and in 25% of the cases, the unmarried mother's parents or relative paid the bill. In 22% of the cases, the putative father paid for confinement costs, and in 20% of the cases, the city, town, or some charitable institution took care of the expenses (*Study of Children Born out of Wedlock in Connecticut*, p. 36).

31. Annie Lee Davis, "Attitudes toward Minority Groups and Their Effect on Social Services for Unmarried Mothers," p. 9, unpub. ms., 1948, Box 122, KFH.

32. Salvation Army homes seemed more inclined than Crittenton homes to accept African-American women. A United Charities of Chicago study found that the Salvation Army Booth Memorial Home "is the only one making regular provision for Negroes, serving a maximum of eight and an average of six" ("Unmarried Mother Study: Major Findings," 1942, p. 3, Box 52, Folder 3, UCC). Marian Morton finds that the Salvation Army Rescue Home in Cleveland "routinely took black women, the only Cleveland home to do so" (Morton, "'Go and Sin No More,'" p. 132). Maternity home services to African-American women remained scarce into the early 1960s. See Solinger, *Wake Up Little Susie*, pp. 50–51.

33. Margaret Bovil to Emma Lundberg, January 25, 1919, Box 68, Fol. 7-4-4-0, CB.

34. R. Barrett, *Care of the Unmarried Mother*, pp. 8–9. See also John O'Grady, "Ethical Aspects of Illegitimacy," *Catholic Charities Review* 11 (Jan. 1927): 15; Hilda Hertz and Sue Warren Little, "Unmarried Negro Mothers," p. 78; Reed, *Negro Illegitimacy*, p. 110.

35. E. Smith, "Study of Twenty-Five Adolescent Unmarried Mothers in New York City," p. 45.

36. Ibid.

37. Ibid., p. 54. Smith found that "seven out of the ten colored girls studied made a distinction between the attitude of the colored and the white people in regard to unmarried motherhood, and consequently those seven colored girls did not consider motherhood out of wedlock disgraceful" (p. 63).

38. Ibid. Few early-twentieth-century commentators noted the irony of judging a "colored attitude" toward illegitimacy when African-Americans' history of legally sanctioned marriages was only several decades old.

39. Admissions Policy, 1922, Door of Hope, Jersey City, New Jersey, RG 14.5, SAARC.

40. Haven's Fund Report, 1948, p. 1, Box 125, KFH.

41. Ibid. See also Haven's Fund Report, 1952, Box 125, KFH.

42. H. Edwina Connell, Family and Children's Society of Montclair, New Jersey, to Miss P. Kelly, February 13, 1947, "Correspondence—Inquiries for Admission," Box 125, KFH.

43. Smith, "Study of Twenty-Five Adolescent Unmarried Mothers," p. 43.

44. See case files #1330092, #1320091, Door of Hope, Jersey City, New Jersey, RG 14.5, SAARC.

45. Case file #1350097, Door of Hope, Jersey City, New Jersey, RG 14.5, SAARC.

46. *Study of Children Born out of Wedlock in Connecticut*, p. 12. Women were referred to the Jersey City Door of Hope by many local social welfare agencies, including the Social Service Bureau, the Church Mission of Help, the Charity Organization Society, the Jewish Child Guidance Center, the Special Service Bureau, and the Children's Aid and Protective Society. See case files, Door of Hope, Jersey City, New Jersey, RG 14.5, SAARC.

47. "I Was an Unmarried Mother," *True Story* 35 (Sept. 1936): 22. See also "Results of Magazine Publicity," *Florence Crittenton Bulletin* 12 (Jan. 1937): 8. In 1926, seven years after its first publication, *True Story* magazine reached over 2 million readers (Theodore Paterson, *Magazines in the Twentieth Century* [Urbana: University of Illinois Press, 1964], p. 300.

48. See Robert South Barrett to Colonel Milton Ochs, October 6, 1936, Box 8, Folder 86, NFCM.

49. "Results of Magazine Publicity," p. 8. The Crittenton article was so successful that Dr. Valeria Parker began to run a monthly column in *True Story* that was devoted to directing unmarried mothers to homes and services near them. Although the Children's Bureau was initially wary of appealing to unmarried mothers through a popular magazine, Morlock concluded that "my own opinion is that Dr. Parker is reaching many girls who at this stage of social work development would not be reached in any other way" (Maud Morlock to Lucille Cairns, August 14, 1942, Box 176, Fol. 7-4-3-1-4, CB). The Children's Bureau arranged for Dr. Parker to send the letters to them, and an officer from the bureau replied to the unmarried mothers. See Morlock, "Letters from Unmarried Mothers—What Answer?" December 29, 1941, Box 208, Folder 4, WC.

50. Virginia Reid, "Black Market Babies," *Woman's Home Companion* 71 (Dec. 1944): 30–31.

51. Letter to Maud Morlock, December 16, 1944, Box 176, Fol. 7-4-3-1-4, CB.

52. Letter to Maud Morlock, November 21, 1944, Box 176, Fol. 7-4-3-1-4, CB.

53. Joan Younger, "The Unwed Mother," *Ladies' Home Journal* 64 (June 1947): 105.

54. Jersey City Door of Hope residents between 1920 and 1945, for example, averaged around 20 years old, but ranged in age from 12 to 39, with a sizable minority under 17 and over 25. The quantitative information on unmarried mothers from the Jersey City Door of Hope used in this chapter was calculated from a systematic sample of 500 cases, drawn from 1,500 cases from the years

between 1922 and 1945. On the age of unmarried mothers, see Parker, *"Follow-Up Study of 550 Illegitimacy Applications,* p. 22; Bingham, "Determinants of Sex Delinquency," p. 25; Watson, "Philadelphia's Problem," p. 46; Reed, *Social and Health Care of the Illegitimate Family,* pp. 20–24; Trounstine, "Illegitimacy in Cincinnati," pp. 194–95; *Study of Children Born out of Wedlock in Connecticut,* p. 5; Reed, *Negro Illegitimacy,* p. 21.

55. The list of jobs held by unmarried mothers before coming to the Door of Hope reflected those available to working-class women generally. Shifts in the occupations reported by unmarried mothers in maternity homes from the early to the mid-twentieth century reflected larger changes in occupational opportunities for women. Many investigators noted the preponderance of unmarried mothers in domestic service in the late nineteenth and early twentieth centuries. In the 1920s, while unmarried mothers continued to report jobs as domestics and factory operatives, many began to come from jobs in offices and stores, reflecting the shift to clerical and service work for white women in this period. On the employment backgrounds of unmarried mothers, see *Study of Children Born out of Wedlock in Connecticut,* p. 6; Puttee and Colby, *Illegitimate Child in Illinois,* pp. 99–100; U.S. Children's Bureau, "Illegitimacy as a Child-Welfare Problem," Part 2, p. 46; Watson, "Philadelphia's Problem," p. 52; Guibord and Parker, *What Becomes of the Unmarried Mother?* p. 27; Maxfield, "The Social Treatment of Unmarried Mothers," p. 212; Trounstine, "Illegitimacy in Cincinnati," p. 195; Parker, "A Follow-Up Study," pp. 30–31. The growing middle-class clientele in the 1940s will be discussed more fully in chapter 6.

56. Thirteen percent of the residents of the Jersey City Door of Hope between 1922 and 1945 had graduated from high school. A little more than half (59%) had less than a ninth-grade education. Less than a third (29%) had some high school education, and 4% had attended some college.

57. Sixty-seven percent of the women at the Door of Hope claimed to live with parents or relatives, and 13% either boarded, lived with friends, or lived alone. The remainder lived with employers, with men they were involved with, or in institutions or foster homes.

58. "Door of Hope Home and Hospital Brief," n.d., n.p., RG 14.5, SAARC. On religious affiliation of unmarried mothers in New York City in 1932 see Reed, *Social and Health Care,* pp. 34–36. Homes in areas where Catholic, Jewish, and Episcopal organizations sponsored their own homes may have been more religiously homogeneous.

59. The number of Italian unmarried mothers may surprise historians who have noted the conservative cultural traditions regulating Italian women's familial roles and curtailing their social participation, especially with regard to courtship. Yet their numbers seem to bear out historian Kathy Peiss's observation that "even in Italian families, young women carved out spaces in their lives for privacy, independence, and unsupervised social interaction" (Peiss, *Cheap Amusements,* p. 70).

60. Letter from judge, Juvenile Court, Bergen, New Jersey, included in case file #1320091, Door of Hope, Jersey City, New Jersey, RG 14.5, SAARC.

61. Marie Hibbard to Major Duffey, case file #122002, Door of Hope, Jersey City, New Jersey, RG 14.5, SAARC.

62. See case files #1230079, #1260080, #1250081, #1250019, #1400103, Door of Hope, Jersey City, New Jersey, RG 14.5, SAARC.

63. My argument that maternity home culture was characterized as much by tension and conflict as by solidarity runs counter to that offered by Rickie Solinger, who contends that single pregnancy after 1945 was a "leveling experience" that rendered "status differences that had meaning and would have separated girls from each other . . . meaningless in the home" (Solinger, *Wake Up Little Susie*, p. 139). Our different arguments may in part be informed by the different periods we study—after 1945, maternity homes may have housed more homogeneous communities of single mothers—as well as by our respective sources. I suspect that case records are more likely to reveal conflict than other sources of maternity home culture, such as maternity home newsletters.

64. Case file #1450075, Door of Hope, Jersey City, New Jersey, RG 14.5, SAARC.

65. Case file #1430065, Door of Hope, Jersey City, New Jersey, RG 14.5, SAARC.

66. Case file #1430061, Door of Hope, Jersey City, New Jersey, RG 14.5, SAARC.

67. Elza Virginia Dahlgren, "Attitudes of a Group of Unmarried Mothers toward the Minnesota Three Months' Nursing Regulation and Its Application" (M.A. thesis, University of Minnesota, 1940), p. 108.

68. Case file #1390102, Door of Hope, Jersey City, New Jersey, RG 14.5, SAARC.

69. "Case Work Services for 1945," Box 127, KF.

70. "Correspondence—Inquiries for Admission," Katy Ferguson Home, Box 125, KFH.

71. "I Kept My Baby," p. 27.

72. I owe my understanding of this distinction between "roughness" and "respectability" as it operated in maternity homes to Sherri Broder. Drawing on Ellen Ross's study of respectability in pre–World War I working-class London neighborhoods, Broder finds that the distinction between "roughness" and "respectability" permeated relationships between unmarried mothers in the Sheltering Arms home in Gilded Age Philadelphia (Broder, "Politics of the Family: Political Culture, Moral Reform, and Family Relations in Gilded Age Philadelphia" [Ph.D. diss., Brown University, 1988], chap. 5).

73. Lucy Abbott to Robert South Barrett, February 5, 1939, Box 10, Folder 108, NFCM.

74. Letter to Mrs. Gail Bosworth, State Department of Social Welfare, Lansing, Michigan, May 28, 1943, Box 175, Fol. 7-4-3-1-1, CB.

75. "I Kept My Baby," p. 139. Rickie Solinger discusses what she terms "home culture" in postwar maternity homes in *Wake Up Little Susie*, pp. 134–44.

76. "Grateful Letters from 'Our Girls,'" *Florence Crittenton Bulletin* 5 (April 1930): 9.

77. Salvation Army officer Evelyn Skinner recalled that "the Army to me now is like my family. It's like a sisterhood" (Skinner, oral history, June 30, 1987, p. 88, Accession No. 88–18, SAARC). Kathy Peiss argues that "as middle-class women internalized the homosocial ordering of their world, defining their status and character in terms of it, they also sought to spread these ideas. . . to women of the laboring classes" (Peiss, *Cheap Amusements*, p. 7).

78. Kate Waller Barrett, letter addressed to "My Dear Girls," December 10, 1919, Box 3, Folder 4, KWB.

79. "A Refuge for the Erring: A Few Facts about the Salvation Army Rescue Home in New York," *Social News* 4 (Feb. 1914): 14.

80. Cowden, "Finds Hope for the Unfortunate Girl," p. 8.

81. "Romance in the Out of Love Club," p. 6.

82. Major John Milsaps, "Chicago Rescue and Maternity Home," *Social News* 2 (July 1912): 10.

83. Cowden, "Finds Hope for the Unfortunate Girl," p. 8.

84. "Romance in the Out of Love Club," p. 6.

85. Ibid. See also "A Refuge for the Erring," p. 14.

86. F. A., "My First Impressions and Adjustment at Lakeview," in Edlin, *The Unmarried Mother in Our Society*, p. 74.

87. Helen Welsh to Julia Lathrop, December 23, 1919, Box 68, Fol. 7-4-4-1, CB.

88. K. Barrett, *Some Practical Suggestions on the Conduct of a Rescue Home*, p. 17.

89. "In a Superintendent's Office," *Florence Crittenton Bulletin* 10 (Oct. 1935): 23.

90. "Essay Contest of Florence Crittenton Mission, Scranton, Pennsylvania," *Girls* 18 (March 1915): 52–53.

91. Rusty Brown, "Always Me," in *Long Time Passing: Lives of Older Lesbians*, ed. Marcy Adelman (Boston: Alyson Publications, 1986), p. 145.

92. Case file #1230005, Door of Hope, Jersey City, New Jersey, RG 14.5, SAARC. Historian James Mohr has found "some evidence that women shared abortifacient information with one another and assisted their friends in attempted self-abortions. . . . Female undergrounds, if that phrase does not stretch the notion too far, even eliminated literacy as a necessary prerequisite for practicing abortion" (Mohr, *Abortion in America*, pp. 106–07). The Door of Hope superintendent in 1946 suspected one woman of attempting to induce an abortion while a resident in the home. "I may be wrong," she wrote, "but I have an idea that Doris has tried to get rid of her baby. She says the baby is not alive so there is no use of her staying here. She roams around the house all during the night and has been found sitting on the cold tile floor in the shower room in the basement" (Case file #1460106, Door of Hope, Jersey City, New Jersey, RG 14.5, SAARC).

93. E. Smith, "Unmarried Mothers," p. 22.

94. Charles S. Birtwell to Mrs. Redfern, 1890, quoted in M. Smith, "Changing Emphases in Case Work with Unmarried Mothers," p. 311.

95. Baylor, "The Necessary Changes to Be Effected," p. 147.

96. Murphy, "Mothers and—Mothers," p. 175.

97. Reed, *Social and Health Care*, p. 56.

98. See, e.g., Meyerowitz, *Women Adrift;* Judith Smith, "Our Own Kind: Family and Community Networks in Providence," *Radical History Review* 27 (Spring 1978): 99–120; Ardis Cameron, "Bread and Roses Revisited: Women's Culture and Working-Class Activism in the Lawrence Strike of 1912," in *Women, Work, and Protest,* ed. Ruth Milkman (Boston: Routledge and Kegan Paul, 1985).

99. Case file #1370042, Door of Hope, Jersey City, New Jersey, RG 14.5, SAARC.

100. See, e.g., case file #1290023, Door of Hope, Jersey City, New Jersey, RG 14.5, SAARC; "Luella," March 1910, "Patient Histories," Booth Memorial Home and Hospital, Pittsburgh, PA, RG 14.8, SAARC.

101. Letter from resident to "Sweetheart," September 17, 1925, case files, Booth Memorial Home and Hospital, Des Moines, Iowa, RG 14.2, SAARC.

102. Superintendent's Report, April 4, 1898, Florence Crittenton Home, Norfolk, Virginia, Box 17, Fol. 60, FCS.

103. See George Chauncey, Jr., "From Sexual Inversion to Homosexuality: Medicine and the Changing Conceptualization of Female Deviance," *Salmagundi* 58–59 (Fall 1982–Winter 1983): 114–46; Nancy Sahli, "Smashing: Women's Relationships before the Fall," *Chrysalis* 8 (Summer 1979): 17–28.

104. K. Barrett, *Some Practical Suggestions*, pp. 10–11. Barrett's concern regarding same-sex relationships was part of a larger fear that focused on same-sex institutions, ranging from reformatories to women's colleges. For examples, see Margaret Otis, "A Perversion Not Commonly Noted," *Journal of Abnormal Psychology* 8 (1913): 113–16; Charles A. Ford, "Homosexual Practices of Institutionalized Females," *Journal of Abnormal Psychology* 23 (1929): 442–48.

105. Board minutes of the Chicago Florence Crittenton Anchorage, November 7, 1912, FCA.

106. Constitution of the NFCM, c. 1934, p. 1, Box 1, Folder 1, NFCM.

107. *Florence Crittenton Bulletin* 14 (Aug. 1939): 44.

108. Case file #1420058, Door of Hope, Jersey City, New Jersey, RG 14.5, SAARC.

109. Dahlgren, "Attitudes," p. 107.

110. Ibid.

111. Case file #1390100, Door of Hope, Jersey City, New Jersey, RG 14.5, SAARC.

112. Case file #1440074, Door of Hope, Jersey City, New Jersey, RG 14.5, SAARC.

113. Marie Winokur to Katherine Lenroot, n.d., Box 295, Fol. 7-4-4-1, CB.

114. "Message from the President," *Florence Crittenton Bulletin* 20 (Sept. 1945): 2.

115. Case file #1440105, Door of Hope, Jersey City, New Jersey, RG 14.5, SAARC.

116. Superintendent's Report, July 1898, Florence Crittenton Home, Norfolk, Virginia, Box 17, Fol. 60, FCS.

117. Superintendent's Report, May 8, 1898, Florence Crittenton Home, Norfolk, Virginia, Box 17, Fol. 60, FCS.

118. *Florence Crittenton Bulletin* 14 (Aug. 1939): 9.

119. On medical care provided to unmarried mothers in maternity homes, see George W. Kosmak, "Committee on Obstetrical Care of Unmarried Mothers," NCSW, *Proceedings* (1920), p. 116; U.S. Census Bureau, "Study of Maternity Homes in Minnesota and Pennsylvania," p. 3.

120. Case file #1460106, Door of Hope, Jersey City, New Jersey, RG 14.5, SAARC.

121. Case file #1370041, Door of Hope, Jersey City, New Jersey, RG 14.5, SAARC.

122. Case file #1370039, Door of Hope, Jersey City, New Jersey, RG 14.5, SAARC.

123. Case file #1440017, Door of Hope, Jersey City, New Jersey, RG 14.5, SAARC.

124. Case file #1290086, Door of Hope, Jersey City, New Jersey, RG 14.5, SAARC.

125. Door of Hope Home and Hospital Brief, 1943, n.p., Door of Hope, Jersey City, New Jersey, RG 14.5, SAARC.

126. "The Salvation Army Home and Hospital, Door of Hope," March 2, 1937, Door of Hope, Jersey City, New Jersey, RG 14.5, SAARC.

127. Quoted in Anne Cohn, "Survey of Services Given to Fifty Unmarried Mothers by the Jewish Board of Guardians" (M.S.S. thesis, Smith College School for Social Work, 1938), p. 50.

128. See Brenzel, *Daughters of the State;* Schlossman, *Love and the American Delinquent;* Mary Odem, "Single Mothers, Delinquent Daughters, and the Juvenile Court in Early Twentieth Century Los Angeles," *Journal of Social History* 25 (Fall 1991): 27–43.

129. Case file #1440072, Door of Hope, Jersey City, New Jersey, RG 14.5, SAARC.

130. Case file #1230007, Door of Hope, Jersey City, New Jersey, RG 14.5, SAARC.

131. Robert South Barrett to Mrs. Coleman, August 10, 1943, Box 8, Folder 92, NFCM. See also "Message from the President," *Florence Crittenton Bulletin* 17 (Oct. 1942).

132. Maud Morlock to Miss Wood, October 21, 1944, Box 173, Fol. 7-4-0-7-6, CB.

133. Morlock drew the connection between restrictive policies in maternity homes and "the number of empty beds" (Morlock to Alice B. Huling, Boston Council of Social Agencies, December 31, 1940, Box 746, Fol. 7-4-0-7-6, CB).

134. Mrs. J. E. Collier, "The Challenge of Present Day Conditions in Florence Crittenton Work," *Florence Crittenton Bulletin* 9 (July 1934): 18. Increasingly, the "modern" girl that maternity home workers were so eager to accommodate was also middle class. These changes initiated during World War II were probably intended, in part, to make maternity homes more attractive to middle-class girls and women who began to apply in greater numbers during and after the war. The shift to a middle-class maternity home clientele will be discussed in chapter 6.

135. Hester Brown to Robert South Barrett, October 17, 1942, Box 2, Folder 15, NFCM.

136. Edlin, *Unmarried Mother in Our Society*, p. 50.

137. Hanna, "Changing Care of Children," p. 166.

138. "The Residence Period in a Maternity Home," *Florence Crittenton Bulletin* 12 (Oct. 1937): 29.

139. "Message from the President," *Florence Crittenton Bulletin* 17 (Oct. 1942): 1.

140. Marion Baker Callsen to Robert South Barrett, September 30, 1942, Box 4, Folder 2, NFCM.

141. Ruth Pagen to Maud Morlock, August 10, 1944, Social Services—Homes and Hospitals collection, SAARC.

142. Martha M. Dore attributes these changes to professionalization and argues that local homes were moving away "from a traditional Crittenton ideology to embrace a professional social work approach to service delivery" (Dore, "Organizational Response to Environmental Change," p. 131). Not all homes could get away with defying the NFCM. In 1936, President Barrett announced that the Indianapolis home would no longer be allowed to use the Florence Crittenton name, since they had been "carrying out a policy that was not consistent with that of the National. One of the cardinal principles of Florence Crittenton work is that every effort should be made to keep mother and child together, and that the adoption of babies was the last recourse" ("Message from the President," *Florence Crittenton Bulletin* 11 [Jan. 1936]: 2).

143. Clarence R. Preston to Robert South Barrett, June 18, 1926, Box 6, Folder 59, NFCM.

CHAPTER 4 "PROBLEM GIRLS": DOCILITY AND DISSIDENCE IN MATERNITY HOMES

1. Quoted in Edlin, *Unmarried Mother in Our Society*, p. 69.

2. "Essay Contest of the Florence Crittenton Mission, Scranton, Pennsylvania," p. 53.

3. Ibid., p. 52.

4. See, e.g., Elizabeth Stuart Phelps, *Hedged In* (Boston: Fields, Osgood, 1870); Edgar Fawcett, *The Evil That Men Do* (New York: Belford Co., 1889).

5. T. M., "What Lakeview Means to Me," in Edlin, *Unmarried Mother in Our Society*, pp. 74–75.

6. *Madeleine: An Autobiography* (New York: Persea Books, 1986), p. 30.

7. Quoted in Edlin, *Unmarried Mother in Our Society*, pp. 67–68. See Solinger, *Wake Up Little Susie*, p. 134.

8. Younger, "Unwed Mother," p. 105.

9. Dahlgren, "Attitudes," p. 11.

10. Case file #1350033, Door of Hope, Jersey City, New Jersey, RG 14.5, SAARC.

11. "A Mother" to Grace Abbott, February 14, 1928, Box 295, Fol. 7-4-4-1, CB, NA.

12. Younger, "Unwed Mother," p. 105.

13. Edlin, *Unmarried Mother in Our Society*, p. 53.

14. Evangeline Booth, "Rescue Work: Our Part in the Struggle for Purity," pp. 8–9. Peggy Pascoe discusses the relationship between rescue home matrons and inmates in *Relations of Rescue*, pp. 100–111.

15. J. B., "Living and Learning at Lakeview," in Edlin, *Unmarried Mother in Our Society*, pp. 75–76.

16. Quoted in Edlin, *Unmarried Mother in Our Society*, p. 67.

17. Dahlgren, "Attitudes," p. 107.

18. Letter to Major, November 27, 1925, case files, Booth Memorial Home and Hospital, Des Moines, Iowa, RG 14.2, SAARC.

19. Florence Crittenton League, New York City, *Annual Report* (1917): 10.

20. "A Florence Crittenton Girl Who Was Given a Chance and Made Good" to Mrs. Collier, February 22, 1933, Box 4, Folder 31, NFCM.

21. Brenner, "What Facilities Are Essential?" p. 430.

22. Case file #1390044, Door of Hope, Jersey City, New Jersey, RG 14.5, SAARC.

23. Quoted in Preston, "Good Care of Unmarried Mothers," p. 98.

24. Superintendent's Report, Nov. 1904, Florence Crittenton Home, Norfolk, Virginia, Box 18, Fol. 2, FCS.

25. Case file #1440073, Door of Hope, Jersey City, New Jersey, RG 14.5, SAARC.

26. Case file #1450064, Door of Hope, Jersey City, New Jersey, RG 14.5, SAARC.

27. Case file #1400050, Door of Hope, Jersey City, New Jersey, RG 14.5, SAARC. See also case files #1390044, #1410052, #1360035; "Florence Crittenton Work in Texas," *Girls* 12 (Oct. 1909): 226.

28. Case file #1230006, Door of Hope, Jersey City, New Jersey, RG 14.5, SAARC.

29. Case file #1340030, Door of Hope, Jersey City, New Jersey, RG 14.5, SAARC.

30. Case file #1370039, Door of Hope, Jersey City, New Jersey, RG 14.5, SAARC.

31. Case file #1450078, Door of Hope, Jersey City, New Jersey, RG 14.5, SAARC; case files, 1910, Booth Memorial Hospital, Pittsburgh, Pennsylvania, RG 14.8, SAARC.

32. Matron's Report, Detroit Florence Crittenton Home, NFCM, *Annual Report* (1925): 95.

33. Case file #1400047, Door of Hope, Jersey City, New Jersey, RG 14.5, SAARC.

34. Interview with Agnes Wright Dickinson, conducted by Christine Simmons, July 28, 1982, p. 41.

35. Louise K. Trout, "Services to Unmarried Mothers," *Child Welfare* 35 (Feb. 1956): 24.

36. Case file #1400048, Door of Hope, Jersey City, New Jersey, RG 14.5, SAARC.

37. Edna B. Waugh, Warren County Board of Supervisors, Child Welfare Service to Major Bartlett, November 21, 1939, in case file #1390045, Door of Hope, Jersey City, New Jersey, RG 14.5, SAARC.

38. Case file #1450078, Door of Hope, Jersey City, New Jersey, RG 14.5, SAARC.

39. Case file #1410054, Door of Hope, Jersey City, New Jersey, RG 14.5, SAARC.

40. Case file #1440071, Door of Hope, Jersey City, New Jersey, RG 14.5, SAARC.

41. Quoted in Edlin, *Unmarried Mother in Our Society*, p. 69.

42. Case file #1440069, Door of Hope, Jersey City, New Jersey, RG 14.5, SAARC. Pauline Leader complained about the library in the home in which she was a resident: "There were no books here; only the books, pollyannaish in tone, that nobody read" (Leader, *And No Birds Sing*, p. 262). On the popularity of confessional magazines in the early twentieth century, see Russel Nye, *The*

Unembarrassed Muse: The Popular Arts in America (New York: Dial Press, 1970), pp. 210–15; Meyerowitz, *Women Adrift*, p. 133.

43. Matron's Report, Detroit Florence Crittenton Home, NFCM, *Annual Report* (1925), p. 95.

44. Ibid.

45. Case of Dorothy, February 1, 1942, p. 3, Box 1, Folder 3, Dorothy Hutchinson papers, Columbia University Archives.

46. Case file #1390101, Door of Hope, Jersey City, New Jersey, RG 14.5, SAARC.

47. See, e.g., case files #1350096, #1290024, #1260018, #1250014, #1250012, Door of Hope, Jersey City, New Jersey, RG 14.5, SAARC.

48. President's Report, March 15, 1897, p. 2, Box 17, Fol. 41, Florence Crittenton Home, Norfolk, Virginia, FCS.

49. Superintendent's Report, July 1898, Florence Crittenton Home, Norfolk, Virginia, Box 17, Fol. 60, FCS.

50. Dahlgren, "Attitudes," p. 108. The unmarried mothers in Dahlgren's study were compelled by Minnesota law to stay in maternity homes three months after delivery. Known as the "Three-Month Nursing Regulation," this law was justified in part by the value of breast milk to the infant. Dahlgren documents a remarkable act of resistance in maternity homes, however, in which unmarried mothers refused to consume liquids, "thereby actually showing a disapproval of their refusal to nurse the child" (Dahlgren, "Attitudes," p. 99).

51. Case file #1410056, Door of Hope, Jersey City, New Jersey, RG 14.5, SAARC.

52. Case file #1340031, Door of Hope, Jersey City, New Jersey, RG 14.5, SAARC.

53. Common in many homes, escape was well-documented in the Door of Hope case records. See, e.g., case files #1360036, #1350034, #1250013, #1340031, #1250012, #1240010, #1440074, #1300088, Door of Hope, Jersey City, New Jersey, RG 14.5, SAARC.

54. Case file #1440074, Door of Hope, Jersey City, New Jersey, RG 14.5, SAARC.

55. "Their Freedom Was Brief," *Arkansas Democrat*, August 29, 1941, clipping in Box 5, Folder 35, NFCM.

56. Mrs. Reubye Edwards to Robert South Barrett, September 10, 1941, Box 5, Folder 35, NFCM.

57. Hester Brown to Reba Barrett Smith, March 15, 1942, Box 2, Folder 15, NFCM.

58. Case file #1410055, Door of Hope, Jersey City, New Jersey, RG 14.5, SAARC.

59. Russell Cooper, director, Florence Crittenton Home, Phoenix, Arizona, to NFCM, March 19, 1937, Box 4, Folder 31, NFCM.

60. Clarke, *Story of an Invisible Institution*, p. 5.

61. Younger, "Unwed Mother," p. 105.

62. Case file #1360036, Door of Hope, Jersey City, New Jersey, RG 14.5, SAARC.

63. Murphy, "Unmarried Mother at Work," p. 642.

64. Case file #1360038, Door of Hope, Jersey City, New Jersey, RG 14.5, SAARC.

65. Case file #1410051, Door of Hope, Jersey City, New Jersey, RG 14.5, SAARC.
66. Reed, *Negro Illegitimacy*, p. 55. Peggy Pascoe discusses the placement of rescue home inmates in domestic service in *Relations of Rescue*, pp. 166–71.
67. Baylor, "The Necessary Changes to Be Effected," p. 146.
68. Cohn, "Survey of Services," p. 53.
69. This argument is informed by recent efforts by historians to engage theoretical questions about the ways in which identities are socially constructed and to explore the relationship between the material and the discursive. Joan Scott has considered these questions most directly, writing that "treating the emergence of a new identity as a discursive event is not to introduce a new form of linguistic determination, nor to deprive subjects of agency. It is to refuse a separation between 'experience' and language and to insist instead on the productive quality of discourse. Subjects are constituted discursively, but there are conflicts among discursive systems, contradictions within any one of them, multiple meanings possible for the concepts they deploy." She moves further to ask that historians focus on "processes of identity production, insisting on the discursive nature of 'experience' and on the politics of its construction" (Scott, "Evidence of Experience," pp. 793, 797). See also Smith-Rosenberg, *Disorderly Conduct;* Walkowitz, *City of Dreadful Delight;* Jennifer Terry, "Theorizing Deviant Historiography," *Differences* 3 (Summer 1991): 55–74; Esther Newton, "The Mythic Mannish Lesbian: Radclyffe Hall and the New Woman," *Signs* 9 (Summer 1984): 557–75; Hayden White, "The Value of Narrativity in the Representation of Reality," in *On Narrative*, ed. W. J. T. Mitchell (Chicago: University of Chicago Press, 1988), pp. 1–23.
70. This argument draws on Foucault's observation of confession as "the general standard governing the production of the true discourse on sex," and the widening of its domain from a ritualized and localized practice to one "employed in a whole series of relationships: children and parents, students and educators, parents and psychiatrists, delinquents and experts" (Foucault, *The History of Sexuality*, vol. 1, *An Introduction*, trans. Robert Hurley [New York: Random House, 1978], p. 63).
71. Letter to Maud Morlock, March 8, 1944, Box 176, Folder 7-4-3-2-1, CB.
72. Case file #1250017, Door of Hope, Jersey City, New Jersey, RG 14.5, SAARC.
73. Case file #1320028, Door of Hope, Jersey City, New Jersey, RG 14.5, SAARC.
74. Case file #1260019, Door of Hope, Jersey City, New Jersey, RG 14.5, SAARC.
75. Minutes of the Section on Illegitimacy of the Child Welfare Division of the Chicago Council of Social Agencies, March 8, 1928, Box 207, Folder 1, WC. Anna Clark finds that unmarried mothers who applied for admittance to the Foundling Hospital in the early nineteenth century invoked the melodramatic image "of the innocent maiden who *always* faints when ravished." Clark argues that "if a woman admitted she had been raped she revealed her loss of the sexual innocence so prized in the early nineteenth-century feminine soul, but if she

claimed she fainted, she retained this blissful ignorance and avoided the necessity of describing a confusing and painful experience" (Clark, *Women's Silence, Men's Violence,* pp. 81–82).

76. Case file #1420057, Door of Hope, Jersey City, New Jersey, RG 14.5, SAARC.

77. In her study of prostitution in Victorian England, Judith Walkowitz finds that "certain segments of the working class had also internalized the values of social purity in the late nineteenth century. Thousands of respectable workingmen were recruited into white-cross armies throughout the nation and dedicated themselves to promoting the single standard of chastity and attacking public and private vice" (Walkowitz, *Prostitution and Victorian Society,* p. 253).

78. Unmarried mothers who prized respectability did not necessarily imbibe the middle-class version that permeated maternity homes. As historian Ellen Ross argues, "Among the working class, 'respectability' was not a filtered down version of its bourgeois form, but a fluid and variable idea. The contrast between working-class and middle-class definitions of respectability, of course, reflects great class differences in income and life situation, but also working-class culture's capacity for reorganizing and transforming concepts from the dominant culture" (Ross, "'Not the Sort that Would Sit on the Doorstep'").

79. Helen W. Papashvily discusses popular seduction novels written by American women in the nineteenth century in *All the Happy Endings* (New York: Harper and Row, 1951). See also Nye, *Unembarrassed Muse,* pp. 25–29.

80. Charlotte Henry, "Objectives in Work with Unmarried Mothers," *Family* 14 (May 1933): 76.

81. Thomas, *Unadjusted Girl,* pp. 125–26.

82. "Results of Magazine Publicity," p. 8. Historian Michael Denning offers some suggestions as to how to interpret the different meanings of seduction and abandonment narratives in dime novels, in *Mechanic Accents,* pp. 93–99, 190–92. See also Jochen Schulte-Sasse, "Can the Dispossessed Read Mass-Produced Narratives in Their Own Voice?" *Cultural Critique* no. 10 (Fall 1988): 171–99.

83. Frazier, *Negro Family in the United States,* p. 264.

84. "The Story of a Repentant Woman," *True Romances* 1 (Oct. 1923): 46.

85. "The Price of Silence," *True Story* 10 (April 1924): 57.

86. "The Baby I Never Saw," *True Romances* 30 (Jan. 1940): 25.

87. "When Passion Misleads," *True Romances* 25 (May 1937): 45.

88. These stories appeared in *True Romances* 2 (Sept. 1924).

89. Case of Maria, March 1, 1943, p. 2, Box 1, Folder 3, Dorothy Hutchinson papers, Columbia University Archives.

90. Thomas, *Unadjusted Girl,* pp. 125–26.

91. Kammerer, *Unmarried Mother,* p. 222.

92. Frances Q. Holsopple, "Social Non-Conformity: An Analysis of Four Hundred and Twenty Cases of Delinquent Girls and Women" (Ph.D. diss., University of Pennsylvania, 1919), p. 36.

93. Case file #1320029, Door of Hope, Jersey City, New Jersey, RG 14.5, SAARC.

94. Reed, *Negro Illegitimacy*, pp. 114–15.

95. Case file #1340095, Door of Hope, Jersey City, New Jersey, RG 14.5, SAARC.

96. Cohn, "Survey of Services," p. 53.

97. Mrs. Emma Booth Tucker, "Rules and Regulations for Rescue Officers," 1897? Pamphlet collection, SAARC. See also W. Bramwell Booth, *Orders and Regulations*, p. 287.

98. At the Jersey City Door of Hope, 45% of the unmarried mothers who stayed in the home between 1922 and 1945 claimed that the father of their child had promised to marry them.

99. Reed, *Negro Illegitimacy*, p. 98.

100. Miss Elsie Lynton to Reba Barrett Smith, November 17, 1939, Box 10, Folder 108, NFCM.

101. It was not, however, risk-free. Christine Stansell describes earlier courtship patterns and the potential for danger that they held for women: "Courtship was one part of a system of barter between the sexes in which a woman traded sexual favors for a man's promise to marry. Premarital intercourse then became a token of betrothal. This was, however, a problematic exchange for the woman, since she delivered on her part of the bargain—and risked pregnancy—before the man came through with his" (Stansell, *City of Women*, p. 87). See also Clark, "Politics of Seduction," pp. 53–54; Clark, *Women's Silence, Men's Violence*, p. 86; Hobson, *Uneasy Virtue*, p. 59; Fairchilds, "Female Sexual Attitudes," pp. 641–42.

102. See Lunbeck, "'A New Generation of Women,'" p. 521; Peiss, *Cheap Amusements;* Stansell, *City of Women*, p. 189.

103. Case file #1260083, Door of Hope, Jersey City, New Jersey, RG 14.5, SAARC.

104. Case of Rachael, 1942, p. 2, Box 2, Folder 18, Dorothy Hutchinson papers, Columbia University Archives.

105. Cohn, "Survey of Services," p. 56.

106. Case file #1240008, Door of Hope, Jersey City, New Jersey, RG 14.5, SAARC. Linda Gordon argues that social workers who first cited cases of incest as "too revolting to publish" and later labeled victims of incest "sex delinquents" were complicit in maintaining this silence (Gordon, *Heroes of Their Own Lives*, p. 215).

107. Walkowitz, *City of Dreadful Delight*, p. 114.

108. Thomas, *Unadjusted Girl*, pp. 125–26. Many investigators linked "treating" and out-of-wedlock pregnancy. See Kammerer, *Unmarried Mother*, chap. 5; Groves, *Social Problems and Education*, p. 198; Howard Moore, *Care of Illegitimate Children in Chicago*, p. 27; Queen and Mann, *Social Pathology*, p. 165; Bingham, "Determinants of Sex Delinquency," pp. 24–25.

109. Smith, "Study of Twenty-Five Adolescent Unmarried Mothers," p. 42.

110. Case of Jean, pp. 3–4, 1939, Box 208, Folder 1, WC.

111. Meyerowitz, *Women Adrift*, p. xxiii; chap. 5.

112. Smith, "Study of Twenty-Five Adolescent Unmarried Mothers," p. 53.

113. Included in the 21% are women who reported meeting men at dances, movie theaters, amusement parks, skating rinks, nightclubs and bars, the beach, and on the street.

114. Case file #1290025, Door of Hope, Jersey City, New Jersey, RG 14.5, SAARC.

115. Smith and Cabot, "A Study in Sexual Morality," p. 540.

116. Reed, *Negro Illegitimacy*, pp. 88–89.

117. *Study of Children Born out of Wedlock in Connecticut*, pp. 5–6.

118. Quoted in Smith, "Study of Twenty-Five Adolescent Unmarried Mothers," p. 49.

119. Case of Marjorie, July 26, 1946, p. 1, Box 1, Folder 3, Dorothy Hutchinson papers, Columbia University Archives.

120. These findings on unmarried mothers support those historians who argue that the early-twentieth-century change in sexual mores, rather than being a postwar middle-class phenomenon, was forged by young urban working-class women, who set the patterns that middle-class women later followed and "helped chart the modern sexual terrain" (Meyerowitz, *Women Adrift*, p. 116.) See also Peiss, *Cheap Amusements;* Lunbeck, "'A New Generation of Women'"; John Modell, "Dating Becomes the Way of American Youth," in *Essays on the Family and Historical Change*, ed. Leslie P. Moch and Gary D. Stark (College Station: Texas A. and M. University Press, 1983), pp. 91–126.

121. Laughlin, "Condemned Mothers and Babies," p. 234.

122. R. Barrett, *Care of the Unmarried Mother*, p. 37.

123. Case presented to the Committee on the Study of Illegitimacy, April 12, 1939, Box 208, Folder 1, WC.

124. Case of Mary, August 18, 1943, p. 5, Box 1, Folder 3, Dorothy Hutchinson papers, Columbia University.

125. Edlin, *Unmarried Mother in Our Society*, p. 38.

126. R. Barrett, *Care of the Unmarried Mother*, p. 36.

127. Younger, "The Unwed Mother," p. 45.

128. Letter to Maud Morlock, November 22, 1944, Box 176, Fol. 7-4-3-1-4, CB.

129. Kammerer, *Unmarried Mother*, p. 114.

130. Case file #1360036, Door of Hope, Jersey City, New Jersey, RG 14.5, SAARC.

131. Younger, "Unwed Mother," p. 44.

132. Smith, "Study of Twenty-Five Adolescent Unmarried Mothers," p. 25.

133. "Superintendent's Report," Boston Florence Crittenton League of Compassion, *Annual Report* (1915): 13.

134. Florence Crittenton Anchorage, Chicago, *Annual Report* (1920): 3; K. Barrett, *Some Practical Suggestions*, p. 28.

135. Case presented to the Committee on the Study of Illegitimacy, April 12, 1939, Box 208, Folder 1, WC.

136. Linda Gordon has most thoroughly theorized social control and complicated and criticized arguments based on it in "Family Violence, Feminism, and Social Control"; See also Pascoe, *Relations of Rescue;* Meyerowitz, *Women Adrift;*

Lunbeck, "'A New Generation of Women'"; Walter I. Trattner, ed., *Social Welfare or Social Control? Some Historical Reflections on* Regulating the Poor (Knoxville, Tenn.: University of Tennessee Press, 1983).

CHAPTER 5 "CASE WORKERS HAVE BECOME NECESSITIES"

1. Clara E. Marshall, "Unused Power in Florence Crittenton Homes," *Florence Crittenton Bulletin* 12 (Oct. 1937): 16.
2. Murphy, "What Can be Accomplished through Good Social Work in the Field of Illegitimacy?" p. 130.
3. Anita Robb, oral history conducted by Nikki Tanner, p. 140, Accession No. 88-13, SAARC.
4. "The National Conference of Florence Crittenton Workers at Boston," *Girls* 14 (May 1911): 33.
5. Muncy, *Creating a Female Dominion in American Reform*, p. 38. Muncy argues that the Children's Bureau headed what she terms the "child welfare dominion" in the 1920s, an institutional nexus dominated by women from both voluntary and professional organizations. See also Nancy Pottisman Weiss, "Save the Children: A History of the Children's Bureau, 1903–1918" (Ph.D. diss., UCLA, 1974); Louis Covotsos, "Child Welfare and Social Progress: A History of the U.S. Children's Bureau, 1912–1935" (Ph.D. diss., University of Chicago, 1976); Parker and Carpenter, "Julia Lathrop and the Children's Bureau"; Rosenthal, "The Children's Bureau and the Juvenile Court"; James A. Tobey, *The Children's Bureau: Its History, Activities, and Organizations* (Baltimore: Johns Hopkins University Press, 1925).
6. See U.S. Children's Bureau, *Infant Mortality: Results of a Field Study in Johnstown, Pa., Based on Births in One Year*, Pub. No. 9 (Washington, D.C.: Government Printing Office, 1915). On Children's Bureau investigations on infant mortality, see Parker and Carpenter, "Julia Lathrop and the Children's Bureau," p. 63; Bremner, *From the Depths*, pp. 158–59; Abbott, "Ten Years' Work for Children," p. 191; Richard A. Meckel, *Save the Babies: American Public Health Reform and the Prevention of Infant Mortality, 1850 to 1929* (Baltimore: Johns Hopkins University Press, 1990).
7. June Hill to Ethel Waters, May 5, 1923, Box 60, Fol. 20-66-5, CB.
8. U.S. Children's Bureau, "Illegitimacy as a Child-Welfare Problem," Part 3, p. 1. In her survey of illegitimacy in Philadelphia, Children's Bureau investigator Amey Watson stated that her primary purpose was "to put before the social agencies . . . a standard of diagnosis and treatment," and "second, to provide a scientific basis for comparing Philadelphia's problem with the work of other cities" (Watson, "Philadelphia's Problem and the Development of Standards of Care," in U.S. Children's Bureau, "Illegitimacy as a Child Welfare Problem," Part 3, p. 17).
9. A. Madorah Donahue to Ethel Waters, July 15, 1924, Box 60, Fol. 20-66-5, CB.

10. June Hull to Ethel Waters, June 4, 1923, Box 60, Fol. 20-66-5, CB.

11. Trolander, *Settlement Houses and the Great Depression*, p. 59. Historian Michael Sedlak draws attention to the importance of the major shift in the way private welfare services were funded to the professionalization of those agencies, and specifically to Florence Crittenton Homes, in "Young Women and the City," p. 13. See also Aiken, "The National Florence Crittenton Mission," p. 198.

12. Whittemore, *Mother Whittemore's Records*, p. 48.

13. "Report from Spokane, Washington, Florence Crittenton Home," *Girls* 12 (Oct. 1909): 245; "Report from New Haven Florence Crittenton Home," *Florence Crittenton Magazine* 8 (July 1906): 672. See also Claudia Tharin, "How to Get City Appropriations," *Florence Crittenton Magazine* 2 (1900): 60–61; Tharin, "Why Should the Florence Crittenton Home Receive Public Money?" *Florence Crittenton Magazine* 6 (July 1904): 220–21; "List of Florence Crittenton Homes Receiving Public Money, Per Annum," *Girls* 15 (1912): 126–28.

14. See, e.g., "Report from Spokane, Washington, Florence Crittenton Home," *Girls* 12 (Oct. 1909): 245–46.

15. Reba Barrett Smith to Martha Morgan, March 5, 1941, Box 10, Folder 105, NFCM.

16. "Report of the President," NFCM, *Biennial Report* (1922–24): 6.

17. "Door of Hope Home and Hospital Brief," M.S., 1937, n.p., RG 14.5, SAARC. The Door of Hope noted that in 1937 the $694.88 they received monthly from the Community Chest in addition to the $150 monthly from the divisional headquarters of the Salvation Army did not come close to meeting their monthly expenses, which totaled $1,960. Many maternity home workers were particularly galled by the suggestion of Chests to limit maternity home services to unmarried mothers from the local area to cut costs. See U.S. Children's Bureau, "The Nonresident Unmarried Mother," March 1941, Box 49, Folder 1, CWLA; Robert W. Kelso, "Problem of the Non-Resident Unmarried Mother," *Child Welfare League of America* 8 (Sept. 1929): 7–8; *Florence Crittenton Bulletin* 4 (Jan. 1929): 8.

18. Hester Brown to Robert South Barrett, June 10, 1941, Box 2, Folder 14, NFCM.

19. Although social work leaders were well represented among leaders of the federated charities movement and the Chests represented the interests of the social work establishment, not all social workers approved of the Chests. Daisy Lee Worthington Worcester, for example, chronicled the changes in social work in the 1920s when, "without a protest, the Community Chest was imposed upon them. With scarcely a murmur, they watched it reach the zenith of its power, boasting of a concerted war against want which it never seriously attempted, employing metaphors instead of measures, substituting a military technology for the fighting spirit of the social workers of an earlier day" (Worcester, *Grim the Battles*, p. 231).

20. Evelyn Skinner, oral history conducted by Nicki Tanner, June 30, 1987, p. 69, Accession No. 88–18, SAARC.

21. Judith Ann Trolander argues that the Chest served to inhibit "controversial" projects in settlement houses and to push the settlements toward more conservative goals, in *Settlement Houses and the Great Depression*.

22. Mrs. Ward Williams to Robert South Barrett, October 14, 1939, Box 5, Folder 35, NFCM.

23. Although President Barrett assured Crittenton workers that "despite bank closings, financial depressions, unemployment, and all the ills that seem to have settled on the American people, our work goes on unabated," the view from local maternity homes was more distressing ("Message from the President," *Florence Crittenton Bulletin* 8 [April 1933]: 1). See, e.g., "The Florence Crittenton Mission and Home in Kansas City, Missouri, Report," July 20, 1933, unpublished report, Box 7, Folder 65, NFCM. Evelyn Skinner recalled that matrons had to beg for food for some Salvation Army maternity homes (Skinner, oral history conducted by Nicki Tanner, June 30, 1987, p. 30, Accession No. 88-18, SAARC).

24. Mrs. Thomas E. Robertson, "How Can a Florence Crittenton Home Best Cooperate with the Community Chest?" *Florence Crittenton Bulletin* 10 (Oct. 1935): 45.

25. "Annual Report of the General Superintendent," *Florence Crittenton Bulletin* 12 (June 1937): 3.

26. Michael Sedlak provides an account of this conflict in "Young Women and the City."

27. See memo from Edwina M. Lewis, Chicago Council of Social Agencies, March 12, 1941, Box 318, Folder 5, WC.

28. Major A. E. Ramsdale to Edwina M. Lewis, November 13, 1937, Box 397, Folder 1, WC.

29. Smith, "Message from the General Superintendent," *Florence Crittenton Bulletin* 13 (May 1938): 3–4.

30. Memo from Edwina M. Lewis, November 1, 1940, Box 318, Folder 5, WC; Hester Brown to Robert South Barrett, March 3, 1942, Box 2, Folder 15, NFCM.

31. Minutes of Meeting with Edwina Lewis and Mrs. Eaton, June 19, 1940, Box 208, Folder 3, WC.

32. Minutes of Committee on Study of Illegitimacy, May 22, 1939, Box 208, Folder 1, WC.

33. Minutes of the Committee on the Referral Center, February 10, 1939, Box 208, Folder 1, WC. On the Referral Center, see Helen Renald and Frances H. Higgins, "A Description of the Development of a Referral Center for Unmarried Mothers," March 1942, Box 52, Folder 5, UCC.

34. *Florence Crittenton Bulletin* 10 (Oct. 1935): 58–59.

35. Gladys Revelle to Robert South Barrett, August 19, 1943, Box 2, Folder 11, NFCM.

36. Gladys Revelle to Hester Brown, December 12, 1940, Box 2, Folder 10, NFCM.

37. "Social Welfare: An Introductory Course Given by the Salvation Army," n.d., n.p., SAARC. See also Grace Mehling, "A Study of Salvation Army Principles and Practices Seen in Relation to Case Work" (M.A. thesis, New York School of Social Work, 1946), pp. 2–3. The eagerness of Crittenton and Salvation Army workers to jump on the bandwagon of professionalism clearly had more to do with external pressure than with a strong commitment to its ethos. Reba Barrett Smith pointed out to Crittenton workers that the very survival of their homes "depends upon our understanding of present day requirements and a willingness to become part of the existing program of social service" (Reba Barrett Smith to Martha Morgan, March 5, 1941, Box 10, Folder 105, NFCM).

38. NFCM, *Annual Report* (1923): 25.

39. "Superintendent's Report," Boston Florence Crittenton League of Compassion, *Annual Report* (1915): 8.

40. Hester Brown to Robert South Barrett and Reba Barrett Smith, August 20, 1940, Box 2, Folder 13, NFCM.

41. Minutes of Meeting with Mrs. Lewis and Mrs. Eaton, June 19, 1940, Box 208, Folder 3, WC.

42. *Florence Crittenton Bulletin* 9 (April 1934): 4.

43. Wilson, *Fifty Years' Work with Girls*, p. 74.

44. Ione Ross to Reba Barrett Smith, December 11, 1934, Box 9, Folder 101, NFCM.

45. Estelle Jewett to Reba Barrett Smith, December 5, 1939, Box 9, Folder 99, NFCM.

46. Reba Barrett Smith to Margaret Hinchliff, July 8, 1942, Box 9, Folder 103, NFCM.

47. Reba Barrett Smith to Mrs. Abbott, January 27, 1937, Box 8, Folder 96, NFCM.

48. Reba Barrett Smith to Eva Gore, March 3, 1936, Box 8, Folder 96, NFCM.

49. "Application for NFCM Training School," 1930, Box 9, Folder 100, NFCM; "Application for Employment in the NFCM," 1940, Box 9, Folder 103, NFCM.

50. Irene Hunter to Reba Barrett Smith, November 12, 1941, Box 9, Folder 104, NFCM.

51. Morlock, "Address," p. 3; Murphy, "Mothers and—Mothers," p. 172.

52. Puttee and Colby, *Illegitimate Child in Illinois*, p. 140.

53. "Discussion of Some Phases of Casework with Unmarried Mothers," prepared by the Committee on Problems Related to Unmarried Parenthood, Family Service Section, Division on Family and Child Welfare, Council of Social Agencies of Chicago, April 1941, pp. 16–17, Box 52, Folder 1, UCC.

54. Murphy, "Mothers and—Mothers," p. 172.

55. Reed, *Modern Family*, p. 141.

56. Yeo, *Inasmuch*, pp. 9–10; Mildred P. Carpenter, "Viewpoints on Maternity Home Care," CWLA, *Bulletin* 7 (March 1928): 8.

57. "Discussion of Some Phases of Case Work with Unmarried Mothers," p. 16. See

also U.S. Children's Bureau, *Maternity Homes for Unmarried Mothers*, p. 19; Brisley, "The Illegitimate Family and Specialized Treatment," p. 72; Watson, "Illegitimate Family," p. 110.

58. Catherine Mathews, "Case Work with Unmarried Mothers," *Family* 13 (Oct. 1932), p. 190.

59. "What Has the National Movement Done for the Homes?" *Florence Crittenton Magazine* 1 (March 1899): 6.

60. Reba Barrett Smith to Lena Cook, July 31, 1930, Box 8, Fol. 97, NFCM.

61. Salvation Army Home and Hospital, New York City, General Report and Statements of Account, 1925, p. 6, SAARC.

62. "The Maternity Home: How It Is Operated," *Social News* 12 (Sept. 1922): 15.

63. Maryland passed this law, popularly known as the "six months' law," in June 1916. See U.S. Children's Bureau, *Welfare of Infants of Illegitimate Birth in Baltimore*, Pub. no. 144 (Washington, D.C.: Government Printing Office, 1925), p. 1; U.S. Children's Bureau, "Children of Illegitimate Birth and Measures for Their Protection," Emma O. Lundberg, Pub. no. 166 (Washington, D.C.: Government Printing Office, 1926), pp. 8–9. North Carolina passed a statute similar to that of Maryland in 1917, forbidding separation except with the consent of the superior court and the county health officer. For examples of social workers in favor of keeping mother and child together, see Katherine Lenroot, "Recent Developments in Provision for Children Born out of Wedlock," paper delivered at the NFCM conference, May 20, 1929, pp. 2–3, Box 2, Folder 2, Katherine Lenroot papers, Columbia University Archives; Maxfield, "The Social Treatment of Unmarried Mothers," p. 214.

64. Watson, "Illegitimate Family," p. 107.

65. Barrett, *Some Practical Suggestions on the Conduct of a Rescue Home*, p. 47; Minutes of the Committee on the Study of Illegitimacy, January 11, 1939, p. 2, Box 208, Folder 1, WC. See also U.S. Children's Bureau, *Maternity Homes*, p. 25. In her study of the history of social services, early childhood education, and the mental health profession during the first half of the twentieth century, Sonya Michel explores the relationship between children's interests and mothers' rights and argues that social workers' concern for children blinded them to the needs of mothers (Michel, "Children's Interests/Mothers' Rights: Women, Professionals, and the American Family, 1920–1945" [Ph.D. diss., Brown University, 1986]).

66. Cole, "The Need of Case Work Method in Dealing with Illegitimacy," p. 434. See also Colcord, "The Need of Adequate Case Work with the Unmarried Mother," p. 22.

67. Solinger discusses in detail what she terms the "postwar adoption mandate" during and after World War II, in *Wake Up Little Susie*, chap. 5. In a review of maternity home disposition records, Michael Sedlak finds what "whereas perhaps two babies in ten were adopted between 1890 and 1930, at least eight out of ten were being adopted by the early 1950s" (Sedlak, "Youth Policy and Young

Women," p. 456). On the trend toward adoption taken by social workers, see "Social Workers Look at Adoption," *Child* 10 (Jan. 1946): 110–12; A. H. Stoneman, "Social Problems Related to Illegitimacy," NCSW, *Proceedings* (1924): 144–50; Helen S. Trounstine, "Illegitimacy in Cincinnati," in *Studies from the Helen S. Trounstine Foundation* 1 (Sept. 1919): 216; Louise Waterman Wise, "Mothers in Name," *Survey* 43 (March 20, 1920): 779–80; Clothier, "Problems of Illegitimacy").

68. Clothier, "Problems of Illegitimacy," p. 581.

69. Case file #1430062, Door of Hope, Jersey City, New Jersey, RG 14.5, SAARC.

70. Quoted in Rose Bernstein, "Are We Still Stereotyping the Unmarried Mother?" *Social Work* 5 (1960): 28.

71. See Tiffin, *In Whose Best Interest?*

72. Mangold, *Children Born out of Wedlock*, pp. 92–93. In her study of social workers' surveys on illegitimacy, Lillian Ripple noted that "the focus of attention in illegitimacy cases during the 1920s had been almost wholly upon the child and the agencies assuming major responsibility were the child-caring agencies" (Ripple, "Social Work Studies of Unmarried Parenthood as Affected by Contemporary Treatment Formulations, 1920–1940" [Ph.D. diss., University of Chicago, 1953], pp. 107–08).

73. See Brumberg, "'Ruined Girls,'" p. 262; Trounstine, "Illegitimacy in Cincinnati," pp. 200–07; Michael Grossberg, *Governing the Hearth*, chap. 6; Tiffin, *In Whose Best Interest?*, pp. 175–80; Lydia Allen DeVilbiss, "Who Is the Father?" *Survey* 41 (March 29, 1919): 923–24; Harry M. Fisher, "The Legal Aspects of Illegitimacy," NCSW, *Proceedings* (1917): 294–99; Hanna, "Changing Care of Children Born out of Wedlock"; Reed, *Social and Health Care of the Illegitimate Family*, p. 9; U.S. Children's Bureau, *Illegitimacy Laws of the United States*, Ernest Freund, Pub. no. 42 (Washington, D.C.: Government Printing Office, 1919).

74. U.S. Children's Bureau, *Maternity Homes*, p. 22.

75. Young, "The Unmarried Mother's Decision," p. 27.

76. Clothier, "Problems of Illegitimacy," p. 579. See also Trounstine, "Illegitimacy in Cincinnati," p. 216. Linda Gordon finds that single mothers were consistently overrepresented as neglectful parents in "Single Mothers and Child Neglect."

77. Trounstine, "Illegitimacy in Cincinnati," p. 16.

78. Morlock, "Address," *Florence Crittenton Bulletin* 14 (Aug. 1939): 45.

79. Ronald C. Howard argues that "the family remained the central focus of concern for social work throughout this period, and the preservation of the family became the major justification for the existence of family case work," in "Sociology and the Family in the Progressive Era," p. 42.

80. Mary Willcox Glenn, "The Growth of Social Case Work in the United States, *Family* 9 (Dec. 1928).

81. Elsa Castendyck, "Helping to Prevent Sex Delinquency," NCSW, *Proceedings* (1943): 146–47.

82. Van Waters, "The New Morality and the Social Worker," NCSW, *Proceedings* (1929): 73.

83. Gillin, *Social Pathology*, p. 213.

84. Queen and Mann, *Social Pathology*, p. 158. See also Brisley, "The Illegitimate Family and Specialized Treatment," p. 71.

85. Bertha B. Howell to Maud Morlock, April 6, 1944, Box 174, Fol. 7-4-0-7-6, CB.

86. Maud Morlock to Josephine Deyo, June 10, 1944, Box 173, Fol. 7-4-0-7-3, CB.

87. Robb grew up in the Salvation Army but received training as a social worker at Ohio State University. From there, she went to the University of Chicago to study psychiatry. She worked for the United Charities of Chicago before becoming a Salvation Army officer in 1936. When Robb decided to become a Salvationist, her father warned her that "it will be very difficult for you because you are a social worker and the Army is not ready to accept professional people" (Anita Robb, oral history, pp. 11, 16–17, Accession No. 88-13, SAARC.)

88. Jane E. Wrieden, quoted in Beulah Amidon, "Front-Line Officer," *Survey Graphic* 37 (Oct. 1948): 430.

89. National Committee on Service to Unmarried Parents, notes for meeting, January 16, 1959, Box 47, Folder 1, CWLA; U.S. Children's Bureau, *Children of Illegitimate Birth Whose Mothers Have Kept Their Custody*, A. Madorah Donahue, Pub. no. 190 (Washington, D.C.: Government Printing Office, 1928), p. 4. The Inter-City Conference was established in 1915 at the meeting of the NCSW in Baltimore. On the conference, see "Background History of the National Conference Committee on Unmarried Parenthood," 1944, Box 47, Folder 1, CWLA; Smith, "Changing Emphases in Case Work with Unmarried Mothers"; Maud Morlock, "The Future of the Inter-City Conference," CWLA *Bulletin* 10 (April 1931): 8.

90. Josephine Deyo to Maud Morlock, July 20, 1944, Box 173, Fol. 7-4-0-7-3, CB.

91. *Florence Crittenton Bulletin* 4 (Jan. 1929): 10.

92. Florence Crittenton League of Compassion, Boston, *Annual Report* (1933): 1.

93. "President's Statement," Florence Crittenton League of Compassion, Boston, *Annual Report* (1915): 7.

94. "Message from the General Superintendent," *Florence Crittenton Bulletin* 4 (Jan. 1929): 3.

95. "Victoria and Frances and Albert," pamphlet, Boston Florence Crittenton League of Compassion, n.d., n.p., FCL.

96. Reba Barrett Smith to Mrs. Kerby, October 2, 1937, Box 5, Folder 40, NFCM.

97. Reba Barrett Smith, "Cooperation between Professional and Volunteer Social Workers," *Florence Crittenton Bulletin* 15 (July 1940): 38.

98. Reba Barrett Smith to Grace Knox, January 28, 1947, Box 8, Folder 88, NFCM.

99. Mrs. A. J. Wilson, letter to Mr. Sam Grunfest, president of Little Rock Community Chest, October 20, 1939, Box 5, Folder 35, NFCM. Evangelical women's resistance to the incursions of professional social workers closely parallels the "traditionalist" nurses described by Barbara Melosh who defended nursing as

womanly service and who saw professionalization as an assault on their legitimacy and authority (Melosh, *The "Physician's Hand,"* chap. 1).

100. *Florence Crittenton Bulletin* 14 (Aug. 1939): 26.

101. Whittemore, *Mother Whittemore's Records*, p. 63.

102. "Minutes of the Forty-Fourth Annual Conference," NFCM, *Annual Report* (1926): 22.

103. Hazel J. Tuck, "Discussion of 'Case Work,'" NFCM, *Annual Report* (1929): 26–27.

104. Maud Morlock to Genrose Gehri, Sept. 13, 1940, Box 744, Fol. 7-4-0, CB.

105. Genrose Gehri, "The Case Work Function of the Maternity Home," Child Welfare League of America, *Bulletin* (Dec. 1939): 7.

106. *Crittenton Capers* (Nov. 1, 1955), Florence Crittenton home, Norfolk, Virginia, Box 28, Fol. 27, FCS.

107. U.S. Children's Bureau, *Maternity Homes for Unmarried Mothers: A Community Service*, pp. 19–20.

108. Morlock, "Letters from Unmarried Mothers: What Answer?" December 29, 1941, pp. 1–2, Box 208, Folder 4, WC.

109. Ada Sheffield, "Questionnaire Regarding an Unmarried Mother," in Mary E. Richmond, *Social Diagnosis* (New York: Russell Sage Foundation, 1917). See also Cole, "The Need of the Case Work Method in Dealing with Illegitimacy," p. 431; Reed, *Social and Health Care*, pp. 49–50; Watson, "The Illegitimate Family," pp. 106–7.

110. Leader, *And No Birds Sing*, p. 242. When unmarried mothers in Cleveland in 1937 were asked why they did not go to social agencies immediately on discovering that they were pregnant, the interviewer "found an almost unanimous feeling on the part of the unmarried mothers that they wanted more privacy; they did not want to go through the interviewing system, etc., of the social agencies" (Minutes of the Committee on the Study of Illegitimacy, April 1, 1937, Box 207, Folder 5, WC). Some social workers were sensitive to the intrusiveness of casework. Maud Morlock, for example, questioned Salvation Army Brigadier Pagen regarding the type of questions asked unmarried mothers in their first interview: "It seems to me that many girls would be bewildered by some of this information as to why it was being asked and the purpose that anyone would have in asking it. . . . I doubt very much whether she would see the necessity of your asking many of these items that have been included, particularly the details in regard to her mother and father, addresses and details about all her brothers and sisters, etc., previous marriage of her parents" (Maud Morlock to Brigadier Pagen, December 21, 1944, Box 173, Fol. 7-4-0-7-3, CB).

111. U.S. Children's Bureau, "Maternity Homes for Unmarried Mothers: A Community Service," p. 42.

112. Hazel J. Tack, "Discussion of 'Case Work,'" NFCM, *Annual Report* (1929): 27.

113. Hazel Tack wrote of casework with unmarried mothers, "it is very necessary to have first-hand information about the home from which she came, some knowledge of the type of people she has chosen for friends, her choice of recreation, all these things are immeasurably helpful in making a plan for her" (Tack, "Discussion of 'Case Work,'" pp. 27–28). This troubled some social workers, who wrote, "social agencies must consider . . . whether they are really living up to their promises to keep the girl's story secret if she must tell it to half a dozen different people in the course of working out the problem" ("Social Workers Look at Adoption," *Child* 10 [Jan. 1946]: 112).

114. Watson, "The Illegitimate Family," p. 105.

115. Case file #1420058, Door of Hope, Jersey City, New Jersey, RG 14.5, SAARC.

116. Leader, *And No Birds Sing*, p. 242.

117. Case of Marjorie, presented to the Committee on the Study of Illegitimacy, March 9, 1939, Box 208, Folder 1, WC.

118. Hildegarde Dolson, "My Parents Mustn't Know," *Good Housekeeping* (May 1942): 158.

119. "Report of the Unmarried Mothers Committee," United Charities of Chicago, December 9, 1936, Box 52, Folder 4, UCC. See also Cole, "The Needs of Case Work Method," p. 431; Baylor, "Social Agencies and Unmarried Mothers," p. 146; Ripple, "Facilities," p. 162.

120. Brenner, "What Facilities Are Essential?" pp. 438–39.

121. Frances M. Potter, "The Subjective Element in Interviewing," *Survey* (Nov. 15, 1927): 226.

122. "Social Workers Look at Adoption," p. 111. Their insistence that subjectivity was the handmaiden of objectivity led some social workers into confusing theoretical positions. Assuming that case records contained objective and subjective material, Thomas D. Eliot wrote, "the important thing is that subjective material should not be recorded *as if* it were objective, but should be recorded as objectively as anything else" (Eliot, "Objectivity and Subjectivity in the Case Record," *Social Forces* 6 [June 1928]: 444).

123. Murphy, "Mothers and—Mothers," p. 172.

124. Brisley, "The Illegitimate Family and Specialized Treatment," p. 68; Brisley, "'Humble and Distracted,'" *Family* 15 (Nov. 1934): 230.

125. "Discussion of Some Phases of Case Work with Unmarried Mothers," p. 9, prepared by the Committee on Problems Related to Unmarried Parenthood of the Family Service Section, Division on Family and Child Welfare of the Council of Social Agencies of Chicago, April 1941, Box 52, Folder 1, UCC.

126. Elizabeth H. Dexter, "The Social Case Workers' Attitudes and Problems as They Affect Her Work," *Family* 7 (Oct. 1926): 179.

127. Marjory Embry, "Planning for the Unmarried Mother," p. 11, pamphlet, Child Welfare League of America, 1937, New York Public Library.

128. Robinson, *Changing Psychology*, p. 101. On the functional school of social work, of which Robinson was a leading theorist, see Ehrenreich, *Altruistic Imagination*, pp. 123–27; Germain, "Casework and Science," p. 17; Lora Kasius, ed., *A Comparison of Diagnostic and Functional Case-Work Concepts* (New York: Family Service Association of America, 1950); Ruth E. Smalley, "The Functional Approach to Casework Practice," in *Theories of Social Casework*, ed. Robert W. Roberts and Robert H. Nee (Chicago: University of Chicago Press, 1970), pp. 77–128.

129. Potter, "The Subjective Element," p. 226.

130. Dexter, "The Social Case Worker's Attitudes and Problems," p. 195.

131. Brenner, "What Facilities Are Essential?" p. 428.

132. Erma C. Blethan, "Case Work Services to a Florence Crittenton Home," *Family* 23 (Nov. 1942): 251.

133. Case of Maria, March 1, 1943, p. 1, Box 1, Folder 3, Dorothy Hutchinson papers, Columbia University Archives.

134. Brenner, "What Facilities Are Essential?" p. 434.

135. Reed, *Negro Illegitimacy*, p. 87.

136. Ibid., p. 115. This explanation, of course, drew on popular cultural representations of black motherhood through the stereotype of the Mammy. See Karen Sue Jewell, *From Mammy to Miss America and Beyond: Cultural Images and the Shaping of United States Social Policy* (New York: Routledge, 1992).

137. Parker, "A Follow-Up Study," p. 17.

138. Mattingly, "Unmarried Mother and Her Child," p. 49.

139. Case of Marjory, presented to the Committee on the Study of Illegitimacy, April 12, 1939, Box 208, Fol. 1, WC.

140. Quoted in Brenner, "What Facilities Are Essential?" p. 430.

141. Gordon Hamilton, "Basic Concepts in Social Casework," NFCM, *Proceedings* (1937): 161.

142. Larson, *Rise of Professionalism*, p. 31.

143. Fern Lowry, "The Clients' Needs as the Basis for Differential Approach in Treatment," in Lowry, *Differential Approach in Case Work Treatment* (New York: Family Welfare Association of America, 1936), p. 2.

144. Mathews, "Case Work with Unmarried Mothers," p. 185.

145. "Report of the Unmarried Mothers Committee," December 9, 1936, Box 52, Folder 4, UCC. In her study of Cleveland maternity homes, Marian Morton comes to a similar conclusion, arguing that "although Cleveland maternity homes conformed to some pressures from the federated charities to modernize policies and practice, the homes retained their nineteenth-century religious commitments and mission for at least sixty years" (Morton, "Fallen Women," p. 62).

146. Puttee and Colby, *Illegitimate Child in Illinois*, p. 136.

147. Minutes of the Trenton, New Jersey, Florence Crittenton Home Annual Meeting, May 11, 1945, Box 7, Folder 70, NFCM.

CHAPTER 6 WHITE NEUROSIS, BLACK PATHOLOGY, AND THE IRONIES
OF PROFESSIONALIZATION: THE 1940s

1. "Annual Report of the National Officers," *Florence Crittenton Bulletin* 16 (Sept. 1941): 10.

2. Solinger, *Wake Up Little Susie*. In this thoughtful and thorough analysis, Solinger traces the relationship of postwar racialized constructions of out-of-wedlock pregnancy to social policy regarding black and white single mothers. In this chapter, I am more concerned with the ways that those constructions became legitimizing vehicles for social workers and policymakers in their struggles for cultural authority during and after the war. I also intend to begin the project of exploring the interdependence of ideologies of gender and race; to that end, I hope to show that these constructions of out-of-wedlock pregnancy depended upon and were in dialogue with each other.

3. The Bureau of the Census reported a decrease in illegitimate births in 1942, from 40.8 per 1,000 in 1941 to 37.2 in 1942. This represented a decrease of 8.8% from that of 1941 and was the lowest reported proportion since 1931 (Bureau of the Census, Vital Statistics—Special Report, *Illegitimate Births by Race, United States, 1942*, vol. 19 [April 27, 1942], p. 142).

4. *Florence Crittenton Bulletin* 15 (Oct. 1940): 1. The United Charities of Chicago reported a 23% increase in the number of unmarried mothers under their care from 1942 to 1943 ("Twenty-Three Per Cent Increase in Unwed Mothers," *Family Service* 8 [Oct. 1943]: 1).

5. Illegitimacy rose from 82,586 in 1943 to 87,001 in 1944 (Bureau of the Census, Vital Statistics—Special Report, *Illegitimate Births by Race: United States and Each State, 1944*, vol. 25 [Oct. 31, 1946], p. 255).

6. Helen Harris Perlman, "Unmarried Mothers," in *Social Work and Social Problems*, ed. Nathan E. Cohen (New York: National Association of Social Workers, 1964), p. 301.

7. Solinger, *Wake Up Little Susie*, p. 93.

8. Young, *Out of Wedlock*, p. 1.

9. J. Kasanin and Sieglinde Handschin, "Psychodynamic Factors in Illegitimacy," *American Journal of Orthopsychiatry* 11 (Jan. 1941): 68. See also Edlin, *The Unmarried Mother in Our Society*, p. 85; *Florence Crittenton Bulletin* 22 (July 1947): 36; Edith Balmford to Maud Morlock, February 21, 1944, Box 173, Fol. 7-4-0, CB.

10. Kasanin and Handschin, "Psychodynamic Factors," pp. 71, 68.

11. Edlin, *The Unmarried Mother in Our Society*, p. 85.

12. Bernstein, "Are We Still Stereotyping the Unmarried Mother?" p. 24.

13. Young, *Out of Wedlock*, p. 241. Rickie Solinger provides an excellent analysis of psychiatric diagnoses of white unmarried mothers in *Wake Up Little Susie*, chap. 3.

14. Grace Marcus used this phrase in "The Status of Social Case Work Today,"

Compass 16 (1935): 8. Historians since have adopted it to describe the influence of psychiatry on social work in the 1920s. See, e.g., Kathleen Woodroofe, *From Charity to Social Work in England and the United States* (Toronto: University of Toronto Press, 1962), chap. 6.

15. Many historians argue that psychiatry served to deflect social work from its former concern with social reform. See Chambers, "Creative Effort in an Age of Normalcy," pp. 257–58; Ehrenreich, *Altruistic Imagination;* Lubove, *Professional Altruist;* Herman Borenzweig, "Social Work and Psychoanalytic Theory." Not all social workers embraced psychiatric social work. Florence Day remembered a colleague's remark that "the depression would have at least one good result if it whacked 'this psychiatry business' out of case work" (Day, "Changing Practices in Case Work Treatment," in *Readings in Social Case Work,* ed. Fern Lowry [New York: Columbia University Press, 1939], p. 333).

16. Mary K. Jarrett, "The Psychiatric Thread Running through All Social Case Work," NCSW, *Proceedings* (1919): 1.

17. Rose Hahn Dawson, in recorded interview with Vida S. Grayson, July 22, 1978, p. 52, Social Work Archive, Sophia Smith Collection, Smith College, Northampton, Massachusetts.

18. Jessie Taft, "The Relation of Psychiatry to Social Work," *Family* 7 (Nov. 1926): 201.

19. Bertha Reynolds, "Rethinking Social Casework," Social Work Today Pamphlet no. 1, May 1942, p. 16, Box 7, Folder 104, Bertha Reynolds papers, Sophia Smith Collection, Smith College, Northampton, Massachusetts.

20. Leslie B. Alexander, "Social Work's Freudian Deluge: Myth or Reality?" *Social Service Review* 46 (Dec. 1972): 517–18. See also Ehrenreich, *Altruistic Imagination,* p. 123.

21. Gottesfeld and Pharis, *Profiles in Social Work,* p. 111. See also Marcus, *Some Aspects of Relief in Family Case Work,* p. 46.

22. On the expansion and popularization of psychiatry during World War II, see Burnham, "Influence of Psychoanalysis upon American Culture"; William C. Menninger, *Psychiatry in a Troubled World* (New York: Macmillan, 1948); Walter Bromberg, *Psychiatry between the Wars, 1918–1945: A Recollection* (Westport, Conn.: Greenwood Press, 1982), pp. 102–22.

23. Doris P. Brooks, "Future Trends in Work with the Unmarried Mother," CWLA, *Bulletin* 17 (Jan. 1938): 1.

24. Mandel Sherman, "The Unmarried Mother," 1938, Box 52, Folder 3, UCC. See also Clothier, "Psychological Implications," p. 548.

25. Field, "Social Casework Practice," pp. 494, 496.

26. Case of Marjorie, July 26, 1946, p. 6, Box 1, Folder 3, Dorothy Hutchinson papers, Columbia University Archives.

27. Case of Jennie, May 13, 1942, p. 13, Box 2, Folder 18, Dorothy Hutchinson papers, Columbia University Archives.

28. Amidon, "Front Line Officer," pp. 439–40.

29. See Babette Block, "The Unmarried Mother: Is She Different?" NCSW, *Proceedings* (1945): 283; Scherz, "'Taking Sides,'" pp. 57–58; Bernard, "Psychodynamics," p. 40. Young devoted chap. 3 of *Out of Wedlock* to "The Mother Ridden," and chap. 4 to "The Father Ridden."

30. Deutsch, *Psychology of Women*, 2:345, 369.

31. Young, *Out of Wedlock*, p. 36; Young, "Personality Problems in Unmarried Mothers," *Family* 26 (Dec. 1945): 7.

32. Deutsch, *Psychology of Women*, 2:349.

33. Bernard, "Psychodynamics," p. 40. See also Young, *Out of Wedlock*, p. 40.

34. Robert Fleiss, "Foreword," in Young, *Out of Wedlock*, p. v.

35. Young, *Out of Wedlock*, p. 21.

36. Sherman, "The Unmarried Mother," p. 17.

37. Powell, "Illegitimate Pregnancy in Emotionally Disturbed Girls," p. 173.

38. Elaine Tyler May documents the "widespread endorsement of this familial consensus in the cold war era," in *Homeward Bound*, p. 20.

39. Marynia Farnham and Ferdinand Lundberg, *Modern Woman: The Lost Sex* (New York: Harper and Brothers, 1947), p. 280.

40. Young, *Out of Wedlock*, p. 37.

41. Morlock, "Foster-Home Care," p. 55. Social workers who advocated foster homes for unmarried mothers include Erma C. Blethan, "A Foster Home Program for the Unmarried Mother," *Family* 23 (Dec. 1942): 291–96; Mary S. Brisley, "Parent-Child Relationships in Unmarried Parenthood," NCSW, *Proceedings* (1939): 435–45; U.S. Children's Bureau, "Maternity Homes for Unmarried Mothers," pp. 27–28; Trout, "Services to Unmarried Mothers," p. 26; Young, *Out of Wedlock*, pp. 229–33.

42. Blethan, "Foster Home Program," p. 294.

43. Perlman, "Unmarried Mothers," pp. 288, 301.

44. Bernard, "Psychodynamics," p. 39.

45. Young, *Out of Wedlock*, p. 22.

46. Deutsch, *Psychology of Women*, 2:374, 338.

47. Dolson, "My Parents Mustn't Know," p. 159.

48. Deutsch, *Psychology of Women*, 2:355. Of the unmarried mothers in her study, Miriam Powell noted that "one girl was said to go out with 'pick ups,' usually sailors, almost nightly. Another girl would 'pick up' men in Times Square. . . . Another girl was 'always with men,'" and "she frequently stayed out until early morning and sometimes all night" (Powell, "Illegitimate Pregnancy in Emotionally Disturbed Girls," p. 172). Young, too, found that "an astonishing number of unmarried mothers met the fathers of their babies in casual, unconventional fashion. They 'pick up' a man in trains, hotels, at dances and large parties, or they meet him on 'blind dates' with casual acquaintances" (Young, *Out of Wedlock*, p. 22).

49. In 1915, George Mangold noted the disproportionate representation of domestic servants among the unmarried mothers he studied and asked, "is domestic

service a morally extra-hazardous occupation? Is the class of women employed in this branch of industry mentally and morally inferior?" (Mangold, "Unlawful Motherhood," p. 342). Most social workers believed in some combination of the two and closely linked domestic service and sex delinquency. See, e.g., U.S. Senate, "Relation between Occupation and Criminality of Women," pp. 86–87; Ida Parker, "Follow-Up Study," pp. 30–31; Aronovici, *Unmarried Girls*, p. 27; Reed, *Social and Health Care*, pp. 38–39.

50. Sherman, "The Unmarried Mother," p. 13.

51. Young, *Out of Wedlock*, p. 50. See also Scherz, "Taking Sides," p. 59.

52. The metaphor of "containment" is developed by Elaine Tyler May in her analysis of the "containment" of sexuality within the family during the Cold War (May, *Homeward Bound*, chap. 5).

53. Young, "The Unmarried Mother's Decision about Her Baby," p. 33. See also Young, *Out of Wedlock*, p. 39; Deutsch, *Psychology of Women*, 2:376; Scherz, "'Taking Sides,'" p. 61; Bernard, "Psychodynamics," p. 43; Ruth F. Brenner, "Case Work Services for Unmarried Mothers," *Family* 22 (Nov. 1941): 218.

54. Solinger discusses what she terms the "postwar adoption mandate" in *Wake Up Little Susie*, chap. 5.

55. Young, *Out of Wedlock*, pp. 7, viii.

56. American Social Health Association, "The Social Challenge of Prostitution: An Outline for Communities Fighting Prostitution and Venereal Disease," 1945, p. 14, Box 129, Folder 3, ASHA. Elaine Tyler May discusses this fear of premarital female sexuality that resurfaced during World War II and the postwar period and points out that the wartime fear of promiscuity extended to include all forms of nonmarital sexual behavior, including prostitution and homosexuality, in *Homeward Bound*, chap. 4. See also D'Emilio and Freedman, *Intimate Matters*, chap. 11; Anderson, *Wartime Women;* John D'Emilio, *Sexual Politics, Sexual Communities: The Making of a Homosexual Minority in the United States, 1940–1970* (Chicago: University of Chicago Press, 1983), chaps. 2, 3; Estelle B. Freedman, "'Uncontrolled Desires.'"

57. See Brandt, *No Magic Bullet*, esp. pp. 165–69.

58. Merrill, *Social Problems on the Home Front*, p. 99. The American Social Hygiene Association proposed a redefinition of prostitution to include "all sex relations which are indiscriminate or without sincere emotional content" (American Social Health Association, "The Social Challenge of Prostitution," pp. 2–3).

59. Helen D. Pigeon, "Effect of War Conditions on Children and Adolescents in the City of Hartford, Connecticut," Connecticut Child Welfare Association, New Haven, Connecticut, p. 24. See also Venereal Disease Control Conference, March 5, 1945, San Antonio, Texas, pp. 23–24, Box 129, Folder 1, ASHA.

60. James Gilbert observes that "social class had become, by the end of the fifties, a major element in both structural and cultural interpretations of delinquency" (Gilbert, *A Cycle of Outrage: America's Reaction to the Juvenile Delinquent in the 1950s* [New York: Oxford University Press, 1986], p. 18).

61. Venereal Disease Control Conference, pp. 24, 25.
62. Ibid., p. 33. See Anderson, *Wartime Women*, pp. 103–11. Many discussions of the unwholesome influence of war on girls focused on illegitimacy. See, e.g., U.S. Children's Bureau, "Services for Unmarried Mothers and Their Children" (Washington, D.C.: Government Printing Office, 1945), p. 1; Dorothy Ellsworth, "Precocious Adolescence in Wartime," *Family* 25 (March 1944): 3–13; Merrill, *Social Problems on the Home Front*, pp. 89–124; Castendyck, "Helping to Prevent Sex Delinquency," pp. 140–48; Morlock, "Unmarried Mothers in Wartime."
63. See Reed, *Social and Health Care of the Illegitimate Family*, p. 17; Trounstine, "Illegitimacy in Cincinnati," p. 221; Reed, "Illegitimacy among Negroes," *Journal of Social Hygiene* 11 (Feb. 1925): 73–91; Hertz and Little, "Unmarried Negro Mothers in a Southern Urban Community"; Frazier, "Analysis of Statistics on Negro Illegitimacy"; Olive Davis Streater, "Some Aspects of Illegitimacy among Negroes," Inter-City Conference on Illegitimacy Bulletin, in Child Welfare League of America *Bulletin* 10 (May 1931): 8; Hertz, "Negro Illegitimacy in Durham, North Carolina," (M.A. thesis, Duke University, 1944), pp. 14–15, 101.
64. Melville J. Herskovits, *The Myth of the Negro Past* (New York: Harper and Brothers, 1941), p. 167.
65. Frazier won a research fellowship in 1920 at the New York School of Social Work, where he took several courses. From 1922 to 1927, he served as acting director of the Atlanta University School of Social Work. For a discussion of Frazier's career in social work, see Anthony M. Platt, *E. Franklin Frazier Reconsidered* (New Brunswick: Rutgers University Press, 1991), chap. 7.
66. Knapp, "Attitudes of Negro Unmarried Mothers toward Illegitimacy," p. 153.
67. Young, *Out of Wedlock*, p. 121. See also Hertz, "Negro Illegitimacy"; Maurine Boie LaBarre, "Cultural and Racial Problems in Social Case Work with Special Reference to Negroes," in *Cultural Problems in Social Case Work* (New York: Family Welfare Association of America, 1940), pp. 1–20.
68. Reed, *Negro Illegitimacy*, p. 7. See also R. Barrett, *Care of the Unmarried Mother*, pp. 8–9. The relative silence in social work on black illegitimacy before the late 1930s was part of a larger silence in the profession on the lives of African-Americans. Anthony Platt finds that "between 1920 and 1928, *The Family* carried only three articles that addressed the specific problems of Afro-American families. The National Conference of Social Work regularly devoted a whole section to the problems of European immigrants but rarely included panels on African Americans" (Platt, *Frazier Reconsidered*, p. 70).
69. Charles S. Johnson, *Shadow of the Plantation* (Chicago: University of Chicago Press, 1934), p. 49. See also Hertz and Little, "Unmarried Negro Mothers in a Southern Urban Community," p. 78. Maternity home workers used the "cultural acceptance" of illegitimacy to justify denying their services to African-American unmarried mothers. See, e.g., *Florence Crittenton Bulletin* 4 (Jan. 1929): 5; Abbey, "Illegitimacy and Sex Perversion," p. 29.

70. Frazier, "Analysis of Statistics on Negro Illegitimacy," p. 255. On the rural-urban transmission of black illegitimacy, see also Drake and Cayton, *Black Metropolis*, p. 590; Hertz, "Negro Illegitimacy," p. 35.

71. Carby discusses the ways in which this characterization legitimized the policing and disciplining of black women by both black and white institutions and intellectuals, in "Policing the Black Woman's Body," p. 739.

72. Frazier, *Negro Family in the United States*, p. 267.

73. Frazier, "Analysis of Statistics on Negro Illegitimacy," p. 256.

74. Frazier, "Traditions and Patterns of Negro Family Life in the United States," in *Race and Culture Contacts*, ed. Edward Byron Reuter (New York: McGraw-Hill, 1934), pp. 194–95.

75. Frazier, *Negro Family in the United States*, p. 265. See also Reed, *Social and Health Care*, p. 17; Trounstine, "Illegitimacy in Cincinnati," p. 198; Hertz, "Negro Illegitimacy," p. 87.

76. Frazier, *Negro Family in the United States*, p. 265. This condemnation of the black unmarried mother who did not want to keep her baby coincided with the diagnosis of the white woman who wanted to keep her child as "neurotic."

77. See Platt, *Frazier Reconsidered*.

78. Young, *Out of Wedlock*, p. 120.

79. LaBarre, "Cultural and Racial Problems in Social Case Work," p. 3. See Platt, *Frazier Reconsidered*, p. 139.

80. Hertz, "Negro Illegitimacy," p. 75. See also Margaret Brenman, "Urban Lower-Class Negro Girls," *Psychiatry* 6 (Aug. 1943): 308.

81. Hertz, "Negro Illegitimacy," p. 77; Brenman, "Urban Lower-Class Negro Girls," p. 316. See also Drake and Cayton, *Black Metropolis*, p. 593. Many social historians have also been interested in the dynamics of class divisions within black urban communities. See Joe William Trotter, Jr., *Black Milwaukee: The Making of an Industrial Proletariat, 1915–1945* (Urbana: University of Illinois Press, 1985); Gilbert Osofsky, *Harlem: The Making of a Ghetto, 1890 to 1930* (New York: Harper and Row, 1966); Allan Spear, *Black Chicago: The Making of a Negro Ghetto, 1890 to 1920* (Chicago: University of Chicago Press, 1967); Kenneth Kusmer, *A Ghetto Takes Shape: Black Cleveland, 1870 to 1930* (Urbana: University of Illinois Press, 1976); Thomas Philpott, *The Slum and the Ghetto* (New York: Oxford University Press, 1978).

82. Hertz, "Negro Illegitimacy," pp. 76–77.

83. Hazel Carby characterizes this period as one of "ideological, political, and cultural contestation between an emergent black bourgeoisie and an emerging black working class" (Carby, "Policing the Black Woman's Body," p. 754).

84. Drake and Cayton, *Black Metropolis*, p. 593. G. Franklin Edwards points out that "The concepts of social disorganization and social reorganization as related aspects of a process were first used by W. I. Thomas and Florian Znanieski in *The Polish Peasant* to analyze the problems encountered by peasant commu-

nities as their contacts with the wider community increased in number, variety, and intensity. A period of social disorganization . . . is followed by a period of social reorganization or social reconstruction, in which new rules and institutions, better adapted to the needs of the group, are fashioned from preexisting elements of the peasant culture" (Edwards, "E. Franklin Frazier," in *Black Sociologists in Historical and Contemporary Perspectives*, p. 101).

85. Southern, *Gunnar Myrdal and Black-White Relations*, p. 55.

86. Myrdal, *An American Dilemma*, pp. 930–31. On the influence of Frazier on Myrdal, see Jackson, *Gunnar Myrdal and America's Conscience*, esp. pp. 245–70.

87. Daniel P. Moynihan, *The Negro Family: The Case for National Action* (Washington, D.C.: U.S. Department of Labor, 1965).

88. Anthony Platt argues that Moynihan actually misused Frazier's scholarship (Platt, *Frazier Reconsidered*, pp. 115–20). See also Jackson, *Gunnar Myrdal and America's Conscience*, p. 303.

89. Frazier, *Negro Family in the United States*, p. 100.

90. On the association of African-Americans and venereal disease, see Brandt, *No Magic Bullet*, pp. 116, 157–58, 169–70; Fee, "Venereal Disease: The Wages of Sin?" pp. 181–83.

91. Rickie Solinger traces the turning point in public attitudes toward black single pregnancy in the 1940s to the uneasiness of whites toward ADC and other forms of public assistance (Solinger, *Wake Up Little Susie*, pp. 29–34, 56–76). See also Winifred Bell, *Aid to Dependent Children* (New York: Columbia University Press, 1965).

92. Schumacher, "The Unmarried Mother; a Socio-Psychiatric Viewpoint."

93. Jean Thompson, *House of Tomorrow* (New York: Harper and Row, 1967), pp. 7–8.

94. Drake and Cayton, *Black Metropolis*, pp. 592–93.

95. Solinger, *Wake Up Little Susie*, p. 16.

96. Rickie Solinger describes in detail "a two-tiered service system, coercive and humiliating to white and black women, but particularly threatening to blacks," in *Wake Up Little Susie*, p. 34. Although many black unmarried mothers were sterilized, Solinger notes that efforts to pass sterilization legislation on the state level were largely unsuccessful (pp. 53–57).

97. Kenworthy, "The Mental Health Aspects of Illegitimacy," p. 507. Henry Schumacher envisioned a similar professional team in "The Unmarried Mother," p. 782.

98. Neilson, "Smith College Experiment," p. 2.

99. Esther Cook, in recorded interview by Vida S. Grayson, July 22, 1978, p. 48, Social Work Archives, Sophia Smith Collection, Smith College, Northampton, Massachusetts.

100. Reynolds, "The Relationship between Psychiatry and Psychiatric Social

Work," p. 1, paper given before the American Association of Psychiatric Social Workers, 1934, Box 5, Folder 79, Reynolds papers, Sophia Smith Collection, Smith College, Northampton, Massachusetts.

101. Reynolds, *An Uncharted Journey*, p. 62.
102. See Elizabeth Lunbeck, "Psychiatry in the Age of Reform: Doctors, Social Workers, and Patients at the Boston Psychopathic Hospital, 1900–1925" (Ph.D. diss., Harvard University, 1984). In many ways, the dilemma of social workers' relationship to psychiatrists resembles that which Barbara Melosh describes in nursing. The push to professionalize nursing situated nurses in a professional hierarchy in which they would always remain subordinate to doctors (Melosh, *"The Physician's Hand"*).
103. Brenner, "What Facilities Are Essential?" p. 430.
104. Schmideberg, "Psychiatric-Social Factors in Young Unmarried Mothers," p. 7.
105. Young, *Out of Wedlock*, pp. 177–78.
106. Scherz, "'Taking Sides,'" p. 22. See also Block, "The Unmarried Mother—Is She Different?" p. 2; Deutsch, *Psychology of Women*, 2340; Jane K. Goldsmith, "The Unmarried Mother's Search for Standards," *Social Casework* 38 (Feb. 1957): 74.

Bibliography

MANUSCRIPT AND ARCHIVAL COLLECTIONS

Chicago Historical Society, Chicago, Illinois
  United Charities of Chicago Collection
  Welfare Council Collection
Columbia University Library, Manuscripts Division, New York, New York
  Katherine Fredrica Lenroot papers
  Dorothy Hutchinson papers
  Emma Octavia Lundberg papers
Crittenton-Hastings Home, Boston, Massachusetts.
  Florence Crittenton League of Compassion Collection
Library of Congress, Manuscripts Division, Washington, D.C.
  Kate Waller Barrett papers
National Archives, Washington, D.C.
  U.S. Children's Bureau Collection
Old Dominion University Archives, Norfolk, Virginia
  Florence Crittenton Services of Norfolk, Virginia, Collection
Rutgers University Library, Special Collections, New Brunswick, New Jersey
  Katy Ferguson Home Collection, in Sheltering Arms Collection
  Florence Mission Collection
Salvation Army Archives and Research Center, Alexandria, Virginia
  Booth Memorial Hospital, Des Moines, Iowa, Collection
  Catherine Booth Home and Hospital, Cincinnati, Ohio, Collection
  Evangeline Booth Home and Hospital, Cincinnati, Ohio, Collection
  Door of Hope, Jersey City, New Jersey, Collection
  Booth Memorial Hospital, Wauwatosa, Wisconsin, Collection
  Booth Memorial Hospital, Buffalo, New York, Collection
  Booth Memorial Hospital, Pittsburgh, Pennsylvania, Collection
  Salvation Army Oral History Project

Social Welfare History Archives, University of Minnesota, Minneapolis, Minnesota
  American Social Health Association Collection
  National Florence Crittenton Mission Collection
  Child Welfare League of America Collection
University of Illinois, Chicago, Circle Library, Chicago, Illinois
  Florence Crittenton Anchorage, Chicago, Illinois, Collection

ANNUAL REPORTS AND PERIODICALS

Catholic Charities Review
Child Welfare League of America, *Bulletin*
The Family
Florence Crittenton Bulletin
Florence Crittenton Magazine
Girls
Intercity Conference on Illegitimacy, *Bulletin*
Journal of Social Hygiene
National Conference of Charities and Corrections, *Proceedings*
National Conference of Social Work, *Proceedings*
National Florence Crittenton Mission, *Annual Reports*
Social News
Survey
Survey Graphic
War Cry

GOVERNMENT DOCUMENTS

United States. Census Bureau. *Protective Case Work for Young People and Mater-
nity Homes.* By Glenn Steele. Pub. No. 209. Washington, D.C.: Government
Printing Office, 1932.
———. *Study of Maternity Homes in Minnesota and Pennsylvania.* By Ethel
Waters. Pub. No. 167. Washington, D.C.: Government Printing Office, 1926.
———. *Vital Statistics—Special Reports.* "Illegitimate Births by Race; United
States, 1942." Vol. 19 (April 27, 1942).
United States. Department of Labor. Children's Bureau. *Children of Illegitimate
Birth and Measures for Their Protection.* By Emma O. Lundberg. Pub. No. 166.
Washington, D.C.: Government Printing Office, 1926.
———. *Children of Illegitimate Birth Whose Mothers Have Kept Their Custody.* By
A. Madorah Donahue. Pub. No. 190. Washington, D.C.: Government Printing
Office, 1928.
———. *Illegitimacy as a Child-Welfare Problem, Part II: A Study of Original
Records in the City of Boston and in the State of Massachusetts.* By Emma O.
Lundberg and Katherine F. Lenroot. Pub. No. 75. Washington, D.C.: Govern-
ment Printing Office, 1921.

———. *Illegitimacy as a Child Welfare Problem, Part III*. Pub. No. 128. Washington, D.C.: Government Printing Office, 1924.

———. *Illegitimacy Laws of the United States*. By Ernst Freund. Pub. No. 42. Washington, D.C.: Government Printing Office, 1919.

———. *Maternity Homes for Unmarried Mothers: A Community Service*. By Maud Morlock and Hilary Campbell. Pub. No. 309. Washington, D.C.: Government Printing Office, 1946.

———. *Services for Unmarried Mothers and Their Children*. Washington, D.C.: Government Printing Office, 1945.

———. *The Welfare of Infants of Illegitimate Birth in Baltimore as Affected by a Maryland Law of 1916 Governing the Separation from Their Mothers of Children under Six Months Old*. Pub. No. 144. Washington, D.C.: Government Printing Office, 1925.

United States Congress. Senate. *Report on the Condition of Women and Child Wage Earners in the United States*. Doc. No. 645. 61st Cong., 2d sess., 1911. Vol. 15. *Relation between Occupation and Criminality in Women*. Washington, D.C.: Government Printing Office, 1911.

DISSERTATIONS AND THESES

Aiken, Katherine Gertrude. "The National Florence Crittenton Mission, 1883–1925: A Case Study in Progressive Reform." Ph.D. diss., Washington State University, 1980.

Antler, Joyce. "The Educated Woman and Professionalization: The Struggle for a New Feminine Identity, 1890–1920." Ph.D. diss., State University of New York at Stony Brook, 1977.

Cheyney, Alice S. "A Definition of Social Work." M.A. thesis, University of Pennsylvania, 1923.

Cohn, Anne. "Survey of Services Given to Fifty Unmarried Mothers by the Jewish Board of Guardians." M.S.S. thesis, Smith College School for Social Work, 1938.

Dahlgren, Elza Virginia. "Attitudes of a Group of Unmarried Mothers toward the Minnesota Three Months' Nursing Regulation and Its Application." M.A. thesis, University of Minnesota, 1940.

Davenport, Isabel. "A Study of the Trends of Sexual Interest and Status of Knowledge of Young Women in Their Late Adolescence." Ph.D. diss., Columbia University, 1923.

Dore, Martha M. "Organizational Response to Environmental Change: A Case History Study of the National Florence Crittenton Mission." Ph.D. diss., University of Chicago, 1986.

Hertz, Hilda. "Negro Illegitimacy in Durham, North Carolina." M.A. thesis, Duke University, 1944.

Holsopple, Frances Quinter. "Social Non-Conformity: An Analysis of Four Hundred and Twenty Cases of Delinquent Girls and Women." Ph.D. diss., University of Pennsylvania, 1919.

Ladd-Taylor, Mary Madeline. "Mother-Work: Ideology, Public Policy, and the Mothers' Movement, 1890–1930." Ph.D. diss., Yale University, 1986.

Lunbeck, Elizabeth. "Psychiatry in the Age of Reform: Doctors, Social Workers, and Patients at the Boston Psychopathic Hospital, 1900–1925." Ph.D. diss., Harvard University, 1984.

Mattingly, Mabel Higgins. "The Unmarried Mother and Her Child." M.A. thesis, Western Reserve University, 1928.

Mehling, Grace. "A Study of Salvation Army Principles and Practices Seen in Relation to Casework." M.A. thesis, New York School of Social Work, 1946.

Michel, Sonya Alice. "Children's Interests/Mothers' Rights: Women, Professionals, and the American Family, 1920–1945." Ph.D. diss., Brown University, 1986.

Netting, Florence Eleanor. "The Church-Related Social Service Agency and the Meaning of Its Religious Connection: Three Case Studies." Ph.D. diss., University of Chicago, 1982.

Peterson, June. "Dr. Kate Waller Barrett: A Friend of Girls." M.A. thesis, Seattle University, 1969.

Reed, Ruth. "The Negro Women of Gainesville, Georgia." M.A. thesis, University of Georgia, 1920.

Ripple, Lillian. "Social Work Studies of Unmarried Parenthood as Affected by Contemporary Treatment Formulations: 1920–1940." Ph.D. diss., University of Chicago, 1953.

Shnayerson, Hilda B. "History of the Florence Crittenton League in New York City, 1883–1956: The Evolution of an Agency Dedicated to Meeting Changing Community Needs." M.S. thesis, New York School of Social Work, 1957.

Sibley, Eloise Pearce. "A Study of the Vocational Success of Fifty Unmarried Mothers." M.A. thesis, Ohio State University, 1938.

Smith, Enid Severy. "A Study of Twenty-Five Adolescent Unmarried Mothers in New York City." Ph.D. diss., Columbia University, 1935.

Trudel, Ruth Elizabeth. "The Religious Aspect of Case Work in the Family and Personal Service Department of the Salvation Army." M.A. thesis, Buffalo School of Social Work, 1946.

Watson, Amey Eaton. "Illegitimacy: Philadelphia's Problem and the Development of Standards of Care." Ph.D. diss., Bryn Mawr, 1923.

Wriedan, Jane E. "Growth of a Case Work Agency toward Full Participation in the Life of Its Community." M.S.S. thesis, University of Buffalo, 1945.

PRIMARY SOURCES: BOOKS AND ARTICLES

Abbey, Charlotte. "Illegitimacy and Sex Perversion." In *A Child Welfare Symposium*. Ed. William H. Slingerland. New York: Russell Sage Foundation, 1915.

Abbott, Grace. *The Child and the State*. Vol. 2. Chicago: University of Chicago Press, 1938.

———. *The Immigrant and the Community*. New York: Century Co., 1921.

———. "Ten Years' Work for Children." *North American Review* 218 (July 1923): 189–200.

Adams, Elizabeth Kemper. *Women Professional Workers*. New York: Macmillan, 1921.

Additon, Henrietta. *City Planning for Girls*. Chicago: University of Chicago Press, 1928.

Adkins, Frances L. *Illegitimacy in Cook County*. Chicago: Council of Social Agencies of Chicago, 1935.

Anderson, V. V. "The Immoral Woman in Court." *Journal of Criminal Law and Criminology* 8 (1918): 902–10.

Aronovici, Carol. *Unmarried Girls with Sex Experience*. Philadelphia: Bureau for Social Research of the Seybert Institution, 1922.

Barnes, Annie F. "The Unmarried Mother and Her Child." *Contemporary Review* 112 (Nov. 1917): 556–59.

Barrett, Kate Waller. *Some Practical Considerations on the Conduct of a Rescue Home*. Washington, D.C.: National Florence Crittenton Mission, 1915.

Barrett, Robert South. *The Care of the Unmarried Mother*. Alexandria, Va.: National Florence Crittenton Mission, 1929.

Bartlett, Harriet. "Medical Social Work with the Unmarried Mother." *Child* 2 (May 1938): 235–38.

Baylor, Edith M. "The Necessary Changes to Be Effected in the Methods of Social Service Agencies Working with Unmarried Mothers." *Hospital Social Service* 6 (1922): 144–56.

Beane, James C. "A Survey of Three Hundred Delinquent Girls." *Journal for Juvenile Research* 15 (July 1931): 198–208.

Bernard, Viola W. "Psychodynamics of Unmarried Motherhood in Early Adolescence." *Nervous Child* 4 (Oct. 1944): 26–45.

Bernstein, Rose. "Are We Still Stereotyping the Unmarried Mother?" *Social Work* 5 (1960): 22–28.

Bibring, Grete L. "Psychiatry and Social Work." *Journal of Social Casework* 28 (June 1947): 203–11.

Billingsley, Andrew, and Amy Tate Billingsley. "Illegitimacy and Patterns of Negro Family Life." In *The Unwed Mother*. Ed. Robert W. Roberts. New York: Harper and Row, 1966.

Bingham, Anne T. "Determinants of Sex Delinquency in Adolescent Girls." *Journal of Law and Criminology* 13 (Feb. 1923).

Blanchard, Phyllis, and Carlyn Manasses. *New Girls for Old*. New York: Macaulay, 1930.

Bliss, Nettie Stray. *A Glimpse of Shadowed Lives in a Great City*. Chicago: N.p., 1913.

Booth, W. Bramwell. *Orders and Regulations for Officers of the Women's Social Work of the Salvation Army*. New York: Salvationist Publishing, 1920.

Bowen, Louise DeKoven. *The Public Dance Halls of Chicago*. Chicago: Juvenile Protective Association of Chicago, 1917.

Bowler, Alida C. "A Study of Seventy-Five Delinquent Girls." *Journal of Delinquency* 2 (May 1917): 156–68.

Breckenridge, Sophinisba P. *The Family and the State: Selected Documents*. Chicago: University of Chicago Press, 1934.

———. *Family Welfare Work in a Metropolitan Community: Selected Case Records*. Chicago: University of Chicago Press, 1929.

Breckenridge, Sophinisba P., and Edith Abbott. *The Delinquent Child and the Home*. New York: Russell Sage Foundation, 1912.

"Brief Sketches Taken from the Record of Thirty-One Years in Redemption Home." *There Is Hope* 21 (1934): 1–3.

Brown, Esther L. "Social Work against a Background of the Other Professions." In *Readings in Social Case Work, 1920–1938: Selected Reprints for the Casework Practitioner*. Ed. Fern Lowry. New York: Columbia University Press, 1939.

———. *Social Work as a Profession*. 4th ed. New York: Russell Sage Foundation, 1942.

Bruno, Frank J. *Trends in Social Work, 1874–1956*. New York: Columbia University Press, 1957.

Cabot, Richard C., ed. *The Goal of Social Work*. Cambridge, Mass.: Houghton Mifflin, 1927.

Cheyney, Alice S. *The Nature and Scope of Social Work*. New York: American Association of Social Workers, 1926.

Clarke, Lilian Freeman. *The Story of an Invisible Institution: Forty Years Work for Mothers and Infants*. Boston: George H. Ellis, 1913.

Clothier, Florence. "Problems of Illegitimacy as They Concern the Worker in the Field of Adoption." *Mental Hygiene* 25 (Oct. 1941): 576–90.

———. "Psychological Implications of Unmarried Parenthood." *American Journal of Orthopsychiatry* 13 (July 1943): 531–49.

Colby, M. Ruth. "The Unmarried Mother and Her Baby." *Welfare Magazine* 17 (June 1926): 5–8.

Colcord, Joanna C. "A Study of the Techniques of the Social Case Work Interview." *Social Forces* 7 (June 1929): 519–27.

Cole, Lawrence. "The Need of the Case Work Method in Dealing with Illegitimacy." *Hospital Social Service* 13 (May 1926): 430–42.

Crittenton, Charles N. *The Brother of Girls*. Chicago: World's Events Co., 1910.

———. "From Lips Usually Sealed to the World." *Ladies' Home Journal* 26 (Jan. 1909): 23.

Davis, Kingsly. "The Forms of Illegitimacy." *Social Forces* 18 (Oct. 1939): 77–89.

———. "Illegitimacy and the Social Structure." *American Journal of Sociology* 43 (Sept. 1939): 215–33.

DeSchweinitz, Karl. *The Art of Helping People out of Trouble.* Boston: Houghton Mifflin, 1924.

Deutsch, Helene. *The Psychology of Women: A Psychiatric Interpretation.* Vol. 2. New York: Grune and Stratton, 1945.

Devine, Edward Thomas. *The Spirit of Social Work.* New York: Charities Publication Committee, 1911.

————. *When Social Work Was Young.* New York: Macmillan, 1939.

Dickinson, Robert Latou, and Lura Beam. *The Single Woman: A Medical Study in Sex Education.* New York: Williams and Wilkins, 1934.

Dietrich, Ellen Battelle. "Rescuing Fallen Women." *Women's Journal* (May 27, 1893): 162.

Dinwiddie, Emily W., and Maxwell Ferguson. *The Social Workers' Handbook.* New York: Greenwich House, 1913.

Dolson, Hildegarde. "My Parents Mustn't Know." *Good Housekeeping* (May 1942): 29, 158–59.

Donahue, A. Madorah. "Children Born out of Wedlock." *Annals of the American Academy of Politics and Social Science* 151 (Sept. 1930): 162–72.

Dorr, Rheta Childe. "Reclaiming the Wayward Girl." *Hampton's Magazine* 26 (Jan. 1911): 67–78.

Drake, St. Clair, and Horace R. Cayton. *Black Metropolis: A Study of Negro Life in a Northern City.* New York: Harcourt, Brace, 1945.

Du Bois, W. E. B., ed. *Efforts for Social Betterment among Negro Americans.* Atlanta: Atlanta University Press, 1909.

Edholm, Charlton. *Traffic in Girls and Florence Crittenton Missions.* Chicago: Women's Temperance Publishing Association, 1893.

Edlin, Sara B. *The Unmarried Mother in Our Society.* New York: Farrar, Straus, and Young, 1954.

Eliot, Thomas D. "Objectivity and Subjectivity in the Case Record." *Social Forces* 6 (June 1928): 439–44.

Elliott, Mabel A., and Francis E. Merrill. *Social Disorganization.* New York: Harper and Row, 1934.

Falconer, Martha P. "Causes of Delinquency among Girls." *Annals of the American Academy of Political and Social Science* 36 (July 1910): 77–79.

Farmer, Gertrude L. "Case Work with the Unmarried Mother." *Hospital Social Service* 4 (Nov. 1921): 285–88.

Fink, Arthur E. *The Field of Social Work.* New York: Henry Holt, 1942.

Fisher, Lettie. "The Unmarried Mother and Her Child." *Contemporary Review* 156 (Oct. 1939): 485–89.

Fletcher, Ralph Carr. "The Problem of Illegitimacy in Pittsburgh." *Federator* 14 (Oct. 1939): 236–45.

Frazier, E. Franklin. "An Analysis of Statistics on Negro Illegitimacy in the United States." *Social Forces* 11 (Dec. 1932): 249–57.

———. *The Negro Family in the United States.* Rev. ed. New York: Citadel Press, 1948.

———. *Negro Youth at the Crossways: Their Personality Development in the Middle States.* Washington, D.C.: American Council on Education, 1940.

———. "Traditions and Patterns of Negro Family Life in the United States." In *Race and Culture Contacts.* Ed. E. B. Reuter. New York: McGraw-Hill, 1943.

Garrett, Annette. "Historical Survey of the Evolution of Casework." *Social Casework* 30 (June 1949): 219–29.

———. *Interviewing: Its Principles and Methods.* New York: Family Welfare Association of America, 1942.

Gillin, John Lewis. *Social Pathology.* New York: Century, 1933.

Groves, Ernest R. *Social Problems and Education.* New York: Longmans, Green, 1925.

Guibord, Alberta, and Ida R. Parker. *What Becomes of the Unmarried Mother? A Study of Eighty-two Cases.* Boston: Research Bureau on Social Case Work, 1922.

Halbert, L. A. *What Is Professional Social Work?* New York: Survey, 1923.

Halton, Mary. "America's Disgrace: One Hundred Thousand Illegitimate Babies Yearly." *True Story* 40 (March 1939): 4–5, 76–78.

Hanna, Agnes K. "Changing Care of Children Born out of Wedlock." *Annals of the American Academy of Political and Social Science* 212 (Nov. 1940): 159–67.

———. "Maternity Homes." *Mother* (April 1942): 11–12.

Hatcher, O. Latham, ed. *Occupations for Women.* Richmond, Va.: Southern Women's Educational Alliance, 1927.

Healy, William. *The Individual Delinquent.* Boston: Little, Brown, 1915.

Hertz, Hilda, and Sue Warren Little. "Unmarried Negro Mothers in a Southern Urban Community." *Social Forces* 23 (Oct. 1944): 73–79.

Hickey, Margaret. "The Crittenton Program." *Ladies' Home Journal* 75 (Aug. 1958): 23.

———. "Unmarried Mothers . . . Salvation Army Care." *Ladies' Home Journal* 14 (1949).

Howland, Goldwin W. "Illegitimate Mothers." *Hospital Social Service* 16 (July 1927): 6–10.

Hurlin, Ralph G. *The Number and Distribution of Social Workers in the United States.* New York: Russell Sage Foundation, 1933.

———. *Social Work Salaries.* New York: Russell Sage Foundation, 1926.

Hutzel, Elenore L. "Social Treatment of the Unmarried Mother." *Hospital Social Service* 6 (Sept. 1922): 156–64.

"I Kept My Baby." *American Magazine* 130 (Aug. 1940): 27+.

"Illegitimacy during the Depression." *Child* 1 (Sept. 1936): 17–18.

Interviews: A Study of the Methods of Analyzing and Recording Social Case Work Interviews. New York: American Association of Social Workers, 1931.

Jameson, Augusta T. "Psychological Factors Contributing to the Delinquency of Girls." *Journal of Juvenile Research* 22 (Jan. 1938): 25–32.

Jarrett, Mary C. "The Significance of Psychiatric Social Work." *Mental Hygiene* 5 (July 1921): 509–18.

Judge, Jane G. "Casework with the Unmarried Mother in a Family Agency." *Social Casework* 32 (Jan. 1951): 7–15.

Kammerer, Percy Gamble. *The Unmarried Mother: A Study of Five Hundred Cases*. Boston: Little, Brown, 1918.

Karpf, Maurice J. *The Scientific Basis of Social Work: A Study in Family Case Work*. New York: Columbia University Press, 1931.

Kasanin, J., and Sieglinde Handschin. "Psychodynamic Factors in Illegitimacy." *American Journal of Orthopsychiatry* 11 (Jan. 1941): 66–84.

"Kate Waller Barrett: Nurse, Doctor, and Sociologist." *Trained Nurse and Hospital Review* 24 (April 1925): 387.

Kellog, Foster S. "The Unmarried Mother before and after Confinement." *American Journal of Obstetrics and Gynecology* 1 (Dec. 1920): 292–93.

Kenworthy, Marion E. "The Mental Hygiene Aspects of Illegitimacy." *Mental Hygiene* (July 1921): 499–508.

Knapp, Patricia. "The Attitudes of Negro Unmarried Mothers toward Illegitimacy." *Smith College Studies in Social Work* 17 (Dec. 1946): 153–54.

Konopka, Gisela. "Changing Definitions and Areas of Social Work Research." *Social Work Journal* 36 (April 1955): 55–59.

LaBarre, Maurine Boie. "Cultural and Racial Problems in Social Case Work with Special Reference to Negroes." In *Cultural Problems in Social Case Work*. New York: Family Welfare Association of America, 1940.

Lauder, Ruth. "No Longer Alone: An Intelligent Approach to the Unmarried Mother." *Trained Nurse and Hospital Review* 107 (Dec. 1941): 423–25.

Laughlin, Clara E. "Condemned Mothers and Babies." *Pearson's Magazine* (Feb. 1915): 227–37.

Leader, Pauline. *And No Birds Sing*. New York: Vanguard Press, 1931.

Lee, Porter R. *Social Work as Cause and Function*. New York: Columbia University Press, 1937.

Lee, Porter R., and Marion E. Kenworthy. *Mental Hygiene and Social Work*. New York: Commonwealth Fund, 1929.

Lenroot, Katherine F. "Case Work with Unmarried Parents." *Hospital Social Service* 12 (Aug. 1925): 69–76.

Lesik, Vera. "Bachelor Mothers." *Magazine Digest* (Sept. 1940): 34–39.

Leyendecker, Gertrude T. "Generic and Specific Factors in Casework with the Unmarried Mother." In *Services to Unmarried Mothers*. New York: Child Welfare League of America, 1958.

Lowe, Charlotte. "The Intelligence and Social Background of the Unmarried Mother." *Mental Hygiene* 11 (Oct. 1927): 783–94.

Lowell, Mrs. Charles Russell. "Houses of Refuge for Women: Their Purposes, Management, and Possibilities." New York State Conference of Charities and Corrections. *Proceedings* (1900): 245–61.

Lowry, Fern. "The Client's Needs as the Basis for Differential Approach in Treatment." In *Differential Approach in Case Work Treatment*. New York: Family Welfare Association of America, 1936.

Lowry, Fern, ed. *Readings in Social Case Work, 1920–1938: Selected Reprints for the Case Work Practitioner*. New York: Columbia University Press, 1939.

Lundberg, Emma O. "The Illegitimate Child and War Conditions." *American Journal of Physical Anthropology* 1 (July–Sept. 1918): 339–52.

———. *Unmarried Mothers in the Municipal Court of Philadelphia*. Philadelphia: Thomas Skelton Harrison Foundation, 1933.

———. *Unto the Least of These: Social Services for Children*. New York: D. Appleton-Century, 1947.

McClure, W. E. "Intelligence of Unmarried Mothers, II." *Psychological Clinic* 20 (Oct. 1931): 154–57.

McClure, W. E., and Bronnett Goldberg. "Intelligence of Unmarried Mothers." *Psychological Clinic* 18 (May–June 1929): 119–27.

Magee, Edith D. "Illegitimacy as a Medical Social Problem." *Hospital Social Service* 25 (April 1932): 287–306.

Mangold, George. *Children Born out of Wedlock: A Sociological Study of Illegitimacy, with Particular Reference to the United States*. Columbia: University of Missouri Press, 1921.

———. "Unlawful Motherhood." *Forum* 53 (Feb. 1915): 335–43.

Marcus, Grace F. *Some Aspects of Relief in Family Case Work*. New York: Charity Organization Society of New York, 1929.

"Maternity Home Care during 1937." *Child* 2 (June 1938, supp.): 3–9.

Mathews, Julia. "A Survey of Three Hundred and Forty-one Delinquent Girls in California." *Journal of Delinquency* 8 (May–June 1923): 196–231.

Maxfield, Francis N. "The Social Treatment of Unmarried Mothers." *Psychological Clinic* 9 (Dec. 15, 1915): 210–17.

"Medical Social Work with the Unmarried Mother." *Child* 2 (May 1938): 235–38.

Menken, Alice D. "A Social Aspect of the Unmarried Mother." *Journal of Delinquency* 7 (March 1922): 99–103.

Menninger, William C. *Psychiatry in a Troubled World*. New York: Macmillan, 1948.

Merrill, Francis E. *Social Problems on the Home Front: A Study of War-Time Influences*. New York: Harper and Brothers, 1948.

The Milford Conference Report: Social Case Work Generic and Specific. New York: American Association of Social Workers, 1929.

Miner, Maude. "The Woman Delinquent." New York City Conference on Charities and Corrections. *Proceedings* (1911): 152–65.

Moore, Howard. *The Care of Illegitimate Children in Chicago*. Chicago: Juvenile Protection Association of Chicago, 1912.

Moore, Katherine. "The Relation of Social Worker and Patient." *Social Syndrome* 2 (1922): 10–12.

Morlock, Maud. "Foster-Home Care for Unmarried Mothers." *Child* 3 (Sept. 1938): 51–55.

———. "'Shall I Keep My Baby?'" *Trained Nurse and Hospital Review* 109 (July 1942): 21–24.

———. "Social Treatment of the Unmarried Mother Separated from Her Child." *Hospital Social Service* 6 (1922): 68–75.

———. "Wanted: A Square Deal for the Baby Born out of Wedlock." *Child* 10 (May 1946): 167–69.

Moxcey, Mary E. *Girlhood and Character.* New York: YWCA, 1916.

Murphy, J. Prentice, "Illegitimacy and Feeblemindedness." *Mental Hygiene* 1 (1917): 591–97.

———. "What Can be Accomplished through Good Social Work in the Field of Illegitimacy?" *Annals of the American Academy of Political and Social Science* 93 (Nov. 1921): 129–35.

Myrdal, Gunnar. *An American Dilemma: The Negro Problem and Modern Democracy.* New York: Harper and Brothers, 1944.

Neilson, W. A. "The Smith College Experiment in Training for Psychiatric Social Work." *Mental Hygiene* 3 (Jan. 1919): 59–64.

Nottingham, Ruth D. "A Psychological Study of Forty Unmarried Mothers." *Genetic Psychology Monographs* 19 (May 1937): 155–228.

O'Conner, Eileen. "Baby or Abortion—Which?" *She* (Dec. 1944).

Odencrantz, Louise C. *The Social Worker in Family, Medical, and Psychiatric Social Work.* New York: Harper and Brothers, 1929.

Ordahl, Louise E., and George Ordahl. "A Study of Delinquent and Dependent Girls." *Journal of Delinquency* 3 (March 1918): 41–73.

Paddon, Mary E. "A Study of Fifty Feeble-Minded Prostitutes." *Journal of Delinquency* 3 (Jan. 1918): 1–11.

Palmer, Agnes L. *1904 to 1926: The Time Between.* New York: Salvation Army, 1926.

Parker, Ida R. *A Follow-Up Study of Five Hundred and Fifty Illegitimacy Applications.* Boston: Research Bureau on Social Case Work, 1924.

Parsons, Katherine Corbin. *The Unmarried Mother and Her Child.* Boston: Christopher Publishing House, 1951.

Peirce, Adah. *Vocations for Women.* New York: Macmillan, 1933.

Perlman, Helen Harris. "Unmarried Mothers." In *Social Work and Social Problems.* Ed. Nathan E. Cohen. New York: National Association of Social Workers, 1964.

Phelps, Harold A. *Contemporary Social Problems.* New York: Prentice-Hall, 1933.

Pigeon, Helen D. *Effect of War Conditions on Children and Adolescents in the City of Hartford, Connecticut.* New Haven: Connecticut Child Welfare Association, 1944.

Pinckney, Merritt W. "The Delinquent Girl and the Juvenile Court." In *The Child in the City.* Ed. Sophinisba Breckenridge. Chicago: Department of Social Investigation, 1912.

Potter, Ellen C. "How Shall We Plan for Children of Unmarried Mothers in Correctional Institutions?" *Hospital Social Service* 23 (April 1931): 403–12.

Powell, Miriam. "Illegitimate Pregnancy in Emotionally Disturbed Girls." *Smith College Studies in Social Work* 19 (June 1949): 171–79.

Pruette, Loring. "Conditions Today." In *The Sex Life of the Unmarried Adult*. Ed. Ira Wile. New York: Vanguard Press, 1934.

Puttee, Dorothy Frances, and Mary Ruth Colby. *The Illegitimate Child in Illinois*. Chicago: University of Chicago Press, 1937.

Queen, Stuart Alfred. *Social Work in the Light of History*. Philadelphia: J. B. Lippincott, 1922.

Queen, Stuart Alfred, and Delbert Martin Mann. *Social Pathology*. New York: Thomas Y. Crowell, 1925.

Railton, George. *Talks with Rescuers: Being a Review of the Work during 1898, under the Direction of Mrs. Bramwell Booth*. London: Salvation Army, 1898.

Reed, Ruth. *The Illegitimate Family in New York City: Its Treatment by Social and Health Agencies*. New York: Columbia University Press, 1934.

———. *The Modern Family*. New York: Alfred A. Knopf, 1929.

———. *Negro Illegitimacy in New York City*. New York: Columbia University Press, 1926.

———. *The Social and Health Care of the Illegitimate Family in New York City*. New York: Research Bureau Welfare Council of New York City, 1932.

Reeves, Margaret. *Training Schools for Delinquent Girls*. New York: Russell Sage Foundation, 1929.

Reid, Virginia. "Black Market Babies." *Woman's Home Companion* 71 (Dec. 1944): 30–31.

Reynolds, Bertha C. *Social Work and Social Living*. New York: Citadel Press, 1951.

———. *An Uncharted Journey: Fifty Years of Growth in Social Work*. New York: Citadel Press, 1963.

Rich, Margaret E., ed. *Family Life To-Day*. Cambridge, Mass., Riverside Press, 1928.

Richmond, Mary E. *Friendly Visiting among the Poor: A Handbook for Charity Workers*. New York: Macmillan, 1899.

———. *Social Diagnosis*. New York: Russell Sage Foundation, 1917.

Richmond, Winifred. *The Adolescent Girl*. New York: Macmillan, 1930.

Robinson, Virginia P. *A Changing Psychology in Social Case Work*. Philadelphia: University of Pennsylvania Press, 1930.

———. *Supervision in Social Case Work*. Chapel Hill: University of North Carolina Press, 1936.

Robinson, William J. *Sexual Problems of To-Day*. 12th ed. New York: Critic and Guide Co., 1923.

Roror, Emily F. "A Survey of Illegitimacy of Unmarried Negresses Who Were Delivered at the Lying-In Hospital of Philadelphia, 1927–28." *Medical Woman's Journal* 39 (Jan. 1932): 8–13.

Rubinow, I. M. "Social Case Work—A Profession in the Making." *Journal of Social Forces* 4 (1925): 286–92.

Schatkin, Sidney B. *Disputed Paternity Proceedings*. Albany, N.Y.: Matthew Bender and Co., 1944.

Scherz, Frances H. "'Taking Sides' in the Unmarried Mother's Conflict." *Journal of Social Casework* 28 (Feb. 1947): 57–61.

Schmideberg, Melitta. "Psychiatric-Social Factors in Young Unmarried Mothers." *Social Casework* 32 (Jan. 1951): 3–7.

Schumacher, Henry C. "The Unmarried Mother: A Socio-Psychiatric Viewpoint." *Journal of Mental Hygiene* 11 (Oct. 1927): 775–82.

Service: An Exposition of the Salvation Army in America. Clinton, Mass.: Colonial Press, 1937.

Sheffield, Ada E. *The Social Case History: Its Construction and Content*. New York: Russell Sage Foundation, 1920.

———. "What Is the Case Worker Really Doing?" *Journal of Social Forces* 1 (May 1923): 362–66.

Slawson, John. "The Adolescent in a World at War." *Mental Hygiene* 27 (Oct. 1943): 531–48.

Smith, Edith Livingston. "Unmarried Mothers." *Harper's Weekly* 58 (Sept. 6, 1913): 22–23.

Smith, R. G., and Harry Gauss. "Serologic Survey of the Denver Florence Crittenton Home." *Journal of the American Medical Association* 78 (Feb. 1922): 535–36.

"Social Workers Look at Adoption." *Child* 10 (Jan. 1946): 110–12.

Stevens, Raymond B. "Illegal Families among the Clients of Family Agencies." *Social Forces* 19 (Oct. 1940): 84–87.

Study of Children Born out of Wedlock in Connecticut. New Haven: Connecticut Child Welfare Association, 1927.

Taft, Jessie. "The Relations of Function to Process in Social Case Work." *Journal of Social Work Process* 1 (Nov. 1937): 3.

Taylor, Eleanor. "Nobody's Child." *Woman's Journal* 15 (May 1930): 20–21, 35–36.

Thomas, William I. *The Unadjusted Girl*. Boston: Little, Brown, 1923.

Tobey, James A. *The Children's Bureau: Its History, Activities, and Organization*. Baltimore: Johns Hopkins University Press, 1925.

Todd, Arthur James. *The Scientific Spirit and Social Work*. New York: Macmillan, 1919.

Trounstine, Helen S. "Illegitimacy in Cincinnati." *Studies from the Helen S. Trounstine Foundation* 1 (Sept. 1919).

Trout, Louise K. "Services to Unmarried Mothers." *Child Welfare* 35 (Feb. 1956): 21–26.

Tufts, James H. *Education and Training for Social Work*. New York: Russell Sage Foundation, 1923.

Turner, E. S. "An Equal Standard of Morals—Some Plain Words on a Forbidden Subject." *Philanthropist* (May 1894): 1–3.

Vincent, Clark E. "The Unwed Mother and Sampling Bias." *American Sociological Review* 19 (Oct. 1954): 562–67.

Walker, Sydnor H. *Social Work and the Training of Social Workers*. Chapel Hill: University of North Carolina Press, 1928.

Watson, Amey Eaton. "The Illegitimate Family." *Annals of the American Academy of Political and Social Science* 77 (May 1918): 103–16.

White, R. Clyde. "A Strategy for Social Workers." *Compass* 25 (Nov. 1943): 21–23.

Whittemore, Emma. *Mother Whittemore's Records of Modern Miracles*. Toronto: Missions of Biblical Education, 1931.

Wiley, Mabel A. *A Study of the Problem of Girl Delinquency in New Haven*. New Haven: Documents of the Civic Federation of New Haven, 1915.

Wilson, Otto. *Fifty Years' Work with Girls, 1883–1933*. Alexandria, Va.: National Florence Crittenton Mission, 1933.

Wolbarst, Abr. L. "The Unmarried Mother and the Wasserman Reaction." *Hospital Social Service* 5 (May 1922): 281–88.

Woods, Robert A., and Albert J. Kennedy. *Young Working Girls: A Summary of Evidence from Two Thousand Social Workers*. Boston: Houghton Mifflin, 1913.

Worcester, Daisy Lee Worthington. *Grim the Battles: A Semi-Autobiographical Account of the War against Want in the United States during the First Half of the Twentieth Century*. New York: Exposition Press, 1954.

Worthington, George E., and Ruth Topping. *Specialized Courts Dealing with Sex Delinquency*. New York: Frederick H. Hitchcock, 1925.

Yeo, Lillian M. *Inasmuch: A Résumé of Twenty-two Years in the House of Mercy*. New York: Edwin S. Gorham, 1923.

Young, Leontine R. *Out of Wedlock*. New York: McGraw-Hill, 1954.

———. "The Unmarried Mother's Decision about Her Baby." *Journal of Social Casework* 28 (Jan. 1947): 27–34.

Younger, Joan. "The Unwed Mother." *Ladies' Home Journal* 64 (June 1947): 102+.

Zarefsky, Joseph L. "Children Acquire New Parents." *Child* 10 (March 1946): 142–44.

SECONDARY SOURCES

Abir-Am, Pnina G., and Dorinda Outram, eds. *Uneasy Careers and Intimate Lives: Women in Science, 1789–1979*. New Brunswick, N.J.: Rutgers University Press, 1987.

Abramovitz, Mimi. *Regulating the Lives of Women: Social Welfare Policy from Colonial Times to the Present*. Boston: South End Press, 1988.

Achenbaum, W. Andrew. "An Agenda for Future Research in American Social Welfare History." In *Social Welfare in America: An Annotated Bibliography*. Ed. Walter I. Trattner and W. Andrew Achenbaum. Westport, Conn.: Greenwood Press, 1983.

Agnew, Jean-Christophe. "A Touch of Class." *Democracy* 3 (Spring 1983): 59–72.

Aiken, Katherine G. "From Mission to Hospital: The Detroit Florence Crittenton Organization, 1897–1930." *Detroit in Perspective: A Journal of Regional History* 6 (Spring 1982): 50–64.

Alexander, Leslie B. "Social Work's Freudian Deluge: Myth or Reality?" *Social Service Review* 46 (Dec. 1972): 517–38.

Allen, David G. "Professionalism, Occupational Segregation by Gender and Control of Nursing." *Women and Politics* 6 (Fall 1980): 1–24.

Anderson, Karen. *Wartime Women: Sex Roles, Family Relations, and the Status of Women during World War II*. Westport, Conn.: Greenwood Press, 1981.

Ashby, LeRoy. *Saving the Waifs: Reformers and Dependent Children, 1890–1917*. Philadelphia: Temple University Press, 1984.

Bailey, Beth L. *From Front Porch to Back Seat: Courtship in Twentieth-Century America*. Baltimore: Johns Hopkins University Press, 1988.

Baxter, Annette K., and Barbara Welter. *Inwood House: One Hundred and Fifty Years of Service to Women*. New York: Inwood House, 1980.

Becker, Dorothy G. "Exit Lady Bountiful: The Volunteer and the Professional Social Worker." *Social Service Review* 34 (March 1964): 57–72.

Bledstein, Burton J. *The Culture of Professionalism: The Middle Class and the Development of Higher Education in America*. New York: Norton, 1976.

Borenzweig, Herman. "Social Work and Psychoanalytic Theory: A Historical Analysis." *Social Work* 16 (Jan. 1971): 7–16.

Brandt, Allan M. *No Magic Bullet: A Social History of Venereal Disease in the United States since 1880*. New York: Oxford University Press, 1985.

Bremer, William W. *Depression Winters: New York Social Workers and the New Deal*. Philadelphia: Temple University Press, 1984.

Bremner, Robert H. *From the Depths: The Discovery of Poverty in the United States*. New York: New York University Press, 1956.

———. "'Scientific Philanthropy,' 1873–1893." *Social Service Review* 30 (June 1956): 168–73.

———. "The State of Social Welfare History." In *The State of American History*. Ed. Herbert J. Bass. Chicago: Quadrangle, 1970.

Brenzel, Barbara M. *Daughters of the State: A Social Portrait of the First Reform School for Girls in North America, 1856–1905*. Cambridge, Mass.: MIT Press, 1983.

Brown, Jo Anne. "Professional Language: Words that Succeed." *Radical History Review* 34 (Jan. 1986): 33–51.

Bruel, Frank R., and Steven J. Diner, eds. *Compassion and Responsibility: Readings in the History of Social Welfare Policy in the United States*. Chicago: University of Chicago Press, 1980.

Brumberg, Joan Jacobs. "'Ruined' Girls: Changing Community Responses to Illegitimacy in Upstate New York, 1890–1920." *Journal of Social History* 18 (Winter 1984).

————. "Zenanas and Girlless Villages: The Ethnology of American Evangelical Women, 1870–1910." *Journal of American History* 69 (Sept. 1982): 347–71.

Brumberg, Joan Jacobs, and Nancy Tomes. "Women in the Professions: A Research Agenda for American Historians." *Reviews in American History* 10 (June 1982): 275–96.

Burnham, John C. "The Influence of Psychoanalysis upon American Culture." In *American Psychoanalysis: Origins and Development.* Ed. Jacque M. Quen and Eric T. Carlson. New York: Brunner/Mazel, 1978.

————. "Medical Specialists and Movements toward Social Control in the Progressive Era: Three Examples." In *Building the Organizational Society.* Ed. Jerry Israel. New York: Free Press, 1972.

Carby, Hazel V. "Policing the Black Woman's Body in an Urban Context." *Critical Inquiry* 4 (Summer 1992): 738–55.

Chambers, Clarke A. "Creative Effort in an Age of Normalcy, 1918–33." *Social Welfare Forum.* New York: Columbia University Press, 1961.

————. *Seedtime of Reform: American Social Service and Social Action, 1918–1933.* Minneapolis: University of Minnesota Press, 1963.

————. "Social Service and Social Reform: A Historical Essay." *Social Service Review* 30 (June 1956): 158–67.

————. "Toward a Redefinition of Welfare History." *Journal of American History* 73 (Sept. 1986): 407–33.

————. "Women in the Creation of Social Work." *Social Service Review* 60 (March 1986): 1–33.

Chesham, Sallie. *Born to Battle: The Salvation Army in America.* Chicago: Rand McNally, 1965.

Clark, Anna. "The Politics of Seduction in English Popular Culture, 1748–1848." In *The Progress of Romance: The Politics of Popular Fiction.* Ed. Jean Radford. London: Routledge and Kegan Paul, 1986.

————. *Women's Silence, Men's Violence: Sexual Assault in England, 1770–1845.* London: Pandora Press, 1987.

Connelly, Mark Thomas. *The Response to Prostitution in the Progressive Era.* Chapel Hill: University of North Carolina Press, 1980.

Costello, John. *Virtue under Fire: How World War II Changed Our Social and Sexual Attitudes.* Boston: Little, Brown, 1985.

Costin, Lela B. *Two Sisters for Social Justice: A Biography of Grace and Edith Abbott.* Chicago: University of Illinois Press, 1983.

Cott, Nancy F. *The Grounding of Modern Feminism.* New Haven: Yale University Press, 1987.

Cumbler, John T. "The Politics of Charity: Gender and Class in Late Nineteenth Century Charity Policy." *Journal of Social History* 14 (Fall 1980): 99–112.

Davis, Allen F. *Spearheads for Reform: The Social Settlement and the Progressive Movement, 1890–1914.* New York: Oxford University Press, 1967.

D'Emilio, John, and Estelle B. Freedman. *Intimate Matters: A History of Sexuality in America.* New York: Harper and Row, 1988.

Demos, John, and Virginia Demos. "Adolescence in Historical Perspective." *Journal of Marriage and the Family* 31 (1969): 632–38.

Denning, Michael. *Mechanic Accents: Dime Novels and Working-Class Culture in America*. London: Verso, 1987.

Diamond, Irene, ed. *Families, Politics, and Public Policy: A Feminist Dialogue on Women and the State*. New York: Longman, 1983.

Drachman, Virginia. *Hospital with a Heart: Women Doctors and the Paradox of Separatism at the New England Hospital, 1862–1969*. Ithaca: Cornell University Press, 1984.

Dudden, Faye E. *Serving Women: Household Service in Nineteenth-Century America*. Middletown, Conn.: Wesleyan University Press, 1983.

Edelman, Murray. "The Political Language of the Helping Professions." *Politics and Society* 4 (1974): 295–310.

Ehrenreich, Barbara, and John Ehrenreich. "The Professional-Managerial Class." *Radical America* 11 (March–April 1977): 7–31.

Ehrenreich, Barbara, and Deirdre English. *For Her Own Good: One Hundred and Fifty Years of the Experts' Advice to Women*. Garden City, N.Y.: Anchor Press, 1978.

Ehrenreich, John H. *The Altruistic Imagination: A History of Social Work and Social Policy in the United States*. Ithaca: Cornell University Press, 1985.

Epstein, Barbara Leslie. "Family, Sexual Morality, and Popular Movements in Turn-of-the-Century America." In *Powers of Desire: The Politics of Sexuality*. Ed. Ann Snitow, Christine Stansell, and Sharon Thompson. New York: Monthly Review Press, 1983.

––––––. *The Politics of Domesticity: Women, Evangelism, and Temperance in Nineteenth-Century America*. Middletown, Conn.: Wesleyan University Press, 1981.

Epstein, Cynthia Fuchs. "Encountering the Male Establishment: Sex Status Limits on Women's Careers in the Professions." *American Journal of Sociology* 75 (May 1975): 965–82.

––––––. *Woman's Place: Options and Limits in Professional Careers*. Berkeley: University of California Press, 1970.

––––––. *Women in Law*. New York: Basic Books, 1981.

Etzioni, Amitai, ed. *The Semi-Professions and Their Organization*. New York: Free Press, 1969.

Fairbank, Jenty. *Booth's Boots: Social Service Beginnings in the Salvation Army*. London: Salvation Army, 1983.

Fairchilds, Cissie. "Female Sexual Attitudes and the Rise of Illegitimacy: A Case Study." *Journal of Interdisciplinary History* 8 (1978): 627–67.

Fee, Elizabeth. "Venereal Disease: The Wages of Sin?" In *Passion and Power: Sexuality in History*. Ed. Kathy Peiss and Christina Simmons. Philadelphia: Temple University Press, 1989.

Field, Martha Heineman. "Social Casework Practice during the 'Psychiatric Deluge.'" *Social Service Review* 54 (Dec. 1980): 482–507.

Fitzpatrick, Ellen. "Childbirth and an Unwed Mother in Seventeenth-Century New England." *Signs* (Summer 1983): 744–49.

Franklin, Donna L. "Mary Richmond and Jane Addams: From Moral Certainty to Rational Inquiry in Social Work Practice." *Social Service Review* 60 (Dec. 1986): 504–25.

Freedman, Estelle B. "Separatism as Strategy: Female Institution Building and American Feminism, 1870–1930." *Feminist Studies* 5 (Fall 1979): 512–29.

———. *Their Sisters' Keepers: Women's Prison Reform in America, 1830–1930.* Ann Arbor: University of Michigan Press, 1981.

———. "'Uncontrolled Desires': The Response to the Sexual Psychopath, 1920–1960." *Journal of American History* 74 (June 1987): 83–106.

Fuchs, Rachel G., and Leslie Page Moch. "Pregnant, Single, and Far from Home: Migrant Women in Nineteenth-Century Paris." *American Historical Review* 95 (Oct. 1990): 1007–31.

Galambos, Louis. "Technology, Political Economy, and Professionalization: Central Themes of the Organizational Synthesis." *Business History Review* 57 (Winter 1983): 471–93.

Garrison, Dee. *Apostles of Culture: The Public Librarian and American Society, 1876–1920.* New York: Free Press, 1979.

Germain, Carol. "Casework and Science: A Historical Encounter." In *Theories of Social Casework.* Ed. Robert W. Roberts and Robert H. Nee. Chicago: University of Chicago Press, 1970.

Gettleman, Marvin E. "Charity and Social Classes in the United States, 1874–1900." *American Journal of Economics and Sociology* 22 (April 1963): 313–29.

———. "Philanthropy as Social Control in Late-Nineteenth-Century America: Some Hypotheses and Data on the Rise of Social Work." *Societas* 5 (Winter 1975): 49–59.

Gillis, John R. "Servants, Sexual Relations, and the Risk of Illegitimacy in London, 1801–1900." *Feminist Studies* 5 (Spring 1979): 142–73.

Ginzberg, Lori D. *Women and the Work of Benevolence: Morality: Politics, and Class in the Nineteenth-Century United States.* New Haven: Yale University Press, 1990.

Giovannoni, Jeanne M., and Margaret E. Purvine. "The Myth of the Social Work Matriarchy." In *Social Welfare Forum.* New York: National Conference on Social Welfare, 1974.

Glazer, Penina Migdal, and Miriam Slater. *Unequal Colleagues: The Entrance of Women into the Professions, 1890–1940.* New Brunswick, N.J.: Rutgers University Press, 1987.

Gordon, Linda. "Black and White Visions of Welfare: Women's Welfare Activism, 1890 to 1945." *Journal of American History* 78 (Sept. 1991): 559–90.

———. "Family Violence, Feminism, and Social Control." *Feminist Studies* 12 (Fall 1986): 453–78.

———. "Feminism and Social Control: The Case of Child Abuse and Neglect." In

What Is Feminism? Ed. Juliet Mitchell and Ann Oakley. New York: Pantheon, 1986.

———. *Heroes of Their Own Lives: The Politics and History of Family Violence: Boston, 1880–1960.* New York: Viking, 1988.

———. "Single Mothers and Child Neglect, 1880–1920." *American Quarterly* 37 (Summer 1985): 173–92.

———. *Woman's Body, Woman's Right: A Social History of Birth Control in America.* New York: Grossman, 1976.

Gottesfeld, Mary L., and Mary E. Pharis. *Profiles in Social Work.* New York: Human Sciences Press, 1977.

Grimm, James W. "Women in Female-Dominated Professions." In *Women Working: Theories and Facts in Perspective.* Ed. Ann H. Stromberg and Shirley Harkness. Palo Alto, Calif.: Mayfield, 1978.

Grimsted, David. *Melodrama Unveiled: American Theater and Culture, 1800– 1850.* Chicago: University of Chicago Press, 1968.

Grossberg, Michael. *Governing the Hearth: Law and the Family in Nineteenth-Century America.* Chapel Hill: University of North Carolina Press, 1985.

Gullett, Gayle, "City Mothers, City Daughters, and the Dance Hall Girls: The Limits of Female Political Power in San Francisco, 1913." In *Women and the Structure of Society.* Ed. Barbara J. Harris and JoAnn R. McNamara. Durham, N.C.: Duke University Press, 1984.

Gutman, Herbert. "Mirrors of Hard, Distorted Glass: An Examination of Some Influential Historical Assumptions about the Afro-American Family and the Shaping of Public Policies, 1861–1965." In *Social History and Social Policy.* Ed. David J. Rothman and Stanton Wheeler. New York: Academic Press, 1981.

Haller, Mark H. *Eugenics: Hereditarian Attitudes in American Thought.* New Brunswick, N.J.: Rutgers University Press, 1963.

Harris, Barbara J. *Beyond Her Sphere: Women and the Professions in American History.* Westport, Conn.: Greenwood Press, 1978.

Haskell, Thomas L., ed. *The Authority of Experts: Studies in History and Theory.* Bloomington: Indiana University Press, 1984.

———. *The Emergence of Professional Social Science: The American Social Science Association and the Nineteenth-Century Crisis of Authority.* Urbana: University of Illinois Press, 1977.

Haug, Marie R., and Marvin B. Sussman. "Professional Autonomy and the Revolt of the Client." *Social Problems* 17 (Fall 1969): 153–60.

Hays, Samuel P. "The New Organizational Society." In *Building the Organizational Society.* Ed. Jerry Israel. New York: Free Press, 1972.

Hewitt, Nancy A. *Women's Activism and Social Change: Rochester, New York, 1822–1872.* Ithaca: Cornell University Press, 1984.

Hill, Patricia R. *The World Their Household: The American Woman's Foreign Mission Movement and Cultural Transformation, 1870–1920.* Ann Arbor: University of Michigan Press, 1985.

Hobson, Barbara Meil. *Uneasy Virtue: The Politics of Prostitution and the American Reform Tradition.* New York: Basic, 1987.

Hochschild, Arlie Russell. "Emotion Work, Feeling Rules, and Social Structure." *American Journal of Sociology* 85 (May 1979): 551–75.

Hollinger, David A. "Inquiry and Uplift: Late-Nineteenth-Century American Academics and the Moral Efficacy of Scientific Practice." In *The Authority of Experts.* Ed. Thomas Haskell. Bloomington: Indiana University Press, 1984.

Howard, Ronald L. "Sociology and the Family in the Progressive Era, 1890–1920." In *A Social History of American Family Sociology, 1865–1940.* Ed. Ronald L. Howard. Westport, Conn.: Greenwood Press, 1981.

Hudson, Kenneth. *The Jargon of the Professions.* London: Macmillan, 1978.

Hummer, Patricia M. *The Decade of Elusive Promise: Professional Women in the United States, 1920–1930.* Ann Arbor: UMI Research, 1979.

Ignatieff, Michael. "Total Institutions and the Working Classes: A Review Essay." *History Workshop* 15 (Spring 1983): 167–73.

Irigaray, Luce. "Is the Subject of Science Sexed?" *Cultural Critique* 1 (Fall 1985): 73–88.

Israel, Jerry, ed. *Building the Organizational Society: Essays on Associational Activities in Modern America.* New York: Free Press, 1972.

Jackson, Walter A. *Gunnar Myrdal and America's Conscience: Social Engineering and Racial Liberalism, 1938–1987.* Chapel Hill: University of North Carolina Press, 1990.

Jones, Gareth Stedman. "Class Expression versus Social Control? A Critique of Recent Trends in the Social History of 'Leisure.'" *History Workshop* 4 (Autumn 1977): 163–70.

Kaminer, Wendy. *Women Volunteering: The Pleasure, Pain, and Politics of Unpaid Work from 1830 to the Present.* Garden City, N.Y.: Anchor Press, 1984.

Katzman, David M. *Seven Days a Week: Women and Domestic Service in Industrializing America.* New York: Oxford University Press, 1978.

Keller, Evelyn Fox. *Reflections on Gender and Science.* New Haven: Yale University Press, 1985.

———. "Women Scientists and Feminist Critics of Science." *Daedalus* 116 (Fall 1987): 77–91.

Kett, Joseph F. *Rites of Passage: Adolescence in America, 1790 to the Present.* New York: Basic Books, 1977.

Kirschner, Don S. *The Paradox of Professionalism: Reform and Public Service in Urban America, 1900–1940.* New York: Greenwood Press, 1986.

Klaassen, David. "The Provenance of Social Work Case Records: Implications for Archival Appraisal and Access." *Provenance* 1 (Spring 1983): 5–30.

Klegon, Douglas. "The Sociology of Professions: An Emerging Perspective." *Sociology of Work and Occupations* 5 (Aug. 1978): 259–84.

Kremer, Gary R., and Linda Rea Gibbens. "The Missouri Home for Negro Girls: The 1930s." *American Studies* 24 (Fall 1983): 77–93.

Kusmer, Kenneth L. "The Functions of Organized Charity in the Progressive Era: Chicago as a Case Study." *Journal of American History* 60 (1973): 657–78.

Larson, Magali Sarfatti. "The Production of Expertise and the Constitution of Expert Power." In *The Authority of Experts: Studies in History and Theory*. Ed. Thomas Haskell. Bloomington: Indiana University Press, 1984.

———. *The Rise of Professionalism: A Sociological Analysis*. Berkeley: University of California Press, 1977.

Lasch, Christopher. *Haven in a Heartless World: The Family Besieged*. New York: Basic Books, 1977.

Leavitt, Judith Walzer. *Brought to Bed: Childbearing in America, 1750 to 1950*. New York: Oxford University Press, 1986.

Leff, Mark H. "Consensus for Reform: The Mothers'-Pension Movement in the Progressive Era." *Social Service Review* 47 (Sept. 1973): 397–417.

Leiby, James. "Charity Organizations Reconsidered." *Social Service Review* 58 (Dec. 1984): 523–38.

———. *A History of Social Welfare and Social Work in the United States, 1815–1972*. New York: Columbia University Press, 1978.

Leighninger, Leslie. *Social Work: Search for Identity*. New York: Greenwood Press, 1987.

Lloyd, Gary A. *Charities, Settlements, and Social Work: An Inquiry into Philosophy and Method, 1890–1915*. New Orleans: Tulane University Studies in Social Welfare, 1971.

Lubove, Roy. *The Professional Altruist: The Emergence of Social Work as a Career, 1880–1930*. Cambridge, Mass.: Harvard University Press, 1965.

Lunbeck, Elizabeth. "'A New Generation of Women': Progressive Psychiatrists and the Hypersexual Female." *Feminist Studies* 13 (Fall 1987): 513–44.

McConnell, Nancy Fifield, and Martha Morrison Dore. *1883–1983: Crittenton Services: The First Century*. Washington, D.C.: National Florence Crittenton Mission, 1983.

McGovern, Constance M. "The Myths of Social Control and Custodial Oppression: Patterns of Psychiatric Medicine in Late-Nineteenth-Century Institutions." *Journal of Social History* 20 (Fall 1986): 3–23.

McGovern, James R. "The American Woman's Pre-World War I Freedom in Manners and Morals." *Journal of American History* 55 (Sept. 1968): 315–33.

McKinley, Edward H. *Marching to Glory: The History of the Salvation Army in the United States of America, 1880–1980*. San Francisco: Harper and Row, 1980.

———. *Somebody's Brother: A History of the Salvation Army Men's Social Service Department, 1891–1985*. Lewiston, N.Y.: Edwin Mellen Press, 1986.

Magnuson, Norris. *Salvation in the Slums: Evangelical Social Work, 1865–1920*. Metuchen, N.J.: Scarecrow Press, 1977.

May, Elaine Tyler. *Homeward Bound: American Families in the Cold War Era*. New York: Basic Books, 1988.

Mayer, John E., and Noel Timms. *The Client Speaks: Working Class Impressions of Casework*. New York: Atherton Press, 1970.

Meier, August. "Black Sociologists in White America." *Social Forces* 56 (Sept. 1977): 259–70.

Melosh, Barbara. *"The Physician's Hand": Work Culture and Conflict in American Nursing*. Philadelphia: Temple University Press, 1982.

Meyerowitz, Joanne J. *Women Adrift: Independent Wage Earners in Chicago, 1880–1930*. Chicago: University of Chicago Press, 1988.

Modell, John. "Dating Becomes the Way of American Youth." In *Essays on the Family and Historical Change*. Ed. Leslie P. Moch and Gary D. Stark. College Station: Texas A. and M. University Press, 1983.

Mohl, Raymond A. "Mainstream Social Welfare History and Its Problems." Review of *A History of Social Welfare and Social Work in the United States*, by James Leiby. *Reviews in American History* 7 (Dec. 1979): 469–76.

Mohr, James C. *Abortion in America: The Origins and Evolution of National Policy, 1800–1900*. New York: Oxford University Press, 1978.

Moldow, Gloria. *Women Doctors in Gilded-Age Washington: Race, Gender, and Professionalization*. Urbana: University of Illinois Press, 1987.

Morantz-Sanchez, Regina M. "The Many Faces of Intimacy: Professional Options and Personal Choices among Nineteenth- and Early-Twentieth-Century Women Physicians." In *Uneasy Careers and Intimate Lives*. Ed. Pnina G. Abir-Am and Dorinda Outram. New Brunswick, N.J.: Rutgers University Press, 1987.

———. *Sympathy and Science: Women Physicians in American Medicine*. New York: Oxford University Press, 1985.

Morton, Marion J. "Fallen Women, Federated Charities, and Maternity Homes, 1913–1973." *Social Service Review* 62 (March 1988): 61–82.

———. " 'Go and Sin No More': Maternity Homes in Cleveland, 1869–1936." *Ohio History* 93 (Autumn 1984): 117–46.

———. "Seduced and Abandoned in an American City: Cleveland and Its Fallen Women, 1869–1936." *Journal of Urban History* 11 (Aug. 1985): 443–69.

Muncy, Robyn. *Creating a Female Dominion in American Reform, 1890–1935*. New York: Oxford University Press, 1991.

Neal, Harry Edward. *The Hallelujah Army*. Philadelphia: Chilton Co., 1961.

Neverdon-Morton, Cynthia. *Afro-American Women of the South and the Advancement of the Race, 1895–1925*. Knoxville: University of Tennessee Press, 1989.

Parker, Jacqueline K., and Edward M. Carpenter. "Julia Lathrop and the Children's Bureau: The Emergence of an Institution." *Social Service Review* 55 (March 1981): 60–77.

Parr, G. J. "Case Records as Sources for Social History." *Archivaria* 4 (Summer 1977): 122–36.

Pascoe, Peggy. *Relations of Rescue: The Search for Female Moral Authority in the American West, 1874–1939*. New York: Oxford University Press, 1990.

Peiss, Kathy. *Cheap Amusements: Working Women and Leisure in Turn-of-the-Century New York*. Philadelphia: Temple University Press, 1986.

Pivar, David J. *Purity Crusade: Sexual Morality and Social Control, 1868–1900*. Westport, Conn.: Greenwood Press, 1973.

Piven, Frances Fox, and Richard A. Cloward. *Regulating the Poor: The Functions of Public Welfare*. New York: Pantheon, 1971.

Platt, Anthony M. *The Child Savers: The Invention of Delinquency*. Chicago: University of Chicago Press, 1969.

———. *E. Franklin Frazier Reconsidered*. New Brunswick, N.J.: Rutgers University Press, 1991.

Pleck, Elizabeth. "Feminist Responses to 'Crimes against Women,' 1868–1896." *Signs* 8 (Spring 1983): 451–70.

Pumphrey, Ralph E. "Compassion and Protection: Dual Motivations in Social Welfare." *Social Service Review* 33 (March 1959): 21–29.

Pumphrey, Ralph E., and Muriel W. Pumphrey, eds. *The Heritage of American Social Work: Readings in Its Philosophical and Institutional Development*. New York: Columbia University Press, 1961.

Rains, Prudence M. "Moral Reinstatement: The Characteristics of Maternity Homes." *American Behavioral Scientist* 14 (Nov.–Dec. 1970): 219–36.

Rauch, Julia B. "Women in Social Work: Friendly Visitors in Philadelphia, 1880." *Social Service Review* 49 (June 1975): 241–59.

Reagan, Leslie J. "'About to Meet Her Maker': Women, Doctors, Dying Declarations, and the State's Investigation of Abortion, Chicago, 1867–1940." *Journal of American History* 77 (March 1991): 1240–64.

Reverby, Susan. *Ordered to Care: The Dilemma of American Nursing, 1850–1945*. New York: Cambridge University Press, 1987.

Roberts, Robert W., ed. *The Unwed Mother*. New York: Harper and Row, 1966.

Roberts, Robert W., and Robert H. Nee, eds. *Theories of Social Casework*. Chicago: University of Chicago Press, 1970.

Rochefort, David A. "Progressive and Social Control Perspectives on Social Welfare." *Social Service Review* 55 (Dec. 1981): 568–92.

Rosenthal, Marguerite G. "The Children's Bureau and the Juvenile Court: Delinquency Policy, 1912–1940." *Social Service Review* 60 (June 1986): 303–18.

Ross, Ellen. "'Not the Sort that Would Sit on the Doorstep': Respectability in Pre–World War I London Neighborhoods." *International Labor and Working Class History*, no. 27 (Spring 1985): 39–59.

Rossiter, Margaret W. *Women Scientists in America: Struggles and Strategies to 1940*. Baltimore: Johns Hopkins University Press, 1982.

Roth, Julius A. "Professionalism: The Sociologist's Decoy." *Sociology of Work and Professions* 1 (Feb. 1974): 6–23.

Rothman, David J. *Conscience and Convenience: The Asylum and Its Alternatives in Progressive America*. Boston: Little, Brown, 1980.

Rothman, Ellen K. *Hands and Hearts: A History of Courtship in America.* New York: Basic Books, 1984.

Rothman, Sheila M. *Woman's Proper Place: A History of Changing Ideals and Practices, 1870 to the Present.* New York: Basic Books, 1978.

Ruether, Rosemary Radford, and Rosemary Skinner Keller, eds. *Women and Religion in America.* Vol. 3. San Francisco: Harper and Row, 1986.

Ruggles, Steven. "Fallen Women: The Inmates of the Magdalen Society Asylum of Philadelphia, 1836–1908." *Journal of Social History* 16 (Summer 1983): 65–82.

Sandall, Robert. *The History of the Salvation Army.* Vol. 3. London: Thomas Nelson and Sons, 1955.

Scanzoni, Letha Dawson, and Susan Selta. "Women in Evangelical, Holiness, and Pentacostal Traditions." In *Women and Religion in America.* Vol. 3. Ed. Rosemary Radford Ruether and Rosemary Skinner Keller. San Francisco: Harper and Row, 1986.

Scharf, Lois. *To Work and to Wed: Female Employment, Feminism, and the Great Depression.* Westport, Conn.: Greenwood Press, 1980.

Schlossman, Steven L. *Love and the American Delinquent: The Theory and Practice of "Progressive" Juvenile Justice, 1825–1920.* Chicago: University of Chicago Press, 1977.

Schlossman, Steven L., and Stephanie Wallach. "The Crime of Precocious Sexuality: Female Juvenile Delinquency in the Progressive Era." *Harvard Educational Review* 48 (Feb. 1978): 65–94.

Scott, Joan W. "The Evidence of Experience." *Critical Inquiry* 17 (Summer 1991): 773–97.

———. *Gender and the Politics of History.* New York: Columbia University Press, 1988.

Sedlak, Michael W. "Young Women and the City: Adolescent Deviance and the Transformation of Educational Policy, 1870–1960." *History of Education Quarterly* 23 (Spring 1983): 1–28.

———. "Youth Policy and Young Women, 1870–1972." *Social Service Review* 56 (Sept. 1982): 448–64.

Smith, Daniel Scott. "The Dating of the American Sexual Revolution: Evidence and Interpretation." In *The American Family in Social-Historical Perspective.* Ed. Michael Gordon. New York: St. Martin's Press, 1978.

———. "The Long Cycle in American Illegitimacy and Prenuptial Pregnancy." In *Bastardy and Its Comparative History.* Ed. Peter Laslett et al. Cambridge, Mass.: Harvard University Press, 1980.

Smith, Daniel Scott, and Michael S. Hindus. "Premarital Pregnancy in America, 1640–1971: An Overview and Interpretation." *Journal of Interdisciplinary History* 5 (Spring 1975): 537–70.

Smith-Rosenberg, Carroll. "Beauty, the Beast, and the Militant Woman: A Case Study in Sex Roles and Social Stress in Jacksonian America." In *Disorderly Conduct: Visions of Gender in Victorian America.* New York: Knopf, 1985.

———. "The New Woman as Androgyne: Social Disorder and Gender Crisis, 1870–1936." In *Disorderly Conduct: Visions of Gender in Victorian America.* Ed. Carroll Smith-Rosenberg. New York: Knopf, 1985.

Solinger, Rickie. *Wake Up Little Susie: Single Pregnancy and Race before Roe v. Wade.* New York: Routledge, 1992.

Southern, David W. *Gunnar Myrdal and Black-White Relations: The Use and Abuse of "An American Dilemma," 1944–1969.* Baton Rouge: Louisiana State University Press, 1987.

Stansell, Christine. *City of Women: Sex and Class in New York, 1789–1860.* New York: Knopf, 1986.

Staves, Susan. "British Seduced Maidens." *Eighteenth-Century Studies* 14 (Winter 1980–81): 109–34.

Taylor, Peter L. "'Denied the Power to Choose the Good': Sexuality and Mental Defect in American Medical Practice, 1850–1920." *Journal of Social History* 10 (1976–77): 472–82.

Teeters, Negley K. "The Early Days of the Magdalen Society of Philadelphia." *Social Service Review* 30 (June 1950): 158–67.

Tiffin, Susan. *In Whose Best Interest? Child Welfare Reform in the Progressive Era.* Westport, Conn.: Greenwood Press, 1982.

Tilly, Louise A., and Joan W. Scott. *Women, Work, and Family.* New York: Holt, Rinehart, and Winston, 1978.

Tilly, Louise A., Joan W. Scott, and Miriam Cohen. "Women's Work and European Fertility Patterns." *Journal of Interdisciplinary History* 6 (Winter 1976): 447–76.

Trattner, Walter I. "Introduction: The State of the Field—and the Scope of This Work." In *Social Welfare in America: An Annotated Bibliography.* Westport, Conn.: Greenwood Press, 1983.

Trattner, Walter I., ed. *Social Welfare or Social Control? Some Historical Reflections on Regulating the Poor.* Knoxville: University of Tennessee Press, 1983.

Trolander, Judith Ann. *Professionalism and Social Change: From the Settlement House Movement to Neighborhood Centers, 1886 to the Present.* New York: Columbia University Press, 1987.

———. *Settlement Houses and the Great Depression.* Detroit: Wayne State University Press, 1975.

Ulrich, Laurel Thatcher. *A Midwife's Tale.* New York: Knopf, 1990.

Veysey, Lawrence. "Who's a Professional? Who Cares?" *Reviews in American History* 3 (Dec. 1975): 419–23.

Vicinus, Martha. "'Helpless and Unbefriended': Nineteenth-Century Domestic Melodrama." *New Literary History* 13 (Autumn 1981): 127–43.

Vinovskis, Maris A. *An "Epidemic" of Adolescent Pregnancy? Some Historical and Policy Considerations.* New York: Oxford University Press, 1988.

Walkowitz, Daniel J. "The Making of a Feminine Professional Identity: Social Workers in the 1920s." *American Historical Review* 95 (Oct. 1990): 1051–75.

Walkowitz, Judith R. *City of Dreadful Delight: Narratives of Sexual Danger in Late-Victorian London*. Chicago: University of Chicago Press, 1992.

———. "Male Vice and Female Virtue: Feminism and the Politics of Prostitution in Nineteenth-Century Britain." *History Workshop* 13 (Spring 1982).

———. *Prostitution and Victorian Society: Women, Class, and the State*. Cambridge: Cambridge University Press, 1980.

Walton, Ronald G. *Women in Social Work*. London: Routledge and Kegan Paul, 1975.

Wells, Robert V. "Illegitimacy and Bridal Pregnancy in Colonial America." In *Bastardy and Its Comparative History*. Ed. Peter Laslett et al. Cambridge, Mass.: Harvard University Press, 1980.

Wertz, Richard W., and Dorothy C. Wertz. *Lying-In: A History of Childbirth in America*. New York: Schocken, 1979.

Wilding, Paul. *Professional Power and Social Welfare*. London: Routledge and Kegan Paul, 1982.

Wilensky, Harold L. "The Professionalization of Everyone?" *American Journal of Sociology* 70 (Sept. 1964): 137–58.

Wilensky, Harold L., and Charles N. Lebeaux. *Industrial Society and Social Welfare*. New York: Free Press, 1965.

Willis, Sabine. "Made to Be Moral—at Parramatta Girls' School, 1898–1923." In *Twentieth-Century Sydney*. Ed. Jill Roe. Sydney, Australia: Hale and Iremonger, 1980.

Wimshurst, Kerry. "Control and Resistance: Reformatory School Girls in Late-Nineteenth-Century South Australia." *Journal of Social History* 18 (Winter 1984): 273–87.

Windshuttle, Elizabeth. "Discipline, Domestic Training, and Social Control: The Female School of Industry, Sydney, 1826–1847." *Labour History* 39 (1980): 312–24.

Withorn, Ann. *Serving the People: Social Services and Social Change*. New York: Columbia University Press, 1984.

Woodroofe, Kathleen. *From Charity to Social Work in England and the United States*. Toronto, Canada: University of Toronto Press, 1962.

Wyman, Margaret. "The Rise of the Fallen Woman." *American Quarterly* 3 (Summer 1951): 167–77.

Zaretsky, Eli. "The Place of the Family in the Origins of the Welfare State." In *Rethinking the Family: Some Feminist Questions*. Ed. Barrie Thorne and Marilyn Yalom. New York: Longman, 1982.

Index

FROM THESE ROOTS

FROM
THESE ROOTS

THE IDEAS THAT HAVE MADE
MODERN LITERATURE

BY

MARY M. COLUM

LIBRARY OF
JBT
JOHN BELLAMY TAYLOR

CHARLES SCRIBNER'S SONS · NEW YORK
CHARLES SCRIBNER'S SONS · LTD · LONDON
1938

Copyright, 1937, by
CHARLES SCRIBNER'S SONS

Printed in the United States of America

*All rights reserved. No part of this book
may be reproduced in any form without
the permission of Charles Scribner's Sons*

TO
my friend
DR. W. J. M. A. MALONEY
my editor
HENRY GODDARD LEACH
my husband
PADRAIC COLUM

CONTENTS

vii

CONTENTS

FROM THESE ROOTS

Chapter One

WHAT IS CRITICISM?

I

FOR AT LEAST one hundred and fifty years criticism has been increasingly operative on literature, yet, as a literary mode it is still in its infancy, though, as Anatole France predicted, it may end by swallowing up all the others. When George Sand wrote to Flaubert, on the death of Sainte-Beuve, that she believed criticism had come to an end, Flaubert, a man of enormously penetrating perceptions, answered, "I think, on the contrary, that it is at most only at its dawning. They are on a different tack from before, but nothing more. At the time of La Harpe they were grammarians; at the time of Sainte-Beuve and Taine they were historians. When will they be artists—really artists?" In these few words Flaubert, who, like Anatole France, was a fine critic himself though he expressed that talent chiefly in his correspondence, stated a truth not even now generally recognized. Literary criticism is now only at its dawning in spite of great and transforming critics like Taine and Sainte-Beuve, whom Flaubert erred in not recognizing as artists.

I

The older critics—that is, those who made a trade of criticism before Lessing came and gave it wings—were grammarians, rule-makers, analyzers, commentators, pedagogues, and it is these most people have in mind instead of the artist-critics like Lessing and Herder, Wordsworth and Coleridge, Taine and Sainte-Beuve— transformers of literature, all of them; men who made a new channel for the current of literature. It is still a notion fairly widespread that criticism of any kind is simply the action of one mind upon the work of another. This, in essence, would mean that criticism is a secondary sort of writing which does not invent or transform its material but is rather a kind of parasite on other minds and other forms of writing—a stepchild and handmaiden of the other arts and the other literary modes, as romances in their earlier forms were regarded. Any sort of literary genre in its lower forms is a parasite on other minds and modes. In its higher forms, criticism is as much creative literature as a fine novel, or a play or a poem; it is not the form or character which is the decisive factor in determining whether any kind of writing is creative literature or not—it is the quality of the mind behind it. Creative writing is simply writing produced by a creative mind regardless of the form or genre the writer uses for his expression: in fact, any fine critic can write finely in what the popular mind regards as the creative form: Lessing was a dramatist, Boileau, Herder, Sainte-Beuve and Matthew Arnold were poets. So many great literary critics have been great poets—Dryden, Coleridge, Poe, Goethe—that there is good ground for believing that there is a close relation between poetry and criticism. All poets have to be critics, and they can fitly be called great critics when the theories they evolve about their own work influence others, as Wordsworth's Preface to the *Lyrical Ballads* influenced generations of poets.

However, the creative mind is exceptional and there is no more reason for describing a successful piece of criticism as creative writing than for so describing a successful novel. But of all the rare forms of creative writing, creative criticism is the rarest, and those who have accomplished it to any extent might be counted on the fingers of one hand. One of the reasons why this is so is that the writing of criticism is very arduous and, in general, the rewards are sparse compared with the rewards for other forms of literature, and this in spite of the fact that the man or woman who writes criticism has less competition from the great dead and the great living than any other type of writer. Another reason for the rarity of fine criticism is the number of difficulties in the way of learning the job thoroughly. Other writers may be able to learn their trade alone, but critics, because they have to be familiar with writing of all kinds, are best developed when, during their formative periods, they are surrounded by writers, saturated in literature, rocked and dandled to its sounds and syllables from their earliest years, as composers have to be rocked and dandled to the sounds of music. Because the nature and province of criticism is still somewhat of a puzzle, particularly in the English-speaking world, an attempt to formulate a definition of it is not out of place, but is even the business of anybody engaging seriously in the craft.

2

The popular idea of criticism is that it is some form of abuse, or attack, or harsh judgment, and doubtless it was as some form of attack that criticism took its beginning. It is necessary also to ask the general reader to dissociate the term criticism as a literary mode from its meaning in practical life, where it commonly denotes a form of censure. With the lapse of time it may be concluded that there will be no more confusion between the meanings of the word than there is between the word "essay" as a literary form and the practical meaning of the word. At present, however, the confusion exists. Recently, in New York, a distinguished physician asked a patient how he earned his living: on being told that it was by writing criticism he warmly recommended him to abandon his job, for, said the doctor, criticism springs from a virus, an irritant in the mind which prevents a person from adapting himself to life. With this astonishing dictum the invalid, a simple-minded man who wrote reviews for a Sunday paper and who suffered from indigestion, seemed to concur, for he had never thought about his profession at all.

Criticism is in itself neither praise nor blame, neither attack nor judgment: as an intellectual force it represents a principle through which the world of ideas renews itself, which prunes and trims old ideas to satisfy new desires or aspirations. Purely literary criticism, which, of course, is only one branch of criticism, represents, in the work of its highest practitioners, that branch of literature whose most important office is the originating of the ideas, the discovery of the circumstances, the foreseeing of the lines that other branches of literature follow.

Besides its major rôles, criticism has many secondary ones, and, therefore, it may ordinarily be described as a literary force put at the service of another force. In relation to art, criticism is a literary force put at the service of art; social or sociological criticism is a literary force put at the service of society; literary criticism is a literary force put at the service of literature. As a force put at the service of literature, criticism can be exercised in various ways according to the nature of the talent that makes up the force. It may be literary history like Saintsbury's or Brunetière's, where the critic has to have the mind of an historian; it may be pure theorizing like Croce's or Alain's, where the critic has to have the mind of a metaphysician; it may be the sort of criticism that deals with the sources and genesis of a work of art, like that of Joseph Bedier, or Victor Bérard, where the critic has to be a specialized scholar, and of which a remarkable example in America is the work of John Livingston Lowes, whose book *The Road to Xanadu* is a production of genius in this class. Or criticism may be simply sensitive and brilliant and informing chatter about books, and to this class belong not only the witty, distinguished criticism of Anatole France and Lemaître and Oscar Wilde, but also the criticism of the best of our present-day columnists. It may be, and it most commonly is, a talent which expresses itself in explaining the work of authors past and present, and in passing judgment on them. Book reviewing, as commonly practised, is seldom criticism, being simply book news in which the writer gives some information about the book considered and passes some judgment on it. The book reviewer, to use Sainte-Beuve's phrase, is the secretary of the public and not necessarily a critic at all.

For, at its highest, literary criticism is the creation of profound, informing, and transforming ideas about literature and life—about life as well as literature, for no one can understand literature without a comprehension of life, which is the matter of literature. Hence the great primary critics have been those whose work had or has, not merely an effect on the understanding and assessing of writing, but a continuous influence on the creation of literature. According to this definition one would have to begin any list of primary critics with Aristotle: however, as I am dealing with criticism in the modern world, where it has preceded great literary movements, I would list as the great creative critics Lessing and Herder, Wordsworth and Coleridge, Sainte-Beuve and Taine: these were the critics who changed and revitalized, in a way that critics had not done before, literature and the matter of literature. In any anthology of creative criticism one would have to include pieces by other writers—by Dryden, Matthew Arnold, Samuel Johnson, by Goethe, by Dante, and by the numerous writers of the Arts of Poetry since the beginning of literature—writers the main direction of whose work would not entitle them to a place with the transforming critics.

To the small number of the great critics there are the strongest reasons for adding the name of Madame de Staël, whose book *Literature in Relation to Social Institutions* is not only the basis of all the conceptions of literature put forward recently as Marxist, but is also one of the bases of the theories of Sainte-Beuve and Taine. She was a social rather than a literary critic and regarded literature as an expression of society—a theory, no matter how interesting in itself, which would, in practice, banish a great portion of the imaginative literature of the world, would banish nearly all lyric poetry and also such literatures as reflect a purely fantastic, imaginative, or psychic life. She influenced, not literature generally, as the great critics had done, but thinking *about* literature, and this makes her a passion with critics rather than with other kinds of writers.

Her importance—her very great importance—was in the fact that it was she who formed the bridge between the two great French critics, Taine and Sainte-Beuve, and the two great Germans, Lessing and Herder. It was she who discovered that German literature had been born of criticism and that it was Lessing who had given life to it.

3

Eighteenth-century Germany, the Germany into which Lessing brought his transforming ideas, was culturally sufficiently like the America we have known to make a parallel enlightening. A learned culture had been built up in the universities, at the courts, and among the literati in general, which was remote from the life actually lived and the language actually spoken, and its proponents, as in America, resisted the upthrust of other forces and the newer vitalities. In America in our time the last fight of the learned culture was made by Babbitt and More, who lost the fight as all such fights have to be lost. The leader of the learned culture who preceded Lessing in early eighteenth-century Germany might stand as typical of all the leaders that the fight against the newer, more confused forces brings forth.

This leader was a professor with various interests,

named Gottsched. His stock-in-trade was not exactly the same as that of the proponents of the learned culture in America, but his mind and theirs were of a like pattern. Like all such leaders—they are generally high-minded men—he believed that the Greeks were the one people who had produced a genuine literature and who knew the ways and means whereby it was done. He was one of a line of savants who had decided that the Greeks had every virtue, that Greek literature was powerfully moral, and that the characters in it represented the height of ethical achievement. To this standard notion was added the other notion that the continual reading of the Bible, with its accounts of the violent passions and emotions of barbarous, lusty men, naturally made people disciplined, restrained, and virtuous and likely to keep the Commandments. Gottsched, equipped with such convictions, reinforced with Leibnitzian rationalism and Lutheran ethics, looked through his learned spectacles at the Greeks and Latins, and especially Aristotle and the Aristotelian Poetics, and perceived that poetry was a branch of scholarship, a rational pursuit meant to add to the moral improvement of man; he perceived likewise that after the ancients, the people who knew most about poetry and drama were the French. To guide his fellow countrymen he made translations from Racine, and taking the old tag from Aristotle, which is so hard to interpret, about poetry being an imitation of nature, he proceeded to write an Art of Poetry on his own account, in which he expounded the necessary rules for writing, showed the part that regularity, intelligence, reason, and common sense should play, and explained that the aim of poetry was to teach by giving pleasure. When a literary group in Switzerland, whom he had imagined to be his followers, wrote with extravagant admiration of the English poet, Milton, and went so far as to talk about the "wonderful" in poetry, it seeemed to Gottsched as if the end of all good taste, of all standards, was coming.

It was in the university where Gottsched professed philosophy according to Leibnitz, in his own university of Leipzig, that the very man was bred who undid him and all he stood for—Gotthold Ephraim Lessing. But the type is recurrent, and Gottscheds belong to every country with an undeveloped culture. This sort of professional critic and legislator of Parnassus is not likely to have much influence in a country with a long and highly developed literary tradition. But the Germans at this time were, to use a phrase of J. G. Robertson's, "as a literature-producing people of no consequence at all." Something similar might be said of Americans nearly up to our own time. The domination in Germany of a diluted classicism and the ascendancy of French culture corresponded to colonialism in America, with a similar theological background. In both countries there was a lack of focus of intellectual life: neither had a capital.

All peoples who have too few models of their own in

art and literature, and who are not familiar with the recorded expression of human experience, are likely to be pedantic in their writing or vacuously dull—this though at times they may show a streak of life and of genius. Sometimes a great political event will arouse such a people out of their tutelage to the pedants, and from dullness into some sort of life. Occasionally a sudden ferment of ideas will accomplish the miracle and start a real expression in literature. There had been in the past of Germany, as in the past of America, certain outstanding figures, but not many: Germany at the time of Gottsched was hardly a nation at all, and this forms a parallel with America. In Germany there had been a few poets, there had been theologians, and there had been the philosopher Leibnitz. Preceding our day in America, there had been a few poets, a few novelists, a few theologians, and, particularly, there had been the two Jameses—the one with his transforming psychology and the other with his transforming material and technique of the novel. There had been in both countries now and again an isolated masterpiece; there had been outstanding intellects, and there had been poets who were worth while, though, for the most part, in the literature produced, there had been dismal stretches of dullness: the minds of the writers, though sometimes filled with learning, had not awakened to complete awareness; they were not really deeply touched by life, for they met life at too few points. When their speculations were most transcendental they were hardest to get at: what is now read, in the one country, of Klopstock and Gellert, and in the other, of Emerson and Whittier, outside a small amount of exciting lyricism, is limited to a few specialists in literature.

It is patent that when literature is in this condition what especially is needed is something that will arouse people, or a section of them, to a state of self-criticism. First of all, there is the necessity for giving them sufficient racial and national pride to make them stop swallowing whole other cultures; then, if the country has the materials of literature, they have to be shown where these materials lie. If America had to make only in a limited degree the same fight against pedants that Lessing had to make in Germany, it had, on the other hand, developed very much less of the sort of life and the sort of human being that could be made into literature, for Germany had in its past a deeply rooted folklore and mythology which had given some of its richness to the commonest man in his every-day life. Therefore, in America, what was needed first of all was a vigorous social criticism in place of the refinement of literary criticism that was Lessing's contribution. And it is precisely in social criticism that America has excelled.

Lowell, fifty years ago, knowing perhaps only subconsciously what he meant, said, "We must have a criticism before we can have a literature." In America there is a new kind of society, a society built out of elements that have never previously come together, and a genuine literary expression of that society has to be preceded by a criticism of it. To produce works like *Main Street* and *An American Tragedy* a criticism is needed, but an even deeper criticism is needed before we can produce works like "Kubla Khan" or the "Ode to a Nightingale," or *Faust,* or *Les Fleurs du Mal.* Old homogeneous countries can evolve their literatures from their mythology and their folklore and their traditional life, but a new country which has neither folklore, nor mythology, nor much fertile tradition in life, has, first of all, to mold its society into shape and take stock of its values, before that society becomes material for literature. In the older countries, where literature was an evolution, the human values that were important in art were those always of powerful significance in actual life, but such values were not always significant in America. Too much psychical and physical energy had to go into conquering the soil and making it fit for habitation to leave overmuch of that sort of energy that goes into the making of a passionate or interesting personality, or into the developing of strong emotions and vigorous sensitivities and sensibilities.

In some of the frontier States, or even those last settled, one can encounter highly intelligent and even highly educated people of a blankness of spirit, a temperamental vacuity, which give the impression that one has met that wraith which some of the old philosophers used to talk about—a human being without a soul, one in whom the breath of the Creator, that breath that gives consciousness, has not entered. Their spirits and emotions are anemic through lack of that long interchange between man and the soil, that daily, almost unconscious contact with the recorded experience of man, which, in an old civilization, can make a rich, subtle, highly sensitized human being of even an illiterate peasant. For this reason, in spite of resemblances, the conditions critics had to cope with in America were not identical with, though in some respects similar to, those that Lessing had to cope with in Germany. He had to struggle to create a literature in a country where a literature of a kind already existed, and where, outside the foreign, learned culture, there was a folk-culture and a warm, rich life and language, native and of the people's own making. In spite of the fact that the learned, like Leibnitz and others, wrote in Latin or French, all this was to be found in Germany. But in America the language was the language of another people, the English, and, to begin with, the culture was transplanted seventeenth-century English, that later became a miscellany of all the cultures of Europe.

There was little art at first. The chief reason why new countries have little art is that the people do not want it—it is not that the potential artist is not born there, but that too few people feel the need of expression for that need to make an impression upon the artist's mind.

While life was a conquering physical adventure, as it had to be for long in America, people's energies were too much absorbed for them to demand anything from life except living. But there came a time when they began to wonder what there was besides. Out of this state there emerged with surprising suddenness a civilization in America different from anything the world had seen before, and, more surprising still, there emerged men who gave tongue to it—men whose spirits passed through the gates of utterance apparently without any of the preparation such spirits need in older countries. These artists, no matter in what form they expressed themselves—whether as novelists, like Sinclair Lewis, in *Main Street* and *Babbitt,* or Dreiser, in *An American Tragedy* and *Sister Carrie,* or as poets, like Frost, in *North of Boston,* or E. A. Robinson, in *The Man Against the Sky,* or Edgar Lee Masters, in *Spoon River Anthology,* or the amazing creators of the comic strips, with their satiric reproduction of every type in the country, or Mencken with his assault on the "booboisie"—were, every one of them, devastating social critics. The caricaturists of the daily papers, concerning themselves with the narrowness, aridity, and philistinism of American domesticity, a domesticity more enclosed inside family life than any in the Old World, made themselves part of the experience of the every-day men and women who take the subway or the commuter's train to their work. So that criticism in America not only affected the life of those interested in art and literature, but also the lives of people who read little except the newspapers. Whatever was overlooked by the literary men was savagely satirized by these caricaturists, by Briggs, Sidney Smith, and others. And whatever escaped the notice of the native critics the visiting critics made up for. Some of these outside critics, like Count Keyserling and André Siegfried, had many prcfound intuitions, but others were merely patronizing humbugs and chatterers.

No one who has made a study of American life, or who is familiar with the anemia, woolliness and narrowness of its intellectual life even as recently as twenty years ago, can fail to realize all that criticism has accomplished for it. So that we are justified in saying that American literature started, as Madame de Staël showed German literature to have started, with criticism—criticism that was the first wave of a strong, violent, productive life. However, not all the critics were equally effective: some of them were made arid by New England gentility; some had but short-lived vitality; some of those who set out to be literary critics especially were, like that typical champion of a learned culture, Gottsched, apostles of the notion that only the Greeks knew anything about literature, and that both literature and life should be conducted according to principles drawn from their work. Still, it must not be overlooked that their intervention was also valuable—they brought to people's attention the necessity for cultivation, for taste and scholarship. Their main fault was in thinking that these were the only ingredients that a literature needed. But what American literature and American civilization owe to the whole body of critics is tremendous; it is not easy to formulate; in fact, it cannot be formulated until it is looked at from the perspective of time.

It is also not easy to formulate for the reason that American critics started out without any theories except those they evolved as they went along or those they adopted wholesale from European writers. This adoption was inevitable, for both in life and in literature these were the ideas that had helped to make the world as we know it; they were the ideas behind modern literature, for, as distinct from the older literatures, modern literature was dependent on ideas which gave it a direction, and these had been evolved by a few men to whom the revelation came that, for a time, anyway, literature had to be about the ordinary man because civilization was developing around him, and modern literature and modern civilization were bound up with each other. It is with these ideas, the men who formulated them as a literary philosophy, and the men who applied them in literature, that this book is concerned.

Chapter Two

MODERN LITERATURE BEGINS: THE IDEAS OF LESSING AND HERDER

I

MODERN CRITICISM as a literary force began in Germany in the middle of the eighteenth century and began with Lessing, who laid the foundation on which all critics since have worked. In what way did this new instrument differ from what had previously been called criticism? It differed chiefly in this, that its major business was not rule-making or judgment-passing but the evaluation of the body of literature of the time. Literature in all countries was in a dreary condition: if in Germany real expression had not begun, in other countries it had lost the breath of life and was dying of anemia. A drying wind of reason, wit, rules, good sense, artificial language, had done its work; spontaneity, emotion, life, and lyricism were gone. The job the new critics had to tackle was that of changing literary taste, and they set themselves to it, first by showing up the weaknesses of literature as it stood, then by propounding new theories, and finally by persuasion, force, and example, showing how the change could be accomplished and life brought back to literature. Each of them as he came along took over a stock of literary ideas from his predecessor and added a particular contribution of his own, for in criticism, as in all the other works of men, each originating mind adds to a sequence of already existing ideas: every writer who contributes ideas that revivify literature and that release the minds of other writers to fresh expression is a critic and generally a great one. Every great writer of any kind, even though the general direction of his work may not be criticism, is a critic: the critical mentality, and, one may add, the lyrical mentality, is a fundamental part of the outfit of every writer of the first rank. The most important writers of any period, whether poets, dramatists, or novelists, are very likely to be amongst its greatest critics in their own genre if they have the time or the energy to reduce their literary principles and theories to writing. The best critic of poetry in his own time, for example, was Goethe; the best critic of the novel in his own time was Flaubert. On the other hand, those writers the general direction of whose work is criticism express themselves likewise in other literary forms—in fact it is difficult to imagine how anybody can be a literary critic without that all-round comprehension of literature that comes from the practice of writing in many forms.

Aside from all this, there are certain definite tendencies in criticism and critics that must be taken note of:

one is that, at times of sweeping literary changes, the great transforming critics, consciously or unconsciously, work in pairs—thus we have Lessing and Herder, Wordsworth and Coleridge, Taine and Sainte-Beuve, where in each case one mind is the complement of the other. Then, running through what first-rate literary criticism we have, there will be found in evidence two kinds of minds: the poetical-critical mind and the philosophical-critical mind. Among the critics mentioned, Herder, Wordsworth, and Sainte-Beuve represent the poetical-critical mind, while the philosophical-critical mind was that of their co-workers, Lessing, Coleridge, Taine—for it should be noted that no matter how distinguished a poet Coleridge was, his criticism was philosophic rather than poetic. Finally, it must be repeated that the critical mind and the creative mind are not two distinct kinds of minds, but the same sort of mind developing through different outlets according to circumstances and the needs of the time.

Of the three pairs of critics mentioned above, all except Taine worked in several literary forms. Lessing's great interest was drama and controversy, so he wrote dramas, controversy, verse, and criticism; he was the first outstanding German dramatist and one of the greatest of controversialists. Herder's great literary interest was poetry, and he wrote poetry, history, and criticism. Sainte-Beuve's great literary interests were poetry, biography, history, and fiction, and he wrote all of them as well as criticism. The great literary interest of Wordsworth and Coleridge was poetry, so they wrote poetry and criticism. Wordsworth's criticism, to be sure, was small in bulk, but it was tremendous in its import: it has influenced nearly all poetry written since in Western countries.

The literary ideas these critics put in circulation were not always discoveries: sometimes they were the novel application of old ideas. Lessing, in addition to his own discoveries, gave a new application to the dramatic theories of Aristotle; he had made a study of the Greek text of the Poetics and left the interpretation of it that is now generally accepted by literary critics. The theory to which Taine's name is most commonly attached, that which explains all literary production by the influence of race, milieu, and moment, was taken over from Hegel, who expressed it in language almost word for word with Taine. Hegel wrote in his *Aesthetik: "So dann gehört jedes Kunstwerk seiner Zeit, seinem Volke, seiner Umgebung."* "Every work of art belongs to its time, its people, and its environment." A like formula was gropingly applied by Herder almost a century before Taine had made an extensive explanation of this part of his method, in his Introduction to his *History of English Literature.*

Apart from the difficulty of disentangling what each critic's special original contribution was, it is difficult, and, I am inclined to believe, impossible, to formulate with precision the literary discoveries of the great critics, for what they contributed was not so much a systematic philosophy of literature as a ferment of ideas. This phrase "a ferment of ideas," used by Lessing about his own *Laocoön,* is equally applicable to the work of all the critics considered in this chapter—to the *Biographia Literaria,* to Wordsworth's epoch-making Preface, to Herder's conception of poetry. In spite of Sainte-Beuve's effort to organize some of his ideas into the semblance of a system in his essay on Chateaubriand, and in spite of Taine's orderly *Philosophy of Art,* what these two critics also contributed was an exciting ferment of thought that aroused a ferment of thought in others. This is also true of all those important critics whose main reputation is in another literary medium, like Goethe, like Poe, like Flaubert, and, in our own day, like Yeats and Valéry and Eliot. These writers contribute a whirl of fertilizing ideas without which literature would become desiccated or even impotent as a vehicle of artistic expression.

2

In the case of Lessing, who, in the estimation of the present writer, was the most original and the most originating mind in modern criticism, though not the greatest, it happened that he aroused a whole nation to literary expression. Through the energy of his ideas and his practice he gave release to minds that without him would either never have found a voice or only

piped a feeble note. Saintsbury said of him that the
Germans owe him Goethe and the English, Coleridge.
Goethe, who was never tired of telling what he owed
to him, wrote, in *Dichtung und Wahrheit,* of the effect
of Lessing's *Laocoön* on himself and his contemporaries, "As if by a lightning-flash, the consequences of
his splendid thought lighted up the way before us, and
all previous criticism was thrown away like a worn-
out coat." Not only did his splendid thought light up
the way for his own countrymen, his influence spread
to all European literature. It is even true to say that
not only the seeds of contemporary literary ideas, but
the seeds of contemporary technical inventions in writing are to be found in Lessing's criticism, for the most
recent developments in technique are an outcrop of his
special notion of "action" in literary composition.

The two main principles with which his name in
criticism is associated are the conception of literature
as an expression of national or racial genius, and, secondly, the notion that each of the arts has a boundary
beyond which it is best not to pass, and that the highest development of any art takes place inside its own
boundary. The conception of literature as an expression of racial or national genius derives from the German philosophy of racism and is valid only to a degree: it does not cover the total range of literature in
any country or in any period. However, in the heyday
of its popularity it represented a high truth and was

potent with inspiration until almost the year before last; it played an awakening rôle in many of the new European literatures—in Norwegian literature, in Russian literature, in Flemish literature and Irish literature. But in the world that in our time is coming into being, this conception has not the same power of influencing the creative imagination. In every country there is to be observed a cleavage between the intellectual and artistic life on the one side, and the racial and national tradition. Art, due in part to the purely prosaic influence of the ease and swiftness of transportation and transmission, is becoming international as well as national. The international conception is not crowding out national art, but is taking its own share of the field. Some of the newer writers are as national as writers ever were, but at the same time there are a number of others in every country who express in their work something outside of race and national genius.

The stressing of this idea, the racial and national idea, was a powerful force in exciting Lessing's readers; it was the first time in literary history that it had been put forward as a doctrine of literary production. And as any idea that has once been powerful may, in suitable soil, again be a source of power, it is worth while considering why it was powerful and why the soil was suitable. For one thing, Lessing put it forward both forcibly and convincingly, both in precept and practice; he was that figure who sometimes appears in lit-

24

erary history, the man with a new idea which, when it is expressed, goes straight to the minds and hearts of his readers as a form of nutriment for which they were longing. Before Lessing came and before his precept and example took effect, the Germans had been trying to make themselves over in imitation of the French and to give themselves French culture, as did the Russians later, and as the Roumanians have done in our time, and as the Irish and the Americans, until recently, tried to give themselves an English culture. Things had reached such a pass in Germany that all writing was an imitation of the French, and the educated classes spoke only French amongst themselves. The conquering king, Frederick the Great, made no secret of his contempt for the German language, and his own literary performances, such as they were, and they are not contemptible, were entirely in French. Now, this king was the ruler of the country in which Lessing in his young manhood tried to start a literature, and though Frederick despised the language as much as Lessing venerated it, and had the limited notions of a man of action of what made a country's greatness, yet if there had been no Frederick, Lessing's task would have been impossible. For although the great king never spoke the German language at all if he could help it, psychically he was one of the forces that made that language, and the literature in it, one of the greatest in modern Europe. It was this Germany that Frederick had created—invented, one might say—that Lessing willed to turn into the paths of literary expression.

When Lessing was a boy of eleven, Frederick ascended the throne of Prussia, and when, as a young man, after a false beginning, he turned to writing his first startling essays on literature, they were addressed to a people into whose blood the king had put life and iron. Twenty years before, they would have been addressed to a people whose minds had long gone stagnant under floods of theological argumentation and the despair of lost wars, invaded territory and wasted life, for during generations these had been the chief experiences of the German nation. For all outcropping of spiritual fruit there has to be a physical and material preparation. Nothing in literary history is more psychologically interesting than the influence of Frederick. We are not concerned here with the details of the wars and battles that he won, for we are only interested in certain of their effects. It had been the habit of other nations to hire as their fighting-men those foreign mercenaries who made a trade of war, but when Frederick took the field, with a large proportion of the powers of Europe against him, his forces were his own countrymen. When they, the long-beaten, found themselves conquerors in many battles, they began to reach a stage of consciousness that needed some other outlet than the battlefield. "The exploits of the great Frederick," wrote Goethe, in *Dichtung und Wahrheit,* "were the first living, genuine, heroic foundations of German poetry. All national poetry is empty, or risks becoming so, unless it rests on what is most profoundly human—on the destiny of peoples and their leaders, when they are identified with one another."

This was all true, but the great Frederick himself only believed in the future of Germany politically; he had no faith in it artistically. The poets who sang of his victories he treated with either scorn or indifference; for him his countrymen were intellectually slow and ponderous people who could never produce finely in art or literature. The best destiny he could think out for them was that they should become imitators of the French. For himself, he thought and spoke and wrote in French. He had an acquaintance of a kind with literature, got from books read between battles and drillings and from the society of the literary men he collected around him. The sort of literary knowledge he had bears a curious resemblance to that of Trotzky in our day: his interest in it was genuine; he could write fairly well himself, though he never understood the circumstances out of which literature came. This did not prevent him, however, from taking it upon himself to write criticism. Like Trotzky he wrote a work on literature remarkable for its directness, its common sense, its mixture of ignorance, superficial knowledge, and second-hand literary opinions. Naturally he wrote it in French. It was entitled *De la Littérature Alle-*

mande; therein he made an assault on the efforts of his countrymen to produce a literature, singling out in particular *Goetz von Berlichingen,* a work by a young nursling of Lessing's and Herder's, Johann Wolfgang Goethe, which he termed a vulgar imitation of Shakespeare. However, in this book of his he announced his belief that the great days of literature were to come, but that he himself would not live to see them. He did not know that these great days were upon him and that the makers of literature had sprung up all around him, a product of the seeds he himself had sown with his victories, and that the greatest of them all, indeed the greatest of the moderns, was that identical young man whose *Goetz von Berlichingen* he had so rashly attacked.

3

But if Frederick had no intuitions about the psychic life around him, there was another German ruler who had. Frederick's youthful fellow sovereign, the life-loving, poetry-loving Duke of Weimar, had not much territory to rule over and his name had cut no figure in the Gazettes, and he did not, perhaps, know a great deal about either conquering or ruling a kingdom, but he was a great aristocrat and he knew intuitively that art of aristocrats, the art of enriching life. And so he made the author of *Goetz von Berlichingen* his high priest, his chancellor, his boon companion. To Weimar also came Herder and Schiller and many others, until

28

the little Duchy became a sort of Athens, alive with great intellects and great emotions. But all this outburst of creative life represented intellectual conquests by Lessing and Herder that were as marvellous as those of Frederick on the field of battle.

It was the fashion at that time for kings and rulers to have at their courts poets, littérateurs, men of genius. For life is dull for the politically great as well as for the financially great unless it is somehow lightened or made more meaningful and profound by contact with those who are in touch with the emotional and spiritual strivings of man. In spite of his bit of artistry, Frederick had no power of communication with the developing interior life of his people, for the writer he invited to his court was Voltaire. The King of Denmark might ask to Copenhagen, as a representative of culture, the German poet Klopstock, who wrote the *Messiah,* but Frederick would have no Germans. "I find myself in France here," wrote Voltaire after his arrival at Frederick's court; "they speak only our language; German is for soldiers and horses. I find that the cultivated people at Königsberg know my verses by heart."

Now this and similar was what Lessing had to cure his countrymen of—the contempt for their own language and culture and their mania for quoting the verses and dramas of the French poets, and in particular the poetry of Voltaire, which did not happen to be poetry at all, and his dramas, which did not happen to be dramas at all. When Voltaire arrived in Berlin, Goethe was a babe in arms; Herder, who later was to become Lessing's aide and disciple, was a little boy in petticoats, and Lessing himself was only twenty-two. But though Lessing earlier had, like everybody else, floundered around in imitations of the French, he soon outgrew this immaturity, and with the instinct of a man of genius, he perceived that if he was ever to rouse his countrymen to genuine literary expression, one of the first things to be fought was the influence of Voltaire. Voltaire had written in verse more than fifty plays; they had been enormously successful, as are the plays of Bernard Shaw in our own time and for much the same reason: they were brilliant; they were witty; they were amusing. But he had only slight power of creating character; his personages, like Shaw's, were mostly types on which he hung his philosophy; in general, his dramas were propaganda for his ideas—his mocking, brilliant, and sometimes noble ideas. His following all over Europe was an immense one, and to Frederick and his court and all educated Germany he represented the highest literary genius and the last word in intellectual sophistication. Lessing had to fight vigorously against all this, and he was well equipped for the battle: he was learned; he was witty; he was satirical; he could be profound; he could himself illustrate his own critical theories. In controversy he was a master. His literary attacks have been described as lacking in urbanity. But urbanity, which is a virtue in personal quarrels, has, it may be, no more place in a fight for intellectual convictions than it has in a statement of the theory of relativity; urbanity is a necessity in social intercourse, but truth, to quote Lessing himself, is a necessity of the soul.

4

In the realization of his theory that literature was an expression of national being, one of the first things Lessing had to cope with was the language of the literature he was trying to create. The language according to Frederick should be French, and according to Gottsched might be German, but only the German of savants, a language different from that of every-day life. Lessing, in spite of his passion for the Greeks, was, like Coleridge after him, like all the writers sprung from the blood of the old Teutons, by temperament more akin to the spirit of the Hebrew Bible than to that of the Greeks or Latins, or that of any people working in their tradition. He turned back to Luther's Bible, and to those long-despised sources from which Luther said he got the language that he used for his writing—"the mother in the house, the children in the street, the man in the market-place." The language, literature, and emotions of that other great Teutonic or part-Teutonic people, the English, had been profoundly influenced by the Bible, and Lessing now announced that the German mentality was subject to much the same influences as the English. All literatures influence each other, but a choice of influences had to be made and those chosen which were in accord with the national genius. But the only art the ordinary man among Lessing's fellow countrymen came in contact with was the artificial tragedy made in imitation of Racine and Corneille and staged by strolling players all over the country. This art, with its fantastic heroes and sceptered kings stalking across the boards and orating pages of rhetoric, was remote from any life the audiences knew.

It will be remembered that at this period, the middle eighteenth century, the novel was at its beginning: it had, as a matter of fact, appeared in English and French; in other literatures there were only odd picaresque romances that came out under Spanish influences. So that, for the average person interested in character, literature meant a play, generally a play in verse —when people spoke of literature they generally meant a composition in verse. It was for this reason that when Lessing started his literary reforms he began with the drama: with his versatile mind he was not only able to invent the principles of reform but to carry them into practice. The art the people came in contact with, he said, should reflect the people's life, and so he wrote a play, *Minna von Barnhelm,* that, for the first time in German literary history, brought German life on the stage. The audiences were delighted to see, on the boards, themselves and their problems, their life and their language, the contemporary history of their country. It was the first conscious and deliberate experiment in making literature national expression—an expression of the people. This has been done in other places since Lessing's day, and has its great popular success in countries where, for one reason or another, literary expression has been dominated by alien influences or is remote from the life of the people. One of the striking examples of its success in contemporary literature has been with that school of writers who formed what was called the Irish Renaissance, under the leadership of William Butler Yeats, Douglas Hyde, and Æ.

When the bulk of the people see their every-day life portrayed in literature there is a new stirring of vitality among them, even when they protest, as they frequently do, against the manner in which the artist has depicted them. However, as can easily be imagined, the portrayal of ordinary, every-day life may degenerate into a form of photographic realism from which all art and inspiration have been excluded. At this stage in our own day a theory the exact opposite of Lessing's, something that demands a purely fantastic or stylized expression, might have the best stimulus for the reviving of literature. But a literary theory, if it has ever been really effective, never becomes moribund; it is always capable, when the need is felt, of taking a fresh form of life; a newer theory causes a re-arrangement of values, but that does not mean that the old one has been made completely obsolete.

About the same time that he produced *Minna von Barnhelm,* Lessing published his classic in criticism, *Laocoön.* This is one of those books like, in science, Darwin's *Origin of Species;* in criticism, Taine's *De l'Intelligence;* in psychology, Freud's *Interpretation of Dreams,* which turn men's minds in a new direction. Its subject was the boundary between literature or poetry and the plastic arts; its effect was the overthrowing of the rococo formalism, the conventionalism that had had a strangle hold on literature, and the release of the minds of his countrymen to literary expression. *Laocoön* was not only the first piece of real modern criticism—it was the first extensive piece of criticism since Aristotle. By showing that each art has its laws, its boundary beyond which it is possible to pass, but that each art achieves the best results inside its own boundary, that each art has a special function and that it cannot trespass on the functions of the other arts, he introduced into criticism a wholly new principle. *Laocoön* was not limited to the theme proposed: it was filled with exciting ideas about life, psychology, methods of writing.

5

There has always been a tendency in the minds of the art-conscious to confuse the various arts, to suppose that the effects of one art can be produced in another. Sometimes, it has been thought that the effects of a landscape as presented in a painting can be reproduced in words. From this notion sprang the long descriptions of places, or things, that have from time to time been the fashion in both poetry and prose. From this confusion, also, sprang the literary painting, the painting which tried to produce the effect of a story or a poem. And again, writers have believed that they could achieve in literature, especially in poetry, the effects of music, and the present-day attempt at these effects amongst certain modernistic writers is not so new as has been supposed: on the contrary, it is an ancient heresy. In his great attempt to define the boundaries of the arts, to show the limits of expression in each art, Lessing brought into criticism a wholly new principle, and if only this principle were put into general practice it would be a liberation for every art. The picture that tries to tell a story can never be anything but an illustration for a piece of literature; the literary passage that tries to produce the effect of a painting loses its natural verve; the poem that insists on being pure music is neither music nor poetry. Lessing meant the *Laocoön* to be only a first volume, the volume in which he delimited the provinces of poetry and the plastic arts; he had meant to write a second volume which would deal with the relations of music and literature and which would delimit the provinces of these two arts, but he did not get down to it—perhaps through lack of sufficient knowledge or simply through lack of time: he lived only to be fifty-two. The fact is that whereas he delivered a lasting blow to the sort of literature that imitated painting and the sort of painting or sculpture that imitated literature, the notion that poetry can reproduce the effects of music still has a sturdy life in literary cliques. The boundary between poetry and music has never been defined—perhaps it really is too intangible to define. In the lifetime of Lessing himself there was born a man, Novalis, who by precept and example did considerable to confuse the boundary of poetry and music, and who provided rallying cries that were taken over into French by Verlaine, and, later and especially, by Mallarmé. Mallarmé not only adopted Novalis's theory that poetry was the more excellent in proportion as it produced the effects of music, but also his notion that poetry was the conversation of the soul with itself. From this we can see the evolution of the idea popular in certain modern coteries that literature expresses but need not communicate. In fact, it cannot be too often emphasized that the contemporary world has invented no new ideas with regard to literary expression.

To return to *Laocoön:* Lessing hung his ideas on the Laocoön in sculpture and the Laocoön in literature: the Laocoön of the Greek sculpture and the Laocoön of Virgil. He developed certain ideas of his predecessor, Winckelmann. It would have been against the laws of plastic beauty to show faces with muscles violently and permanently distorted; therefore, in the group of the sculptor, while we have Laocoön and his children entwined in a death grip by the serpent, in the midst of most frightful sufferings, we see on each face the expression of a soul at rest. This was, Lessing explained, because a statue or a picture can show us only a moment of time, whereas in poetry we have the development of an action. Virgil, therefore, could represent Laocoön as crying out with pain, not because he had a different conception of his character, but because he was working in a different art, a different medium. That is, plastic art deals with things coexistent in space—bodies; poetry (or literature in general) represents things sequent in time—actions. Plastic art is confined to immobility; poetry (literature in general) lives on movements and contrasts. In poetry, for example, Homer does not describe Helen's beauty, but shows how the sight of her affected the elders of Troy; he does not describe the completed shield of Achilles, but shows it to us in the making, and makes us, as it were, participators in its devising.

6

Without the aid of his younger contemporary, Herder, it might not have been so easy for Lessing to carry out his idea of literature as national expression. For

Herder had what Lessing lacked—the lyrical mind. Lessing was learned, witty, satirical, profound: he could analyze to the depths any type of literature except the lyrical, and this drawback made him somewhat lacking in the comprehension of every kind of poetry. He was never the equal of Herder in understanding the workings of the poetic mind. In spite of his spontaneity, in spite of the fact that he published a book of what he called lyrics, his mind was incapable of lyrical flights. This deficiency caused some of the younger critics of his later years to deny him the creative mind, though it is plain that he possessed one of the great creative minds of the eighteenth century—a mind that sowed ideas which have since cropped up in all sorts of places and have influenced the whole development of European literature. In his later days, in the hey-day of the great German lyric, the creative mind and the purely lyrical were confounded, as in our day the creative mind is popularly supposed to be the one which expresses itself in character creation or narrative making. Lessing could not be denied the power of character creation or of idea creation, but he was no lyric poet. Herder, on the other hand, no matter how one may estimate his own poetry, had the lyrical mentality, and because of this was naturally the poetic-critical mind as Lessing was the philosophical-critical mind. The aims of both critics were the same: to create a new German literature, to free the minds of their countrymen from the shackles of pseudo-classicism and the rule-making criticism of pedants. Both had the same belief that literature was the product of national conditions, both had the same dislike of classical French drama, the same passion for English literature and for Shakespeare. But where Lessing was guided by reason, Herder, who had a fiery, eager poet's mind, was guided by flashes of intuition; it was his glory and his defect that his mind worked in flashes. Where Lessing gave up his mind to the study of drama and the development of literary and æsthetic ideas, Herder gave his chiefly to the study of poetry, which he declared "ought to be the most impetuous and self-assured daughter of the human soul."

Lessing, for all his hatred of the rule-makers, had a passion for Aristotle. In spite of his belief in what he called "the inner rule" he thought that absolute canons of art could be arrived at and that the way to reach them was through a study of the Greeks. The rules expounded by Aristotle, he maintained, were as infallible as the elements of Euclid, and when he wished to praise Shakespeare highly he said he was truer to the Aristotelian principles than were the French classical dramatists. Herder, however, announced that the Greeks, after all, were only the Greeks, and that they had never been brought into the world to furnish artistic norms for all men to the end of time. The literature of the Greeks was like every other literature: a product of national conditions which could not be duplicated in another country, in another age. That literature was the product of national conditions formed the chief matter of his agreement with Lessing. On other points they differed as much as did Sainte-Beuve and Taine. Herder did for poetry a service that Lessing was not capable of doing: he awakened the latent lyricism of the Germans. He announced that poetry was the mother tongue of mankind, that the first authors of every nation are its poets, that the earliest poetry in a nation's history, being the most spontaneous, is the greatest: that is, the poetry of Homer, of the Bible, and, he added, the newly discovered poetry of Ossian.

Herder wanted poetry to be said or sung, not read silently in a printed book. Homer, the first great poet, did not write; he sang. Of Homer he said, "Long centuries have knelt before him as before a god or a messenger of the gods." His conception of poetry as the mother tongue of mankind led him naturally to the study of the folk song; he brought out a collection of folk songs translated from many languages, in which he exhibited not only his own poetic gifts but his great power of penetration into the minds of primitive peoples. It was in his writing on primitive poetry that he showed his disagreement with Lessing and with Lessing's great friend, the soldier-poet Kleist, both of whom were inclined to regard poetry as composition.

"Do not be surprised," wrote Herder, in a paragraph that set many minds on fire, "do not be surprised that a young Lapp who does not know his letters, has never been to school and hardly has a god, sings better than Major Kleist. For the Lapp sang his song on the wing as he was gliding over the snow with his reindeer, impatient to see Lake Orra where his sweetheart lived, but Major Kleist made his song by imitation from a book."

The young Goethe, studying law and trying to Frenchify himself in the Alsatian town of Strassburg, met in that city this fiery literary revolutionary, just five years his senior, and this meeting was one of those lucky chances that befell Goethe all his long, lucky life. "Study the superstitions and the sagas of the forefathers," said Herder to him, and the saying passed not only into the soul of Goethe but, later, into the soul of Wagner. And Goethe, in studying the legends of the forefathers, attached himself particularly to the legend of Doctor Faustus, who sold his soul to the devil, and he made it into the history of the eternal struggle of the creative mind, and he made it also the history of the strivings of the modern man. Under Herder's influence he too became a collector of folk songs; he got the rhythm into his blood, the rhymes into his measures, and like Herder's Lapp he, too, began to sing his songs on the wing as he rode to see his sweetheart, and he got into them the earth and the sunshine, the clouds and the mountains, and the lyricism and spontaneity of the folk song.

> Wie herrlich leuchtet
> Mir die Natur!
> Wie glänzt die Sonne,
> Wie lacht die Flur!
> O Lieb', O Liebe
> So golden-schön
> Wie Morgenwolken
> Auf jenen Höh'n!

7

Herder's translations of the old spontaneous songs and poems aroused and quickened the lyrical genius of the poets around him. Among his other gifts was that curious power, sometimes noticeable in critics, of being able to form a conception of a whole work from a very small fragment of it—give him a line or two of an old song, a piece of a work of literature, and he knew the spirit, the structure of the whole. Strongly as he believed that literature, and especially poetry, was national and racial expression, it can be deduced from his work that there was one form of literature, at least, which from its very nature had to be international, and that was criticism. Literary ideas, no matter where they have had their rise, are equally the inheritance of all literatures that can avail themselves of them. Starting from this thought he became the initiator of the study of comparative literature, a necessary outgrowth of modern criticism. Even now the interdependence of literary and critical ideas is not sufficiently realized. Brunetière's *History of Criticism* is only a history of French criticism; he seems to think that only French criticism is of any import; Saintsbury, too, took very little stock in the interdependence of literary ideas: one would suppose that all the great modern critics were English, from his *History of Criticism* and his passages illustrative of critical theory and practice from Aristotle downwards, which he called *Loci Critici*.

Not only did Herder start the study of comparative literature, he was one of the initiators of the modern manner of studying history, and his *Philosophy of History* played a great rôle in the method of writing history. No doubt he was influenced in this work by the ideas of that strange seventeenth-century philosopher, Vico. However, while no one can pretend that any new idea comes into being without antecedents, the fact remains that Herder exerted the greatest influence in starting people's minds on a new conception of history. "History has been transformed," said Taine, writing nearly a hundred years afterwards, "within a hundred years in Germany [that is, since Herder's *Philosophy of History*], within sixty years in France, and that by a study of their literatures." That is to say, the transformation was brought about by the application of Herder's thought. It is true that he was never able to

43

outline his ideas with precision as Lessing could and did: his intuitions were often expressed in loose, cloudy, flowery language. Yet in its own loose way his mind sowed the seeds of as many ideas as did Lessing's. All those later critical theories explaining literature by the time and place, or accounting for it as an expression of society, are to be found in germ in Herder's work. His influence on the philosophers was marked; some of Hegel's æsthetics being simply certain ideas of Herder's, pondered over, systematized, and philosophically stated—notably, the idea of the race, milieu, and moment referred to previously, and which was taken over by Taine. Both Herder and Lessing powerfully influenced a series of German philosophers, beginning with Hegel and Fichte—Fichte's famous *Addresses to the German Nation* being simply a metaphysical and political expression of the literary theories of these two great critics.

In Lessing, who gave his mind especially to the study of form, we have in germ very many of the most modern developments of literary forms—the abolishing of transitions, the revelation of physical traits of people or landscape or things by showing them in action. After two hundred years, sentences from *Laocoön* are still literary sign-posts taking one away from swamps and jungles. Nothing has been said about emotional extravagance in art better than Lessing's—"In the whole gamut of emotion there is no moment less advanta-

geous than its topmost note." For, as he said, "Beyond
the top there is nothing more and nothing is left to
arouse the imagination." It may equally be said, however, that there is nothing below the lowest note, and
that the common habit of the moderns of expressing
emotion on its lowest note makes an unfair demand
upon the imagination. And who better than Lessing
has noted the necessity for the extension of the boundaries of art beyond the notions of the Greeks, to include not only the naturally beautiful but the whole
of nature and humanity, of which the beautiful is only
a part? For, as he remarked, an ugliness of nature can
be transformed into a beauty of art. And how clear
and emphatic are his objections to the use of propaganda in art! "I should like the name Works of Art
to be reserved for those alone in which the artist could
show himself actually as artist. All the rest, in which
too evident traces of religious dogma appear, are unworthy of the name. Art here has not wrought on her
own account but has been auxiliary to religion." In
Lessing's day, it should be noted, religious propaganda
was the one most generally encountered in art, as in
our day the propaganda most likely to be encountered
would be political and social. "The frigid delineations
of physical objects," to which Lessing objected, were
effectively banished from poetry in his own day, but
it is only in our own time that they are being banished
from the prose narrative. In addition to attacking

French neo-classicism Lessing made a study of the Greek text of Aristotle's *Poetics* and gave the interpretation that is now generally accepted.

While stressing the originality and power of both Herder and Lessing, it is not to be denied that they were deeply influenced by certain of their predecessors —Lessing by Winckelmann's studies of the Greek plastic arts, and Herder by Hamann's discourses on English and on primitive poetry. In spite of their opposition to French influences they were themselves influenced by Rousseau and Diderot—Lessing noticeably by Diderot—and Herder was easily won over to the doctrine of the goodness of the natural man. Where they found ideas that fitted in with theirs or could be used to help along the creation of the new literature they had in mind, they took them over and formed their own construction on them. This is what all the important critics have done: those who came after Lessing and Herder in their turn used the ideas of these first modern critics as a foundation for their own contribution. For these two were the founders of a new school of literature, and that means the revealers of a new side of life; they emphasized a different side of man from the one which for so long had been exploited in literature: that product of the Enlightenment, the uniformitarian man, went into the background. A great renewal of life and literature had suddenly begun.

Chapter Three

THE ENGLISH CONTRIBUTION: COLERIDGE
AND WORDSWORTH

I

THE CONCEPT of literature as racial and national became so universalized, not only during their lifetime but all through the nineteenth century down to the Great War, that it is not easy for us to comprehend the sweeping extent of Lessing's and Herder's reforms and the nature of the struggle against seventeenth and eighteenth-century Enlightenment and Uniformity. There are in humanity a set of deeply rooted desires towards uniformity and standardization that in suitable soils and periods can be developed to an alarming extent. These tendencies towards pattern and standardization are sometimes confused with discipline, sometimes confused with high ethical and political aspirations, and while they have been responsible for much that is great and stately, they are also responsible for those regimentations of ideas that, if carried far enough, are ruinous to all forms of vigorous life and art.

But seldom is any idea carried too far, for ideas, like creatures when their usefulness is past, are shelved or die, or, rather, they die to that extent that some other idea generated by them is started on its career and in its turn influences humanity. The standardization, the uniformity that Lessing and Herder successfully combated, gave way in their turn to a set of ideas that have ruled men's minds down to our time. How all-embracing was the uniformity of that period sometimes called the eighteenth century, but in reality partly the seventeenth and partly the eighteenth, how this uniformity was operative in movements of the period which at first sight seem totally dissimilar in temper and orientation, has been shown by Arthur O. Lovejoy in a paper called *The Parallel of Deism and Classicism*. Uniformitarianism, to use Lovejoy's term, was the first and fundamental principle of the Enlightenment. When the outstanding men of the period talked about "nature," whether it was Spinoza, or Fénelon, or Voltaire, or Rousseau, the common element of the meaning of the word as it was understood by all of them was uniformity. All the history of civilized mankind for them had been a long tale of departure from the uniformity and simplicity of nature. In theory the æsthetic of neo-classicism was fundamentally an æsthetic of uniformitarianism. "The fact is writ large," to quote Professor Lovejoy, "in all the most famous expositions of neo-classical doctrine." The objection to the *differentness* of men was also extended to the *differentness* of races and nations. The rebellion against this uniformitarianism has been the motive principle in literature and art generally, from the time of Lessing down to our own time.

In the Enlightenment the object of the reformer, religious, moral or social, as well as of the literary critic, was to standardize men—their beliefs, their likings, their activities, and their institutions. But there was in the Enlightenment, as in everything else, an admixture of many opposed ideas, and some of these contained the seeds of racism, nationalism, and romanticism. Lessing himself, forecasting modern developments in psychology, said that there does not exist a single unmixed feeling in nature. Nor, may it be said, does there exist a single unmixed idea: each idea contains the seeds of its opposite or of what can be developed into its opposite. In both Lessing and Herder themselves there were the vestiges of many of the ideas they were out to combat. Lessing thought that by logic one always arrived at true conceptions, and while out against the rule-makers he was all for the Aristotelian rules, though Aristotle as a critic represented the opposite kind from Lessing, being the critic who coming after a great period in literature draws from masterpieces handed on to him the laws for creating others. Lessing, on the other hand, was the sort of critic who foresees and directs great movements in literature—the sort of critic that is considered in these chapters. If he had vestiges of the rule-makers in him, Herder, in spite of his attachment to folk songs and primitive poetry, had strong vestiges of eighteenth-century pedantry.

2

The more remote heirs of the thought of Lessing and Herder were the great French critics, Sainte-Beuve and Taine; the nearest heirs were Wordsworth and Coleridge, who, between them, did in England exactly what Herder and Lessing had done in Germany—changed the course of literature by making people realize that another phase of human experience and of the mind of man had to be expressed.

These two, Wordsworth and Coleridge, are, I hold, the greatest minds in English criticism—both nearly the same age, both younger contemporaries of the great German critics. They worked even more closely together than did their older contemporaries. As is well known, they brought out jointly the volume *Lyrical Ballads* illustrating their literary ideas. It has been commonly said of them, and especially of Wordsworth, that their literary principles represented an æsthetic statement of the Rights of Man as proclaimed by the French Revolution: this, I think, is a great mistake. There is no doubt that their minds were influenced by this social upheaval, but it was a transitory influence. Their æsthetic principles were very similar to those of

Lessing and Herder, but on many points they represented a development of the German ideas. Lessing wanted ordinary life and the ordinary man expressed in the drama; Wordsworth wanted him expressed in poetry. Lessing wanted the speech of drama reformed so as to be the actual speech of men; he wanted to have the eighteenth-century poetic diction and rhodomontade banished and to have every-day life and speech upon the stage. These are the same literary principles that Wordsworth advances in his Preface, developed several degrees further and applied, not to the drama, but to lyric and narrative poetry. It has been said that originally the seeds of these ideas were supplied to Wordsworth by Coleridge, and very likely they were. But the fact remains that it was Wordsworth and not Coleridge who developed them, reduced them to vigorous and simple language, and who wrote the famous Preface—the one solitary example, in English literature, of a poetic manifesto that started a school of poetry, which school, it should be added, lasted down to our own time. Both Coleridge and Wordsworth had the same notion of what constituted poetry as Herder had and the same recognition of the necessity for turning to old songs and ballads. Many of Herder's ideas are explicit in the famous Preface—his passion for the primitive, for folk poetry, all poetry that was the expression of natural passions.

These four critics, Lessing, Herder, Wordsworth, and

Coleridge, had an identical object in mind: to destroy the deliberate style of the neo-classicists, to abolish artificial and "poetic diction," to extend the boundaries of literature so that it could express familiar life and the ordinary man's passions and desires; they had the same desire to get rid of "gaudiness and inane phraseology," to awaken an interest in Shakespeare and in all spontaneous and lyric writing. This lyricism was, it should be noted again, less a passion with Lessing, who had no great comprehension of lyric poetry, than with the other three. The two great English critics had no such struggle against the ravages and extravagances of neo-classicism and uniformity as had the two Germans; English literature had been classicist and uniformitarian for a brief period only. On the other hand, the English writers had not the same virgin field to work in: Germany had produced practically no literature; England had already produced one of the great literatures of the world, and though Wordsworth and Coleridge might and did start literature on a new track, they could never surpass the great age. The lyricism and spontaneity of that age they could restore; they could, in the estimation of some of their admirers, equal the great figures; they could and did extend the bounds of expression; they could and did explore the path to new material. All this, to be sure, amounted to a great reform—a reform which started English literature on a new course. With Lessing and Herder, on the other hand, the great age of German literature, the age of modern literature, began.

As is well known, the Preface was not prefixed to the first edition of *Lyrical Ballads,* but to the second, and was written after the return of Wordsworth and Coleridge from Germany, where Coleridge already had fallen not only under the spell of Lessing and Herder, but also of Schelling, one of the philosophers influenced by the new critics. That the Preface was really not a preface at all but was written long after the poems and was partly a rationalization, an apologia, for work already done, makes no difference; that the ideas themselves were, to some extent, already current in Germany, makes no difference in the value of the great manifesto. Wordsworth took to himself the literary ideas that were most akin to his mind, he added new elements to the thoughts of others, and these new ingredients had a virility and a power of life that in their turn gave out the seeds of future ideas. In the *Lyrical Ballads* the two poets, according to Coleridge's account, had two aims in mind: Wordsworth in his subjects and verse was to give "the charm of novelty to things of every day," and Coleridge was to deal with "persons and characters supernatural, or at least, romantic." Wordsworth was to make the familiar wonderful and Coleridge to make the wonderful familiar. Coleridge attempted his part of the enterprise in the "Rime of the Ancient Mariner," and among Wordsworth's attempts to make the familiar wonderful were "Tintern Abbey," "The Idiot Boy," "The Reverie of Poor Susan," "Simon Lee." In the second edition, the edition with the Preface, he added poems he had written in Germany—"Lucy Gray," "Ruth," "Three Years She Grew," "Michael," and others. Thus, some of the greatest of Wordsworth's poems belonged to the *Lyrical Ballads* period.

If we take the Preface as a piece of independent criticism and not, as it is generally taken, a standard to measure whether the poetry does or does not illustrate the principles laid down, the conclusion must be that it is one of the most powerful and influential critical statements of the last hundred and fifty years and Wordsworth one of the greatest of critics. Its influence, as Coleridge tells us in his *Biographia Literaria,* began almost immediately. "Not only," said Coleridge, "in the verses of those who had professed their admiration of his genius, but even of those who had distinguished themselves by hostility to his theory and depreciation of his writings, are the impressions of his principles plainly visible."

3

Let us now consider the salient points of the Preface. The most familiar of these is the one relating to language, which he returned to again and again, expressing it in slightly different ways. This was that the language of poetry should, as far as possible, be a selection

54

of the language really used by men. When he expresses this idea with a slight variation he tells us that his purpose was to imitate, and, as far as possible, to adopt, the very language of men. He rejected the sort of language that had come to be called "poetic diction" because it was used only in poetry. In addition, he rejected what was associated with poetic diction—personifications of abstract ideas, which he called "an ordinary device to elevate the style and to raise it above prose."

This theory of language is, in some of its facets, a very old one: we have Luther's version of it in his statement that he took the language he used in his version of the Bible from "the mother in the house, the children in the street, the man in the market-place," and Dante's consideration of "the illustrious vernacular" and "the vulgar tongue which, without any rules at all, we get by imitating our nurses," and which he called "noble" because it is in common human employment and is not academic or literary. Wordsworth stated his theory of language with the passion of one who had discovered it anew. Round it he hung a conception of poetry that speedily made its way into the minds of readers and writers, and it is this general conception of his, rather than his much-debated theory of language, about which there is really nothing to debate, that has made him such a force—in fact, his theory of language is but a natural consequence of his general conception. Poetry was not to be metaphysical

Essays on Man or on Criticism, or dissertations on the Pleasures of Hope or the Progress of the Mind or the Vanity of Human Wishes; it was to be about "the essential passions of the heart." And these passions, in Wordsworth's mind, found a better soil to mature unrestrainedly "in humble and rustic life" because "in that condition of life our elementary feelings co-exist in a state of greater simplicity, and consequently may be more accurately contemplated and more forcibly communicated." The subject of poetry, therefore, was to be "the incidents and situations of common life," but at the same time the poet was "to throw over them the coloring of the imagination, whereby ordinary things should be presented to the mind in an unusual aspect."

To make the incidents and situations of common life the subject of poetry was, at this period, a literary principle of vast revolutionary import. Wordsworth wanted, what all the literary revolutionists wanted, an extension of the boundaries of literary expression; he designed a more extensive expression of life as it is really lived. For literature, it cannot be too often said, has expressed only a limited amount of the experiences of men, and one of the ways for revealing in words a wider area of life is first of all to envisage something that has been left out of literary expression, and then, if necessary, to invent new technical devices for expressing this. Any one literary principle has many antecedents, and the fact is that Wordsworth repeated a demand that Lessing had made—with Lessing it was for drama, with Wordsworth for lyrical and narrative poetry. The short appendix to the *Lyrical Ballads,* published two years after the publication of the Preface, dealt again with the language of poetry and reproduced the Herder conception of poetry and language, and in similar words, but Wordsworth made it more precise and intense, and gave it a new coloring, and added new elements from his own mind.

In addition to what Coleridge called his "literary principles," Wordsworth devoted his Preface not only to the subject and language of poetry but to a consideration of what poetry is, of what a poet is, and to what degree he differs from the ordinary man. He did not mind repeating himself and reiterating his major ideas, for literary principles always need to be repeated in the same or similar words until they make themselves a part of the reader's mind and imagination. "All good poetry," he said, "was the spontaneous overflow of powerful feelings." And, at the same time, he went on to explain that while this is true, "poems to which any value can be attached were never produced on any variety of subjects but by a man, who, being possessed of more than usual organic sensibility, had also thought long and deeply." He said, in effect, that the spontaneity and powerful feelings were directed and modified by thoughts—thoughts, he said, which are indeed the representatives of past feelings. This statement is in itself a clue to the mind of Wordsworth, whose thoughts all sprang from past feelings—sometimes, as some of his critics have declared, from dead feelings, feelings that had no more life. Continuing to develop his theory, he maintained that poetry takes its origin from "emotion recollected in tranquillity; the emotion is contemplated till, by a species of reaction, the tranquillity gradually disappears and an emotion kindred to that which was before the subject of contemplation is gradually produced." In this way he gives us what is in actual fact an account of the workings of his own creative personality, of what happened in his mind before he wrote a poem, during the writing of it, and what he conceived to be the result when finished. He turned the powerful critical side of his genius to an analysis of his own mind, and while it is, perhaps, true, that he was too much inclined to regard his own as the norm of the poet's mind, the fact remains that his revelations apply to the workings of a great many poets' minds. Substantially the same account has been given of their creative processes by many others since, including our contemporaries Paul Valéry and Robert Frost.

Some of the definitions and descriptions of poetry which are in the Preface are, in effect, the same as Coleridge's, who, in spite of minor disagreements with Wordsworth about the language of poetry, was in agreement with him as to its nature. "Poetry is the image of man and nature," said Wordsworth, "its object is truth . . . carried alive into the heart by passion. . . . Poetry is the breath and finer spirit of all knowledge." Compare these with Coleridge's "Poetry is the fragrancy of all human knowledge, human thoughts, human passions, emotions, language. . . . No man was ever yet a great poet without being, at the same time, a profound philosopher." If their poetry differed, their literary principles were almost the same, and one must remember that with Wordsworth and Coleridge, as with Lessing and Herder, as with Boileau, as with Dante, as with Aristotle, the word Poetry stood for practically everything in imaginative literature.

Wordsworth's description of a poet could stand for that of any creative writer of any type. "What is a poet?" he asks. "He is a man speaking to men, a man, it is true, endowed with more lively sensibilities, more enthusiasm and tenderness, who has a greater knowledge of human nature and a more comprehensive soul than are supposed to be common among mankind. . . . One who rejoices more than other men in the spirit of life that is in him. . . . To these qualities he has added a disposition to be affected more than other men by absent things as if they were present. He is chiefly distinguished from other men by a greater promptness to think and to feel without immediate external excitement, and a greater power in expressing such thoughts and feelings." What are these thoughts and feelings that the poet expresses? Are they something peculiar and personal to himself? No, they are the passions, thoughts, and feelings of men, for poets do not write for poets alone, but for men. From these general literary principles of Wordsworth's was derived that special one about the language of poetry being a selection of the language spoken by men, which, though it has aroused more discussion than all the others, was really but a minor part of his whole poetic creed. It was not even an essential part as practised by himself, for of all his literary and poetical principles it was the one he most often left out in actual writing. Others following him carried out this particular one much more readily than they did his great and major ones. There have been many poets who have spoken forcibly to men in their own language without really having very much to communicate to them, while great poets, men speaking to men, have spoken clearly and lastingly without using at all the ordinary language of men.

All writers in a new literary era or a new literary movement have to cope with the problem of language. It is one that comes up when the language of writing becomes worn out or becomes too exclusively literary, or has not been revivified from the actual speech of men. The problem arises again if this actual speech has become but conventional symbol and not a real medium of emotions and thoughts. Wordsworth's principles penetrated more widely and more rapidly than his poetry, and often to places where his poetry never penetrated at all. His poetry, great as it was, was like Milton's in that it was too peculiarly English to have a ready following in other countries. The admirers of his poetry abroad, like his admirers at home, were inclined to exalt him for what they believed to be the philosophy that they extracted from his work, especially from his long poems.

The French exiles who returned from England to France with volumes of English poetry in their baggage brought, amongst others, the poetry of Wordsworth, but they more especially brought the Preface, the doctrine of which was rapidly disseminated. Sainte-Beuve made his own of it: in France it became the poetical doctrine associated with his name. Something similar happened at a later date in the case of the poetic doctrines of Poe. We know that Baudelaire was influenced by Poe, though, as he tells us, he had never read a line of him until after the *Fleurs du Mal* was written: it happened simply that Poe's ideas had infiltrated into many coteries. In Wordsworth's lifetime people quarrelled about the Preface who never read the poetry, or who read it only to see how he put his principles into effect. The audience for the Preface has been an enormous one; the audience for the great poems has been much more limited, for the Preface, his manifesto, satisfied the greater need at the time, the need for a new æsthetic doctrine, the need for rejuvenating and transforming ideas, in all the mature European literatures. It was a masterpiece of literary criticism.

In that secondary form of criticism, the criticism of judgment, Wordsworth was equally outstanding. His estimate of Gray, of Johnson, of Cowper, though it occupies only a few succinct pages, is a masterly example of the art of judging poetry, and especially of the art of judging the poetry of an age that was going out by a practitioner of the poetry of an age that was coming in. The manner in which he picks out the lines that have the quickness of life in them and discards the lines that belong merely to an outmoded convention, reinforcing his intuition with his carefully worked-out literary principles, is an unforgettable example of the application of insight and principle to the evaluation of poetry. One's decisions upon poetry, he held, conduced to the improvement of one's own taste, "for an accurate taste in poetry is an acquired talent which can only be produced by thought and a long-continued intercourse with the best models of composition." Coleridge, on the side of the criticism of judgment, made mistakes in estimating his contemporaries that it would be difficult to imagine Wordsworth committing, such as, for example, the rhapsodies on the sonnets of Bowles and the work of Southey, which we find in the *Biographia:* no one can doubt that it is Coleridge's praise that has kept Southey's name alive in the anthologies. On the other hand, Wordsworth's mind was narrower; he had not that diversity of intellectual interests—psychology, philosophy, politics—that helped Coleridge to evolve all those principles for estimating literature and analyzing the creative mind, and which have gone to make him the first English writer to give criticism a metaphysical framework.

4

The age of Coleridge and Wordsworth was one of extraordinary interest in literature, in England. An early training in it was more possible then than now, as we can see from Coleridge's own account of the manner in which he was taught as a schoolboy to compare various works of literature. One of the reasons why the *Biographia Literaria* is one of the greatest books on literature in any language is that it was written for an age, in a country, that was at the time capable of appraising the ideas it presented and of discussing them with excited interest, of attacking some and accepting others. This book of his, Coleridge said, represented "a statement of his principles in politics, religion, and philosophy, and an application of the rules deduced from philosophical principles to poetry and criticism." The result was, not only the biography of his mind, of his religion and his philosophy, not only a statement of his own politics, but of the politics of the time, in which he as literary and political editor of *The Morning Post* had played an active part. In this

63

rôle he was an ardent admirer of Burke; he launched vigorous onslaughts upon the administration of the day, and showed the same hostility to "French principles and ambition" that he showed to French literature, though I am inclined to believe that he caught his dislike of the literature from Lessing and Herder, the influence of whose ideas is very apparent in the *Biographia.*

Fox went so far as to accuse *The Morning Post,* and the ideas circulated through it by Coleridge, of causing the war with Napoleon. In short, the part he played, not only in literature but in journalism, in politics, gives no ground for the charges against him of bamboozling his mind with idlenesses, with dreaming, with laudanum. It is true that he idled, that he dreamt, that he took laudanum, that he was a metaphysician in a country that had but little use for metaphysicians, but through all of these impracticalities, or through some of them, he made of his mind a marvellous and subtle instrument. John Livingston Lowes's great piece of criticism, *The Road to Xanadu,* in which are charted the mind of Coleridge and the influences which went to the making of it, has done much to remove the effect of those foolish aspersions that marked him as a man who never finished anything and who dreamed his life away. Carlyle is sometimes judged responsible for this characterization of Coleridge, but as a matter of fact these charges were all brought against him early in his life-time, and, as he records in the *Biographia,* caused him serious injury. "By what I effected," he said himself, "am I to be judged by my fellow men. What I could have done is a question for my own conscience." What he did effect is imposing: in mere bulk his work both in prose and verse is large. It would have been to the gain of literature if he had worked less diligently, if he had not tried to make a living by writing, but had, like Wordsworth, procured a sinecure to provide for himself and his family. Out of Coleridge's work, when winnowed, there come enough poems of the highest quality to fill a fair-sized volume, and a volume of criticism that belongs to the half-dozen or so great works of the kind ever written. These two collections belong to the first order of genius: in his work of the secondary order there are a dozen or so more volumes of all kinds, some of poetry, some translations, some dealing with politics, fine arts, philosophy. In the poems, as Saintsbury has remarked, "the poetry of the nineteenth century is almost wholly suggested and, to a very great extent, contained after the fashion of the oak and the acorn," though this, of course, is equally true of Wordsworth, of both of them together.

Certain of his admirers regard Coleridge as greatest in his poetry, others as greatest in his criticism. But the truth is he is great in everything he has touched—poetry, criticism, psychology, philosophy. He was the first

English writer to evolve an æsthetic, and as a critic, as has been said before, his work belongs to the philosophic-critical group. Of the two conditions on which great literature depends—the action of significant mind on significant material—he, more than any of the six chief critics discussed here, comprehended that mind and all the elements that compose it. I am willing even to hazard the statement that he comprehended it better than any critic who wrote before or since. The philosophers who dealt with æsthetics too seldom understood sufficiently the conditions under which literature is actually produced—not only the external conditions of place and time, but the subjective conditions peculiar to the writer—to realize the several elements that go into literary creation. Coleridge knew them and everything connected with the production of literature; he charted the mind, marked it with signposts, illuminated it with definitions, and turned a blaze of light on all the summits. He explained, for all the writers who came after him, the difference between genius and talent, imagination and fancy, prose and poetry, art and nature, consciousness and mysticism. When he distinguished genius and imagination from talent and fancy he did not maintain that genius should be without talent or imagination without fancy: on the contrary, he said that genius needed talent properly to manifest itself. Lessing would have said that genius needed the critical mentality properly to manifest it-

66

self, and in his investigation of the literary mind he concluded that all men of genius were naturally critics, but that the converse was not equally true—the critic was not always a genius, for the critical talent in some degree could exist without any other sort of talent in literature.

5

On what did Coleridge ground his literary principles? Over and over again he tells us, in somewhat varying language: on the nature of man, on the nature of the whole being of man. There were some points, to be sure, in this nature, some common points, some common emotions, that a great poet, of necessity, shared to some extent with all his fellows, and these common points Wordsworth understood better than Coleridge, for he had explored very thoroughly the bit of life given him to experience or that he chose to experience. It was in the comprehension of the uncommon emotions, the uncommon flights of the mind without which there can be no literature, that Coleridge went beyond Wordsworth and beyond the others. He understood these, not merely in individuals, in men of great genius like Shakespeare or Chaucer or Dante, he understood these in whole ages of time. He was able to put his understanding into short, clear definitions such as his definitions of imagination, genius, and fancy, into his discoveries that genius and intellect, imagination and judgment were all equally powerful in the writers of the first order such as Shakespeare, Chaucer, and Fielding. He was able to show the especial points of difference between the literature of the Greeks in the pagan age and the literature of the moderns in the Christian age, in a way that metamorphosized thinking on the subject. The Greeks and the moderns really represented opposed ideas—"The Greeks receiving the names of their gods from Egypt soon deprived them of what was universal; they changed the ideas into finites, and these finites into anthromorphi or forms of men. Hence their religion, their poetry—nay, their very pictures—became statuesque; with them the form was the end." He showed that the effect of Christianity had been the reverse of all this. In a Christian age, finites, even the human form, must, in order to satisfy the mind, be brought into connection with, and be, in fact, symbolic of the infinite. The two great effects of Christianity on poetry, he deduced to be a combination of poetry with doctrine and a combination of poetry with sentiment —the latter combination being brought about by turning the mind inward on its own essence instead of letting it act only on its outward circumstances and communities. In short, literature became more subjective, and "it is this subjectivity which principally and most fundamentally distinguishes all the classic from all the modern poetry."

In these conclusions of Coleridge we have his explanation of the difference between the classical spirit and that which came to be called the romantic; we have, in fact, the beginning of that discussion about classical and romantic literature, and about the very terms themselves, which Goethe said were the invention of Schiller and himself. This discussion renews itself every time the expression of the mind in literature takes on a new phase, and always finds support in academic circles. It figured for a brief space a couple of years ago during the temporary excitement over the New Humanism, the rule-making critics writing then, as always, on the assumption that classical literature was something that a writer could produce if he put himself into a proper state of mind, learnt the technique, read Aristotle and the Greeks, changed his conduct.

Coleridge forestalled Spengler and recent historians of culture in showing that the two types of literature, classical and modern, represented essentially different forms of civilization—two differing ages, two differing cultures. Greek literature represented one form of religious experience and aspiration; the modern European, down to our own time, represented another. From our time a new era begins, and while it is impossible to affirm anything about the future, it can be said of the bulk of current literature that the religious mentality and religious aspiration in any shape or form are generally absent.

He anticipated many modern conclusions and discoveries, particularly those dealing with the association of ideas and with the conscious and the unconscious. He divided "all human knowledge into those on this side and those on the other side of the spontaneous consciousness," and as the Romans talked of Cis- and Trans-alpine Gaul, he talked of "the *citra et trans conscientiam communem.*" Of this knowledge on the other side of consciousness he made the distinction between that which was controlled by the intellect, and which he called philosophy, and the second, which he condemned as "flights of lawless speculation which, abandoned by all distinct consciousness, because transgressing the bounds and purposes of our intellectual faculties, are justly condemned as *transcendent.*" A similar distinction between these two kinds of thinking is made by the psychoanalyst, C. J. Jung, who terms them "directed thinking" and "fantasy thinking"; "the first, working for communication with speech elements, is troublesome and exhausting, the latter, on the contrary, goes on without trouble, working spontaneously with reminiscences." Coleridge, however, did not foresee that these "flights of lawless speculation, abandoned by all distinct consciousness," would become, a century later, an element in literature of great import and an element that is in literature to stay, though it will assuredly be forced to become less lawless, more subject to form, and therefore less monotonous than it is today.

The majority of people, Coleridge thought, could not and did not penetrate far *trans conscientiam;* "the first range of hills that encircle the scanty vale of human life is the horizon for the majority of its inhabitants. On *its* ridges the common sun is born and departs; from *them* the stars arise and, touching *them,* they vanish. By the many, even this range, the natural limit and bulwark of the vale, is but imperfectly known. Its highest ascents are too often hidden by mists and clouds from uncultivated swamps, which few have the courage or curiosity to penetrate." It may be noted here that one of the differences between our own era and those eras that Coleridge divided into pagan Greek and modern Christian is this obstinate attempt to penetrate beyond consciousness into regions uncontrolled by the intellect, to surmount not only "the first range of hills that encircle the scanty vale of human life," but any other possible ranges that may be beyond them. The chapter of the *Biographia* from which are taken the above quotations, the marvellous Chapter Twelve, entitled "A Chapter of Requests," which contains his famous explanation of the "subjective" and "objective," so irritating to many of his countrymen, is one that can be more readily comprehended in the light of modern discoveries in psychology than it was in his own day.

"All knowledge," he said, "rests on the coincidence of an object with a subject. . . . The sum of all that is merely objective we will call nature . . . the sum of all that is subjective we may comprehend in the name of

the self, of intelligence. . . . During the act of knowledge itself the objective and the subjective are so in-
stantly united that we cannot determine to which of
the two priority belongs." "Self-consciousness," he declared (and we would use the term consciousness), "is
not a kind of being but a kind of knowing."

The truth concerning Coleridge's struggle with the
subjective and objective, with self-consciousness and
beyond-consciousness, with transcendent and transcendental, was that he was trying to arrive by speculation
at a conception of the conscious and unconscious or
subconscious which was not possible to reach by mere
speculation. In other words, he was trying to explain
the unconscious life of the mind, the existence of
which we have only come to understand since the experiments and investigations of Charcot, William
James, Breuer, Janet, Freud, Jung, and the other psy-
choanalysts, all of which will be dealt with in a later
chapter.

It was not only his speculations on the subjective
and objective and beyond-consciousness—*extra-consci-
entiam*—that were considered "formless digressions"
but also his speculations on philosophy, on Kant, on
Fichte, on Schelling, and on those whom he called the
unlearned mystics whose writing "contributed to keep
alive the heart in the head." To those whose only
conception of the function of criticism was the action
of one mind on the work of another the important

chapters in the *Biographia* were those on Wordsworth's
poetry—these are the ones commonly treated in the histories of literature and generally the only ones students
read; the other chapters are considered as a digression.
But if any, it is the chapters on Wordsworth that may
be said to be the digression, for in the book as a whole
he is always consistently carrying out the intentions
that have their statement on the first page—"A statement of my principles in Politics, Religion, and Philosophy, and an application of the rules, deduced from
philosophical principles, to poetry and criticism." However, he was as careful as Herder to point out the limits of all rules, and in a sentence that forms a striking
parallel to Herder's on the same subject, he shows the
great mistake made by writers like Pope and the eighteenth-century classicists in condemning Shakespeare
for not following the Greek dramatists. These writers
mistook for the essentials of the Greek stage "certain
rules which the wise poets imposed on themselves in
order to render all the remaining parts of the drama
consistent with those that had been forced on them by
circumstances independent of their will." The circumstances in the time of Shakespeare, which it was equally
out of his power to alter, were different; consequently,
all these comparisons of Shakespeare with the Greeks,
in which he was judged by the rules that accidental
circumstances imposed on them, were simply futile.
"Critics are apt to forget," he said, "that rules are but

a means to an end, and where the ends are different, the rules must likewise be so." "The ultimate end of criticism," he maintained, "is much more to establish the principle of writing than to furnish rules how to pass judgment on what has been written by others." As Arthur Symons, himself in his day one of the most interesting of modern critics, said of him, "In this he is defining that form of criticism in which he is supreme among critics."

When Coleridge himself comes to the judgment of certain great writers it is no longer the mere reasonings and conclusions commonly associated with the criticism of judgment, it is an intuition into the processes of the writers' minds; it is that rarest of all rare powers in literature, the ability to penetrate into the genesis of a man's genius, which, along with the power of creating new literary ideas, is the mark of that unique figure, the creative critic. In spite of the cumbersomeness of his prose style he had the faculty of making concise generalizations which are truly memorable. For example, the following as a definition of poetic genius would, if learned by heart, save many writers from imagining they were poets and many critics from being deluded about what poetry is. "The sense of musical delight with the power of producing it . . . together with the power of reducing multitude into unity of effect, and modifying a series of thoughts by some one predominant thought or feeling." And who more concisely than he has noted certain of the curses that afflict literature from the inside, in every age? There are the writers "who mistake an intense desire to possess the reputation of poetic genius for the actual powers and tendencies which constitute it," and, "those popular writers who have raised themselves into temporary fame and reputation with the public at large by that most powerful of all adulation, the appeal to the bad and malignant passions of mankind." "Of all trades," he lamented, "literature at present demands the least talent or information—men who first become scribblers from idleness and ignorance next become libellers from envy and malevolence." And we have this insight into fanaticism and superstition, which, he says, spring from "a debility and dimness of imaginative power, and a consequent necessity of reliance on the immediate impressions of the senses; having a deficient portion of internal and proper warmth, minds of this class seek in the crowd for a warmth in common. Cold and phlegmatic in their own nature, like damp hay they heat and inflame by co-acervation." The vigor, and even violence, of these remarks was aroused by the irresponsibility of criticism in his day, a transition period in literature, and for that reason abounding in "arbitrary and sometimes petulant verdicts." In the great critical reviews like the *Edinburgh* and the *Quarterly,* the reviewers seemed to be possessed, not so much of any literary principles as of a personal resentment against the authors they were dealing with. This aroused Coleridge to the point of even suggesting the formation of a sort of society of critics or an academy—a "number of learned men in the various branches of science and literature," who would "pledge themselves inwardly, as well as ostensibly, to administer judgment according to a constitution and code of laws . . . grounding this code on the twofold basis of universal morals and philosophic reason, independent of all foreseen application to particular works and authors."

Easily as one can see why Coleridge and the other poets of the new movement, harassed by ignorant and sometimes malignant reviewers, would demand an organization of critics who would base their judgments on literary knowledge, it is difficult now to see how such a proposal could be carried out. What he meant by "universal morals and philosophic reason" is now hard to get at, nor can we very well figure how he could expect "Kubla Khan" or the "Ancient Mariner" or "Christabel" to be judged and explained according to such a code. It shows something of that tendency stressed by Taine as being especially English, the tendency to moralize that came in with the Puritan domination of England. Taine describes English writers as engaged in giving a moral background to everything; he represents their public as saying to them, "Be moral. We have practical minds and we would not have literature corrupt practical life. We believe in family life and we would not have literature paint the passions that attack family life. We are Protestant and we have preserved something of the severity of our fathers against enjoyment and passions." The literary taste of the nation certainly imposed moral intentions, and Taine shows the difference between Balzac, who was interested in all passions, all life, neither praising nor blaming, who regarded men and women as interesting in themselves, and Dickens and Thackeray, who, instead of penetrating the depths of a character, preferred to weep over it or rail at it or satirize it. We remember that Coleridge commended Southey because as a writer "he has uniformly made his talents subservient to the best interests of humanity, of public virtue and domestic piety." A like concern with moral intention obtrudes itself here and there in Wordsworth's Preface.

Chapter Four

DE STAËL BRINGS THE NEW IDEAS
TO FRANCE

I

Now AT THE end of the eighteenth century or at the beginning of the nineteenth a new sort of literature based on certain new freedoms was well on its way. And this new literature took its beginning not out of the French Revolution, but at the moment when Lessing recognized and forcibly expressed the fact that every-day man and every-day life had not been revealed in literature, and that it was the business of the new writers to deal with the every-day man and the every-day life. Great literature in the past had, of course, sprung from life, out of man's mind, but had very seldom been about ordinary life or ordinary man: it had been about life stylized, emotions stylized, human relations and human aspirations stylized, and characters stylized into types. It had, of course, always touched life and the passions of life at some point, but life as lived by the generality it had treated only incidentally. Even English literature, the most human of all literatures up to this time, had seldom dealt with ordinary men and women. Shakespeare had revealed all the passions but not all men; his characters were mainly kings and heroes and conquerors, great lovers, strange women, people outside the ruck of humanity. The common man, in Shakespeare, was likely to be a grave-digger or a clown; general life was as rarely touched upon as it was in Sophocles, or Æschylus, or Dante.

But from this period on, from the latter part of the eighteenth century, what was meant by progress in literature was to be progress towards the revelation in language, in poetry and prose, of the mass of men, of their lives and experiences. From this time on, too, the history of literature was to become the history of the adventures of ideas and doctrines through the imagination of men. Complex philosophical ideas and doctrines were to have a tremendous motive power both in life and in literature: civilization took on a new movement, literature took on a new movement. While it would be ridiculous to try to explain any separate work of literature by this or that idea, this or that doctrine, yet the large movements of the mind, the literary schools, the new techniques, were all the outcome of ideas and doctrines.

The revolution in literature was in being in both Germany and England before it spread to France, and this though some of the most fruitful seeds had originally come from that country. But in France literature had been more stylized than in any other country; it was a major interest to a greater percentage of the population, so that a larger movement was involved in the change; more hard-and-fast ideas had to be loosened; wider sections of society had to be affected. The influences, however, that finally set it going became concentrated in a woman, Madame de Staël; many ramified tendencies, social, political, literary, philosophical—French, German, and English—came to a focus in her work: she represented the strong currents of the eighteenth century that were passing away, as well as the new currents of the nineteenth century that were just setting in. From the side of the eighteenth century her mind had been formed by the Encyclopedia and the Encyclopedists, above all by Diderot, Voltaire, Rousseau and Helvetius—in fact, it may be said that the general tendencies of their thought became fused in her enfranchised and strongly intuitive intellect so that something new and prophetic of the new forces came out of it.

On the negative side these general tendencies were a desire to break away from the authority of tradition, from old forms of government, old social stratification, from the classical school in literature and from organized religion. On the positive side they stood for a belief in reason, in progress, in the continuous development of the mind and of the arts. They stood for joy in the delights of the senses, in the present time and in the passing moment. From Diderot and Rousseau, especially, among the Encyclopedists, came the questioning of the value of European civilization and the doctrine of the primacy of strong feelings. From Rousseau came the plea for the exaltation of the heart over the intellect, for a trust in instincts and natural passions, and for the freedom of the individual; the whole inclination on one side was towards praise of life and what Wordsworth called "the natural passions of the heart." On the other side, perhaps as an outcome of this, there was a strong trend towards materialism and towards a belief in the almighty power of the fact, which later became systematized in the criticism of Taine, and which eventually had the result of affecting minds with a profound pessimism. From Helvetius came the theory which, in the nineteenth century and our own day, was to have a powerful effect on every art and which was, at the same time, responsible for many vagaries—the theory that the mind grows with the passions and that one becomes stupid when one ceases to be passionate.

Out of these influences together came the conviction that the way to progress was to shake off the authority of the past, and this notion has grown in prestige and takes on a new importance every time there is in the world a considerable change of any kind. All these trends and doctrines, some more securely than others, found a place in the mind of de Staël and urged her towards the evolution of those theories that made her work such a vitalizing force in the general thought of her own time and later. This brilliant and sophisticated cosmopolite was somewhat older than the two English poets and critics and had a vast experience, not only of the social world but of the intellectual world in all its facets.

2

Though born in Paris, Germaine de Staël was not a Frenchwoman but a Genevan married to a Swede, the daughter of Necker, the finance minister of Louis XVI, and included among her ancestry German, French, and Irish strains, which gave her a more natural sympathy with cosmopolitan and especially with German ideas than was customary in France at the time. She paid a visit to England just after the publication of the *Lyrical Ballads* had definitely turned English literature on a new path; she visited Germany a couple of years after Coleridge and Wordsworth had been there, and when the new German literature was rising to its ripest development, when the change in taste effected by Lessing and Herder was bearing its noblest fruit. She had early, as her book *De la Littérature* showed, been strongly stirred by English and German literature; her first work had appealed to both Schiller and Goethe, and Goethe had translated portions of it for publication in the periodical that the two poets were running in the interest of the new school. When she went to Germany, therefore, de Staël's mind was prepared to fall completely under the sway of ideas with which she had always sympathized. In fact, it was after this visit, and as a result of it, that her mind really began to bloom. To her the criticism of Lessing and Herder, the poetry and dramas of Goethe and Schiller, represented the literature of the future, and as such she put them forward to her countrymen.

In her book *De la Littérature* she had already criticized the shackled condition of French drama and poetry, which she declared had lost vigor under the domination of the salons; their endeavor to conform to the spirit of good society had placed grace and taste before originality and power. In addition, French tragedy had for the most part confined itself to the same subjects as the Greek and to the same laws of composition, though lending to the personages French sentiments, customs, and gallantries. Like Lessing she demanded that the dramatists give up treating of kings and gods and get down either to subjects from their own history, as did the English dramatists and Schiller, or to subjects from every-day life, as did Lessing. Not only the limitations of the subject but the unities and the verse-form, the Alexandrine, had been an obstacle to getting actual life on the stage. A master like Racine had, she was willing to admit, conquered all these obstacles, but while decrying any idea that she was attacking the great French tragic dramatists, she declared the time had come for a different type of literature.

French literature had stood in the same place too long, and this chiefly because of continual imitation of the masterpieces, both its own and the ancient Greek and Roman. Nothing in life ought to be stationary, and when art does not *change* it becomes petrified. Life had *changed;* the Revolution had altered the foundations of society, and now on the threshold of the nineteenth century, she perceived that a new sort of life was coming into being, and this new sort of life needed a new sort of literature. She offered to her countrymen as the type of this innovation the literature that was being produced in Germany, with its originality, its individuality, its free form, its philosophic depth, its independence of social conventions: this was what she called the literature of the North, modern literature, in contra-distinction to the literature of the South, classical literature.

In *De la Littérature* she had talked of what she called the two distinct literatures that Europe had produced, that which came from the South and that which came from the North. The Greek, the Latin, the Italian, the Spanish, and the French of the century of Louis XIV belonged, she stated, to the literature of the South; the English, the German, the Teutonic literature generally, the Scandinavian, the Icelandic, the Celtic, belonged to the literature of the North. The differences between these literatures she explained, according to the central theory of her book, by the climate, the na-

ture of the soil, the political and social conditions—
in short, according to her doctrine that literature was
an expression of society. She indicated a new basis for
criticism, a new principle by which literature was to
be evaluated, when she wrote an explanation of her
purpose. "I propose to examine the influence of religion, customs, and laws on literature, and also to examine the influence of literature on religion, customs, and
laws. It seems to me that the moral and political causes
which affect literature have never been sufficiently analyzed. . . . Religion and laws decide almost entirely
the resemblance or difference between the minds of nations. . . . The climate accounts for some differences,
but the general education of the leading classes of society is always the result of political institutions. The
government being the center of the greater portion of
the interests of men, customs and ideas follow the
course of the interests." This view of literature proved
to have rousing effects and brought to her, not only in
her lifetime but even to a greater degree since, many
disciples. It represented a fresh discovery, a fresh portion of truth, and like all such discoveries affected a release of minds of differing tendencies—politicians, historians, and poets, critics like Schlegel, historians like
Prosper de Barante.

Immediately after de Staël came Sainte-Beuve and
the whole group of the *Globe* newspaper, who based
their criticism on her theories. In our own day all the

theories by which she related literature to society and made it an expression of society have been taken over by that school of critics who call themselves Marxists, but with a more narrow interpretation of the possibilities of man and the perfectibility of the human spirit, and with the substitution of the economic man for the Rousseauan natural man. In fact, she is the originator of a school of social criticism which, especially in America, has had a noteworthy influence on life and literature. Her thesis that literature is an expression of society is also the thesis of every social and sociological critic since her time.

As a social critic Madame de Staël was the most stirring and the most original of the train of those who are her descendants. Like all social critics she had serious limitations on the purely literary and æsthetic side, which have to be taken into account in all applications of her theories, particularly her early theories as expressed in *De la Littérature*. She understood best the sort of writing that was the expression of society and thought that all literature was neither more nor less than this. In spite of her ardent espousal of the poetic theories of Herder she appears to have got little out of poetry except its intellectual and emotional content, a weakness of all social critics since her time, including the Americans. The poetic utterance itself, the apprehension of the form, all that really made the process of poetry different from the process of poetic, or imaginative, or lyrical prose, she seemed either constitutionally incapable of grasping, or, it may be, she was determined to measure all writing by the eighteenth-century standards of reason and logic.

3

And so it happened that, much as Goethe and Schiller admired her, we have evidence that they did not think she really understood their poetry. Her theory of literature as an expression of society works very well when applied to memoirs, diaries, certain kinds of drama and fiction; it was to work very well when applied to the new form of writing that was coming in and which, to some extent, she practised herself—the novel. Applied to literature of other types, the highly imaginative or the deeply philosophic, or to most types of poetry, it creaks ominously. To state its defects, however, is not to deny the great influence of the challenge that it gave, or to limit the enduring influence her own explanation of it has had on literary thought. It stirred new writers to the study of the actual life around them with the object of expressing this life and this society in literature, it started off whole movements in technique, especially in prose. But like all literary doctrines its limitations became clearly visible when applied wholesale to literature by too literal minds, which happened almost immediately. Her theory, like Lessing's, explains some traits in all kinds of literature including the ancient Greek; it explained almost completely that new form of literature that was coming in—the novel —as well as the new drama of contemporary life; she herself showed that it could be applied with revealing results even to the sort of drama that was going out, the classical theatre of Racine.

But, after all, the work that was to have the most thrilling influence on her immediate successors was her book on Germany for which all her early work was a preparation and which represented the highest flight of her mind. The thought of Lessing roused her as it had roused Coleridge, but that side of her mind which had been formed by Rousseau and Diderot was most strongly drawn to Herder. Those two ideas of Herder's that especially fascinated his followers, the one about the significance of primitive poetry, including the notion that poetry came from the primitive side of the imagination (though she had little understanding of what primitive imagination was), and the other about the difference between the literature of the North and the literature of the South, between the literature of the moderns and the literature of the ancients, took possession of her mind. Coleridge had also seized on this notion of Herder's and had attached it to a metaphysical idea, by asserting that the Greeks changed ideas into finites and these finites into anthromorphi or forms of men. He also explained it more simply by a comparison of Paganism with Christianity, of Greek architecture with Gothic architecture, and of the *Antigone* of Sophocles with the *Hamlet* of Shakespeare. But de Staël was to illuminate it with a more direct light.

After her sojourn in Germany she proceeded to identify the literatures she had previously divided into those of the North and those of the South, with Romantic and Classical literature. The expressions "Romantic" and "Classic," though put into currency by de Staël, appear to have been first used in his lectures by William Schlegel, who became a great friend of hers. Goethe, in his *Conversations with Eckermann,* said that it was he and Schiller who were the originators of these terms. "This division of poetry into Classic and Romantic comes originally from Schiller and me. It was my principle in poetry always to work objectively; Schiller, on the contrary, wrote nothing that was not subjective. The Schlegels got hold of the idea, developed it, and little by little it has spread throughout the world." Now the idea that lay behind the terms, as we have seen, was first put forward by Herder and later worked over by Coleridge. But it was de Staël who took the terms out of the realm of speculative ideas and attached to them something ardent and related to life.

"The name Romantic," she said, "has been newly introduced in Germany to designate the poetry which was born of chivalry and Christianity. If one admits nothing except Paganism and Christianity, one can say that the North and the South, chivalry on the one side, and the Greeks and Romans on the other, divide the empire of literature between them. One sometimes uses the word Classic as a synonym of perfection; for myself, I use the term in another meaning—considering Classical poetry as that of the ancients and Romantic poetry as that which proceeds in some way from chivalrous traditions. This division relates equally to two periods of the world—that which preceded Christianity and that which followed it." In addition, she went back to her old claim that the modern Latin nations, of which the French were the most cultivated, leaned towards the Classical and imitation of the Greek and Latin, whereas the Teutons, of which the English were the most illustrious representatives, produced Romantic literature. This diversity of taste, this divergence of literary orientation, she believed, sprang not from accidental causes but from primitive sources of imagination and thought. With this latter sentence, according to certain critics who followed her, she changed the object of criticism by relating literature to the states of civilization of which it is, in her idea, the natural product.

Her comparison of the simplicity of Greek civilization, where men carried the action of the soul outwards, personifying nature and ideas, with the modern tendency towards continually turning the mind inwards, influenced people to take this complex modernity of mind more and more into account; so this had the effect of increasing the mood of introspection and subjectivism. Romantic literature, she believed, was the only type of literature natural to this modern mood, because it alone had, according to her conception, the potentiality of growth and renewal.

Through her power to foresee the trend that civilization and literature were taking, she was able to define in advance the character of the prose and poetry that were to be dominant in Europe for the next century. The qualities she saw in this new literature, "the sorrowful sentiment of the incompleteness of human destiny, melancholy, reverie, mysticism, the sense of the enigma of life," became the qualities pursued by the new writers. She pointed out the main defects of French literature: that in type, form, and content it belonged to a civilization that had become obsolete; that besides being a reflection of the Greek, it had been developed too much according to the demands of good society. The brilliant company that had congregated in the salons required above all a form of writing that could be easily read and understood. Profundity, the power of meditation, of brooding on life, all had been sacrificed to grace and good taste, qualities which ended in sterility, lack of fervor and monotony.

Literature, as she maintained, can stand only as much grace, taste, and refinement as is compatible with genius. Not only was the artist shackled by the precepts of good taste that made originality and individuality undesirable, but he was shackled also by the Aristotelian unities, by the rigid verse forms, and by the convention of taking the same themes as the Greek and Roman dramatists. Break away from all these conventions, she advised; give up depicting kings and heroes on the stage, and easily delineated qualities like jealousy, ambition, and the like, and depict the complex characteristics of the modern man. The great classical drama was not enjoyed by the common people as were the dramas of Shakespeare and Schiller; they were too remote from any life the ordinary man experienced, understood, or could imagine. Contemporary German writers had produced a literature that shook the imaginations and emotions of men, a strong, violent, and original literature, because, unlike the French, they were not absorbed in the life of society and had not to consider the taste and tone of society. In explaining all this, she made careful studies of the work of Lessing, Herder, Klopstock, Goethe, and Schiller: she had encountered their work and some of them personally at the moment when literary expression and artistic productiveness had reached their height in Germany. The qualities that marked their work she wanted brought, not only into French but into all contemporary literatures, for her great desire was for a common European literary art, national and at the same time international.

What she actually succeeded in bringing about was

a fusion of the qualities of the Teutonic and the Latin literatures, a fusion not entirely relished by some of her French critics: she has indeed been accused by them of diverting the national literature from its native direction. But, like Lessing, she affected profoundly the minds of the writers who came after her, and this in spite of a curious moralizing tone in her criticism, which belonged to her Genevan background rather than to the country she was addressing. Her emancipated literary ideas were frequently interlarded with such assertions as, that it was not in the power of a poet to draw forth a tragic effect from an incident which admitted the smallest tendency to an immoral principle, or that "literary criticism is not infrequently, indeed, a sort of treatise on morality," and she was sure that "perfect virtue" is the *beau idéal* of the intellectual world.

The main defect, however, in her criticism is her attitude to poetry. Schiller, indeed, went so far as to say "of what we call poetry, she has no perception." Yet, as a good disciple of Herder, she asserted the primacy of lyric poetry—that song on the wing that he said all real poetry was, and that all early poetry had been. She re-stated Herder's remarks about poetry, perhaps without really comprehending them; she even put forward the strange statement, very strange in a champion of lyricism, "poetry is, of all the arts, that which belongs closest to reason." Still, in spite of such limitations, she,

more than any of the other critics up to her time, made
ideas and literatures seem the common possession of
all men and of all countries; she led the European spirit
across national frontiers, even though she was not able
to lead it across class frontiers. The new writers took
as guide-posts watchwords and talismanic phrases
drawn from her books. Hugo and Lamartine devoured
all she had written: she gave the former the intellectual background necessary to shape the elemental force
that was his genius. As Brunetière has pointed out,
there is nothing in Hugo's famous preface to *Crom-
well,* around which so much of the Romantic Movement eddied, that did not come from her book on
Germany. There is, indeed, almost nothing in any of
his literary ideas of which she is not the parent. He, like
Walter Scott, went straight for inspiration to those Middle Ages, to the Troubadours, to Chivalry, out of which,
as she declared, modern romantic literature had proceeded. Sainte-Beuve, the friend and critic of Hugo—
they were both about the same age, having been born in
the dawn of the nineteenth century—was so deeply influenced by de Staël and her name comes so frequently
into his criticism, that she has been called the heroine
of his *Lundis.*

4

The great affair of all the critics whose work has
been discussed in these chapters had been to change the

course of literature in their respective countries, to change its orientation; for long the sap had been drying up, and the writers were ceasing to provide spiritual nutriment. Each modern literature from this time on had to take graftings from the others, for countries were becoming intellectually interdependent, and the old frontiers, the old national prejudices, the old literary prejudices, had to be broken down. To turn into literature new springs of such strength that the old bed was re-channelled—that was what they all had labored for.

The French was the last of the great European literatures to change its course, to attune itself to the rhythm of the new civilization, the new attitude towards life. The German had come first, the English next, and then the French. But the ideas that came in the train of the change in French literature brought with them more developments than came from the change in any of the others: developments in poetry, in the novel, in biography, in psychology and, especially, in that study which was the inevitable outcome of the work of the new critics, the study of comparative literature.

Several conclusions emerged from the changes in the great literatures. First of all, as has been said above, it became obvious that literary ideas were interdependent, they spread from country to country. It became clear that modern literature, unlike early literature, no longer developed unconsciously around certain inherited tales, fables, and traditions, and without guides or charts. The unconscious stage was passed. Now it was plain that a few men with a dream and an idea could turn literature on to a new path, could deliberately say, "This side of life or man has not yet been expressed; this or this tendency, this or this attitude to life, which was not in the ancient world, has not yet been revealed —let us find a way to do it." They could say, too, "Language, from over-use, through its employment by everybody in every-day life, has become worn and dull—let us put life and iron into it."

In effect, all these critics said the same thing; the services to literature of all of them were of the same kind; they revealed a new attitude towards civilization, towards the development of man; they extended the bounds of what could be expressed in literature; they brought in new subjects; they revivified language; they tried to make literature the possession and the instrument of the ordinary man. Herder and Lessing, Goethe and Schiller, Coleridge and Wordsworth, Hugo and Lamartine, brought in emotions, passions, characters, that until then had been ignored or even scorned as material. They started new rhythms in language; they changed, as it were, the very sound of it; they made it respond to the new ideas that were surging in. There is a sentence in Zola's *Lettre à la Jeunesse* in which he sums up what Hugo had achieved, and this summing-up applies to all these innovators. "He renewed the language; the classical language was dying of anemia; he put into circulation a vocabulary that had been scorned; he wrote verses that had the sheen of gold and the sonority of bronze."

Chapter Five

THE IDEAS ON THE MARCH:
SAINTE-BEUVE AND TAINE

I

AT THE OUTSET of the movement towards the renewal of literature and the extension of its boundaries, the men who evolved the theories were also those who put them into practice. As time went on, there arose the necessity for a label that would differentiate the new kind of writing from the older productions: there became annexed to it somehow the label "Romantic." It was the label that Madame de Staël had taken over from the Germans as suitable for distinguishing what she called the literature of the North from the literature of the South, and the literature of the ancients from that which came out of modern minds given another orientation by the Christian religion and the traditions of Chivalry. Acrimonious discussion rose round the use of the term "Romantic," which was really a misnomer and has thrown innumerable difficulties in the way of understanding the trend of literary expression all through the nineteenth century and up to our own day. But owing to the innate passion of men for attaching a name to a thing once it comes into existence, regardless of whether the naming is suitable or not, the label "Romantic," in spite of all protests, quickly effected an entrance into people's imaginations; not only the early innovators but the whole change that swept in with the new era came to be described as "The Romantic Movement." Yet even those to whose work the label seemed most appropriate—Victor Hugo, for instance—objected to it. Others thought that a loose label like "Modernism" was better fitted to describe the new trend. The Germans, even, who were originally responsible for the designation, had for the most part been content with calling their own production "the newest literature." It was not easy for the innovators themselves to comprehend exactly what was happening, but now, looking back on it, we can perceive that it all was simply a strong impulse towards bringing into literature a larger variety of human experience, more and more of humanity, and greater complexity of emotion.

Madame de Staël had said that the distinguishing mark of the new literature was the sorrowful sentiment of the incompleteness of human destiny and the complexity of the modern man. Coleridge had declared that it was "subjectivity" which principally and most fundamentally distinguished all modern from all classic poetry. As divergent notions of literary technique and literary expression developed, varied and sometimes fantastic labels were devised, especially in France, to define the various stages of the new literary doctrines. Some of the most practical of these, such as "Realism" and "Naturalism" in prose, or "Symbolism" in poetry, are still vital enough, or are, at least, handy and convenient critical terms. The word "Romantic" itself, however, is now so hazy in its significance that it has no possibilities of conveying any clear-cut meaning in regard to the whole literary trend; in our every-day vocabulary the expression has followed the fate of the word "genteel," and is now somewhat derogatory in meaning.

With the literature that grew out of the new doctrines came a whole new attitude to life, a new trend of civilization, based partly on the evolution of history, partly on the evolution of expression. The minor movements that came out of the main one were from time to time regarded as reactions against it, when, as a matter of fact, they were specific developments of it. Actually, there was no reaction against the movement as a whole until our own time, and this, at the moment, is in some degree a reaction and in some degree, as will be shown later, a fresh development of the main doctrines.

2

When Sainte-Beuve, the next of the great minds that kept ideas on the march, appeared on the scene as a young critic of the *Globe* newspaper and as a member of the Poets' Club, the *cénacle* that surrounded Hugo, the earlier shape of the movement, in all countries where it was in being, was beginning to change. It kept growing and growing and, at times, some of the forms of its development, as of the opposition to it, became a trifle ridiculous. The limits of absurdity in the opposition were reached in France when seven writers of the older school petitioned the King, Charles X, to banish the new romanticism from the Comédie Française.

Many of the major figures of the movement in various countries were alive and producing at the same time: Herder was still living when Wordsworth and Coleridge visited Germany and when Madame de Staël wrote her book on literature; Goethe and Schiller were in their prime when Sainte-Beuve and Victor Hugo were born. Wordsworth, one of the chief instigators of the change, lived through many different phases of it to become Queen Victoria's poet-laureate; he lived long after his creative period had come to a close; he survived to find himself regarded as out of fashion, but at the same time he saw, or could have seen, all his ideas bear fruit—sometimes an unpredictable sort of fruit—and, oddly enough, rather more on the Continent than in England. The greatest carrier of his ideas to the Continent was, of course, Sainte-Beuve, who was not only intimately acquainted with the poetry of Wordsworth, but with that of the whole Lake School.

He had a passion for translating Wordsworth, Southey, and Coleridge, for translating and quoting them, which was to affect French poetry all through the nineteenth century. Not only did he attach himself as a critic to the Wordsworthian doctrine of poetry, but in his own verse he put the doctrine into practice. A good portion of Sainte-Beuve's own poetry was an attempt to write of humble life, and the humblest things in life, in terms of the Wordsworthian ideal. He presented little stories in verse, little dramas of nature, simple pictures of real life, and these started in France at least two schools of poetry the developments of which will be dealt with later.

After writing three collections of poems, Sainte-Beuve abandoned not only poetry but all other sorts of writing except criticism, into which he put all his variety of talents. He was the first figure in literature to become the critic-specialist, the all-round literary expert. One may have one's preference as between these two vastly influential critics, Sainte-Beuve and his successor Taine, but it is not easy to decide which of them was the greater critic, for their influences on literature were from differing angles: the two were contrasting mental types; to go back to the distinction previously made, Sainte-Beuve was the poet-critic, Taine, the philosopher-critic. We have Sainte-Beuve's own dictum that the critic ought to be part poet: *Il est mieux qu'il y ait dans le critique un poète: un poète a le sentiment*

plus vif des beautés, et il hésite moins à les maintenir.
The poet in Sainte-Beuve gave a perpetual fresh life
to his criticism; for him, the artist-critic, a book is the
expression of an individual, the fruit of his mind and
personality. The leading principle of his method, the
identity of the man with his work, *tel arbre, tel fruit,*
was a translation into terms of criticism of one of the
great guiding motives of the new dispensation—the
primacy of the individual, the importance of the personal, the ego, in literature.

Very early in his career, at the height of his friendship with Hugo, at the time of his first enlistment with
Romanticism, Sainte-Beuve began to evolve his distinctive method of criticism. Originally it was sketched out
in his portrait of Corneille in the *Globe* newspaper to
which he was attached as literary critic. Sainte-Beuve
was quite aware that in epochs when literature was
less personal, or even impersonal, his method would
not have had such fruitful results, for, as he said himself, in the case of the older writers, anyway, very little
data about their personal lives existed, so that their
biographers devoted their thought to their work, and
little or none at all to the man behind the work. In
this, the first bare outline, Sainte-Beuve declared that
a writer must be studied, not merely in his work, but
in his private and domestic relations as well. As to his
product, it was important to get a revelation of him
at its source, that is, at the moment when he brought

out his first significant work. When you have unravelled the circumstances which led to this work, when you have discovered that region where his genius first took up its abode and thrived, then you understand your writer.

This essay on Corneille, however, showed only Sainte-Beuve's groping after his method: it was as late as thirty years afterwards, when he had experimented with it all his life and worked it out to perfection, that he described it fully in his essay on Chateaubriand. Here it appears so clearly and is described so succinctly that it is almost as if tabulated into rules. A literary product is not separable from the one who produces it; it is difficult to judge it without a knowledge of the man who wrote it; therefore, real criticism of the work of the ancients is not possible because there are not sufficient data about their lives. . . . To know a work, to study it, you must first know its author, you must study him; after this, comes the study of the type of mind to which he belongs, for there are families of minds, Sainte-Beuve thought, as there are families of plants and animals. But with men, of course, he added, one could never draw an exact conclusion. Literature for him was the product of certain great and superior minds which it was the duty of the critic to understand and explain. It was well, therefore, to begin with the race and native country of this man of superior mind, to study him physiologically in his ancestors and in his descendants. His family, his brothers, sisters,

children, should be carefully considered; special attention should be paid to the mother as the more direct
parent. This study of his blood relations will often
reveal important lineaments of the writer's personality,
which were masked, in the man himself, and which are
extremely important to know about.

After his family, the next important subject in the
study of a writer should be the group of which he first
formed a part. A group, par excellence, would be such
a one as surrounded Racine or Molière, or, in English
literature, the Wordsworth group or the Shelley group,
or, in America, the Emerson Concord group, or, in Germany, the Goethe-Schiller Weimar group. By examining, from all known data, the quality of the minds of
the group, one gets another light on the mind one is
endeavoring to reveal. It might be noted here that
Sainte-Beuve himself, when at the age of twenty-four
he gave the first outline of his method, was a member
of a group, the group of critics on *The Globe,* who devoted themselves largely to disseminating the ideas
of Madame de Staël. It is the group, to continue Sainte-
Beuve's account of his method, the fellowship, the
active exchange of ideas, which enables a man of talent
or genius to find himself and develop. His earlier idea
of the importance of grasping the man at the moment
of his first important work he stressed all through his
career as a critic. In addition, he said, there is always
in the life of every writer a period to be studied with

equal care—it is when the promise of the first real work either never fructifies or when it surpasses the earlier promise. Then, again, the critic must likewise take note of the moment when the great talent begins to waver, to grow old or to weaken. This does not necessarily mean that it is age that brings the weakening of the talent: on the contrary, Sainte-Beuve believed that few talents survive to old age at all. Fifteen years, he maintained, was the length of the average literary life, the average period during which a man was at the height of his power. Sainte-Beuve himself seemed to be at the height of his power for over thirty years. Yet his own criticism of himself was "I lost early, not my fire, but my wings." But the reader, in Sainte-Beuve's last as well as in his first work, is apt always to hear the beating of wings.

In the general estimation of a man and his work, Sainte-Beuve believed no question too insignificant, no sort of information too unimportant, even information which has no apparent connection, or but the slightest, with his actual production. The questions he lists that should be asked by a biographer and a critic about his subject are: What were his religious views? What was his attitude towards women? Towards money? Was he rich? Was he poor? Was he affected by scenery? What was his daily manner of living? What was his vice? His weakness—for every man has one? What were his physical characteristics, and were these translated into his writing? The answers to all these are important unless the book the subject has written is a treatise on geometry. Finally, who were a man's friends? His enemies? His disciples? His admirers? Nothing shows better the nature of a talent than the point at which the revolt against a writer begins, for in nearly every author's life there comes a period when his own, or a younger generation, begins to find him inadequate. Now we can arrive at a comprehension of Sainte-Beuve's most characteristic definition of criticism, the one, of all those descriptions of its function, scattered through his work, which most clearly defines his own kind of criticism: "Real criticism, as I define it, consists in studying each person, that is, each author, each talent, according to the conditions of his nature, in order to make a vivid and pregnant description of him so that he can later be classified and put in his proper place in the hierarchy of art."

The word "classified" in this definition is one of those recurring and guiding words that serve as a key to Sainte-Beuve's thought. It was his ambition to make what he called a "natural history of minds" and to classify them in families. "I am a naturalist of minds," he remarked of himself; "what I should like to establish is a natural history of literature. Some day," he said, "there will come a great observer, a natural classifier of minds; meanwhile the work of the most humble of us is to prepare the elements and to describe the individuals, relating them to their true type—that is what I am trying to do more and more. . . . The genuine and natural families of minds are not so numerous. . . . When one has observed and worked over sufficient examples, one recognizes how many diverse kinds of minds, of organizations, are related to certain types, come under certain leading heads. Any noted contemporary whom one has well observed and understood will explain and evoke a whole series of figures of the past, from the moment the real resemblance between them becomes manifest and certain family characteristics have compelled your attention. It is exactly as a botanist works with plants or a zoölogist with animals. . . . An individual carefully observed is related promptly to the species, which one has only noted in a general way, and throws light on it." However, he did not believe that human beings could be classified with the same exactness as animals and plants.

In addition to these leading ideas, he had all sorts of ancillary notions—how one age grows out of a previous age; the relation of a man to his age; how any man, even the greatest, is partly plunged into the prejudices of his time, though great men, unlike the common run, are not imprisoned in their time. And there is that sentence of his, pondered over by so many novelists, including Proust and Joyce, about the mobility, the changefulness of men and life and the mind, which are always in flux. "Every day I change; my tastes of yesterday are no longer my tastes of today; my friendships themselves wither up and are renewed; before the final death of the mobile being that bears my name, how many men have already died within me?" Then there was his notion of the master faculty, now chiefly identified with Taine, the notion that in every man, and in particular in every genius, there is one quality of mind —*la qualité principale—le trait dominant*—which dominates all the others. But with regard to this, too, he was certain that no great result could be obtained until psychological knowledge was more advanced. Himself a great natural and intuitive psychologist (he had received, he said, the fatal gift of reading the secret of souls), he worked without any of the data that modern psychological research has placed at the disposal of our contemporaries who have taken over his method. Nevertheless, he remains the only complete master of the method.

And the only perfect workings-out of it are still his. That method has its most revealing results in his *Port-Royal* and his *Chateaubriand;* the one, the critical history of a group, and the other, the critical history of an individual. In his *Port-Royal* he refers again and again to the points of his method, remarking that he is applying it to the group as he would to an individual, following the succession of happenings, the developments, step by step, on all sides—theological, philosophical, literary, and in the individual careers—not only of the great men of the group, Pascal, Racine, Arnauld, Jansenius, but even of the minor figures associated with it.

In *Chateaubriand* we have an example of the method at its best, when applied to an individual, and likewise an example of the very type of writer to whom the method could be most revealingly applied. Chateaubriand was precisely one of those writers whose work could be explained by his life, his ancestry, his family, his personal relations, and by the answers to all those questions which Sainte-Beuve had listed as significant to ask. In the case of Sainte-Beuve's imitators, the results depended on the nature of their abilities, on their particular temperament, experience, and psychological insight. It must likewise be said that the successful working out of the formula depended greatly on the user's ability to adopt a critical attitude towards his own personality and on his power to keep it from intruding on the study of his subject. The procedure gives a great deal too much leeway, to an uncritical or personal-minded writer, to work off his own complexes, experiences, or temperamental twists, on his subject. Its inventor never intended it to be used in the manner of a hostile judge or prosecuting attorney, which has been the manner of so many biographers who are his disciples—often unknowingly his disciples, because his ideas, like those of all real initiators, have become part of the common stock.

In contemporary writing the best examples of the

method are seen where the subject is a public figure about whose private life and ancestry intimate details are easily discoverable, as, for instance, in Lytton Strachey's *Queen Victoria,* or Stefan Zweig's *Marie Antoinette* or *Mary Queen of Scotland.* But where the subject is an artist, the biography frequently turns out to throw more light on the writer of it than on the subject. For example, in John Middleton Murry's *D. H. Lawrence* and in Van Wyck Brooks's *Mark Twain,* the result is a work as exciting as any novel, with interesting psychological and historical judgments, but with a private-minded interpretation of the subject's work and personality. A dubious use of the method is exhibited in André Maurois's book on Shelley, called *Ariel,* where the author concentrates on Shelley's private life and leaves out of account altogether Shelley's poetry—the *raison d'être* of any biography of him. The most deliberate application of it is that by Gamaliel Bradford in his portraits or psychographs. In this case the great drawback in the results came first of all from the second-rate mind of the writer, and secondly, from the fact that he works out the problems in the lives of his characters from data given by books, without any of that fullness of life which made Sainte-Beuve himself the only real master of his own method, and without any of his power of relating them to living families of minds. Yet in spite of the defects of the method and the difficulties of fully applying it, it revolutionized biography, for of course Sainte-Beuve is the father of modern biography and very largely also of the modern autobiographical novel. No one now starts out to write the life of any personage without first of all asking concerning his subject all those questions and seeking that information which Sainte-Beuve sets out as of first importance.

3

The effect of his method was to bring into literature new types of writers: Sainte-Beuve opened the gates of literary expression for a lot of men and women who heretofore had no way of expressing themselves, or who had done so only in elementary ways. There was, for example, the intuitive psychologist, the character reader, who in the past had set forth his talent in humble ways like astrology and palm reading; there was the prosecuting attorney, who might have to expend his gifts in a law court or in displays of oratory; now he could bring a human being before the bar in a book, examine him, present him to the public, and pass judgment on him; there were, besides, all those who could create neither character nor ideas but who could exercise an analyzing and psychological talent on persons who had actually lived. In this way it was possible for mediocre minds without any great sense of life to attain a passable success in writing, and indeed it was this type that the Sainte-Beuve procedure frequently equipped with a method and a scalpel for dissecting the great. Our contemporaries have had an extra weapon placed in their hands, a sort of scientific weapon that the modern discoveries in psychology provided. In short, ever since Sainte-Beuve the sharply investigating biography has become a common feature of the literary landscape, though the bulk of this sort of writing must be described as of passing interest only. For the great biographer, like the great critic, is a very rare figure in literature; only once have the two been united in the same man—Sainte-Beuve.

What made him a master on both counts was his vast knowledge of both life and literature, his profound psychological insight, his all-round gifts as a writer, his great love for the interior lives of men—a love that often made him as interested in the second-rate as in the first-rate mind. Supporting all his natural gifts was his training, and as part of this training his medical studies. "It was to medicine," he said, "that I owed the spirit of philosophy, the love of exactitude, the physiological reality, whatever of good method has passed into my writing." In addition to his gifts of imagination and interest, and his extraordinary training, there was his reverence for the superior man, his respect for the great individual who added to the achievements of the race. But a whole array of the new biographers who imitated him concentrated less on what made their subjects great and superior than on those qualities that made it possible for other people to patronize them. It would have been of little interest to the public at large to be given an account of the mental discipline, the searing meditation and emotions, that went into the making of the *Divine Comedy* or the *Fleurs du Mal* or *Faust*. But the love-affairs of great men, their futilities, their petty degradations, their inferiority as citizens to their fellow citizens, some concealed or reserved incident in their lives, something that could make other men pleasantly familiar with them or condescending to them—these were what too many of the Sainte-Beuve imitators seized upon.

Many of the great Victorian writers have been made comic to the point of buffoonery through a biographer's placing a wrong emphasis on some trait. Thus, their discipline has been made to appear hypocrisy, their loves childish or sordid. Those temporizings, those adaptations which all men, and especially men of genius, have to make with their surroundings and with conventions originally made for the greatest good of the greatest number, have been presented as cowardly subterfuges. And this has been done by unduly stressing the answer to some one of Sainte-Beuve's questions, when he meant all of them to be part of the general pattern, and subsidiary to it. It has been said of some of these biographers that they wormed their way into the subject, and the figure of speech is excellent, for in many cases they left the subject worm-eaten and with little remaining of one who had been a great figure in life: they ate him away as parasites would.

In spite of the fact that it revolutionized criticism, the method had its defects, and the first to admit it would have been its initiator. While he stuck closely enough to it, he never let it master him. "I have never ceased to follow it," he said, "or to vary it according to the subject." But his own mind was too complex, he was too great a man of genius, to believe that the mind can always be gauged by any measuring rod invented by man. He drew back before a too logical application of it. With all his allegiance to his idea, it represented to him simply the best plan for working that he could devise, and like all plans for working, he was aware that it had drawbacks even though he did not himself fully realize what they might lead to. As a matter of truth, his famous method applied to some writers could explain almost everything; applied to others, it explained but little. Applied to certain men of great genius like Shakespeare or Keats or Racine, even if there had existed enough information about them to supply all the answers to Sainte-Beuve's questions, it was likely to explain nothing except a few minor phenomena. Applied to others like Rousseau or Chateaubriand or Byron, concerning whom the known information is extensive and to whom dramatic events happened, it could explain and interpret so much that we can comprehend why Sainte-Beuve himself believed that it could explain nearly everything—a belief that he shares with every originator of a critical or psychological method.

As to his well-known dictum, *tel arbre, tel fruit,* there does not seem to have entered into his calculations the notion that the fruit is sometimes not like the tree, and that the book is sometimes different from the man who wrote it. An action is generally like the one who performs it: it comes out of the life he lives: but a book, a picture, a poem, a statue, a symphony, can be a dream, a journey into a land where the author has never set foot, an escape into emotions he has no outlet for in life. A writer often expends in a book quite other energies than those he uses in every-day life. In fact, his daily life and experiences may prevent him from tapping again the energy he has already used or exhausted once and for all. It is only in the case of a certain type of writer that it can be assumed that his life explains his work, or that his work reveals the sort of life he lived. In some cases, the creative life seems to have so little relation to the every-day life that the answer to the Sainte-Beuve questionnaire would be sure to fall short of any great revelation concerning the work. The great myth-makers like Shakespeare and Balzac, perhaps indeed most great artists of any kind, had an every-day personality and a creative personality, and as creators they could make worlds and people them with beings, human and otherwise, that they never encountered in life.

The truth about Sainte-Beuve's method, as about all methods and systems that aim at explaining men, their works and days, is that, employed with mere literalness and without the corrective of genius and disinterested intuition, it most successfully explains the second-rate: no method is completely adequate to the first-rate. Even when used by Sainte-Beuve himself, it worked out most interestingly and fruitfully in the case of those in whom the imponderables of genius and creative power were not too vast. However, when all is said and done, the fact remains that the process thoughtfully elaborated can explain something of every writer and nearly everything of some. There have been a few ingenious additions to the method, notably the one employed by a French biographer, Bazalgette, based on the notion of key words in phrases, where the subject was presented by the biographer in sentences and phrases abstracted from his own writing. But, on the whole, the additions have meant nothing worth while, though they have been borrowed by imitators of imitators of the master.

One of the curious influences exercised by the method was the conclusion by Sainte-Beuve's contemporaries, and those who came after him, that if a writer's life explains his work, then a writer might deliberately live the sort of life that might be supposed to be inspiring for his writing—cultivate the passions, the emotions, the senses; try all sorts of experiences, all sorts of intoxications and *paradis artificiels,* including those brought on by drugs. And so there came into existence the type of artist who abandoned himself to tasting life to the lees. Sainte-Beuve had explained the dryness and impersonality of Boileau's style and of his art *poétique* by the dryness of his life, and it seemed as if the new school, Baudelaire, De Musset, Verlaine, were determined at all costs not to have a dry life.

It was Sainte-Beuve's theories of poetry, and his own poetry, as much as his general criticism (relating the writer to his work), that deeply affected the new writers, and, in turn, their successors until our own day. He had two theories of poetry, which, like his theories of criticism, had far-flung effects. His own special theory, which he put into practice in his verse, was the one he developed from Wordsworth and from the famous Preface. He believed that he himself belonged to the same family of minds as the Lake School, and his ambition as a poet was to be the French Wordsworth, to be the poet of nature, of the hearth, of domestic things, of humble and ordinary life. His muse, he said, was no grand lady, no brilliant odalisque or young and vermillioned Peri, but a poor, coughing girl, living in a cabin, washing her clothes in a stream and keeping her old blind father whose reason was gone. The people who populated his poetry, his little stories in verse, were, he explained, not the grand and romantic heroes and heroines of Byron and Chateaubriand, with aristocratic lineages and splendid castles; they were the poor people of the *faubourgs,* the suburbs, and the countryside, who had no choice in their woes as did Childe Harold or Manfred or René; their woes were those that every-day life thrust upon them. He used his hospital experiences in these poems, and we have realistic accounts of the illnesses and miseries of the humble. Believing profoundly, himself, in the poetry of ordinary life, of the common man and woman, he gave currency to such poetry. The reign, he said, of the older poets is over; their work is incapable of satisfying the new needs of the imagination and of the heart; poetry must be about the lives of the men and women we meet. To Wordsworth's famous rustic as the subject of poetry, he added the small-town man and the suburban, crushed with work and illness. Some of his poetic work was regarded as morbid, and both in its morbidity and in its subjects, as well as in the every-day language employed, it was the antecedent of the work of Baudelaire and of La Forgue and of their imitators in all lands.

If this first theory of his was evolved or taken over from Wordsworth, the second came from Hugo, Byron, Chateaubriand, from all the Romantics, in fact. It was this, that poetry was the expression of the individuality of the poet, of his ego, of his personality, of his personal emotions and experiences—in short, the expression of the man himself. He could not find this personality, this necessary personal emotion, in Boileau, or in others of the French classical school, but he claimed to find it in the older French poets. He once went so far as to seek, for the new literature, an ancestry in the poets of the Pléiade, whose lyricism seemed to have something in common with the modern Romantics. This conclusion of his was meant to do something to take away from the imputation that all these new literary ideas were a foreign importation, taken over from Germany and England, and alien to the French spirit.

As a great writer, as a contributor of revolutionizing literary ideas, as an influence of wide significance covering more than a century, Sainte-Beuve is a personage of the greatest importance in modern literary history. He was the first literary critic who brought to criticism the most complex variety of literary gifts; he could and did excel in many kinds of writing, but a power of creating ideas and of analyzing minds and works urged him to turn all his gifts to criticism. His influence still goes on; to many he is the greatest purely literary critic that has ever appeared, and with this conclusion it is hard to disagree.

4

The critic who attempted to carry on Sainte-Beuve's ideas, who developed them in his own way and added his own distinct and remarkable contribution, was Hippolyte Taine. As an influence on all literary output since their time, the effect of the ideas of these two men is still extraordinary; no new ideas have sprung up strong enough to displace theirs or even to seem a development of them, though Sainte-Beuve is nearly seventy years dead and Taine nearly sixty. Sainte-Beuve's influence is still active in criticism, in poetry, in biography, and in the autobiographical novel; Taine's in the realistic novel, in history, and in social criticism. All except a minority of living writers pursue a path marked out for them by Sainte-Beuve and Taine. Though the literature of emotion and of rhapsodic imagination gives to the majority more eager and lasting delight, yet it is the literature of ideas which, in the modern world, has the profoundest effect on the originating of other forms of literature.

The forces of literature may be compared to an army composed of divisions, general staff, an advance guard, and right and left wings. It is the main duty of criticism to foresee which way the army ought to take so that it may proceed to the best advantage; it is its duty to know when it is time to make new roads and build new bridges. The objective of the forces is the achievement of the complete expression of man in language: very little of this objective has yet been achieved; the total experience of the most ordinary man, woman, or child has never yet been expressed in literature. We do not even know how it can be done, or if it can be done. If complete expression can be achieved, such expression will take men a long way on the hard road to complete consciousness. We make a little advance in expression from one century to another; our advance in literature has not been towards making a greater literature than the ancients achieved, but towards one that gives a more comprehensive expression to humanity. No modern literature, that is, no literature based on the ideas started by Lessing and developed by all these critics, can get on without that directing force, that idea-creating force, that he called criticism. The older literatures, literature at its dawn, when its business was to create a few powerful masterpieces broadly expressive of a few outstanding emotions, or symbolic of a few adventures, could do without it. A literature like the English in the past got on without much of this sort of leadership, or at least without the leadership organized. But a literature like the German could not have come into being without it, and there was hardly a period in French literature when it was not a powerful directing force.

Where Taine, who liked to think of himself as Sainte-Beuve's successor, differed in purely literary ideas from his predecessor, is, as the latter himself said, very hard to discover. But the intellectual structure of their minds was totally different: as Sainte-Beuve would say, they belonged to different families of minds: one was the poet-critic, the other the philosopher-critic. Taine's philosophy was a materialistic determinism which, as he worked it out in literature, had points in common with the manner in which Marx applied the dialectic of materialism to history. Literature, the mind of the author, the master-faculty, were determined by three forces: the race, milieu, and moment. He himself said that "every man and every book can be summed up in three pages, and these three pages can be summed up in three lines." His method can, in fact, be summarized, if not completely stated, in a line or two, in more or less the original formula from Hegel's *Aesthetics,* plus the chief details of the Sainte-Beuve method.

But if one supposes that all of Taine could be included in this, one would come to very wrong conclusions. The combination gave him a working base. After passing the Hegel formula and the Sainte-Beuve formula through his mind, he developed them in this way: a work of art is not isolated; it belongs to the total work of the artist who is its author, and is definitely related to and linked with his other works. The artist himself is not isolated; he belongs to an ensemble greater than himself, which is the school or family of artists of the same country, of the same period, to which he belongs.

Shakespeare, Taine notes, seemed a wonder fallen from the sky, a meteor from another world. Actually, he was one of a group of great dramatists, Webster, Ford, Massinger, Marlowe, Ben Jonson, Fletcher, who wrote in the same style and spirit; their plays had the same sort of characters. Likewise, in the domain of painting, Rubens seemed a unique personage, but he really was one of a group whose talents were similar to his—Van Dyck, Jordaens, Van Thulden, Van Roose, and others who painted in the same spirit, and who, with all their differences, still keep the air of belonging to the same family.

These great artists belonged, in turn, to a vaster ensemble, which was the world around them, the public. The state of mind, manners, and habits of the time are the same for the public as for the artists, but it is the artist's voice alone that we hear across the centuries. Below this clear, penetrating voice there is the low hum, the multiple voice of the people singing in unison around him. This is true of all periods and of all the arts. The men who made the Parthenon and the Olympian Jupiter were, like the other Athenians, educated in the Palaestra; like them they had wrestled, exercised, voted, and deliberated in the public square; they had the same habits, the same ideas, the same interests; they were men of the same race, the same education, the same language; they were like their public in all the important parts of their lives: therefore, to under-

stand any work of art with exactitude we must picture
to ourselves the general state of the manners, public
spirit, and mind of the time to which it belongs. If we
look at the principal epochs of history, we find that the
arts appear, then disappear, at the same time as certain
states of mind and manners to which they are attached.
The greatest artists are men who possess in the highest
degree the faculties, the sentiments, and the passions
that the public surrounding them possesses in some degree. The products of the mind, like those of nature,
can be explained only by their environment. As there
is a physical temperature which determines the appearance of such and such a species of plant, so there is a
spiritual or psychic temperature which, by its variations, determines the appearance of such or such a
species of art.

All these points of his method Taine maintained as
laws, and he worked out their application with a perfection of logic which makes them convincing, to the
reason at least. It was the business of a critic, he said,
to concern himself with the laws, not to impose precepts on the artist. Anyhow, he explained, there are
only two precepts: the first is, to be born with genius;
the second is, to work hard so as to be a master of one's
art.

As to the famous scientific system with which he applied his method, it can all be discovered in his *De
l'Intelligence,* that first important contribution to mod-

ern psychology, which Pierre Janet has described as his *livre de chevet*. There could be no real criticism, no real history, no real study of anything relating to the mind of man without scientific psychology. "The basis of history," he said, "ought to be scientific psychology. What historians do with the past, great novelists and dramatists do with the present." But on what was this scientific psychology to be based? In the preface to the book, Taine announced that "the matter of all knowledge was little facts, well chosen, important, significant, amply circumstantiated, and minutely noted." The great thing to know was how these little facts could be combined and the effects of the combination. For instance, he conceived of personality as made up of little facts which formed the phenomena of consciousness, and nature as formed of little facts which made up the phenomena of motion. Even poetry he described as the art of transforming general ideas into *petits faits sensibles*.

Of his own critical procedure he stated: "The modern method, which I try to follow, consists in considering the works of man as facts and products of which it is necessary to mark the character and seek the causes." And as for the man responsible for the works, "One can consider man as an animal of superior species who produces philosophies and poems somewhat as the silkworm makes cocoons and the bee cells." But this animal, man, has been described by Comte—who, after Hegel and Sainte-Beuve, was the great influence on Taine's mind—as "a continuation of nature, a being like the other guests of the universe called animals." Taine, continuing this conception and applying the formula taken from Hegel, declared that this animal, man, was subject to conditions of race, climate and milieu. "Discover, therefore, the conditions of race, climate and milieu, education, customs, in which he lived, and you can deduce with a certainty the nature of his talent and of his work, and the diverse conditions that establish the master-faculty, both the causes and the consequences at the same time. Art, therefore, is a product which can be explained like any other product, if we have the data to go on, all the little facts. In fact, vice and virtue are products like sugar and vitriol."

Of the little facts that make up personality, there is a system of inner impressions and operations that form an artist, a musician, a religious man. Each has his own special structure; in each the connection of ideas and emotions is different. But the structure of all of them has some dominating trait, some essential characteristic, as would be shown in natural history. This essential, in natural history, carries with it all the others, and its presence determines or regulates the constitution of the entire animal. In man, this force, the great motive power to which all others are subordinate, he called the master-faculty. This central force, this determining force, is also, on its part, conditioned by the race—by the

characteristics transmitted by the blood; by the milieu—
that is, by the ensemble of circumstances and influences
to which the individual is subjected; by the moment—
that is, by the drive of the past on the present. If you
uncover the master-faculty in a man, then you have
uncovered the man himself, and you can define his
mind through its most fundamental trait.

The master-faculty, the dominant trait, Taine sought
for, not only in individuals, but in whole epochs of
civilization. "In periods and centuries likewise," he said,
"there is a dominant trait which determines each of the
parts. For in each period, first of all, there is a surface
characteristic, surface manners which last two or three
years; the variations of fashion or dress reveal this sort
of spirit; below that lies a layer of more solid characteristics, lasting twenty, thirty or forty years, half an epoch
in history; below that again, is another layer of characteristics, lasting the entire epoch, which remains itself
through all the changes and renewals of the people—
this is the dominant characteristic."

The dominant characteristic, and the influence of the
race, milieu and moment in an individual, he worked
out in detail, and what he would call scientifically, in
the case of La Fontaine the fabulist. As a naturalist,
working on a natural history of minds, he proceeds to
examine La Fontaine. As bees make cells, he had said,
man makes philosophies and poems. Imagine, therefore,
that in the presence of the fables of La Fontaine you are

before one of these hives. We shall want to know how, given a garden and bees, a hive is produced. What are the intervening operations? and what general forces act on each step of the operation? Given France and La Fontaine, what were the general forces that determined the nature of the *Fables?* Behind the fact of the *Fables* there is the fact of the man who produced them; he was a Frenchman of Gallic race, a Gaulois speaking to other Gaulois, with the innate and hereditary dispositions common to all of them. He had, in fact, these dispositions to an exaggerated degree—that is, he was not very strict as to morals; his dignity was only passable; he was exempt from the grand passions and inclined to pleasure; he was middle-class, well-connected, living the gay life of a provincial bourgeois before the Revolution; he gambled; he loved wine and the pleasures of the table; he read books and made verses; he never took marriage seriously, neither his own nor that of his friends; he had affairs with women of all kinds and degrees; his feeling for them was neither passionate nor gross; he was inclined neither to strong emotions nor to brute enjoyments; he simply wanted happiness and pleasure—a good time generally, and so he avoided the disagreeable and the irksome as much as possible. This is the hereditary Gaulois. Then he was a poet; he had in a high degree the two great traits of a poet, "the faculty of forgetting the real world and that of living in an ideal world, the gift of not seeing matter-of-fact things and that of following the life of his dreams." . . . "He gave to himself the harmony that his verses bring to us. . . . His mind moved among a multitude of sentiments, fine and gay and tender; he traversed the range of human sentiments, occasionally among the most elevated, generally among the gentlest." "I think," Taine writes, "that of all Frenchmen, it is he who has been most truly a poet." So much for the man and the racial background; now for the milieu. He was born in Champagne, in that area of France which is most thoroughly French, which has conquered and molded all the others. Everything there is temperate; the climate is neither warm nor cold; there are neither excesses nor contrasts; the mountains are ranges of hills and the woods clumps of thickets; everything is on a small scale, with a tendency towards delicacy and refinement rather than strength—narrow rivers wind between clumps of alder trees; a row of lonely poplars in a grayish field; a fragile birch tree trembling in a glade of firs; a flash of a stream through hampering duckweed; the delicate colors of distant woods—this was the scenery that formed La Fontaine; this was the soil and the climate that fashioned him and the race he came from; this was the scenery that appeared in the *Fables,* for he had taken the imprint of this soil and sky. Now, for the moment. It was the period of the Grand Monarch, Louis the Fourteenth, when France was the greatest country in Europe, with the most magnificent court life and a galaxy of the greatest writers, which included La Fontaine's fellow Champagnois, the great Racine. The animals of the *Fables* were the people of the Court, as Racine's Greeks and Romans were so often the ladies and gentlemen of the Court; the characteristic types of the period also appeared in the skins of animals. In addition to the courtiers and the noblesse, there appeared the monk, the bourgeois, the provincial squire, the merchant, the peasant—every one was there; the *Fables* had the profusion of an Iliad; "they form our epic," Taine declares, "our only epic." The King was the Lion; the chief courtier, the Fox, the hypocrite of the Court, as the Cat was the hypocrite of religion; elephants, bears and the larger clumsy beasts symbolized the country squires and squireens; the Master Rat was the Burgomaster; the Ant was the small bourgeois, and so on; there was a whole gallery of characters, a whole array of events and emotions.

5

As Sainte-Beuve's study of Chateaubriand is the clearest and most characteristic example of his method applied to an individual, so Taine's *La Fontaine* is the perfect example of his. Both these critics chose from their native literature the writers who suited their investigations in every detail. The answers to Sainte-Beuve's questions explain Chateaubriand; Taine's investigations worked out with most excellent results in the case of La

Fontaine, whose life and work exemplified his formula and could illustrate his dictum: "Recover the conditions of the country, climate, race, milieu, education, habits in which a man has lived, and you will deduce unquestionably the nature of his talent and his work, and from the diverse conditions of his life you will establish the master-faculty with its causes and consequences."

Although, in *La Fontaine,* Taine worked out the master-faculty as a part of the study, he made it his main study in his work on Livy, the Roman historian. As was usual with Taine, in his preface he stated the problem he proposed to answer: Can a man of genius or of outstanding ability be described in a formula? Are the faculties of a man like the organs of a plant, interdependent on one another? Are they all governed by a single law? Is there in us a master-faculty whose uniform action is communicated differently to our different mechanisms and which impresses on our machine a necessary system of predetermined movements? He replies by an example, and the example worked out by him is the historian Livy.

"The difficulty for me in an investigation," Taine said, "is to find some characteristic and dominant trait from which everything may be deduced geometrically; in a word, to discover the formula of the thing. It seems to me that the formula for Livy is as follows: an orator who becomes an historian." This, then, was Livy's master-faculty, the gift of oratory, and from this spring both the merits and the faults of his work as an historian; it accounts for the beauty and the eloquence of his style; it accounts for his indifference to material that might have been available from the study of the remains of early Rome. But Livy was not interested in perusing ancient treaties or bronze tablets, or the moldy writings in old temples. Within the limits of his temperament he was accurate, and had authorities for every statement he made, but the dominant traits of his mind make him chiefly interested in such facts as were material for eloquent utterances. Anything that would have the effect of making his style dry he avoided; what he liked to write about were battles, decrees of the Senate, quarrels in the Forum. Dramatic action was what interested him; he was more interested in the story of Virginia than in new legislation; he did not care, in his search for facts, to wade through the enormous pile of superstitious puerilities that made the earliest records of Rome; he did not dig into family archives or check up sham genealogies. With the orator's concern for moving us and convincing us, he treats facts as mediums for oratory; he was always representing the characters in his history as making speeches, delivering harangues, exhorting armies. When he faced the facts of history he tried to bring back to life the long-dead passions and emotions that had animated them.

Taine shows us, in fact, a Livy who is one of the fathers of romanticized and dramatized history. In this study of Livy, the most often repeated words are his favorite "facts" and "laws"—the word "fact" sometimes occurring five times on a page. Facts are the material of all knowledge, and when you have enough facts, he seems to be always telling us, you can make a law; even from a single general fact you can deduce a law, as Newton deduced the law of gravity from the falling apple.

In these two early books we have the basic points of Taine's method in its application to individuals; we have also the first emphasizing of other ideas in his system: the primacy of the fact and the document, and the importance of the master-faculty. In his *La Fontaine and His Fables,* Taine had said, in effect, "Here is the work; let us re-create the conditions of race, climate, country, milieu, in which La Fontaine lived, and see how his work is conditioned by them." In his *Livy,* as we have seen, he posed and answered the question, Can a man of genius be circumscribed in a formula? Is there such a thing as a master-faculty that imposes itself on all the others? His formula for Livy was: an orator becomes an historian; Livy's master-faculty, therefore, was oratory; this was the dominating trait in his *History,* and he sought naturally such facts as were the best material for this to work on. So much for the application of Taine's method to individuals.

6

But as you can construct the spiritual and psychological history of an individual writer from his work, so you can construct the spiritual and psychological history of a people from its literary production. And as Sainte-Beuve applied his method to a whole group, the Port-Royal group, Taine proceeded to apply his, in its entirety, to the whole literature of a people. But for his experiment he had, first of all, to find a great and complete literature which had kept its life and vitality through the vicissitudes of its people's history. Of this type of literature, he believed there were only three great and complete examples: the English, the French, and the Greek, and of these three, Greek literature and civilization were over. Of the living literatures, he did not feel that the Italian and Spanish were complete, because, as he believed, they had ended in the seventeenth century. He did not accept the German as complete, because of the gaps in its production and because, in fact, as a great literature it was only beginning. But the English had been continuous; its difference from French literature made a special appeal to a Frenchman; being living, it was subject to direct examination and could be studied more easily than a dead literature or a dead civilization. Taine, therefore, set out to deduce from their literary production the moral and psychological history of the English people.

For the purpose of this study he thought that a people's literature supplied more fruitful facts and documents than its legal or religious codes; for politics are made alive in speeches, and religion in sermons, and both speeches and sermons belong to literature. He set out to arrange the literary product in periods, to study the climate and the soil; to show how the race was formed, to show the effect of the Norman conquest, on which he laid great stress. He traced the development of the language; he studied the dominating characteristic of each period, the dominating characteristic of the outstanding writers, their psychological mainsprings, their connection with the surrounding society and with their epoch. The result was a psychological and sociological study of English literature that cast a powerful light on English civilization.

If he did not explicitly say that the *raison d'être* of literature was an expression of society, his attitude was that it so largely had that result that he was justified in studying it to discover the dominant traits of the civilization, the psychological history of the people and their social trends. In his study of epochs he was extraordinarily illuminating, but when he found himself confronted with great single figures like Shakespeare, Swift, or Wordsworth, his refusal to see literature as anything but predetermined by forces, his refusal to face the fact or the mystery of individual genius, led him to some strange conclusions. Like Madame de

Staël, he comprehended best such literature as was really an expression of society. He incorporated in his critical system all the discoveries of his predecessors, not only de Staël's theory of literature as an expression of society, but Lessing's theory of it as an expression of national genius; he likewise included Herder's theories of history, applying them to literary history, and he took over Sainte-Beuve's procedure of seeking the man behind the work.

On the other side, he was blind to the genius of Wordsworth and Coleridge in creating ideas that gave a new direction to literature. Coleridge he barely mentions, and that in passing; Wordsworth he considered inferior to Cowper, and was frankly bored by his poetry; he did not see, as Sainte-Beuve saw, that imbedded in it lay the beginnings of a new trend in literary expression, the expression of a new trend in civilization even, a new trend in human history. What he saw in Wordsworth was a philosophical moralist; he saw but little of the poet and nothing of the critic whose ideas had such a transforming effect on poetry. Wordsworth's molds, he said, are of bad, common clay, cracked, unable to hold the noble metal that they ought to contain. Like those admirers of Wordsworth about whom Matthew Arnold complains, he was looking for a philosophy instead of for poetry, and for moralizings instead of æsthetic ideals.

Equally strange were his conclusions about Swift,

whom he considered an example *par excellence* of the positive mind, and whom he represents as "inspired and consumed by the excess of his English qualities," with the intensity of desire "which is the main feature of the race." He also describes him as showing "preeminently the character and mind of his nation." In reality, Swift was an Anglo-Irishman, possessed of the Anglo-Irish mentality in one of its most typical manifestations, endowed with wit, satire, combativeness, strong emotion, social indignation and political insight; Swift was intensely affected by the country in which he was born and by the unsettlement of his milieu; also, his peculiar kind of literary talent has not been uncommon in Irish literature. But Taine regarded him as an example of the positive mind, the mind which, he says, wishes to attain, not to eternal beauty, but to present success. Swift does not address men in general, but certain men; he does not speak to reasoners, but to a party; he does not care to teach a truth, but to make an impression; his aim is not to enlighten the mind, but to stir feelings and prejudices. As is usual with Taine, his whole study of Swift, wrong-headed as it is, in detail, is full of the wisest and profoundest critical generalizations, and contains all of the arguments as to why special pleading and propaganda in themselves cannot be literature. It is only that his arguments, applied to Swift, do not even present a half-truth.

His study of Shakespeare has sometimes been described as the least successful in his *History,* but, as a matter of truth, in its general effect and largely even in its detailed criticism of the characters and the plays, it is, in spite of some strange conclusions, one of the most illuminating studies of Shakespeare and of the English mind of the period that has ever been written. Taine brings his force and passion, all his critical imagination, all he had learned of life and psychology, to bear on Shakespeare. His psychologizings make credible and human the author of the plays and the sonnets, and that by presenting him as a man of extreme humanness, ardent in thought, bewildered in love, mighty in feeling, equally overcome by man's greatness, his piteousness and his twisted nature. The other artists of the age had the same kind of mind, the same idea of life, but in Shakespeare it was stronger and in more prominent relief.

Great works of art, Taine tells us, can be interpreted only by the most advanced psychological systems; Shakespeare himself can be comprehended only by the aid of science, and so, by his own psychological system and his own science, he tries to interpret him. What was the master-faculty in Shakespeare's case? Taine finally decides that it is an impassioned imagination freed from the shackles of reason and morality, though we can observe him wavering around the idea of describing it as love and passion. In going through the plays and observing the ease and subtlety with which

Shakespeare can depict not only the highest grade of the creative imagination and the reasoning mind but also all the grades of the unreasoning mind and the disordered imagination, in observing his power in depicting *idées fixes,* hallucinations, the caprices of the mind, Taine imagines Shakespeare writing a treatise on psychology and he concludes that if Shakespeare had framed a psychological system he would have said with the French psychiatrist, Esquirol: Man is a nervous machine governed by mood, disposed to hallucinations, carried away by unbridled passions, essentially unreasoning, a mixture of animal and poet, having, instead of mind, rapture, instead of virtue, sensibility, with imagination for prompter and guide, led at random by the most determinate and complex circumstances to sorrow, crime, madness and death.

7

Taine's own major interest, like Sainte-Beuve's, was psychology, and he piled up all the facts that he could collect, about the mind of man and its development from the cradle to the grave, including all that was available in his time from doctors and students of insanity.

His *De l'Intelligence* is really the first modern treatise on psychology, the first account of the structure of the mind based on experiment and observation, on facts that could be examined and related. It is, therefore, a work in experimental psychology; in some ways it is the most important of all his works: he himself considered that it contained the roots of his ideas, for he had reflected over it for twenty years. Taine worked on all the facts made available through the discoveries of physicians and physiologists, by studies of *idées fixes,* illusions, psychic hallucinations, troubles of memory. He studied the developing speech of children, dreams and the phantasies of opium-eaters, and the talk of people affected by mental maladies. As for psychological research, consciousness, our principal instrument, he showed is no longer of any more value than the naked eye is in optics; the range of consciousness is not great; its illusions are numerous; the greater part of ourselves remains beyond our grasp. The visible personality (*Le moi*) is incomparably smaller than the hidden personality. William James, ten years later, put this observation in a striking image when he compared personality to the iceberg, the unconscious being the greater part which is submerged and out of sight.

Amongst Taine's studies, too, were the question of the existence of more than one personality in the same individual, automatic writing, spiritism. All special states of intelligence, he considered, should be the subject of monographs; every painter, poet, novelist, of exceptional lucidity, ought to be interrogated and observed by a psychologist-friend; one should learn from the artist the way in which figures form themselves in his mind; his manner of mentally visualizing imaginary objects and the order in which they come before him, whether by involuntary fits and starts or in regular procedure. He thought, for example, that if Poe, Balzac, Hugo, and other men of genius, had been questioned and had left memoranda, we should have had information of the greatest value. The observations extant about persons suffering from mental maladies, the limited amount of transcripts or stenographic accounts of their conversation that were available, he made use of. He considered that the reach of consciousness was so limited that it needed the extension of whatever microscope or telescope a study of the abnormal could provide. He regarded himself as doing in psychology only some pioneer work. But it would surprise a good many readers to find that a psychological method which they consider especially to be the fruit of the twentieth century belongs in reality to the middle nineteenth.

Chapter Six

THE COMING OF THE REALISTS

1

THESE, THEN, were the different literary ideas and doctrines that provided the philosophy and the working inspiration for modern literature, that is, for the literature that began when Lessing proceeded to break down the old æsthetic. For modern literature really had its beginning when Lessing perceived that the boundaries of literature would have to be extended far beyond what the Greeks and the Middle Ages thought was beautiful and what the seventeenth and eighteenth centuries regarded as good taste in literary accomplishment. The whole of nature and humanity, of which the beautiful was only a part, had to be expressed.

That the ordinary man had to be given in literature was a well-organized idea before the rights of the ordinary man in politics came to be recognized. Undoubtedly the men who played a rôle as the precursors of the political idea—Rousseau, Diderot—influenced Lessing, but there is no reason to suppose that he would not have propounded the idea without them. For a new world was coming in, and of this new world the idea-makers were the movers and shakers; some of the old dreams that had kept civilization together were dying; the art, the literature, the social ideas that had dominated the world were changing. The old dreams, in fact, were dying too quickly, long before sufficient new ones to take their place had been envisioned. Still, in the beginning of the change, anyway, and even up to the death of Taine, the last great idea-maker in literature, it seemed as if it were bliss "within that dawn to be alive, and to be young were very heaven." The new epoch had need of a new literature and there were plenty of writers to make it: there were Goethe and Schiller; Wordsworth and Coleridge; Keats and Shelley; Byron and Chateaubriand and Pushkin; Scott and Balzac; there was a great chorus of voices in every country. The new literature represented a conquest, though the extent of the conquest, as happens in a new age, was exaggerated. But walls were down, and there were fewer and fewer barriers against experience; ideas and emotions could take flight in expression, no longer bound down by the rule-makers. The notion, too, was abroad that the life that was a great adventure was at hand. When Taine came and gathered all the ideas into one receptacle there seemed to be no limit to the adventures that the mind might seek. He brought the conviction that there were to be no more mysteries, that science and a proper study of facts would explain all things.

It must not be taken for granted, however, that the old notion of the beautiful, that *only* the beautiful should be expressed in art and literature, was finished. What happened was that the new ideas caused a re-arrangement of values. The very fact that the whole new movement to extend expression had been called the Romantic Movement showed the persistence of the older æsthetic ideals. What was actually the "beautiful" side of the movement, its romantic side in its earlier manifestations, was what gave it its name. But the lasting core of the change, the inner dominating idea, was that which stood for the expression of everything in life, everything that touched men, whether this was beautiful or ugly, beneficent or evil, whether it repre-sented noble human passions or base ones, sordid hu-man experiences or grand ones.

In the first flush of the movement, with its devotion to the blue rose, to grand, wrecking passions, and with a lyric production the greatest the world has ever wit-nessed, what was really new was more or less covered, only groping its way; it was hidden for long by the label. Yet romanticism had always been in literature, and the lyric was the oldest form of literary expression; both romanticism and lyricism had been in Greek literature and in Roman literature; the greatest of all English poets and dramatists had been romantic through and through, as was indeed all but a minor part of English literature. But romanticism and lyricism did not express the bulk of humanity, and to express the bulk of humanity was really what these reformers started out to do: romanticism was only one side of the shield or one stage of the progress or one part of the whole objective. The real goal of the movement—the expression of every man and every side of him—made headway only in proportion as the technique for accomplishing this was discovered. Even Wordsworth himself, who had written the poetic manifesto and who had made a determined attempt to express the common man in an art alien to him—the art of poetry—and in a language considered alien to that art, the language of every-day speech, was himself more deeply enmeshed in the romantic side of the movement than in the everyday-life side of it. His was the mind, it will be remembered, that, in addition to constructing the poetic manifesto for the revolutionary age, had also discovered that "it was bliss within that dawn to be alive." Imaginations, emotions and longings took a great leap, regardless of where they landed, and they generally landed at a long distance from ordinary life.

In England, the lyrical and romantic side was carried to its highest point by a group of younger contemporaries of Coleridge and Wordsworth, Byron, Shelley, Keats, all of whom represented the new passion for freedom and the hatred of injustice, and manifested it in different ways. Both Byron and Shelley showed that passion which might be said to be common to international romanticism, the desire to construct the interior life on the idea of freedom of emotion. Byron in England, Chateaubriand in France, evolved the type of the proud, free, unhappy, heroic aristocrat, half sincere, half poseur, devoted to lost causes, chivalrous and unself-seeking, "present on the day of danger, absent on the day of rewards"—a type which captivated the imagination down to the Great War and was a model for imitation in life and in fiction. Byron made literature out of his sins and misfortunes, was a believer in freedom, and at the same time was convinced that grand, free, generous emotions, courage and magnanimity were the birthright of the aristocracy alone, as indeed was Chateaubriand. At heart, Byron believed Wordsworth to be a prosy rustic and, like Matthew Arnold, he regarded Keats as a druggist's apprentice, great poet though he might be. Byron was one of the representatives of international romanticism, as was Goethe in his *Werther* and in his *Faust,* as was Chateaubriand in his *René,* as was Victor Hugo in his dramas and lyrics. With his dashing, aristocratic vulgarity, in his poetry and in his dramas, he represented something that was really new in English literature. Great lyricists, like Shelley and Keats, had been in English before. The lyric was peculiarly suited to the English mind and there were not wanting those who insisted that the lyricists of the new age be described as a continuation of the Elizabethans. Byron, with his *Manfred,* his *Cain,*

however, was different. There was something in him
that the new Europe understood. His energy, his sense
of adventure, his realism, his scorn were all more comprehensible to the ordinary man than the shuddering
lyricism of Shelley, than the winged idealism of "Laon
and Cythna" and "Epipsychidion," or the emotion, at
once passionate and luminous, of Keats. There were no
winging skylark song, no charmed magic casements or
foam of perilous seas, or faerylands forlorn, in Byron.
But his loves and his lusts, his scorn, his aristocratic
dash, the activity of his life, his chivalrous defense of
the Greeks, all made him easy to understand. Shelley
and Keats did not live long enough to make themselves understood in their own lifetime, though they
were, as a matter of fact, more in the ancient tradition
of English poetry than was Byron. Their ancestry went
far back, whereas whatever of Byron did not belong
to the spirit of his age went no farther back than the
eighteenth century.

Byron and Goethe in poetry, Scott in the novel, were,
in the movement's early days, the most familiarly
known figures in Europe. As we look back on the
modern mind in literature, the first really great and
universal one was Goethe's: in his work were focussed
all the trends that went with the new order—lyricism,
nationalism, mysticism, symbolism, criticism, scientific
investigation; he worked in every literary form—lyric,
drama, novel, autobiography, criticism, not to speak of

his scientific essays; he wrote subjectively, romantically, at one part of his career, and objectively, classically, at another. His mind was one of those comprehensive ones that are really above the tendencies of the time, though they include them. The biases of any movement are generally best observed in its men of secondary genius, the first being above all tendencies and influences. Goethe, infected as he was by Lessing's ideas, yet made very little attempt to translate the every-day man into writing; he essayed to write novels that are, however, treasure-houses of poetic imagination rather than revelations of the common mind. But the time spirit was moving steadily towards bringing this mind into literature, and it became evident that with the development of the novel this was going to become easier to achieve.

2

Novels of any kind, it has been said, were, before Balzac, happy accidents, but when he came, he worked out a conscious scheme both for subject matter and technique; the novel was to be a study of society, a sort of testament, of historic and documentary value. The historic and documentary value had, before him, to some extent, been achieved by Scott, to whom it had brought European homage. In our day it is perhaps difficult to understand the vast admiration given to Scott in his own time, but the fact is that he was one of those writers, representative of a new age, who seem extremely important to their contemporaries. Goethe even was sufficiently dazzled by the contemporary spirit to say of him "a great mind unequalled anywhere." And to Balzac he was the standard-bearer in the art of the novel, who elevated it, as he said, to the philosophical value of history, who united in one form narrative, drama, dialogue, portrait, landscape, description; who brought in, side by side, the epic elements of the marvellous and of the real. To people whose literary diet had been classical tragedy and high-flown romances, the novels of Scott seemed to portray recognizable life with some relation to the lives of men. Nevertheless, the man who really tried to bridge the pass between romance and realism, between the romantic and the every-day, between the dream and the reality, was Balzac himself.

Greatly influenced by Scott, Balzac, who had begun with sensational romances, worked out in detail a project for putting life, as common experience, into literature, under the general title of the *Comédie Humaine, The Human Comedy,* as against *The Divine Comedy* of Dante, the common life as against the life of vision. He determined to make himself the historian of French society as he saw it. As he himself said, French society would be the historian, he would be only the secretary, and he would thus achieve the history overlooked by so many historians—that of manners. Having made up his mind as to what he wanted to do, he worked out a

plan and an æsthetic that represented a halfway house
between the ideas of the first romantics and of the later
realists. In his theoretic outlook on society, akin to that
of Taine, on whose mind he exercised a marked influence, Balzac decided that men and women should be
studied for literary purposes as a naturalist studies
animals or plants; in fact, he declared, there is only one
animal; the Creator used one and the same pattern
for all creatures, and all the differences in animals come
from the milieux to which they have to adapt themselves. With a mixture of that simple and astounded
admiration for the new science of zoölogy, and for the
work of Buffon and other naturalists, which affected so
many French writers of the time, and with a combination of naïveté and powerful critical intuition, Balzac
set about explaining what he wanted to do and rationalizing what he had already done.

There were different species of men, Balzac announced, as there were different species of animals, and
he proposed to write a work which should do for
society what Buffon had done for zoölogy—exhibit the
different types of men that make up society, as Buffon
had exhibited the animals. Thus, for the first time, what
was known as "Naturalism" came in as a literary ideal.
The *Comédie Humaine,* he said, would deal with men,
women and things—that is to say, with persons and
with the whole environment they created for themselves. What might be called the pre-romantic ideas of

the movement, such as de Staël's notion of literature as an expression of society, and Lessing's that a beauty of art was not the same as a beauty of nature, made a strong appeal to Balzac. Examining society, he estimated that there were at any period about four or five thousand people who represented the whole of it, and these four or five thousand he proposed, in his capacity as secretary of society, to get into his work. While he put forward many theories that later became part of the canon of realism, he himself should not be described as a realist, for he created a world of his own rather than made a description of the one around him. To the critics who accused him of not being true to life according to the new literary notions that were just coming in, or of not representing life as it is, he replied that real life is either too dramatic or dramatic in ways that would not seem probable in literature; the novelist should go beyond nature, improve on its crudities, transfigure his characters and make of them types.

Balzac really had no interest in painting directly from life or in depicting every-day people; in fact, when he was taken to task for not doing so, he protested that to write about ordinary people whose life was without drama would make his work unreadable. He tells how he kept his sketch of the character of César Birotteau for six years, despairing of ever being able to make an interesting figure out of a mediocre little shopkeeper with his common misfortunes, his stupidity, until it suddenly dawned on him that he could transfigure him by making him the image of probity, that is, by elevating him to a type. Like Taine, he believed in the master-faculty, or rather in a master-passion, or a master-quality, and his chief personages are all moved by a dominating passion, so that they become typical and representative of that passion, as characters in the older classical literature were typical and representative. His Père Grandet as a miser is as typical as Molière's Harpagon; the daughters of Père Goriot are the types of filial ingratitude; Cousine Bette the type of jealousy. In his pursuit of this master-quality he was led into exaggerating personages and milieux to the extent of making them marvellous and sometimes even fabulous. In actual life he said one would have to study several characters to create a single one in fiction; the writer had to proceed like a painter, take the hands of one model, the feet of another, the bust of a third. For instance, in creating the characters of Père Goriot and his daughters, each fact or incident taken separately was from life, though some of the actual happenings in the lives of the living models he considered too frightful and too improbable for a novel. The writer, he agreed, might or should take his facts from life, but he would have to reassemble them to suit the pattern he had in mind. For example, he might have to take the beginning of one incident, the middle of another, and the end of a third, to create a single incident in literature.

Balzac's art, as has often been said, especially by realists, was a sort of gigantization of life. What he actually did was to create a world of his own out of patterns he had picked out in the world of reality. No writer studied the mainsprings of human motives or actions as carefully as he did, and few writers in the whole course of literature had such powers of observation, such intuition as to what was happening in people's minds. His power of insight became so acutely developed that he could pierce through the exterior into the interior life of others, identifying himself with them. He tells us in memorable words how, dressed like one of themselves, he would mingle with workingmen in the streets and watch them concluding their bargains or quarreling as they left their work. Again, he tells us how he would follow a workingman and his wife as they came home from a theatre, listen to their conversation as they talked of the play, of the way they spent their money, of the price of potatoes, of the dreariness of winter, of their debts to shopkeepers, becoming angry in sympathy with them as they talked of a domineering boss. Listening to them he was able to merge his personality with theirs, and he himself considered that he had a power in all this that was strange and unique. The people he created out of this sort of observation he confused with the world of reality; he had difficulty in getting outside the world he himself made. As Sainte-Beuve said, he had created them so powerfully that, once he got them going, he and they could never part again.

Balzac's ideal of himself as the secretary of society, in the *Comédie Humaine,* gave him principles outside his purely literary ones: a writer who was something more than a mere entertainer ought to have fixed opinions in morals and politics and to be able to make a decision on human affairs; he ought to be able not only to depict life but to come to conclusions about it. He himself based his opinions and conclusions on his convictions as a Catholic in religion and as a monarchist in politics. "I write," he said, "under the ægis of two eternal truths, religion and monarchy." As a historian of manners he considered that a writer should be, not only a delineator of human types, a recorder of dramas of intimate life, but that he ought to include in his work such descriptions of professions and occupations, of towns, streets, houses, furniture, as would be a record, for the future, of the state of civilization in the epoch he was describing; in short, he considered that the novelist should get down all the accessories of existence, of whatever period he was dealing with, which might seem of importance to future readers. In addition to all this, he thought the writer should try to bring to light the reasons behind events, the motive powers behind society. Outside its task of painting society, he believed that literature should attempt to make a better world; that a writer ought to make moral comment, to accompany his revelation of the passions with instructive lessons, and point a moral by the juxtaposition of good and evil.

A realistic novelist making his work a representation of life, Balzac was not—in spite of all his passages about copying life and studying men and women as a naturalist studies animals. Every emotion, every action, every personage in the *Comédie Humaine* is, to be sure, drawn from a careful observation of the motive powers behind life and a superhuman insight into them, but Balzac enlarged everything in his work to the scale of the gigantic or the eccentric or the demoniacal. "No delineation of character or of surroundings," says Croce, "but he exaggerates to the extent of making it altogether marvellous and fantastic. . . . He gives an extraordinary aspect to what is ordinary." And Baudelaire wrote of him, "all his characters are endowed with the same vital ardor that he himself had . . . all are more eager for life, more active and wily in combat, more voracious of joy, more angelic in devotion, than the human comedy of the real world shows us."

3

But the very year before the death of Balzac, the year 1849, another step was taken towards getting the human being, as he actually existed in the real world, into literature, and it was taken by Flaubert. How strikingly literary opinion had advanced to the next step on that road is evident from the account of what led Flaubert to the writing of *Madame Bovary*. He had finished a first version of *The Temptation of St. Anthony*, on which he had spent three years, and had invited some literary associates to a reading of it. Its lyricism and romanticism belonged to an age that was passing, and to the up-to-date young men who listened to the reading, the *Temptation* seemed so old-fashioned that they thoroughly discouraged him from continuing in that vein. "Give it up," they said. "Starve out your lyricism! Take a feet-on-the-ground subject like those of Balzac, like his Cousine Bette!" This verdict was a blow to Flaubert, but it meant a turning point in his work, and when, the next day, one of his auditors suggested as a subject the story of a country doctor who had been an interne under Flaubert's father in the hospital of Rouen, whose wife after love affairs had poisoned herself, the author accepted the suggestion. The novel, thus projected, it was decided, should follow real life in its smallest details. Following a habit of his mind, Flaubert allowed the characters, the plot and the theme to develop slowly in his imagination, and the novel itself was not begun until about two years later. The writing of it took some four and a half years, during which he lived in tranquil isolation in the small town of Croisset, near Rouen, because, as he said, a complete immobility of existence was necessary for him before he could write.

Finally, in the year 1857, was published the first realistic novel, *Madame Bovary*. Balzac had given a foretaste of what it might be, so, in a measure, had Stendhal, so had Mérimée; it was left to Flaubert to accomplish it. In fact this year, 1857, saw the publication of two books of the kind that had been dreamed of since Lessing's criticism had first burst on Europe. One was Flaubert's *Madame Bovary;* the other was a book of verse, Baudelaire's *Les Fleurs du Mal.* Realism in both prose and verse, the Comédie Humaine of the actual world, long envisaged, long struggled towards, was in literature at last. Here the older symbolism was exchanged for shapes and symbols from every-day life; here, instead of the older dramatic effect, was real life in a series of pictures.

The two books were startling in every way—in outlook on life, in subject matter, in technique, in style, in language. In each, personages were presented with reality of a kind hitherto unknown in literature—their characters, their souls were revealed with complexity and subtlety; the language of both the prose writer and the poet had a sharp intensity; both showed a like concern for the absolutely correct word; with each of them the inspiration, or genius, or talent was intense and penetrating, rather than large or exuberant. The novelist was far from the loose abundance of Balzac or Walter Scott; the poet far from that of Hugo or Wordsworth or Byron. To their readers they offered the essence of their minds. The result was a grave and careful art, the fruit of labor and deliberation, and of an integral observation—an observation that represented the very height of emotional and intellectual communication with the life they were drawn to express. What they put into writing was experience, winnowed until the necessary kernel was shaken free. The poetry was as realistic, as ironic, as the novel, but with the deeper subtlety and concentration of verse. What Sainte-Beuve said of one of them is equally true of both, "a severe and pitiless verity has entered into art as the last word in experience."

The story of *Madame Bovary* is familiar to practically all seasoned novel readers, as it is to all accomplished novel writers. We are led through the life experiences of the two major characters, Charles and Emma Bovary, from their childhood until their deaths, and are brought into intense contact with a number of people who abut on the lives of these two. While Flaubert took the outlines of the plot and of the chief characters from actual happenings and personages in his own neighborhood, these really represented only the framework, and he kept making careful notes, suggested by many sources, for the events, the emotions, the characters he was going to reveal. Here, in these jottings for the character of Charles Bovary, is a sample of his note-taking: "Intimate vulgarity even in the manner in which he carefully folds his napkin . . . in which he eats his soup . . . animality of his organic functions. He wears in winter knitted waistcoats and gray woollen socks with a white border, good boots, habit of picking his teeth with the point of his knife, habit of whittling the corks of bottles so that he can put them back in the bottle."

We first meet Charles at school, a commonplace youth of the small bourgeoisie; then we see him studying for his medical examinations; then practising medicine in the small town of Yonville; then entering into a marriage, arranged for him by his parents, with an elderly widow supposed to have a dot. That Bovary was a widower who had first been married to an elderly plain wife was one of the little insignificant facts that made for the realism of his character, the ordinariness of his life. During the lifetime of his first wife he encounters Emma when, as a doctor, he is called in to visit her father. She has been educated in a convent boarding school, has graces of appearance, dress and manner which captivate him. After his wife's death he marries Emma and takes her from her father's farm to his house in the small town where he practises. Flaubert himself lived for the most part in a similar town—in fact, he lived in it all through his·writing of the novel—and he had meticulously observed and documented the life around him. What had he seen there? asked Sainte-Beuve, in his study of the novel—littleness, sordidness, pretentiousness, stupidity, routine, monotony, ennui. And as for the people, they were vulgar, flat, stupidly ambitious, entirely ignorant or semi-literate, and when they loved, they were lovers without delicacy—they loved grossly. Among these people Flaubert placed Emma Bovary and her dreams of love.

There were, as has already been indicated, originals who were models to some extent for the principal characters and for the incidents of their lives, and the other personages were composites of people Flaubert was acquainted with. Nevertheless, the author said of Emma, as he also said of Frédéric, in *L'Education Sentimentale,* as perhaps every novelist can say of his chief character, "Madame Bovary c'est moi." That is, she symbolized one of the personalities of which his own personality was made up. He revealed, in her, certain potentialities of his own mind and of his own emotions. The school days, the youth, that had been his own were partly the youth, the school days, that he now gave Emma. "I believed in the poetry of life, in the plastic beauty of the passions. . . . I do not know what may be the dreams of schoolboys nowadays, but ours were superbly extravagant. . . . Those with romantic hearts sighed for dramatic scenes of love with obligatory accompaniment of gondolas, masks, and ladies swooning in postchaises on Calabrian hills. We ruined our eyes reading novels in the dormitory." Emma, too, read novels in the dormitory of her convent school; she, too, sighed for the dramatic scenes of love; she dreamed of the romantic life and was resolved to attain it. She tried to make life correspond to these dreams, her own dreams, as well as those in the romances she had borrowed from her sewing teacher. The ennui of her life with her good, commonplace, stupid husband became unbearable; she succumbed to two lovers, and during her relations with them experienced all the gamut of emotions and temptations connected with physical love. Finally, beaten down by a series of events, she slowly disintegrates and dies a suicide.

4

Madame Bovary not only crystallized the literary genre, but fixed the novel as the primary literary form, the one most favored by writers and readers for nearly a century; it also set the pattern for novel writing in subject, theme and construction down to our time, and still shows signs that it may continue into the future, side by side with new patterns that may be brought in. It is very important to note the theme of this first realistic novel—that is, the theme as apart from the plot and the content—for we find it repeated over and over again by realistic novelists. The theme of *Madame Bovary* is the attempt to make life, every-day life, conform to one's youthful dreams, and after the vain attempt to make it conform, the renunciation of all dreams. This is not only the theme of Flaubert's other realistic novel *L'Education Sentimentale,* but is the theme of all the great realistic novels. Sometimes the renunciation of the dream comes violently as in *Madame Bovary* and *Anna Karenina,* and it is well to remember that not only the theme of Tolstoy's novel but also the plot is the same as Flaubert's. However, for Tolstoy every-day life was the life of the aristocracy, and so the personages are aristocrats, while Flaubert's are middle-class. The renunciation comes violently in Theodore Dreiser's important novels. Sometimes there is a compromise between the life of dream and reality as in George Moore's *Esther Waters,* Somerset Maugham's *Of Human Bondage,* Arnold Bennett's *The Old Wives' Tale,* Sinclair Lewis's *Main Street.*

The theme and the pattern are substantially the same with all the practitioners of the Flaubertian novel, which means that "facts," with the great realists, concern the interior life as well as the exterior. There were the "facts" of the imagination, the "fact" that life was dream as well as actuality, and they took both sides of life into consideration. This novel was the reversal of the old English themes of romance: it was almost a reversal of the Balzacian theme or subject, for Balzac, in spite of his efforts at imitating life, made his characters extraordinary, doing extraordinary and even fabulous things, whereas Flaubert's were ordinary people with only a dream of being extraordinary that passed with youth. What had happened in this book was that a writer for the first time in the history of literature had turned all his gifts, not to poetry or high romance or great drama, but to the revelation of people who might be encountered in any small town or any little suburb. The chief character, in spite of some flights of imagination beyond those of the majority of her acquaintances, in spite of expectations from life a little beyond theirs, was, at the same time, not more distinguished from the others than one woman might be among the inhabitants of the street of a small town and yet remain quite within the ordinary and the commonplace. Nothing happens to her beyond the possibility of happenings in any little community. All the personages could be duplicated in any town, village or suburb, and none of them do or say anything that had not been done or said a million times before in the world. They were created out of Flaubert's observations and experience; very completely indeed were the personages and appurtenances of romance replaced by every-day life, the gods and heroes, the kings and princesses, the lords and ladies, by the bourgeoisie—and, according to Flaubert's own definition, the bourgeoisie was now all mankind, including the people. The carefulness of his observation, his note-taking, showed itself not only in the personages, the incidents, the conversation, the habits and customs, but also in such details as the way the first Madame Bovary wore her little shawl, the details of the Agricultural Show, the stores, the pharmacy, the village church, the wedding festivities. The world in which the personages moved was not only their own world, perfectly created for them, but was, besides, the world lived in by the bulk of the reading public, who consequently understood and appreciated the book on its first appearance more rapidly than did the intelligentsia.

The personages who, whilst we are reading the novel, give the impression of being individuals become, in retrospect, types—that is, they are at once individual and typical. Emma Bovary herself, considered in turn by critics as the most complete feminine portrait in literature, as one of the most fascinating revelations of the soul of a woman, and—especially by Anglo-Saxon critics, like Percy Lubbock—as the portrait of a common, silly little person, foolishly romantic, meanly ambitious, in conflict with her environment, is in reality such an exceedingly subtle portrait that she is in some respects every woman. The portrait of Charles Bovary, good, stupid, with even a more limited expanse of consciousness than the average man, living a common, semi-animal, semi-plant life, with no desires or ambitions that his environment cannot more than satisfy, betrayed by his wife, represents the character of more men than any other type that up till then had appeared in literature. In the same way the character of Homais, the druggist, fairly intelligent, determined to get on in the world, using the environment and his adherence to all the social and tribal laws to advance himself, having some acquaintance with literature, having even a faint touch of artistry, a faint, but not too disturbing sense that there are great men in the world whom it is well to admire at a distance of both time and place, is to be found by the score in every community. It is he, observing all the laws, habits and customs, keeping all the moralities, fulfilling all the ambitions of the ordinary man, who is the one happy person in the book, a contented husband and father, a success all round in his business and in his community. The vast irony of the portrait could not have been apparent to more than a fraction of the first readers of the novel; it is, perhaps, not apparent to the bulk of readers even now. The curé, Bournasien, to whom Emma went for comfort, is also both an individual and a type. According to Flaubert's own notes, as the son of a peasant he thought only of the physical, of the sufferings of the poor, their lack of bread and fuel, and never divined the spiritual wants, the vague mystical aspirations of his fellow men. There is no portrait in *Madame Bovary* created with less irony than that of Emma herself: there is indeed less of Flaubert's well-known and often expressed contempt for humanity in his delineation of her than in that of any other character he has built up.

It has often been said of Flaubert, and he thought and said it himself, that the whole life depicted in this book was so alien to his temperament and mentality that he had to evolve an anti-self to enable him to write it and to devote himself persistently to a sort of life and to a type of humanity that he despised with a patient and all-embracing hatred. In reality, he was the first author whose mentality represented strongly and clearly the two goals that the whole modern movement in literature, beginning with Lessing, was moving towards—the romantic and the every-day, the dream and the reality. A writer could depict the reality only if he thoroughly knew the dream, and he could realize the significance of the dream only by coming into conflict with reality. Flaubert was, like the bulk of humanity, a dreamer and a realist. In addition, he was a man with a lyrical temperament and an analytic mind, part idealist, part materialist, in his philosophic outlook a scholar with a profound knowlege of literature, an artist born with the sense of form, the very type of those who create new modes of expression.

At the same time, far from being the pure lyric and romantic he sometimes thought himself, he only understood the romantic and lyrical temperament when it was well anchored on one side to common sense and every-day realism. Hence his harsh criticism of men like de Musset, lyricists without being realists, whom Flaubert liked in his lyrical moments because, as he said, his own spiritual vices of lyricism, vagabondage, and temperamental swagger were flattered by this type of work. "He never could separate poetry," Flaubert wrote of de Musset, "from the sensations it arises from;

music for him was made for serenades, painting for portraiture, and poetry for the consolation of the heart. . . . Poetry is not a debility of the spirit, and these nervous susceptibilities are. . . . This faculty of feeling beyond measure is a weakness. . . . Passion does not make poetry, and the more personal you are the weaker you are." And of Leconte de Lisle, he said, with a master craftsman's contempt for one who has not the accomplishments essential to his job, "He has not read the classics of his language sufficiently, and so has neither swiftness nor clarity." In these comments, carefully examined, will be found the basis of Flaubert's æsthetic, an æsthetic which, with that of Baudelaire, was adopted by a great portion of the modern accomplished literary world.

Working out the theories he put into practice in his realistic novels, *Madame Bovary* and *L'Education Sentimentale,* Flaubert expressed his conclusions in a series of convictions for the most part stated in his correspondence with Louise Colet, to whom he wrote half of the letters in the published correspondence; with George Sand, who had only a limited admiration for the new realistic novel and was too much immersed in her own ideals of writing for Flaubert's to be entirely sympathetic or even quite comprehensible to her. Some of the more salient of these conclusions have passed into the common stock of literary and critical ideas, not only in relation to the novel, but to poetry; for, as with all significant writers, the basic construction of Flaubert's mind was poetic. "The author in his work," he said, in a well-known sentence, in which he expressed his theories about the type of novel he had invented, "ought to be like God in the universe, present everywhere but visible nowhere. . . . Art being a second nature, the creator of this nature ought to act by analogous proceeding. I do not believe that the novelist should express his own opinions. . . . According to the ideal of art that I have, I think that an artist should not manifest anything of his own feelings, and that he should not appear any more in his work than God in nature. . . . The man is nothing, the work is everything."

In his realistic novels, Flaubert deliberately turned away from the accidental, the extraordinary and the dramatic which had so beguiled Balzac; he created neither remarkable persons nor heroes, though he did not blame anybody who did, for, as he said, "Art is what one can make it; we are not free. Each follows his own path in spite of his own desires." As for the meticulous power of observation shown in his books, he, like most men of genius, did not place too high a degree of importance on it; it was valuable, but subsidiary. "If I have arrived at some knowledge of life," he wrote, "it is by dint not of chewing a great deal of it but of having ruminated a lot on it." A little experience well pondered over—that gave him the matter for his novels. Other general theories of his have been repeated over and over again and re-created in a form that now represents the most advanced literary ideas of our age, such as are being enunciated by Valéry and T. S. Eliot. "The less one feels a thing, the more apt one is to express it as it is, as it is in itself, in its universality, freed from accidental ephemera." But he added that one must have the faculty of making oneself feel it, that is, one must have the potentiality of feeling what one expresses, even if one has never actually experienced it in life. "One does not write with one's heart, but with one's head, and no matter how well endowed one may be, one always has need of that concentration which gives vigor to the thought, luster to the expression."

That "form and matter were two subtle qualities, neither of which could exist without the other," was the first article in Flaubert's artistic creed. He weighed sentences and phrases, and he carved and filed until he got the exact words in the exact order with the sound that he felt expressed what he wanted to say. Because, as he said, the words fitted for expressing an idea have a predetermined relation to the facts that gave rise to the idea, the discovery of the inevitable word, phrase, or sentence required from him great travail. Working seven hours a day, he would manage to produce in a month about twenty pages or even less. "To write a book is for me a long voyage," he said, and for the voyage that was *Madame Bovary,* between the conception, the working-out and the writing, he took more than seven years in all. But when the voyage was ended and the completed book reached the public, it produced an excitement similar to that caused in our day by the publication of Joyce's *Ulysses,* for another milestone on the road to expressing in literature the totality of human experiences had been passed, and the ordinary man, or to use Flaubert's own phrase, "the bourgeois that is now all mankind," was to be the hero of literature for a long time to come.

Strange and even startling as was Flaubert's achievement, he was in form, even in technique, the heir of a long line not only of French writers but of the whole Latin tradition; in the psychological construction of his characters, as well as in his carefully wrought style, he showed himself of the same line as Racine: the shape of his plot, with its beginning, its crisis, its conclusion, was clearly in the classical manner. He used the old splendid tools on new material and as a new practitioner.

5

Inclined towards determinism, which was the accepted philosophy of the age, Flaubert was akin to Taine on one side of his mind, but on another he had a singular kinship with the author of the second great literary sensation of 1857, with the poet of *Les Fleurs du Mal.* Baudelaire, on his side, felt the kinship, and after the appearance of *Madame Bovary,* wrote one of the two understanding critiques of that novel, the other having been written by Sainte-Beuve.

The two books broke on a startled public, accustomed to regarding the established literary works and their subjects as representing the perpetual standards of art, with a moral shock—the novel differed from all preceding novels and romances and the volume of poems from all preceding poetry. Looking backwards, one cannot avoid the conviction that the ensuing legal prosecution of the two books, *Madame Bovary* for immorality and *Les Fleurs du Mal* for immorality and blasphemy, resulted as much from mental shock, caused by a blasting of existing conceptions of literature, as from any moral or religious scruples.

As *Madame Bovary* changed the shape and content of the narrative, so *Les Fleurs du Mal* changed the shape and content of poetry: together, the two modified, all over Europe, the attitude towards literature and literary form of the great bulk of the writers who came after them. It was not that narrative was never again to be written as it was before Flaubert, or poetry as it was before Baudelaire, but that materials and values, persons and things, whose expression had been dimly longed for, hazily struggled towards since Lessing, were now definitely emergent in literature.

The two who had accomplished this were subject to many of the same influences: what Taine would call the intellectual climate was very similar for both, with the difference in final effect that one was a prose writer and the other a poet, dowered differently in imaginative quality and nature of expression. The effect, on writing, of Flaubert's work was immediate; that of Baudelaire's was slower except in the case of a small group of the younger poets, particularly those who later were to call themselves Symbolists, the group around Verlaine and Rimbaud. At the period, the dominating trend in writing was towards the utmost care in form and style, towards an impersonal attitude to material, towards a cult of objectivity, towards keeping the personality of the author out of his work. These were the aims of a group of poets who called themselves Parnassians, with the leader of whom, Théophile Gautier, Baudelaire felt strong enough kinship, strong enough common aims, to dedicate to him *Les Fleurs du Mal*.

Flaubert's aims in prose were, in theory anyhow, the same as those of Gautier and the Parnassians in verse. The same rays of influence poured on all of them from the milieu and the moment, but each took what best suited his temperament, what best developed his own originality. Apart from the peculiar differentiation of their genius, Baudelaire's resemblance to Flaubert was sufficiently striking. To begin with, both were born in the same year, 1821; both produced their epoch-making books in the same year, 1857; both were realists in the only sense in which a man can be a realist and be a great artist, in their sharp consciousness of the struggle between the dream and the reality, between the aspiration and common happenings. The nervous structure of their personalities had much in common: a similar dread of life was manifested by both at an early age. As a child of thirteen, Flaubert could write to a friend about a story he was weaving around Queen Isabeau, "If I had not in my head and at the end of my pen a French queen of the fifteenth century, I should be totally disgusted with life and a bullet would deliver me from the buffoonery that one calls living." And Baudelaire wrote in one of his journals, "As a child I felt in my heart two contradictory sentiments, the horror of life and the ecstasy of life." Nevertheless, Baudelaire did not continually display that hatred for the folly and futility of mankind which goes like a refrain through Flaubert's correspondence, through his life, and which he made the groundwork of his art.

The attitude of both to life and art was, in great part, the result of a highly strung temperament, subtly attuned nerves, and an inherited lack of that sort of physical force and vital abundance that made Hugo and Balzac at once objects of admiration and something of ironic mockery to both. Their nervousness, their irony, their general outlook on life, gave their writing a sharpened sense of reality. This sense of reality made Baudelaire incapable of making poetry out of mere reverie or fantasy: his utmost fantasies, his strangest emotions, were well winnowed by his intellect before they were transmuted into art and were always made definite through being brought into touch with some common experience, some familiar occurrence. His attitude in this respect is characteristically revealed in that remark of his about de Musset—that he never understood the process by which a reverie became a work of art: de Musset was satisfied when he had versified the reverie.

Baudelaire expressed his passion for form and style in terms akin to Flaubert's: for both, the writing of a book was a long travail; the coupling of the right adjective with the right noun a matter for laborious experimentation. For the poet, the significant adjective or noun sometimes came from analogy, sometimes from incongruity. In their care for form and style they were not only part of a reaction against the carelessness and flamboyance of the more exuberant romantics like de Musset, Sand and Hugo, they were the heirs of the long line of masters of French literature. In addition, Baudelaire was the inheritor from Lessing, Herder, Wordsworth, Coleridge, through Sainte-Beuve, of all the innovating ideas about poetry. The strong effect on him of Sainte-Beuve's verse is one of those not uncommon instances of a poet of rare genius receiving an influx of energy and ideas from one of lesser caliber, one who, in this particular case, was supreme in a field of literature that included the intuitive perception of new poetic directions. We must keep in mind that Sainte-Beuve's *Ra-*

yons Jaunes and *The Poetry of Joseph Delorme,* of which Baudelaire described himself as an incorrigible lover, were in their day a new species of poetry and remained a new species of poetry for a generation younger than that of Baudelaire, Verlaine's.

But to get to the root of Sainte-Beuve's sway over a couple of generations of poets, we must go back to those influences that made him. He was one of the few great critics in all literature—an idea-carrier, an innovator, a shaker-up of old conventions, a man who foresaw the motive forces in literature. The new wave of poetic ideas had come from England and was to return to England in another form, in later time. Sainte-Beuve was steeped in English literature, and he brought into French not only the ideas and poetry of Wordsworth and Coleridge, but of Lamb, Kirk White and Cowper, and even of the Bowles who is so strangely praised in the *Biographia Literaria.* The hearth-and-family school represented by Cowper in England never made much headway on the Continent; it was, however, cherished by Sainte-Beuve, who conceived that if he failed in his ambition to become the French Wordsworth he might become the French Cowper. The bulk of the poetic principles that he strove to turn into terms that could be assimilated by French genius came from Wordsworth and the Lake School, especially from the powerful summons of the Preface to the *Lyrical Ballads.* "The principal object," Wordsworth had written, "proposed in these poems was to choose incidents and situations from common life and to relate or describe them throughout, as far as possible, in a selection of the language really used by men." Sainte-Beuve accordingly took on the ambition to be the French Wordsworth and proceeded to write about incidents and situations and people chosen from common life; made, in fact, a considerable effort to be a realist in verse. As he said, his muse was no brilliant odalisque, no young and vermilion peri, but a "poor girl washing clothes by a stream." So he chose themes suited to the "poor girl" and these occasionally were difficult to make poetry out of; some of the poems derived from Wordsworth had more of the famous prosiness of the master than of his high poetry. Nevertheless, there can be no doubt that Sainte-Beuve was a poet both in mind and performance, even though it is in his influence on poetry rather than in his poetic achievement that his importance lies. Wordsworth had said that he had chosen humble and rustic life for his poems "because in that condition the essential passions of the heart find a better soil in which they can attain their maturity."

The humble and rustic life that gave him the matter for his poems Wordsworth found in his daily walks. Sainte-Beuve proceeded to find subjects in his walks. The walk, in fact, became an inciter of inspiration, and "Promenade," as a title, acquired a vogue. But common life for Sainte-Beuve was not rustic life: it was such as he could find in the streets of Paris, and he describes the promenades of his "Joseph Delorme" and the sights and scenes he encountered "in that vast cemetery that is called a great city." The holes in the hedges through which could be viewed the mean little vegetable gardens, the monotonous side streets, the elm trees gray with dust, an old woman crouching on the ground with children, a belated soldier going back to barracks with tottering steps, a workman's party. His Sunday evenings in Paris he described in the poem called "Rayons Jaunes," and this poem, in spite of its touches of prosiness, had repercussions in poetry that affected not only Baudelaire, but Laforgue and Laforgue's followers in every country, and among these we can reckon many of our own contemporaries, and, outstandingly, T. S. Eliot and Ezra Pound.

Baudelaire could write to Sainte-Beuve, "I hope to be able to show one of these days a new Joseph Delorme grappling at each incident of his promenade with his rhapsodic thought and drawing a distasteful moral from everything." Sainte-Beuve himself spoke of his *Rayons Jaunes* as the *Fleurs du Mal* of the day before, and he adopted Baudelaire as his son in Apollo, addressing him as "my dear son." But in spite of all this mutual interest and admiration, this undoubted kinship, it is clear that the author of *Les Rayons Jaunes* never really became an appreciator or even a comprehender of the stronger and stranger music, the more heady wine of *Les Fleurs du Mal.* He was even a trifle nonplussed at some of the subjects exploited in that volume, and suggested that Baudelaire should have written certain of his verses in Latin. And with all his admiration for Sainte-Beuve, Baudelaire could write to him the following: "In certain places in 'Joseph Delorme' I find too many lutes, lyres, harps and Jehovahs. This is a blemish on the Parisian poems; besides, you have come to destroy all that." It was true, he had come to destroy all that. But it was Baudelaire who was really destined to accomplish the destruction. He sought for his material where Joseph Delorme had looked before him, "in that vast cemetery that is called a great city." His muse was far from being Sainte-Beuve's "poor girl washing clothes by a stream," and the life he found in Paris was other than what Joseph Delorme discovered in his daily promenades.

Baudelaire's common humanity was neither Sainte-Beuve's nor Wordsworth's; it comprised the castaways of a great city—beggars, tramps, prostitutes, assassins, drunkards, lesbians, rag-pickers, the old men and old women of the parks and the quays; his scenery was destitute of running brooks, singing birds, primroses by a river's brim; it was, instead, dawn on the Seine, fogs, rain, hospitals, cemeteries, the streets, the cafés of Paris. Parisian life, he affirmed, was full of marvellous subjects, and he took what he called "the bath of multitude," for to the poet belonged "the incomparable privilege of being both himself and others," of being able to "enter at will the personality of any man." That he deliberately chose to find poetry in subjects where nobody thought of looking for it before is clear not only from his work but from his own comments on it. For, he declared, as the great poets of the past had divided among themselves the happier provinces of the domain of poetry, he set himself to extract beauty from evil and misfortune, or, in his own words, "extraire la beauté du mal," and Sainte-Beuve wrote to him, "You, the latest comer, said to yourself, 'Well, I will find poetry where no one thought of culling it before.'"

Baudelaire could, apparently, draw poetry from anything in life that came to his attention, for there were depths of reverie and emotion and memory in his being, that could couple themselves with any experience. His daily experience, intermingled with his indestructible memories, with the nervous complexity of his emotions and the sharp power of his senses, formed the groundwork of his poetry. He expressed the conviction that art ought to be a revelation of modern life, that contemporaries were more important than the men of the past, and so he placed Balzac above Homer, Wagner above previous musicians; he considered that Manet and Delacroix were painting the modern world's pictures; the age of gods and goddesses was gone by; the great artist, he wrote, would be the one who could seize from every-day life its epic side and show us how great and poetic we were in our neckties and polished shoes. He himself, to be sure, did not always seek greatness and poetic emotions in neckties and polished shoes, but was fond of inducing other emotions and sensations by drinking strange potions, by eating hashish and opium, by means of which he entered what he called his artificial paradises. But he did seize, from every-day life, its epic side and he seized the epic side of the morbid, the exotic, the neurotic, the unwholesome, the disintegrated, the bored, the exasperated and the lonely. The Goncourts said that both language and literature had been formed by men who were too healthy and well-balanced to be really representative of humanity. They concluded that the instabilities of the ordinary man, his vagaries, his experiences, his bewilderments, his sins and his suffering, must be expressed in a different style of writing and in a language and syntax susceptible of taking on the coloring of the modern world and the shapes of the many complex human types that compose it.

The Goncourts believed that they themselves were to be the first to accomplish this in prose, for the old Titans of literature had expressed the few and not the many, the uncommon, simple emotions instead of the common, complicated ones. But their contemporary and friend, Baudelaire, was doing it in poetry in their lifetime with a complexity and completeness which no one, either in prose or verse, has since equalled. He got into poetry emotions, thoughts, spasms of the mind and senses, that people recognized to be theirs only after he had expressed them. For, as has been said of him, he modified the sensibility of generations of intellectuals; he gave voice to the complexity of sentiments and sensations embodied in one emotion; he manipulated language and language-combinations and sounds so that a single line or a couplet could convey layers and layers of experience that lay outside the realm of the older poetry.

Les morts, les pauvres morts ont de grandes douleurs.
(The dead, the poor dead, have great sorrows.)

.   .   .   .

L'Irréparable ronge avec sa dent maudite
Notre âme.
(The Irreparable gnaws our soul with his cursed teeth.)

.   .   .   .

La Maladie et la Mort font des cendres
De tout le feu qui pour nous flamboya.
(Illness and Death make ashes of all the fire that flamed
    for us.)

.   .   .   .

Ma jeunesse ne fut qu'un ténébreux orage,
Traversé çà et là par de brillants soleils.
(My youth was only a tenebrous storm, traversed here and
    there by brilliant suns.)

.   .   .   .

O douleur! O douleur! Le Temps mange la vie,

Et l'obscur Ennemi qui nous ronge le cœur,
Du sang que nous perdons croît et se fortifie!
(O sorrow, sorrow! Time eats life away, and the obscure
 Enemy that gnaws our heart, grows and is fortified by
 the blood we lose.)

. . . .

J'ai plus de souvenirs que si j'avais mille ans.
(I have more memories than if I had a thousand years.)

. . . .

     mon triste cerveau,
C'est une pyramide, un immense caveau,
Qui contient plus de morts que la fosse commune.
(My sad brain is an immense cave that contains more dead
 than the potter's field.)

. . . .

Rien n'égale en longeur les boiteuses journées,
Quand sous les lourds flocons des neigeuses années
L'Ennui, fruit de la morne incuriosité,
Prend les proportions de l'immortalité.
(Nothing equals in length the limping days, when, under
 the heavy flakes of the snowing years, Ennui, fruit of
 gloomy incuriosity, takes on the proportions of im-
 mortality.)

When he wrote the poem "La Servante au Grand
Cœur," a commemoration of the dead, of a servant who
had attended him as a child, it was not just the expression of a simple emotion accompanied with a little
philosophic reflection, as it might have been in a Wordsworth poem or even in one by any poet preceding Baudelaire; it became laden with memories, with medita-

tions on life, love and death, with visions of cold October winds shearing the leaves off the trees, the memory of his mother's jealousy, the forgetfulness of the living, the sadness of the dead in their isolation—the restlessness and loneliness of the grave.

La Servante au Grand Cœur

La servante au grand cœur dont vous étiez jalouse,
Et qui dort son sommeil sous une humble pelouse,
Nous devrions pourtant lui porter quelques fleurs.
Les morts, les pauvres morts, ont de grandes douleurs,
Et quand Octobre souffle, émondeur des vieux arbres,
Son vent mélancolique à l'entour de leurs marbres,
Certe, ils doivent trouver les vivants bien ingrats,
De dormir, comme ils font, chaudement dans leurs draps,
Tandis que, devorés de noires songeries,
Sans compagnon de lit, sans bonnes causeries,
Vieux squelettes gelés travaillés par le ver,
Ils sentent s'égoutter les neiges de l'hiver
Et le siècle couler, sans qu'amis ni famille
Remplacent les lambeaux qui pendent à leur grille.

Lorsque la bûche siffle et chante, si le soir,
Calme, dans le fauteuil je la voyais s'asseoir,
Si, par une nuit bleue et froide de décembre,
Je la trouvais tapie en un coin de ma chambre,
Grave, et venant du fond de son lit éternel
Couver l'enfant grandi de son œil maternel,
Que pourrais-je répondre à cette âme pieuse,
Voyant tomber des pleurs de sa paupière creuse!

The Servant of the Great Heart

The servant of the great heart, that you were jealous of,
And who sleeps her last sleep under an humble sward,

We should nevertheless bring her a few flowers—
The dead, the poor dead, have great sorrows,
And when October blows its melancholy wind—
Shearer of old trees—around their marble tombs,
Certainly they must find the living very ungrateful
To sleep as they do warmly between their sheets,
Whilst, devoured with black broodings,
Without bed-companion, without good conversation,
Old frozen skeletons wrought upon by the worm,
They hear the snows of winter dripping,
And the century go past, without friends or family
Replacing the tatters that hang on the railing.

When the log whistles and sings, if in the evening
I should see her placidly sitting in the armchair,
If, in the blue and cold night of December,
I found her crouched in a corner of my chamber,
Grave, coming from the depths of her eternal bed
To look tenderly at the child grown from her maternal eye,
What could I reply to this faithful soul,
Seeing the tears fall from her hollow eyelids!

(Literal translation by M. M. C.)

6

With Baudelaire, came into poetry the civilized man of the cities, with the sort of life experience of the man of the cities, with the nervous reactions of one whose life is complicated with happenings, with people and with sufferings, with sorrow and sin. He dowered misery, sordidness, dissolution, with a beauty shocking to the vigorous, to the happy, the optimistic, to those accustomed to think that contemplating the bright side of things was alone worthy of a man. He sought for poetry in the story of the drunkard who had killed his wife, from the sight of a corpse rotting on the highway, a beggar girl, an old ragpicker livened by wine—"the people harassed with care, ground down by toil, plagued by old age." He told us their dreams when they escaped from misery through wine or sleep. He revealed death in all its shapes, the fear of death, the victory of death, the relief of death, the death of lovers, of the poor, of artists. He revealed love, if not in all its shapes, at least in more shapes than any single poet had ever done before. Assassins and damned women, beggars and vampires, and emotions and sensations, and even senses, that had never before appeared in poetry were in this single volume of his. It was indeed said of him that he had transfixed in his verse all sorts of fleeting states of mind and body, passing loves, fugitive melancholy, the fugitive loves and melancholies and joys of men and women who were not at all like the characters in the work of the older masters. In "La Passante" the poet meets a woman passing by in the street, meets her eyes for a minute, falls in love with her for a minute, and out of it he makes a poem of a moment that leaves an immortal mood. Opposite as his temperament and life were to Wordsworth's, many of his subjects are the exact city parallels of the rustic subjects that Words-

worth treated. Wordsworth has a meditation on the
country girl:

> Three years she grew in sun and shower;
> Then Nature said, "A lovelier flower
> On earth was never sown;
> This child I to myself will take;
> She shall be mine, and I will make
> A lady of my own.
>
> "Myself will to my darling be
> Both law and impulse; and with me
> The girl, in rock and plain,
> In earth and heaven, in glade and bower,
> Shall feel an overseeing power
> To kindle or restrain.
>
> "She shall be sportive as the fawn
> That wild with glee across the lawn
> Or up the mountain springs;
> And hers shall be the breathing balm,
> And hers the silence and the calm
> Of mute insensate things. . . .
>
> .   .   .   .
>
> "The stars of midnight shall be dear
> To her; and she shall lean her ear
> In many a secret place
> Where rivulets dance their wayward round,
> And beauty born of murmuring sound
> Shall pass into her face. . . ."

Baudelaire has a meditation on a girl of the city
streets.

FROM THESE ROOTS

A Une Mendiante Rousse

Blanche fille aux cheveux roux,
Dont la robe par ses trous
Laisse voir la pauvreté
    Et la beauté,

Pour moi, poète chétif,
Ton jeune corps maladif,
Plein de taches de rousseur,
    A sa douceur.

Tu portes plus galamment
Qu'une reine de roman
Ses cothurnes de velours
    Tes sabots lourds.

Au lieu d'un haillon trop court,
Qu'un superbe habit de cour
Traîne à plis bruyants et longs
    Sur tes talons;

En place de bas troués,
Que pour les yeux des roués
Sur ta jambe un poignard d'or
    Reluise encor;

Que des nœuds mal attachés
Dévoilent pour nos péchés
Tes deux beaux seins, radieux
    Comme des yeux;

Que pour te déshabiller
Tes bras se fassent prier
Et chassent à coups mutins
    Les doigts lutins

THE COMING OF THE REALISTS

Perles de la plus belle eau,
Sonnets de maître Belleau
Par tes galants mis aux fers
    Sans cesse offerts,

Valetaille de rimeurs
Te dédiant leurs primeurs
Et contemplant ton soulier
    Sous l'escalier.

Maint page épris du hasard,
Maint seigneur et maint Ronsard
Epieraient pour le déduit
    Ton frais réduit!

Tu compterais dans tes lits
Plus de baisers que de lis
Et rangerais sous tes lois
    Plus d'un Valois!

—Cependant tu vas gueusant
Quelque vieux débris gisant
Au seuil de quelque Véfour
    De carrefour;

Tu vas lorgnant en dessous
Des bijoux de vingt-neuf sous
Dont je ne puis, oh! pardon!
    Te faire don.

Va donc, sans autre ornement,
Parfum, perles, diamant,
Que ta maigre nudité,
    O ma beauté!

FROM THESE ROOTS

To a Brown Beggar-Maid

White maiden with the russet hair,
Whose garments, through their holes, declare
That poverty is part of you,
    And beauty too,

To me, a sorry bard and mean,
Your youthful beauty, frail and lean,
With summer freckles here and there,
    Is sweet and fair.

Your sabots tread the roads of chance,
And not one queen of old romance
Carried her velvet shoes and lace
    With half your grace.

In place of tatters far too short
Let the proud garments worn at Court
Fall down with rustling fold and pleat
    About your feet;

In place of stockings, worn and old,
Let a keen dagger all of gold
Gleam in your garter for the eyes
    Of roués wise;

Let ribbons carelessly untied
Reveal to us the radiant pride
Of your white bosom purer far
    Than any star;

Let your white arms uncovered shine,
Polished and smooth and half divine;
And let your elfish fingers chase
    With riotous grace

THE COMING OF THE REALISTS

The purest pearls that softly glow,
The sweetest sonnets of Belleau,
Offered by gallants ere they fight
　　For your delight;

And many fawning rhymers who
Inscribe their first thin book to you
Will contemplate upon the stair
　　Your slipper fair;

And many a page who plays at cards,
And many lords and many bards,
Will watch your going forth, and burn
　　For your return;

And you will count before your glass
More kisses than the lily has;
And more than one Valois will sigh
　　When you pass by.

But meanwhile you are on the tramp,
Begging your living in the damp,
Wandering mean streets and alleys o'er,
　　From door to door;

And shilling bangles in a shop
Cause you with eager eyes to stop,
And I, alas, have not a sou
　　To give to you.

Then go, with no more ornament,
Pearl, diamond, or subtle scent,
Than your own fragile naked grace
　　And lovely face.

(*Translation by F. P. Sturm.*)

FROM THESE ROOTS

The next quotations, where both poets write of seeing an old man on their morning's walk—Wordsworth on a country walk in the moors, Baudelaire in the city streets—show even more strikingly the likeness of the theme and at the same time the opposed temperaments of the two poets.

Les Sept Vieillards

Fourmillante cité, cité pleine de rêves,
Où le spectre en plein jour raccroche le passant!
Les mystères partout coulent comme des sèves
Dans les canaux étroits du colosse puissant.

Un matin, cependant que dans la triste rue
Les maisons, dont la brume allongeait la hauteur,
Simulaient les deux quais d'une rivière accrue,
Et que, décor semblable à l'âme de l'acteur,

Un brouillard sale et jaune inondait tout l'espace,
Je suivais, roidissant mes nerfs comme un héros
Et discutant avec mon âme déjà lasse,
Le faubourg secoué par les lourds tombereaux.

Tout à coup, un vieillard dont les guenilles jaunes
Imitaient la couleur de ce ciel pluvieux,
Et dont l'aspect aurait fait pleuvoir les aumônes,
Sans la méchanceté qui luisait dans ses yeux,

M'apparut. On eût dit sa prunelle trempée
Dans le fiel; son regard aiguisait les frimas,
Et sa barbe à longs poils, roide comme une épée,
Se projetait, pareille à celle de Judas.

THE COMING OF THE REALISTS

Il n'était pas voûté, mais cassé, son échine
Faisant avec sa jambe un parfait angle droit,
Si bien que son bâton, parachevant sa mine,
Lui donnait la tournure et le pas maladroit

D'un quadrupède infirme ou d'un juif à trois pattes.
Dans la neige et la boue il allait s'empêtrant,
Comme s'il écrasait des morts sous ses savates,
Hostile à l'univers plutôt qu'indifférent.

Son pareil le suivait: barbe, œil, dos, bâton, loques,
Nul trait ne distinguait, du même enfer venu,
Ce jumeau centenaire, et ces spectres baroques
Marchaient du même pas vers un but inconnu.

A quel complot infâme étais-je donc en butte,
Ou quel méchant hasard ainsi m'humiliait?
Car je comptai sept fois, de minute en minute,
Ce sinistre vieillard qui se multipliait!

Que celui-là qui rit de mon inquiétude,
Et qui n'est pas saisi d'un frisson fraternel,
Songe bien que malgré tant de décrépitude
Ces sept monstres hideux avaient l'air éternel!

Aurais-je, sans mourir, contemplé le huitième,
Sosie inexorable, ironique et fatal,
Dégoûtant Phénix, fils et père de lui-même?
—Mais je tournai le dos au cortège infernal.

Exaspéré comme un ivrogne qui voit double,
Je rentrai, je fermai ma porte, épouvanté,
Malade et morfondu, l'esprit fiévreux et trouble,
Blessé par le mystère et par l'absurdité!

FROM THESE ROOTS

Vainement ma raison voulait prendre la barre;
La tempête en jouant déroutait ses efforts,
Et mon âme dansait, dansait, vieille gabarre
Sans mâts, sur une mer monstrueuse et sans bords!

The Seven Old Men

Ant-hill city, city full of dreams,
Where the specter in broad daylight accosts the passer-by,
Everywhere mysteries flow like sap
In the narrow arteries of the powerful Colossus.

One morning, whilst in the sad street
The houses, whose height the fog steepened,
Were like the embankments of a river receded,
And which, a setting akin to the soul of the player,

A dirty yellow fog inundated, all the space,
I followed, steeling my nerves like a hero,
And holding speech with my soul, already wearied,
The purlieus shaken by the heavy wagons.

All at once an old man, whose yellow tatters
Imitated the hues of the rainy sky,
And whose looks would have made alms rain
Except for the villainy which gleamed in his eyes,

Appeared to me. One would have said that his eyeballs
    were steeped
In gall; his glance made keen the winter,
And his overgrown beard, stiff as a sword,
Protruded like the beard of Judas.

He was not bent but broken, his backbone
Making with his leg a right angle
So true that his stick, finishing his appearance,
Gave him the gait and awkward step

194

THE COMING OF THE REALISTS

Of a lamed quadruped or a three-legged Jew.
In the snow and the mud he went hobbling
As if he were stamping the dead under his old shoes,
Hostile to the universe rather than indifferent to it.

His fellow followed him—beard, eye, back, stick, tatters,
No sign made them different, come from the same hell,
These centenarian twins, these grotesque apparitions
Marched with the same step towards an unknown goal.

What infamous game was being played on me,
Or what mischievous chance thus humiliated me?
For I counted, minute to minute, seven times
This sinister old man multiplying himself.

Let any one who laughs at my uneasiness,
And who is not gripped with a sympathetic shiver,
Consider that in spite of so much decrepitude
These seven hideous monstrosities seemed immortal.

Would I have, without dying, looked on the eighth,
Inexorable, ironic, deadly counterpart,
Disgusting Phœnix, son and father of himself?
But I turned my back on the hellish procession.

Exasperated as a drunkard who sees double,
I turned home; I shut my door, affrighted,
Sick and benumbed, my spirit feverish and troubled,
Wounded by the mystery and the absurdity.

Vainly my reason strove to take the helm.
The tempest, frolicking, baffled its efforts,
And my soul danced, danced, an old hulk
Without masts, on a monstrous and shoreless sea.

(*Literal translation by M. M. C.*)

FROM THESE ROOTS

Wordsworth's old man is a leech-gatherer, and in his walk on a beautiful morning after a night of rain he sees the old man standing by a pool.

I thought of Chatterton, the marvellous Boy,
The sleepless Soul that perished in his pride;
Of Him who walked in glory and in joy
Following his plough, along the mountainside:
By our own spirits are we deified:
We Poets in our youth begin in gladness;
But thereof comes in the end despondency and madness.

Now, whether it were by peculiar grace,
A leading from above, a something given,
Yet it befell that, in this lonely place,
When I with these untoward thoughts had striven,
Beside a pool bare to the eye of heaven
I saw a Man before me unawares:
The oldest man he seemed that ever wore grey hairs.

As a huge stone is sometimes seen to lie
Couched on the bald top of an eminence;
Wonder to all who do the same espy,
By what means it could thither come, and whence;
So that it seems a thing endued with sense:
Like a sea-beast crawled forth, that on a shelf
Of rock or sand reposeth, there to sun itself;

Such seemed this Man, not all alive nor dead,
Nor all asleep—in his extreme old age:
His body was bent double, feet and head
Coming together in life's pilgrimage;
As if some dire constraint of pain, or rage
Of sickness felt by him in times long past,
A more than human weight upon his frame had cast.

* * * * * * * * * * * * *

THE COMING OF THE REALISTS

At length, himself unsettling, he the pond
Stirred with his staff, and fixedly did look
Upon the muddy water, which he conned,
As if he had been reading in a book:
And now a stranger's privilege I took:
And drawing to his side, to him did say,
"This morning gives us promise of a glorious day."

. . . .

He told, that to these waters he had come
To gather leeches, being old and poor:
Employment hazardous and wearisome!
And he had many hardships to endure;
From pond to pond he roamed, from moor to moor;
Housing, with God's good help, by choice or chance;
And in this way he gained an honest maintenance.

The old Man still stood talking by my side;
But now his voice to me was like a stream
Scarce heard; nor word from word could I divide;
And the whole body of the Man did seem
Like one whom I had met with in a dream;
Or like a man from some far region sent,
To give inhuman strength, by apt admonishment.

. . . .

While he was talking thus, the lonely place,
The old Man's shape, and speech—all troubled me:
In my mind's eye I seemed to see him pace
About the weary moors continually,
Wandering about alone and silently.
While I these thoughts within myself pursued,
He, having made a pause, the same discourse renewed.

. . . .

These poems, while characteristic of the minds of the authors, contain some lines that are examples of the famous prosiness of which both have been accused. In Wordsworth's case that prosiness came from a commonplace streak in his mind, from a wingless literalness, from a didacticism, from the Country Curate temperament that sometimes dominated his faculties as it dominated his existence; it also came from an occasional undue application of his formula for language. In Baudelaire's case the accusation arises from a conventional attitude in the reader's mind, and this is based on the fact that some of his poems present a picture deliberately filled in with details like the details on a Dürer woodcut, for as the French critic Charles Du Bos has pointed out he executed an engraving with words.

It must be repeated that Wordsworth and Baudelaire were the oustanding poets of the nineteenth century who made poetry out of the people and spectacles that every-day life presented, so that some of their readers, used to the older content of poetry, sometimes had difficulty in believing that their work was poetry at all. As with the poet-dramatists, it was humanity itself and the souls of men and women that stirred their imagination: they were poet-psychologists, "with a greater knowledge of human nature and a more comprehensive soul than are common." Wordsworth, to be sure, like all the great English poets, sometimes made an ascent into a region where the ordinary man could get little foothold, but when Baudelaire took flight into the upper air he peopled it with the nerves and emotions of humanity; he gave a tongue to senses, to anguishes and ennuis that until then had been voiceless. At least one half of Wordsworth's verse is of little value as poetry and might have been composed by a country curate with a turn for versifying and moralizing on life. There is not a single line of Baudelaire, with the exception of one experiment in conversational verse, that is not sheer poetry. He was the first of the poets who deliberately eliminated from poetry anything that he thought might be just as well or almost as well expressed in prose. All his work is of such density and intensity that it seems as if a world of concentrated thought and emotion went into every verse, even every line. Into that one book of poetry he put the essence of his mind: truly enough he believed that a man could put all of himself into one or two books; in comparison with him, as with Catullus, other poets seem intolerably long-winded. Put within the covers of one book, as was done by Matthew Arnold, Wordsworth gives a more real impression of the great poet that he was than in his collected works.

7

Almost the whole of modern poetry has sprung from roots dug up to the common sight by these two oddly affiliated poets, Baudelaire and Wordsworth, so apart from each other in temperament, environment and life experience; almost the whole of it has come out of territory explored by them, out of theories evolved by them, and from the special sort of revolt their work led to. It is well to remind those who figure them as apart from each other in time that when Baudelaire was writing *Les Fleurs du Mal,* Wordsworth was Queen Victoria's laureate. And as to the much-publicized influence of Edgar Allan Poe on Baudelaire, as far as the poetry is concerned there is not much reason to take it into serious consideration. A resemblance can be pointed out to some of Poe's poems, as for instance to "Ulalume," the poem beginning—

> The skies they were ashen and sober;
> The leaves they were crispèd and sere,
> The leaves they were withering and sere;
> It was night in the lonesome October
> Of my most immemorial year.

Or to certain lines of "Dream-Land," or of "The City in the Sea." We know that the greater part of *Les Fleurs du Mal* was written before Baudelaire had any acquaintance with the work of Poe, for the book was already announced for publication twelve years before it actually appeared, that is in 1845, and it is not till a year or two later that we have any record of Baudelaire's reading Poe. Though all the poems that finally appeared in *Les Fleurs du Mal* were not finished at that early date, yet many of the most striking were, and some had been given magazine publication.

Baudelaire has left a record of the effect on his mind of his first encounter with the work of Poe. In a letter to a friend, one Armand Fraisse, he wrote, "In 1846 or '47 I made the acquaintance of a few fragments of Poe; I experienced a strange excitement. His complete works having been collected in a single edition only after his death, I took the trouble of making myself acquainted with Americans living in Paris, so that I might be able to borrow collections of journals that had been edited by Edgar Poe. And then I found, believe me if you will, poems and tales of which I had had the thought, vague and confused and badly arranged, and which Poe had been able to combine and bring to perfection." As is well known, Baudelaire translated the *Tales* and thus brought into French literature a whole new influence. We can truly say that if Baudelaire had written tales or short stories they would have been akin to Poe's. We can also say that what might be termed the Poetic Principles of both had many points in common, though Poe's idea of the content of poetry was conventional and traditional when compared with that of Baudelaire, who had the large variety of emotions, the extensive communication with life, of the very great poets.

But Poe's æsthetic, as defined in "The Poetic Principle," might conceivably have been known in French literary circles long before his general work, and if so, it certainly influenced Baudelaire in his conception of poetry, and all the more so as his mind was already working in the same direction. Poe had come out strongly and sensationally against the long poem, maintaining definitely that the phrase "a long poem" was a contradiction in terms; the value of a poem lay in its elevating excitement, and as all excitements are, through a psychical necessity, transient, no excitement could last all through a long poem. The poem should be written for the poem's sake, regardless of how the result affected readers. This is very like what Baudelaire, who never wrote a long poem, has said about poetry. He had the same abhorrence of a didactic element, the same belief in the importance of music, for the preoccupation with the music of verse was very intense with both poets. "Music," Poe said, "in its various modes of meter, rhythm and rhyme, is of so vast a moment in poetry that he is simply silly who declines its assistance." And Baudelaire was not only concerned with the musical structure of lines, but with the interior music of words. "Any poet," he wrote, "who does not know exactly what rhymes each word allows, is incapable of expressing any idea whatever. The poetic phrase (and in this it touches the art of music) can imitate the horizontal line, the straight line ascending and the straight line descending. . . . It can express every sensation of sweetness or bitterness, of bliss or of horror, by coupling such a noun with such an adjective, analogous or opposite." And these two poets had similar notions of what constituted the beautiful: Poe believed that a certain taint of sadness is "inseparably connected with all the higher manifestations of true beauty"; and Baudelaire defined beauty as "something ardent and sad, something slightly vague, giving conjecture wing. . . . Mystery, regret, are also characteristics of beauty. . . . Mystery, and finally, let me have the courage to confess to what degree I feel myself modern in æsthetics, misfortune. . . . I can scarcely conceive a type of beauty in which there is no misfortune." Here it may be noted that the title of his book, *Les Fleurs du Mal,* might with just as much accuracy be translated "Flowers of Misfortune."

Like Poe, Baudelaire believed that the supernatural was a fundamental literary quality, but to this he added others of which Poe was incapable—irony, macabre humor, qualities few poets other than Baudelaire and Swift have ever got into poetry. On the whole, it has to be said that Poe's influence on Baudelaire's successors, especially on Verlaine and Mallarmé, was greater than ever it was on Baudelaire himself. Baudelaire's intense sympathy and admiration for Poe, a similarity in some of their experiences, in their misfortunes, their poverty, their pursuit of artificial paradises through drugs and drink, a similar breaking away from old literary and social traditions, have caused their names to be joined. But Poe made no such experiments with life as did Baudelaire, who pursued exotic experiences and emotions, whose mind and senses registered a hundred responses to the most common incidents of life, whose senses had a score of points of contact where the average man has only one, and even great poets not many more. The acuteness of his senses and his nerves, his undoubted touch of manic depressiveness, his somewhat pathological concern with remorse, with death, his ennui, his obsession with the tedium of existence, his melancholies, are responsible for the popular attitude towards what was called "la folie Baudelaire." The terrible complexities of a civilization that had grown without the control of man, and without consideration of him, as registered on the mind of one who was one of the most subtle products of that civilization, were expressed in his verse. As both the product and the victim of such a civilization, he expressed its miseries and its despairs at every point at which he touched them, the natural miseries and despairs like death and disaster and balked love, the unnatural ones like corruption and vice, and with them the escape, the search for artificial paradises.

Baudelaire's special use of the word "artificial" has been commonly and perhaps deliberately misunderstood. By it he meant simply a creation of art in contradistinction to the creations of nature. In this he was at the opposite pole from Wordsworth, for whom the artificial was something not only contrary to what was natural but inferior to it. For Baudelaire, to whom the Church's doctrine of original sin was one of the profound ideas that enabled one to understand the universe, the artificial was a discipline by which one improved on nature. He had none of the eighteenth century's belief in the natural goodness of man. Good, he thought, was always the product of art, whereas evil was done naturally without effort. "Analyze," he said, "all that is natural, all the actions and desires of the natural man, and you will find nothing but what is horrible." Virtue for him was artificial and supernatural. Out of his belief in this duality, good and evil, he wrote that sentence since adopted into the philosophy of Paul Valéry and embodied in one of his greatest poems, "Ebauche d'un Serpent": "What is the Fall? What is meant by the Fall? It is unity become duality, it is God who has fallen. In other words, is not creation the Fall of God?"

> Comme las de son pur spectacle,
> Dieu lui-même a rompu l'obstacle
> De sa parfaite éternité;
> Il se fit Celui qui dissipe
> En conséquences, son Principe,
> En étoiles, son Unité.
>
> Cieux, son erreur! Temps, sa ruine!
> Et l'abîme animal, béant! . . .
> Quelle chute dans l'origine
> Etincelle au lieu de néant! . . .

Baudelaire's philosophy, though it included belief in God and, in a bizarre fashion, belief in the Church and the Church's doctrine, was one of profound and even perverse pessimism. Yet no poet has produced a book more profoundly philosophical in the sense of being a vast meditation on life and man and man's miserable fate in the universe, none has produced a book more under the guidance of the intellect, the intellect interwoven with the senses and the emotions. In sheer modernity, expressing the modern world and modern pessimism, no book written since has gone beyond it. It was the first in that genre to which the bulk of the great modern books, whether in verse or in prose, belong— the literature of memory. It was a complete confession, in essence, of all that life, art, love, despair, ennui, had done to a modern man of the subtlest emotions and senses, who could not feel or think except in a complex manner. When he loved, his love had not only, like Catullus's, a mixture of hate, but of a score of other emotions. His concern with life was suffused with a perpetual concern with death; his love of goodness was mixed with a perpetual desire to experiment with evil. Some of his perverse opinions were undoubtedly due to a desire to *épater le bourgeoisie,* or else to that vast ironic attitude, in life and in art, which is the last gift or curse of the gods for the too subtly civilized. The title of his book, *Les Fleurs du Mal,* was adopted with a mixture of irony and of a desire to shock, while at the same time he permitted himself to believe that this provocatively titled volume would bring him and the publisher fame and fortune. Previously he had considered other titles, such as "Les Lesbiennes," "Les Limbes," which were equally calculated to disturb the average reader, and which were even more unrepresentative of the contents of the book as a whole. A friend finally suggested "Les Fleurs du Mal," but as far as the contents were concerned, "Fleurs de Beauté" would have been more accurate.

The provocative title, on a work published in the middle of the nineteenth century, in itself invited attack, though even without the label the courts would probably have prosecuted the author, on religious and moral grounds, for some of the contents. Flaubert got freed by the courts because, after all, there was really nothing in *Madame Bovary* that was uncommon or abnormal, but the sins to which some of Baudelaire's poems were devoted, like "Les Femmes Damnées: Delphine et Hippolyte," "L'Une Qui Est Trop Gaie," were abnormal, and "Le Reniement de Saint Pierre" was regarded as blasphemous. While the prosecution of *Madame Bovary* was the result of nineteenth-century Puritanism, the prosecution of *Les Fleurs du Mal,* or at least the demand for the withdrawal of certain of the poems, was based on a profound instinct of men— the desire to hold on to the slowly and painfully constructed plan of life that humanity has evolved for itself. It is but fair to realize that there can be two attitudes towards a work of art, the attitude of the artist and the attitude of the moralist. A work may be entirely justified in the eyes of the artist and the critic, yet seem unjustifiable to a large section of the people. It is these two attitudes that will be considered in the next chapter.

Chapter Seven

THE TWO CONSCIENCES

I

LITERATURE, like every other art, is produced for a minority of the human race; the masses in any country have no great direct interest in it because they have neither the time nor the vitality, apart altogether from the question as to what proportion of the people have the intellectual or emotional equipment for understanding any art. The vitality of men in the mass is engaged primarily in all the activities and organizations and labors connected with that major concern of humanity, handing life on to others. They are so busy trying to live, trying to earn the necessities, real or imaginary, connected with providing a home and the rearing of offspring, that they have little energy left over for the comprehension of life or of any art. They make the most of what forms of life or art come their way, provided these do not make too great demands on them, preferring those that either give entertainment and recreation, or are a help in the management of their lives. The mass of men, now as always, prefer forms of art related to spectacles, pageants and dramas, such as are given in theatres, or arenas. In certain periods and in certain countries, like ancient Greece or Shakespearian England, the people were better conditioned to the understanding of art, or else were less spoiled and worn out by their occupations, so that the drama produced was great literature written for a people who demanded it and understood it.

Art is the direct concern of only a minority in any country, and it is for this minority that all the books are written, all the pictures painted, and all the music made. There is nothing strange about this: all high products of the human mind, whether science or philosophy or theology, are for minorities and interest the majority only as something that will either amuse them or help them, with the difference that from science they demand some form of material help, from art or literature, as from religion or philosophy, some form of immaterial help—from the one, something for the body; from the other, something for the spirit. Sheer disinterestedness in the pursuit of these occupations is not of any great import to them, for they are engaged in "making the world go round," in the simple living of physical life or that part of it which can be lived according to anybody's potentialities and opportunities. No one can, with any conviction, set about saying whether the majority or the minority is more important in what is termed "the final scheme of things." One only asks that the labors of each be recognized in their place and importance and according to their own rules and laws.

Man, however, to whom material things have such tremendous importance, has nevertheless decided that the human achievements most worthy of remembrance come from the spirit, and these are what the race really values—indeed, it is these that set up the ideal values by which other values are measured. These spiritual achievements are attached to or spring from religion, art, philosophy. Though art and religion and art and philosophy have frequently worked hand in hand, there has never been a time when morals, which is both a branch of religion and a branch of philosophy, has not been at loggerheads with art. This is simply stating that the two main consciences of the human race, the ethical conscience and the æsthetic conscience, contemplate man from standpoints which are often completely incompatible: the ethical conscience contemplates the human passions as moral qualities, the æsthetic conscience, as an array of poetic and psychological powers. The ethical conscience evaluates man not only as a creature of abstract vices and virtues but by the manner in which he fits himself into society and obeys the rules that society has formed for the convenient and orderly arrangement of living; it summarizes man as good or bad, virtuous or vicious, as he keeps these rules and laws and codes. The æsthetic conscience summarizes man as a creature of passions and aspirations the history of which is the history of life itself. Naturally enough, more people understand the ethical conscience in its ordinary every-day manifestation than understand the æsthetic conscience in any manifestation. A man who keeps conscientiously the laws and codes may seem to the every-day ethical conscience a virtuous person, yet the same man may conceivably appear, when viewed by the æsthetic conscience, a very poor creature indeed, bereft of all psychological interest. Morals are the fruit of the ethical conscience, art of the æsthetic conscience; each has its own rules, and while in actual practice neither ethics nor art can be at all times judged exclusively by its separate laws, just as nothing in life can be so judged, it is the desire of every artist that his work should be judged by purely æsthetic laws.

Life is the subject of all the arts, but literature more than any of the others has the power to express life and to be the history of life and human relations. As no definition of literature can be fully explanatory, no apology is made for the numerous definitions or explanations or repetitions that are scattered through these pages. Literature is not, as many professors of it assume, the history of the moral laws man has evolved, or of the regulations he has invented for the control of the passions. It is not the history of the best that has been known and thought in the world: it is, as far as possible, the history of everything that has been known and thought in the world; it is the attempt of man to express all human experiences that have inherent in them sufficient emotion, imagination, vitality to make them significant. All the arts, of course, are an attempt to express human experience, everything that the race and the individual have undergone, but the other arts are limited by the nature of their medium. Brass and marble, paint and canvas limit the life of the work of art expressed in them to the life of the medium; the picture can live only as long as the canvas it is painted on; the sculpture and the monument as long as the marble or the bronze they are made of. But literature is made with words and sounds and these, once recorded, can endure to the limits of time. The artist who chooses to express himself in words has chosen, not only an everlasting medium, but the one most universally understood. Of all the arts it alone is unlimited and has in itself the potentiality of revealing the whole history of man—his emotions, his passions, his longings, ordered or disordered, tutored or untutored, good or bad.

Such a history of life is both disinterested and interested—disinterested in that it is a search for truth, as science is. Its authors are under the necessity of regarding as psychological forces and poetic powers those human passions that are the pivots around which their history moves; they do not regard them merely as moral qualities, in the manner of theologians or moralists. This history of life which is literature is, on the other hand, interested in that it is colored, re-created, re-arranged according to the personality, temperament, intellectual and emotional powers of the recorder. Every work of genius is a new creation, as every human being is, made up of elements of which the material—that is, the external life which the author had to deal with— is one element, and the other the author's individual mind.

2

Art includes both the material and the manner in which the material is worked and used. The most luminous and, at the same time, the most practical definition of art is the one abstracted from scholastic philosophy by the French philosopher Jacques Maritain—"Recta ratio factibilium," which may be freely rendered into English as the right ordering, or the right arrangement of the work to be done or the thing to be made. A book by a popular ephemeral writer might be concerned with the same material as a work by Flaubert or Tolstoy or Hardy, but would not, on that account, be comparable to the work of these great artists, for the popular writers in general have not the emotional, intellectual, or imaginative power to accomplish the right arrangement, the right revelation of the material. In addition to not having the power to produce a work of art, the bulk of the popular writers have not that aim: themselves and their work carefully looked into, it will be found that their aim is to produce a salable article which, in addition to bringing them money, may bring amusement, a sense of well-being, or even of moral uplift, to their readers. It would be difficult to think of such authors producing a work which would not be in response to the desire of a great number of people and agreeable to them in manner and treatment.

On the other hand, it may happen that an artist like Baudelaire, wishing to transmute into poetry his responses to life, to the life he felt urged to live and express, will find that, for the right revelation of the material, he may have to express emotions disagreeable or even shocking to a number of people. Similarly, an artist wishing to create a character like, for example, that of Mrs. Bloom in *Ulysses* may find that for the perfection of his creation, for the right revelation of the character, he has to give her lines of thought and a vocabulary also disagreeable, or even shocking, to a great number of people—so shocking, in fact, that the book is banned in many countries, even though it has attained that highest virtue in the work of an artist, the right revelation of the material. In the case of *Les Fleurs du Mal,* six poems were ordered to be excised by the court. With these cancelled, Baudelaire was still violently attacked for expressing emotions and sensations shared by a great number of human beings.

It can happen also that an artist, a man with a gift for producing a work of art, may, through desire for money or popularity, deliberately omit from his work qualities that are necessary for the right revelation of the material. In that case he is doing what is called prostituting his art, producing something for the greatest entertainment of the greatest number, or pandering to their prejudices.

Often a work of art needs no fight whatever against received ideas or prejudices; opposing received ideas or accepted moralities is, in itself, no sign of originality or artistry; it may in fact be a sign of weak-mindedness or neuroticism. The originality of a work of art is in the material, the ideas, and the just expression of them. The material, the arrangement, and the final form are all inseparably bound together; not the matter alone, or the form, or the style, but all together make a work of literature.

A work of literature is not destined for such or such a particular end, or for such or such a common good of humanity; it is not meant to serve the greatest good of the greatest number; it is its business simply to express the piece of life the author knows or understands, or has discovered, or can reveal. As a scientist cannot be turned away from the pursuit of truth in his discovery, let us say, of the nature of time or the nature of man because he happens to be confronted with the idea that existing knowledge will receive a dangerous shock or existing notions will be dangerously uprooted, so an artist cannot allow himself to be turned from the pursuit of truth as he sees it by the notion that the way he sees it is not for the happiness or the well-being of his fellow men. He has to make his work as sincere and as fine as he can, without allowing other provinces of human achievement to shove their laws or rules onto him. Pure literature, therefore, can never be propaganda, for propaganda is the turning aside of literature from the expression of life, which is its field, to the praise or advertisement of some policy, some endeavor, some side line of life, which may represent a public good. It is the subjection of one form of human endeavor to another, and frequently in practice is the submission of men of mind to men of action. Some great literary artists have applied themselves to propaganda of a kind and become pamphleteers, but it is not for the object of the propaganda they are remembered but for some revelation of life that they could not help but give. The right of any artist to work according to the eternal laws of his art does not at all imply that any public, if it is so moved, cannot criticize harshly, and condemn as much as it pleases, a work of art. The right of the public to condemn the work of an artist is as valid as the right of the artist to produce it, but no more valid. No public or law ought, in a civilized country, to have the right to suppress or destroy a work of art, although it has the right to censure and condemn it, or even, in cases, to limit its circulation.

In the case of *Les Fleurs du Mal,* the order of the court to excise from the next edition particular poems, six of them, might be regarded as justifiable from the point of view of the general public and its *mores.* But what really aroused hostility to the book was not these incidental poems but the whole startling newness in literature of the material that the author welded into poetry. He was attacked most frequently for expressing emotions and tendencies, nervousnesses and morbidities, transitory movements of the soul, common to at least half of mankind.

Works of art are attacked by the general public for one thing mainly—freedom or frankness in treating matters connected with sexual relations. They are commonly attacked by philosophers and theologians if they display subversive tendencies in politics or religion. Sometimes they are attacked for what is called false logic, from the idea that what is logically sound or dialectically proved must be true in life—an idea contradicted by experience. However, most of these attacks and criticisms are perfectly legitimate. The public in all periods has objected to descriptions of emotions connected with sexual relationships, and for the psychologically sound reason that for only a small proportion of the human race has the sex relation in itself been a poetical and transforming experience. The vast majority think, and have always thought, that all manifestations of sex love, except such as take place within legal or conventionally arranged bonds, represent an undignified, if not a low form of animal life, and that sex is a dignified experience only when settled down and veiled with domestic affection, with a legal relationship for the woman and children. As nudity was supposed to suggest sex, nudes have been very generally disapproved of. One must remember that Michelangelo's statue of the naked young David was as gravely attacked in the Italy of his time as any piece of frank contemporary art by Anglo-Saxon Puritans.

Man has arrived but slowly at the conception of love, as he has arrived but slowly at thought, and only a minority understands either one or the other of these, the most ecstatic and at the same time the most profoundly mournful experiences of humanity. Every one has the right to defend his own comprehension or lack of comprehension of them, the ordinary man as much as the artist or thinker. If the artist has a right to choose any material he wishes and the right to employ every means he can to make a lasting thing and to defend it, the public also has the same right to defend what it has made, its rules and regulations for the convenient conduct of life. One must remember that there are many battles to which there can be no end, which in their very nature must be perpetual. There have to be such conflicts; if there were not, the world would become static and in a static world both art and morality would lose their meaning.

Chapter Eight

THE RUSSIAN CONTRIBUTION TO
REALISM

I

IN THE MIDDLE of the nineteenth century realism was
definitely in the public domain and it still had half
a century or so of inspiration-giving power before it
grew away from the men of genius and down to the
men of talent. One must remember, however, that
realism in literature was in the main limited to that
comparatively new form, the novel, and to the drama:
realism in poetry, what there is of it, is in descent from
Wordsworth and Baudelaire; it made but limited headway, though in our own time it has influenced several
schools of poetry. Making poetry out of every-day life,
making it realistic, was always destined to be a rare
achievement, attainable in the isolated poems of a few
poets. The literary genre that was easiest to make the
vehicle of the realistic doctrine was the novel, and so
it was the novelists, chiefly, who proceeded to put into
practice the Taine dictum—to note facts, to choose important and significant ones, and to circumstantiate

221

them fully. The author, in short, began to keep a notebook and to set down all his observations and experiences of every-day life, and from this notebook procedure came the bulk of our great realistic novels, short stories and plays. For a time, all other theories of art were displaced by this new one, which set out to show "real" life in literature. It was in vain that certain writers pleaded that other theories of art had at least equal validity and that which of them he gave allegiance to depended on the writer's temperament.

The doctrine of realism spread quickly from one literature to another until it took in all the literature-producing countries of Europe, with one great exception. Pure realism made little and spasmodic advance in England, where literature has always been predominantly romantic, or, to apply one of the terms that Zola used to denote a literature opposite to realism—idealistic. It would almost seem as if any other type of literature was alien to England, where the classicism of the eighteenth century was no more than an interregnum, and realism, with some few exceptions, something brought in by the outside writers of English, like the Irish or the Americans. It should be noted, however, that whereas George Moore is generally regarded as the first realistic novelist in English, actually the first realistic English novel written was Samuel Butler's *The Way of All Flesh,* which was not published until after the author's death. But the most romantic

THE RUSSIAN CONTRIBUTION TO REALISM

English literature always had enough common humanity to make a literary revolution uncalled for. In the highest realism there has to be romanticism, for that is natural to human life and human imagination.

Is it possible to give a definition of realism in literature? No single definition, of course, can be fully explanatory, but realism may be described as the attempt to give a reproduction of life as actually lived by the average person, or by what, in the author's experience, is the average person, and it was the natural accompaniment in literature of the new scientific discoveries that rocked the world in the nineteenth and the beginning of the twentieth century—in fact, the literary doctrine of the new material civilization which had been given the world by science. It was in the early nineteenth century that it first seemed credible that the experimental study of facts, of data, would in the end explain everything—man, nature, God and the universe—that it would not only explain everything but bestow everything humanity longed for—happiness, health, security. Facts, which began by being the matter of science, proceeded to become the matter of literature, and Taine with his doctrine of the "little facts" became, from about 1865, the most celebrated and influential of the legislators of ideas.

The great realists and semi-realists—Balzac, Gogol, Dickens, Thackeray, Flaubert, Turgenev, Dostoevsky, Tolstoy, Ibsen, Zola—were all living at the same time and were not too far apart in age; all of them, except Balzac, being born in the beginning of the nineteenth century, all of them, except Tolstoy and Zola, in the first quarter of it. It is safe to say that every one of them was influenced by Balzac, and that, in spite of differences of talents and temperaments, they have in common the desire to depict life as it presented itself to them, and men and women as they knew them. Balzac, Dickens and Gogol, the great semi-realists, had this intention, as well as the other realists, but when they sat down to write, the marvels and wonders of the world they could invent would sometimes sweep the every-day world from their minds, and the whims and oddities of the human beings with whom their imaginations teemed would overshadow the common every-day personages in their pages; they created worlds that touched the real world at points, some-times firmly, sometimes hardly at all, but which were more fascinating to their readers than the every-day world, giving them both the desired contact with it and a desired escape from it. In point of time, the earlier of the great novelists were the semi-realists, who carried over from older literary doctrine certain con-ventions of structure and character but who also pos-sessed a good deal of the abundance and extravagance of temperament characteristic of the romantic side of the movement. Balzac, Dickens and Gogol satisfied their minds and imaginations by putting things into their books in the excessive measure which it would have pleased them to find in actual life, and in this way they were related to the great romantics. Balzac's personages, their emotions and actions, were, as has been said in a previous chapter, exaggerated to the point of being larger than life. He patterned them on what he encountered in the real world, but he made them more gigantic, more marvellous. The characters of Dickens and Gogol, both writers of less tremendous genius than Balzac, were exaggerated, not in the sense of being made larger than life, but of being caricatured; they were given traits more grotesque, more humorous, more pathetic than actual people had. These three representatives of different literatures were all prodigious creators, men of indeliberate genius, not always careful in their workmanship, not always conscious of what they were doing, as were the bulk of the more thoroughgoing realists who came later. But the thorough realists, those who created people life-sized, were sometimes regretful that the Time-spirit, or their own temperament, trimmed their talents. "Some things," said Flaubert, "I can do better than Hugo; some better than Balzac; some better than Rabelais. But I lack their thrusts of power beyond the reach of conscious art."

2

Although realism spread rapidly through the literatures of Europe, there were two countries that stood out from the others in the production of the realistic novel—France and Russia. The French and the Russians, with marked differences in the type of novel they produced, became the masters of all the others; developments of the realistic novel, which might have been distinguished in many countries, were dwarfed by the achievements of the Russians, Turgenev, Dostoevsky, Tolstoy, and by the technique and the doctrines of the French. The new movement in literature, especially the realistic side of it, awoke Russia into conscious and extensive expression. The romantic side had little soil to take root in, although Byron and the German romantics had had their effect. It was about 1840 that Carlyle uttered his famous sentence, "Russia has not spoken," though, unknown to him, there had been several remarkable writers, including the great Pushkin. But when Russia finally spoke out strongly enough to make all Europe listen to her voice, it was with the tongue of realism. Turgenev, Dostoevsky, Tolstoy, with a bound, brought Russia and Russian psychology into the consciousness of Western Europe, and their names became household words and their works so widely read that people all over the world began to speak of the characters in their books, as they spoke of the characters in Dickens and in Balzac. Turgenev was a sort of half-way house to the comprehension of the others: he was half way between the French objective novel and the Russian analytical one. More Western in his outlook, he provided a halting-place for the mind before it could encompass Tolstoy and Dostoevsky, writers immensely different from those of the West. One who had read *A Nest of Gentlefolk,* or *On the Eve,* or *Smoke,* had, as it were, the necessary ground-work of Russian literature and psychology to get on with *The Brothers Karamazov,* or *War and Peace,* or *Resurrection.*

Russia, which had been regarded contemptuously as a barbarous country that could be symbolized by an English poet as "the bear that walks like a man," broke into expression, in the complacent Victorian age, in a startling manner. The Russians who were putting forth novels seemed not only men of vast imagination and intellectual powers, but the diversity and complexity of their emotions, their experience of life and humanity, the profound level at which they themselves had lived before writing at all, made the Western writers seem a little complacent, or, to use a word that was then generally coming in, bourgeois. They were, in addition, all melodramatic; none of them, not even Turgenev, had the Western objection to striking an emotion on its topmost note. Tolstoy, in *Resurrection* and *Anna Karenina,* could write scenes parallel to those in *L'Education Sentimentale,* or in *Madame Bovary,* with an intensity, with a pity mixed with moral ardor, with a high coloring, that made the Western novel seem too restrained. The Goncourts' complaint that language and literature had been made by men who were too healthy and well-balanced could never, after Dostoevsky, seem such a valid criticism as before, for the characters in his books were sick in body and mind, and a touch of madness seemed to the author to be the norm of humanity. His people felt no emotion in its singleness; they loved where they hated and hated where they loved; they were cruel and pitying, fearful and ecstatic, all at the same time. Yet whatever they felt they felt with such intensity, such diversity and complexity, that they seemed to embody all the emotions and fears of mankind.

The manner in which a modern literature began in Russia was parallel to the way it began in Germany, though the Russians had no such literary past as Germany, just as Germany had no such literary past as France, England, Spain, and Italy. The first great influence in starting a modern literature in Russia came from her great monarch Catherine, who corresponded to Frederick the Great in being one of the psychic forces that brought about the expression, in literature, of a nation. Like Frederick, Catherine wrote in French because the culture of her educated subjects, the culture of the aristocracy, was French. Like Frederick she was a great admirer of Voltaire, and like him also she encouraged pseudo-classical writing in imitation of the French, so that it was not surprising that in Russia, as in Germany before Lessing, literature and French classicism seemed almost interchangeable terms. But Catherine had a wider knowledge of Western literature than had Frederick; her mind was more open to the currents that were coming in; intellectually she belonged to a later age. She set up a corps of translators to put Western works into Russian, and she herself set about providing the Russian stage with a repertoire of plays from her own pen, imitating any playwright whose works came into her mind at the moment, Shakespeare, Molière or Voltaire. That her mind was more awake to the age that was coming in is shown by the fact that whereas Frederick had Voltaire at his court, Catherine had Diderot, to whom so many modern ideas can be traced. However, about the time of the French Revolution the Empress's ardor for things French dampened considerably, partly because of the effects of the Revolution, partly because, with all her Liberalism, she was an absolute monarch, and partly because a strong wind of ideas, ever increasing in force, was coming from Germany. The success of Lessing and Herder in ridding Germany of French classical and pseudo-classical influence, in initiating a new order of literary ideas, and in starting a German national literature, made itself felt in Russia, reinforcing the desire for a Russian national literature. Those two ideas of Lessing, then so fresh and vital, that literature was national and racial expression and that it should reflect contemporary life, quickly made headway in Russia and went in with the newborn Slavophile movement which was attracting the devotion of the young intellectuals and writers. Russian students in German universities returned with the works of the new German literature in their baggage, and, what was even more important, with the works of the philosopher Hegel.

Catherine herself lived long enough to hear of what was happening in Germany; she was a German herself. As she corresponded to Frederick, so the Russian critic, Belinsky, corresponded to Lessing, in the rôle he played in a dawning national literature. Without a knowledge of the Russian language we are in no position to appraise the importance that has been claimed for Belinsky in Russian thought and Russian progress generally. But there seems to be no doubt that his was one of the shaping minds of the nineteenth century. He held many conflicting literary theories from time to time, but the literature he understood thoroughly, by temperament, was the literature of realism. He knew that his was the age of realism in literature, and the literary form he understood and advanced was the novel. If the new national literature of Germany took shape in poetry and drama, the new national literature of Russia took shape in the realistic novel. Belinsky made no mistake in this: he knew that realism had an affinity with the Russian spirit; he had qualities by no means universal among important critics, a power of stirring up a ferment of creative activity and a sound sense of the value of the work produced in his own time. When Dostoevsky's first book, *Poor Folk,* written at the age of twenty-two, reached Belinsky's editorial desk, he saw, through all its faults, the great writer, the mighty genius, who was making his beginnings, and the enthusiasm of Belinsky's praise was said to have made the young Dostoevsky intolerably vain for a while.

Like all the men of outstanding mentality in the beginning of the nineteenth century, Belinsky's mind was roused by Hegel, and like most of them, he was able to find a backing in Hegel's philosophy for his own ideas, even when he switched from one line of thought to another. The Hegelian "concrete reality," the Hegelian "reality in experience" became for him the philosophic support of the literary doctrine of realism. Very familiar with the literature and literary doctrines of the West, he thoroughly accepted de Staël's conception of literature as an expression of society; like hers, his understanding of poetry, in spite of, in later life, an appreciation of Pushkin, seems to have been incomplete.

Belinsky gave the writers grouped around him a philosophy, ideas that roused their creative power and afforded a focus for their work. The dominating idea of his critical work was that reality, for a writer, was to be found in the life, the problems, the events, the people of his own time. It was a program that was

bound to have the maximum influence on his contemporaries. This critic was essentially a man of his
own time, understanding really, perhaps, only the tendencies, scientific, social and literary, that were potent
in his own time. He died before the century in which
he was born was half way through, having fostered
and cherished most of the great Russians of his day.
Belinsky's mind finally hardened into something very
like the conclusion that the function of literature was
to serve society and to help solve social and political
problems. This sort of attitude is really indigenous to
the Russian mind; afterwards, it reached its most noble
as well as its most absurd expression in Tolstoy's *What
Is Art?*, where all the literature that does not propa-
gate directly the ideal of human brotherhood is considered wanting and where the bulk of the great artists
of the time are arraigned because they do not conform
to the ideals of Tolstoy's later period. Belinsky's special
conception of the social function of literature, reinforced by Tolstoy's, grew to be a sort of canon with
a later school of writers and is the basis, with some even
the total doctrine, of what has come in our day to be
called "Marxist" literary criticism.

There have not been wanting recent Russian critics
who hold that the social doctrines of Belinsky were
mainly responsible for the decline of Russian literature
that came about after the passing of the great realists.
With them, the social doctrines had been mingled with

the moral doctrines of Christianity, especially with those that had to do with atonement and expiation, the equality of souls and the brotherhood of man. On such subjects, if he is a great genius, a writer can be didactic without any deep injury to his work, because invariably his power of giving spontaneous life to his characters is in the ascendant. The urge to be preachers, not uncommon in writers, was strong in the Russians. Even in the case of a great genius like Tolstoy, whose gift might be supposed to be powerful enough to carry it along, the didacticism is too evident, so that the second part of *Resurrection* reads like a tract dealing with atonement and expiation.

All the great Russian realistic novels—the very greatest are Turgenev's *Fathers and Sons,* Dostoevsky's *The Brothers Karamazov,* Tolstoy's *War and Peace*—came after *Madame Bovary,* but not one of them equalled it in technical perfection, or in the perfectly convincing feeling that real every-day life was being depicted; we believe in Flaubert's novel completely, from start to finish, as in something that has happened since the world began and will go on happening until its end. But in details the Russians made a deeper penetration into life, even if all around they were not so convincing. They were not hampered by Western conventions of life or art, and before they wrote their greatest work they had seen forms of life, experienced forms of emotion, closed to the Western mind. Life had touched them all at so many points before they set themselves to produce their masterpieces that, in comparison with their immense human experience, the bulk of Western writers seemed to have led the existence of small-town bourgeoisie.

The life around the Russian writers was touched with the barbaric, the savage and the cruel, yet all of them, in spite of serfdom and feudalism, particularly Tolstoy, gave the impression of being intimate with all sorts and conditions of men. They were so sensitized to experience that they gave the impression of feeling with their intellects and thinking with their hearts. Of Dostoevsky it has been said that he felt ideas as others feel cold or hunger or thirst: more than this, his senses responded to ideas as those of others did to passions. In his case, we wonder, not so much that he was psychopathic and subject to fits of epilepsy, as that he ever had the strength to assume the responsibilities of existence, the fortitude and endurance to work so hard and to produce so many masterpieces after his shaking experiences. The author of the first realistic novel, Flaubert, also an epileptic, lived a carefully guarded life, away from the battle, with an assured income on which to do his books and put his literary theories in practice; as he said himself, he knew life by tasting it a little and ruminating on it a lot. It was very different with the Russians; even Turgenev, the gentlest of them, gave to his French writer-friends the impression of a man with an immense background of experience. Dostoevsky had all the harassments that make up the life of a writer who lives by the sweat of his brain on advances from editors: he had to have work in at fixed periods and had not always time to write with careful art. In addition to disturbing if illuminating love affairs and two marriages, he spent years as a political prisoner in Siberia, having been at first condemned to death only to be reprieved at the last moment as he was standing in his shirt waiting to be executed. When he was in his teens his father had been murdered by serfs: this episode may have been responsible for his interest in murder, and the marvellous intuition in depicting incentives to murder, displayed in his two great books, *The Brothers Karamazov* and *Crime and Punishment*. With all this, he himself was subject to a practically uncontrollable temptation to gamble, to satisfy which he would sometimes pledge everything he and his wife had.

Tolstoy had as wide a life experience as Dostoevsky, though it went along different paths altogether. As a young man he lived a life not unlike Byron's and went in for what he conceived to be the natural existence of a young aristocrat, satisfying all his desires, which included women, drinking, gambling, and hunting. Being both more of a sensualist and more of a puritan than Dostoevsky, every passion satisfied brought sooner or later an immense moral crisis in his life. He fought through the Crimean War, where he was able to note all the psychological motives that possess men on the battlefield, motives which he afterwards developed into his great novel, *War and Peace.* A man of great genius and great atonements, he was composed of a number of contradictory personalities, but at the same time, as a writer, a leader, a prophet and a preacher, he was the most towering personality in modern literature.

3

The impact of the Russian novel had significant effects on Western literature; it saved the realistic novel, at its greatest period, anyhow, from becoming an indictment of mankind, an attack and a denigration. The discoveries of science had diminished man's place in the universe; Taine and the whole philosophy of determinism and materialism were situating him in the animal world; the later minor realists were bent on diminishing him more and more. But the immense sympathy and dynamic emotional characterization of the Russians, their faith in mankind in spite of sins, crimes and crazinesses, gave a new scope to the realistic movement, helped, in fact, to make it one of the really great movements in literature. Raskolnikoff, in *Crime and Punishment,* might be a half-crazed, hallucinated creature; Prince Muishkine, in *The Idiot,* might be a moron and an epileptic; the brothers Karamazov might be all deranged; but nevertheless they were subtle creations of the spirit, far above the brute-beasts to which the later realists degraded men and women. Tolstoy's heroes, the most realistic men in literature, were all conceived on a high plane, caring intensely for moral perfection and struggling unceasingly towards it; they were very different from the males of almost purely physiological reactions who came to be the standard characters in the decline of realism.

But it was not only the content and personages of the Russian novel that had a vast influence: the technique played a great rôle in the evolution of the present-day novel. The Russians knew French literature and French technical developments well; they not only read Balzac, Flaubert and Hugo, who were the vogue, but we know that Tolstoy studied the work of a writer whose vogue did not come in until much later, Stendhal, whose *Le Rouge et Le Noir* and *Chartreuse de Parme* influenced his *War and Peace*. Turgenev was an intimate of the great French realists, not only of Flaubert, but of the Goncourts and Zola. They took what they needed from the discoveries of the French realists, but what they took they gave back in new combinations. One outstanding characteristic, however, of the Western novel, its narrative construction, they treated with scant respect; the Aristotelian and classical ideal, that a work should have a beginning, a crisis and a conclusion, was no appreciable part of the Russian literary canon. Instead of rising to a crisis, as in *Madame*

Bovary, the Russian novels had a way of beginning with a crisis, and very often they had no conclusion in the Western sense at all. Then, instead of being all-knowing creators making disclosures about their characters, the authors gave the impression that their knowledge of the characters was not something fixed but something unfolding; they built them up with happenings, emotions and background, so that we got to know them gradually as we get to know people in life; in any chapter the personages might surprise us with something unexpected. Instead of description, the Russians, particularly Dostoevsky, went in for evocation—that is, instead of laying out before us the scene or the character, they evoked them in the manner since made familiar to us by very modern writers. All of them, but Dostoevsky markedly, dealt with the unconscious springs of action in personality in a new way: they were all, probably, aware of contemporary psychological findings, and Tolstoy shows in his books an acquaintance with the recent discoveries of the then well-known French psychologist, Charcot. The devices by which the subconscious groundwork of a personality is suggested, the psychological exploration taking the place of narrative development, the use of characters and episodes that had not much connection with the main theme but which revealed some spring of personality, and, finally, the inconclusive ending, all played a revolutionary part, for good or for ill, in the technique of the novel as we know it in our own day. But with all this, the primary influence, and the most widespread, remained that of Flaubert; the realistic novel in general so thoroughly kept to the Flaubert model, and especially to the pattern that is in *Madame Bovary,* that the modern novel, except as written by certain recent innovators, is, and has to be thought of as, the Flaubertian novel.

In less than half a century after the publication of *Madame Bovary* all the outstanding realistic novels had been written; the movement swept through the literatures of the world bringing the novel form into great popularity, a sort of popularity that often had but little to do with literary value. It is noticeable that the movement was in its decline, and that the reaction against it had set in, before the realistic novel had made its appearance in English. It is highly probable that Samuel Butler's *The Way of All Flesh* was the first written, in point of date, at the high mark of Flaubert's influence, but the first realistic novels actually given to the public were those of George Moore, who modelled his work by turns on Flaubert, the Goncourts and Zola. In America, the first realistic novel, Dreiser's *Sister Carrie,* did not appear until 1907.

Chapter Nine

THE DECLINE

A LITERARY PRINCIPLE is the sharp crystallization of a number of related impulses and tendencies and gropings towards a new kind of literary expression. No literary principle is ever new in the sense that it has not appeared in literature before in some subsidiary and unchallenging way. It is only that an age comes which picks out and focuses attention on a facet of expression that is suited to its needs. The principle of realism was the sharp crystallization into one point, of the impulses, tendencies and gropings towards the expression of every-day life and modern man. Romanticism and realism represented different groupings of the same related impulses; they did not represent disparate movements but were component parts of the same modern movement. A literary principle should not be confounded with literary opinions which, of necessity, are ephemeral; a principle is something lasting, in the sense that once it is developed it will always exist even though newer and later developed principles may bring about a revaluation of the older ones. Romanticism and realism, for example, which displaced in most modern literatures what was called classicism or pseudo-classicism, have implicit in them a great many of the characteristics and forms of the principles they had displaced. Romanticism, which has been defined as a form of literature in which lyricism dominates—this like every other literary definition is too limited—was merely emphasizing a tendency that was part of Greek classical literature, the lyric tendency. And the form of the bulk of the realistic novels, like the form of *Madame Bovary,* was classical; it followed the old classical formula with its beginning, its crisis, and its conclusion—the form of the old classical plays and the old tales. The plot on such lines, inherited from the older literature, started the notion that the realistic novel was not realistic enough. In the latter part of the nineteenth century the new realistic theorists declared that such a plot, that any plot, was an imposition upon the novel and the short story, and should not be used at all. The plot was actually an encumbrance, in revealing the life of an average human being. After all, it was maintained, the life of such a person has no great crises or excitements; he very seldom has a story; the story is merely a literary convention. The life of the average human being is generally only a string of banal events which have no particular consequences, none of the developments nor the coincidences which the novelist, even the realistic novelist, imposes on his characters. The real art of the novel and the short story should be to present every-day life, which is in the main mediocre, neither especially interesting nor uninteresting, more likely to be ugly than beautiful.

The matter proper to a novel should be "a slice of life," and this "slice" need not have beginning, middle or end, as ordinary careers have no real beginning, middle or end. Neither should this "slice" be about an extraordinary happening in the experiences of a character, since extraordinary happenings in life were so exceptional that to deal with them in literature would contravene the realistic effect. It would likewise be a great mistake to go in for writing about great emotions—ordinary people did not have them. The thing to do was to study scientifically the physical state which gave the impression or the illusion of an emotion. Remorse, for example, was not an emotion; remorse was a disease, and should be studied physiologically. There were a number of theorists who wanted love treated in the same way.

Some of the above theories or some facets of them were, of course, Flaubert's also, especially that concerning the avoidance in art of the extraordinary, of extraordinary people or extraordinary happenings. "I avoid," he said, "the accidental and the dramatic. . . . I try to stick to the greatest generalities; no extraordinary people, no heroes." But many of the realistic developments and the realistic theories he, as an artist, could never accept, for he looked upon them as something alien to art. Nearly twenty years after the publication of *Madame Bovary* he was roused to write: "I curse what they agree to call realism, though they make me one of its high priests. . . . The people that I see often [the Goncourts and Zola were his intimates] cultivate all that I scorn and are indifferently disturbed by what torments me. . . . I am seeking above all for beauty, which my companions pursue but languidly."

The truth was that already in the lifetime of the master the decline had set in. What was happening to the doctrine of realism is what happens to every idea once powerful in the world—it began at a high level, rose in the work of its greatest practitioners to a distinguished development; then it began to deteriorate to a type of writing that expressed only the side of people susceptible to external observation. Every new member of the realistic school—and some of them, to Flaubert, regarded as the founder of it, were not writers at all—developed a few theories of his own. The attaching to literature of scientific and medical theories went further and further. The neo-realists decided that the realism of *Madame Bovary* and *L'Education Sentimentale* was not scientific enough or physiological enough, though their author had devoured medical literature for all it could tell him of soul and body and their disorders, and though he had submitted all his characters to physiological and psychological examination. But Flaubert made no bones about saying that though he regarded accuracy in technical details, in local exactness, the precise side of things—in fact, observation—as important, yet it was only of secondary importance.

2

As the progress of the realistic novel followed the same path in every country, even in those countries where its appearance was comparatively recent, a general description of its course is applicable to every literature. The æsthetic on which the new literary doctrines were based, and which was displacing the old æsthetic of the beautiful, held that nothing human was alien to literature, and with this in the forefront of their minds the writers evolved more and more theories. The French were the most unmitigated theory-spinners and *nomenclateurs* of all. As soon as they evolved a theory they proceeded to attach a new name to it, with the result that any petty movement, in the shape of a reaction against realism or a development of it or a degradation of it, was given a new title, and new *isms* and *ists* were manufactured for every phase. "Things have to be given new names," Zola explained, "so that the public will think they are new," and this was said when he tried to replace the name Realism with the older name Naturalism. But every theory in connection with realism has had a persistent if fevered life and is in circulation all the time, for the reason that realism opened the way for a rush of people into writing who could previously have had no place at all there.

The general theorizing started with the question, What has not yet been expressed in literature? Among other things, it was obvious that, owing to the older ideals of the spiritual and emotional content of literature, the physiological side of man had not been given any great rôle, and that what were called "the lower classes" had had very little showing. After all, the neo-realists argued, one did not ordinarily meet doctors' adulterous wives or young gentlemen of independent means, any more than one met Walter Scott's heroes or heroines, or Balzac's millionaire misers. The ordinary person was none of these; the ordinary person was the working man or the working woman; the "fact," the great, the significant "fact" that the older realists were leaving out of account, was that ordinary life was the life of the greatest number; consequently, the proper subject for literature was the life of the populace, or, as we should name them in present-day parlance, the proletariat.

The Goncourts were the first experimenters in the proletarian novel, and Zola and his followers, in addition, set about revealing the physiological man, and what they called "the fœtid and palpitating sources of life." The Goncourts put forward both a literary and a social reason for tackling the working classes in literature. Living in the nineteenth century in a time of universal suffrage, of democracy, of liberalism, in a country without caste or legal aristocracy, could the people, they asked—the lower class, that world under a world—be ignored any longer by writers? Tragedy, an art form belonging to a dead society, might not in itself be dead. It might now, instead of dealing, according to the Aristotelian convention, with people above the common and with actions of magnitude—it might deal with the little miseries of the poor, in the new expanding form of the novel. The Goncourts made no pretense of thinking that their novels of the working class would be read by the working class—no, their novels of the *canaille* would let the upper classes know how the majority lived. As for themselves, they were, as they said, gentlemen, attracted—they surmised frankly enough—to lower forms of civilization as to something exotic; interested, by way of contrast to their own lives, in those of the *basses classes,* their radicalism, their working-class sympathy being, as it were, a reaction against their own genteelnesses and delicacies. As a relief from taking notes about the working classes and delving into facts, into real life, they took refuge, as another form of reaction, in the study of delicate Oriental art. They were very careful of their style, which they tried to make artistic and striking, experimenting with grammar, with phrases and sentences, to make language more suitable for expressing the sick, the miserable, the hallucinated, the debilitated people of modern life. Like all the other realists, they made perpetual appeal to science and demanded that the novel be "scientific," based on a careful study of facts and documents. They put into general circulation expressions such as "human document," "reportage," to describe the type of writing they would have take the place of the novel of romance and adventure and what they called "anodyne and consoling works."

Zola, the youngest of the first group of realists—he died at the beginning of the present century—enthusiastically attached himself to all these theories, and after stewing them around in his own mind, and adding a few more to them, put the lot forth in a form which is still popular and which we are likely to hear, in some shape, at all discussions of "proletarian" literature. He attached himself to Taine's literary doctrines, and took over Taine's particular psychological determinism; he believed that he was incorporating Taine's ideas in his practice of the novel, especially in the Rougon-Macquart series, in which he claimed to encompass "the natural and social history of a family under the Second Empire." This family was composed of the descendants of a neurotic and delinquent woman by a healthy husband and an alcoholic lover, and the volumes of the series were supposed to exhibit scientifically and clinically the effects of heredity and of "the race, milieu and moment."

More voluminously than any writer before or since, Zola filled notebooks with "the little significant facts, minutely noted and amply circumstantiated."

Taine had written a famous essay in which he had agreed with Balzac's own thesis that a novelist should deal with men and women as a naturalist with animals and plants, and he had put into currency the expression "naturalism" to describe this new practice of literature and the new literature itself. But with Zola the expression came to include things that had not gone into the Balzac *Comédie Humaine,* and especially the "physiological man." He considered himself Balzac's successor and accepted eagerly the conclusions that Balzac had extracted from Buffon, that there is only one animal, that man is a variety of it; therefore, the revelation of the human animal was the all-important affair for the new novelists, the naturalists. Given a puissant man, Zola postulated, and an unassuaged woman, the problem is to find the animal in them, even to find only the animal. Finding the animal in man soon came to be looked on as an end to be worked towards, and it was not long until the conclusion was reached that as the real man, the natural man, was the physiological man, the ultimate in naturalism was to be found, not in the lowest social and economic order, to which the great number belonged, but to the lowest moral order. To depict the lives of rudderless men and women, their miseries, their follies, their passions, "feeble but uncontrollable," to use a phrase of Doctor Carrel's, their vices, their trickery, their inability to cope with life except by ruses—this became one of the aims of the neo-realists. The more brutal, the more revolting, the facts, the more they dealt with the waifs and strays of society, the better material they were considered for literature.

The physiological man was deemed such an important subject that Zola annexed the realm of medicine to the novel, and as Balzac had attached his speculations to the discoveries in natural history and the animal realm of Buffon the naturalist, so Zola attached his speculations to the findings of the medical scientist, Claude Bernard. His gifts as a novelist entitle Zola to a place among the great realists, for when he got down to writing his talents got the better of his more extreme theories, yet in comparison with his great predecessors his intellectual and reasoning power was limited: his attempts to attach science to literature and to make literature scientific frequently resulted in fantastic conclusions, all of which, however, were swallowed eagerly by his followers. Claude Bernard had discussed experimental medicine; Zola proceeded to discourse on the experimental novel, attaching to it all the phraseology that Bernard had used about medicine, and announcing, "Since medicine, which is an art, is becoming a science, why should not literature also become a science, by means of the experimental method? . . . We naturalistic novelists submit each fact to the test of observation and experiment." The novelist experimented on dangerous sores that were poisoning society; in the same way as the "scientific" doctor he tried to find the initial causes. By pursuing this method the realists would construct in time what Zola called a "practical sociology" and their work would be an aid to political and social science; they would thus be "among the most useful and the most moral workers in the human workshop." Finally, he summed up what was to be the result of this moral work—"to regulate life, to regulate society, to solve in time all the problems of Socialism . . . when society becomes putrified, when the social machine gets out of order, the rôle of the observer and thinker is to note each new sore, each unexpected shock. . . . We are living in the ruins of a world, our duty is to study the ruins."

It was in vain, as far as Zola's followers in every country were concerned, for gentlemen in the higher courts of literature to maintain that devotion to such subjects was not likely to result in literature—his followers for the most part were not much concerned about literature, anyhow. Zola went ahead. He uttered pronunciamentoes in a style imitated from Taine's more dramatic declarations. "Finding the formula of the thing" was one of Taine's well-known approaches to the solution of difficult problems, and this, together with the observation of the "little facts," was assumed by his disciples to be a technique for solving riddles of all kinds as well as illumining obscurities. Zola cast around for a formula that would describe the new literature and make its aims clear: he said he had extracted it or evolved it from a reading of *L'Education Sentimentale*. "Naturalism," he announced, "is a formula of modern science applied to literature." This was received as an illumination and it had the advantage that it could be re-arranged, without changing it much, to fit any new notions that might come in. His German disciples were soon able to improve on the famous definition. In Germany, French influence, which Herder and Lessing had banished, came back with a rush; Flaubert, Maupassant, Zola—all the French realists —made a new conquest of German literary thought, as they did of Italian literary thought, but no writer rose out of it who could be compared with the great French or Russian realists. It was noticeable that the German trend, for the most part, was towards Zolaism and naturalism, the Italian trend towards Flaubertian realism. The manifesto of the Italian realists—they called themselves the Verists—put forward by Giovanni Verga, was completely derived from Flaubert.

In Germany, along with the influence of the new scientific discoveries, there was being developed a sort of scientific sociology and political economy, all owing much to English and French thought. The outstanding figures connected with these developments were Lasalle and Marx, and, affected by these, Zola's German followers were able to recast the formula; it became in turn a formula of modern sociology or a formula of modern politics applied to literature. Except for Gerhardt Hauptmann, whose work, however, belongs more closely to our own time, the bulk of the German realists were minor practitioners of Zola's doctrine, and their work suffered, to quote Professor J. R. Robertson, from a "too exclusive application to the lower life of the great cities and from a tendency to exploit the proletariat in the interest of radical political doctrine." That Zola himself was familiar with the Communist Manifesto and the writings of Engels and Marx on the class struggle in France, and on the new materialism, is clear from the enthusiastic if somewhat hashed version of their doctrine which he was able to attach to his conception of the naturalistic novel. He hated not only the bourgeoisie but the socially ascendant classes of all kinds; only the workingman, the proletariat, the people, had virtue, goodness and true appreciation; the upper classes were wicked, cruel, obtuse, without real understanding. As he usually did, he forgot such theories when he sat down to write, and he has left delineations of the working class and the peasants that are devastating. Nevertheless, he was for every political idea that had for aim the augmenting of the people's power.

Zola's convictions were powerful, more powerful than his reasoning powers, his sympathies warm and generous; he was for everything that he believed would tend towards the general good. His political and social passions—he was a republican, a socialist, a communist, and an anti-cleric, in the fashion of these things sixty years ago—his discourses on how writing could help society were at least as responsible for his large following as were the literary value of his novels, the lyricism and imaginative power of which were beyond the appreciation of a good portion of his public. It was the very part of his theories that flew away from him when he started to write his novels, that had the widest influence. The influence continued unabated; it passed from one country to another, becoming tied up with all the radical and socialist movements; it reached writing in English only in our own time, and it is within the last twenty-five years that these doctrines have been brought to America by European radicals.

3

The British Islands were almost immune to these particular literary doctrines, which scorned the supernatural, the mystical and the mysterious—all those hidden worlds of thought, the expression of which had been the glory of English literature. These doctrines, materialistic, physiological, sociological, had ardent welcomers, however, among the ranks of a type of writer who was coming in. With the spread of elementary education, the development of capitalism and industrial life, this type catered to the newly literate readers. The new type of writer had for the most part no interest in literature as an art; writing for him was a trade like any other trade; it was utilitarian; it served the definite purpose of amusing people or of instructing them, of conveying opinions of all kinds and propaganda for social and political doctrines. This type of writer, in fact, belonged to none of the old orders.

In the past, before the industrial age, a writer was either an artist, a scholar or a pamphleteer: a man entered writing rather as a vocation than as a means of earning a living; in fact, of all the arts, literature was the least likely to furnish a livelihood. Hence the patrons and the sinecures, if the author had no private means. It was so simply taken for granted that a living could not be made by the practice of literature that Coleridge devoted some pages of the *Biographia Literaria* to the problem of the means by which a writer might earn a living while pursuing his art, and ended by suggesting the Church as a sort of parallel vocation that would bring in a living without too great an exhaustion of energy.

From the middle nineteenth century on, especially in the industrial and capitalistic countries, there appeared the trade writer, who produced work as a commodity. Both trade writers and their readers belonged to two well-defined classes: there were those who were interested in romance and adventure, and those who were interested in "facts." In fiction, the commonest of

all literary forms since the advent of realism, one class
of trade writer was the bastard offspring of the old
romance and adventure writer. He generally needed
little for his equipment except a facility in turning a
sentence and enough fancifulness of mind to give him
an unrestrained power for spinning tales of love or
adventure. The second class of trade writer was the offspring of the realists, sometimes of the lower order of
realists who were defective in imaginative power and
who consequently made a rubric of observation and
external reality in every shape and form. The creative
imagination was out of it, as far as they were concerned;
the novel was to be written from documents, not from
imagination; the novelists were not to concern themselves with the interior life but with movements and
happenings around them.

The interpretations of what was meant by *reality*
went to more and more fantastic extremes; to write
nothing but what was "true," but what had happened,
to copy life as it was—that became the watchword. The
older realists, the artist-realists, had been tolerant of
every sort of literary doctrine, but the neo-realists could
not tolerate any writing that was not akin to their own.
The artist-realists had been, as far as their talents went,
like the great writers of the past, dowered in the same
way; it was their material, their doctrine, their theories
of art, that were different. They all were, to be sure,
whether Flaubert, Baudelaire, or Tolstoy, intolerant of

the extremer vagaries of romanticism, but now both Flaubert and Maupassant were just as intolerant of the extremer vagaries of realism. Maupassant—and if ten thousand novelists have imitated Flaubert, at least fifty thousand short-story writers have imitated Maupassant —was roused to criticism of the raw-life group, a group coming into literature for the first time in history, and to a defense and explanation of the older realists. To give an illusion of life, he declared, was the aim of the higher realists, and this illusion could not be given us by presenting a banal photograph of life, but only by giving us a picture more perfect, more striking, more convincing than reality itself. The writer must have the art of eliminating the trivial incidents of every-day life that do not serve his end, the art of setting essential events in a strong light and of using everything else as relief; having chosen his subject he must select only such characteristic details as develop it; he must pick and choose so as to give the illusion of life. Truth for the realistic novelist consists in the production of perfect illusion by following the logic of facts and not by transcribing them from life as they follow one another pell-mell. The realistic novelist must accordingly eschew any concatenation of events which might seem exceptional. The "facts" should be normal and probable.

Maupassant showed as strongly as Flaubert his disapproval of the vagaries of the extremists and their intolerance of any type of writing other than their own.

"All the literary doctrines," he maintained, "should be welcomed. . . . To blame a writer for the way he sees things is to reproach him for not being made on a standard pattern. . . . To dispute an author's right to produce a poetic or a realistic work is to try to coerce his temperament, to take exception to his originality, to forbid his using the eyes and wits bestowed on him by nature. . . . Let him be free, by all means, to conceive of things as he pleases, provided he is an artist." *Provided he is an artist!* But that was the trouble. The new type of writer just coming in, the lower realist, was not an artist; he, they, were tradesmen of letters bent on forcing literature to serve a special end, which end they decided on. The higher realists, being artists, were tolerant of other artists, of other literary principles; the lower realists, being tradesmen of letters, could hardly even afford to be tolerant; to give themselves importance they had to force literature into the service of a practical purpose, a purpose, to be sure, in the importance of which they sincerely believed. But they brought the realistic school far down the decline, and the inevitable reaction against it, and all it stood for, set in.

But, even in its decline, realism was destined to last a long while, and one of the reasons it was destined to last was connected with the development of industrialism. Before the industrial era men and women had all sorts of humble outlets for expression: they wove, they span, they carved, they embroidered, they made chairs and tables. But the machine was soon to take away these outlets and to leave men and women empty-handed, with insistent bits of their minds and emotions dammed up. Civilization was developing recklessly, without guidance, without thought as to how it was serving human beings. There was a greater and greater rush into literary expression. The realistic method of writing, in its lower forms, was not difficult; even its higher forms could be imitated without too much demand upon creative imagination or creative emotions; facts, observation, the human document, reportage (to use the Goncourts' term)—these were a stock-in-trade within reach of a great many. Realism, in fact, admitted to writing a new world of men and women who, without any special talent, if they were literate, persevering, and carried a notebook either literally or mentally, could write a passable novel or short story of the kind that begins in the manner of the American contender for a recent international prize: "Mrs. Salz was dusting the sitting-room." The notion that the accurate observation of every-day life was what made literature became so widespread that in our day it is firmly embedded in the general reader's consciousness that a book, or play, or novel, is of value if it factually renders something in life that he knows has happened or which is within reach of his experience. As a literary doctrine, realism spread all over the literature-producing world;

it became the one literary principle known to everybody; it produced the standard of criticism that dominated all others from the middle nineteenth century until our own time. Realism made fiction so popular that a book in most people's minds was a novel, and of a novel the common criterion was, Is it true to life? Is it even a copy of life? as if there were any such thing as a standardized truth to life.

Chapter Ten

THE OUTSIDE LITERATURES IN ENGLISH: THE IRISH AND THE AMERICAN

I

LITERARY doctrines when they pass from one country to another take the same, or a very similar form of development in their new abode; the human mind is given to following like patterns with but little variation. The two new literatures in English, the Irish and the American, which developed strongly in the last century or so, followed pretty closely the pattern of similar developments in other countries. In Ireland, what was called the Renaissance represented a struggle towards cultural re-nationalization, and it followed almost exactly the same lines as had the first movement of this kind, the German movement. Exactly the same methods were employed as those devised by Lessing and Herder to found a national literature. Their ideas, principles and methods were adopted by a group of young Irishmen known as "The Young Ireland" group, or as "The Nation" group from the name of the newspaper founded by them. The most far-seeing of them, Thomas Davis, began the attempt to rouse his country to expression, with words sometimes taken literally from Lessing and Herder, sometimes in paraphrase. In an address to the young men of a college society in Dublin University in 1840—he was only twenty-six at the time—we have him using the same exhortations that were used by the German literary leaders, and we find him quoting directly from Lessing a sentence that became a rallying cry in Ireland for nearly a century—"Think wrongly if you will, but think for yourselves."

For Thomas Davis the highest poetry was national poetry, and he assessed national poetry in the same terms that Herder did: "National poetry is the very flower of the soul, the greatest evidence of its health, the greatest evidence of its beauty. It binds us to the land by its condensed and gemlike history." It was an age when young men thought they could save the world, or at all events, their own countries, by literature. The methods by which a national literature was produced in Germany, and alien influence banished, were studied in Ireland. Herder's ideas about poetry—primitive poetry, ballad poetry, folk poetry—were hopefully taken over; his utterances about folk songs and traditional poetry were eagerly discussed. That recommendation of Herder's to the young Goethe was, in another country, passed around with what later proved to be potent results, "Study the superstitions and the sagas of the forefathers." This became a credo, for Ireland, like Germany, had both a folklore and a mythology, that glorious possession of some fortunate peoples, which stamps itself so subtly, not only on every form of art they produce but on the racial character.

Of the writers grouped around Davis and "The Nation," James Clarence Mangan was the most authentic poet, and he set himself to make an anthology of the new German poetry, translated into English verse by himself. This anthology included some of Herder's ballads, his renderings of the traditional heroic poetry of other countries. Another of "The Nation" poets, Samuel Ferguson, was later to delve into "the superstitions and sagas of the forefathers," and gave versions of them in English from the native Gaelic language. Herder also had touched on these very sagas—the "Ossian" and the Fianna stories—in an essay, "Ossian and the Poetry of Other Peoples," for MacPherson's flighty renderings of the Gaelic sagas had become known all over Europe. Davis wrote some rousing national ballads, "Fontenoy," "The Sack of Baltimore"; Mangan turned to more deeply native sources, and made such impressive expressions of the national spirit as "Dark Rosaleen," "Cathleen-ni-Houlihan," "The Lament for the Princes of Tyrone and Tyrconnell."

This movement was destined to be cut short in its course; for one thing, two of its founders, Davis and Mangan, died young—the one in his early thirties, the other in his forties—for another, they had not developed a technique which would make an appeal to the two races that called themselves Irish, the Gaelic and the Anglo-Irish. But the great calamity that prevented the movement from realizing itself for another half-century was the famine of 1846–47, one of the greatest disasters that ever befell a European people. Not only national creative vitality, but individual creative vitality, was starved out under the effects of the disaster. The young and the strong flew to America, from the hunger-ridden, plague-ridden country, and the old, who were the custodians of the "superstitions and sagas of the forefathers," went into their graves.

2

It was not until fifty years later that a generation was vigorous enough to take up the movement where Davis and Mangan had left off. Meanwhile, Samuel Ferguson of "The Nation" group had survived and was still living when the next poet to take up the national tradition, William Butler Yeats, reached his young manhood. Ferguson's delving into Celtic myth and legend, his creations from them, *Congal,* and his *Lays of the Western Gael,* were the work of an older contemporary of Yeats. The younger poet knew his rôle from the start, and one of his earliest poems has the lines:

> Know, that I would accounted be
> True brother of that company,
> Who sang to sweeten Ireland's wrong,

> Ballad and story, rann and song;
> Nor be I any less of them,
> Because the red rose-bordered hem
> Of her, whose history began
> Before God made the angelic clan,
> Trails all about the written page.

and again:

> Nor may I less be counted one
> With Davis, Mangan, Ferguson,
> Because to him, who ponders well,
> My rhymes more than their rhyming tell
> Of things discovered in the deep,
> Where only body's laid asleep.

Once more the manifestoes about national literature and a national culture began. Davis's writings were re-read. "Study the superstitions and the sagas of the fore-fathers" once more showed its rousing power. The sagas and the hero tales, the folk songs and the folk tales, were again brought back from obscurity. Standish O'Grady and Lady Gregory proceeded to make modern renderings of the hero tales, Douglas Hyde of the folk tales and the folk songs: Hyde became head of the great popular movement for the restoration of the native language. Yeats, not unself-consciously, occupied a position rather like Goethe's in Weimar, and made himself the head of a theatre that produced national drama in prose and verse. There was indeed in Yeats's mentality something very like Goethe's, without Goethe's comprehensiveness. As in Germany, in the beginning of its national movement, the audiences in the newly created theatre were delighted to see on the boards plays dealing with their contemporary life, as well as renderings of their sagas. The Irish people differed from the Germans in the fact that they were not homogeneous in language and race; the literature they knew and read and understood was in the language of the people whose influence the movement was trying to uproot. It was not only the upper classes who spoke English, as the upper classes in Germany and Russia had spoken French; English was the language of almost the whole population. The native Gaelic tongue was still living and was spoken and written by a minority, but English was in the ascendancy and writers who wanted to be widely read wrote in English. This was true, and has continued to be true, even of those who could have written in Gaelic, for the Celts of Ireland, like the Celts of France, adopted the language of the conqueror, and as the French Celts became part-Latin, so the Irish Celts became part Anglo-Saxon. But though they assimilated the great language and literature of the conqueror, and even became masters of it and creators in it, they had had no part in its making. The literature of their own that they made in English was written in a language colored by their native Gaelic language and idiom. This literature in English owed much of its color and sound to the old literature in Gaelic and to the influence, generally, of the movement for the restoration of the Gaelic tongue.

The product of the writers of the Renaissance was partly lyrical, partly realistic, partly poetic drama and narrative founded on the hero tales. There arose a number of distinguished poets, and among them the greatest poet of his day writing in English, perhaps the greatest contemporary poet writing in any language, William Butler Yeats. On the poetic side of the movement there was not only the Herder-Lessing influence, there were also the influences of every other movement that had arisen in Europe in the nineteenth century, and these became woven in with the native inheritance of folk and hero poetry. On drama, there was the Scandinavian influence; there was the influence of French realism, brought in by George Moore; there was a touch of the French Symbolist movement; there was a Whitman influence, and other American influences generally. But very markedly there was the influence of the Wordsworth-Baudelaire combination. Yeats re-stated Wordsworth's doctrine of the language of poetry, in a paraphrase of the words of the Preface to the *Lyrical Ballads*. "We wanted," he said, "to get rid, not only of rhetoric, but of poetic diction; we tried to strip away everything that was artificial, to get a style like speech, as simple as the simplest prose, like a cry of the heart." John Synge was also profoundly influenced by Baudelaire—not, it should be said, by the erotic side of his genius which swayed the English poets of the 'nineties, but by Baudelaire's power of creating characters at once tragic and grotesque, and by his approach to his subjects, by his whole attitude towards life and death, and by the directness of his language. Synge was not only influenced by Baudelaire but by the older French authors who themselves had affected Baudelaire—Villon, Ronsard, and mediæval writers. But then, it should be noted that a body of Irish poetry seeming to have a Baudelaire derivation is, in reality, derived from Irish mediæval literature, and the literature-producing classes in Ireland were temperamentally attracted to French literature and had, many of them, a French culture.

Among Herder's ideas was one, age-old, to be sure, but given a new life by him—the idea that poetry should be said or sung, not read silently from a printed book. Yeats developed this and encouraged the speaking of verse with a special utterance differentiated from the speaking of prose. With his collaboration, Florence Farr invented an instrument, a sort of lyre, to the accompaniment of which she said or chanted poetry. These experiments influenced the speaking of verse in the Abbey Theatre plays, and the speaking of verse, in turn, influenced the composition of poetry. The direction of Yeats's later poetry, with its direct rhythm and colloquial vocabulary, was strongly affected by hearing his verse spoken in the theatre. The common Irish habit of saying poetry made the verse familiar to audiences before it was printed, and certainly affected the style of the whole poetic production.

The dramatic side, with its national theatre, became the most widely known, but the real glory of the Irish movement was in its poetry. There sprang up about half a dozen genuine poets: following the precedent set by Baudelaire, Verlaine and Mallarmé, they kept their poetic production down to one or two books, but if an anthology were made of the best work of these half dozen, it would with its direct expression make most of the poetry of our ultra-modern poets seem lacking in intensity and experience as well as in poetic invention and that fundamental lyricism which is an essential of all poetry. This new Irish literature lacked the abundance of the great English periods, but what it lacked in abundance it almost made up for in intensity. Though it was distinctly national poetry, it had been fed by many cultures, so that it was lifted out of provincialism. The whole product was very different in mental climate, in spiritual temperature, from English literature; in some cases there could hardly be detected a trace of English influence, although the writers wrote in the English language. The novel, as written by George Moore, was not in the English tradition at all: it was derived, partly from the French realists and partly from the traditional Irish story-tellers, the shanachies, that Moore knew in his childhood and youth in the west of Ireland. The realistic novel that came after George Moore and that is now being written in Ireland was, in addition, influenced by the Russians. There is, to be sure, in the earlier Yeats, an occasional Swinburnian line, like "Autumn is over the long leaves that love us," and in some of his verse-plays, just as in almost all the verse-plays in Europe, since the modern movement began, there is the inescapable sway of Shakespeare; but on the whole, and for a time anyhow, English influence on Irish literature was almost nil.

3

It was far different, for a long time, in the other outside literature in English, the American. The first important American writer, Washington Irving, was not only English in his mental make-up, but English in his writing models; he could have passed for an English writer. In spite of great American publishing houses, publication in England was regarded as the real crown of a writer's success, and the gaining of this was the desired goal down even to our own time, until the time of the Great War. The audience for the first American writers was preponderantly English in blood and tradition; it was a part of the English race cut away from the main branch, but in it there dominated a quality, Puritanism, which the English did not like in themselves and which was indeed at odds with their own great dominant characteristic and the outstanding characteristic of their literature, emotional power. The men and women who made English literature felt all emotions so directly and so strongly that, in emotional force, it is the greatest of all literatures, as in form and intensity the Greek is. They had indeed felt so abundantly and so romantically that they seemed unable for long to tolerate any tendency in their literature in which emotion was not the supreme quality. But the rising American literature, particularly the New England literature, was emotionally thin, and this was one of the qualities that in the end turned it to a different line of expression from the English and into a sort of psychological and social analysis that had not been in English literature at all. Besides, the Puritan temperament, undirected by strong emotions, developed an independent, rational attitude towards life that, limiting as it may have been for literature, was a constructive force in statesmanship and social advance.

The first really American piece of literature was Jefferson's Declaration of Independence, and that had about it a sort of prophetic sweep, as of something appearing out of the future; it was a premonition of a world that was coming to birth under circumstances that the old European world could never really appreciate or assess, and this though it was raised on a foundation of ideas taken over from Europe. It was nearly half a century before the next piece of influential American literature appeared: this was Emerson's "The American Scholar"; the two together gave a pattern to the American dream, gave to America a dream and a philosophy.

But any account of American literature in the nineteenth century begins of necessity with George Ticknor and Edward Everett, those two young men who, having read a glamorous book, about glamorous new poets and philosophers and scholars, called *De l'Allemagne,* decided they would cross the ocean and see the author, Madame de Staël, and as many as possible of the poets and philosophers she had written of; in short, they determined to make a pilgrimage to the men who were creating modern literature and ideas, and to the places where these were being made. In the year of the battle of Waterloo, five years after the publication of *De l'Allemagne,* they started on their pilgrimage. The author herself was still alive—she lived until 1817—and she welcomed the young men as an elder author might welcome two of the younger generation who had been stirred by her ideas and who were to spread them in another country. Goethe was still living, enthroned in Weimar, the greatest writer and the wisest man in Europe; he also welcomed them with interest and even with enthusiasm. All doors were opened to the two young pilgrims from Washington's country. They met all the important figures; they saw the very men de Staël had written about, or all of them that were alive;

they met one, or both, of the brothers Schlegel, they who had been responsible for fastening the name "Romantic" to the new movement, a nomenclature that had spread everywhere in spite of objections from the very writers who were making what came to be known as "Romantic" literature. The younger Schlegel explained that what he meant by "Romantic" was "a progressive universal poetry," which would include all kinds. While the battle about the name went on, the name itself had made an entrance into people's imaginations and stuck there. The two young Americans were destined to become professors at Harvard, and the two Schlegels were admirable models for the progressive scholar with wide interests: they had been trying to develop further the conceptions of Herder and they kept alive, by their writings and discussions, his ideas on folk poetry, on old ballads, on what he had called "wilde poesie" in mediæval romances, in Eastern literature, Homer, Greek literature, in Shakespeare, in Ossian. The elder Schlegel, Wilhelm, did what Herder had thought of doing but had not had the time for—he provided Germany with a real translation of Shakespeare in verse; he also translated Dante and Cervantes, and was an enthusiast regarding the literature of the Spanish peninsula. The younger Schlegel published the first German book on the literatures and wisdom of India.

These were the intellectual orientations, the enthusiasms and the learning that the two young pioneers brought back to New England, and that Ticknor brought to his professorship of Modern Languages at Harvard, a chair destined to have a wide influence and to be a directing force with the New England writers, for Longfellow was Ticknor's successor, and Longfellow's successor was Lowell, and they all followed in Ticknor's path. And it was Ticknor who urged Longfellow to go to Germany and make much the same pilgrimage that he and his companion had made, and to meet those of the great figures who were left, and to read their work. Starting with Lessing, Longfellow read all the writers of the movement down to his own contemporaries. He read Herder's collection of folk songs, and those lines of his, "For a boy's will is the wind's will, and the thoughts of youth are long, long thoughts," he took from Herder's rendering of a Lapland song:

> Knabenwille ist Wind'swille,
> Jüngling'sgedanken lange Gedanken.

He returned with the same enthusiasms as those of Ticknor, and brought them, in his turn, to the Harvard chair, in modernized form.

4

Emerson was a student at Harvard when Ticknor was expounding there the modern literary ideas that he had brought back from Europe, and when the other pilgrim, Edward Everett, was the Harvard professor of Greek. However, these influences might not have done more than provide a general literary culture or a general intellectual direction and might never really have produced a focus for New England literature if Emerson had not decided, in his late twenties, to go to Europe and estimate for himself what was in these ideas, especially as they were shaping in England. When he left he was a young clergyman who had just thrown up his church and his pulpit and was groping towards his path in life; when he came back he knew exactly where that path lay, and which among the ideas were his to use and to make his own.

Not a great writer, in spite of his few fine poems and essays, Emerson was destined to be a great fructifier, a leader of thought. Lowell said of him, "There are staminate plants in literature that make no fine show of fruit, but without whose pollen, quintessence of fructifying gold, the garden had been barren. Emerson's mind is emphatically one of these, and there is no man to whom our æsthetic culture owes so much." His mind really developed only after he had gone to Europe; he was thirty when he met Coleridge and Wordsworth and Carlyle, some of whose work he already knew; he became steeped in the world of their ideas and in the antecedents of these ideas. He was not, like Ticknor, to cherish disinterestedly all the seeds he gathered; he winnowed them and kept what suited his own purpose and what could best take root in the soil of his own country as well as in his own mind. There was not much for New England in some of these European ideas; for the moment anyway, there was no urge towards expressing everyday life or rustic life, though both Whittier and Lowell, later, initiated a rural New England poetry. And attractive as all Lessing's ideas might be, there was not much use in America for his conception of literature as racial expression. But Lessing's demand on his people to shake off slavish foreign influences, to use what they could as bricks but with them to build their own structure, to be self-reliant and independent, to think wrongly if they liked, but to think for themselves—these were all in "The American Scholar," an address Emerson made to the Harvard students soon after his return from Europe, an address very like in spirit to the one Thomas Davis was to make, a couple of years later, to the students of Dublin University. These two college addresses were responsible for starting off the two new outside literatures in English.

Emerson soaked himself in the work of Wordsworth and Coleridge, in Wordsworth's poetry and in his conception of nature and his contemplation of nature. Carlyle, with whom he felt a temperamental kinship, turned him on to Goethe and to Fichte. However, most of what came to be called Emerson's philosophy was built on Coleridge and Coleridge's interpretation of the German philosophers, especially on his interpretation of Schelling, who, like all the other German philosophers of the day, had been started off by the work of Herder and Lessing. Schelling, with his two books, *Ideas Towards a Philosophy of Nature* and *A System of Transcendental Idealism,* had exerted a potent influence on certain phases of the new literature. These two books were spoken of by Coleridge as if they were divine revelations, and they became almost that to Emerson and to the newly born Transcendental Club of Boston.

Emerson's kinship with Schelling is evident: as Sainte-Beuve would say, they belong to the same family of minds. Schelling, like Emerson, was not a systematized thinker; he was an intuitive, glorifying intuition; he was indeed Emerson's own idea of a philosopher— a sort of seer or priest in a temple, listening for revelations from the oracles, which he interpreted in oracular statements. He held what he termed the philosophy of identity—the identity, in the absolute, of the subjective and the objective, of the ideal and the real, of nature and spirit. As Madame de Staël, with a feminine desire to make plain sense of things, explained, his aim was to reduce existence to a single principle: nothing was more absurd, for instance, than the expression, the philosophy of Plato and the philosophy of Aristotle—there was only one philosophy or there was none, according to Schelling. The natural consequence of this philosophy of identity was the conclusion that all wisdom was in ourselves, and that to know the world we had only to look deep into ourselves. In short, intuition was the great revealer. This suited Emerson exactly, as did Schelling's view of the divine origin of man—that man and nature were emanations from God. It also suited the Transcendental Club, and provided a philosophical backing for the Transcendental Movement.

New England Transcendentalism was a combination of every sort of American idealism, based, on one side, on a doctrine of man's divinity and, on the other, on everything that was in the Declaration of Independence and in Emerson's "The American Scholar." All the writers were Transcendentalists, and both the movement and the writers were responsible for impregnating the national character with a peculiar form of idealism and optimism—an almost eccentric idealism, at once disinterested and opportunistic, chivalrous and utilitarian, humanitarian and egoistic, philanthropic and acquisitive. The same subtly excellent components do not belong to the optimism that springs from the vague side of Transcendentalism and the more complacent side of Emerson's teachings. What Transcendentalism provided, on the whole, was a sort of Unitarian substitute for certain of the orthodox doctrines and disciplines of Christianity, which never found a foothold in America, if they ever weathered the Atlantic at all. "Christianity," Thoreau declared, "has hung its harp on the willows and cannot sing a song in a strange land." Irving Babbitt, three-quarters of a century later, was to re-discover some of these lapsed disciplines and to deliver himself of some of the more elementary teachings of Christendom with the air of a man who has fathered a new philosophy.

The Concord group of writers belonged to the Transcendental Club, and it was the Concord group that left the deepest impress on New England literature; it was they whose work provided what may be described as the overture to American literature. After his return from Europe, Emerson had also settled in Concord, and here he, Thoreau and Hawthorne lived a cloister-like life and had the characteristics of an order of monks, of which Emerson was the preaching member, Thoreau the one who retired to his cell in solitude like a desert father, so as to come face to face with spiritual reality, Hawthorne the one who meditated on the sins of men, their lusts and their vengeances, their hatreds and their remorses. Emerson was descended from seven generations of preachers, and his own preaching, given in the form of lectures and essays, related chiefly to the conduct of life or to spiritual possessions. For what he had picked from the new European ideas were those that were especially concerned with the conduct of life and with the emergence of the divine in man; to the doctrines concerned with purely literary expression he had not so much response.

In spite of the fact that he and Thoreau discussed Herder's theories of literature, of "wilde poesie," of early poetry, of ballads, sagas and epics, and his notions of history, Emerson only played with these, for they could have had but little practical influence on America at that time, and Emerson was eminently practical in his selection of the ideas that he was able to make his own.

The interest in Oriental literature, that Ticknor had taken over from the Schlegels, who had taken it over from Herder, was to open to the pantheistically-minded Emerson a world that was of importance for his poetry. From ancient Indian poetry he took the matter and the imagery of his most memorable poem:

> If the red slayer think he slays,
> Or if the slain think he is slain,
> They know not well the subtle ways
> I keep, and pass, and turn again.
>
> Far or forgot to me is near,
> Shadow and sunlight are the same;
> The vanished gods to me appear;
> And one to me are shame and fame.
>
> They reckon ill who leave me out;
> When me they fly, I am the wings;
> I am the doubter and the doubt,
> And I the hymn the Brahmin sings.
>
> The strong gods pine for my abode,
> And pine in vain the sacred Seven;
> But thou, meek lover of the good,
> Find me, and turn thy back on Heaven!

In this, and in half a dozen other poems, and in about a dozen lines and couplets, Emerson produced poetry of a kind unique in English. From Goethe he got the irregular meter that he uses in an artificial poem like "Give All to Love," and in philosophical pieces of this kind:

> The rushing metamorphosis,
> Dissolving all that fixture is,
> Melts things that be to things that seem,
> And solid nature to a dream.

> . . . .

> All forms are fugitive,
> But the substances survive.
> Ever fresh the broad creation,
> A divine improvisation. . . .

His sort of poetry and prose is not unlike the literature left us by the historic saints: the sentiments and reflections of the essays are strikingly like those of Thomas à Kempis's *Imitation of Christ;* there is the same inclination towards the same sort of spiritual maxims, though à Kempis's have more of a narrow prudence and less of an independence than Emerson's. If these essays were winnowed and the most revealing passages in them arranged in an order like that of the *Imitation,* Emerson would be the gainer. In a work edited with such intention his strange lack of discipline and his peculiarly feminine reliance on instinct, the undirected nature of his thought, and his consequent inconsistencies, might pass unnoticed. He had one gift in an almost unexampled degree, a power of intuition, a richness of the sub-conscious, out of which he could draw striking revelations; he had half the outfit of a great writer, a rich inner life, but his emotions were thin, his response to life mild. He thoroughly realized his own lack, for he noted in himself "an absence of common sympathies . . . a want of sufficient bottom to my nature. . . . I have not the kind affections of a pigeon. . . . I was born cold." He noted the coldness and unresponsiveness of the people he knew, remarking on how insulated and pathetically solitary were all his friends. "I spoke of friendship," he wrote, "but my friends and I are fishes in our habits." Concord, in fact, offered a meager world. There were none of the romantic loves and friendships, the unrestrained enthusiasms, of the European literary movements; the writers all went into reveries, betook themselves inside themselves.

Emerson and Hawthorne settled down without glamour to affectionate marriage-relationships that helped rather than hindered them in living in themselves. Emerson made the best of it; he probably got out more of what was in him in that world and in that soil than he could have in any other. But with Hawthorne it was different. Of the three, his was the most varied literary endowment, and it included a talent, the fictional, that needs for its operation a warm relation with humanity. Fate and destiny, however, decreed that he should exist out of life most of the time, without close connections with other human beings. In his own family, his mother and his sisters and himself lived secluded from each other and generally ate their meals in solitude. Though he joined the Brook Farm colony for a while, this did not give him any more facility for mingling with his fellows; though he joined the Transcendental Club, he had no sympathy with the ideas that dominated that group. He himself was a Transcendentalist, in the dictionary meaning of the term. That, in the end, he died of his painful solitude, Emerson, who knew that Hawthorne had never got all his talent into his books, said of him the day of his funeral. He did not know people, so he could not create character; his writing, except in one book where he tried to get down the life of Brook Farm, is almost pure symbolism and the theme is always the effect of sin and evil. His characters are symbols by which he illustrates the sin, the remorse, the revenge that all his books are about, as a Morality Play might be about them. He was, as he himself explained, a romance-writer, not a novelist: by "novelist" he understood the type of writer who dealt with real life. What he was, really, was a narrator of tales, and one can always hear, behind his best work, his lovely, lonely book, *The Scarlet Letter,* the voice of a man telling a story, not of people so much as of the consequences of their sins. Through two of his books, anyway, *The Scarlet Letter* and *The House of the Seven Gables,* he is not only a figure in American literature, he is a figure in nineteenth-century literature. Hawthorne himself knew that he had lost out in this life, that his was a lean world, but, because of his temperament, it was the only world he could cope with.

5

In spite of the fact that Emerson could say of Thoreau, in his general remarks on the coldness of his friends, "I would as soon take the limb of an elm tree as Henry's arm," there is more warmth and ecstasy in one little book of Thoreau's, *Walden,* than in all Emerson's prose put together. Take one or two sentences from a familiar passage, "I went to the woods because I wished to live deliberately, to front only the essential facts of life, and see if I could not learn what it had to teach, and not, when I came to die, discover that I had not lived. I did not wish to live what was not life, living is so dear. . . . I wanted to live deep and suck out all the marrow of life." Here we have that nervous style that has behind it a man of blood and fire, a creature of light; these words are vascular; as Emerson said of Montaigne, cut them and they will bleed. Thoreau's words, indeed, generally walk alive across the page, something that Emerson's very rarely do. This sort of life, this sort of luminousness, makes Thoreau's *Walden* so glamorous that it is one of the great experiences of youth in the 'teens to read it, similar to the great experience of reading *Hamlet* or *Faust,* in the twenties. Youth may only half understand an immortal book, but one that has no appeal to youth at all cannot be said to belong to literature, though it may be outstanding in some other branch of expression, in science or in philosophy.

It would not be surprising if time, the last arbiter, decided that of the three most important early New England writers, Thoreau is the greatest in sheer writing power, in the power of putting life into language. What he meant by life was not, of course, physical life or material life; reality for him was interior. He had neither wife nor child, and there is no record of his ever having been in love; he never seems to have endured that distressful temptation of the desert saints— the temptation of being, in his solitude, "harried by lust," but he was one of their order, not only in the reality of his search for what was his to get out of life, but in his bliss in solitude and in the nervous passion of his writing. His philosophy was a simple one, but its depth was unsoundable; all that men have of their own is themselves, their lives, and a little gift of time, and he made a valiant effort to get what was his to get, out of that little time, and to write down what it was.

Neither Thoreau nor Hawthorne had, to any degree, the conviction that only the Puritans or their Transcendentalist descendants had the secret of the good life, the noble life, a conviction which is at the back of Emerson's writing. Hawthorne, in spite of defects of temperament, had the artist's sense of life; Thoreau, who was of Channel Island descent, had an infusion of the free critical mentality of the French: they had few complacencies, but Emerson's complacence was at times extraordinary, and it enabled him to come to self-righteous conclusions about his European contemporaries, Goethe, Coleridge, Wordsworth, Carlyle, conclusions impossible to either Thoreau or Hawthorne, and which had, like everything else that emanated from Emerson, a great influence.

6

The rest of the New England group, except Melville, who, at the moment, has an extensive reputation and whose *Moby Dick* is described as an epic by those anxious to find all forms in New England literature, have lost out with the present generation. Longfellow, whose command of modern languages and literature did so much for the fine literary culture that was New England's, has lost his once wide reputation. The very bad poetry he wrote at his worst has cast a shadow, not only over his fine poetry, but over all his services to this first American literature—the anthologies by which he made European poetry known, his translation of Dante, which in stretches has never been surpassed in English, the beauty of a large amount of his work, which, if selected in a small, expertly edited volume, would salvage his poetic reputation. Longfellow's subjects, and his virtuosity in verse-technique, fascinated poets remote in place and genius, among whom was Baudelaire, who had no objection to borrowing from him a line or a phrase and who made a sort of version or imitation of part of *Hiawatha*.

Of the critics, Margaret Fuller's services, excellent as they were, were for their day only, but Lowell has produced something that will last. There have been critics since with a more solid knowledge of literature, like Woodberry or Paul Elmer More, and of course Poe's flight was higher, but a better all-round critic than Lowell has not appeared, or one who had more of an intuition regarding what American literature should be or was going to be. He really belonged to the type of what has since been called the impressionistic critic; what he was inclined to give his readers was the adventures of his soul among books, so that his judgments are not always careful conclusions, but quick reactions to temperamental likes or dislikes. His poetic endowment was considerable, and two of his lyrics, "When I Was a Beggarly Boy" and "My Heart, I Cannot Still It," once read, are possessions for a lifetime. His *Biglow Papers* started off the whole school of humorous, satiric, bucolic verse that became rife all over America. He and Whittier together initiated that rural New England poetry from which a poet like Robert Frost stems.

Like all the early New England writers, Lowell left the stamp of his mind and character on his countrymen. Insufficient and one-sided as New England literature might be, as an expression of the New England mind it had the quality of revealing and moulding the people it expressed, and their descendants all over the country; it was like them, like the inhabitants of the village and the countryside, in a way that a great literature, such as the English, is not like the ordinary English people at all but only like a symbolic English people. As far as it went, New England literature was true to the minds of the people, and so strongly did the writers influence the developing American civilization that one can meet in any village a miniature sage who is a vulgarization of Emerson, or a miniature naturalist who is a vulgarization of Thoreau, or a popular satirist such as Lowell, or a brooder on sin such as Hawthorne.

They also passed on to their descendants their own incapacity for close human relationships; their own limited psychic and emotional energy made them incapable of leaving any profound pattern for living or for literature. No tragedy, no love-poetry, no novel of passion, says George Woodberry, came from them. Their loneliness was tremendous except in the case of Thoreau, for whom solitude was a beatitude, as it was to the Desert Fathers, and therefore capable of generating its own warmth. Emerson took refuge from his loneliness in a contemplation of the divine in his own mind and in the angelic messages that he said came to him; in a complacence and a mental irresponsibility that made him happy. Hawthorne alone was aware of the drawbacks of a retreat from the emotional complexities and conflicts of human relationships. He left behind a few pregnant sentences showing his consciousness of the predicament from which he had not the force to extricate himself. Others took refuge from their loneliness in various ways: some, in their European memories; others, in their scholarship; Longfellow, in a yearning Teutonic romanticism; Lowell, in his books. Looking back on their literary product, distinguished as it was, and fine and broad as was their literary culture, we see that they left behind them few seminal ideas such as might yield a harvest for their descendants or for the greater America that was coming in. They worked effectively and even nobly with the ideas they took over and made their own, but they really added little to them, and they produced neither literary philosophies nor speculative philosophies as did the Germans and the French of the same period. Herman Melville, the one man among them who might have come out with a speculative philosophy expressive of a country that persistent men had conquered or half conquered, tamed or half tamed from the wild, had no real contacts with the others or with the life around him; he was more alone, more undirected than any of them. His solitariness, his strange psychic energy, his restless and gloomy speculations on the forces that rule the world, found outlet in an epical and symbolic tale of the pursuit through tumultuous seas of a white whale, a creature surviving from primeval times. The whale Moby Dick was "an incarnation of all those malicious agencies, that intangible malignity, which has been from the beginning." He is pursued by the crew under the leadership of Ahab, whose leg he has torn off, and "for whose vengeful mind all the subtle demonisms of life and thought were personified" in the whale. In the end, the malign creature and the ruthless element are the conquerors. It is hardly surprising that Americans, demanding some profounder view of life out of their history than their literary men as a whole had given them, turned to this anarchical epic and perhaps overestimated its significance.

7

But there were three writers who, though they made far less of an entrance into the minds of their countrymen than did the others, were the ones who left behind them the most penetrating influences, who impregnated their epochs with a set of literary values that have been felt all over the world. These three were Edgar Allan Poe, Walt Whitman and Henry James. It is their work that gives an earnest as to what the rôle of a future American literature is likely to be if minds can spring up equal to the task of making that universal literature of which Goethe and de Staël dreamed, a universal

literature which would overshadow the national literatures which, in their turn, had overshadowed the cul-
ture-literatures that came out of Greece and Rome,
which, again, in their turn, had overshadowed the early
wild literatures, the rhapsodic literatures, the mytholo-
gies, of primeval times. There had been in America,
from the beginning, a tendency to knit in with world-
literatures and world-philosophies; this tendency, far
from expressing subordination or derivativeness, showed
itself possessed of a shaping function. It was a tendency
natural in a people who came into literary expression
after the national literatures had partly run their course,
and who could not produce a national literature in the
sense of one that came out of old racial and national
developments. The Americans were not moulding a
language or intensifying an inherited racial consciousness; they were forming a population out of different
races joined together by a metaphysical idea, given a
tangible meaning by a piece of literature, Jefferson's
Declaration of Independence, and by a geographical
area, and not by "the superstitions and sagas of the
forefathers."

The American direction was towards an internation-
alism in literature, towards a universal stream in which
theirs would be a current—even, in time, the dominating
current; they were taking up where the elder races
halted, but that was all the more reason why they should
know all the roads the elder races had traversed. For

this reason, among others, American literature could never be the almost accidental, instinctive thing the elder literatures had been during most of their course.

The contribution of Edgar Allan Poe, Walt Whitman and Henry James to this conception was salient; another half-dozen minds as originating as theirs would have made American literature a world-force. A striking characteristic of the New England literature was its symbolist quality. The outstanding original works were symbolic—Emerson's poetry, *The Scarlet Letter, Moby Dick*. This inclination towards symbolism was due to several causes: the writers were highly endowed intellectually; they had no large or fecund material to hand; they were meagerly endowed emotionally; they were a new people in an immense unsettled country over which they felt the play of mysterious psychic forces. It was almost inevitable that their literary expression should be in the order of symbolism.

8

When Edgar Allan Poe was still in his 'teens he accomplished a phenomenal thing—he wrote an original poem, in the lines that we know as "To Helen," and a poem original as this poem was is always destined to have far-reaching effects. The originality of "To Helen" was fundamental: that combination of music and imagery had not happened previously; that note of the gamut had not been struck before. The short, ecstatic, intense lyrics had been made either on a singing note or a chanting note, but this was neither singing nor chanting; it was a new mode in lyric poetry. Tennyson, a little afterwards, was also to find that mode when he wrote the lines that Poe was to praise, "Tears, idle tears, I know not what they mean." Poe's poem had other significant elements in it: the obviously logical structure is abandoned and evocation takes its place. The beauty of Helen is conveyed to us by far-brought images—"Nicæan barks," "The agate lamp within thy hand," "The glory that was Greece and the grandeur that was Rome." The poem, in fact, belongs to a type of composition that was to come in about half a century later, in which the thought and emotion were evoked and suggested rather than directly named, and were revealed by a succession of images—that is, "To Helen" was the new kind of symbolist poem. Poe wrote other strikingly original poems, original in content, in structure, in musical effects, "Ulalume," "The City in the Sea," "The Conqueror Worm," "The Raven," but "To Helen," though it has the marks of a youthful effort and may be said almost to have the weakness of a creature of a new species, nevertheless remains the most original poem of a man whose most striking characteristic naturally, as well as the one he most deliberately sought for, was originality.

Poe's other striking distinctions were in his craftsmanship and in his discipline; he is the accomplished craftsman in all his work—in his poems, his stories and his criticism. He knew "the right ordering of the thing to be made," and he was thoroughly aware that the knowledge of "the right ordering" could not come by improvisation, but only by hard training, self-discipline and the equipment of knowledge. It is an instance of the confusion between the two consciences that it is Emerson who is always regarded as disciplined and well-ordered, while Poe is looked on as undisciplined and disordered. On the plane of thought, it was Emerson who was the self-indulgent, loose-disciplined, undirected man, and on that plane Poe was disciplined, precise, reasoning, well-ordered and industrious. This is what has made him the honored master of so many modern poets, from Baudelaire on. He was against the blind furies of improvisation and the more mythological aspects of inspiration. A poet was, especially, a man who knew his job, who guided his art consciously with his mind. His analysis of the psychological conditions from which literature is produced, of the poetic principle in itself, was bound to affect profoundly that school of modern poets who were in revolt against the loose abundance in poetic product, those who believed that poetry "is literature reduced to the essential of its active principle."

Poe had found the basis of his "The Poetic Principle" in certain ideas of Herder, certain ideas of Coleridge, and in Coleridge's practice, but it was only a basis, for on it he raised some ideas of poetry that were so remote from any his age had considered, that his originality must again be acknowledged. Wordsworth, and even Coleridge, had been almost as moralizing in some of their speculations about poetry as the New England group, and so when Poe declared that "the didactic heresy, which Bostonians had developed in full . . . accomplished more corruption of our poetical literature than all others combined," and when he announced that the aim of poetry is the rhythmical creation of beauty, that poetry has only collateral relations with intellect or conscience, that there is no such thing as a long poem, for the value of a poem depends on its elevating excitement, and all excitements, through a psychic necessity, must be short, that melancholy is the most legitimate of all poetical tones, that the higher manifestations of beauty are connected with melancholy, he was saying not only something startling at the time but saying something momentous to a large audience, larger than the America of his day, more numerous than the readers of *Graham's Magazine,* in which the statement was printed: he was saying something, in fact, destined to enter into all future considerations of poetry.

Without laying any stress on the ostensible meaning addressed to the intelligence, Poe stated that a poem should have an undercurrent of meaning, however indefinite, and mocking a little at the Transcendentalist idea of meaning and at the poets who wished it understood that they composed in a species of frenzy, he let his readers into the secret of the processes by which a poem is composed. In his most detached manner he takes his own "The Raven," because he thinks it is the most generally known of his poems, and shows, step by step, how, having decided on the tone, which was to be melancholy, on the refrain, which was to be monotone and in a single word, he settled on the subject, the death of a beautiful woman; then, he explains at what point he changed from the fantastic to the serious, and how, in the last stanzas, he decided to make the raven the symbol of never-ending remembrance: he tells us in detail how he fixed on the meter. By thus making us familiar with his method of composing a poem and with what might be called his rejections, he is responsible for a new angle in criticism —that which takes into account, not only what a writer has put into his work, but what he refused to put in, and what Paul Valéry terms the nature of his refusals.

His critical theories, his lucid analyses, had the significance of a manifesto, not of a manifesto that started a new sort of literature, but of one that initiated a new critical attitude in a writer towards his own product. A considerable amount of modern poetry—that of Mallarmé, of Valéry, of Verlaine, of T. S. Eliot, can only be properly estimated in the perspective of Poe's "The Poetic Principle" and his "Philosophy of Composition."

It is not alone by his poetry or poetic principles that he has exerted an influence; he created a type of tale in which the ratiocinative imagination takes a dominating rôle. The eeriness of his stories was in itself not new; it had been in Hawthorne's tales; it was to appear again in Henry James, a sort of distinctively American eeriness that could hardly be duplicated in another literature, but it was the influence of that ratiocinative imagination that started off the modern detective story. In addition to his stories, his poems and his criticism, Poe managed to produce one of the most astonishing pieces of speculative literature ever written by a poet, that consideration of the universe which he entitled "Eureka," in which he attempts to discover the rationale of the universe, the "plot of God," as he calls it: here he tries to unriddle the universe as if it were a cryptogram. This immeasurably industrious man, with his high gifts, his supreme artistic integrity, his subtle literary knowledge, suffered from hunger and cold, and the illnesses and emotional derangements consequent on them: he died at forty.

9

Some time after Poe's death, a younger contemporary, Walt Whitman, was also to announce that the great poet "does not moralize or make applications of morals," and he claimed for the greatest poets all the magnanimities, all the wisdoms, and all the generosities. His own desire in writing, he said, was "to articulate and faithfully express in literary or poetic form, and uncompromisingly, my own physical, emotional, moral, intellectual, and æsthetic personality . . . and to exploit that personality, identified with place and date [e.g., the America of his time] in a far more candid and comprehensive sense than any hitherto poem or book." His first volume of poetry, written with this aim, appeared two years before that other volume, *Les Fleurs du Mal,* in which another poet very differently but also faithfully expressed his physical, emotional, moral, intellectual, and æsthetic personality. If *Leaves of Grass* shocked as many people in its own way as did Baudelaire's volume, it brought Whitman a following all over the world, from New York to Japan, almost as if he had been the head of a religious cult and the bearer of a new gospel. What was remarkable about Whitman was that he really soaked up something of all the ideas of his age: something of all the literary doctrines, beginning with Lessing's idea of national and racial expression; and something of all the political doctrines, beginning with Jefferson's Declaration of Independence; and of all the philosophic doctrines, including Hegel.

Whitman's aim was to be an American national poet, revealing America and everything American—ideals, scenery, war, its leaders and its men and women—revealing all through what he called "a stock-personality," which was a projection of himself. More of a seer and a prophet than was Emerson, he was at once more egoistic and less so, more complacent and less so; his voice even more than Emerson's was mystical, seer-like, uttering revelations from an oracle. But he gave a realistic note to his oracular and rhapsodic interpretations of the wonders of life and the wonders of America. He was both realist and romantic, national and universal; he contained in himself all the ideas and ideals that the new literature and the new age were struggling towards. He aimed, as he wrote, at "creating an *imaginative* New World, the correspondent and counterpart of the current scientific and political New World." He evoked this imaginative world in a large, loose way, setting himself to write for the average man in a selection of the speech of the average man; he made himself what he conceived to be the pattern of the average man, what he called a composite man and woman of democracy.

With neither private prejudices nor private emotions nor private moralities, Whitman's sensitivities and convictions were those of man as a member of society, not of man as a personal lover or friend; he was sensitive to the emotions themselves, not to their personal aspects; he was sensitive to the fact of death, of love, of universal brotherhood, for the sake of these things in themselves. Where he differed most profoundly from the other poet of his time who wrote of himself was at the point where he was most American: he had no concern with, perhaps no understanding of, the intense personal relationships, the strong complex personal emotions, the ever-present memories, of which *Les Fleurs du Mal* is composed. Baudelaire is always talking to somebody personally, is always writing of people as individuals, individuals about whom he felt intensely and lastingly, while Whitman is always talking *of* people and *to* people in multitude. He is exhorting men in the mass to comradeship, to universal love and brotherhood; he makes a sweeping gesture of acceptance of things in the mass, whatever they are—fatherhood, motherhood, sex, leadership, affection, death. He makes a sweeping get-together appeal; for that reason he speaks in orations. And, for that, he invented the one sort of vehicle suitable: free verse unchecked by rhyme, by regular rhythms, or stanza-formation. It was, for his theme, an inevitable form. The others, the traditional measures, were all locked up with the purely personal experiences, the personal emotions of men.

Whitman was the one poet who made his audience feel that they were a necessary part, almost collaborators in the composition. His reader never feels alone, a lone man listening to another lone man's confidences, but one of a congregation. That sort of poetry, that sort of appeal in poetry, had never happened before and it really, in spite of all Whitman's imitators, has never happened since. He was a pure original. One may easily prefer other poets, one may admit that because he was talking to multitude he repeated himself over and over again, even contradicted himself ("Do I contradict myself? Very well then, I contradict myself—I am large, I contain multitudes"). One must admit, too, that only once or twice in the course of a fairly long poem would he reach the high plane of memorable expression, but when he reached it, it was as memorable as that of any poet who ever lived, and in a different way. Sometimes all that was memorable was a line, but the line was pregnant as few single lines ever were:

I am the man, I suffered, I was there.

or

Agonies are one of my changes of garments.

or

Now we have met, we have looked, we are safe.

or

Whoever you are, I fear you are walking the walk of
      dreams.

On his highest level, his pregnancy and his lyric potency were both unsurpassable and unique:

For my enemy is dead, a man divine as myself is dead,
I look where he lies white-faced and still in the coffin—I
      draw near,
Bend down and touch lightly with my lips the white face
      in the coffin.

or

Come, I will make the continent indissoluble,
I will make the most splendid race the sun ever shone upon,
I will make divine magnetic lands,
    With the love of comrades,
       With the life-long love of comrades.

. . . .

or

When lilacs last in the dooryard bloom'd,
And the great star early droop'd in the western sky in the
    night,
I mourn'd, and yet shall mourn with ever-returning spring.

Ever-returning spring, trinity sure to me you bring,
Lilac blooming perennial and drooping star in the west,
And thought of him I love.

or

Come, said the Muse,
Sing me a song no poet yet has chanted,
Sing me the Universal!

10

Whitman and Poe had two qualities in common—
vitality and originality—and it was these two that
brought them into the current of world-literature in
such a way as to affect that current and to continue
affecting it. They were of their time, if we regard the
time over a long period, and they both reflected an array
of ideas to which they also contributed. Henry James
was more particularly of his time in the sense of be-

longing definitely to some three decades of it during which the novel developed from Flaubertian realism to something else. The evolution of his later work, "made of him," said William Crary Brownell, "perhaps the most individual novelist of his day, who, at the same time, is also in the current of its tendencies."

No writer who was born in the nineteenth or the beginning of the twentieth century can help being dominated, for some part of his career, by the literary ideas of the nineteenth century, especially the ones which announced that literature is an expression of national and racial genius, that it is the expression of society, and that the powerful doctrine of realism is almost unquestionable. But if one is to consider fairly the work of Henry James one must get outside these special theories: much as he himself, like every other writer, was influenced by them, what he accomplished belongs eventually to another conception of literature altogether, a conception which, no doubt, some critic will find a name for.

He was one of the writers who frequented the gatherings of the early realists, the group composed of Flaubert, the Goncourts, Zola, Turgenev, and while, in theory, he subscribed fervently to the new doctrines of realism and learned much from its practitioners, he was never, in their sense, a realist, and when after experimentation he evolved a method peculiar to himself, this method was destined to have an effect in combating realism; it was actually a move in the direction of the reaction. As with all the others, Balzac was his first master, and throughout his work something of Balzac remains—the Balzacian sense of the importance of appurtenances and things, which made a special appeal to Henry James. In spite of his theoretic adherence to realism, he did not believe that after Flaubert any writer could do much for the further development of the realistic novel. "Realism," he declared, "seems to us, with *Madame Bovary,* to have said the last word." So, consciously or unconsciously, after his early period, he set himself to evolve a type of novel that was destined to give those in reaction against the realists a battery of new technical devices.

What James contributed that was new was his method, his material—a small, detached, over-privileged, cultivated international group, and the psychological type that made up such a group. The psychological type to which he attached his powers of intuition and investigation was in itself one which, before him, had not been given any studied presentation in literature, though, of course, it had appeared. But it should be noticed that the kind of human being presented by the great European writers, whether ancient or modern, belonged, on the whole, to one or two broad psychological divisions—they were either the men and women in whom the primitive instincts of early man had evolved to the height of strong emotions, with a consequent dimming of a sense of self-preservation, or else they were people in whom the instincts remained in a crude and untutored state, though with some emotional power. There is a third type, less simple than the other two, and to this belong the men and women in whom the instincts have not been brought to the point of strong or over-mastering emotions but have simply been refined away in motive forces of immense psychological complexity, with the sense of self-preservation very active, sometimes dominatingly so. When this type was given in the older literatures, he or she was presented as a heartless schemer or a cold sensualist— an Iago, a Becky Sharp, or a Joseph Surface.

When Henry James devoted his powers to the representation of this type—and the bulk of his personages belong to it—he presented him or her at a stage of refinement, sophistication and good breeding, that occasionally became a kind of idealism. He had studied the type carefully first, in a Puritan environment—and a Puritan may be said by definition to be one in whom primitive instincts have not developed into strong emotions but have been trimmed and regulated into something else which can in time reach, not only an extreme social refinement and gentility, but even a sort of idealism. Henry James, having encountered and appraised the type early, pursued it in many countries through the same social milieu—that of well-to-do people surrounded by the luxuries of living.

In the group in Paris that he frequented, he had noticed that when he uttered them, his ideas on novel writing made small impression. Flaubert, who had accomplished the realistic revolution, was taking very little stock in the novel-writing theories of a young American who did not seem to him to know what he was talking about; his interest, as well as his disapproval, was centered on Zola, who had nominated himself his disciple; then the Goncourts were off on a line about the novel of the working class, or as they called it, the *basses classes,* which had but little interest for Henry James. But there was also associated with the group Ivan Turgenev—"Mon grand moujik," Flaubert called him—and though James learned a great deal from all the others, it was Turgenev who turned his mind to the special problems in technique that became his lifelong interest, even his obsession. "Henry James went to Paris and read Turgenev; Howells stayed in America and read Henry James," said George Moore, that other subtle technician of the novel.

"A novel, for Turgenev," Henry James told us, "almost always began with a vision of some persons who hovered before him, soliciting him . . . then he had to find out for them the right relations, those that would most bring them out . . . and the situations most useful and favorable to the sense of the creatures themselves." This way of approaching a novel, Turgenev maintained, reduced the "architecture" to a minimum, and he would rather have too little "architecture" than too much. This preference for little "architecture" meant the minimizing of plot and became one of the corner-stones of James's technique. Like Turgenev, he took characters that solicited his interest and he set them moving in their world, using only the amount of plot that would keep them going. Like Turgenev, Henry James, in his early novels, was the narrator, narrating a story in chronological order, as in *Roderick Hudson,* or *Washington Square,* or *The Portrait of a Lady.* But after he had written some twenty or twenty-five novels, and towards 1890, it is clear that he began seriously to question himself both as to his material and his methods. He was intellectually too clear-sighted, too original, not to be aware that unless he could make a contribution of his own he would be merely one more of the numerous diggers in another man's ditch. The first sign of his uneasiness was his dropping his international material for a time and devoting himself to depicting the English society around him. The next move by which he showed his feeling that his work had need of change, of renewal, was a venture into play-writing, into the world of the theatre. This was, as most literary men's are, unsuccessful. Restlessly he turned towards writing short novels; finally, *What Maisie Knew* and *The Awkward Age* showed distinctly the beginnings of his own definitive method. His incursion into the theatre had been the artist's instinctive groping towards self-renewal. George Moore, who had belonged to the same group in Paris as Henry James, had, at the very same time, felt the same need for renewal of his work: in his case, it took the shape of going back to Ireland and turning his attention to the traditional Gaelic narrative forms.

The three novels that revealed James's new manner in complete development are *The Wings of the Dove, The Ambassadors, The Golden Bowl,* and in these we find his deeper and ever deeper concern with psychological reasons. Here he throws over whatever of the objective and direct methods of the realists still remained with him, and devotes himself completely to following clues to the interior lives of his characters, to tracing their stream of consciousness. In these novels we can note definitely the results of his incursion into play-writing. They are constructed as a series of situations, "scenically," he himself says, as if he had started by drafting a scenario, as a playwright does. Probably no novelist before or since has constructed such a complete scenario for a novel as he did, step by step, scene by scene, act by act, for *The Ambassadors.* His dialogue has also changed in character: if we compare the sort of conversation that is in *The Portrait of a Lady* with the conversation in *The Wings of the Dove,* we find in the later novel a conversation directed to the revealing of character and the preparation of situations such as might be constructed by a playwright in a piece of dramatic dialogue. Now, instead of the all-knowing author, the ideal spectator, who can reveal everything in the minds of his characters, we have an indirect device; now he begins to give "not my own personal account of the affair in hand, but my account of somebody's impression of it." In short, he begins to present his characters and his story "through the opportunity and the sensibility of some more or less detached, some not strictly involved, though thoroughly interested and intelligent witness or reporter." In the first volume of *The Golden Bowl* we see the affair in hand, and all the characters, through the mind of the Prince; later, we see it and them through the mind of the Princess. As the author himself states, the Prince opens the door to half the light on Maggie (the Princess) and she opens it to half the light on the Prince. Then, in these last novels, he does not start with the characters soliciting him, as in his early books, but with a sort of metaphysical idea sometimes suggested by an anecdote half told at a dinner table. For instance, the idea that started him on *The Ambassadors* came from the report of a conversation in which somebody had remarked, "One should live all one can," and the essence of the novel is contained in Strether's outbreak, "Live all you can; it's a mistake not to. It doesn't so much matter what you do in particular so long as you have your life. If you haven't had that, what have you had? Live, live!" A similar idea is behind *The Wings of the Dove.*

As he penetrates more and more into the interior lives of his personages, he touches on motives that are barely ponderable, and in trying to carry these over to the reader, he makes the characters themselves extraordinarily analytic, almost forcing them to penetrate into their own unconscious. In this way, the narrative of his later novels becomes an interior narrative with an interior dialogue constantly going on; he has somehow succeeded in making objectivity and chronology seem no longer so important as the realists made them. It is only a step from his interior narrative and interior dialogue to the interior monologue or to the contemporary method of sur-realism. The main thing now for Henry James became the touching of the psychological rhythm at its most significant key, for which reason he frequently begins a novel or a tale or a chapter in the middle of its interest as a story but at the height of its interest as psychological tension.

To understand the twistings and turnings in the technique of the modern novel, to understand the half-notes and the semi-tones, the detectivating attitude towards the interior motives, what Henry James has accomplished must be carefully taken into account, for he was one of the great technical masters in literature, one of those who discover how human experiences can be revealed. Granted that he was one of those to whom the supreme and devastating and transforming human emotions could never happen, yet he invented a way for expressing the infra-motives, the half emotions, the subdued desires that are a motive power with so much of civilized humanity. It is idle to suppose that fundamentally he felt he had made any sort of mistake in exiling himself from his country; to write of international society was his job and to be an exile was his function to which his instinct led him. Like most of the New England writers his instinct about his own destiny was sound; he was one of those destined to lead literature across national frontiers; he did this so well and with a technique so intellectually subtle, so meticulously worked out, that he was decades ahead of his time, as was Stendhal, and like Stendhal he was one of the masters of the distinguished workers in his own art. Also he gathered into his work many of the faint stirrings of the new manners in literature that were being worked up around him; a thorough symbolist, he took in the indirect methods of the Symbolists, and he left behind him a whole armory of technical devices for those writers coming after him who were capable of using them, and among the outstanding students of his work were Marcel Proust and James Joyce.

James was, of course, thoroughly American. When Ford Madox Ford tells us that Henry James was the most American product that New England turned out, he is stating what a critic familiar with both Europe and America, and their literatures, knows to be a simple fact. Whatever the material he used, he handled it as only an American could: only an American could have grasped the international scene as he did. Then, in his mental equipment, he had a strong common likeness to the other New England writers. He was meagerly endowed emotionally; he had a remoteness from everyday life; he had a refinement that was a trifle bewildering to his European confrères. He had the American quality of high intelligence, a penetrating intelligence, and this, attached to an acute psychological curiosity, produced what Taine would call his master-faculty. In common with Hawthorne and Poe, Henry James had a peculiarly American sense of eeriness and terror; he had likewise their inclination towards symbolism. Poe's approach in his stories, and in his "Eureka," is that of an investigator towards the problem of a cryptogram for which curiosity and concentrated intelligence could eventually provide a solution. In regard to his characters and their emotions, Henry James, like Poe, turned a concentrated intelligence onto the solution of a cryptogram.

Chapter Eleven

THE REVOLT

I

IN THE INNER courts of literature, for over fifty years there has been a struggle against the doctrine, the technique, the content, and the language of realism. It began in France, for it was there that the doctrine and the practice had ripened fastest, and the revolt was in full blast before the original doctrine had reached some of the other literatures. The revolters made little headway as far as the novel and drama went, for it was to the interest, not only of the real writers in these forms, but especially of a large group of the new trade writers, to hold the novel and the drama bound to the fact, the document, the observation of external and everyday life. Realism had such sanction that any sort of novel or drama that people could recognize as a transcript of life at first hand was regarded as superior in literary merit to romance and adventure writing of any kind. The documentary novel, with the locale in the lowest social milieu, with the characters treated from the physiological and economic standpoint, that would be welcomed enthusiastically in Paris, say, in 1890, would reach Berlin sometime before 1900, would get to Chicago and New York in the 1930's. And the only difference that the course of time had made between one and another of them would be in the geographical situation and the day-by-day routine of living. But in actual revelation of life there would be no difference at all. All of them would be intelligent and show powers of observation, for the realistic novel of any kind can exist only on these qualities, but of imagination, of sympathetic communication with life, of real creative effort, of power in the moulding of language, there would be little or no evidence. The ideas propounded by the authors, the characters displayed, would be of exactly the same kind, in the 1890's in Paris, the 1900's in Berlin, and the 1930's in Chicago or New York: the same critical vocabulary would be rife in acclaiming them. The Goncourts' term for non-realistic literature, "anodyne," used by them in 1865, became current in America sixty years later as "escapist" literature and was used in the same disparaging sense with regard to any literature of the imagination. A poem like Lindsay's "The Chinese Nightingale," a novel like Thornton Wilder's *The Bridge of San Luis Rey,* were attacked because the authors did not come "to grips with life," and did not deal with strikes, modern industrial life, with economic struggle. A novel about prostitutes and pimps and the moral dregs of society, like Charles-Louis Philippe's

Bubu of Montparnasse, which was received as a distinct revelation in Paris in 1900, would have its American version about 1935. In America, such works were considered the expression of after-war disintegration, whereas they were really the sign of paucity in literary invention and of the belatedness with which literary fashions of the Continent arrive in English-speaking countries. As the radical middle-class intelligentsia, interested in political and social reforms, increased in every country, realistic writing became more and more popular and profitable, for it could be made to reflect the special problems of the moment, and be a sort of history of the day.

There was, as has already been noted, a school of poetry, the Parnassian, which corresponded in a manner to the higher realism in prose. The leader of this school, Théophile Gautier, who called himself "a man for whom the exterior world exists," made an effort to translate into poetry the exterior world that he observed and knew, without injecting into it his own personality. Trained in painting, he tried to reproduce in language the effects of painting; his observations he translated into precise images and words, for he prided himself on the exactitude of his imagery and his vocabulary. He and the other Parnassians tried to produce a poetry that was hard, clear and impersonal. The bulk of the Parnassian theories, mixed with a few theories from the Symbolists, was taken over between 1910 and 1920 by a short-lived school of English and American poets who called themselves "Imagists."

2

The first clear indication of a strong revolt against realism was given in poetry. Of the two who began the revolt, Paul Verlaine and Arthur Rimbaud, both were in descent from Baudelaire, though they started with a leaning towards the Parnassians. Rimbaud had such a powerful originality and was so thoroughly in revolt against objective and realistic literature that, if he had pursued the normal productive life of a writer for about ten or fifteen years, giving his mind a chance to grow and his theories to ripen, he might have been the leader of a school of poetry that, on its side, would have been as forceful as the realists were in prose. But his creative period lasted only a couple of years, and before he was twenty he had deserted literature forever. Had he worked a few years more, his extreme, his anarchical doctrines, might have been moderated, widened, left more inclusive and usable for succeeding poets. Rimbaud's ambition was to overthrow the current ideas of prose and poetry and to start a completely new literary expression based on the idea that the only reality was in the world inside man; the world of external appearances was a snare. For poetry, the dream was the only thing—*le rêve* and the Baudelarian music. Out of the past he would admit nobody to be of any literary importance except

Baudelaire, and with him he believed a new day had begun. "Before Baudelaire," he wrote, "there was no poetry at all; there was only a sort of rhymed prose, the bovine glory of innumerable generations of idiots." In such revolt was he against realism and the external world as a subject for literature, that he forced himself into a state of mind where all was vision. "I say one must be a seer. The poet must make himself a seer by a prolonged, immense, reasoned derangement of all his senses." "I accustomed myself," he wrote, "to a simple state of hallucination. I saw very plainly a mosque in the place of a mill, a drum-band of angels, carriages on the highways of the sky, a salon at the bottom of a lake. . . . Then I explained my magical sophisms with the hallucination of words. I ended by finding sacred the disorder of my spirit. . . . My weakness was leading me to the confines of the world and of Cimmeria, the fatherland of shades and whirlwinds."

By something like a reasoned derangement of his own senses, a dream or an hallucination, Rimbaud produced his astonishing "Bateau Ivre," one of the most remarkable poems in the whole of literature, a completely original poem and of a far more sustained creativeness than that other original poem, also by a young man in his teens, Poe's "To Helen." The "Bateau Ivre" is of such vigor, such thrilling and original imagery, such varied and subtle music, that it is difficult to believe that a young man who could write in such fashion abandoned literature without regret at the age of nineteen, looking back afterwards on his brief literary career as "une saison en enfer"—a term in hell. Like Poe's "To Helen," the "Bateau Ivre" had far-reaching effects, and there have been distinguished men of letters in our day, such as Paul Claudel and Jacques Rivière, who are convinced that Rimbaud was one of the greatest and most original poets who have ever existed.

Part of the "Bateau Ivre" goes back to a boy's dream of adventure, as when in the first stanza he visualizes the boat descending an impassable river in America, attacked by redskins, its haulers seized and nailed to vari-colored totem poles. The boat itself thus left to its own devices staggers down the river to the sea without guidance, like a drunken man. Then we have the dream-like adventures of the boat as it is tossed about by wild storms, drifting through strange seas, touching incredible lands, encountering all the legendary spectacles of the sea, finally, wearily sinking under the waves. All is related in verse of the most marvellous and far-fetched imagery, exhibiting in the very highest degree the seer-like quality that Rimbaud insisted the poet must attain to. While freely using colloquial expressions, he does not employ them in their ordinary meaning but according to some associated meaning that the image he is projecting calls forth. For instance, when he is noting the phosphorescent lights on the tropical sea, he describes them as "des phosphores chanteurs," which means literally "singing phosphorus," suggesting the vibration of the lights through its resemblance to the vibration of a singer's voice. Words are used with the deliberate intention of suggesting more than one meaning: thus, the Indians who have seized the haulers are described as "les Peaux-Rouges criards," which means both "the yelling Red-skins" and "the Red-skins vivid with war-paint." Now and again words are shifted from their normal place in the sentence; sometimes the reader is free to construe whatever meaning his sensibility and imagination can receive from the description of the visionary adventures of the intoxicated boat. With a boy's dream of strange lands and seas there is mixed a man's desolate feeling of the meaninglessness, aimlessness and wastefulness of life. Sometimes the boat loses its identity in the poet, and it is the man who hurtles himself, masterless, rudderless, into unchecked adventures. It is as if the poet at the age of seventeen, when he wrote the "Bateau Ivre," peered into the future and saw the adventurous, exotic, rudderless life that was to be his.

Je sais les cieux crevant en éclairs, et les trombes
Et les ressacs et les courants; je sais le soir,
L'aube exaltée ainsi qu'un peuple de colombes,
Et j'ai vu quelquefois ce que l'homme a cru voir.

J'ai vu le soleil bas, taché d'horreurs mystiques,
Illuminant de longs figements violets,
Pareils à des acteurs de drames très antiques,
Les flots roulant au loin leurs frissons de volets.

THE REVOLT

J'ai rêvé la nuit verte aux neiges éblouies,
Baisers montant aux yeux des mers avec lenteur,
La circulation des sèves inouies
Et l'éveil jaune et bleu des phosphores chanteurs.

. . . .

Or, moi, bateau perdu sous les cheveux des anses,
Jeté par l'ouragan dans l'éther sans oiseau,
Moi dont les Monitors et les voiliers des Hanses
N'auraient pas repêché la carcasse ivre d'eau.

. . . .

Mais, vrai, j'ai trop pleuré. Les aubes sont navrantes,
Toute lune est atroce et tout soleil amer.
L'acre amour m'a gonflé de torpeurs enivrantes.
Oh! que ma quille éclate! Oh! que j'aille à la mer!

. . . .

I know the skies bursting into flashes and the waterspouts,
And the waves' back-wash and the currents; I know the
    evening,
The dawn uplifted like a flock of doves,
And I have sometimes seen what men believed they saw.

I have seen the low sun, stained with mystic horrors,
Lighting up with long, violet curdlings,
Like the actors in antique plays,
The shivering clefts of the waves in the distance.

I have dreamed the green night through with its dazzle of
    snow,
Kisses tardily rising to the eyes of the sea,
The circulation of unheard-of ichors,
And the yellow-blue awakening of the vibrating phosphorus.

. . . .

Now I, a boat lost under the lianas of the creeks,
Flung by the whirlwind into the birdless air,
I, whose drunken carcass neither iron-clads nor the schooners
    of Hansa
Would have fished out of the water.

  . . . .

But truly I have wept too much. The dawns are intolerable,
Every moon is atrocious, and every sun is galling.
Bitter love has filled me with enervating languors.
Oh, let my keel burst, let me go under the sea!

                       (*Literal translation by M. M. C.*)

The imagery of this poem is hardly related to actual
sights or sounds but has correspondences with sight, or
sound, or memory, in the poet's mind, which makes an
appeal, not to the surface intelligence of the reader but
to his imagination, to his sensibility and his associations.
And yet one can believe that this very complicated poem
might have glamorous interest for seventeen-year-olds
who had never read anything except boys' books of adventure.

It is hard to know whether all the creative power
Rimbaud possessed, that "circulation of unheard-of
ichors," came to sudden fruition and an end in a couple
of years, or whether his relation with Verlaine disgusted him forever with all memories of his literary
life, that life which he was to describe as "a term in
hell." It was Verlaine, however, who had the haunting
regret as well as the lasting attachment. While the
great intellectual power, the revolutionary originality,

the transforming force, was Rimbaud's, Verlaine had that sort of unique emotional power which can result in expression of the most direct simplicity. Nothing can show this better than the little poem he wrote while in gaol for wounding Rimbaud with a revolver.

Le ciel est, par-dessus le toit,
Si bleu, si calme!
Un arbre, par-dessus le toit,
Berce sa palme.

La cloche, dans le ciel qu'on voit,
Doucement tinte.
Un oiseau, sur l'arbre qu'on voit,
Chante sa plainte.

Mon Dieu, mon Dieu, la vie est là,
Simple et tranquille.
Cette paisible rumeur-là,
Vient de la ville.

Qu'as-tu fait, ô toi que voilà
Pleurant sans cesse,
Dis, qu'as-tu fait, toi que voilà,
De ta jeunesse?

.   .   .   .

The sky is up above the roof,
So blue, so calm,
A tree above the roof
Rocks its branch.

The bell, in the sky we see,
Softly chimes,
A bird, on the tree we see,
Sings its lament.

O God, O God, life is there,
Simple and sweet,
That peaceful humming there
Comes from the town.

What have you done, O you there,
Weeping without ceasing—
Say, what have you done, O you there,
With your youth?
(*Literal translation by M. M. C.*)

This very great sincerity, this integral expression, is only to be found in a few poems, outside of folk-songs, in the whole of literature, and oftener in English literature than in any other. Both Verlaine and Rimbaud were profoundly influenced by English poetry, and sometimes what their innovations amounted to was an attempt to reproduce in French the half-said, blurred effects of English poetry.

Verlaine, before his meeting with Rimbaud, was a fine poet; after this meeting, he became a great one, for all the potentialities that were in him, of original thought, of emotion, of musical utterance, all his latent sense of revolt against the nullity towards which literature was heading, came to the surface under the influence of this prophetic and penetrating mind and this disrupting personality. All that Verlaine did not of himself understand of the necessity for renewal in literature, this young man made him aware of. Rimbaud was an example of precocious intellect and poetical intuition unparalleled in literature, with perhaps the exception of Chatterton. He was a sort of elemental creative force, bursting to reform everything he touched. In his "L'Alchimie du Verbe"—"Transfiguration of the Word"—he tells us how he wanted to invent not only new poetical forms but a new world with new stars, new flowers, new flesh; he wanted especially to invent a new language, for, as he said, it was impossible to write poetry in words and sentences that had been weighed down by the leaden meanings of practical life. He wanted to reform both God and man, for this astonishing young man thought that the mind could re-create all things; he studied magic and necromancy; he imagined himself, as other poets sometimes have imagined themselves, to be a sorcerer or alchemist, and he thought that by forcing his mind outside everyday existence he might ultimately attain the talisman for changing life. To the bespelled Verlaine, ten years his elder, he taught that letting oneself be involved in the common world of eating, sleeping, begetting and providing for a family was practically the all-inclusive vice, and that the old world of everyday happenings had nothing to do with poetry or with the poet's existence.

Whatever has to be said against their relationship, it was, while it lasted, a period of intense intellectual, poetical, and emotional activity for both Rimbaud and Verlaine. Under the influence of Rimbaud, Verlaine wrote his "Art Poétique," which crystallized the new attitudes towards poetry and which later became a sort of gospel with the Mallarméan symbolists. Most of the theories of this poem were derived from Rimbaud and from English poetry. To write poetry like English poetry in a language like French, which had been developed logically with the avowed intention of becoming an instrument of expression of the greatest clarity, was immensely difficult. To express under-tones and over-tones, hidden meanings, to attain the half-said thing, to make an appeal directly from one sensibility to another, was, in the language and in the existent metres, if not exactly an impossibility, at least a perplexing task. Consequently Verlaine's "Art of Poetry," which, though written during his relation with Rimbaud, became generally known only a decade later, was accepted as a liberation; Verlaine, following Poe and Baudelaire, demanded in poetry *de la musique avant toute chose*—music above all—and he marched haughtily past the great French sign-posts demanding the *mot juste*. The latest of these, it will be remembered, had been set up by Gautier and Flaubert. Verlaine asked the poet to choose his words somewhat carelessly, unprecisely, to join the precise to the unprecise—in short, to achieve, not the exact, but the nuanced. This was more in accordance with Rimbaud's practice than with Verlaine's.

> Car nous voulons la nuance encor,
> Pas la couleur, rien que la nuance!
> Oh! la nuance seule fiance
> Le rêve au rêve et la flûte au cor!

.   .   .   .

> For we want the nuance,
> Nothing of color, only the nuance!
> Oh! the nuance alone weds
> The dream to the dream and the flute to the horn.

In a succeeding stanza he tenders that since often-quoted advice—"Prends l'éloquence et tords-lui son cou!"—"Take eloquence and wring its neck." This manifesto has been taken very seriously by the poets in English since the 1890's, the line about twisting the neck of eloquence being put forward as a poetical principle, though, as a matter of fact, it has very little application for an English poet, for what Verlaine meant by "eloquence" was that deliberate study of rhetoric so usual in France and which had played such havoc with French literature after the great classical period. But eloquence had been a glory in English poetry, especially with the great dramatic poets, and still remains a glory when it does not sink to mere declamation. Verlaine recommended the break-up of the French line into unequal lines, and after a mocking attack on rhyme and a praise

of assonance, he summed up the modern Art of Poetry
in two stanzas that have passed into the literatures of the
world.

> De la musique encore et toujours!
> Que tons vers soit la chose envolée,
> Qu'on sent qui fuit d'une âme en allée
> Vers d'autres cieux à d'autres amours.
>
> Que ton vers soit la bonne aventure
> Éparse au vent crispé du matin
> Qui va fleurant la menthe et le thym . . .
> Et tout le reste est littérature!
>
> . . . .
>
> Music again and ever!
> Let your verse be a thing on wings,
> Which visibly came from a soul in flight
> Towards other skies and other loves.
>
> Let your verse be the gay adventure
> Scattered on the crisp wind of morning
> Which snares the scents of mint and thyme . . .
> And all the rest is literature.
>
> *(Literal translation by M. M. C.)*

Verlaine lived for twenty-three years after the separation from Rimbaud, holding deep in his mind the
memory of his lost friend, his "époux infernal," and
editing an edition of his poems. The "époux infernal,"
on his side, abandoned poetry and Europe; he wandered
in Asia, in Africa, and like his own Bateau Ivre, as a
trader he descended impassable rivers, sailed phosphor-

escent seas, until "every dawn became intolerable, every moon atrocious and every sun bitter." He died at the age of thirty-seven in a hospital in Marseilles, caring nothing at all for the reports which reached him of his increasing fame as a poet. Verlaine died even more miserably than Rimbaud, alone in a dismal room, half falling out of bed, while the trollop with whom he lived deserted him in his dying hour to drink with her cronies in a neighboring bistro. Rimbaud and Verlaine were the last great French poets; there have been distinguished poets since, but no really great ones. When Rimbaud vanished from the literary scene, leaving his small bulk of work behind him, his admirers said that he had left with Verlaine the secret of the poetry of the future.

If a writer of great genius had then appeared, who could have taken over "the secret," who was capable of making a new synthesis of the exterior and the interior life, of the dream life and the everyday life, another new creative age might have been inaugurated. But the men who took it over, the Symbolists, were not able to use it in a way to render any powerful service to literature. The turning away from the exterior and the concentration on the interior world became, in their case, as exaggerated as the concentration of the realists on the physical world. If the realists de-valuated the life of the spirit, the bulk of the Symbolists rejected physical and everyday life as matter for literature in a manner which was destined to be not only limiting but even sterilizing. They were, in the main, accomplished and subtle men of letters, with a gift for poetry, a great flair for theorizing, and an excited interest in anything that seemed to lead to literary reform, such as the verse-forms of Whitman and the poetry and criticism of Edgar Allan Poe.

3

While the Symbolists were the most interesting literary group of the late nineteenth century, interesting for their theories and for their attempts to put them into practice, their chief doctrines did not originate with them, and the ones that did, the minor doctrines, were too esoteric and even eccentric to have vigorous life. Their progenitors in French literature were, of course, Baudelaire, Rimbaud and Verlaine; then they took over many ideas from the criticism and poetry of Edgar Allan Poe. Also, they tried to invent a French verse-form that would correspond to Whitman's: this was variously called free verse, liberated verse, polymorphous verse. This last invention has been claimed by Gustave Kahn, but it may have been initiated by the two Americans who were of the group, Stuart Merrill and Vielé Griffin. What the Symbolists accomplished separately is, in the case of most of them, not of so much importance as the general influence that emanated from the group. They were deliberately in revolt against realism and Parnassianism, more deliberately than were Rimbaud and Verlaine, though the core of their ideas came from these two predecessors. They also believed that inner reality is the only reality, and that the world from which a poet draws his poetry is a transcendent world, outside the everyday world. The whole art of poetry needed to be renewed, and the poetry of the future would be different from the poetry of the past, which had been made—and especially in French—with the same language and according to the same grammatical rules as prose. For the making of *this* poetry, the poetry of the future, the common, logical language, created for practical everyday usage, was no longer suitable; the very words that made up the language were conditioned by everyday employment and were incapable of encompassing ideas from the other world, the transcendent world of dream and poetry. Mallarmé, like Rimbaud, conceived of this language as weighing down poetry with the weight of lead.

What then was to be done with language so that it could be made a fitting vehicle for poetic expression? In the past, every initiator of a literary form had, first of all, to do something with language when it had begun to lose tone and color through being used too long in a particular way. The old way of renewing the literary language was to refresh it from popular speech. This was all very well when Dante took over what he called "the illustrious vernacular," or when Luther took over the language of the housewife and the artisan, or when Wordsworth advocated the language of the common Englishman, the rustic. But in the latter part of the nineteenth century, as in our own time, the spread of popular education meant that "the illustrious vernacular" was disappearing, for the popular language was becoming merely a degeneration of the written one. Faced with the problem of language, Mallarmé advanced a number of ideas, which he himself put into practice and some of which have been upheld by poets and writers ever since. Words, he said, should be deprived of their too obvious meaning; the poet should use words in an evocative and a suggestive instead of a literal and logical sense; the mood, the idea, the emotion should be evoked instead of described. This, it will be remembered, was what Edgar Allan Poe had succeeded in doing, both in verse and prose, and Mallarmé even more than Baudelaire was under the spell of Poe. In an often-quoted sentence Mallarmé declared, "to name an object is to suppress three-quarters of the joy of the poem, which is made of the happiness of guessing, little by little—to suggest, that is to reveal the dream." To achieve this evocative and suggestive effect, words, freed from their every-day meaning, should be given another meaning corresponding chiefly to their sound and their association-value. The sound and association-value of words had been used by Rimbaud and by many other poets before him, in many languages, but this was the first time that this special practice was deliberately advanced as part of an Art of Poetry.

Actually, if we take any words in any language—*house, bridge, love; maison, pont, amour; Haus, Brücke, Liebe; casa, ponte, amore*—each of them has at least three meanings: an ordinary sense-meaning, a sound-meaning and an association-meaning. Rimbaud did not mind using common colloquial or even slang words, but he seldom used them in their ordinary meaning, but to convey a sense of association or correspondence. Mallarmé did not use colloquial words, but he believed that words devitalized by their everyday use could again be made living by giving them an unusual place in the sentence; prepositions, conjunctions and words which marked the transitions, or gave a too commonplace clarity, should be thrown out altogether; punctuation and other marks, like capital letters, which are a logical or a conventional imposition on the line, should be rejected. The poet's business was not to trim his ideas into a logical order; it was the business of the reader to give them such an order. He held that a poem was a mystery, the key to which the reader or hearer had to search for; therefore, it might easily come about that, as each reader would supply a different key, different interpretations of a poem were quite as legitimate as different interpretations of a piece of music, for in music alone was expressed the interior life without the imposition of logical development.

331

These ideas, in practically the same form, had first been put forward as far back as the time of Goethe, by that strange romantic German writer, Novalis (Von Hardenberg, the seeker after the blue rose). Novalis announced that poetry achieved its object in proportion as it approached the art of music, the most all-embracing of the arts; like the later Mallarmé, he held that there could be a poetry which had no intelligible meaning and which might be made up of musical sounds. He held other views, similar to or identical with those which became associated with the Symbolists: that poetry should express the profound and mysterious reaches of the soul, the essence of the interior life; that poetry is an interior language, the conversation of the soul with itself, therefore, it should not be shut up in too precise forms that might hinder the free flight of the mind. Novalis also declared that the art of revealing the interior life of dream demanded something higher than our common logic, which is the art of deliberate thinking. He conceived, too, of a prose literature which would not be logically joined together but where the connection would be through the association of ideas, as in dreams. When we review these conceptions we perceive that Novalis was in possession of most of the reforming theories of the Symbolists.

But what was original with the Symbolists was their attempt to unite these theories with the new philosophies of the unconscious that were then coming in, chiefly the philosophy of Hartmann, but also that of Schopenhauer, which tended to show that intelligence was a by-product of other life-forces and that reason and logic were more or less irrelevant. This gave some of the Symbolists a more metaphysical and cerebral attitude than their predecessors towards the content and structure of a poem. Mallarmé was metaphysical where Novalis was mystical, where Rimbaud was sensuous and ardent, and Verlaine emotional. With Mallarmé, a phase of the interior life of the mind, what he called the transcendent reality, would be translated into an idea, and this idea would then be transposed into a symbol, or several symbols, that would evoke or suggest it, and would contain it as "a plant contains a flower without resembling it." From this came the Symbolist formula, or one of the Symbolist formulas: a work of art is a thought inscribed in a symbol.

To show what Mallarmé meant and how he put the theory into practice, we will take the most often-quoted of his hermetic sonnets, the one entitled "Sonnet en i Majeur," which expresses a common mood of his spirit, the blankness of his mind before a white sheet of paper. In this poem, it will be observed that in spite of its difficulty, the Symbolism though deliberate is comparatively clear. Though there is undoubtedly a secondary meaning, the primary meaning is quite sufficient for a grasp of the poem. Of the virgin day that begins, the poet wonders if it is going to rend from him some expression, but like a swan frozen into the ice, he cannot shake his mind free from the sterility which holds it bound.

Le vierge, le vivace et le bel aujourd'hui,
Va-t-il nous déchirer avec un coup d'aile ivre
Ce lac dur oublié que hante sous le givre
Le transparent glacier des vols qui n'ont pas fui!

Un cygne d'autrefois se souvient que c'est lui
Magnifique, mais qui, sans espoir, se délivre
Pour n'avoir pas chanté la région où vivre
Quand du stérile hiver a resplendi l'ennui.

Tout son col secouera cette blanche agonie,
Par l'espace infligée à l'oiseau qui le nie,
Mais non l'horreur du sol où le plumage est pris.

Fantôme, qu'a ce lieu son pur éclat assigne,
Il s'immobilise au songe froid de mépris
Que vêt parmi l'exil inutile le Cygne.

. . . .

The virgin, the vibrant, the beautiful To-day,
Will it rend for us with a flash of inebriated wing,
This hard, forgotten lake where, under the glaze, abides
Transparent the congealer of wings that have not flown!

A swan of other days remembers that it is he,
Magnificent, but who, because he has not sung
The region to live in when the ennui of sterile winter
Has gleamed, without hope delivers himself.

All his neck will shake off this white agony
By space inflicted on the bird who disowns it,
But not the horror of the ground where his plumage is held.

Phantom, that to this place his pure brightness assigns,
He immobilizes himself in the cold dream of contempt
With which he vests his vain exile, the Swan.

(Literal translation by M. M. C.)

In this poem, as in all of Mallarmé's except the earlier ones which were written under the influence of Baudelaire, like "La Chair Est Triste, Hélas!" and "Las de l'Amer Repos," if you take the lines separately or the words separately, you will make nothing of them. It is essential to get the total meaning of the poem before examining the lines and the words. The "Sonnet en i Majeur," like many of his poems, contains the history of the efforts of his mind, his struggle for themes, for he was somewhat sterile, and getting a poem out of himself could only be accomplished by enormous labor. There is nothing in his writing to show that he ever came to strong grips with life or felt the fiercer forms of love, hate, anger, melancholy, despair or compassion that are in *Les Fleurs du Mal*. But in his best poems, and above all in his wonderful sonnet to Poe, he is able to achieve an expression that does really seem as if it came from some transcendent world, so noble and sweeping it is. However, his deliberate attempt to be obscure gives one a feeling as of a man trying to arrange a cross-word puzzle, and he set the example, or he or his followers gave the formula, for some of the strange verse-concoctions of our time that are considered poetry in certain writing *cénacles*.

Towards his last phase he got to the point where he conceived that poetry should actually be written as music is written, the theme orchestrated instead of developed, the words used like notes in music, grouped in some lines, isolated in others, the whole printed so as to give obscurely the effect of a sheet of music. At this stage he had fallen under the influence of Wagner and Debussy in music, and had reached that old heresy, or old illusion, that a synthesis of all the arts could be achieved and a single art evolved which would convey visual effects and sound effects, suggest plastic effects and color effects, as well as transmit a verbal meaning. The idea of inventing a language which would convey this ensemble occurred to him and to some of his followers; this notion has, in actual fact, been put into practice in our own time by James Joyce, in his strange *Work in Progress*.

4

The poet, sometimes assumed to belong to the Symbolist group, who has had the most influence on writers of our time is Jules Laforgue. While drawing on the ideas of the Symbolists, he can hardly be regarded as one of them, for he was against their favorite doctrine that the interior life represented the only reality, and he considered that they had beaten too complete a retreat from everyday life. He himself evolved a sophisticated realistic poetry in which the two psychic streams, the conscious and the unconscious, were subtly revealed and intermingled. In poems, written in ordinary conversational language, about flirtations, railway stations, pianos playing in the suburbs, the little miseries of winter, or in poems built around the refrains of old songs, he accomplished, in the 'eighties of the last century, almost everything in verse which we consider to be the special expression of this modern, post-war, disintegrated age. He sunk himself in the study of philosophy, and especially in the philosophy of the sub-conscious as, in his pre-Freudian day, it was explained by the German philosopher Hartmann. If he did not succeed in revealing it as Joyce and Proust have done, Laforgue managed to convey, in verse arranged, not logically but according to the association of ideas and with a subtle use of symbolism (not the deliberate symbolism of Mallarmé but a symbolism springing naturally from the subject), the mystery that lies behind the most trivial happenings.

Laforgue's aim was to express in poetry the *homme moyen* of modern civilization, the man who in each country possesses the same sort of apartment, the same sort of piano—in our day it would be a radio—who wears the same sort of clothes, who has fought with the same sort of weapons in the same war. This personage was given by Laforgue a variety of cultivated, sophisticated emotions and ideas, and enough music, art and literature at the back of his mind to color or give a sort of refrain to his experiences of life. Laforgue's influence has been very great, and there have been choruses and choirs of Laforguians in every modern literature. In English, the most important poets who have followed his lead have been T. S. Eliot and Ezra Pound, though there are at least a score or two others in English, Irish and American literature who have tried to achieve the same effects. The following example of a Laforgue poem is an account of a banal flirtation betwen a conventional young woman trying to be profound, and a sophisticated, ironic young man who knows that this appearance of profundity is drawn from whatever little literature the young woman knows.

Elle disait, de son air vain fondamental:
"Je t'aime pour toi seul!"—Oh! là, là, grêle histoire;
Oui, comme l'art! Du calme, ô salaire illusoire
    Du capitaliste Idéal!

Elle faisait: "J'attends, me voici, je sais pas" . . .
Le regard pris de ces larges candeurs des lunes;
—Oh! là, là, ce n'est pas peut-être pour des prunes,
    Qu'on a fait ses classes ici-bas?

Mais voici qu'un beau soir, infortunée à point,
Elle meurt!—Oh! là, là; bon, changement de thème!
On sait que tu dois ressusciter le troisième
    Jour, sinon en personne, du moins

THE REVOLT

Dans l'odeur, les verdures, les eaux des beaux mois!
Et tu iras, levant encore bien plus de dupes
Vers le Zaimph de la Joconde, vers la Jupe!
    Il se pourra même que j'en sois.

.   .   .   .

She said, with her empty transcendental air:
"I love you for yourself alone." Oh, my, my! the old story;
Yes, like a book. O illusory salary of the calm,
    Of the capitalistic ideal!

She went on: "I am waiting, here I am, I don't know" . . .
Her eyes full of the large candours of moons;
Oh, my, my! it is not perhaps for nothing
    That one takes one's college courses, here below?

But, lo, one fine evening, unfortunately,
She dies. Oh, my, my! let us change the subject.
We know that you should arise the third
    Day, if not in person, at least

In the odour, in the verdure, in the waters of the fine
    months.
And you will go levying further dupes,
Towards Giaconda's guimpe, towards the gown!
    Very likely I'll be one of them.
                (*Literal translation by M. M. C.*)

Even more than the official Symbolists Laforgue
broke up the logically arranged lines in verse which
were an imposition from all previous literatures. Even
in the most romantic English poetry, which at times
provided a pattern for the Symbolists, it was the poet's
design to develop his theme logically, in logically ar-

ranged lines. A well-known poem of Shelley's runs like this:

> I arise from dreams of thee
> In the first sweet sleep of night,
> When the winds are breathing low
> And the stars are shining bright.

And proceeds by a logical sequence:

> I die, I faint, I fail!
> Let thy love in kisses rain
> On my lips and eyelids pale.

But the modern poets who wanted to express hitherto unstressed complexities of emotions believed that almost anything of the multitudinous ideas associated with love was matter for a love-poem. As a lover arising from dreams of his belovèd was just as likely to associate his emotion with ideas of how to array himself as with exclaiming, "I die, I faint, I fail," T. S. Eliot, in the "Love Song of J. Alfred Prufrock," wrote:

I grow old. . . . I grow old. . . .
I shall wear the bottoms of my trousers rolled.
Shall I part my hair behind? Do I dare to eat a peach?
I shall wear white flannel trousers and walk upon the beach.
I have heard the mermaids singing each to each.

I do not think that they will sing to me.

. . . .

We have lingered in the chambers of the sea
By sea-girls wreathed with sea-weed red and brown,
Till human voices wake us and we drown.

The influence of Laforgue in breaking up the old logic, the old unity of poetry, was greater than Mallarmé's, and the content and form of his verse, in addition, exercised a considerable influence on the technique of the novel. This was true, however, of all those modern poets who broke off from the older traditions. Baudelaire's peculiar realism, in which he expressed his own personal conflicts with life and the conflict of the interior life with the exterior world, was one of the influences which made for the modern autobiographic, semi-realistic novel, with a strong strain of lyricism running through it. Another persistent and lasting influence towards this kind of fiction was Goethe's *Wilhelm Meister,* which still holds its glamour for most young men and women, and for all young writers.

Among the other forces acting on the technique of the novel was the Symbolist formula: a writer should not describe a scene or a character or an emotion—he must evoke them. This—with Henry James's "minimum of architecture" and his later device of presenting his characters and his story "through the opportunity and the sensibility of some more or less detached, some not strictly involved, though thoroughly interested and intelligent witness or reporter," his habit of dealing with barely ponderable motives—is responsible for the bulk of modern technical reforms in fiction. The idea of giving us the scene, not as Flaubert did, completely objectively, with the novelist like God in the universe the ideal spectator present everywhere, but simply as one or two persons involved see it, was first carried out by Stendhal, who, in his famous account of the battle of Waterloo, describes only so much of it as was apparent to Fabrizio; similarly, in *Ulysses,* when James Joyce is describing a funeral, his method differs fundamentally from that of Flaubert. In the account of the funeral in *Madame Bovary,* we have every significant detail realistically described—the funeral procession, the grave-clothes of Emma, the three coffins, the chanting choristers, the lighted candles, the priest, the lowering of the coffin into the open grave. Through nine or ten pages we have nothing but the funeral. James Joyce takes about thirty pages to present his funeral, but instead of Flaubert's objective description, he presents the streets of Dublin and some people passing along, as they appear, in occasional views through the shaded windows, to the occupants of one of the mourning-carriages. We have the aimless gossip, on all sorts of topics, by the men in the carriage—the half-conscious and subconscious thoughts of the chief character, Leopold Bloom. Similarly, when Virginia Woolf is presenting, in *Jacob's Room,* a party, there is no objective description; she puts the party before us by giving us the conversation of people meeting and passing each other in the ballroom, by remarks thrown out as the partners dance past each other; and the effect, in both cases, of the inconsequent actuality of the conversation is most memorable in bringing to us the funeral and the dance; the reader feels as if he were participating in the events. However, this sort of technique is sometimes bewildering to those accustomed to the realistic, semi-realistic, or romantic novel, for it is often only when the reader has got the impression of a whole chapter in his mind that he knows what is taking place, or where it is taking place.

5

But the great, the overwhelming influences on all literary transformations—on technique, on content, on language—were the new discoveries in psychology, the new knowledge of the mind, arrived at in the last quarter of the nineteenth century and the beginning of the twentieth. When all the old conventions were being shaken to pieces, it was discovered that that universally accepted figure, the conscious man, the man that all laws, governments, civilizations, had been built around, was also a convention. Man was only conscious to a limited degree: the greater part of him was unconscious. This fact had peeped in and out of philosophy for a long time, but as it was very disturbing, the bulk of mankind preferred to ignore it. Hartmann expressed the discovery first, for the Germans, and when his work was translated into French it greatly stirred the writers in reaction against realism, for it seemed then as if this new philosophy would be a pillar of support to those who believed the interior life, the life beyond everyday life, to be the only reality. In the 'eighties, Charcot and Ribot demonstrated the discoveries for the French; and in America, at about the same time, William James, experimenting in psychology, got himself employed as a census-assistant so as to have the opportunity to meet and study a wide variety of human beings. After his census experience he declared, "We all have a subliminal self—that is, a self below the threshold of consciousness, which may at any time make an eruption into our ordinary life. At its lowest, this is only a deposit of forgotten memories; at its highest, we do not know what it is at all." It was James, too, who was responsible for the famous simile of the iceberg—that the conscious mind is comparable to the smaller part that is above water, the unconscious to the greater bulk that is submerged.

Théodule Ribot showed the existence, in us, of unconscious memory. Pierre Janet, Charcot's pupil, who lectured recently at the Harvard Tercentenary, demonstrated how several personalities could exist at the same time in one individual, each now and again breaking through to the other. Freud, a while later, developed the technique by which, he said, the subconscious personality and the hidden memory could be brought to the surface, or partly to the surface. After the conscious man and the unified personality were shown to be conventions, the philosopher, Henri Bergson, came along and said that what we call time is a convention; real time was not hours as measured by a clock, or in days or weeks on a calendar; it, too, was something inward, duration experienced; every moment in life represents our entire past shaping itself into a new creative movement; nothing was fixed or finished; everything was in a state of becoming. For Bergson, also, the unconscious was the source from which flowed, in a thin stream for some, in a wider stream for others, our conscious life.

All the literary philosophies relating to the revelation of life having reached a dead end, the writers had to turn to the experimental and speculative philosophies. Such discoveries as had come through them were eagerly seized upon by that type of mind which initiates new literary modes and ideas. Now the first problem was: Could this subconscious part of man, this part that was now described as the moving force of his being, be expressed in literature? As in poetry the first attempt had been made, in the 'eighties, so now in prose the first attempt also was made, and made by a curiously talented novelist of very limited range, who was a follower of one of the Symbolist groups, Edouard Dujardin, still alive. He attempted to express the undercurrent of the mind of his character by "the interior monologue." Now, what is the interior monologue, which is being so identified with our most advanced novelists, though, like almost every other modern literary device, it dates back to the nineteenth century? I know no better definition of it than Dujardin's own: "The interior monologue is the discourse without auditor, unspoken, by which a person expresses his inmost thought, the thought nearest the unconscious, anterior to any logical organization, by means of sentences with a minimum of syntax. It is done so as to give the impression that it is poured out, and is a slice of the interior life without explanation or commentary."

Dujardin himself had not sufficient clue to the technique to be employed in rendering "the thought nearest the unconscious." But in the interim between him and the writer who took the next step forward, James Joyce, there came all the discoveries of Freud and Freud's technique for getting a patient to pour out his unconscious life. That the interior monologue, which was one of the most discussed features of *Ulysses* on its publication, was managed so successfully was because Freud had actually discovered a method of revealing the subconscious and the twilight stage between the conscious and the unconscious. Freud made the subject lie on a couch while he himself took up a position where he could not be seen, and induced the subject to talk, following step by step anything that came into his mind, one idea leading to another, one memory suggesting another, one association dragging another to the surface of the mind, until the world below consciousness was revealed either wholly or in part. This is really the process followed by Joyce in the celebrated monologue of Marion Bloom with which *Ulysses* ends.

For purposes of illustration, I give a short quotation from this monologue, which is a widely imitated device in recent novels:

> they all write about some woman in their poetry well I suppose he won't find many like me where softly sighs of love the light guitar where poetry is in the air the blue sea and the moon shining so beautifully coming back on the night-boat from Tarifa the light-house at Europa point the guitar that fellow played was so expressive will I never go back there again all new faces two glancing eyes a lattice hid I'll sing that for him they're my eyes as if he has anything of a poet two eyes as darkly bright as love's own star aren't those beautiful words as love's young star it'll be a change the Lord knows to have an intelligent person to talk to about yourself not always listening to him and Billy Prescott's ad and Keyses' ad and Tom the Divil's ad then if anything goes wrong in their business we have to suffer.

Is this actually the way the mind works anterior to consciousness? An extraordinary light was recently thrown on the authenticity of the procedure by the case of a criminal dying in New York. Detectives attached to the criminal bureaus in our large cities are, like writers and doctors, students of psychology, and one of them had the idea of taking down a stenographic report of the utterance of a gangster, Dutch Schultz, while in that state of mind, as the result of a wound, when he was incapable of imposing any logic on what he was saying. The whole stenographic report, not more than a couple of newspaper columns, was a real revelation of the content of the man's mind. Compare the quotation from the novel with the following, from this particular report. Whereas the Joyce extract runs on without punctuation marks, the stenographer has put them into this extract:

Don't put any one near this check; you might have— please do it for me. Let me get up, heh? In the olden days they waited and they waited. Please give me shot. It is from the factory. Sure, that is bad—well, oh good ahead that happens for trying. I don't want harmony. Oh, mamma, mamma! Who give it to him? Who give it to him? Let me in the district—fire—factory that he was nowhere near. It smoldered.

On the publication of *Ulysses,* it was considered by many that it was not possible in literature to carry the expression of the unconscious further and have it keep any intelligible pattern. However, Joyce's new puzzling book, *Work in Progress,* is an attempt to carry the revelation of the unconscious life many stages further than in *Ulyssess* and much further than any other writer has dreamed of bringing it. Proust said of the opening chapter of *À la Recherche du Temps Perdu,* "I have tried to envelope my first chapter in the half-waking impressions of sleep." But Joyce, in this latest work, tries to depict the whole night-life of the mind, and the result, I am afraid, will be intelligible to a very limited number of readers. In *Work in Progress* he is influenced by Novalis's and Mallarmé's theories of

348

the sounds of words, and the work has, in its best-known passage, reproduced so effectively, through the sonority of his words and sentences, the effects of falling night and fluttering river-water that, without the words being even intelligible, the reader can know what the passage is about if it is read aloud and falls on the ear as music does. There are specific points in technique in which it is difficult to believe that any writer can go beyond Joyce. One is the skill with which he evokes a scene, an atmosphere, a personage, a group, without ever once describing them or giving a hint as to who they are or where the scene takes place. He is a master of the evocative method, and if the reader compares the opening of *Ulysses* with the opening of Sinclair Lewis's *It Can't Happen Here,* he will observe immediately and inevitably the difference between the two methods, the evocative and the descriptive. Joyce's mastery of the interior monologue is the second point in his technique in which he is likely to remain unsurpassed, and for this mastery he undoubtedly owes a great deal to Freud.

6

There are a few points in common between James Joyce and the other outstanding modern innovator, Marcel Proust. For Proust, also, the great reality is in the unconscious; he also has an interest in sleep as its great manifestation; for both writers no happening, no event is complete, everything is in a state of becoming.

The work of both represents a reaction against realism, and is at the same time a development of it. Again it should be noted that, in literature, the age that is coming to birth is not only a reaction against the age that is dying but also an outgrowth of it. Both Joyce and Proust subscribe to the fundamental dogma of realism —that literature should be about everyday life; the work of each illustrates certain of the realistic doctrines. Joyce began definitely under the influence of Flaubert, which is patent in the stories in *Dubliners,* and though in the meantime, as can be seen in *Portrait of the Artist,* he was affected by the technique of Henry James, the influence of Flaubert is still traceable in *Ulysses,* especially the pre-realistic Flaubert of *La Tentation de Saint Antoine.* His characters are on the same level as Flaubert's and he has always held to the Flaubertian veto as to the author's commenting on his personages. He has, however, a whole battery of technical devices to reveal what is passing in their minds and what rises up in their memories, of which the interior monologue is but one. Others are the use of scenes parallel with scenes from the Odyssey, of paraphrases of myths and legends, and of parodies of writing representing stages in the development of language. The technique is infinitely more complex than Proust's, the interior life revealed very much less so; in fact, it is comparatively simple, comparatively ordinary, and does not embrace a wide variety of experiences.

The formative periods of the lives of the two writers were totally different. As a student, Joyce lived in Dublin during the most exciting years of the Irish revival and shared the interest of that period in myths, legends, symbolism—not only the particular form of symbolism called the Symbolist Movement, which had a romantic rather than an influential interest, but in all the symbolism of the literature of the past, the symbolism and philosophy of the Catholic Church and the compelling mystery of history. Then, later but still as a very young man, he went to live in Austria, where he encountered the latest manifestations of the philosophy of the unconscious. Proust, a Frenchman, lived in Paris, was influenced by the ideas of French philosophers and psychologists, and also by Freud. He appears to have passed through intense and varied emotional and intellectual experiences, to have sunk himself in music, painting and literature, making a study of the English novelists and of Henry James. The great developing influence on him was that of Bergson. He moulded his work deliberately on the Bergsonian conceptions of Time and Memory; in fact, Time may be called the hero of Proust's *À la Recherche du Temps Perdu*. "This invisible substance of Time," he said, "I have tried to isolate, but to do this the experience had to last." This meant that he had to deal with personages whose lives merged and flowed into each other over a long period, so that every little happening, as he said himself, would indicate the passing of time. Time walks through his book like a personage, transforming things, people, actions, ideas, opinions, social and political groups, from day to day, from year to year. As Time passes, the same personage takes on different aspects in the eyes of others, as, to use Proust's own image, we see different sides of a town from the windows of a train winding through it. Thus, he joined his conception of psychology to his conception of Time, for, as he himself said, "As there is a plane geometry and a geometry in space, so for me the novel is not only plane psychology but psychology in time."

As for Time, real Time, memory is its deposit, but what type of memory? It is what he calls "unconscious memory," as opposed to the memory of the intelligence, to voluntary memory. An odor, a savor, experienced in circumstances quite different, bring back, after the lapse of years, people and things that seem to have been forgotten: this is the unconscious memory, the involuntary memory. For in our lives the Past is that which has ceased to act but has not ceased to exist. It survives in our unconscious and has the potentiality of rising again to consciousness. Marcel Proust produced his work out of this conception of Time and Memory. He called his work in many volumes *À la Recherche du Temps Perdu,* familiar in its English title as *Remembrance of Things Past,* but which, it seems to me, would have been more revealingly translated as *The Search for Lost Time*.

This work unrolls itself as memory brought back to consciousness, Time experienced inwardly, Time made perceptible to the heart. An exact rendering of Bergson's conception of Time is to be found in the final pages of this novel. It is, in fact, probably the first time that there has been put into literature in a moving and imaginative way the central thought, the metaphysics, of a philosopher, during his own lifetime. A sound recalls to the middle-aged man, to Proust himself, the tinkle of the bell which he had heard as a child when his parents were showing their guest, Swann, to the door:

Then, thinking over all the events that necessarily ranged themselves between the moment when I heard those sounds and the Guermantes' reception, I was startled at the thought that it was, indeed, this bell which was still tinkling within me and that I could in no wise change its sharp janglings, since, having forgotten how they died away, to recapture it and hear it distinctly I was forced to close my ears to the sound of the conversations the masks were carrying on around me. . . .

When the bell tinkled I was already in existence and, since that night, for me to have been able to hear the sounds again, there must have been no break of continuity, not a moment of rest for me, no cessation of existence, of thought, of consciousness of myself, since the distant moment still clung to me and I could recapture it, go back to it, merely by descending more deeply into myself. *It was this conception of Time as incarnate, of past years as still close held within us, which I was now determined to bring out into such bold relief in my book.* And it is because they thus contain all the hours of days gone by that human bodies can do such injury to those who love them, because they contain so many past memories, joys and desires, already effaced for them but so cruel for one who contemplates and carries back in the domain of Time the cherished body of which he is jealous, jealous even to the point of desiring its destruction. For, after death, Time withdraws from the body, and the memories—so pale and insignificant—are effaced from her who no longer exists, and soon will be from him whom they still torture, and the memories themselves will perish in the end when the desire of a living body is no longer there to keep them alive.

The novel is an unrolling of life, revealing no crisis, no plot, only the poignant effects of Time on people who, day by day, are inevitably touched by Time, changed by Time, not only in themselves, but in their relation to each other. There is a rendering of an interior life that is not under the control of the intelligence, of an emotional life driven by a mechanism deep in the subconscious and not amenable to laws imposed by logic or rational ethics. "My book," asserted Proust, "is in no manner a work of the reason; the smallest elements of it have been furnished by my sensibility; I first perceived them deep in myself without understanding them, having as much difficulty in converting them into something intelligible as if they had been as foreign to the world of intelligence as, say, a motif in music. What we have not had to clarify for ourselves, what was clear before, as, for example, logical ideas, is not ours at all; we do not know if it is real." This sentence shows that Proust did something for himself that the other modern experimenters did not really do, he passed the speculative philosophies, the philosophy of Bergson and the psychology of Freud, through the medium of his sensibility, through all the furnishings of his own mind, before he used them in his work; that is, he performed the critical task of making a speculative philosophy into a literary philosophy, through first making it usable for himself. If all the modern writers had taken the same pains, or had a like equipment for making speculative philosophies into literary material, we should have much less unintelligibility in modern writing.

This disclaiming of the reason, of the conscious intelligence, this denial of logical ideas as being really our own, is the antithesis of the realist intelligence and objectivity. With its stress on everything that happens in the mind, in the interior life, *À la Recherche du Temps Perdu* is the opposite of a typical realistic work. At the same time, it must not be assumed that because Proust declares his book is not a work of the reason it is not a work of the intellect. It is a highly intellectual book, the work of a comprehensive intellect made luminous by strong emotions and an all-encompassing memory.

Both Joyce and Proust give the same impression, that they have penetrated into reaches of the inner life of men and presented them with far more actuality than has been done before. Yet we feel that this very same impression was given in their day by the creators of Emma Bovary and Anna Karenina, and it is probably the impression given by all innovators in literature. In both *Ulysses* and *À la Recherche du Temps Perdu,* the author is a character in his own work; this is perhaps always necessary in the literature which may be described as the literature of memory, in which the author invokes Time lived through.

This is true of the American writer whose work, likewise, might be described as Remembrance of Things Past and is also made up of Time, myths, legends, history, language—Thomas Wolfe too introduces Time into his titles, and has named one of his books *Of Time and the River.* Like Proust he tells us of his struggles with Time-elements, and has, in addition to the two Time-elements of Proust, the Present and the Past, brought in a third which he calls Time Immutable, the time of rivers, mountains, oceans and the earth. Like Proust he discourses on the powers of his memory to bring back odors, sounds, colors, shapes; like Joyce he has struggled with the mystery of myths and legends; like many modern writers, Aldous Huxley and D. H. Lawrence, he has expressed the convic-

356

tion that all serious creative work must at bottom be autobiographical, a conviction with which it is not necessary to agree, but which is undoubtedly true of all those forms of literature in which Time and Memory are the sources of inspiration.

7

Like all modern theories of literature, these theories about the novel are complex and intellectual. A great deal of modern poetry, also, is dominated by complex philosophical ideas. Poetry, for the distinguished French poet, Paul Valéry, as for the later Yeats, is a luminous revelation of ideas or spiritual perceptions. Poetry, for Paul Valéry, who is a direct descendant of the Symbolists, and like them somewhat sterile in his inspiration and deliberate in his attitude towards composition, is an art in which it is legitimate to use all the effects of the other arts—the sound of music, the composition of painting. In the world from which he draws his ideas, logic is of no more importance than it is in the world of Proust and Joyce, or than it was in the world of Rimbaud and Verlaine. Like theirs, Valéry's is an endeavor, but a far more deliberate endeavor, to get away from the domination of the old literary conceptions, the old literary effects. A few lines from one of his well-known poems will throw a little light, not only on his method but on the method of some other modern poets. Here is the opening of his "Cimetière Marin":

> Ce toit tranquille, où marchent des colombes,
> Entre les pins palpite, entre les tombes;
> Midi le juste y compose de feux
> La mer, la mer, toujours recommencée!
> O récompense après une pensée
> Qu'un long regard sur le calme des dieux!
>
> . . . .
>
> This quiet roof where the doves walk
> Palpitates between the pines, between the tombs;
> Midday appeases with its fires
> The sea, the sea always beginning again!
> O recompense after thought—
> A long gaze on the calm of the gods!

Of course, in this bare rendering, all the beauty of sound of the original is lost. To get at its meaning, poetry of this kind, like the poetry of Mallarmé or the poetry of Rimbaud, demands from the reader an exercise of the intellect and the imagination. The poet takes no trouble to make it easy for the reader; Valéry puts into these lines only the essential points of the scene on which he gazes—the cemetery, the pines, the sea, and the poet's thought brooding on them. The effect of the sun on the sea, of the sails of the boat on the water, is one of pictorial composition—it makes a picture like doves walking on a roof. What a writer out of the older literary tradition would have written would be something of this kind: "The quiet sea, where

the sails of the fishermen's boats move, is like a flat
roof where doves are walking": all that Valéry gives us
is the "quiet roof where the doves walk," and this is an
inheritance from those theories of writing that Rimbaud and Verlaine worked out together.

And here is a passage from the middle:

> Ils ont fondu dans une absence épaisse,
> L'argile rouge a bu la blanche espèce,
> Le don de vivre a passé dans les fleurs!
> Où sont des morts les phrases familières,
> L'art personnel, les âmes singulières?
> La larve file où se formaient des pleurs.
>
> Les cris aigus des filles chatouillées,
> Les yeux, les dents, les paupières mouillées,
> Le sein charmant qui joue avec le feu,
> Le sang qui brille aux lèvres qui se rendent,
> Les derniers dons, les doigts qui les défendent,
> Tout va sous terre et rentre dans le jeu!

. . . .

> They have vanished into a dense absence,
> The red earth has drunk the white generations,
> The gift of living has passed to the flowers!
> Where are the familiar phrases, the personal manner,
> The separate souls of the dead?
> The grub crawls where the tears once formed.
>
> The shrill cries of fondled girls,
> The eyes, the teeth, the moist eyelids,
> The charming bosom playing with fire,
> The blood glowing on lips that surrender,
> The last gifts, the defending hands—
> All go down into earth and back into the game.

(Literal translation by M. M. C.)

"Game" here means nature's vast game of life and death.

To eyes used to taking in the meaning of lines and sentences in a flash, as one passes, in an automobile, hoardings advertising soaps and toothpastes, this sort of writing will on first encounter be unintelligible. It demands not only a glance of the eyes, but an exercise of the intelligence, the imagination, the memory, and a power of meditation that is in itself an attainment; it demands more from a reader than a mere visual exercise. The accustomed combinations of words are not there; adjectives are employed, not for their power of description but for their power of evoking a thought.

Chapter Twelve

WHERE WE ARE

I

THE TRUTH of it is that, in spite of some interesting writers and their technical innovations, we are still living on the ideas, the literary doctrines, the programs of the nineteenth century. We write biography, history, poetry, novels, dramas, as the great critics and writers of the nineteenth century have taught us to write them. All the literary doctrines of whatever nature, whether Lessing's, that literature is the expression of national and racial genius, or de Staël's, that it is an expression of society, or the total trend of the literary ideas of the nineteenth century, that realism was the ultimate goal of literary expression, or the ideas of the later realists, that social reforms were the concern of writers and of writing, all these ideas and all the others—Sainte-Beuve's and Taine's and Wordsworth's and Baudelaire's—all were true, but they represented only a part of the truth, and none of them were meant to be assumed to stand for a dominating regulation of literature at any time. All these ideas, some more than others, have played a great and transforming rôle in literature down to the present day. Some of them have had followers as fanatical as the devotees of religious dogmas. These ideas—because, like all real ideas, they remain alive—might still play some sort of vivifying rôle if vitalized by a transforming mind that could mould them into a new shape and add its own original contribution to them. But the truth is, in their original form they have reached a dead end, and most of them, in the hands of uncreative writers, have become tyrannical platitudes. Writing is no longer re-creating itself; it is simply repeating itself, however this repetition may be masked by the use of adroit technical devices.

What we have added that is new is very slight: the material used by Joyce and Proust was developed in the nineteenth century, though an effective way of using it in literature was not attained to until the present century. The most accomplished mind in literature that we have had in this century has probably been that of Proust; he is unique among modern writers in that he made the first successful effort to translate into literary material and into a literary philosophy the formal philosophies he made use of. The inclination of all other writers who made use of psychological discoveries or social ideas or philosophic speculations was to use them in the raw without transforming them by passing them through the medium of their own sensibility or through the artistic imagination. This lack of transforming power is partly responsible for the unintelligibility of a certain type of modern literary expression: the writers have not known how to mould their material, or the critics have not assisted them to mould it. If enough disinterested and competent minds had devoted themselves to the development of new ideas in art, as has been the case in science, it would not have been possible for literature to have got itself into the rut that it is in at the present time. Nor would it have been possible, laying aside for the moment all consideration of literature as an art, for writing to have been one of the few remaining trades or professions where a man who knows nothing about the job can make an entrance and sometimes even a success. A man nowadays can produce a book that corresponds in content and construction to an early or elementary type of automobile, and yet get it published and even praised. Books that are dead as soon as they are published are turned out as fast as the printing-presses can work; the forests are denuded of trees to make paper to print works of which the world had no need, which were useless from the start, which lived only a feeble life and died without leaving a trace.

This state of affairs is due either to the paucity of first-rate critical minds or to the fact that, owing to economic necessity, such minds may be locked up in remote colleges instructing youth in the elements of literature, or are wasting their powers in the literary reviews trying to decide which third-rate trade-writer has produced a book a trifle better than some other third-rate trade-writer. It is, of course, entirely possible, that we have no first-rate critical minds at all at present. "An age that has no criticism," said Oscar Wilde, "is either an age in which art is immobile, hieratic, and confined to the reproduction of formal forms, or an age that possesses no art at all . . . it is the critical faculty that invents fresh forms . . . it is to the critical instinct that we owe each new mould that art finds ready to its hand. . . . There has never been a creative age that has not been critical also."

2

There are two great problems before the critical intellect at the present time; one is to achieve some liberating ideas that will stir minds to new expression and bring literature out of the dead-end it has reached and once more into the rôle of creation instead of reproduction—to stir minds to new expression as the great critics dealt with in this book stirred them. The other problem is to make some clear and recognizable boundaries between the various kinds of writing, for the critical mind has allowed itself to become overwhelmed by the eruption into writing, during the last fifty years, of a vast mob. Whereas, in the old days, the divisions in which writers could be placed were few—

there were perhaps two of them—we now have many.

In the modern world, writing is both an art and a trade, an art or a trade. As a trade, it came in with the development of capitalism and industrial life and with the spread of elementary education, which brought into existence an audience of the newly literate who demanded reading-matter of their own. Consequently, as a trade, writing is followed by a number of workers to whom all art, including the art of literature, is an unrevealed mystery. It is also followed as a trade, or perhaps as a profession, by writers who, on occasion, can rise to the production of a work of art. Sometimes a man writing what he thinks is a piece of trade-writing, produced for a definite market, consciously or unconsciously achieves a work of art; the other way round may be equally true, and a man aiming at producing a work of art may turn out a piece of trade-writing or merely a piece of literate writing. The line has to be drawn, and it is the critic's immediate responsibility to draw it, not so much between writers themselves as between their products, for the same writer can produce work varying between high literature and the commonest type of trade-writing. As trade-writing came in with the development of capitalism and industrialism, so in the non-capitalistic or industrially backward countries the trade-writer, except as a newspaper writer, is an uncommon figure. In the highly developed capitalistic countries he is common; in a great capitalist country like America, he is very much to the fore, and sometimes makes as large an income as any other sort of manufacturer—a coat and suit manufacturer or a toothpaste manufacturer. The smaller trade-writer is like the small trader of any kind—the house-painter, the carpenter, the small storekeeper—sometimes he makes a decent living, sometimes a starvation wage.

Writing, as a trade, in the hands of competent and talented practitioners is a high-class trade, demanding greater intelligence and broader experience of life than most others, but it should not be confused with literature, the production of a number of rare minds in every generation, a number of minds whose work is, according to Hegel's definition, the production of truth or spiritual reality in sensuous form. Trade-writing has a number of uses, some invaluable, some of little consequence; some trade-writing—and this includes a large slice of fiction-writing—serves the purpose of recreation or escape from ennui; another type conveys instruction, information, opinions, propaganda or advertisement. In a modern magazine, the part which contains the fiction and the formal articles is described as the literary section, and is published in a different way from the advertising section, but in actual fact, in an up-to-date publication, there is hardly a pin's difference between the content, language, and recreation-value of the advertising pages, and the content, language, and recreation-value of the literary section. I will give, as examples, a story from the advertising section of *Harper's Bazaar,* and a story, by a well-known author, in the literary section; no reader unfamiliar beforehand with the matter would be able to recognize, I am sure, which is meant to be the literature and which the paid advertisement.

Quotation I:

Cap'n Sam paused for a dreamy moment. "And now I'll be telling you about the Parsee princes in Bombay," he went on, ". . . and the lovely little folk that live in Bali. Peaceful people, like your mother said." Mrs. Milford looked at her husband, and he returned her smile. They both remembered that day, three months before, when Captain Sam had appeared at the back door of their country home. He had been impressive even in his threadbare clothes, patched with a sailmaker's undisguised stitches. "I'm Captain Sam Johnson," he had introduced himself simply; "and I'm eager to do anything, from gardening to a bit of seafaring." So a gardener he was, now, and a painter of porches that he somehow made to look trim and smooth like the decks of a ship.

And here is Quotation II:

Steven first met Matilda at a friend's coming-of-age party. She was nineteen then, very pretty and eager and determined; and he, of the same age, was a shy, rather sulky-looking youth with red hair and green-blue eyes. They danced together once, but he was not very good at the new steps, so they sat out a second dance and talked about books. He was a medical student and wanted to lend her a new novel he had just been reading. . . .Two days later the novel arrived, and when she wrote thanking him for it he asked her to tea at a restaurant. . . . After a few more meetings they discovered themselves to be in love and became engaged. Steven was working hard for his examinations, and it would have been a pity if Matilda had been the wrong sort of girl for him, and some people thought she might be. "They don't seem to get on very well together," people said.

The author of the advertising story is anonymous, but I really believe it is the better written and shows the more inventive power of the two. The author of what is meant to be the literary story is James Hilton, author of *Goodbye, Mr. Chips*. Both the fiction writer and the advertising writer are trade-writers, producing work to meet a market-demand and using language as a stereotyped, almost algebraicised vehicle of expression. Trade-writing is a commodity produced for a known market in exchange for cash; the market fluctuates, but in the main, in a capitalist country, if a writer produces a piece of work, say, for the market covered by the largely circulated magazines, we can tell its money value beforehand, varying a little according to the product and to the status of its producer.

So much for writing as a trade. Now we come to writing as an art, writing which is literature, the production of truth, the production of new truth in every age, in sensuous form, the sort of writing that this book is concerned with. High literature has no market value of the kind that can be assessed in money; nobody can tell what the cash value of a masterpiece might be in its author's lifetime. Some people can estimate what its value as art is, that is they can tell, roughly speaking, if it has enduring reality, though they may not be able to tell how long it will endure, for a piece of writing can be a work of art—a minor work of art— and have a fleeting life; a great work of art is, of course, one that lasts, one of the realities that forgetful mankind finds worthy of remembrance. A good piece of trade-writing can last for some years, too, but what is a long life for a piece of trade-writing would be a short life for a work of art.

When we say that a great work of art is a work of such revelation, such reality, that it is considered of lasting value by generations of men, we again have to make another distinction, for if the *Divine Comedy* has shown itself possessed of lasting reality so also has Euclid's *Elements* or Darwin's *Origin of Species* or Harvey's *Motion of the Heart and Blood*. What distinguishes a work of art from any of these, what distinguishes the reality that is *Hamlet* from the reality that is Euclid's *Elements,* is that one is spiritual truth in sensuous form and the other is factual truth in logical form; what distinguishes *Hamlet* again from Locke's *Concerning Human Understanding* is the difference between truth in sensuous form and truth in abstract form. A work of philosophy can, of course, be a work of literature as well, when the sensuous imagination enters in an or-

ganic way into its creation, as it does in the works of
Nietzsche or Schopenhauer. There is, of course, imagination shown in the *Elements* of Euclid, there may
even be emotion, but these are of a totally different
kind from those that enter into a work of art. Even
the types of imagination that enter into the composition of various forms of art differ, the one from the
other. The type of imagination that is in lyric poetry
differs from the type of imagination that is in a narrative poem, or a novel, or a biography, or a piece of
criticism. The sort of intelligence that is displayed in
Euclid's *Elements* is dominatingly the reasoning intelligence; the intelligence in *Hamlet* is an emotional-
ized intelligence, what Coleridge called "the heart in
the head." The imagination in Euclid is a formal
imagination; the imagination in *Hamlet* is the rhapsodic imagination, a type of imagination that can be
uncontrolled vision, as it sometimes is in the work of
William Blake, and as Rimbaud aimed at making it.
A work of history, also, can be simple information, or,
like Gibbon's *Decline and Fall of the Roman Empire*,
it may, because of its range of emotion, the nature of
its imagination, its acute sensitivity to historical experience, the manner in which it is thought out into
language, belong to the category of literature.

The confusion that exists at present between literature and all other sorts of writing is partly due to the
uncritical manner in which literary history has been

ganic way into its creation, as it does in the works of
Nietzsche or Schopenhauer. There is, of course, imagination shown in the *Elements* of Euclid, there may
even be emotion, but these are of a totally different
kind from those that enter into a work of art. Even
the types of imagination that enter into the composition of various forms of art differ, the one from the
other. The type of imagination that is in lyric poetry
differs from the type of imagination that is in a narrative poem, or a novel, or a biography, or a piece of
criticism. The sort of intelligence that is displayed in
Euclid's *Elements* is dominatingly the reasoning intelligence; the intelligence in *Hamlet* is an emotional-
ized intelligence, what Coleridge called "the heart in
the head." The imagination in Euclid is a formal
imagination; the imagination in *Hamlet* is the rhapsodic imagination, a type of imagination that can be
uncontrolled vision, as it sometimes is in the work of
William Blake, and as Rimbaud aimed at making it.
A work of history, also, can be simple information, or,
like Gibbon's *Decline and Fall of the Roman Empire*,
it may, because of its range of emotion, the nature of
its imagination, its acute sensitivity to historical experience, the manner in which it is thought out into
language, belong to the category of literature.

The confusion that exists at present between literature and all other sorts of writing is partly due to the
uncritical manner in which literary history has been

tell what the cash value of a masterpiece might be in its author's lifetime. Some people can estimate what its value as art is, that is they can tell, roughly speaking, if it has enduring reality, though they may not be able to tell how long it will endure, for a piece of writing can be a work of art—a minor work of art— and have a fleeting life; a great work of art is, of course, one that lasts, one of the realities that forgetful mankind finds worthy of remembrance. A good piece of trade-writing can last for some years, too, but what is a long life for a piece of trade-writing would be a short life for a work of art.

When we say that a great work of art is a work of such revelation, such reality, that it is considered of lasting value by generations of men, we again have to make another distinction, for if the *Divine Comedy* has shown itself possessed of lasting reality so also has Euclid's *Elements* or Darwin's *Origin of Species* or Harvey's *Motion of the Heart and Blood*. What distinguishes a work of art from any of these, what distinguishes the reality that is *Hamlet* from the reality that is Euclid's *Elements,* is that one is spiritual truth in sensuous form and the other is factual truth in logical form; what distinguishes *Hamlet* again from Locke's *Concerning Human Understanding* is the difference between truth in sensuous form and truth in abstract form. A work of philosophy can, of course, be a work of literature as well, when the sensuous imagination enters in an or-

or economic order, but who are productive in the spiritual and intellectual order. It is not suggested that in what is called the total ordering of things the functioning of this class is more important than that of any other, but if its free functioning is prohibited, civilization will arrive at the ant-heap. And its free functioning can be prohibited by other things than the ukases of individual dictators; at present its free functioning in free countries is partly prohibited by the domination in writing of an uncreative majority the consideration of whose works takes up most of the space in literary journals, and by the tactics of a group who wish to subordinate literature to social and political interests. The members of an intellectual or spiritual order cannot, on penalty of being destroyed and having spiritual values destroyed with them, become servants of any economic or class interest; an artist ought not to let himself be deluded in this matter by his natural sympathies.

All the classes, all the dominant interests, at one time or another, have been in hostility to the free functioning of an intellectual aristocracy, for they have expected it to serve their own interests, or at least, not to oppose them. Socrates, Dante, Galileo, Victor Hugo, Dostoevsky, Unamuno, Thomas Mann, were all persecuted because they did not serve the interests or the ideologies of the powerful classes of their day. The number of lesser men and the names of those in our day who have been persecuted for opposing the classes in power, from Russia to Spain, would make a very long list. Those who wish to preserve literature have to set about preserving it from assaults from all sides. It seems as if there has hardly been a period in history when writers were less independent, less devoted to their own vocation, than they are at present. There are, in our time, even among members of writers' groups, a number of people with a hatred of all spiritual values and with an impassioned desire to destroy literature and every expression of the interior life and of the life of dream. Even the most meanly gifted human beings have a life of dream, though it be the narrowest, most limited dream, a dream of marrying the boss's daughter or being the head of the office. But whatever it may be, while it lasts it takes up a great deal of each life, sometimes to the extent of nearly obliterating the life of external reality.

It is one of the objects of art to mould this life of dream, to shape it into forms that will enable men and women to achieve a greater consciousness, a profounder communication with life, stronger feelings, subtler intelligences, more noble imaginations. Why so many writers should disparage the existence of a dream-life and why a certain type of critic should regard it as having less dimension than the exterior life, is hard to understand. But the widespread development of an uninspired and decadent realism and a flat, impoverished materialist philosophy has brought about a concentration on exterior life, and the routine of exterior life, to the discrediting of all forms of interior life. A great many facets of modern art, and especially of modern literature, that the public find difficult to understand, represent an attempt at a restoration of a part of life that is powerfully existent and, with this, a restoration of myths and legends to their necessary place in the domain of human expression. The combination of materialist and positivist philosophies with literal and sordid realism in literature and the denial that we have any spiritual inheritance has given that minority, that always existing minority which since the beginning of history has had a contempt for spiritual truths and for that side of man immersed in dream, a chance to get into a dominating position.

Yet just as surely as time is composed of night and day, life is composed of dream and external reality, and the advancement and happiness of man depend not only on the elevation of his everyday life, but on the elevation of his dream-life. The displacement and the disowning of the dream-life, the lack of recognition of the fact that it, too, needs vitalizing nutriment, are responsible for a great deal of the despair of the modern world. The tendency has been to concentrate on one half of life, and this has forced men further and further back to the conviction that life and creation are not only mysteries, but dismal mysteries, and that the cosmos, instead of implying beauty and order, implies unintelligibility and anarchism. There are now engaged in writing a number of men who appear to live from day to day in the hope that some obscure disaster will overhelm art and humanity. Any sort of writing, no matter how platitudinous or derivative, that seems to portend this disaster, is greeted by them with fervour. Even from a genuine artist like Paul Valéry comes that lonely, incredibly sad solution: that nothingness is better than life, that the earth, the sun, the moon, the stars, humanity itself, are but an error of the Creator, that the universe is God's fall, a defect in chaos, the original sin. The despair of modern philosophies would be intolerable if one did not know with Proust that Time touches everything, that Time changes everything, that spring succeeds winter, and summer, spring, and that the words of another living poet, William Butler Yeats, are prophetic and true:

> O silver trumpets, be you lifted up,
> And cry to the great race that is to come!
> Long-throated swans upon the waves of time,
> Sing loudly, for beyond the wall of the world
> That race may hear our music and awake.

INDEX

INDEX

INDEX

INDEX

INDEX

INDEX

INDEX

MARY M. COLUM

Mary M. Colum was born in Ireland and received her education there and abroad. She began as a short-story writer, and her short stories were welcomed, amongst others, by Massingham of the London *Nation* and J. C. Squire of the *New Statesman*, and they were admiringly commented on by George Moore, while her literary and dramatic criticism attracted the attention of William Butler Yeats, Lord Alfred Douglas and George Moore. Her first critical article that aroused interest was one on John Synge. As a student she took part in the reunions of the group of well-known Irish writers surrounding the Abbey Theatre, amongst whom was Padraic Colum whom she afterwards married. Since 1914 she has made her home in the United States. Mrs. Colum is regarded, on both sides of the Atlantic, as one of the leading contemporary critics. Her book reviews and special articles in the *Saturday Review of Literature*, the *New York Herald Tribune*, *Scribner's*, and the *Dial* have been widely quoted and she has been a frequent lecturer and a contributor to the *New Republic*, the *Nation*, the *New Statesman* and the *Forum* where in recent years her series of featured articles have delighted a large number of readers.